D0856863

THROUGH A WOMAN'S I

An Annotated Bibliography
of American Women's
Autobiographical Writings,
1946 · 1976

by
Patricia K. Addis

The Scarecrow Press, Inc.
Metuchen, N.J., & London
1983

Library of Congress Cataloging in Publication Data

Addis, Patricia K., 1942-
   Through a woman's I.

   Includes indexes.
   1. Women--United States--Biography--Bibliography.
2. United States--Biography--Bibliography.   3. Auto-
biographies--Bibliography.   I. Title.
Z7963.B6A32   1983   [CT3260]   016.92072'0973   82-10813
ISBN 0-8108-1588-5

"I hope my readers will not think me vain for writing my life ... since there have been many that have done the like, as Cesar, Ovid, and many more, both men and women, and I know no reason I may not do it as well as they: but I verily believe some censuring Readers will scornfully say, why hath this Lady writ her own Life? since none cares to know whose daughter she was or whose wife she is, or how she was bred, or what fortunes she had, or how she lived, or what humour or disposition she was of? I answer that it is true, that 'tis to no purpose to the Readers, but it is to the Authoress, because I write it for my own sake, not theirs."

Margaret Cavendish,
Duchess of Newcastle, 1655
cited in Mary Ellen Chase,
A Goodly Heritage, 1932

Acknowledgments

I am grateful to Professor Linda K. Kerber of the Department of History and to Professor Florence Boos of the Department of English, both at the University of Iowa, for strategically-timed nudges during the early stages of this bibliographical project. I am also grateful to Professor Albert Stone of the American Studies Program at the University of Iowa long a scholar and teacher of autobiographies, for his continuing interest in the project.

I would like to thank Mr. Keith Rageth and his staff at the Interlibrary Loan Department of the University of Iowa Libraries. Their cheerful acceptance of what must have seemed like an unending stream of request cards and their handling of some two-thirds of the books discussed in the bibliography were essential to the completion of this project and will be as essential to its continuation in a companion volume.

I would like to thank my husband and my daughters for their familial assistance, and my father-in-law deserves a very special thank you for his expert typing of the manuscript. I thank as well other family members and friends for their continued interest and encouragement.

And finally I thank the thousands of women who, like Margaret Cavendish before them, knew that their own lives were worthy of being recorded and preserved.

Table of Contents

Women's personal narratives in a wide variety of genres can serve as a superb primary source for research in Women's Studies, for within the past decade the rise of Women's Studies as an interdisciplinary field of inquiry has led to an intense re-examination of previously identified resources as well as to a search for hitherto unexplored primary materials. One may consider a narrative of a single event such as Lael Wertenbaker's account of her husband's dying or several massive narratives covering the sweep of an entire lifetime such as those of Frances Parkinson Keyes; one may consider an account by a cloistered nun such as Mother Catherine Thomas of Divine Providence or a memoir by a world famous figure such as Eleanor Roosevelt; one may consider an account of local success such as Nellie Cornish's story of her teaching or an account of historic import such as Mary White Ovington's story of her work with the N.A.A.C.P. All of these constitute the stuff of which the sociology, the psychology, the history of women in America may be written. I find it a wonderful coincidence but altogether fitting that the final stages of this manuscript were completed during Women's History Week of 1982.

Often thus far, discussion of women's autobiographies has not gone beyond the examination of a small number of well-known and much-analyzed works. Scholars seeking to build a broader base for their research find that many of the existing bibliographies are either chronologically or topically narrow or severely limit their contents by various definitions of "autobiography." An exploration of the widest possible collection of sources is a first step to the reevaluation, expansion, and re-definition of the accepted canon: hence the necessity for a bibliography which is broadly inclusive rather than exclusive.

This bibliography includes books of substantial length (a minimum of twenty-five pages) published between and including 1946 and 1976 and readily available from libraries in

the United States. 1946 was chosen as the dividing date between this volume and a succeeding volume that will include
works published before 1946, because the single most nearly
comprehensive bibliography on autobiographies has been Louis
Kaplan's A Bibliography of American Autobiographies (1961),
which lists only books published prior to 1946.

Rather than offer yet another definition of "autobiography" that would exclude many kinds of personal narratives,
I have included autobiographies, letters, diaries, journals,
memoirs, reminiscences, and travel accounts. I have also
included accounts of specific events which were crucial in the
creation of a particular woman's identity, events such as traumatic illness or handicap, the illness or handicap or death of
a family member, incarceration, pioneering, missionary service, a move "back-to-the-land," spiritual awakening, or religious conversion.

I have included published collections of letters because
they can provide a wealth of detail, an immediacy, and even
an emotional intensity that are not always found in a carefully
crafted autobiography prepared for a public readership. The
correspondence that reveals the self-conscious sacrifice of
Abigail Adams, the political and intellectual passion of Emma
Goldman, the sustained whimsy of Clara Boardman Peck, and
the incredulous agony of Ethel Rosenberg are only a few examples of personal narratives that enrich the autobiographical
canon.

I have included travel narratives even though they
sometimes tend to focus on trivial externals. To a certain
extent, I merely wish to remain consistent with the companion
volume to this bibliography which will list early travel narratives that are often of inherent interest because of the unusual
modes of travel employed or the enterprising spirit of the
traveler. But beyond that structural consideration, I was
interested to find many narratives that illustrate women's
ingenuity, good humor, and receptivity to new experience
when they chose or were required to travel or establish a
home in a country and culture not their own. Undertaking
a traditionally female task--homemaking--in unfamiliar surroundings, women often demonstrated their adaptability as
well as their yen for adventure. Whether it is Kathleen
Trautman following her Foreign Service husband to Afghanistan, or Constance Helmericks taking her two daughters on a
rugged, perilous river journey north to the Arctic Circle, or
Ilka Chase accompanying a small group of congenial friends
on the idyllic canals of France, all of these women present

personal narratives that tell us much about themselves and about the variety of women's experience.

There are a number of accounts that portray with rich detail the intricacies of domestic life on the frontier or on a pioneer homestead. Many were written as family chronicles by grandmothers in order to describe to their grandchildren a way of life that had disappeared. The fact that they are often relatively unsophisticated and straightforward lends a particular value to these kinds of personal narratives--an informal but sincere attempt to provide what should become important elements of social history.

There are a number of "mother's stories," like that of Constance Cameron, which describe a life significantly marked by being the mother of an ill, handicapped, or otherwise exceptional child. In a very real sense, the writer's role as a mother in such special circumstances becomes a career. Often in the face of discouraging or inadequate medical diagnoses, a mother commits herself to doing whatever is necessary to enable her child to reach his or her full potential, and fulfilling that commitment requires the mother to become an expert in a field that may have been neglected by the medical profession.

I would not wish to have to judge these narratives as good or bad, for depending on one's purposes for reading them, the line between good and bad can blur. Certainly, in terms of literary merit alone, these books run the gamut from brilliant to execrable. But what is remarkable and invaluable is the range of human experience represented.

For the purposes of this bibliography, I have defined as "American" any woman who is native-born or who is foreign-born but either married to an American citizen or settled permanently in this country, with or without citizenship.

Names beginning with "Mc" are ordered as if they were spelled "Mac." Middle names, maiden names, and married names are listed in sequence, without parentheses. Complete subtitles of books are noted, for they are often useful preliminary summaries in themselves. Where an autobiographical narrative makes significant mention of another woman who is herself a writer of autobiographical narrative, a cross-reference is supplied. Only the first entry number for the writer in the cross-reference is noted.

The Author Index lists writers under categories that identify them by profession or by salient characteristic. Authors have been placed within the most precise category that is appropriate in each case; for example, "first lady" is more precise than "politician's wife," which is in turn more precise than "wife of famous man," so Julia Dent Grant will be found in the Author Index under "first lady."

Many authors are found in more than one category. Lucy Sprague Mitchell, for example, is a teacher, college administrator, and a writer. The category "writer" is broad, and when an author falls under one of its subdivisions, she will be found more appropriately under "poet," "novelist," etc. However, when a woman is listed under the category "writer," it indicates that she has written things other than or in addition to poems, novels, biographies, translations, cookbooks, or children's works.

Every woman who is noted in this book is of course a "person in her own right," but nevertheless in some instances the fact that a woman is the wife of a particular man is the single most important factor in her life. Thus, in including an index category "wife of famous man" or opening an annotation with the words "the wife of ..." I do not in any way mean to belittle the author but to note immediately a crucial, identifying characteristic that she herself acknowledges.

The Narrative Index lists writers and certain books under categories that characterize them by subject matter, for example, conversion narrative or illness/handicap/death of family member. Again, I have selected the most precise category in each case, so that a narrative which tells of missionary experience in Africa would not also be listed under "travel/householding abroad" but only under "missionary experience."

The Title Index follows and refers the reader to a particular entry number.

A woman for whom there is a biographical entry in Notable American Women (for those who died during or before 1950) or in Notable American Women; The Modern Period (for those who died between 1951 and 1975) has the notation "NAW" or "NAWM" to the right of her name.

This bibliographical project grew out of a small suggested reading list that I gave to my students in a course on American Women's Autobiographies which I taught at the University of Iowa between 1973 and 1975. As I browsed among the possibilities for narratives to include in my course, the supplementary list became longer and longer, and it was clear that what would have been most useful to me would have been an extensive bibliography with annotations of sufficient length to include a summary, evaluation, and sometimes brief quotations to help give a feel for the quality or style of the narrative. What I lacked then I have attempted to provide for others now.

Sources that were most helpful in the preliminary stages of the compilation are the following:

Brignano, Russell C., Black Americans in Autobiography: An Annotated Bibliography of Autobiographies and Autobiographical Books Written Since the Civil War. Durham, N.C.: Duke University Press, 1974.
Jacobson, Angeline, Contemporary Native American Literature. Metuchen, N.J.: The Scarecrow Press, Inc., 1977.
James, Edward T., Janet Wilson James and Paul S. Boyer, eds., Notable American Women: A Biographical Dictionary. Cambridge, Mass.: The Belknap Press of Harvard University Press, 1971.
Lillard, Richard G., American Life in Autobiography; A Descriptive Guide. Stanford: Stanford University Press, 1956.
Mainiero, Lina, ed., American Women Writers. New York: Frederick Ungar Publishing Co., 1979.
Nicholson, Margaret E., People in Books. New York: The H. W. Wilson Co., 1969.
Nogales, Luis G., ed., The Mexican American: A Selected and Annotated Bibliography, 2nd ed. Stanford: Stanford University Press, 1971.
O'Brien, Lynne Woods, Plains Indian Autobiographies. Boise, Idaho: Boise State College, 1973.
Sicherman, Barbara and Carol Hurd Green, eds., Notable American Women; The Modern Period: A Biographical Dictionary. Cambridge, Mass.: The Belknap Press of Harvard University Press, 1980.
Stensland, Anna Lee, Literature By and About the American Indian: An Annotated Bibliography. Urbana, Ill.: National Council of Teachers of English, 1973.
Williams, Ora, American Black Women in the Arts and Social Sciences. Metuchen, N.J.: The Scarecrow Press, Inc., 1978.

In addition, citations were gathered both systematically and serendipitously from general sources including the Cumulative Book Index, the National Union Catalog, and Publishers Weekly for the years 1946-1976.

Until very recently, I have been aided by the beginning bibliographer's naïveté, assuming that there were far fewer books to read and annotate than there actually are. Fortunately this misperception allowed me to approach the task undaunted by the staggering numbers involved.

The bibliographer's nemesis is the search for the ever-elusive last entry. Inevitably, omissions will have occurred in the present volume, and I welcome with enthusiasm any suggestions for additions that could be included in future editions of or companion volumes to this bibliography.

--Patricia K. Addis

A

1   ABBOTT, MAMIE GOULET (1881?-)
Santa Ines Hermosa; The Journal of the Padre's Niece.   Montecito, Santa Barbara, Cal.:   Sunwise Press, 1951.   262pp.

Her journal covers the years from 1904 to 1924 during which she serves with devotion as "helpmate and home maker" to her uncle as they rebuild a historic California mission; she restores the church vestments and linens, offers hospitality to houseguests and tourists, and cares for her uncle, even after his health requires their departure from the mission; she triumphs over frustrations and primitive conditions by a sense of humor and "sheer force of will."

2   ABDALIAN, ZABEL (1886-)
Sa Pwh, Prince of the Air.   New York: Pageant, 1955.   49pp.

The daughter of an American medical missionary killed by the Turks in 1895, she presents a disjointed account of her return to the U.S. after her father's death, her voice study, the death of her mother in 1932, and the publication of several books; she writes in the third person.

3   ABRECHT, MARY ELLEN
The Making of a Woman Cop, with Barbara Lang Stern.   New York: Morrow, 1976.   275pp.

A graduate of Mount Holyoke and a newlywed, she becomes a police officer in Washington, D.C. in 1968; after screening and training, she works with the Youth Division, attends law school, and is given patrol duty as she works to equalize women's roles on the police force; she becomes "Policewoman's Coordinator," then Sergeant in 1972, proud of her profession; after recounting numerous anecdotes of both routine and dramatic cases, she closes with reflections on women in police work.

4   ABZUG, BELLA (1920-)
Bella! Ms. Abzug Goes to Washington, ed. Mel Ziegler.
New York: Saturday Review, 1972.   314pp.

1

Her diary-like entries cover the period from January to December of 1971, beginning with her first term in the U.S. House of Representatives; she describes her struggles with the "system" for anti-war and social welfare measures and the formation of the Women's Political Caucus; she writes a little on the personal rewards and costs of her activism.

5   ACOSTA, MERCEDES de
       Here Lies the Heart. New York: Reynal, 1960. 372pp.

A writer of Spanish heritage, she describes a cosmopolitan upbringing, her lifelong association with famous figures in art, literature, theatre, film; she enjoys especially strong friendships with Isadora Duncan (see entry # 609) and Greta Garbo; she works in Hollywood at its height; sees herself as artist, potential saint, vagabond.

6   ADAMS, ABIGAIL SMITH (1744-1818)   NAW
       The Adams Family in Auteuil, 1784-1785, As Told in the
       Letters of Abigail Adams. Boston: Massachusetts Historical
       Society, 1956. 32pp.

Reunited with her husband, John Adams, after a separation of five years, she describes the trials of keeping a house of "luxury and folly" in a foreign country; she is shocked by expenses and appalled that her husband, a dedicated public official, is in such financial straits; after less than a year she departs to England; her letters are sharp and articulate, as usual.

7   The Adams-Jefferson Letters; The Complete Correspondence
       Between Thomas Jefferson and Abigail and John Adams, ed.
       Lester J. Cappon. Chapel Hill: University of North Caro-
       lina, 1959. 2 vol. 638pp.

Included are twenty-seven letters from Abigail Adams to Thomas Jefferson written between 1785 and 1817; in London when her husband is ambassador, she notes with characteristic wit and sharpness the unfriendliness of the British press and the lack of British "Good Sense, Good Nature, Political Wisdom and Benevolence, " at the same time noting the details of buying London tablecloths for Jefferson; by 1788 she reaffirms her nostalgia for her simple country home; very attached to Jefferson's daughter who had visited in 1787, she sends her condolences in 1804 at the young woman's death; also in 1804 there is an exchange of several candid letters, sharply critical but without malice, concerning political differences between Jefferson and John Adams, after which she gracefully withdraws some of her former resentment.

8   The Book of Abigail and John; Selected Letters of the Adams
      Family, 1762-1784, ed. L. H. Butterfield et al. Cambridge:
      Harvard, 1975. 411pp.

         A delightfully coy "Diana" before her marriage and an
      earnest guardian of home and family as "Portia" after her
      marriage, she endures years of "cruel Seperation" when John
      Adams serves in Continental Congresses and then is posted to
      France and Holland by the new government; she repeatedly
      notes her sacrifice of a normal marriage and domestic tran-
      quillity to the "publick weal" and repeatedly reproaches her
      husband for his epistolary brevity, requesting "some senti-
      mental Effusions of the Heart"; she lodges her famous re-
      minder for women's political representation and comments on
      the necessity for women's education; the collection reveals a
      vivacious, sharply observant woman who triumphs over finan-
      cial, domestic, and physical adversity.

9   New Letters of Abigail Adams, 1788-1801, ed. Stewart Mit-
      chell. Boston: Houghton Mifflin, 1947. 281pp.

         In a series of letters written to her elder sister, she pre-
      sents a combination of rich domestic detail and sharp politi-
      cal observations; as the vice-president's wife, she describes
      George and Martha Washington, notes U. S. relations with
      France, tells of her children and grandchildren, and chron-
      icles family illnesses; in "splendid misery" as the president's
      wife, a position "never envy'd or coveted by me," she con-
      tinues to chat intimately about housekeeping as well as polit-
      ical tensions with characteristic acerbic comments.

10   ADAMS, CINDY HELLER
      My Friend the Dictator. Indianapolis: Bobbs-Merrill, 1967.
      312pp.

         A journalist, she is selected by Indonesia's Sukarno to be
      his official biographer; after struggles with bureaucratic inef-
      ficiency, she travels, conducts interviews, and collects gos-
      sip, delighting Sukarno with her "sassy Americanese" and
      being delighted in turn by the "inside dope"; her account is
      full of anecdotes about the amorous dictator and about his
      wives; she completes her book in spite of political unrest and
      finally flees Indonesia in 1965.

11   ADAMS, EFFIE KAY (1925-   )
      Experiences of a Fulbright Teacher. Boston: Christopher,
      1956. 215pp.

         She offers her observations and experiences in Pakistan

from 1952 to 1953, as a specialist in teacher education and a teacher of English; she works for international understanding; she describes the position of women in Pakistan, tells of sightseeing in Southeast Asia, Japan, India, the Middle East, North Africa, and Europe.

12   ADAMS, LILLIAN LOYCE (1912-)
       The Three T's: Teach, Travel and Tell.   Boston: Christopher, 1960. 203pp.

       In a rambling but enthusiastic account, a business professor explains her desire to expand her experiences to enliven her teaching; she travels in Mexico and in the U. S., then teaches in Heidelberg in 1952, using the opportunity to travel extensively in Europe.

13   ADAMS, LOYCE
       see ADAMS, LILLIAN LOYCE (1912-)

14   ADAMS, RACHEL WHITE
       On the Other Hand.   New York: Harper & Row, 1963.
       242pp.

       After the joy and security of a rural New England childhood, she marries a woodsman and raises four children, enjoying the outdoor, country life; her husband, Sherman Adams, enters New Hampshire politics, becoming governor in 1949, and she adds the excitement of a heavy social schedule to her activities in civic affairs; she accompanies her husband on extensive travels for the Eisenhower campaign; when her husband becomes part of the President's administration, she creates a role for herself that includes painting and writing as well as social obligations; she makes only oblique references to the investigation of her husband before his resignation, emphasizing her continued love and respect for him and their quiet satisfaction at their return to rural New Hampshire.

15   ADLER, POLLY (1900?-1962)   NAWM
       A House Is Not a Home.   New York: Rinehart, 1953.
       374pp.

       This is a slangy, anecdotal account focusing on the 1920's and 1930's by a nationally notorious madam; an immigrant at thirteen, she slides into her occupation as a madam and rises economically and socially; hers is a tale of underworld characters, corrupt policemen, vice investigations, and harassment.

16   ADLOF, VIOLA EBEL (1908-)
      Levi's Grandma Writes.   Austin, Tex.:   San Felipe Press,
      1972.   287pp.

      A Texas newspaper columnist chronicles the "everyday
      little things in life" between 1958 and 1972, after the writ-
      ing of her first autobiography; she draws on her diaries to
      provide the multitudinous details of her civic and church
      activities and anecdotes of her family and friends.

17   Lisa's Texas Grandmother.   Boerne, Tex.:   Highland Press,
      1963.   217pp.

      A journalist presents an anecdotal account of the "plain,
      everyday little things"; in her rural Texas childhood hard
      satisfying work is combined with good fun; she marries at
      eighteen, and in spite of recurrent health problems, she
      enjoys farming, raising two children, engaging in civic
      activities, and working on a local newspaper; she produces
      a family chronicle of significant events.

18   AGNELLI, SUSANNA (1922-)
      We Always Wore Sailor Suits.   New York: Viking, 1975.
      182pp.

      She grows up in fascist Italy, the granddaughter of the
      wealthy head of Fiat, and provides in her first vignettes
      sketches of eccentric relatives, governesses, and maids; at
      the death of her father in 1935, her uneducated, childlike
      mother wrests custody of her seven children from her power-
      ful father-in-law by going to Mussolini; after a delightful,
      disorderly youth, she engages in a desultory social life,
      then serves as a nurse during the war, deeply affected by
      the horrors she witnesses; as Italy collapses, she flees to
      Switzerland, then returns, closing her charming account
      with her marriage in 1945.

19   AIMI, MARGUERITE SITGREAVES
      Pedigree of a Nitwit.   New York: Vantage, 1955.   232pp.

      Her account is a series of rambling, humorous anecdotes
      touching on her strong mother, her genial drinking father,
      her first job as a government clerk, her European travels,
      her brief marriage, her unemployment during the depression,
      her work in advertising and in radio, her pet bluejay, and
      her numerous ancestors.

20   AKELEY, MARY LEE JOBE (1886-)
      Congo Eden.   New York: Dodd, Mead, 1950.   356pp.

In 1947 she is invited to make a pilgrimage to her naturalist husband's grave; she tells of her six-month expedition to the Congo National Parks; much of the narrative is historical and describes the local people, flora, and fauna; she recalls the 1926 expedition on which her husband had died; she describes her great affection for his Congolese friends.

21   ALADJEM, HENRIETTA (1917-)
      The Sun Is My Enemy; One Woman's Victory Over a Mysterious and Dreaded Disease.   Englewood Cliffs, N.J.:
      Prentice-Hall, 1972. 162pp.

      A victim of systemic lupus erythematosus writes so that others may benefit from her experiences; Bulgarian born, married, and the mother of three young children, she notes her first symptoms in 1953 but suffers three depressing years before a diagnosis is made, and seven years of experimentation with various doctors and drugs follow; the disease becomes a career, for she does extensive research on it and is treated by doctors almost like a colleague; it finally moves into a state of remission.

22   ALDRICH, DOROTHY COFFIN
      Musings of a Mother.   Chicago: Moody Press, 1949.   124pp.

      The mother of eight young children offers her religious reflections as she finds religious lessons and parallels in everyday domestic events; she is "Mommie" in this third person narrative which portrays close family ties.

23   ALDRICH, MARGARET CHANLER (1870-)
      Family Vista; The Memories of Margaret Chanler Aldrich.
      New York: William-Frederick, 1958.   233pp.

      After presenting a brief history of her distinguished family, she tells of her childhood on a Hudson River estate where she lives with a large extended family after the deaths of her parents; she is the sister-in-law of Margaret Terry Chanler (see entry #384) and the grand-niece of Julia Ward Howe (see companion volume); she spends her youth in Europe, returning in 1891; she enters New York philanthropic work, works for the Red Cross in Cuba in 1898, is an organizer for the Army Nurse Corps, serves with the Red Cross during World War I, and finds her "niche in women's organizations," campaigning for suffrage; married to a New York music critic and the mother of two, she is also a privately published poet.

24   ALIREZA, MARIANNE
      At the Drop of a Veil.   Boston: Houghton Mifflin, 1971.
      275pp.

      A Californian who married into a prominent Arabian fam-
      ily, she presents lively descriptions of warm family ties and
      of her attempts, successful and unsuccessful, to adjust to
      the role of an Arab woman; her husband divorces her twelve
      years later; she flees with her children.

25   ALLDAY, EVELYN (1903-)
      South Carolina: Evil Shadow; How a Woman's Charges of
      Corruption and Vice Led to Her Commitment to a Mental
      Hospital. New York: Exposition, 1959. 177pp.

      In an emotional, bitter "story of lost freedom," a "Yan-
      kee" tells of her move with her husband to a South Carolina
      boomtown in 1951; a family quarrel with her daughter leads
      to sordid troubles with neighbors and local law officials, and
      malicious rumors culminate in a sanity hearing which results
      in her commitment, degradation, slavery, and torture in a
      mental institution; convinced she's been attacked by a "vice
      ring," she flees to Georgia, unsuccessfully filing complaints
      with the FBI and the Justice Department; while they remain
      unresolved, her life stands still.

26   ALLEN, CATHERINE BLANCHE WARD (1883-)
      Chariot of the Sun, with Harry E. Chrisman.   Denver: Sage
      Books, 1964. 244pp.

      In an account rich in anecdote, she opens with her family
      history, going on to portray the story of her close, idyllic
      family life with her father and stepmother; at six, she tra-
      vels by wagon train to live with an aunt and uncle, but in-
      tense homesickness forces her to join a second wagon train
      to return to her family; in 1893 her family settles on newly
      opened land in Oklahoma, later nearly losing the farm that
      is saved only by her mother's willingness to steal and dis-
      semble for the sake of the family.

27   ALLEN, FLORENCE ELLINWOOD (1884-1966)   NAWM
      To Do Justly. Cleveland: Western Reserve University,
      1965. 201pp.

      A senior U.S. circuit judge tells of her youth and educa-
      tional background which includes school in Berlin, teaching
      in a girls' prep school, earning an M.A. in political sci-
      ence, and being the only woman at the University of Chicago
      Law School; from 1910 to 1920 she campaigns and organizes
      in Ohio for women's suffrage; in 1919 she is the first woman

assistant county prosecutor, in 1922 the first woman on the
Ohio state supreme court, in 1934 the first woman on a
U. S. circuit court of appeals; she describes in detail the
"hard work and many rich rewards" of a distinguished career.

28   ALLEN, GINA
      Rustics for Keeps. New York: Odyssey, 1948. 203pp.

She leaves New York City in 1943 to follow her husband
to his wartime job in Oklahoma; they acquire a farmhouse,
seven acres of land, livestock, and pets; she recounts humorous anecdotes of her initial ignorance but her willingness
to learn leads to a fine sense of satisfaction and belonging
on the land.

29   ALLILUEVA, SVETLANA (1925-)
      Twenty Letters to a Friend, trans. Priscilla Johnson Mc-
      Millan. New York: Harper & Row, 1967. 246pp.

A permanent resident of the U. S., the daughter of Josef
Stalin writes these heartfelt letters in 1963, "bearing witness" to her youth and family life; she describes "fairy
tale" years of innocence and joy with her mother, over-
shadowed by the horror of her mother's later suicide; her
father is a distant figure of authority who becomes further
estranged as his secret police infiltrate the household and
even imprison the man she loves; she tells briefly of the
dreary post-war years, of arrests of family members, of
her flight from Russia leaving behind her son.

30   ALSOP, GULIELMA FELL (1881-)
      April in the Branches. New York: Dutton, 1947. 257pp.

A doctor, she settles in a New England farmhouse with
another professional woman in 1925; the account is a log of
the garden, its beauty and wildness, her intimacy with trees
and flowers and birds, plant collecting; she uses nature as
a source of reflection and contemplation; the account follows
the seasonal progression from April to November.

31   Dear Creek; The Story of a Golden Childhood. New York:
      Vanguard, 1947. 310pp.

She feels a double identity for her vivid family life is
centered both with a Pennsylvania grandmother and with her
parents in Brooklyn; her grandmother's stories evoke the
family's past, and love and security underlie the "great affair of learning to know the world"; she is also devoted to
her minister father who encourages her pursuits in literature

and music and her full enjoyment of the "romantic period" of youth.

32 ALSOP, MARY O'HARA
   see STURE-VASA, MARY ALSOP (1885-1980)

33 ALSOP, SUSAN MARY
   To Marietta from Paris, 1945-1960.   Garden City, N. Y. :
   Doubleday, 1975.   356pp.

   In letters written to her childhood friend, Marietta Tree, from post-war Paris, the young wife of William Patten, the American attaché to the U. S. Embassy, offers lively accounts ranging from dinners with great statesmen to domestic trivia, from gossip to careful political observation.

34 ALTA
   Momma; a start on all the untold stories.   New York:
   Times Change Press, 1974.   76pp.

   Buried in a chronicle of daily minutiae, part of her troubled tale emerges only by "innuendo" as she struggles to be both a writer and a mother; burdened with guilt and insecurity, her frustrations sometimes lead to child abuse; fragmented and expressed in repetitive self-analysis, her impressionistic account "is the photograph of a woman giving birth. "

35 AMES, BLANCHE BUTLER (1847-1939)
   Chronicles from the Nineteenth Century; Family Letters of
   Blanche Butler and Adelbert Ames, Married July 21st, 1870.
   Vol. I.   Clinton, Mass. :   priv. pr. , Colonial Press, 1957.
   719pp.

   Her first letters describe her earnest approach to studies at a Georgetown boarding school, then her concern during the Civil War over her father's safety; in 1870 she sends effusive love letters to her fiancé, then a senator; in marriage she finds a "glorious sense of freedom, " writing long letters to her mother on domestic topics, describing life in the Mississippi governor's mansion after her husband's election in 1873, commenting on her husband's political colleagues, telling of her first two children's development; when she and her husband are apart, she writes daily, interested in his political and business activities; her letters are rich, mature, and highly articulate.

36 Chronicles from the Nineteenth Century; Family Letters of

Blanche Butler and Adelbert Ames, Married July 21st, 1870.
Vol. II.   Clinton, Mass.:   priv. pr., Colonial Press, 1957.
689pp.

Through her nearly daily letters she remains extremely
close to her parents, noting with great pride and joy her
six children's activities and writing with concern about her
husband's political difficulties over racial tensions and weak
colleagues which culminate in his election loss and impeach-
ment; she does not hesitate to give him business and political advice, expressing her disgust in the 1870's with southern white politicians and her concern in the 1880's over
financial matters; in 1898 her husband and two sons serve
in the Spanish-American War, and she nurses them on their
return.

37   AMES, EVELYN PERKINS
        Daughter of the House.   Boston: Houghton Mifflin, 1961.
        241pp.

A writer, she is flooded with memories while closing her
Hartford family home; she journeys through a "world without
time," "meeting herself" as a child, and produces a deli-
cately drawn portrait of her parents and their milieu, a
subtle exploration of the subterranean understandings and
misunderstandings between parent and child; she idolizes her
outgoing father and her volatile mother, enjoying a parade
of literary and cultural figures in her childhood and youth;
the later years of her parents' decline and their deaths are
occasions for cherishing fine memories.

38   A Glimpse of Eden.   Boston: Houghton Mifflin, 1967.
        208pp.

She tells of the East African highlands, "a world, and a
life, from which one comes back changed"; with much sensitivity and reflection, she describes her experiences of the
countryside and her own "atavistic alertness," learning the
land; she tells of extraordinary moments in which she enters
new states of being.

39   In Time Like Glass: Reflections on a Journey in Asia.
        Boston: Houghton Mifflin, 1974.   174pp.

In 1971 she travels extensively with her husband in what
becomes a cultural, inner journey as well as a geographical
one; delighting in human connections, she offers perceptive
descriptions of Eastern religions, deities, temples, and
ceremonies, developing a sense of both a collective conscious and a collective unconscious amid the profound reso-

nances that Iran, Afghanistan, Kashmir, India, and Nepal
hold for her.

40   ANDERSON, CAMILLA MAY (1904-)
      Jan, My Brain-Damaged Daughter.   Portland, Ore.: Dur-
      ham Press, 1963. 188pp.

          An M. D. and psychiatrist, she explores the "meaning of
      Jan's problem" since her family life, social life, and ca-
      reer are all profoundly affected by her daughter's needs;
      free of resentment or self-pity, she devotes much time to
      the child's social and intellectual development and notes the
      indirect effects of the work with her daughter on her own
      psychological theories.

41   ANDERSON, ELIZABETH (1884-)
      Miss Elizabeth: A Memoir, with Gerald R. Kelly.   Boston:
      Little, Brown, 1969. 315pp.

          She describes her childhood and education in Michigan;
      she later becomes the manager of Doubleday's bookstore in
      New York City, and meets many writers; she is the third
      wife of Sherwood Anderson; when she is forty-five, he
      leaves; she moves to Taxco, Mexico and settles permanent-
      ly.

42   ANDERSON, LEILA W. (1898-)
      Pilgrim Circuit Rider, in collaboration with Harriet Harmon
      Dexter. New York: Harper, 1960. 200pp.

          She tells of her love of pioneering and rural life, her
      early desire to become a teacher; after college, teaching in
      Ozarks leads to her ordination and dedication to home mis-
      sionary work; from 1953 she is a circuit rider in Christian
      education in New England, Midwest, on Indian reservations;
      she reveals a combination of common sense and religious
      dedication.

43   ANDERSON, MARGARET CAROLYN (1886-1973)   NAWM
      The Fiery Fountains: The Autobiography: Continuation and
      Crisis to 1950. New York: Hermitage House, 1951. 242pp.

          The book is a sequel to My Thirty Years' War; she re-
      counts her intense inner happiness, living in France with
      singer Georgette Leblanc for over twenty years; much of the
      autobiography is of internal states rather than of external
      events.

44   The Strange Necessity: The Autobiography: Resolutions and
      Reminiscences to 1969.   New York: Horizon, 1970.   223pp.

      Sequel to The Fiery Fountains; she reiterates the theme
      of her life, a war against mundane reality; focus diffused;
      passages on beauty, music, art, friendship, love.

45   ANDERSON, MARIAN (1902-   )
      My Lord, What a Morning.   New York: Viking, 1956.
      312pp.

      A concert and opera singer, she was born in Philadelphia
      and began singing in a church choir; refused admission to a
      conservatory, she begins recital tours; gives first success-
      ful New York concert in 1925; studies in Europe, tours
      Scandinavia; in 1939 she is denied the use of Constitution Hall
      because she is black, sings instead at the Lincoln Memorial;
      closes account with reflections on discrimination, the influ-
      ence of her mother, her debut at the Met in 1955.

46   ANDERSON, MARY (1872-1964)   NAWM
      Women at Work; The Autobiography of Mary Anderson, as
      told to Mary N. Winslow.   Minneapolis: University of Min-
      nesota, 1951.   266pp.

      Having emigrated from Sweden at sixteen, she finds "the
      real beginning of life for me in America" in her organizing
      work with the Women's Trade Union League; an acquaintance
      of Jane Addams (see companion volume), she becomes a
      U.S. citizen in 1915, works for labor legislation in Wash-
      ington, D.C., and is appointed the director of the Women's
      Bureau in the U.S. Department of Labor, working particular-
      ly hard under the New Deal; she discusses unionization,
      equal pay, hours legislation, discrimination, and the Equal
      Rights Amendment; her straightforward narrative illuminates
      "a fine, full life."

47   ANDERSON, OLIVE (1915-   )
      A Wilderness of Wonder.   Minneapolis: Augsburg, 1971.
      160pp.

      With a tone of quiet celebration, she describes her sum-
      mers in the northern Michigan wilderness; building a simple
      cabin with her husband, teen-aged children, and friends, she
      finds deep satisfaction and joy in the solitude and "tremen-
      dous trifles" of forest life and regrets changes brought by
      more building and people; her account, written in the third
      person, includes poems inspired by nature.

48   ANDERSON, ROSA CLAUDETTE
      River, Face Homeward (Suten Dan Wani Hwe Fie): An Afro-
      American in Ghana.   New York: Exposition, 1966.   120pp.

      A black teacher, she reverses her childhood visions of
      an uncivilized Africa when she travels to Ghana with her
      husband and children; in long conversations and dialogues
      with friends, she learns about Ghanian culture, the role of
      women, teaching, churches, and religious life; the account
      ends with her return home.

49   ANDREWS, FANNIE FERN PHILLIPS (1867-1950)   NAW
      Memory Pages of My Life.   Boston: Talisman Press, 1948.
      205pp.

      She is a research scholar and author in international re-
      lations; she tells of her early intellectual impulses and re-
      solve to become a teacher; after six years in teaching, she
      marries and turns to college education at Radcliffe; she en-
      gages in national and international efforts in educational co-
      operation; she earns a Ph. D. in 1923 in international law
      and diplomacy; this is a largely impersonal account of world
      travels and high-level conferences.

50   ANDREWS, GRACE ELEANOR
      The Wind That Blows.   Philadelphia: Dorrance, 1953.
      116pp.

      She writes random memories of pioneering on a series
      of family farms in Missouri and Kansas, and of forty years
      later in Oregon after her marriage; she tells of the dangers
      of loose stock, prairie fire, illness, storms, and adds much
      domestic detail; she begins teaching at sixteen, noting that
      "the school days were golden ones"; after her husband's
      death, she becomes a newspaper reporter.

51   ANGELOU, MAYA (1928-   )
      Gather Together in My Name.   New York: Random House,
      1974.   214pp.

      In this sequel to I Know Why the Caged Bird Sings, she
      sets the scene with post-World War II euphoria; working to
      support her infant son and herself, she is a cook, waitress,
      madam, dancer, and prostitute; she tells of love and dis-
      illusionment against the background of her mother's strength
      and her brother's fierce, supportive love; the account is a
      sensitive story of romantic innocence with an overlay of
      later wisdom.

52   I Know Why the Caged Bird Sings.   New York: Random
        House, 1969.   281pp.

        Some striking vignettes, laced with fine humor and warmth,
        illuminate her early childhood with a revered brother at her
        grandmother's home in Stamps, Arkansas; she later lives
        with her mother and mother's family, powers in St. Louis;
        she moves from a denial of her race and the trauma of
        rape at eight and teen-age doubts about her femininity to
        her strong identity as Black and as Woman; the account ends
        with the birth of her son when she is seventeen; later she
        becomes a writer, dancer, and actress.

53   Singin' and Swingin' and Gettin' Merry Like Christmas.
        New York: Random House, 1976.   269pp.

        In the third volume of her autobiography, she writes
        about her misery separated from her son since she must
        work; she marries a white man but finds marriage limiting
        as her sensuality finds release in the black church; jobs as
        a bar dancer and night club singer lead to sudden popular-
        ity; she is the lead dancer for Porgy and Bess on a Euro-
        pean tour in 1954 and describes the white European response
        to a black company; her career continues in Paris night
        clubs; "music was my refuge."

54   ANGIER, VENA
        At Home in the Woods; Living the Life of Thoreau Today,
        with Bradford Angier.   New York: Sheridan House, 1951.
        255pp.

        A theatrical producer married to a writer, she leaves
        Boston with her husband to pioneer in the Alaska wilderness,
        build her own log cabin, explore, share the work and the
        beauty, and live off the country; she sprinkles appropriate
        quotations from Thoreau throughout; they return permanently
        to the wilderness after a brief visit to "civilization."

55   ANTHONY, ALBA RIEK (1879-   )
        Here Am I: A Christian Autobiography.   New York: Green-
        wich, 1957.   171pp.

        In an account sprinkled with Biblical quotations, she pre-
        sents random recollections of a poverty-ridden childhood in
        the rural South; she joins the Baptist Church in 1896, mar-
        ries in 1899, is widowed in 1937; she notes years of hard
        work, strong family ties, and her unceasing efforts to win
        others to Christianity.

56   ANTHONY, SUSAN BROWNELL (1916-)
      The Ghost in My Life.   Washington Depot, Conn.:   Chosen
      Books, 1971.   221pp.

      An author, journalist, and broadcaster, she describes
      the lifelong influence of her great-aunt and namesake; she
      candidly tells of her struggles with alcoholism; her left-
      liberal activities in the 1940's lead to a McCarthy era sub-
      poena and her rejection of U.S. citizenship; her account
      ends on a note of spiritual revelation.

57   Survival Kit.   New York: New American Library, 1972.
      176pp.

      Noting her "rather stormy personal history" which in-
      cludes alcoholism, several broken marriages, harassment
      during the McCarthy years, threatened deportation, steril-
      ity, and a near-fatal accident, she nevertheless is able to
      transcend suffering through her spiritual awakening; inspired
      by the examples of some acquaintances, she learns positive
      patterns of thought and behavior, prays, and exhorts others
      to avail themselves of the same help.

58   ANTON, RITA
      Pleasant Company Accepted.   Garden City, N.Y.:   Double-
      day, 1964.   213pp.

      Her account is a series of nostalgic vignettes of Catholic
      family life; turning first to her childhood, she portrays her
      mother as "the hub and center of all our activities"; her
      father's affection for Chicago is transferred to his children
      as they absorb museums, sights, movies, and books; she
      has warm memories of a Catholic boarding high school;
      married, with five children of her own, she presents a fond
      portrait of her husband and describes a home full of vitality
      and hospitality.

59   ARMER, LAURA ADAMS (1874-)
      In Navajo Land.   New York: McKay, 1962.   107pp.

      A professional photographer who becomes a writer and
      painter, she is drawn to the dramatic northern Arizona land-
      scape, living first with a trader and later in an isolated
      canyon camp where she is visited briefly by her husband and
      adult son; she absorbs Navajo and Hopi folklore and studies
      Indian art and sandpainting from 1924 to 1928; she earns the
      respect of the Indians with her art and her deep response to
      their culture.

60   ARMS, SUZANNE
       A Season to Be Born.   New York: Harper & Row, 1973.
       112pp.

       This introspective, rhapsodic book consists of a young
       woman's musings during her first pregnancy; she closes
       with the birth of her daughter; the book includes photographs
       by her husband.

61   ARMSTRONG, APRIL OURSLER (1926-   )
       House with a Hundred Gates.   New York: McGraw-Hill,
       1965.   286pp.

       A writer of books on religious topics tells of her two
       lives: her youth and her maturity after joining the Catholic
       Church in 1948; her mother is an actress, writer, and re-
       ligious editor, and her father is a writer and editor; her
       mother's alcoholism marks an end to her stimulating child-
       hood and she buries herself in reading and writing, although
       with little self-confidence; she describes her touching reac-
       quaintance with her mother, and with her father after his
       conversion to Catholicism; she serves a long literary ap-
       prenticeship under her father and becomes a Catholic con-
       vert herself, finding that writing is as necessary to her life
       as are her husband and seven children; she takes great
       satisfaction in her father's legacy, finishing a major book
       of his; she later becomes a member of a Franciscan "third
       order" with her family's support.

62   ARMSTRONG, JANE SOTSFORD
       Discovery in Stone.   New York: East Woods Press, 1975.
       44pp.

       After two marriages and a false start in journalism, she
       becomes a stone carver at forty; she tells of "the joy of
       creativity" and of her feelings for stone, describing various
       pieces; settled in Vermont, she is the recipient of numerous
       awards.

63   ARMSTRONG, JOANNA NEUMAN (1915-   )
       A European Excursion; From the Mediterranean to the Alps.
       New York: Carlton Press, 1966.   85pp.

       This is a largely impersonal account of her travels and
       sightseeing in Greece, Turkey, Italy, Austria, Switzerland,
       France, Spain, and Portugal; she writes in the first person
       plural.

64   ARMSTRONG, RUTH GALLUP
      Sisters Under the Sari.   Ames, Iowa: Iowa State University
      Press, 1964.   498pp.

      In a straightforward account with a wealth of detail, this
      collector of Kashmir shawls tells of her close companionship
      with an Indian woman; adopted as an older sister, she tra-
      vels to India where she receives a warm welcome, makes
      friends "from high to low," and obtains intimate glimpses
      of Indian customs and family life.

65   ARNETT, JEAN
      Out of the Mist.   Detroit: Dramar, 1961.   139pp.

      In an exuberant account of travels with her husband, son,
      and daughter in ten European countries, she tells first of
      her preparations by reading and studying, then of her en-
      thusiastic receptiveness to new sights and experiences, find-
      ing "a simple joy and verve in living," learning and growing
      throughout the trip.

66   ARNOLD, MARY ELLICOTT
      In the Land of the Grasshopper Song; A Story of Two Girls
      in Indian Country in 1908-1909, with Mabel Reed.   New
      York: Vantage, 1957.   313pp.

      Employed by the U.S. Indian Service as "field matrons"
      to "civilize the Indians," she and a companion apply their
      youth and spirit to frontier conditions in northern California;
      uncertain about their duties, they decide to be schoolmarms,
      offer medical assistance when they can, and gingerly intro-
      duce some white customs on Christmas and July 4; they es-
      tablish close friendships with the people, feeling more "In-
      dian" than white and grieving when they must leave; this de-
      lightful account was written in 1909.

67   ARNY, MARY TRAVIS
      Seasoned with Salt.   Philadelphia: Westminster, 1954.
      230pp.

      A naturalist, she portrays her childhood in a vivacious
      extended family for whom "life was meant to be savored and
      enjoyed"; she has intense admiration for her parents, who
      encourage her "hoyden heart"; after gaining a college educa-
      tion, she marries in 1938 and her "passionate affection for
      life and living" carries her through motherhood; she is pro-
      foundly moved by the horror of World War II; the deaths of
      two aunts and her father alter her life's balance.

68   ARTHUR, MARY ELIZABETH HILL (1916-   )
        Rebel Nurse.   New York: Comet Press, 1959.   134pp.

        In an unfocused account with no visible "rebellion," she
        opens with random childhood memories, then tells anecdotes
        from her years in nurses' training; graduating in 1938, she
        continues to be hampered by a frail constitution but joins
        the army and sees duty in England during World War II; she
        closes with a near-fatal illness followed by her marriage in
        1946.

69   ASHLEY, DAISY H.
        A Cowgirl's Ups and Downs.   Philadelphia: Dorrance, 1972.
        107pp.

        A "city girl" with no knowledge of cattle ranching, she
        marries a Colorado rancher and goes on to learn about
        horseback riding, haying, cooking in large quantities,
        weather-related crises, setting hens, livestock, blizzards
        and frostbite, and caring for her seriously ill husband; with
        warmth and good humor, she describes a close partnership.

70   ASTOR, BROOKE RUSSELL
        Patchwork Child: Memoir of Mrs. Vincent Astor.   New
        York: Harper, 1962.   224pp.

        She is the child of a peripatetic career Marine officer;
        a term in pre-revolutionary Peking is recalled with special
        affection; she covers childhood to age 16, just before her
        marriage.

71   ASTOR, MARY (1906-   )
        A Life on Film.   New York: Delacorte, 1971.   245pp.

        Pushed into silent films by her parents and tightly chap-
        eroned, she gives a film-by-film and colleague-by-colleague
        account of her growth into a skilled actress and of her strong
        commitment to work; she covers much the same ground as
        in My Story, but this book is more impersonal.

72   My Story: An Autobiography.   Garden City, N.Y.: Double-
        day, 1959.   332pp.

        An actress recounts her career in films, from silent
        movies to television; she places much emphasis on a suc-
        cession of husbands and lovers; she describes the gradual
        onset of alcoholism and her struggle against it which in-
        cludes her first tentative steps in the Catholic faith.

73   ATHAS, DAPHNE (1923-)
        Greece by Prejudice.   Philadelphia: Lippincott, 1962.
        284pp.

            "A quester," this American daughter combines tourism
        and homecoming when she joins her flamboyant Greek father
        in Greece in 1958; after dizzying explorations, she travels
        to the village of relatives, finding communication of the
        blood amid the complex social life of the extended family;
        writing in short descriptive sentences but with an eye for
        detail, the bizarre, and the symbolic, she recounts the
        drama of a typhoon that brings death and destruction to the
        village; allowed the intimacy of her family's grief, she is
        enmeshed in the family network and finds her final departure
        intensely emotional.

74   ATKINSON, ORIANA TORREY
        Manhattan and Me.   Indianapolis: Bobbs-Merrill, 1954.
        267pp.

            A writer, she presents lively and affectionate descriptions
        of the "vexatious city," her home town; she grows up in
        Greenwich Village when it is a solid, middle-class community
        and her explorations as a young woman give her an intimacy
        with all parts of Manhattan; married to a drama critic, she
        tells of Broadway theater life; she also describes the rigors
        of shopping, the joys of collecting antiques, and the demo-
        cratic appeal of the New York Public Library.

75   Over at Uncle Joe's; Moscow and Me.   Indianapolis: Bobbs-
        Merrill, 1947.   325pp.

            She tells of "ten grubby, tiresome, frustrated and fas-
        cinating months" in Moscow as the wife of a foreign cor-
        respondent; she offers entertaining anecdotes of language
        study, hotel life, shopping, people, women workers, chil-
        dren, but studiously avoids discussion of political matters.

76   The South and the West of It: Ireland and Me.   New York:
        Random House, 1956.   303pp.

            Long fascinated with Ireland, she writes a light, humorous
        account of her trip to Ireland with a friend; she describes
        "leprechaun headquarters," the Irish people, sightseeing in
        Dublin, and she includes some historical notes.

77   ATWILL, MARTHA THORNSBERRY
        Thy Will Be Done.   New York: Carlton Press, 1962.
        118pp.

The daughter of a large pioneer family in the Ozarks, she is constantly reminded that she is "the ugly black sheep"; she is given heavy domestic responsibilities and cares for two invalid brothers, later supporting the thankless family with her millinery business; she marries to find love and establish an independent life of her own; her strong religious faith and shrewd business sense support her through numerous familial trials and tribulations, and she continues her pattern of helping others.

78   ATWILL, MATTIE THORNSBERRY
       see ATWILL, MARTHA THORNSBERRY

79   AUER, FRANCES LEVENIA
       God, the Devil, and the Woman in Between, by Dorothy
       Coffee.   New York: Vantage, 1966.   96pp.

She presents a sordid tale of childhood poverty, violence, and sexual abuse; she marries at sixteen and bears three children to a cruel, drunken husband; "sick in soul and heart," she attempts suicide and can only gain a divorce in desperation by giving up her children, a tactic which leads to years of struggle over child custody; predictably, she is later afflicted with mental illness.

80   AUSTIN, BARBARA LESLIE
       Sad Nun at Synanon.   New York: Holt, Rinehart and Win-
       ston, 1970.   186pp.

She first visits Synanon in 1968 to understand "urban problems," then accepts a job there teaching children; in slangy style, she describes the intensity and verbal violence of group sessions; she explores her own religious vocation, her sexuality, but ultimately returns to the convent and to other commitments.

81   AUSTIN, ETHEL L.
       A Babe in the Woods.   New York: Vantage, 1965.   61pp.

A teacher presents a memoir of herself as a five-year-old written in a childlike style; the daughter of a Swedish minister in rural Michigan, she portrays simple times in a close family, noting a child's misunderstandings of the adult world; family struggles are masked by a child's incomprehension of their magnitude; she closes with the family's move to another pastorate.

82   AVAKIAN, ELIZABETH (1943-)
        To Deliver Me of My Dreams.   Millbrae, Cal.:   Celestial
        Arts, 1975.   91pp.

        Her book begins as a journal, then becomes an M. A.
        thesis in psychology in 1972; she explores her identity as a
        woman in a saga of painful but exciting self-discovery; rec-
        ognizing her need for risk and adventure and passing through
        the crisis of marriage and divorce, she overcomes socially
        imposed barriers to self-fulfillment; she is deeply influenced
        by Anaïs Nin (see entry #1520).

83   AYE, LILLIAN (1909-)
        Iran Caboose.   Hollywood, Cal.:   House-Warven, 1951.
        190pp.

        In a humorous account, she tells of two years as a Red
        Cross worker in Iran during World War II; she tells of "both
        mental and physical adjustments," the stench and filth, des-
        ert heat and winter cold, her own romance and marriage;
        she later suffers from malaria and mental depression but
        returns home with her sense of humor intact.

84   AYRAULT, EVELYN WEST (1922-)
        Take One Step.   Garden City, N. Y.:   Doubleday, 1963.
        310pp.

        A psychologist handicapped by cerebral palsy, she recog-
        nizes as a "precious gift" the strenuous physical training
        and normal life demanded by her parents; she notes her
        drive for perfection yet her intense self-consciousness, the
        tension as she works toward independence, her coping with
        rejection when employers fear her handicap; she gradually
        achieves self-acceptance and finds great personal satisfac-
        tion in her work with cerebral palsied children.

85   BABB, SANORA (1907-)
An Owl on Every Post. New York: McCall, 1970. 217pp.

With a family move to a Colorado homestead in 1913,
she becomes a dugout pioneer, tasting isolation and poverty
as well as "the strange splendor of this vast wild land";
she notes the quiet courage of her mother, the appeal of
her eccentric grandfather, and the hardships that come with
their first harvest and first winter; her later move into
town for school brings great changes as she is thrust "back
into the world."

86   BABITZ, EVE (1943-)
Eve's Hollywood. New York: Delacourt, 1974. 296pp.

She writes a tale of life in Hollywood; her childhood is
spent with her violinist father among musical people; she
breaks away to a teen culture in the 1950's, describing her
youth in vignettes of junior and senior high school; she
writes in an impressionistic, choppy style.

87   BACKUS, HENNY
What Are You Doing After the Orgy?, with Jim Backus.
Englewood Cliffs, N.J.: Prentice-Hall, 1962. 182pp.

An actress, she writes some sections of this light, humorous account of the chaos and misadventures in her marriage to undomesticated actor Jim Backus; included are anecdotes of their appearances on "This Is Your Life" and "Person to Person" as well as tales from parties and from a
European trip.

88   BAEHR, CONSUELO SAAH
Report from the Heart. New York: Simon and Schuster,
1976. 192pp.

The book is a painful account of "an ordinary day in our
life," gradually revealing her emotions as a wife and mother;
she reflects on her relationships with her mother and her
husband, noting "I am the only one who knows I'm not doing
well"; routine events trigger memories, fears, insecurity,

feelings of suffocation, isolation, immobilization, inadequacy, and sexual dissatisfaction.

89   BAER, JEAN L. (1926-   )
      Follow Me! New York: Macmillan, 1965. 302pp.

      She describes the delights of traveling abroad alone, drawing on her experiences from sixteen trips in thirteen years all over the world; an outgoing tourist, succumbing to "the lure of the offbeat," she enjoys her independence, loves meeting people, and offers travel advice to other single women.

90   BAEZ, JOAN
      Daybreak. New York: Dial, 1968. 159pp.

      She offers an impressionistic series of portraits and vignettes, including passages on her mother, her father, spiritual love, her commitment to non-violence, her music, and her dreams.

91   BAGUEDOR, EVE
      Separation; Journal of a Marriage. New York: Simon and Schuster, 1972. 219pp.

      Separation from her husband of twenty years becomes "the central fact of my life"; intensely introspective, she examines the loss of the "delicate balance" of her identity, the panic of financial pressures, her loneliness, her sexuality both within the marriage and during the separation, the effects of the separation on her two daughters, and her courtroom experiences; finally, with greater self-awareness, she decides to rejoin her husband.

92   BAHR, EDITH-JANE
      Everybody Wins, Nobody Loses (Advice from a Mother Who Survived). New York: McKay, 1968. 130pp.

      She offers random humorous reflections on family life after eighteen years of marriage and four children; defending the housewife without a career, she describes housecleaning, discipline, pets, the children's schooldays, illnesses, babysitters, and "the magnificent bewilderment of motherhood."

93   BAILEY, EMMA
      Sold to the Lady in the Green Hat. New York: Dodd, Mead, 1962. 213pp.

After a move to Vermont for her husband's health, she is drawn to local auctions; "America's first woman auctioneer," she enters the profession in 1950 to aid the family finances; she demonstrates a love of auction psychology, atmosphere, and stories.

94   BAILEY, HELEN L.
      Jeep Tracks. New York: Friendship Press, 1954. 87pp.

A Baptist missionary in southern India, she describes "village evangelism" as she travels by jeep to remote areas; her anecdotes reveal a deep respect for the people as she offers portraits of her Indian students and colleagues.

95   BAILEY, PEARL (1918-)
      Pearl's Kitchen; An Extraordinary Cookbook.   New York:
      Harcourt Brace Jovanovich, 1973.   211pp.

The well-known singer and entertainer writes that her kitchen is "a kind of temple for me," a special place for family sharing, shadowed by memories of her mother; noting the emotional satisfactions and joys of cooking, she includes recipes which are embellished by anecdotes of friends, times, and places; a vivacious woman who struggles to moderate her hectic pace, she writes down-to-earth descriptions of managing her career while maintaining the "private sanctuary" of her home.

96   The Raw Pearl. New York: Harcourt, Brace & World,
      1968.   206pp.

The account begins with her childhood and covers her career as a singer and actress beginning with her first amateur night success at fifteen; she marries several times, the last to Louis Bellson, a jazz musician, and raises two adopted children; she comments on entertainment, racism, "some of the things I've learned about life" in this story about drive, warmth, and love.

97   Talking to Myself. New York: Harcourt Brace Jovanovich,
      Inc., 1971.   233pp.

She presents free-wheeling, sometimes preachy observations, vignettes, and poems on life, love, ego, inspiration, and other topics in a loosely organized account.

98   BAIRD, MARGARET E. (1879-)
      The Rainbow My Goal; The Autobiography of Margaret E.
      Baird. New York: Exposition, 1962. 139pp.

After a rural Tennessee childhood, her strong desire for
an education leads her to college and schoolteaching, rejecting marriage because it interferes with her ultimate ambition to clerk in a big city store; later she does marry and
works in a recorder's office to raise and educate her two
sons after she is widowed; her travels in the U.S. and Europe close this awkward account.

99   BAIRD, MOLLIE ELNORA
     Sole Treading.   Fort Worth, Tex.:   Texas Graphic Corp.,
     1964.   228pp.

A missionary in India for nearly thirty years opens her
account with her arrival there in 1926; each chapter is a
vignette, portraying her efforts to bring the message of
Christianity to the Hindu villagers, contrasting Christian
beliefs with "heathen worship" and Indian culture; the account is rather impersonal and she refers to herself as "the
Missionary."

100 BAKER, ADELAIDE N.
     Return to Arcady.   New York: Lawrence Hill, 1973.   162pp.

In her youth, her family buys a Connecticut home to
serve as a summer retreat from New York City, and it becomes a place of peace and joy, a repository of fine memories; she discovers the world of nature which feeds her
creativity; the home serves as a focus for a spirited family
life, a base for her during her college years at Radcliffe,
and a source for continuing family unity when the children
marry and move.

101 BAKER, GLADYS
     I Had to Know.   New York: Appleton-Century-Crofts, 1961.
     309pp.

A southern belle, with a "secret contempt" for social life,
she turns to a "career of international journalism"; she interviews prominent European political figures in the years
from 1936 to 1941; she then finds deep fulfillment in marriage; a serious illness and the "half world of invalidism"
lead to religious searching and her conversion to Catholicism
in 1950.

102 BAKER, LOUISE MAXWELL (1909-   )
     Out on a Limb.   New York: McGraw-Hill, 1946.   213pp.

Flippantly this writer, reporter, and teacher tells of "a
unique adventure in living" after having a leg amputated at

eight; she becomes "energetic and athletic," using an arti-
ficial limb, crutches, or a peg leg at various times, and
swimming, playing tennis, and riding; she writes of travels
in Europe and of two marriages.

103   Snips and Snails. New York: McGraw-Hill, 1953. 202pp.

She writes a warm and humorous account of one year during the depression as the only woman teacher at an Arizona
private boys' school; she notes her maternal flutterings and
"love at first sight" for the boys; her anecdotes describe
the boys' various personalities and problems to which she
responds with attention and affection; she is shattered by the
accidental death of a fellow teacher with whom she is in
love; she closes with commencement.

104   BAKER, TRUDY (pseud.) (1942-   )
        The Coffee, Tea, or Me? Girls' 'Round the World Diary,
        with Rachel Jones (pseud.). New York: Grosset & Dunlap,
        1970. 247pp.

International flight stewardesses, they "continue the man-
hunt at 30,000 feet"; their tantalizing experiences are replete
with sexual opportunity flippantly avoided; they describe adventures in Copenhagen, Paris, Berlin, Moscow, London,
Rome, Tel Aviv; a lightweight account.

105   Coffee, Tea, or Me? The Uninhibited Memoirs of Two Air-
        line Stewardesses, with Rachel Jones (pseud.). New York:
        Bartholomew House, 1967. 288pp.

She attends stewardess school to escape home, and writes
breezy titillating tales of passengers and fellow crew members; "meeting men is the name of the stewardess game."

106   BAKEWELL, MARY ELLA (1868-   )
        What Woman Is Here? New York: Oxford, 1949. 250pp.

A social worker and missionary interested in women's
rights and children's rights, she becomes a minister in her
fifties and settles in a small western town in the 1920's;
she describes the local poverty and dirt, visiting parishioners, participation in holiday celebrations, and her struggles
with male superiors; disillusioned, she is nevertheless sorrowful at having to leave.

107   BALCH, EMILY TAPSCOTT CLARK (1893-1953)
        Ingenue Among the Lions: The Letters of Emily Clark to

Joseph Hergesheimer, ed. Gerald Langford. Austin: University of Texas, 1965. 221pp.

She is a journalist and writer, editor of The Reviewer, a magazine of the 1920's that contributed to the literary renaissance of the South; her letters include gossip and literary opinions, press for advice and contributions; much about Cabell, Mencken, and Van Vechten.

108   BALDRIGE, LETITIA
Juggling: The Art of Balancing Marriage, Motherhood, and Career. New York: Viking, 1976. 270pp.

With immense vitality and phenomenal organizational skills, she copes with the demands, excitement, and rewards of multiple roles; after a series of fortunate jobs (see previous accounts), she settles in her own public relations business and enjoys the challenge of the lecture circuit which keeps her in touch with the world beyond New York City; she is sustained by deliberate periodic self-pampering and a sense of humor.

109   Of Diamonds and Diplomats: An Autobiography of a Happy Life. Boston: Houghton Mifflin, 1968. 337pp.

She holds positions as the social secretary to U.S. ambassadors in Paris and Rome, the publicity director for Tiffany's, and the social secretary to Jacqueline Kennedy at the White House; she later establishes her own public relations firm in Chicago; her account is unabashedly light and lively.

110   Roman Candle. Boston: Houghton Mifflin, 1956. 308pp.

The product of an "extra-happy, highly extroverted, and very secure family," and Vassar educated, she chooses secretarial training as her passport to life in Europe; settling in Paris in 1948, she spends an enthusiastic three years as the social secretary to the U.S. Ambassador to France; in love with Italy, she then becomes the social secretary to newly-appointed Ambassador Clare Booth Luce and describes the grueling pace, the drama, the tragedy, and the gentle comedy of her position; she takes unabashed pleasure in the luxurious, glamorous life and provides a portrait of her extraordinary boss; after eight glorious years abroad, she returns to the U.S.

111   BALDWIN, FAITH
see CUTHRELL, FAITH BALDWIN (1893-1978)

112   BALLARD, BETTINA HILL (1905?-1961)
        In My Fashion.   New York: McKay, Inc. , 1960.   312pp.

        Having "stumbled into fashion," she writes and edits for
        Vogue for twenty years, assigned to the Paris office before,
        during, and after World War II; she works for the Red
        Cross during the war; she focuses on personalities in the
        fashion world.

113   BALLENTINE, FRANCES GRISWOLD
        Tiger at the Door.   New York: Vantage, 1958.   87pp.

        She recalls her years in Malaya from 1926 to 1928, new-
        ly married to a businessman; adaptable and receptive to a
        new culture, she describes local sights and customs, social
        life and entertainment, and her home and servants; after her
        daughter's birth, she moves to Java, noting her observations
        during extensive travels; she and her family return to the
        U. S. in 1929, the "end of an era."

114   BALPH, FLORENCE
        Beyond Romance: A True Story from the Heart of India.
        Rev. ed. , Boston: Christopher, 1954.   134pp.

        She is a missionary in northern India with her husband
        and infant son; accepted by the local Rajah, she tells of
        some conversions but also of her "desperate loneliness"
        when she's ostracized; she returns to the U. S. because of
        failing health.

115   BALSAN, CONSUELO VANDERBILT (1877-1964)
        The Glitter and the Gold.   New York: Harper, 1952.
        336pp.

        Born into New York's "400," her childhood of luxury,
        mansions, and travel is solitary and unhappy, marred by
        the domination of her mother; in 1896 she enters a "mar-
        riage of convenience" to the Duke of Marlborough arranged
        by her mother; lonely and insecure amid the restrictions of
        her social obligations, she bears two sons, but separates
        from her husband after eleven years; she turns to philanth-
        ropy, supporting higher education for women, child welfare,
        and woman suffrage; in 1921 she marries a Frenchman for
        love, continuing her philanthropic activities and upper-class
        social life until the German invasion of France forces them
        to flee to Spain.

116   BANFILL, B. J.
        Labrador Nurse.   Philadelphia: Macrae Smith, 1953.   256pp.

A missionary nurse, she first settles among the coastal fisherfolk in 1928; with a sinking heart, she serves a taciturn people and struggles against ignorance; but she is drawn to the beauty of the wilderness and develops a warm interest in the people; after having left for a time, she returns in 1942 and notes the changes wrought by World War II.

117   BANKHEAD, TALLULAH (1902-1968)   NAWM
       Tallulah.   New York: Harper, 1952.   335pp.

She opens with a breathless, free-form first chapter; claiming she hates the drudgery of acting, she recounts engagements on stage and screen, bad and good, "to get my record straight"; her autobiography is an extended monologue, full of characters, including the legend of Tallulah herself.

118   BARANET, NANCY NEIMAN
       The Turned Down Bar.   Philadelphia: Dorrance, 1964.
       81pp.

A bicycle road racer whose career begins at 18 writes of her coaches, intense self discipline, and "tremendous ego," all leading to the U. S. Women's National Championship in 1953, 1954, 1956, and 1957; she describes in detail her eight days as the only American in a French women's road race, a competitive peak in her career; after her return to the U. S. and her marriage in 1958, she retires from racing but serves the sport in organizations.

119   BARBER, OLIVE
       The Lady and the Lumberjack.   New York: Crowell, 1952.
       250pp.

A schoolteacher on vacation, she succumbs to the "concentrated wooing" of an Oregon logger; married life broadens her respect for differing kinds of knowledge and of people; at home on a "floathouse," she learns logging slang and operations and develops a deep affection for loggers.

120   Meet Me in Juneau.   Portland, Ore.:   Binfords & Mort,
       1960.   175pp.

A writer, she tells of twelve years of Alaskan summers, first engaged in commercial fishing, then living in logging camps and mill towns with her husband after their sons are grown; captivated by the way of life and by the natural setting, she also enjoys the characters among the men and women they meet; she travels alone in northern Alaska on

her first book's royalties; she closes with the unexpected
death of her husband.

121   BARBOSA, DIAN RUY
       Love Is His Co-Pilot; A Jungle-Hopping Honeymoon.   New
       York: Exposition, 1951.   147pp.

       She marries a Brazilian aviator, "sharing danger, adven-
ture" on their honeymoon ferrying a plane across Mexico,
Guatemala, Nicaragua, Panama, Colombia, and Venezuela;
she closes with their arrival in Brazil.

122   BARD, LORI
       Hello! World.   Los Angeles: Mara Books, 1970.   112pp.

       In a pleasant account, written partly in the present tense,
a young schoolteacher gives in to her "passion to live in
Europe" and tells of two years abroad; she teaches in Paris,
and travels in France, Scandinavia, Tunisia, Spain, Yugoslavia, Greece, Israel, and Holland; she welcomes new
sights and people, missing the usual tourist spots to soak
up the details of European daily life.

123   BARD, MARY
       The Doctor Wears Three Faces.   Philadelphia: Lippincott,
       1949.   254pp.

       In an entertaining account, she describes her courtship
and marriage to a young doctor; she soon learns the draw-
backs of being a doctor's wife which include constant dis-
ruptions, automatic membership in a group of doctors' wives
known as the "Neglected Ones," and a woeful lack of drama
in her first pregnancy; she focuses on the domestic details
of being a harried but earnest wife and mother.

124   Forty Odd.   Philadelphia: Lippincott, 1952.   353pp.

       The wife of a doctor writes a humorous account of life
after forty; with no audience for martyrdom, she prepares
for the "Change of Life," and throws herself into community
service, exercise, new clothes, sports, Brownies, Great
Books, and piano lessons.

125   Just Be Yourself.   Philadelphia: Lippincott, 1956.   255pp.

       A doctor's wife and mother of three daughters finds her-
self inexorably drawn into her post as a Brownie leader in
this humorous account; in the midst of active young girls,

she is alternately charmed and exasperated, noting the rewards and psychic costs of working with the children and
their mothers.

126   BARKINS, EVELYN WERNER (1918-   )
       The Doctor Has a Baby.   New York: Creative Age, 1947.
       230pp.

       Determined to retain her identity through the experiences
       of motherhood, she tackles tradition and the experts--books,
       doctors, nurses, and grandmothers--with the strong arm of
       common sense; she describes child-rearing, infant sociali-
       zation, nursery school, illnesses, and vacations with a light
       touch.

127   The Doctor Has a Family.   New York: Pellegrini & Cudahy,
       1950.   211pp.

       In this humorous look at the "All-American Family" and
       the "American Home," this former lawyer and mother of
       three attacks the pronouncements of the experts with wit and
       exaggeration, offering the antidote of "common sense and
       love"; her anecdotes touch on demand feeding, progressive
       education, and the suburban dream house; she tells of "end-
       less detours" when writing her first book (see above).

128   Four Children for the Doctor.   New York: Frederick Fell,
       1955.   223pp.

       A lawyer, wife, and mother presents an entertaining ac-
       count of her fourth pregnancy, presided over by her three
       children with "excruciating interest"; she is overwhelmed by
       advice from her daughters, "maddening meddlers"; prepara-
       tion of baby equipment brings a flood of memories, under-
       scoring the uniqueness of each pregnancy and birth; her fourth
       child is truly the family's baby.

129   I Love My Doctor.   New York: Crowell, 1948.   238pp.

       In this lighthearted account, the wife of a struggling young
       intern notes that "being married was lots of fun"; she makes
       gentle jibes at lapses in marital bliss, "playing house," wait-
       ing for patients; the book ends with her first pregnancy.

130   BARKLEY, JANE RUCKER (1912?-1964)
       I Married the Veep, as told to Frances Spatz Leighton.
       New York: Vanguard, 1958.   316pp.

In a lively, unpretentious account, she describes the intense courtship of Vice President Barkley after their meeting in 1949; widowed with two daughters to support and a
modest, guarded person, she finds the glare of publicity
upsetting and is concerned by the great difference in their
ages; she takes on "new and awesome responsibilities" as
the Vice President's wife and enjoys friendships among the
prominent; after her "political baptism" in the 1950 campaign, she supports both his brief retirement and his subsequent term as a senator; her chronicle of "seven years
of happiness" ends with his death from a sudden heart attack.

131   BARLOW, LEILA MAE
        Across the Years: Memoirs.   Montgomery, Ala.:   Paragon,
        1959.   84pp.

        A black teacher tells of 32 years on the English depart-
        ment faculty at Alabama State College beginning in 1924;
        she recounts fond memories of students, extension work,
        struggles to raise the educational standards for blacks, work
        with a drama club, community and church work, travels in
        the U.S. and in Europe; she writes at the time of her re-
        tirement.

132   BARLOW, SANNA MORRISON
        Light Is Sown. Chicago: Moody Press, 1956.   188pp.

        She is one of a team of three missionary women who
        produce tapes and records of gospel messages in numerous
        languages for non-literate people; working in Africa in 1954
        and 1955, she responds vigorously to the challenge posed in
        Kenya by Mau Mau activities; with unbounded enthusiasm she
        travels by jeep to remote tribes, contacting speakers and
        playing recordings, searching for new languages with which
        to continue the crusade.

133   BARNARD, MAUDE EDMUNDSON BANISTER
        Within the Walls of Peking. New York: Vantage, 1973.
        62pp.

        The wife of an army attaché at the U.S. legation writes
        of the "joyous years" from 1923 to 1927 in Peking; after a
        brief historical sketch, she writes of the city's combination
        of poverty and charm, of international social life, of her
        relations with the servants, and of civil unrest during their
        stay.

134   BARNES, RUTH
       Pleasure Was My Business, by Madame Sherry (pseud.), as
       told to S. Robert Tralins.   New York: Lyle Stuart, 1961.
       220pp.

       In a brash, slangy style, she tells of her twenty-five
       years as "undisputed Queen of all the Madams"; opening
       her first house in 1929 in Miami, she caters to royalty,
       professional men, and politicians; as a shrewd business-
       woman, she handles raids, publicity, "hard work and long
       hours" with self-proclaimed honesty and flair; ultimately she
       admits that the luxury masks some disreputable activities.

135   BARNETT, IDA B. WELLS (1869-1931)   NAW
       Crusade for Justice: The Autobiography of Ida B. Wells,
       ed. Alfreda M. Duster.   Chicago: University of Chicago
       Press, 1970.   434pp.

       Born into slavery and orphaned at fourteen, she cares
       for her younger siblings, teaches school, is a "voracious
       reader"; she becomes a Memphis journalist, then a news-
       paper owner and editor but loses her paper in the fight
       against lynching; she is a public speaker and an early or-
       ganizer for the black women's club movement and the
       NAACP; she travels in England speaking against lynching;
       after marriage and motherhood, she continues her career
       in journalism and public life; she vigorously protests the
       treatment of black soldiers during World War I.

136   BARNEY, MAGINEL WRIGHT (1877-   )
       The Valley of the God-Almighty Joneses.   New York: Apple-
       ton-Century, 1965.   156pp.

       The sister of architect Frank Lloyd Wright presents a
       superb evocation of her Wisconsin valley "magnificently
       peopled with the grown-ups of our family"; she provides
       some background on her Welsh grandparents, then describes
       her mother, "emancipated" and "formidable," who focuses
       her obsession with education on her son, although both chil-
       dren spend their formative years on the combination home-
       school-farm.

137   BARRETT, FLORENCE E.
       A Pocket in a Petticoat: Memoirs.   Hicksville, New York:
       Exposition, 1974.   80pp.

       Each chapter is a nostalgic vignette of childhood in a
       small midwestern village, written with great affection; she
       tells of her family's routines and adventures; she provides

a sensitive portrait of her grandmother around whom family
legends center and who typifies independent "country women."

138   BARRETT, RAINA (1936-)
       First Your Money, Then Your Clothes; My Life and Oh!
       Calcutta! New York: Morrow, 1973.   166pp.

       This former high school English teacher, divorced and
       the mother of two sons, writes an account of rewards and
       pains of being in the cast of Oh! Calcutta!; she includes a
       brief note on her childhood and later marriage.

139   BARRETT, RONA (1936-)
       Miss Rona; An Autobiography.   Los Angeles: Nash Publish-
       ing, 1974.   281pp.

       A Hollywood columnist and television interviewer contrasts
       her outward success and her "crummy" personal life; crip-
       pled as a child, she vows to be famous, gaining the spotlight
       through determination and nerve; her anecdotes reveal the
       dark side of Hollywood glitter, her destructive relationships
       with men, her struggles with bitter loneliness, her suicide
       attempt; she is finally able to risk marriage, risk revealing
       herself through autobiography.

140   BARRIE, JANE (pseud.)
       see SAVAGE, MILDRED SPITZ (1919-)

141   BARRINGER, EMILY DUNNING (1876-)
       Bowery to Bellevue; The Story of New York's First Woman
       Ambulance Surgeon.   New York: Norton, 1950.   262pp.

       With the moral support and financial backing of her cou-
       rageous family, she pursues a college degree and medical
       training before the turn of the century; trained privately for
       a year by Dr. Mary Putnam Jacobi (see companion volume)
       and supremely confident of her intelligence and skill, she
       fights to become in 1902 the first woman on a general hos-
       pital staff on New York City's East Side; she becomes
       "shrewd and hard" struggling against the harassment of her
       male colleagues and newspaper publicity, but she appreciates
       the "priceless opportunity to know our old East Side" through
       her pioneering emergency work among the poor.

142   BARRY, ANNE (1940-)
       Bellevue Is a State of Mind.   New York: Harcourt Brace
       Jovanovich, 1971.   178pp.

She fakes insanity to "explore life at Bellevue," "an observer disguised as a patient" for a week in 1969; she examines her own emotions, difficulties maintaining perspective, relations between the "patients and the institution"; at her release, she has difficulty readjusting to the outside world.

143   BARRYMORE, DIANA (1922?-1960)
Too Much, Too Soon, with Gerold Frank.   New York: Holt, 1957.   380pp.

The daughter of writer Michael Strange and actor John Barrymore recounts a lonely childhood and her agonized worship of her father; she endures three disastrous marriages; she works in theatre and films, then declines into heavy drinking; the account ends on tentatively hopeful note.

144   BARRYMORE, ELAINE JACOBS
All My Sins Remembered, with Sandford Dody.   New York: Appleton-Century, 1964.   274pp.

She is the fourth and last wife of actor John Barrymore; while a student at Hunter College, she meets him; the book is a tough and violently romantic account of love and battles that ends with Barrymore's death.

145   BARRYMORE, ETHEL (1879-1959)   NAWM
Memories, An Autobiography.   New York: Harper, 1955. 310pp.

She writes of life among the legends of a theatrical family; financially on her own in her teens, she engages in early touring which leads to half a century of success and honor; she combines her career with marriage and the rearing of three children; her account is told with literate, gentle modesty and reveals total dedication to her work.

146   BARTEL, IRENE BROWN
No Drums or Thunder.   San Antonio: Naylor, 1970.   83pp.

She provides an account of homestead life in the early twentieth century; one of six children, she describes in rich detail her family home, butchering, her school day, farm animals, church activities, community entertainments, country "pride and ethics," women's work; she combines nostalgia with realism, standing "in reverence" for her parents' heritage.

147   BARTELL, JAN BRYANT (-1973)
       Spindrift: Spray from a Psychic Sea.   New York: Haw-
       thorn, 1974.   245pp.

       An actress and writer, she describes a "true paranormal
       experience" living in what had been Mark Twain's Greenwich
       Village town house; beginning in 1957, she endures "seven
       troubled years" of noises, lights, and eerie incidents; she
       reads avidly on the occult, searching for explanations, con-
       sulting a medium; her apprehensions increase as she notes
       several sudden deaths among building residents; writing the
       book is "an exercise in personal exorcism," yet it fails
       when her own death becomes the tenth in the ten families
       in the building.

148   BARTHOLOMEW, CAROL
       My Heart Has Seventeen Rooms.   New York: Macmillan,
       1959.   177pp.

       In 1954 she settles in India with her engineer husband and
       three small sons and keeps a journal of her years there;
       keeping house and adjusting to the novelty of servants, she
       establishes relationships of affection and respect; she volun-
       teers in a local hospital and the unconventional role of a
       white woman nurse frees her to do what she wishes for the
       patients; the hospital becomes her "consuming interest," al-
       though she finds the pace alternately peaceful and frustrating;
       after over two years, she notes that departure is like leav-
       ing members of a family.

149   BARTON, BETSEY ALICE
       As Love Is Deep.   New York: Duell, Sloan & Pierce, 1957.
       144pp.

       Particularly close to her mother due to her own physical
       handicap, she keeps a journal beginning in 1949 and records
       "the story of her death and of my relationship to it and to
       her"; she struggles to use the experience of death for growth,
       and notes her profound love at her mother's courage; her
       relationship with her father and brother is intensified, and
       she exhibits the will to accept a new phase of life through
       rebuilding.

150   BASS, CHARLOTTA A. SPEARS (1880?-1969)   NAWM
       Forty Years: Memoirs from the Pages of a Newspaper.
       Los Angeles: the author, 1960.   198pp.

       She moves to Los Angeles in 1910 and serves for forty
       years as the editor of "California's oldest Negro newspa-
       per"; she dedicates the paper to reform issues; she relates

the details of numerous campaigns and tells of her travels
in 1950 to Europe and the U. S. S. R. for international peace
conferences; she sells the newspaper in 1951; she is the
1952 vice-presidential candidate for the Progressive Party.

151   BASSETT, AMY GILLETTE
        Red Cross Reveries, on the Home Front and Overseas.
        Harrisburg, Pa.: Stackpole, 1961.   108pp.

        A Red Cross volunteer in 1914, she describes her work
as the assistant director of a New Jersey embarkation point
and her later work in England and France in 1918; after the
war, she continues her dedication to serving others with rehabilitation work; in the Washington of the 1930's, she testi-
fies before Congress and lobbies for "national defense"; she
closes her anecdotal account with the onset of World War I.

152   BATES, DAISY LEE GATSON (1922-)
        The Long Shadow of Little Rock: A Memoir.   New York:
        McKay, 1962.   234pp.

        She tells of her childhood in Arkansas and the murder of
her mother by whites; she and her husband are newspaper
publishers, active in the NAACP; she is important in the
struggle to integrate schools in Little Rock in 1957 and
later.

153   BAUER, EVELYN SHOWALTER
        Through Sunlight and Shadow.   Scottdale, Pa.: Herald
        Press, 1959.   221pp.

        After receiving a college education, she marries a fellow
Mennonite missionary and tells of their preliminary language
studies in India; she feels inadequate to the tasks of their
first post, noting the difficulties of mental and emotional
adjustments and her mistakes due to ignorance of Indian
language and customs; changing times in the missionary effort also contribute to her insecurity; she enjoys touring
and proselytizing, but shortly after the birth of her son,
she is felled by polio; sustained by her religious faith, she
acknowledges the blessings of suffering, adjusting to her
severe handicap and the rigors of rehabilitation.

154   BAUER, HANNA
        I Came to My Island; A Journey Through the Experience of
        Change.   Seattle: Bernie Straub, 1973.   142pp.

        A psychologist, teacher, wife, and mother of two keeps
a journal of a three-week interlude alone during which she

explores her own inner experience with a "divine egotism"; she observes nature, describes a variety of moods, reflects on doing and being, and meditates on the points of the compass, each with its reverberations; she includes poetry created during this "self-exploration."

155 BAUM, VICKI (1888-1960)
It Was All Quite Different: The Memoirs of Vicki Baum.
New York: Funk & Wagnalls, 1964. 372pp.

In a richly drawn account, a writer describes her upper-class childhood in Vienna, colored by her deep fear and hatred of her father and disturbed by her mentally ill mother; she loses herself in the discipline of music; married twice and the mother of two sons, she recounts her memories of World War I; she takes an editing job in post-war Berlin and then achieves fame after writing The Grand Hotel; in 1931 she emigrates to the U.S.

156 BAUS, RUTH
Who's Running This Expedition!, with Emily Harvin. New York: Coward-McCann, 1959. 256pp.

In a humorous tale of travel adventure, she tells of accepting the challenge of a jungle river expedition in Nicaragua in 1957, going to photograph and film the area; she is the first white woman to attempt the remote river, traveling with "the Explorer," forming a company of two "independent, lone-wolf individualists"; plagued by insects, delays, poor planning, and amorous local Latins, she nevertheless succumbs to the jungle's beauty and "river ecstasy."

157 BAXTER, ANNE (1922?-)
Intermission; A True Story. New York: Putnam, 1976.
384pp.

An actress on location in Australia, she meets and marries an American rancher and forsakes her career to accept the challenge of creating a home in the Australian bush; the vast personal adjustments required and the lack of social stimulation lead to growing resentment; she leaves several times to make films, juggling home, career, and motherhood, but the juxtaposition of her two lives is disastrous for her marriage; at the close of her Australian interlude, she returns to the U.S. and to her career, having learned much about her inner limitations and resources.

158 BEACH, MARJORIE MARSHALL
First the Seed. Santa Barbara, Cal.: Rowny Press, 1963.
264pp.

In 1939, a trip around the world after her husband's death
helps "to heal my heart"; traveling in spite of the "war
scare," she plants seeds from Missouri wherever she goes
to promote international communication and understanding;
she observes war preparations in several countries; she enjoys people and willingly assumes leadership of her tour;
after a delay in Shanghai at the beginning of World War II,
she finally returns home with a new sense of purpose.

159   BEADLE, MURIEL
       These Ruins Are Inhabited.   Garden City, N.Y.:   Doubleday,
       1961.   359pp.

       A newspaper reporter tells of her year in Oxford with her
       professor husband; she describes adjustments, exploring,
       traveling within England, and discusses the English educa-
       tion system in detail; later she accompanies her husband to
       Sweden for his Nobel prize, and elsewhere in Europe for his
       lectures.

160   Where Has All the Ivy Gone?   A Memoir of University Life.
       Garden City, N.Y.:   Doubleday, 1972.   395pp.

       In an articulate account which "celebrates the academic
       life in general," she writes of her duties and activities after
       her husband becomes President of the University of Chicago
       in 1961; she learns much about urban problems and politics,
       thoroughly enjoying the women engaged in civic work while
       enduring the sometimes killing pace of social obligations;
       noting the rise of the student movement and protests, she
       gains insights into the university's structure and its rela-
       tionship to the city; after her husband's retirement, she
       mixes "housewifery with writing and civic dogoodery."

161   BEAM, LURA (1887-   )
       He Called Them by the Lightning; A Teacher's Odyssey in
       the Negro South, 1908-1919.   Indianapolis: Bobbs-Merrill,
       1967.   230pp.

       After graduation from Barnard, she becomes a mission-
       ary teacher of English in the South; she notes the intense
       wariness between blacks and whites, the "family heroism"
       of her pupils, her own experience of a "dual culture," her
       frustration with "conditions I could not affect"; a sensitive
       observer and participant.

162   A Maine Hamlet.   New York: Wilfred Funk, 1957.   236pp.

       In vivid detail, she paints the portrait of an isolated rural
       community between 1894 and 1904, noting the end of an era

of proud, self-sufficient people; local "man and woman" are represented by her grandparents, who establish her early childhood base characterized by deep ancestral roots and a passion for the land; much of the book, however, remains impersonal.

163   BEARD, CARRIE HUNT (1881-)
       Colorado Gold Rush Days; Memories of a Childhood in the
       Eighties and Nineties. New York: Exposition, 1964. 144pp.

She writes to record her mother's and grandmother's pioneer stories and to record the stories she tells to her children, grandchildren, and great-grandchildren; her lively childhood anecdotes tell of pioneering, her "tomboy" youth, school days, and interesting local characters; she marries in 1898 but does not carry the account past the turn of the century.

164   BEARDSLEY, HELEN BRANDMEIR
       Who Gets the Drumstick? The Story of the Beardsley Fam-
       ily. New York: Random House, 1965. 215pp.

She recounts death of her first husband, leaving her with eight children; she meets a widower with ten children and they marry; a warm story of domestic adjustments, organizational triumphs, and love.

165   BEATON-TROKER, KATHERINE
       Psychic Experiences. New York: Vantage, 1962. 62pp.

She writes disconnected and brief descriptions of various premonitions, including those of her brother's death, events during World War I and World War II; she also tells of dreams, séances, visions, communications with spirits.

166   BEATTIE, CAROL
       For Goodness' Sake. New York: Prentice-Hall, Inc., 1952.
       242pp.

She describes "a conservative, though busy life" after marrying a young Episcopal priest; they serve five churches, enjoy warm support and friendship, and participate in increased community activities during the World War II years; although her sphere is circumscribed by two sons, she notes her deep satisfaction and joy in rectory life.

167   BEATY, JEANNE KELLAR
       Lookout Wife. New York: Random House, 1953. 311pp.

When she marries, she and her husband accept fire look-
out duty in Idaho; her romantic expectations give way to the
reality of the hard work which characterizes a "simple and
exhilarating life"; she describes their duties, their colleagues, and their return to a more isolated post the following summer.

168   BECK, DAISY WOODWARD (1876-)
       All the Years Were Grand. Chicago: Erle Press, 1951.
       257pp.

A musician and minister's wife tells of "adjusting my life
and thought and ways of living" to the demands of her role;
she maintains a lively interest in people through her husband's varied assignments, demonstrating a broad tolerance
in her service as a counselor to the Chicago Boys' Court.

169   BECK, FRANCES
       The Diary of a Widow. Boston: Beacon, 1965. 142pp.

Widowed with three young children, she keeps a diary in
which the entries recount the first four years of pain, adjustment, loneliness, and coping; alternately emotional and
self-controlled, she addresses some passages to her deceased husband.

170   BEEBE, ELSWYTH THANE RICKER (1900-)
       The Bird Who Made Good. New York: Duell, Sloan and
       Pearce, 1947. 61pp.

Having picked up an injured purple finch and dutifully
cared for him, she finds that he has insinuated himself into
her affections; cheerfully anthropomorphic, she presents her
amused observations of his behavior at her Vermont summer
home and her New York City winter apartment, acknowledging her own "foolish devotion."

171   Reluctant Farmer. New York: Duell, Sloan and Pearce,
       1950. 208pp.

A novelist and biographer admits her initial impatience
with "back to the land" accounts, yet presents her own tale
of seven years of joyful ownership of a Vermont farm with
her naturalist husband; at first casual about country life,
she finds herself "turning into a farmer," proud of her hay
and maple syrup; she mentions her research and writing,
and tells more about her pet purple finch (see above).

172   The Strength of the Hills. Chappaqua, N.Y.: Christian
       Herald House, 1976. 219pp.

This narrative is the same as Reluctant Farmer with a brief postscript after her life permanently "shifted to the country."

173 BEERS, LORNA DOONE
Wild Apples and North Wind. New York: Norton, 1966.
219pp.

A writer presents "a kind of tone poem" illuminating her first year on a Vermont farm, a permanent resident after her husband's retirement; her taciturn neighbors become part of her life, as she describes with sensitivity her gardening struggles, the drama of finding water, her "great respect for stones," her abandonment of "clock time," and a New England snow storm.

174 BELFRAGE, SALLY (1936-)
Freedom Summer. New York: Viking, 1965. 246pp.

This is an engrossing, vivid documentary of her work as a librarian in Mississippi during the summer of 1964; with other young, white, middle-class idealists, she struggles to overcome the fear, lethargy, and intimidation of local black people; she teaches literacy, registers voters, observes the racism and violence of the local police when her colleagues are jailed and beaten; at the end of the summer, she attends the Democratic convention to support the Mississippi Freedom Democratic Party.

175 A Room in Moscow. New York: Reynal, 1958. 186pp.

The daughter of radical parents and "always too personally involved in the world's problems," she spends five months in Russia in 1957 "to discover the living realities beneath the symbols"; she takes a job editing translations, socializes with a young people's set, copes with bureaucracy and inefficiency, and is immersed in Russian daily life; leaving, she notes the inadequacy of generalizations and pleads for increased international understanding.

176 BELL, CLARE
And Then We'll Be Rich. New York: McGraw-Hill, 1951.
284pp.

In a lively, entertaining account she describes her abandonment of a comfortable life in suburban Long Island when her lawyer husband wants to side-step the depression by running an apple packing business in the Ozarks; she emerges as the pioneer, the realist, and the capable orchard mana-

ger after two seasons of hard work and "dearly-bought
knowledge" which result in a deep love of the land.

177   BELMONT, ELEANOR ROBSON (1879-   )
       Fabric of Memory.   New York: Farrar, Straus and Cudahy,
       1957.   311pp.

       The daughter and granddaughter of actresses, she comes
       to the U. S. at seven and enters the theater as a teen-ager,
       acting for thirteen years; she marries in 1910, adjusting to
       life as a wealthy matron; she serves as an organizer and
       fund-raiser for the American Red Cross during World War
       I; she works for prohibition, on behalf of the unemployed
       during the depression, and for the Metropolitan Opera Com-
       pany.

178   BENARY-ISBERT, MARGOT
       These Vintage Years.   Nashville: Abingdon, 1968.   223pp.

       An author of children's books, she writes a "book about
       old age" in her late 70's; tells of her thirty-eight years of
       marriage, reflects on a couple's growing old together, adjust-
       ments to widowhood, satisfactions being a mother and grand-
       mother, travels; random memories feed reflections.

179   BENEDICT, RUTH FULTON (1887-1948)   NAW
       An Anthropologist at Work; Writings of Ruth Benedict, ed.
       Margaret Mead.   Boston: Houghton Mifflin, 1959.   583pp.

       The account, which reveals a highly articulate and per-
       ceptive woman, includes her correspondence from 1922 to
       1923, her diaries from 1923 to 1926, an incomplete but ex-
       tremely analytical autobiographical sketch written in 1935,
       journals from 1912 to 1934 which include profound reflec-
       tions on life and on woman's place, her correspondence
       from 1924 to 1934 from the field and telling of her anthro-
       pological colleagues, and her correspondence from 1923 to
       1940 with "Papa Franz" Boas.

180   BENEFIELD, JUNE
       Laughing to Keep from Crying.   Houston, Tex.:   Gulf Pub-
       lishing, 1972.   116pp.

       Most of this journalist's account was originally published
       in the Houston Chronicle; she leaves reporting for "suburbia,
       motherhood, and good housekeeping"--her first career
       choice; she then becomes the "victim of a horrible myth";
       her short anecdotal chapters are humorous vignettes of
       family life.

181   BENET, LAURA (1884-1979)
       When William Rose, Stephen Vincent and I Were Young.
       New York: Dodd, Mead, 1976. 111pp.

       Herself a poet and biographer, she offers a reminiscence
       of "a childhood full of warm memories" with her two broth-
       ers; her earliest recollections are of images and small in-
       cidents; as her father is transferred among military arsenals,
       she adjusts to several family homes, finds new friends who
       join in impromptu games; her parents, a source of enter-
       tainment and education, make youth a "constant and imagina-
       tive adventure."

182   BENETAR, JUDITH
       Admissions; Notes from a Woman Psychiatrist.   New York:
       Charterhouse, 1974.   219pp.

       In her second year as a psychiatric resident in a New
       York City hospital, she describes her patients, including a
       suicide, as well as their psychological and emotional effect
       on her; flashbacks offer glimpses of her personal life, a
       broken marriage and fragmented joy with a transatlantic
       lover; sustained by her toughness and dedication, she en-
       dures loneliness, anger, and frustration, both personally
       and professionally.

183   BENGIS, INGRID (1944?-)
       Combat in the Erogenous Zone.   New York: Knopf, 1972.
       260pp.

       Defining her own truth out of her own varied and incon-
       sistent experiences, she explores hatred of men and the
       "veritable war zone" of sexuality, the "crossfire between
       mind, body, and feelings" fed by the tension between puritan-
       ism and romanticism, and the stability and permanence of
       love.

184   *I Have Come Here to Be Alone.*   New York: Simon and
       Schuster, 1976.   268pp.

       After the breakup of an affair, she seeks retreat on a
       Greek island, wishing to come to terms with her past, "the
       fits, starts and fizzles of my life"; in a documentary style,
       she records the details of her present existence, shifting to
       imaginative flashbacks of her childhood, of the mysterious
       undercurrents of her Russian Jewish immigrant parents' re-
       lationship, of her sessions with a psychiatrist, of her love
       for an Austrian artist; she resents the myth of independence,
       "conspiring against myself."

185   BENNETT, JEAN FRANCES (pseud.)
       see DORCY, SISTER MARY JEAN (1914-)

186   BENNETT, JOAN (1910-)
       The Bennett Playbill, with Lois Kibbee.   New York: Holt,
       Rinehart and Winston, 1970.   332pp.

       This straightforward account emphasizes her fear and
       adoration of her father, love of her mother; her own turn
       to acting in 1929 comes out of economic necessity; a long
       middle section focuses on preceding three theatrical gener-
       ations; a devoted mother of four, and a grandmother, she
       writes partly to provide a family history.

187   BENNETT, KAY
       Kaibah: Recollection of a Navaho Girlhood.   Los Angeles:
       Westernlore, 1964.   253pp.

       Written in the third person, the account covers the period
       from 1928 to 1935 and tells of "an average Navaho girl" in
       New Mexico; raised by her widowed mother, she develops
       an independent spirit as she takes on responsibilities; she
       describes shyness at tribal gatherings, details of daily life,
       close extended family ties, desire to go to government
       boarding school at 10; because she is the youngest, her
       mother passes on family and tribal knowledge to her; she
       tells of hardship during drought of 1935; account ends with
       her decision to go with missionaries to California.

188   BENTLAGE, MARY KAY (1903-)
       My Name Was Kay. New York: Exposition, 1965.   59pp.

       The daughter of German immigrants who settled in rural
       Iowa in the late nineteenth century, she tells of various
       farm tasks, Sunday visiting, butchering time, Christmas
       celebrations, threshing time, and school; in 1915 they move
       to town; her account focuses on her youth, mentioning her
       marriage and motherhood only briefly at the close.

189   BENTLEY, ELIZABETH (1908?-)
       Out of Bondage; The Story of Elizabeth Bentley.   New York:
       Devin-Adair, 1951.   311pp.

       In 1934 she is drawn to anti-Fascist ideals and joins the
       Communist Party in 1935; marriage to a party leader com-
       plicates her underground work; as a spy for the Soviet Un-
       ion, she is hunted by the F. B. I. but Soviet secret police
       offer no support, only "ugly intrigue"; disillusioned and at-
       tempting to protect her American friends in the party, she

becomes an F. B. I. informant and double agent to "help
smash the Soviet espionage machine"; eventually a fervent
anti-communist, she is the subject of lurid newspaper
stories and congressional investigations in 1946.

190   BENZIGER, BARBARA FIELD
       The Prison of My Mind. New York: Walker, 1969. 171pp.

       The account consists of extracts from a journal kept dur-
ing and after severe mental depression; she experiences ter-
rifying claustrophobia, delusions, panic; she suffers from
unsympathetic doctors and institutional indignities before she
finds a "good" hospital; she describes her gradual transition
to health and offers realistic reflections on the experience
of mental illness and the needs of the mentally ill and their
families.

191   BERG, GERTRUDE (1899-1966)   NAWM
       Molly and Me, with Cherney Berg. New York: McGraw-
       Hill, 1961.   278pp.

       She describes life in a New York City Russian Jewish
immigrant family full of warmth and love; her later childhood is spent with family working at a country hotel; she
marries at nineteen; she creates the radio character Molly
Goldberg and is a writer and actress for radio, theater,
and television.

192   BERG, NORAH SULLIVAN (1897-   )
       Lady on the Beach, with Charles Samuels. New York:
       Prentice Hall, 1952. 251pp.

       After being widowed with two sons, she takes to drink
and then meets a retired Marine whom she marries; they
both resolve to fight their alcoholism and become beach-
combers on the Pacific coast of Washington; she describes
their derelict, dropout neighbors, and the satisfaction she
ultimately finds in their "poor man's paradise."

193   BERKELEY, MARY EMLEN LLOYD (1887?-   )
       Winking at the Brim.   Boston: Houghton Mifflin, 1967.
       172pp.

       The descendant of several prominent Boston families and
a "Bohemian at heart" presents a multitude of brief episodes, revealing a keen sense for the idiosyncratic and
ridiculous and a never-failing zest for life; after a brief
first marriage, she is drawn to Italy, paints professionally
but not seriously, and marries a British lord, unaccustomed

to but delighted with her life of luxury and a parade of houseguests; widowed in 1942, she does Red Cross work in London during the war, then returns to her beloved Italy where she raises three orphan boys and, a Catholic convert, restores a cathedral.

194   BERKELEY, MOLLY
      see BERKELEY, MARY EMLEN LLOYD (1887?-)

195   BERKOWITZ, SARAH BICK (1924?-)
      Where Are My Brothers?   New York: Helios Books, 1965.
      127pp.

      Born a Jew in Poland, she describes the German occupation of her village, the persecution of Jews, the hunger and fear in the Jewish ghetto, "horrible scenes" including her father's starvation; horrors and degradation of concentration camps at Auschwitz and Bergen-Belsen; the "unforgettable day" of liberation; she later becomes a U.S. citizen.

196   BERNAYS, DORIS ELSA FLEISCHMAN
      see FLEISCHMAN, DORIS ELSA (1891-)

197   BERNHEIM, MOLLY (1902?-)
      A Sky of My Own.   New York: Rinehart, 1959.   252pp.

      A teacher of medical students tells how her own fascination with flying is fired by her husband's acquiring a pilot's license; eager to learn and to prove that she is not "too old," she begins in 1946; she experiences the loneliness of solo flight, the exhilaration of ever-longer trips, the pride of becoming a flight instructor, and the thrill of a cross-country journey; flying brings her renewed spirit, delight, and confidence.

198   BERRY, KATHERINE FISKE (1877-)
      Katie-San; From Maine Pastures to Japan Shores.   Cambridge, Mass.:   Dresser, Chapman & Grimes, 1962.   285pp.

      The daughter of a missionary doctor to Japan, she includes childhood letters sent to a friend in the U.S. and a diary begun at thirteen in which she notes in detail the weather, a weekly sermon, her family's activities, and her lessons; writing of herself in the third person, she adds editorial comments; she has a "protected and isolated upbringing," interacting little with the Japanese; after leaving Japan in 1895 for her education, she returns in 1919, again keeping a journal, seeing Japan from new perspectives and "retrieving one's childhood."

199   BERRY, RUTH MUIRHEAD
       To Enjoy God: A Woman's Adventure in Faith.   Philadel-
       phia: Muhlenberg Press, 1956.   228pp.

          She examines the fundamentalist religious views and prac-
       tices of her rural Iowa childhood in her "quest for a per-
       sonal relationship with God"; in 1916 she is a missionary
       teacher among black people in Alabama, but after her mar-
       riage in 1921, she feels her faith weaken; widowed suddenly
       in 1941, she becomes the director of a servicemen's center
       during World War II and continues to work with church pro-
       jects, loyal to "ecumenical Protestantism."

200   BERTO, HAZEL DUNAWAY (1907?-)
       North to Alaska's Shining River.   Indianapolis: Bobbs-
       Merrill, 1959.   224pp.

          She makes her first journey to the Seward Peninsula in
       1925 as a newlywed, to serve as a teacher of Eskimos for
       the Indian Bureau; she combines teaching, pioneer house-
       keeping, and child-rearing, making major but necessary ad-
       justments and coping with the hard winter isolation and the
       poverty and illness of the natives; she rises to the challenge
       and responsibility of her teaching position and feels it is a
       "proving ground" whose important values remain with her
       after she makes the difficult decision to leave.

201   BERTRANDE, SISTER
       Devotedly Yours.   Chicago: Empire-Stone, 1951.   400pp.

          She shares her experiences of a Holy Year pilgrimage to
       Rome, including side visits to Israel, Europe, North Africa,
       and the Middle East; she gives lively descriptions of sight-
       seeing "as Sisters do it," enjoying the hospitality of reli-
       gious communities in many locales; she demonstrates a vast
       affection for her sisters.

202   BESTON, MRS. HENRY
       see COATESWORTH, ELIZABETH JANE (1893-)

203   BETENSON, LULA PARKER (1884-)
       Butch Cassidy, My Brother, as told to Dora Flack.   Provo,
       Utah: Brigham Young University Press, 1975.   265pp.

          She writes this memoir to correct the distorted history,
       the legend, and the movie about her brother, breaking her
       "sworn silence"; she offers family history, tells of a "quite
       normal" family life and her parents' burden having an outlaw
       son; in 1925 she enjoys a reunion and reminiscences with

her brother; the account includes correspondence concerning
her brother after his death.

204   BEVINGTON, HELEN SMITH (1906-)
       Along Came the Witch: A Journal in the 1960's.   New York:
       Harcourt Brace Jovanovich, 1976.   223pp.

       Cast in the form of monthly journal entries, her account
       includes much quotation of and comment on her favorite lit-
       erary passages; she presents some fine vignettes, telling of
       her mother, husband, grandchildren, teaching, poetry; the
       book covers the same period in which three earlier volumes
       of autobiography were written.

205   A Book and a Love Affair.   New York: Harcourt Brace &
       World, 1968.   183pp.

       She meets her husband-to-be, a fellow English student at
       Columbia, in a class in 1927 and their love is fed by liter-
       ary quotations; in this story of her marriage, she recounts
       a trip around the world, her teaching, her motherhood,
       friendships, life as a faculty wife, and verse writing; after
       the onset of World War II, she escapes from New York City
       to Durham, North Carolina.

206   Charley Smith's Girl: A Memoir.   New York: Simon and
       Schuster, 1965.   255pp.

       A poet and English professor, she offers a sensitive,
       beautifully written story of her childhood and youth; the
       daughter of divorced parents, she grows up between her
       mother's disciplined loneliness and her father's intense but
       contradictory nature; the book contains many fine prose por-
       traits.

207   The House Was Quiet and The World Was Calm.   New York:
       Harcourt Brace Jovanovich, 1971.   174pp.

       The third volume of her autobiography covers the years
       from 1942 to 1956; at Duke University she is offered a war-
       time teaching position; her account focuses on her domestic,
       professional, and private lives, including her reflections on
       poetry and teaching and her description of a sabbatical stay
       in England; the book is a charming, compassionate story of
       survival through the chaos of war, illness, and accident.

208   BIDDLE, CORDELIA DREXEL
       My Philadelphia Father, as told to Kyle Crichton.   Garden
       City, N.Y.: Doubleday, 1955.   256pp.

Her background includes two prominent and wealthy Philadelphia families, the "Drexel-Biddle combine" and an adored
father, noted for his "surging enthusiasms," a writer, amateur boxer, and amateur singer; her marriage to an im-
mensely wealthy New Yorker, her two sons, her ties with
her in-laws the North Carolina Dukes, her divorce, are all
secondary to the vivid portrait she presents of her father,
an "elemental force" until his death in 1948.

209   BINGLE, ALICE (1879-)
       The Best Years. N. p. : 1961. 61pp.

Thinly disguising herself as "Agnes Shingle," she presents
a third-person narrative which opens in 1907 with her grueling nurse's training in London; she tells of private and public cases and of nursing soldiers during World War I; in
1919 she emigrates to the U. S. and establishes her home
and career at Antioch College, delighted to care for students.

210   A Woman's Diary. New York: Vantage, 1958. 91pp.

In diary entries from 1954 to 1955, written as if addressed to a friend, the sprightly British-born author notes
running errands, visiting, writing letters, attending lectures
and concerts, and working on her memoirs; she reveals a
quick, sympathetic concern for others and enjoys many warm
friendships, some dating from her years with the Antioch
College infirmary.

211   BIRD, BARBARA KEPHART (1897-)
       Calked Shoes; Life in Adirondack Lumber Camps. Prospect,
       N. Y. : Prospect Books, 1952. 141pp.

Married in 1920 to an Adirondack forester, she "defied
convention" and "followed my husband into the woods" in
1922; fond of the outdoors, she begins as camp cook and
tells of life in a logging camp, a "man's world."

212   BISHOP, NELL FOLEY (1906-)
       The Path, A True Story of Christian Service to the Unfor-
       tunate Inmates of a County Penal Farm. New York: Green-
       wich Book Publishers, 1957. 112pp.

Her account covers the six-year period during which she
works with her superintendent husband as his secretary; her
anecdotes demonstrate a warm interest in the prisoners; she
closes with her husband's sudden death and her departure
from the farm.

213   BJORN, THYRA FERRE (1905-)
       Mama's Way. New York: Rinehart, 1959. 214pp.

       A Swedish-born author offers a religious account, includ-
       ing stories from her life as a child, wife, mother, and
       grandmother; told in random way, unified by theme of prayer.

214   This Is My Life. New York: Holt, Rinehart and Winston,
       1966. 181pp.

       A Swedish-born author, she recounts events which happen
       after the publication of her first book; she describes the ten-
       sion between domestic affairs and her love of writing; she
       accepts numerous invitations to lecture and takes several
       trips to Sweden; she notes readers' responses to her books.

215   BLAIR, MAUDE HALL
       A World of Travel and Fun. Philadelphia: Dorrance, 1956.
       487pp.

       She reconstructs her record of six extended trips between
       the 1920's and the 1950's from diaries and letters to her
       family; traveling in style with her husband, she writes with
       enthusiasm of the sights and people in visits to Mediterranean
       countries, central Europe, Asia, southern Africa and South
       America, northern Europe, and the Near East.

216   BLAKE, ALMA CARWILE (1909-)
       Of Life and Love and Things. Parsons, W. Va.: McClain
       Printing Co., 1971. 119pp.

       A "confirmed optimist" writes a bland account of her ex-
       tended family, childhood pastimes, and abbreviated school
       career; married at sixteen, she raises three daughters while
       doing volunteer work for her church and the Girl Scouts; she
       concludes "life is good and I am happy."

217   BLAKESLEE, HELEN VIRGINIA
       Beyond the Kikuyu Curtain. Chicago: Moody Press, 1956.
       267pp.

       A missionary doctor in Kenya for over forty years begin-
       ning in 1911, she writes to justify continued missionary ef-
       forts in spite of the rise of the Mau-Mau; she discusses
       much about Kikuyu culture with a special concern for wom-
       en's position; she establishes a girls' training school, aware
       of the cultural conflicts that result from her medical and
       educational efforts; she notes the political unrest of the
       1920's, growing hostility to missionaries in the 1930's, post-

war lawlessness in the 1940's, and the rise of Mau-Mau
terrorism; she leaves with sorrow in 1954.

218   BLANCHARD, PEARL
The Voyage of the Marauder; A Woman on the Go--in a
Trailer.   New York: William-Frederick, 1951.   41pp.

Over forty and motivated by the desire to escape housekeeping and city life, she tours for eight years, making
diverse friends and "just now getting an education."

219   BLANKENSHIP, MARY ALMOR PERRITT (1878-1955)
The West Is for Us; The Reminiscences of Mary A. Blank-
enship, ed. Seymour V. Connor.   Lubbock, Texas: West
Texas Museum Association, 1958.   125pp.

In a straightforward, enthusiastic pioneer account, she
describes being the only woman on her 1901 journey to a
homestead in west Texas; dedicated to the land, she tells
in detail of a self-sufficient domestic life, in which isolation
is mitigated by homemade entertainments, nearby kin, and
church and school activities; the tempo of life increases with
the coming of the railroad, telephones, and cars.

220   BLAUSTEIN, ESTHER GORDON
When Momma Was the Landlord.   New York: Harper &
Row, 1972.   201pp.

A teacher and journalist recalls her New Jersey childhood
in a large apartment house, "my domain," run firmly by her
mother, the "homemaker and managing agent"; she writes
vivid anecdotes of the eccentric characters among the various tenants, of her extended Jewish family all living nearby,
and of her friends and their entertainments; outgrowing her
adolescent resentment of the demands of the apartments, she
moves on to work, college, and dreams of future adulthood.

221   BLONDELL, JOAN
Center Door Fancy.   New York: Delacorte, 1972.   312pp.

The daughter of a vaudeville actor and a beautiful, im-
mature woman who resents her children, she endures an
unsettled childhood on the road; minor acting jobs lead to
an opening on Broadway in 1929, then to Hollywood films;
thrice married, she chronicles an unhappy series of abor-
tions, love affairs, and breakdowns, repeating her childhood
pattern of chaos in her search for a stable family and home
life.

222   BLOODGOOD, LIDA FLEITMANN (1894-   )
Hoofs in the Distance.   New York: Van Nostrand, 1953.
131pp.

A prominent horsewoman in the U.S. and in Europe during the 1920's describes her New York City childhood amid
wealth and elegance; the riding club is her "second home,"
and her passion for riding leads her to hunting, tandem
driving, showing, and owning a farm of her own; she evokes
an era now gone.

223   BLUM, ELSA PROEHL
They Pleased World Stars; A Memoir of My Parents.   New
York: Vantage, 1960.   58pp.

Growing up in Chicago of German-born parents, she is
the daughter of a father who is a gourmet cook and a mother
who is a pianist and conductor; she follows her mother into
a musical career and becomes a composer; anecdotes illustrate a life of lavish entertaining and cosmopolitan culture.

224   BODELL, MARY
Gullible's Travels.   New York: Dodd, Mead, 1963.   212pp.

A mother of six describes the family saga of summer
camping from Norway to Spain following their year in 1956-
57 in Copenhagen for her husband's Guggenheim fellowship;
she notes the perils of renting a furnished home, their adjustments to the long Scandinavian winter, and their attempts
to learn Danish, closing with their return to the U.S.

225   BODGER, JOAN
How the Heather Looks; A Joyous Journey to the British
Sources of Children's Books.   New York: Viking, 1965.
276pp.

She and her husband and two young children take a summer holiday in England in 1958, exploring out-of-the-way
locales made meaningful by their connections to British
children's authors and illustrators; bringing along much historical and literary knowledge as well as lively imaginations,
they seek out King Arthur's haunts, Robin Hood's Notting-
ham, Winnie the Pooh's countryside, finding delightful "little
countries of the mind."

226   BOGAN, LOUISE (1897-1970)   NAWM
What the Woman Lived; Selected Letters of Louise Bogan,
1920-1970, ed. Ruth Limmer.   New York: Harcourt Brace
Jovanovich, 1973.   401pp.

A distinguished poet, critic, and translator, she writes
to and about other prominent literary figures in intensely
private letters characterized by wry wit, toughness, perception, sharp critical comments, and a passionate independence; she endures several breakdowns and recoveries,
achieving a "second blooming" with the young poet Theodore
Roethke; she serves as the poetry consultant with the Library of Congress, teaches at several colleges, and ac-
cumulates literary honors.

227   BOHNER, OLIVINE NADEAU
       The Long Long Trial.   Mountain View, Cal. :   Pacific
       Press, 1960.   167pp.

       This light, anecdotal account opens with her "determina-
tion to get an education," taking domestic work for tuition;
she attends a missionary college on a shoestring, marries
in 1949, taking an Adventist teaching post in the Far East
with her husband.

228   BOLAND, PEG
       Don't Panic, Mother.   Milwaukee: Bruce, 1964.   101pp.

       She writes humorous short chapters on family pets, sail-
ing, gardening, cooking, her children's activities, a religious study group, and memories of her own college years
generated by her children's entering college; some chapters
were originally published in magazines.

229   BOLES, ANTONETTE
       Women in Khaki.   New York: Vantage, 1953.   240pp.

       This exposé was written by a disillusioned woman who
served in the WACs from 1943 to 1945; she criticizes the
poor food, disorganization, arbitrary authority, hard work,
senseless assignments, and inefficiency; overwork weakens
her own health yet she is considered psychopathic for being
critical.

230   BOLLING, RUTH JAMERSON
       Tales of a Texas Ranch.   San Antonio: Naylor, 1959.
       130pp.

       A former schoolteacher presents the story of "just an
ordinary American family," focusing on the early years of
her marriage in 1907; she tells of her extended family,
raising four children, hard ranch work, visiting with neighbors, and family modes of entertainment in their relative
isolation; she closes with her husband's death in 1958.

231   BOLT, VELMA
        Our Cow. New York: Carlton Press, 1965. 40pp.

        In a series of random recollections written in a raw,
        crude style, she describes growing up in a large, poor
        family in which the cow "means life to us kids"; she re-
        ceives little education, and after her marriage she works
        in a cotton mill while raising four children.

232   BOLTON, ISABEL (pseud.)
        see MILLER, MARY BRITTON (1883-1975)

233   BOND, MARY WICKHAM
        Far Afield in the Caribbean; Migratory Flights of a Natural-
        ist's Wife. Wynnewood, Pa.: Livingston, 1971. 142pp.

        A novelist who "welcomes adventure," she writes sketches
        from her "romantic point of view" of a series of expeditions
        to some forty islands over a period of eighteen years; adjust-
        ing to her husband's "vagabond habits," she describes in vivid
        detail exotic natural settings and colorful, eccentric people.

234   BONHAM, VALERIA LANGELOTH
        Utopia in the Hills; The Story of Valeria Home and Its Found-
        ing. New York: McBride, 1948. 219pp.

        Valeria Home, opened in 1924, is a convalescent center
        for people of refinement; she establishes her background,
        telling of her marriage in 1903 to a cultured, wealthy busi-
        nessman; when she is widowed in 1914, she establishes the
        center in her palatial Long Island home; she is honored for
        her community service.

235   BONN, MARJORIE FAULKNER (1902?-   )
        Hogback. New York: Vantage, 1954. 35pp.

        She tells of homesteading in Washington state beginning
        in 1907; her memories are brief and scattered, but they
        portray a close, simple family life.

236   BOONE, SHIRLEY
        One Woman's Liberation. Carol Stream, Ill.: Creation
        House, 1972. 230pp.

        The daughter of Grand Ole Opry star Red Foley tells of
        her early marriage to singer Pat Boone, and of their four
        daughters; Hollywood life brings tension and unhappiness; an
        account of her new identity through religion relates its effect
        on their family life.

237   BOOZER, CELINA LuZANNE
       Our Brother Red (and His "Bull"), by Liny Lu (pseud.).
       Brooklyn, N. Y. :   Theo. Gaus' Sons, 1962.   198pp.

       In the vernacular of rural Georgia, she tells a story of
       peaceful provincialism, "an ideal community life"; with her
       focus on the family, in which she and her brother are a
       close pair, national events like the Mexican revolution and
       World War I remain shadowy; she offers anecdotes of kin
       and of the family's relationships with local blacks; she
       closes with the family's dispersal when her father dies.

238   BORLAND, MARY BERNICE
       Star of the Sea; A Marian Year Pilgrimage Through Europe
       and the British Isles for Armchair Travelers.   Philadelphia:
       Dorrance, 1956.   190pp.

       Traveling as part of a pilgrimage group, she goes to
       Rome, London, Paris, Cologne, Dublin, Florence, Genoa,
       Venice, Wiesbaden, Amsterdam, Monte Carlo, Cork, and
       Lucerne, visiting numerous shrines of Our Lady and sight-
       seeing with enthusiasm.

239   BOROWSKY, MARCIA C. R.
       A Journey Between Two Wars.   New York: Vantage, 1951.
       253pp.

       Setting her narrative in the first person plural, she de-
       scribes travels in Spain, France, Italy, the Near East,
       North Africa, Russia, Greece, Yugoslavia, and Switzerland
       between World War I and World War II; she includes his-
       torical material, local color, and literary references to
       illuminate her observations; she calls for peace upon her
       return.

240   BOULTON, AGNES
       Part of a Long Story.   Garden City, N. Y. :   Doubleday, 1958.
       331pp.

       A perceptive writer, she evokes the atmosphere and per-
       sonalities of Greenwich Village in 1918; she is drawn to the
       dark, brooding playwright Eugene O'Neill; married, she
       finds happiness and joyful work in "safe" Provincetown dur-
       ing the summer, although she is troubled by his drinking;
       she describes the pattern of their "aloneness," closing her
       narrative with the birth of their son.

241   BOURKE-WHITE, MARGARET (1904-1971)   NAWM
       Portrait of Myself.   New York: Simon and Schuster, 1963.
       383pp.

A fine account of her photography career; her love of industrial pictures leads to jobs with the new Fortune magazine and the new Life magazine; notes two brief marriages, one
to Erskine Caldwell; she is a war correspondent during World
War II; she closes with some intimation of her struggle with
Parkinson's disease.

242   BOURLAND, MARGARET
       Without Gloves.   New York: Vantage, 1950.   84pp.

       In a slangy narrative, played for laughs, she portrays
herself as a "lone wolf" afflicted with "spaced teeth" and an
inferiority complex; random memories lead to various humorous reflections; she finally achieves love and marriage.

243   BOURNE, EMMA GUEST (1882-   )
       A Pioneer Farmer's Daughter of Red River Valley, North-
       east Texas.   Dallas: Story Book Press, 1950.   265pp.

       Opening with a family history, she then relates random
memories from her childhood; in many short chapters, she
describes the details of sewing, cooking, farm animals,
amusements, school days, religious meetings, family illnesses; she marries in 1902, teaches school, and raises
three children.

244   BOURNE, EULALIA
       Woman in Levi's.   Tucson: University of Arizona Press,
       1967.   208pp.

       An independent non-conformist, she teaches in a remote
Arizona country school and homesteads, "serving children
and cattle"; with "three old men" she shares love of the
ranch; describes veterinary medicine, marketing cattle, injuries, dependence on the weather, range language, all in
good humor.

245   BOWEN, CATHERINE SHOBER DRINKER (1897-1973) NAWM
       Adventures of a Biographer.   Boston: Little, Brown, 1959.
       235pp.

       In a perceptive and charming account of "the biographer's
way of life," she describes the people and places in her research; she first tells of a frustrating stay in Russia in
1937, searching for anecdotal detail to enrich a biography
and to enhance the transition "from the present to the past";
later denied the use of letters for a biography of Holmes,
she goes to Boston for interviews with Holmes' acquaintances
who can evoke a vanished way of life; absorbed for five years

in the life of John Adams, she notes the differences between
biographers' and scholars' approaches.

246   Family Portrait.   Boston: Little, Brown, 1970.   301pp.

This writer and biographer tells of growing up in Haver-
ford and Bethlehem, Pennsylvania; her father a lawyer and university president; possessed by the enigma of the lives of
four older brothers and a beautiful sister, she describes intimate family relationships, including a section on her aunt,
artist Cecilia Beaux (see companion volume); a fine, sensitive, moving account.

247   BOWEN, LOUISE HADDUCK DE KOVEN (1859-1953)   NAWM
Open Windows: Stories of People and Places.   Chicago:
Ralph Fletcher Seymour, 1946.   272pp.

Her amusing reminiscences are told in the form of favorite, self-contained stories; she relates anecdotes about her
wedding trip, her children's nurses, an extended trip abroad;
in addition, she relates anecdotes from her thirty-five years'
work with the Juvenile Protective Association and with Hull
House, her acquaintance with famous figures, her political
activities, her war work during World War I; she devotes
two chapters to stories about her long friendship with Jane
Addams (see companion volume).

248   BOWLES, CYNTHIA (1936-   )
At Home in India.   New York: Harcourt, Brace, 1956.
180pp.

In an account drawn from letters and diary entries, the
daughter of the U. S. Ambassador describes her two years
in India; initially unenthusiastic and filled with misconceptions, she attends a public school and makes close friendships; she enjoys informal travels, does volunteer work in a
hospital, and continues her public service work in villages
near her college; numerous visits to the homes of friends
provide insights and understanding; she leaves India determined to return as a public health nurse.

249   BOWMAN, NORA LINJER
Only the Mountains Remain.   Caldwell, Idaho: Caxton,
1958.   322pp.

A city girl enters "this storybook life" in 1919 when a
Nevada ranch vacation leads to a sudden proposal by a ranch
superintendent; her "Viking love of adventure" carries her
through as she learns the ways of the West and earns the

acceptance of ranchers; her anecdotes focus on family
events, colorful Western characters, neighbors, hired hands,
roundups, camping, entertainments, and maternal pride as
her daughter grows to adulthood.

250   BOWNE, ELIZABETH
      Gift from the African Heart.   New York: Dodd, Mead, 1961.
      272pp.

      The book opens with the death of her husband, a pilot,
flying over west Africa; she travels to a mission in the Lib-
erian back country to find his grave and learn the cause of
accident; she moves from horror at local conditions to understanding and acceptance of natives' compassion.

251   Their Silent Message.   New York: McGraw-Hill, 1968.
      215pp.

      A lecturer, traveller, and supporter of the U. N. , she
writes a sequel to Gift from the African Heart; she tells of
her return to an African village to better understand the
needs of the people and their dispensary; she is troubled by
missionary methods and the apathy of the villagers, but is
buoyed by her friends and the hope offered by self-help.

252   BOYD, MAMIE ALEXANDER (1876-   )
      Rode a Heifer Calf Through College.   Brooklyn: Pageant-
      Poseidon, 1972.   253pp.

      A Kansas journalist writes at ninety-two about her long
and productive life; her revered parents provide a heritage
of security and love and a belief in the dignity of hard work;
ambitious for a college education she graduates in 1902;
stricken with tuberculosis, she marries a fellow journalist
in 1905 and in a comprehensive partnership they cure her,
raise two sons, and run a newspaper business; intensely
family centered, she is nevertheless honored many times
for her contributions to Kansas women's club work and to
Kansas journalism.

253   BOYLE, SARAH PATTON
      The Desegregated Heart; A Virginian's Stand in Time of
      Transition.   New York: Morrow, 1962.   364pp.

      "Raised as a typical white Southerner, " she tells of her
"awakening" in 1950 and her inner upheaval caused by the
integration issue; she becomes disillusioned with her community and the subtleties of prejudice; she describes her
first, tentative, sometimes misguided efforts; she publishes

much on integration, and is saddened by the silence of liberals and a lack of leadership during a decade of struggle.

254   BOYNTON, WINIFRED CASE (1887-)
Faith Builds a Chapel; The Story of an Adventure in Craftsmanship. New York: Reinhold, 1953. 135pp.

She describes nine years of work toward the fulfillment of an ideal begun in 1939: the building of a Norwegian chapel near her Wisconsin summer home; a family project, the chapel offers her opportunities for research, carving and painting, as well as inner peace during the anxiety of World War II.

255   BRACKEN, PEG (1918-)
But I Wouldn't Have Missed It for the World! The Pleasures and Perils of an Unseasoned Traveler. New York: Harcourt Brace Jovanovich, 1973. 270pp.

In a light, humorous vein, she records her personal impressions in scatter-gun anecdotes covering all aspects of her worldwide travels, enjoying her encounters with "splendid things and remarkable people."

256   I Didn't Come Here to Argue. New York: Harcourt, Brace & World, 1969. 210pp.

The author of The I Hate to Cook Book writes what she knows, has noticed, has suspected, or has surmised in a light style; she spoofs consumerism, lists her trivial hates, and reflects on pain, travel, books, and growing older.

257   BRAD, JACOBA BAKKER BOOTHMAN (1879-)
Homestead on the Kootenai. Caldwell, Idaho: Caxton, 1960. 180pp.

She settles in Montana as a newlywed in 1898, learning about the countryside and about ranch life; she recalls domestic activities, the births of her five sons, and small-town socializing.

258   BRADEN, ANNE (1924-)
The Wall Between. New York: Monthly Review, 1958. 306pp.

A journalist and public relations worker for trade unions, she recounts with rare understanding the chronology of a racial incident in 1954; her decision to help a black friend

buy a home in a white Louisville suburb leads to "far-
reaching repercussions," which include a cross-burning and
city-wide attention; ashamed by the inaction of liberals and
of the churches and terrified by threats against her children,
she is further horrified when the official investigation becomes an attack on her and her husband and they are jailed
for sedition; she closes her account of civic hysteria with a
call for mutual trust.

259   BRAGGIOTTI, GLORIA
      Born in a Crowd.   New York: Crowell, 1957.   311pp.

      She tells of growing up in a large, close, vivacious, ar-
tistic, creative family; at home in Italy, her parents are
vocal instructors and are interested in health food and dress
reform; after her mother's death in 1919, they return to
Boston and are "plunged into American life"; she joins her
older sisters as a professional dancer; in 1926 she returns
to Italy.

260   BRAIDWOOD, LINDA S.
      Digging Beyond the Tigris: An American Woman Archeolo-
      gist's Story of Life on a "Dig" in the Kurdish Hills of Iraq.
      New York: Henry Schuman, 1953.   296pp.

      She tells of an expedition to search for the "early stages
of settled village life" and offers details of settling into her
workshop home with two children; she describes her work
schedule, digging techniques, cataloguing, local workers, and
camp holidays; she abandons camp as funds run out.

261   BRASHER, NELL
      Angel Tracks in the Cabbage Patch.   New York: William-
      Frederick, 1972.   101pp.

      In numerous brief vignettes, an Alabama newspaper col-
umnist savors seasonal changes, the beauty of nature, family
incidents, domestic tasks, and other delightful minutiae of
daily living; the chapters are drawn from her columns.

262   BRAUDY, SUSAN
      Between Marriage and Divorce: A Woman's Diary.   New
      York: Morrow, 1975.   252pp.

      A journalist, she analyzes her adolescence and sexual
awakening, concluding that "when I got married I was lost";
her dual career as a writer and as a professor's wife raises
tensions, and she comes to use her journalistic interviews
as potential sexual events; after a painful confrontation with

her husband, she enters the "orgy of dismarriage" followed
by numerous sexual encounters; with intense self-conscious-
ness, she feels an increasing independence, stating "I have
survived and probably grown. "

263   BRAZER, MARJORIE CAHN
       Wind Off the Dock. New York: Macmillan, 1968. 206pp.

       She opens with her family's decision to buy a 32-foot
boat, and continues with anecdotes of voyages with her husband and three children along the eastern seaboard and in
the Great Lakes; they experience treacherous seas, bad
weather, inadequate charts, boating hospitality, and "unexpected discoveries. "

264   BRECKINRIDGE, MARY (1881-1965)   NAWM
       Wide Neighborhoods; A Story of the Frontier Nursing Service.
       New York: Harper, 1952. 366pp.

       After having spent portions of her youth in Russia and
Switzerland and after a haphazard education, she marries
but is soon widowed; she is trained as a nurse in New York,
then studies in England and organizes nursing assistance for
France after World War I; she returns to the U. S. and establishes the Frontier Nursing Service, bringing maternal
and infant health care and a hospital to the Kentucky hills in
the 1920's; her devotion to the mountain folk results in a
major medical achievement.

265   BREMSER, BONNIE (1939-   )
       Troia: Mexican Memories. New York: Croton Press, 1969.
       209pp.

       Writing in a confessional but deeply ambiguous tone, she
tells of an unsuccessful attempt at communal living in Mexico with her husband and young daughter; her flippant style
masks "an internal growing hardness" as she becomes a
prostitute with her husband's approval, abuses drugs, is
forced to give up her child, endures beatings by her husband, and has an abortion; her sordid, rambling tale ends
in despair and capitulation when she rejoins her husband,
freed from jail, in the U. S.

266   BRENNAN, MAEVE
       The Long Winded Lady; Notes from The New Yorker. New
       York: Morrow, 1969. 237pp.

       "A traveller in residence" in New York City and a close
observer of people, she writes forty-seven vignettes original-

ly published in The New Yorker between 1953 and 1968;
these "snapshots" capture small, delicate human moments
of defeat, hope, death.

267   BREWSTER, MILDRED (1900-   )
       Red Leaves. New York: Pageant Press, 1959.   105pp.

       A newspaper editor, she offers "memories" from her in-
fancy, contrasting the restrictiveness of her parents to her
own later mothering; she describes domestic activity from
a baby's perspective, gradually discovering a wider world;
she has "the stamina of a man," and becomes a strong
feminist at an early age; she notes that the "most interesting thing in life was action and more action."

268   BRICKER, GERTRUDE DeWEESE (1876-   )
       Preacher's Girl. Philadelphia: Dorrance, 1957.   157pp.

       She describes her childhood as "a simple girl in a much
simpler world"; as a minister's daughter, she experiences
frequent transfers from one "country preacher's" post to
another and grows up under strict discipline and the re-
stricted activities and entertainments of proper young womanhood; she notes adults who influence her life, including a
teacher and Frances Willard; choosing with difficulty between
two suitors, she marries, after a brief fling at college.

269   BRIGGS, MARGARET YANG (1917-   )
       Daughter of the Khans. New York: Norton, 1955.   285pp.

       Born in China of Mongol ancestry, she is the daughter of
a well-to-do scholar and government official; "only" a girl
yet allowed to go to high school, she is influenced by a
Harvard-educated brother and, drawn to the west, seeks an
American college education; fiercely independent, she leaves
her family at seventeen, forbidden to return, and begins to
write feminist magazine articles; she gains sophistication
through a series of jobs and travel, serving during the war
with Chinese intelligence and with the American O.S.S.; at
the end of the war, she meets and marries an American
correspondent, finding her destiny in the west; her narrative
is perceptive and articulate.

270   BRIGHAM, GERTRUDE RICHARDSON
       The Road to the Western Isle. Boothbay Harbor, Maine:
       Boothbay Register, 1963.   180pp.

       An artist, she spends two years traveling, studying, and
sketching in Ireland; she notes the places she visits, the

people she meets, and the hosts with whom she stays; she
includes some historical material as well as her own reflections on Irish painting, literature, songs, and historical
landmarks in an often impersonal style.

271 BRINTON, MARY WILLIAMS
My Cap and My Cape; An Autobiography. Philadelphia:
Dorrance, 1950. 262pp.

A visiting nurse, an industrial nurse, and a missionary
nurse, she tells of her training in Philadelphia in 1917; her
career leads to intimate glimpses of a wide variety of people, the adventure of different posts, and the "great camaraderie" of mission personnel; she travels in Europe and
South America, visiting hospitals; in 1936 her marriage
leads to a fifteen-year "detachment" from her career.

272 BRISTOW, KATIE S.
Moro Magic in Mindanao. Fresno, Cal.: Academy Library
Guild, 1958. 95pp.

She joins her dentist husband in the Philippines, worrying
immediately over threats of Moro rebel attacks on whites;
nevertheless, she opens a small school for the local children; ignoring local tension, she establishes close friendships with her servants and with a Moro leader from whom
she learns Spanish.

273 BROCK, ALICE MAY
My Life as a Restaurant. Woodstock, N. Y.: Overlook,
1975. 142pp.

The child of parents "obsessed with food," she grows up
with a palate trained to the sensual pleasures of food; captive as a "hippy housewife," she escapes in her first restaurant and in the second finds creativity, excitement, chaos,
and success; she is critical of the exploitation of the film
Alice's Restaurant; the book includes recipes.

274 BROOKS, ANN
South on Rolling Wheels; Trailer Adventures in the South.
New York: Exposition, 1956. 136pp.

She describes three winters in Florida for "fun and adventure": with her husband, nine-year-old daughter, and
father-in-law; they find warm hospitality and the excitement
of new and varied sights, enjoying the life of "gypsies" on
the road; each year they return to Illinois to welcome spring.

275   BROOKS, GLADYS RICE BILLINGS
       Boston and Return. New York: Atheneum, 1962. 272pp.

       In this sequel to Gramercy Park; Memories of a New
       York Girlhood, she continues to swing between "informality,
       and the values of an artist's world"; this account opens with
       memories of childhood visits to France, the horror of a
       term at boarding school, then the hiatus between girlhood
       and womanhood; she studies landscape gardening; marries a
       Saltonstall of old New England stock, makes uneasy adjust-
       ment to upper-class conventions; continues playing violin
       between births of four children; describes the joy of cham-
       ber music, especially in World War I Washington, D. C. ; the
       book ends with her separation from her husband after fifteen
       years; presently the wife of Van Wyck Brooks.

276   Gramercy Park; Memories of a New York Girlhood.   New
       York: Dutton, 1958.   220pp.

       Each chapter forms a revealing vignette, moving from
       impulsive childhood, through the growing pains of adoles-
       cence; daughter of a doctor ambitious for his children and
       an idealistic mother devoted to culture, she gradually weighs
       their values against those of her friends and acquaintances.

277   If Strangers Meet; A Memory.   New York: Harcourt, Brace
       & World, 1967.   342pp.

       An intimate, perceptive, moving memoir of 16 years of
       marriage with Van Wyck Brooks; attracted by the quiet in-
       tensity of his presence, she marries him in 1947, and he
       becomes "the pivot of my life"; describes the serenity of
       summers on Martha's Vineyard, settling into a Connecticut
       home, the rhythm of their lives moving from mornings of
       study, writing, "mingled silence," to afternoons and evenings
       with friends; account closes with Brooks' final illness and
       death.

278   BROOKS, GWENDOLYN (1917-)
       Report from Part One.   Detroit: Broadside Press, 1972.
       215pp.

       She presents a series of disconnected impressions and
       images leading to her "know-nows," realizations built on
       past experience; she tells of writing her early poems, of
       her marriage, of her children, and of the exuberance of her
       literary life as a poet and reviewer; she finds joy in teach-
       ing; in 1967 she comes to a realization of her Black identi-
       ty; her account includes fragments about a trip to East Af-
       rica and about several interviews.

279   BROOKS, LORETTA E. (1908-   )
Along the Hudson; Sketches of Childhood Life in a Catskill
Town.   New York: Exposition, 1959.   44pp.

Noting that she "came from simple folks ... all river
men," she writes a nostalgic account of favorite family and
community activities and of her school days; she also mentions community patriotism during World War I.

280   BROOKTER, MARIE (1931-   )
Here I Am--Take My Hand, with Jean Curtis.   New York:
Harper & Row, 1974.   248pp.

An articulate, assertive black woman, she first describes
her childhood as one of twelve children of a Louisiana tenant
farmer; growing up with prejudice, she nevertheless gains a
high school education and later a B.A.; her work with the
NAACP in the post-war push for civil rights gives her life
purpose and direction; widowed, she works in Democratic
Party politics, and becomes a press aide for Kennedy in the
1960 campaign; she works for the EEOC and the OEO, describing the rewards and frustrations of government service;
she produces programs on black history for Chicago public
television, then works for the McGovern campaign in 1972,
disappointed by unexpected racial tensions; her struggle for
civil rights continues.

281   BROWN, BERTHA BENDER (1878-1962)
A Tale of Three Cities: Reno, Carson, San Francisco;
1863-1930; The Saga and Humor of an Old Pioneer Family,
ed. Vinson Brown.   Healdsburg, Cal.:   Naturegraph, 1964.
96pp.

In a nostalgic account, she recounts random memories of
her family's pioneering days in Reno; she is one of the first
two women to complete a twelve-day bicycle trip from San
Francisco to Los Angeles in 1894; family anecdotes include
the 1906 San Francisco earthquake, her career as a professional shopper in San Francisco, and her marriage and
motherhood.

282   BROWN, CLARA LEE
Beating Around the Bush.   Boston: Christopher, 1967.
136pp.

Although she and her husband are settled, middle-aged
grandparents, they are drawn by adventure and go on safari
in 1966; she tells of sightseeing with a congenial group of
people and of observing animals in the wild; she leaves,
"forever grateful for the experience."

283   Voyage Into Danger.   North Quincy, Mass.:   Christopher,
       1972.   128pp.

       In her 50's, she and her husband join an international
       Antarctic expedition in 1972; their visits to research sta-
       tions and enthusiastic observations are cut short when they
       are shipwrecked and forced to evacuate in a blizzard; she
       closes the account with their rescue by a Chilean ship on
       which, in spite of crowded, makeshift accommodations, in-
       ternational goodwill flourishes.

284   BROWN, ELEANOR GERTRUDE (1887-)
       Corridors of Light.   Yellow Springs, Ohio: Antioch Press,
       1958.   186pp.

       A teacher, lecturer, and writer who has been blind from
       infancy tells of her childhood years at a state school for the
       blind; encouraged by her mother to become independent, she
       chooses freedom over security throughout her life; she vigor-
       ously pursues her education, becoming the first blind gradu-
       ate of Ohio State University; she meets the challenges of
       public school teaching, travels, and the pursuit of her M. A.
       and Ph. D. in English at Columbia; a guide dog provides new
       freedom as she continues teaching and summer study.

285   BROWN, ESTELLE AUBREY (1876?-)
       Stubborn Fool; A Narrative.   Caldwell, Id.:   Caxton, 1952.
       309pp.

       Asserting her independence, she enters the Indian Service
       in 1902 as a teacher in a South Dakota school, determined
       to be "an entity in my own right"; indignant, she finds the
       children overworked, underfed, ailing, and struggling with
       an inappropriate education; at other schools in Colorado and
       Arizona she finds injustice, interfering missionaries, incom-
       petent teachers; after sixteen years of vigorous protest, she
       resigns, her health broken, and writes her powerful book as
       an indictment of the Bureau of Indian Affairs.

286   BROWN, HELENE
       Yesterday's Child.   New York: M. Evans, 1976.   209pp.

       An interior decorator, editor, columnist, and lecturer,
       she describes twenty "years of suffering, learning, and
       growing" caring for her daughter who is afflicted with cere-
       bral palsy, mental retardation, and deafness; a single par-
       ent, she suffers periods of despair over the crushing re-
       sponsibility she feels but establishes a successful career to
       satisfy her personal needs and to provide a secure future
       for her daughter.

287   BROWN, MRS. HUGH
       see BROWN, MARJORIE MOORE (1885?-)

288   BROWN, JULIA CLARICE
       I Testify: My Years as an Undercover Agent for the FBI.
       Boston: Western Islands, 1966. 293pp.

            A black woman describes how she unwittingly joins the
       American Communist Party in 1947 while working for civil
       rights in Cleveland; naïve and confused, she goes to the
       FBI and becomes a secret agent for them from 1951 to
       1960; describing her political activities as an agent, she
       argues vehemently against the evils of communism and notes
       her patriotic pride as a key witness for the House Un-
       American Activities Committee in 1962.

289   BROWN, LILIAN MacLAUGHLIN
       Bring 'em Back Petrified. New York: Dodd, Mead, 1956.
       277pp.

            Married to a paleontologist, she accompanies him to the
       Guatemala interior; she establishes a camp home, is a good
       "expedition wife" whose "most important duty is the husband";
       she describes the digging, the local people.

290   Cleopatra Slept Here. New York: Dodd, Mead, 1951.
       248pp.

            A paleontologist's wife, she accompanies her "explorer
       husband" to the Greek island of Samos and humorously de-
       scribes housekeeping, their camp crew, servants, the local
       village and its people, sightseeing, and a holiday in Athens;
       her account contains a light overlay of history and mythol-
       ogy.

291   I Married a Dinosaur. New York: Dodd, Mead, 1950.
       268pp.

            Married to a prominent paleontologist, she tells anecdotes
       of her honeymoon at a campsite in India; her romantic hopes
       are frustrated by "a conniving fossil," and she must travel
       and explore on her own, "husbandless and adventurous"; she
       welcomes the exotic with good humor, enjoying dinner with a
       maharaja, a safari in Burma, and a village women's party.

292   BROWN, MARGERY FINN
       Over a Bamboo Fence; An American Looks at Japan. New
       York: Morrow, 1951. 239pp.

An army wife with four daughters describes living in occupied Japan from 1947 to 1948; she meets a wide variety
of people as a reporter for a Japanese newspaper; the conflict of two cultures proves to be at various times amusing,
grotesque, and depressing; she travels and tells of Japanese
women's lives and of the lives of her close friends.

293   BROWN, MARJORIE MOORE (1885? -)
      Lady in Boomtown; Miners and Manners on the Nevada
      Frontier.   Palo Alto, Cal.:   American West, 1968.   127pp.

      Focusing her spirited account on the years from 1903 to
1922, she describes "the sunset rays of the old romantic
West," the exhilaration of the boom and the sorrow of the
bust; married to a lawyer, she maintains the styles and
amenities of city living amid pioneer conditions; she enjoys
the open country, mining tales, a cattle roundup, and "flamboyant characters" of the early days; she includes a vivid
account of the 1906 San Francisco earthquake and fire, there
to visit her family near the end of a pregnancy; after local
Red Cross work during World War I, she leaves Nevada as
her two sons enter college.

294   BROWN, MARY JANE (1895? -)
      American Panorama; The Memoirs of a Peripatetic Midwest-
      erner.   New York: Exposition, 1962.   229pp.

      Presented as "the life history of an average American
citizen," the account describes her rural childhood and her
high school and college years including zoological studies at
Woods Hole in 1917; she teaches, earning her M.A. in 1921
and her Ph.D. in 1928, later becoming a university professor; her extensive travels, often for study, enable her to
add regional and historical material to the account; she
joins the WAC's for patriotic reasons to do World War II
laboratory work.

295   Around the World in 219 Days.   New York: Vantage, 1957.
      241pp.

      A teacher, she travels in 1939 to Hawaii, Japan, the
Philippines, Indonesia, India, Palestine, Egypt, Greece,
England, and Ireland; she provides notes on schools she
visits, sightseeing, and historical and cultural background
in this "record of places, people and conditions."

296   BROWN, OPAL HARTSELL
      Loose Nuts on the Wheel.   San Antonio, Tex.:   Naylor,
      1963.   279pp.

In this bouncy, bubbly travel account, "two middle-aged, middle-classed and middle-western couples" begin a series of "summer wanderings" soon after World War II; she finds material for her newspaper column in their sightseeing, adventures, and misadventures on the road in the continental U. S. , in Canada, and in Mexico.

297   BROWNE, ROSE BUTLER (1897-)
Love My Children, An Autobiography, with James W. English. New York: Meredith, 1969. 246pp.

A black teacher earnestly engaged in the long struggle to improve education for blacks, she recalls her childhood "in the slums of south Boston," growing up with high aspirations and strong family pride; an aggressive, bright student, she meets with little discrimination, earning an M. A. in 1921 and a Ph. D. in 1937; her teaching in the South brings experiences with prejudice and concern for her students, her "acquired children. "

298   BRUCKNER, LEONA S.
Triumph of Love; An Unforgettable Story of the Power of Goodness. New York: Simon and Schuster, 1952. 213pp.

The mother of a congenital amputee tells of her initial horror and rejection of her son's handicap, and of her later dedication to learn all she can to aid him and to promote his self-sufficiency; with inner strength the family accepts the challenge of his growth and development and offers help and encouragement to other parents.

299   BRYAN, HELEN (1894-)
Inside. Boston: Houghton Mifflin, 1953. 305pp.

Having worked for the Y. W. C. A. , the American Friends Service Committee, and the Spanish Aid Committee, she is sentenced to three months in the Alderson federal women's penitentiary in 1948 for contempt of Congress; she feels "compassion and tenderness" for other inmates who lack her past and future; overcoming her initial fears, she adjusts to prison life and teaches briefly, establishing friendships in spite of her age and education; she leaves with mixed emotions.

300   BRYANT, ALICE FRANKLIN
The Sun Was Darkened. Boston: Chapman & Grimes, 1947. 262pp.

Wrenched by Pearl Harbor from the comfortable life of a Philippine planter's wife, she and her family become refugees

in a camp hideaway during the Japanese occupation; discov-
ered, they are interned and she tells of concentration camp
conditions from 1943 to 1945; she closes with their liberation and repatriation to the U. S.

301   BRYANT, ANITA (1940-)
       Amazing Grace. Old Tappan, N. J. : Revell, 1971. 127pp.

       A popular singer describes both the pressures of televi-
sion performance, record production, and extensive travel
and the exaltation she experiences when her performances
are combined with religious witness; her family life with her
husband and four young children is suffused with strong
evangelical religious faith, and she describes her children's
salvation and her husband's encouragement to continue wit-
nessing in spite of her sense of spiritual inadequacy; she
chronicles the conversions of several friends.

302   Bless This House. Old Tappan, N. J. : Revell, 1972.
       156pp.

       A prominent singer and entertainer presents a candid dis-
cussion of some of the problems she faces in her marriage,
child rearing, and business transactions; she describes the
impact of a religious reawakening in her daily home life as
she learns how to submit to her husband's authority, to take
full responsibility for her four children, and to make Christian friendships; she and her husband write separate, alternating chapters.

303   Fishers of Men, with Bob Green. Old Tappan, N. J. : Re-
       vell, 1973. 156pp.

       Asserting that "witnessing has turned my life around, "
she describes the "power of Christian witness" in anecdotes
drawn from her daily life and her work as a Sunday school
teacher and an organizer of a summer camp for talented
Christian girls; she writes six of the book's thirteen chapters.

304   Light My Candle, with Bob Green. Old Tappan, N. J. :
       Revell, 1974. 159pp.

       She tells how her religious faith sustains her during times
of mental and emotional stress; crises include her tense relationship with her father, her husband's heart trouble, her
own surgery, estrangement in her marriage, the death of a
close friend, and her emotional exhaustion and breakdown;
she uses her own painful experiences as examples to strength-

en the faith of others; she writes ten of the book's fifteen
chapters.

305   Mine Eyes Have Seen the Glory.   Old Tappan, N. J.:   Re-
        vell, 1970.   159pp.

        Born and raised in Oklahoma and a singer since childhood,
        she becomes a finalist in the Miss America Pageant and a
        recording star; success is followed by marriage, motherhood,
        and a continuing career; the account is suffused with reli-
        gious conviction.

306   Running the Good Race, with Bob Green.   Old Tappan, N. J.:
        Revell, 1976.   157pp.

        She notes a parallel between physical exercise and spiritu-
        al exercise, pointing out the similarities in commitment and
        self-discipline, and she undertakes tithing as a form of fi-
        nancial self-control; she reflects on the meaning of submis-
        sion to her husband and to God; she is moved by her father-
        in-law's religious conversion; she writes eight of the book's
        thirteen chapters.

307   BUBLITZ, DOROTHEA E. (1895?-)
        Life on the Dotted Line.   New York: Vantage, 1960.   110pp.

        Nostalgic for the "thrilling life" of the pioneer, she tells
        of her family's move from the U. S. to a Saskatchewan home-
        stead in 1910; after her marriage in 1916, she raises three
        sons on another prairie homestead, recalling her domestic
        tasks, neighbors, hired hands, and the glories of farm life;
        she adds bits of local history to her account.

308   BUCK, PEARL SYDENSTRICKER (1892-1973)   NAWM
        A Bridge for Passing.   New York: John Day, 1961.   256pp.

        A prolific writer, she tells with exquisite sensitivity of
        her return to Asia to film her book The Big Wave; she jux-
        taposes the old and new, the Japan of her memories and
        contemporary Japan; at her husband's death, she experi-
        ences "the final loneliness," recalling twenty-five years of
        an unusually close married life; incidents during the filming
        renew the sorrow of her loss, but she learns to move on
        with strength, to accept a "profound insurge of peace."

309   The Child Who Never Grew.   New York: John Day, 1950.
        62pp.

A noted writer, she describes the sorrow of her gradual realization that her first child, born in the vigor and hope of her young womanhood in China, is severely retarded; learning to accept the burden is a long, painful process, but she is determined that her daughter's "life must count" through her open discussion of the needs and rights of the retarded to security and happiness.

310   My Several Worlds: A Personal Record. New York: John Day, 1954. 407pp.

Her highly articulate account is told in numerous flashbacks; she is the child of missionaries in China; she begins what becomes a prolific writing career at thirty; later she makes a permanent move to the U. S. , establishing her roots in farm and family life; she provides a sensitive combination of cultural and historical perspective on Chinese and American values, fine portraiture, and story-telling.

311   BUECHELE, ELLONA M.
Always Carry a Rabbit's Foot; A Story of Adventures in Everyday Living. New York: Exposition, 1953. 137pp.

She writes light, humorous anecdotes opening with a furnace explosion and continuing with stories about the radio recording business she shares with her husband, building a new home, and travels to Hawaii; it is largely a collection of misadventures.

312   BULIFANT, JOSEPHINE CHRISTIANA (1897-   )
Forty Years in the African Bush. Grand Rapids, Mich. : Zondervan, 1950. 185pp.

She travels as a missionary to the Central Sudan in 1929 and organizes two girls' schools, teaching religion and practical education; she describes native culture, and, noting that "Satan seeks to keep woman down," she is particularly concerned with the conditions for women; she illustrates native "heathenism" and describes converts.

313   BULLE, FLORENCE
Lord of the Valleys. Plainfield, N. J. : Logos International, 1972. 206pp.

Discussing a religious rebirth that changes "the whole course of my life," she tells of a total commitment to faith that sustains her through years of trials and suffering, including severe lung disease, numerous operations, chronic pain, and emotional stress.

314   BURGE, DOLLY SUMNER LUNT (1817-1891)
       The Diary of Dolly Lunt Burge, ed. James I. Robertson,
       Jr.   Athens: University of Georgia Press, 1962.   141pp.

       In a diary that covers the years from 1847 to 1879, she
       is revealed as a woman of great strength, character and
       religious earnestness; having lost her first husband and both
       children, she remarries, and when she is again widowed,
       she raises five stepchildren and a daughter and struggles to
       administer plantation affairs during the Civil War; after the
       war she rebuilds the plantation and finds domestic comfort
       in a third marriage; she is thankful for three "blessed"
       marriages and a beloved daughter; two previous editions in
       1918 and 1927 present only excerpts.

315   BURKE, BILLIE (1886-1970)
       With a Feather on My Nose, with Cameron Shipp.   New
       York: Appleton-Century-Crofts, 1949.   272pp.

       The daughter of a famous clown, she is pushed into act-
       ing by her mother; she describes her early work in London
       and her move to the U.S. in 1907, where she performs
       numerous roles on stage and screen; she marries theatrical
       impresario Flo Ziegfeld; her account closes with the death
       of her husband in 1932, noting only very briefly later events.

316   BURKE, CLARA HEINTZ
       Doctor Hap, as told to Adele Comandini.   New York: Cow-
       ard-McCann, 1961.   319pp.

       Traveling to Alaska in 1907 to regain her health and as
       a companion to a missionary nurse, she responds to the
       challenge of pioneering, learning to cook, nurse, and teach;
       full of "youthful idealism," she meets and marries a young
       doctor, returning only briefly to the U.S. after seven years
       to lecture and raise funds for a hospital; she regrets the
       necessity of sending her sons to her mother for their school
       years but remains totally dedicated to her husband, the Yukon
       hospital, and its people; she closes her touching account with
       the death of her husband, "no ordinary man."

317   BURMEISTER, EVA
       Forty-five in the Family: The Story of a Home for Children.
       New York: Columbia University Press, 1949.   247pp.

       The superintendent of an orphan asylum describes her
       daily routine, her experiences with children, her desire to
       provide a secure refuge and center for identity for orphaned
       children; the narrative focuses throughout on children.

318   BURNHAM, ELEANOR WARING
        Rome: Then and Now.   New York: Vantage, 1951.   228pp.

        This anecdotal narrative is presented through letters; the
        wife of a sculptor, she settles in Rome in 1911 and de-
        scribes her domestic arrangements, the local customs, her
        social life within the American colony there; her descriptions
        include notes on Roman architecture and are detailed and
        lively.

319   BURNS, ANNALEE
        Gone Are the Days.   San Antonio: Naylor, 1960.   95pp.

        Unabashedly sentimental, she portrays her rural Texas
        childhood with lively detail; chapters focus on the visits of
        "summer kin," harvest time, children's pastimes, "oldtime
        religion," home remedies, an old-fashioned Christmas, local
        characters; each nostalgic vignette, suffused with love and
        security, provides a contrast to the present, poorer by
        comparison.

320   BURNS, ELIZABETH
        The Late Liz; The Autobiography of an Ex-Pagan.   New
        York: Appleton-Century-Crofts, 1957.   342pp.

        A slangy, tough, vehement account of an early rebellious
        marriage leading to a five-year nightmare of drink; a second
        marriage includes wealth, boredom, and dissipation; a third
        marriage is disastrous and sons are estranged; she attempts
        suicide, begins "to know God" with the help of her son, a
        minister; she becomes a counselor, works with A. A.

321   BURROW, BRUNETTIE
        Angels in White.   San Antonio: Naylor, 1959.   132pp.

        A private nurse, she describes "true incidents out of
        twenty-five years of nursing experience"; at 24, a broken
        marriage leaves her with a daughter to support, so she en-
        ters nurses' training in 1912; she tells of poverty and hard
        work, laced with a little fun; memorable cases including
        those in the 1918 flu epidemic bring her "life in the raw,"
        and nursing enables her to "redeem the wreck of my early
        life."

322   I Lay Down My Cap.   San Antonio, Texas: Naylor, 1961.
        96pp.

        Written at 73, this account tells of her years as a nurse;
        she supports herself and a daughter with "heartache, humor

and a never-ending sense of self-satisfaction"; she describes
various cases, and spirited exchanges with some doctors in
random anecdotes.

323   BURROWS, DOROTHEA GIBSON
        Heart Cry, as told to Spencer W. Burrows.   Mountain View,
        Cal.:   Pacific Press, 1964.   82pp.

        She writes to encourage others similarly suffering from
        heart disease; a victim of childhood rheumatic fever, she
        pursues work and college to the point of exhaustion, com-
        pleting nurses' training in 1944; the added strains of her
        duties as a minister's wife, as the mother of two, and as
        an occasional nurse result in severe heart damage followed
        by a stroke; her struggle to return to an active life is bol-
        stered by her religious faith and her family's love.

324   BURTON, KATHERINE KURZ (1890-1969)
        The Next Thing; Autobiography and Reminiscences.   New
        York: Longmans, Green, 1949.   246pp.

        She tells of "the steps that brought me into the Catholic
        Church"; she describes a typical childhood and youth, fol-
        lowed by years as a serious student but not marked by
        strong religious feelings; she marries in 1912 and her fam-
        ily prospers with three children; at her husband's nervous
        breakdown, she turns to a Catholic rector for support; she
        writes for religious magazines and for a time wavers be-
        tween the Episcopal and Catholic faiths, but finally converts
        to Catholicism; she writes several biographies of Catholic
        subjects.

325   BURTON, NAOMI (1911-   )
        More Than Sentinels.   Garden City, N.Y.:   Doubleday, 1964.
        346pp.

        A writer and editor traces her reasons for becoming a
        Catholic in a sensitive, thoughtful journal; English-born, she
        sees the dispersal of her family at the end of World War I
        culminate in her mother's death; after boarding school, she
        works for years with a London literary agency, struggling
        against the "slide into inaction"; her passion for the U.S.
        and for New York leads to an editorial position there and
        her gradual Americanization; deeply influenced by the young
        Thomas Merton's autobiography, she moves to Catholicism,
        recognizing its profound effect on her daily life.

326   BUSCH, BETTY
        Eastern Easter in the Holy Land.   New York: Comet Press
        Books, 1955.   104pp.

In 1954 she travels to the Middle East with her husband; her narrative presents detailed descriptions of places and of religious ceremonies and is sprinkled with Bible quotations.

327   BUSH, MARIAN SPORE (1892-1946)
      They. New York: Beechhurst, 1947.   158pp.

      A painter claims that her work is guided by supernatural forces; she tells of psychic experiences which begin in childhood and shift from communications with her deceased mother and automatic writing to automatic drawing and painting; after autobiographical anecdotes, she reveals "teachings of the other world."

328   BUSHAKRA, MARY WINIFRED
      I Married an Arab. New York: John Day, 1951.   246pp.

      "Itching for adventure" after twelve years of marriage, she settles happily with her husband in his native Lebanon; she describes the effusive welcome and the close family ties she finds there; she adopts her husband's granddaughter; she describes the effects of a war in 1939 and of a locust plague.

329   BUTCHER, FANNY
      Many Lives--One Love. New York: Harper & Row, 1972. 463pp.

      A journalist for the Chicago Tribune for forty-nine years, she presents an account structured by topic: her childhood, her journalistic assignments, her great friendships, her lifelong love of books; she includes anecdotes of literary friends and acquaintances.

330   BUTLER, JOYCE
      Pages from a Journal. Kennebunkport, Me.: Mercer House Press, 1976.   171pp.

      Her account is drawn from essays written between 1968 and 1975 for a local Maine newspaper; the quiet, reflective vignettes focus on family activities and country living, treating the seasons, satisfactions of old houses, grief, motherhood, civic concerns, housekeeping, visitors, holidays, and having a room of one's own.

331   BUXBAUM, KATHERINE (1885-   )
      Iowa Outpost. Philadelphia: Dorrance, 1948.   253pp.

      The first three chapters of this book are autobiographical while the remaining chapters are partly fictitious; the daughter of a store owner, she evokes the atmosphere of the family store, the community Moravian Church, and the post-pioneer "mellowness" of a small rural Iowa town.

332   BUYUKMIHCI, HOPE SAWYER
      Hour of the Beaver.   Chicago: Rand McNally, 1971.   173pp.

A conservationist, writer and lecturer, she engages in "intensive beaver-watching" in her New Jersey wildlife sanctuary and finds the camaraderie of the beaver "deeply satisfying"; she enjoys a "growing intimacy" with the trusting second generation of young; she personally confronts hunters, campaigns against the open season on beavers.

C

333 CABEZA DE BACA, FABIOLA
see GILBERT, FABIOLA CABEZA DE BACA (1895-)

334 CAHILL, SUSAN
Earth Angels; Portraits from Childhood and Youth. New
York: Harper & Row, 1976. 213pp.

The youngest daughter in a "not very holy" Catholic family describes growing up in New York City, rebellions and
adventures in parochial school, adolescent "orgies," fascination with nuns; she attends a Catholic girls' college, and
under the pressure of her last year and a search for a major commitment, she decides to become a nun; the contrasts
of the narrow religious community and the upheavals of the
1960's prove too great, and she returns to the secular world.

335 CAINE, LYNN
Widow. New York: Morrow, 1974. 222pp.

The author tells of her husband's dying of cancer, his
death, and her adjustment to widowhood and a new identity;
she discusses the stages of her grief, the effects of their
father's death on her two small children; her account is
written partly to aid other women in the same situation.

336 CALISHER, HORTENSE (1911-)
Herself. New York: Arbor House, 1972. 401pp.

A writer, she tells of the "pure, carnal leap" of achieving her first publication; she produces poetry amid marriage
and domesticity, following an inner compulsion to write, her
"life-habit"; a fellowship in 1952 offers time to explore the
implications of being a woman artist with a conventional
family life; she includes a journal kept during travels in the
Far East; she searches for continuity between living and
writing through long reflective essays, "fugitive soundings"
of a complex personality.

337 CALKINS, FAY G. (1921-)
My Samoan Chief. Honolulu: University Press of Hawaii,
1971. 207pp.

This is a humorous, entertaining account of her marriage
to a Samoan whom she met in the stacks of the Library of
Congress; she describes their return to Samoa, the lavish
hospitality, her vast extended family, the incomprehensible
local economics, the beauty of nature; she organizes a wom-
en's craft co-op, a food co-op; raising her children in two
cultures, she is alive to the differences in "ideas of property, propriety, child raising, and the purpose of life."

338   CALL, HUGHIE FLORENCE (1890-   )
       The Little Kingdom. Boston: Houghton Mifflin, 1964.
       134pp.

       She describes her life on a Montana sheep ranch, her
       daughter's "little kingdom"; with loving detail, she tells of
       the close tie between her daughter and a horse and of her
       daughter's numerous pets; she closes with the death of her
       daughter.

339   CALVERLEY, ELEANOR JANE TAYLOR (1886-   )
       My Arabian Days and Nights. New York: Crowell, 1958.
       182pp.

       "Kuwait's first woman doctor," she describes her twenty
       years as a medical missionary; impressed by the Muslim
       religion and enthusiastic about the area's natural beauty, she
       earns the respect and confidence of the people while raising
       three daughters; she tells of her work in a women's clinic
       and in a women's hospital constructed in 1919, offering anec-
       dotes of patients and her "years of rich privilege"; after
       leaving in 1929, she returns in 1955 and notes many changes.

340   CAMERON, CONSTANCE CARPENTER (1937-   )
       A Different Drum. Englewood Cliffs, N.J.: Prentice-Hall,
       1973. 241pp.

       She tells of the shock and grief that accompany the diag-
       nosis of her son's brain damage and aphasia; she reads ex-
       tensively, resolving to become an expert on aphasia and to
       commit herself totally to the slow, systematic education of
       her son, basing her ideas on the close observation of his
       capabilities and responses; her dedication and courage are
       rewarded by a unique depth of knowledge.

341   CAMPBELL, ELIZABETH WARDER CROZER (1893-   )
       The Desert Was Home. Los Angeles: Westernlore, 1961.
       265pp.

       A professor and archaeologist, she and her husband home-
       stead in the California desert in 1924, settling there for his

health; they build a permanent home with their own hands
and contribute to the development of a community in spite
of attacks by anti-homesteader forces; she tells of her desert education, relishing the nature lore and adventures
unique to the desert, and experiencing her "richest living"
during her homestead years.

342   CAMPBELL, MRS. KEMPER
       see CAMPBELL, LITTA BELLE HIBBEN

343   CAMPBELL, LITTA BELLE HIBBEN (1886-)
       Here I Raise Mine Ebenezer.   New York: Simon and Schus-
       ter, 1962.   256pp.

       A lawyer in practice with her husband, she remarks
       "good fortune has followed me all my life"; raised in a de-
       vout family in decent poverty, she is ambitious, graduating
       from law school with honors, becoming a Deputy District
       Attorney in 1916, joining faculties of both law and medical
       schools; an assertive woman, she describes legal cases and
       crusades, and the pleasures left in her "declining years."

344   Marching Without Banners and Other Devices.   New York:
       Simon and Schuster, 1969.   192pp.

       She writes random reflections on past events and experi-
       ences, from politics to "the tyranny of machines" to char-
       acter to education; each short anecdote contains a moral
       lesson.

345   CAMPION, ROSAMOND
       The Invisible Worm.   New York: Macmillan, 1972.   96pp.

       A writer tells of her encounter with breast cancer; she
       is greatly disturbed by the experiences of others with radi-
       cal mastectomy and by the cavalier attitudes and thoughtless
       procedures of her doctors; she refuses to consent to radical
       mastectomy and travels to the midwest for less radical
       treatment by a sympathetic doctor; with sensitivity, she ex-
       plores her own thoughts and feelings and discusses the issues
       of personal and informed choice.

346   CANDLIN, ENID SAUNDERS
       The Breach in the Wall; A Memoir of the Old China.   New
       York: Macmillan, 1973.   340pp.

       Daughter of a businessman in China, she establishes her
       childhood setting with a wealth of detail and fond memories

of Shanghai; she engages in research work during the 1930's and travels much with her colleagues; she enjoys a "halcyon period" before she is forced to flee during the Sino-Japanese War in 1937; in spite of the bombing in Shanghai, she recalls some "happy hours" within the war; World War II marks "the end of an era."

347   CANNON, AGNES
       About My Father's Business; The Adventures of a Roving
       Minister and His Wife in Arkansas.   New York: Exposition,
       1959.   75pp.

       Opening with her marriage, she tells in flowery prose of "the labors of two itinerants in eleven parishes" beginning in 1925; her anecdotes describe a mixture of trials and rewards in their home mission work, revivals, and the response of the people.

348   CANNON, POPPY (1906?-1975)
       A Gentle Knight: My Husband, Walter White.   New York:
       Rinehart, 1956.   309pp.

       She first meets White in 1931 through her activities in the NAACP of which he's a black officer; a professional author of cookbooks, she travels throughout the South gathering material for a book on cooking "as a Negro art" and comes to her first understanding of racism, a sensitivity made more profound by her interracial marriage in 1949; deeply in love with a "great man," she enjoys a rich social and intellectual life among whites and blacks, finding staunch friends and relishing "a big and exciting world"; she closes her narrative with her beloved husband's death in 1955.

349   CAREY, ERNESTINE MOLLER GILBRETH (1908-   )
       Belles on Their Toes, with Frank B. Gilbreth, Jr.   New
       York: Crowell, 1950.   237pp.

       In a sequel to Cheaper by the Dozen, she tells "the story of Mother," who takes over the family business at the death of her husband and becomes a leading management engineer while raising eleven children and seeing them each through a college education; she describes mass chicken pox, the children's organizational hierarchy on a summer trip to Nantucket, the complications of enjoying the social whirl with numerous siblings, her mother's public lectures which include illustrative but mortifying family anecdotes.

350   Cheaper by the Dozen, with Frank B. Gilbreth, Jr.   New
       York: Crowell, 1948.   245pp.

The daughter of prominent industrial engineers and raised in a family of twelve children, she writes a delightful account of her childhood; her parents' pioneering motion studies carry over into domestic organization, bringing efficiency and form to the boundless energy and chaotic activities of the entire family; after recounting family council meetings, assembly-line tonsillectomies, and summers in Nantucket, she closes with her father's death in 1924.

351   Rings Around Us. Boston: Little, Brown, 1956. 240pp.

Opening her entertaining family chronicle with the story of her courtship and marriage, she tells of juggling work and domesticity with less finesse than her mother, an industrial engineer (see Cheaper by the Dozen); mother of a daughter and a son, she copes with a succession of nurses and homes, finally establishing roots in suburban Long Island and abandoning work for the joys of child rearing, described in numerous amusing anecdotes.

352   CAREY, MICHAEL (pseud.)
        see JOHNSON, JOHNILE CURRY

353   CARL, ELLA LANE
        The Letters of a Texas Oil Driller's Wife. New York:
        Comet Press, 1959. 222pp.

Including some recollections of her childhood, she focuses on the years after 1927, writing to allay her homesickness and dismay at the barren country and her "tar-papered shack"; noting the wind, dust, storms, and dangers from rattlesnakes, prairie fires, and gas explosions, she portrays her domestic situation with four small children and embellishes it with bits of Texas history and lore; she describes hard times as the depression deepens and closes with her departure from Texas.

354   CARLISLE, KATHLEEN SMITH
        The Rampant Refugees. New York: Dutton, 1946. 251pp.

After a peripatetic childhood, she marries a British official in Shanghai and enjoys a frivolous social life; caught in Manila by the Japanese occupation following Pearl Harbor, she is allowed to return to Shanghai only to be interned in a concentration camp with her husband and daughter; eventually repatriated, she arrives in New York without her husband; her flippant style masks anxiety and hardship.

355   CARLSON, AVIS DUNGAN
Small World, ... Long Gone; A Family Record of an Era.
Evanston, Ill.: Schori Press, 1975. 154pp.

A perceptive writer, she describes the self-contained life
at the turn of the century in rural Kansas, having "survived
the changes" from the frontier to contemporary times; part
of a "noisy, disputatious" extended family, she portrays a
spirited grandmother, an ambitious father, and a fiercely
independent mother; she is sensitive to the subtleties of sib-
ling relationships and to the pervasive effects of living on
an isolated farm; a voracious reader, she is introduced to
wider worlds in college, exploring literature with her future
husband; she closes with her wedding in 1917.

356   CARLSON, BETTY
The Unhurried Chase.   Rock Island, Ill.: Augustana, 1962.
145pp.

She describes a background of highly varied interests including teaching, athletic gymnasium supervising, U.S.O.
volunteer work, studies for an M.A. degree, service in the
WAVES, and travels in Europe in 1947; for two years she
lives in a family-like Swiss pension and studies at a music
conservatory; aware of a nagging lack at the center of her
ceaseless activities, she visits the home of missionaries in
Switzerland and finds warm friendship, inner peace, and religious faith.

357   [No entry]

358   CARPENTER, EDNA TURLEY (1872-   )
Tales from the Manchaca Hills; The Unvarnished Memoirs
of a Texas Gentlewoman, ed. Jane and Bill Hogan.   New
Orleans: Hauser Press, 1960.   221pp.

In a lively style spiced with a colorful personal vocabu-
lary, she tells of her childhood in a large, close-knit family; after high school and teaching, she seeks a college education against her mother's wishes and marries in 1897 also
against her mother's wishes; she describes her church activities and her joint management of a county poor farm with
her husband; after "blissful years" farming and raising a
family, she copes with hard times and later, widowhood.

359   CARPENTER, IRIS
No Woman's World.   Boston: Houghton Mifflin, 1946.
338pp.

Struggling against special discrimination as a woman war correspondent, she covers American troops in England before D-Day, the French Maquis, the German occupation of France, Paris after the liberation, the Battle of the Bulge, and the liberation of Nazi concentration camps; an aggressive reporter, she provides many human interest anecdotes, some in horrific detail.

360   CARPENTER, LIZ
       Ruffles and Flourishes.   Garden City, N.Y.:   Doubleday, 1969.   341pp.

       A Texas journalist in post-war Washington, D. C., and "a political animal by nature," she is thrilled by the "excitement and majesty" of the capital; she joins the Lyndon Johnson presidential campaign and becomes press secretary to Lady Bird Johnson; she relates anecdotes of hard work, travels with the First Lady, campaigns, two White House weddings, all marked by her exhilaration and good humor.

361   CARR, LORRAINE
       To the Philippines with Love.   Los Angeles: Sherbourne, 1966.   254pp.

       A journalist, she settles in the post-war Philippines for five years with her doctor husband; she establishes an unconventional friendship with her servants and sees to their education, teaches in an American school, travels with her husband, and describes in detail the hardships, danger, and beauty she encounters; her friendships include the later president Magsaysay; she returns to the U.S. due to her husband's ill health, and sorrowfully notes both his and Magsaysay's deaths.

362   CARRIGHAR, SALLY (1905-   )
       Home to the Wilderness.   Boston: Houghton Mifflin, 1973. 330pp.

       This is a moving, introspective account of her tortured childhood; hated by her mother, gradually alienated from her father, she survives the shock of being beaten and strangled by her mother; she finds some solace in the power of music and in icy self-control; her intense loneliness is broken by brief relationships with adults; her two years at Wellesley in the 1920's are euphoric, but her health breaks; after a series of jobs, she is near suicide during the depression and finds an understanding analyst; while recuperating from illness she is inspired to write about animals and nature, and she moves at last to the California wilderness.

363   Moonlight at Midday.   New York: Knopf, 1958.   389pp.

A naturalist, she settles for a year in an Alaskan Eskimo village to study Arctic wildlife, gradually adjusting to a
life without pressure; hoping to achieve the "quiet mind" of
the natives, she admires Eskimo culture and finds Eskimos
"a people to cherish"; she finds heightened awareness in a
land fraught with daily danger, and the satisfactions of
"Northern living" lead to her prolonged residence.

364   Wild Voice of the North.   Garden City, N.Y.:   Doubleday,
1959.   191pp.

A naturalist, she goes to Alaska to do research on lemmings; finding the North congenial, she lives for five years
in Nome; this account focuses on a Husky dog to which she
is drawn by his leadership, his dignity, his "startling initiative"; she acquires the dog as a companion, observing
his behavior closely and learning the subtleties of co-exist-
ence and mutual courtesy, building remarkably sensitive
communications with him; she closes with his death.

365   CARROLL, GLADYS HASTY (1904-)
Only Fifty Years Ago.   Boston: Little, Brown, 1962.   276pp.

She writes a memoir of the Hasty family members and
the neighbors she knew during her Maine childhood; the
chapters are organized according to the yearly cycle; nature
sets the scene for family vignettes; she notes her discovery
of the joys of writing, and of imaginary worlds.

366   To Remember Forever; The Journal of a College Girl, 1922-
1923.   Boston: Little, Brown, 1963.   306pp.

Finding it "wonderful" to be an aspiring young writer in
America and hoping to become a "local laureate" in her native Maine, she conveys the intense excitement of college
life, continuing her earlier interests in writing by contributing to the campus newspaper and joining a literary club;
her vignettes include charming portraits of her extended
family; the journal closes with her plans to marry and to
remain dedicated to writing, taking as a model Sarah Orne
Jewett (see entry #1050).

367   Years Away from Home.   Boston: Little, Brown, 1971.
373pp.

She describes "the House," her childhood home, as the
center of family life with great domestic detail; she has a

large capacity for deep attachment to places; after college,
she marries and spends years writing for adults' and children's magazines and enjoys major success with her novel
As the Earth Turns; she describes the joy of her son's
first year; the account includes much quotation from her
correspondence.

368   CARSON, MARY
       Ginny: A True Story.   Garden City, N. Y. :   Doubleday,
       1971.   215 pp.

       The mother of eight, she tells of her six-year-old daugh-
ter's struggle for survival after being hit by a truck in
1966; her strong religious faith supports her vigil during
her daughter's coma and slow recovery; she is buoyed by
the support of friends and the dedication of health workers;
her detailed record notes the effects on many lives of her
family's trial.

369   CARTER, SARA ELIZABETH WOODS
       It Happened to Us.   Keene, Tex. :   College Press, 1959.   175pp.

       She calls her description of whirlwind travel and sight-
seeing "The Thrill of Winning a Free Trip to Europe and
the Middle East on KLM Royal Dutch Airlines. "

369a   CARUSO, DOROTHY PARK BENJAMIN (1893-1955)
       A Personal History.   New York: Hermitage House, 1952.
       191pp.

       Her book consists of vignettes, impressionistic images
from "the austerity of my convent, the severity of my family,
the protective isolation of my marriage"; intensely devoted
to her husband, the famous tenor Caruso, her world collapses
when she is widowed with a daughter in 1921; two brief marriages and the birth of a second daughter follow; she recounts
starvation times in France at the beginning of World War II
and the death of a beloved brother; she writes a biography of
Caruso; her search for inner certainty continues.

370   CARVER, SONORA (1905?-)
       A Girl and Five Brave Horses, as told to Elizabeth Land.
       Garden City, N. Y. :   Doubleday, 1961.   208pp.

       Her intense love of horses changes her life when she
joins a diving horse act at nineteen; with unlimited nerve
and "a craving for life, " she submits to grueling training,
deeply influenced by the eighty-four-year-old impresario who
becomes a father figure for her; after his death, she mar-

ries his son, a colleague in the act; damages to her eyes
render her blind at twenty-seven, but she courageously returns to diving horses, riding blind for another eleven years
until her retirement in 1942.

371   CASE, MABEL HAMM (1883-1952)
        The Singing Years. New York: Vantage, 1953.   105pp.

   After a happy country girlhood in Missouri, she becomes
a minister's wife in 1908 and exploits her love of music as
a singer and choir director; in a series of random recollections, she tells of her church work and her leadership of a
YWCA choir after her husband's breakdown following World
War I.

372   CASERTA, PEGGY (1940?-   )
        Going Down with Janis, as told to Dan Knapp.   Secaucus,
        N.J.: Lyle Stuart, 1973.   298pp.

   She writes a lurid account of degradation, jealousy, violence, and drug addiction, played out against a background
of blues and the heyday of Haight-Ashbury; her detailed descriptions of sexual encounters with Janis Joplin are laced
with underlying tension and dissatisfaction, yet she describes
her "reborn love affair" the week before Joplin's death.

373   CASKEY, JESSIE JANE HUSSEY (1875-   )
        Journalizing Jane. New York: Exposition, 1960.   143pp.

   In this rambling chronicle of "a lot of ups and downs,"
she tells of unhappy childhood memories, wishes that she
"had been born a boy"; after a disrupted family life, she
runs away at 15, marries at 18, suffers the death of a
two-year-old son, is deserted by her husband; random memories of housekeeping, odd jobs, and nursing do not reveal
much about her career as a writer and poet.

374   CASSINI, MARGUERITE (1882-   )
        Never a Dull Moment: Memoirs of Countess Marguerite
        Cassini. New York: Harper, 1956.   366pp.

   A fine raconteuse, Russian born, she recalls being torn
between the privileges of her father's life as a diplomat and
the Bohemian leanings of her mother; she describes eight
magical childhood years in China, years in Paris amid the
European aristocracy, and her serving as official hostess
for her father when he is Ambassador to the U.S. in 1898;
ignorant yet precocious, she is thrown into "the limelight"
of social circles; failing as a singer, she enters forty

tempestuous years of marriage to a frivolous fanatic; a survivor of intrigue and chaos during World War I, she finds
"the hard new discipline of work" in Italy as a dress designer, gaining financial success; she settles in the U.S.
in 1937, proud of her famous sons' careers in fashion de-
sign and journalism.

375   CASTLE, IRENE FOOTE (1893-1969)   NAWM
Castles in the Air, as told to Bob and Wanda Duncan. Garden City, N.Y.: Doubleday, 1958.   264pp.

After telling anecdotes of a spirited family life, she describes her "theatrical fever" and her marriage in 1911 to
Vernon Castle; after their appearances in musical comedies,
they begin dancing together in a Paris revue, riding the
American dance craze in "our champagne days" with their
joyful, intuitive dancing; later they teach, appear in vaudeville, and make films; constantly on display, setting fashions,
she maintains a hectic pace, throwing herself into movies
after her husband's accidental death; after two bleak and
stormy marriages and two children, she finds happiness with
a fourth husband.

376   CATES, TRESSA R.
The Drainpipe Diary.   New York: Vantage, 1957.   273pp.

Her perceptive account is taken from a secret diary kept
from 1941 to 1945; a civilian nurse in the Philippines, her
"glorious life" of work, travel, and socializing ends with the
Japanese invasion just before her wedding date; interned with
her fiancé, she recounts the details of prison camp life, her
survival techniques, her swings of morale from high to low,
and her coping with filth, illness, uncertainty, and stress;
she shifts from spirited rebellion to resignation under the
"corroding influence of boredom, hunger, and helplessness";
she describes the horror of the camp's final days, the drama
of liberation, and her long-delayed marriage, rebuilding her
life in Manila.

377   CATHER, WILLA SIBERT (1873-1947)   NAW
Willa Cather in Europe; Her Own Story of the First Journey.
New York: Knopf, 1956.   178pp.

In fourteen travel articles written for a Nebraska newspaper, she records her impressions; at first shocked by the
slovenly appearance of the people, she later offers vivid
portrayals of life on the English canals and "the hideous
distortions of a nightmare" in London's East End, as well
as details of "the beautiful surfaces and the beautiful life of
London"; although she visits several sites with literary as-

sociations, she is at her most charming and revealing in her detailed observations which illuminate common people's lives.

378 CATHERINE THOMAS OF DIVINE PROVIDENCE, MOTHER
My Beloved; The Story of a Carmelite Nun. New York: McGraw-Hill, 1955. 252pp.

She discusses her family background and her decision to become a "contemplative cloistered nun"; her strong sense of vocation overrides her parents' objections and a temporary setback when she develops tuberculosis; her description of the cloistered life counters stereotypes with its illustrations of the sense of discipline, loving obedience, "peace of soul," "austere simplicity," and her companionship with sisters who are full of life and good humor.

379 CATTELL, ANN (1893-   )
Sixty Miles North; Saga of a Country Schoolteacher. New York: Comet Press Books, 1953. 178pp.

She returns to teaching due to a shortage of teachers during World War II and describes one year in rural California, adjusting to inconveniences and small town ways; "bewildered by changed standards and values," she nevertheless meets her students' families, learns some local history, joins a women's social circle, survives the daily "little comedies and tragedies," and gains a deeper understanding of the people.

380 CATTELL, CATHERINE DeVOL (1906-   )
Till Break of Day; Pen Sketches of Life in Bundelkhand, Central India. Grand Rapids, Mich.: Eerdmans, 1946. 214pp.

A missionary who serves with her husband in India, she provides vivid descriptions of the people, their culture, and their surroundings--"scattered pictures of village life"; she travels, holds camp meetings, offers simple health remedies, and chronicles the struggle as well as some victories.

381 CAUDILL, REBECCA (1899-   )
My Appalachia; A Reminiscence. New York: Holt, Rinehart and Winston, 1966. 90pp.

Her account is steeped in nostalgia for the simplicity, wisdom, and strength of the people; she remarks, "in our childhood, there was time, and there was freedom"; she describes the neighborhood social institutions and places rich with family memories; she recoils at the "sinister change" she feels in 1938 upon her return; another return in 1953 reveals disquieting poverty and she protests conditions, asserting "I am one with the mountain people."

382   CAULFIELD, GENEVIEVE (1888-)
      The Kingdom Within, ed. Ed Fitzgerald.   New York: Harper, 1960.   278pp.

      Blind from infancy, educated at Columbia Teacher's College, she goes to Japan in 1923 as an English teacher; she adopts a Japanese daughter; in 1938 she moves to Bangkok and opens a school for the blind; she describes the Japanese occupation; after World War II she returns to Japan with her son-in-law and twin grandchildren; at all times the account breathes confidence and capability.

383   CHAMBERS, MARY JANE
      Here Am I! Send Me.   Atlanta: Forum House, 1973.
      169pp.

      A journalist, she writes of her sudden call to a religious vocation; after recalling her adolescent longing for religious certainty and her years as a wife and mother, she notes that a decision to teach an adult Sunday school class is a turning point; she describes the influence of religion in her daily activities and friendships and her continuing "search for a workable faith."

384   CHANLER, MARGARET TERRY (1862-)
      Memory Makes Music.   New York: Stephen-Paul, 1948.
      171pp.

      She writes of "a long life of faithful music loving" from her childhood resolution to be "a pianist or nothing" to her adult years as "a respectable amateur"; she relates her personal, intimate responses to music and describes her acquaintances among musicians and composers; she includes historical material on some composers and gives "an outline of the changes in taste and fashion as I have lived through them."

385   CHAPELLE, DICKEY (1918-1965)
      What's a Woman Doing Here?   A Reporter's Report on Herself.   New York: Morrow, 1962.   285pp.

      A journalist and photographer for Life and Look, she describes her youthful enthusiasm for aviation which later leads to writing books on aviation as well as to her magazine as-

signments covering military operations, particularly in the
Pacific, during World War II; after the war, she and her
husband produce photos and write for humanitarian agencies,
noting the "paradox of poverty and publicity"; while covering
the Russian invasion of Hungary in 1956, she is captured
and imprisoned; later she covers the Algerian revolution
from the rebel side; still later work on urban unrest and
the Korean War mark her as an articulate and sensitive
"interpreter of violence."

386   CHAPELLE, GEORGETTE MEYER
       see   CHAPELLE, DICKEY (1918-1965)

387   CHAPLIN, LITA GREY (1908-   )
       My Life with Chaplin; An Intimate Memoir, with Morton
       Cooper.   New York: Bernard Geis, 1966.   325pp.

          A Hollywood child, she first attracts Chaplin's attention
       at twelve when she appears with him in a film; protected by
       her mother, to whom she is very close, she is nevertheless
       "created" and then seduced by Chaplin at fifteen; her family
       insists on marriage, and she describes two bitter, destruc-
       tive years with some interludes of real passion as Chaplin's
       wife and the mother of two sons; after a vengeful divorce, she
       searches for an identity, building a career as a singer and
       entertainer but suffering through several marriages, a drink-
       ing problem, and ill health; her pride in her sons, however,
       remains constant.

388   CHASE, CHRIS
       How to Be a Movie Star, or, A Terrible Beauty Is Born.
       New York: Harper & Row, 1974.   208pp.

          An actress, she writes a conversational, flippant book
       about her decision after high school to become a star; her
       anecdotes focus on method acting, theatrical agents, and her
       infrequent jobs on stage and in television.

389   CHASE, EDNA WOOLMAN (1877-1957)   NAWM
       Always in Vogue, with Ilka Chase.   Garden City, N.Y.:
       Doubleday, 1954.   387pp.

          This is the story of her career with Vogue magazine;
       first hired in 1895, she becomes editor in 1914; she writes
       of her long and warm friendship with Condé Nast; her ac-
       count is written in collaboration with her daughter, Ilka
       Chase.

390   CHASE, ILKA (1905-1978)
        Around the World and Other Places.   Garden City, N. Y. :
        Doubleday, 1970.   300pp.

        Aided by a sharp eye and a sharp tongue, she describes
        over two months of travel through North Africa, the Middle
        East, India, and the Far East; she enjoys the hospitality of
        prominent acquaintances, and discusses shopping, architec-
        ture, food, and her various guides, occasionally adding his-
        torical notes.

391   Elephants Arrive at Half-Past Five.   Garden City, N. Y. :
        Doubleday, 1963.   269pp.

        A prolific travel writer, her interest is aroused by read-
        ing about Africa and by her love of animals; she travels
        with her husband in 1962 to Kenya, Zanzibar, Uganda, Ethi-
        opia, and Egypt; eager to learn, she enjoys a safari, her
        observations of animals in several Kenya game reserves,
        her meetings with L. S. B. Leakey and Joy Adamson, and
        her tours of the monuments and museums of Egypt; she de-
        lights in the people she meets, from ambassadors to native
        chauffeurs.

392   The Carthaginian Rose.   Garden City, N. Y. :   Doubleday,
        1961.   429pp.

        A "travel addict," she presents a chronicle of several
        trips with her husband, including visits to France, Spain,
        and England in 1949, a Caribbean cruise in 1953, a stay in
        Monaco in 1956 to cover Grace Kelly's wedding, and another
        visit to England in 1960; her descriptions are articulate and
        brightened with a smattering of history.

393   Free Admission.   Garden City, N. Y. :   Doubleday, 1948.
        319pp.

        In a sequel to Past Imperfect, the actress, writer, and
        radio personality writes a witty, entertaining, anecdotal ac-
        count of the early and middle 1940's; she describes her war
        work and her completion of an unsuccessful play, but focuses
        on a love affair carried on by letter during the war; her ac-
        count ends with divorce and remarriage.

394   Fresh from the Laundry.   Garden City, N. Y. :   Doubleday,
        1967.   230pp.

        An actress and prolific author, she describes a two-month
        tour which begins in Germany and continues to Prague, Vi-

enna, Budapest, Romania, Bulgaria, Yugoslavia, and Greece; traveling with her husband, she provides wry comments on some of the rigors and discomforts of travel, comparisons of capitalism and communism, notes on her extensive sightseeing, and observations on the people she meets.

395   Second Spring and Two Potatoes.   Garden City, N. Y. :   Doubleday, 1965.   302pp.

In typically breezy style, she recounts her travels with her husband to the South Pacific, southern and eastern Africa, and Europe; she notes visits with far-flung acquaintances, wining and dining, and sightseeing with upper-class flair.

396   The Varied Airs of Spring.   Garden City, N. Y. :   Doubleday, 1969.   262pp.

Travelling in style, she begins in Rome and covers Italy, Greece, East Africa, and the Middle East, including a safari in Kenya; she describes sightseeing, with a gloss of historical comments.

397   Worlds Apart.   Garden City, N. Y. :   Doubleday, 1972. 273pp.

A prolific writer with a sharp, observant eye, she calls 1971 "the year of the Conducted Tour," telling of travels to Central America, South America, Russia, and Africa; touring in the former countries with other members of the Theatre Guild, she produces delightful sketches of the people she meets; writing of Africa, she describes a series of comfortable lodges and tent camps; she writes at length of Russia and its pleasant and unpleasant surprises; she enjoys her contacts with the Russian Writers' Union, but finds the atmosphere for the most part drab and oppressive.

398   CHASE, LUCILLE (1933-)
Skirts Aloft.   Chicago: Louis Mariano, 1959.   84pp.

In a light, bouncy style, a domestic flight attendant writes amusing anecdotes of "unusual experiences" with passengers and fellow crew members.

399   CHASE, MARY ELLEN (1887-1973)
The White Gate: Adventures in the Imagination of a Child.
New York: Norton, 1954.   185pp.

She presents a series of finely written vignettes, including passages on those who pass by the white gate of her childhood home; she provides a child's perspective on her siblings, her parents, her relatives in a loving evocation of domestic atmosphere.

400   CHESHAM, SALLIE
       Trouble Doesn't Happen Next Tuesday.   Waco, Texas: Word
       Books, 1972.   160pp.

A minister with the Salvation Army, she serves in a Chicago inner-city storefront project in Christian work; her involvement springs from having written a history of the U. S. Salvation Army; she brings trust, love, and hope to her work against tremendous odds, describing incidents that illustrate the dangers and hardships of street life.

401   CHESNEY, INGA L. (pseud.) (1928?-)
       A Time of Rape.   Englewood Cliffs, N. J. :   Prentice-Hall,
       1972.   255pp.

She recounts her experience of the "Russian conquest" of Berlin in 1945 in a "document of survival"; writing in the present tense with a child's hazy realization of the politics of war, nevertheless the horrors of murder, rape, and starvation are vivid; the end of the war does not bring the end of fear and hunger when she returns to her devastated home; employed by the British occupation forces, she comes to a hard-earned "acknowledgment of good and evil" in human nature.

402   CHICAGO, JUDY (1939-)
       Through the Flower: My Struggle as a Woman Artist.
       Garden City, N. Y. :   Doubleday, 1975.   226pp.

She opens with an account of her Chicago childhood and her early interest in art, then describes the impact of the death of her father; she attends U. C. L. A. , is married but is soon widowed; she turns inward and focuses on art; feminism gradually permeates her teaching and her painting, and she works to establish a woman's art community and to create forms which express her own femaleness.

403   CHIPPS, GENIE
       see   JESSUP, CLAUDIA

404   CHISHOLM, SHIRLEY (1924-)
       The Good Fight.   New York: Harper and Row, 1973.   206pp.

This is an account of her 1972 presidential primary campaign, undertaken to open the political process; she provides
a shrewd political analysis of the 1968-1972 political atmosphere; she discusses the problems of campaign financing, organization, racism, and sexism within politics; she reflects
on black alternatives and coalition politics; she emerges as
an articulate, strong politician.

405   Unbought and Unbossed.   Boston: Houghton Mifflin, 1970.
        177pp.

Born of working-class parents, she spends part of her
childhood with her grandmother in Barbados; she returns to
New York City and is educated at Brooklyn College; she
marries; her political activity leads to offices in the state
legislature and the U. S. Congress; she recounts her struggles against sexism, racism, the war in Vietnam, and
abortion laws; a tough and independent woman.

406   CHOU, CYNTHIA L. (1926-)
        My Life in the United States.   North Quincy, Mass. :   Chris-
        topher, 1970.   274pp.

Born, educated, and married in China, she settles in the
U. S. in 1955; she describes with sensitivity her early mis-
apprehensions as she adjusts to a new culture, a new language, altered values, and the implications of all these for
herself as a woman; following her "career woman's spirit,"
she earns advanced degrees at Columbia University and becomes a teacher; later in Michigan she does much community speaking, devoting herself to writing after 1962; she
closes with reflections on American culture.

407   CHRISTIAN, LINDA
        Linda; My Own Story.   New York: Crown Publishers, 1962.
        280pp.

She describes her interests centered on "home, family,
children, love, work, fidelity"; her childhood is spent in
Mexico, Jerusalem, Holland, and South Africa; brought to
Hollywood by Errol Flynn, she is disappointed in her attempts to establish a film career; she marries Tyrone Power, has two daughters, and goes through a painful divorce
which is followed by other lovers and much unhappiness;
she describes numerous incidents involving clairvoyants' accurate predictions.

408   CIRILE, MARIE
        Detective Marie Cirile: Memoirs of a Police Officer.   Gar-
        den City, N. Y. :   Doubleday, 1975.   222pp.

As a "hapless housewife" she falls into her job as a policewoman and is sworn in in 1957; she tells of sex differentials in training and utilization; in 1963 she works with the Detective Division; her account is organized by cases; she is the mother of two.

409   CLAPP, ESTELLE BARNES
       One Woman's India: Experiment in Living.   DeLand, Fla. :
       Everett/Edwards, 1966.   268pp.

A writer on educational, religious, and children's topics, she tells of a stay in India from 1961 to 1963 to organize for the Experiment in International Living; she produces sharp and sensitive observations of "a land of unbelievable contrasts"; she notes the emotional impact of poverty and hunger and demonstrates her deep commitment to human understanding and friendship; she closes with comments on a return visit in 1965.

410   CLAPPE, LOUISE AMELIA KNAPP SMITH (1819-1906)
       The Shirley Letters from the California Mines, 1851-1852.
       New York: Knopf, 1949.   216pp.

Indulging in her "passion for wandering" and much taken by "this wild and barbarous life," she describes in rich detail her life in a gold rush camp; the scenic grandeur contrasts with the human violence, primitive conditions, and danger that surround her; these lively letters, signed "Dame Shirley," were first published in local California newspapers.

411   CLAPPER, OLIVE EWING (1896-   )
       One Lucky Woman.   Garden City, N. Y. :   Doubleday, 1961.
       503pp.

The account sets her life against the background of contemporary affairs; impulsively marrying a newspaperman at 17, she trains in settlement houses as a social worker; she settles in Washington, D. C. and describes her private life with her husband's very public career; she raises two children; widowed during World War II, she turns to lecturing and writing, carrying on in the tradition of her husband; she later works and travels extensively for CARE.

412   Washington Tapestry.   New York: McGraw-Hill, 1946.
       303pp.

A journalist and the wife of a Washington newspaper and radio reporter, she writes of the years from 1917 to 1944; her recollections are set against the backdrop of world events and prominent political leaders; critical of Hoover's administration, she supports Roosevelt and the New Deal, providing anecdotes of the 1932 and 1936 campaigns; she closes at the end of the "Roosevelt era" with the death of her husband in 1944.

413   CLARK, EUGENIE (1922-   )
        Lady with a Spear.   New York: Harper, 1953.   243pp.

An ichthyologist, she notes that her interest in fish begins at nine; she does her graduate work at Scripps Institute; she discusses various research projects which take her to Micronesia and Egypt; she closes her account with her marriage, return to the U.S., and the task of publishing the results of her research.

414   CLARK, JANET (pseud.) (1929-   )
        The Fantastic Lodge; The Autobiography of a Girl Drug Addict, ed. Helen MacGill Hughes.   Boston: Houghton Mifflin, 1961.   267pp.

The slangy account is based on recordings made by a twenty-three year old heroin addict as part of a research project; combining insight and inarticulate groping, she recounts her childhood misery, adolescent awkwardness and pain, "unpleasant early sex experiences," the terrors of solitary childbirth, and her anguish at the necessity to give up her baby; she endures beatings, neurotic affairs, an unstable marriage, and jail--all part of her unbreakable pattern of men, sex, and drug abuse.

415   CLARK, MAURINE DORAN (1892?-1966)
        Captain's Bride, General's Lady; The Memoirs of Mrs.
        Mark W. Clark.   New York: McGraw-Hill, 1956.   278pp.

She describes her courtship in 1923 and her marriage in 1924 to a career army officer; she tells of her adjustments to the obligations of an army wife and offers anecdotes about the various posts to which they are assigned; she is alone during World War II as her husband is overseas and her children are in college; she travels, speaking on behalf of war bonds in 1943, 1944, and 1945; she travels to Europe at the close of the war and joins her husband in the Far East when he is commanding general in the Korean War; she tells of the strong family ties maintained throughout moves and separations.

416   CLARK, SEPTIMA POINSETTE (1898-   )
        Echo in My Soul, with LeGette Blythe.   New York: Dutton, 1962.   243pp.

A black school teacher, she tells of her own education
and her mother's insistence that she finish high school before becoming a teacher; she takes her first job in 1916 and
tells of primitive conditions in black schools on the South
Carolina sea islands; widowed with a son in 1925, she returns to teaching; she challenges the status quo, fights for
the equalization of salaries, and engages in YWCA and black
women's club work; she is fired in 1956 over the issue of
integration; she turns to work for adult literacy and voter
registration, is a director in the Highlander Folk School,
and works for the Southern Christian Leadership Conference.

417   CLARKE, LOUISE
       see PURTELL, THELMA C.

418   CLAUSEN, CONNIE
       I Love You Honey, But the Season's Over.   New York:
       Holt, Rinehart and Winston, 1961.   240pp.

       This is a humorous account of her only season with the
Ringling Brothers Barnum and Bailey Circus as one of the
"North starlets"; joining them in their Florida winter quar-
ters, she notes her colorful colleagues, "our new education
in manners and morals," her Italian romance, appearances
in Madison Square Garden and on the road, the conflict between her "feminist training" and the macho circus men; she
closes with a serious decision not to marry and not to remain with the circus.

419   CLAWSON, BERTHA FIDELIA (1868-1957)
       Bertha Fidelia, Her Story, as told to Jessie M. Trout.
       St. Louis, Mo.: Bethany, 1957.   128pp.

       She is a Methodist missionary, "idealistic and ambitious,"
who settles in Japan in 1898; in 1905 she founds an evangel-
istic girls' school, and her life parallels "the life of an institution"; she retires in 1935, but is forced to end her
residence in Japan by the onset of World War II.

420   CLAWSON, MARY
       Letters from Jerusalem.   New York: Abelard-Schuman,
       1957.   224pp.

       This is an account of a non-Jewish woman who lived in
Jerusalem with her husband and two young sons for a year
from 1953 to 1954; her letters provide much general cultural
information and details of domestic life for friends back
home.

421   CLEMENS, CLARA
       Awake to a Perfect Day; My Experience with Christian Science. New York: Citadel, 1956. 159pp.

       The daughter of Mark Twain opens with her father's views on Mary Baker Eddy (see companion volume); her own "marked propensity for hyper-emotionalism" and several bouts with illness lead her to seek calm and cure, first in Oriental meditation, with a "practitioner" of Christian Science; exercising strenuous thought control, she slowly improves after years of severe mental and physical illness, and she reflects at length on the "truths" and efficacy of Christian Science.

422   CLEMENS, MARIE LOUISE (1863-   )
       Autobiography of Marie Louise Clemens.   Boston: Bruce Humphries, 1953.   316pp.

       After her humble birth and a precocious and happy childhood in New England, she has "ambitions for knowledge"; married in 1895, she turns her great organizational abilities to promotional and charity work; at fifty-five, her interests shift to spiritualism, reincarnation, faith healing, and lecturing for an astrological society.

423   CLEMENTS, EDITH GERTRUDE SCHWARTZ
       Adventures in Ecology; Half a Million Miles ... from Mud to Macadam.   New York: Pageant Press, 1960.   244pp.

       A botanist and author of scientific works, she describes her work with her husband, a distinguished ecologist; they establish a Colorado alpine laboratory for summer research, enjoying the strenuous outdoor life; she serves as driver, artist, and note-taker on their later summer scientific adventures in the Colorado mountains, Nebraska prairies, North Dakota badlands, and Arizona desert, from the teens to the 1930's; she always views ecology in the service of the public good.

424   CLEMSON, FLORIDE
       see LEE, FLORIDE CLEMSON

425   CLIFTON, BERNICE
       None So Blind.   Chicago: Rand McNally, 1962.   253pp.

       She recounts twenty years of blindness, forced by necessity to find employment to support herself and her mother; she continues a typing career, cooks professionally; aided by a guide dog, she becomes a widely travelled and nationally

known lecturer on blindness; her intense mental discipline,
courage, and inner peace sustain her through the deaths of
her fiancé, her mother, and her beloved dog.

426   CLIFTON, LUCILLE (1936-   )
       Generations: A Memoir.   New York: Random House, 1976.
       79pp.

       A black poet and writer of children's books, she opens
       with a family history dating back to slavery and a line of
       strong and proud "Dahomey women"; the past related by
       her father is woven with her recollections of events sur-
       rounding his death; her college years and portrayal of fam-
       ily and community follow, "lives become generations made
       out of pictures and words just kept."

427   CLINKINBEARD, PHILURA VANDERBURGH (1851?-   )
       Across the Plains in '64, by Prairie Schooner to Oregon,
       comp. by Anna Dell Clinkinbeard.   New York: Exposition,
       1953.   97pp.

       She leaves her Iowa farm after elaborate preparations and
       crosses the plains with her parents and her six children;
       they join other wagon trains for safety, and endure several
       Indian scares before their friendship with a Sioux chief pro-
       tects them from real danger.

428   CLOETE, REHNA
       The Nylon Safari.   Boston: Houghton Mifflin, 1956.   276pp.

       A humorous "factual, autobiographical, unvarnished--
       merely feminized" account of a "city slicker" married to a
       "mad Englishman"; they take a three-week safari in Kenya,
       marked by her mock reluctance and slowly growing enjoy-
       ment of the beauty of nature and of danger deftly avoided;
       she notes her joyous return to civilization's luxuries.

429   COATESWORTH, ELIZABETH JANE (1893-   )
       Maine Memories.   Brattleboro, Vt.:   Stephen Greene, 1968.
       165pp.

       A novelist, she describes her farm home, local country
       stories, the interplay of "the wild and the tame," local
       fauna, the ghosts and witches of local legend, and her neigh-
       bors; she offers "the accumulation of tales remembered," and
       establishes "the emotional background" of the place.

430   Maine Ways.   New York: Macmillan, 1947.   213pp.

She opens with her acquisition of a Maine farm before
World War II and goes on to offer numerous brief vignettes
of the small pleasures of local country life, including hay-
ing, Decoration Day celebrations, animal neighbors, human
neighbors, "the country sense of excitement"; she includes
bits of local Indian heritage, tradition, and folklore.

431   Personal Geography; Almost an Autobiography.   Brattleboro,
       Vt.: Stephen Greene, 1976.   192pp.

A poet, novelist, essayist, and children's author, she offers selections from her private journals; "Each piece in
this book is a moment in my life"; from the perspective of
old age, but noting that "inwardly I am every age," she reflects on childhood, Vassar years, travel, marriage to a
fellow writer, motherhood, life on a Maine farm, widowhood,
her "addiction" to writing.

432   COBB, ELAINE
       see WRIGHT, COBINA

433   COBB, JERRIE (1931-   )
       Woman into Space; The Jerrie Cobb Story, with Jane Rieker.
       Englewood Cliffs, N.J.: Prentice-Hall, 1963.   223pp.

A strong, assertive pilot, "privileged to know the sky,"
she tells of recognizing her destiny as a flyer when she is
twelve; she earns her first license in 1948, later becomes
a commercial pilot and a ground and flight instructor; she
participates in women's transcontinental racing and does air
ferry work to South America and Europe; she sets several
non-stop and altitude records and is named the 1959 Woman
of the Year in Aviation; she is the first woman to undergo
exhaustive physical and psychological astronaut testing, and
she argues for women's role in the space effort, taking her
case from NASA to Congress, a vigorous proponent of wom-
en's capability.

434   COCHRAN, BESS WHITE (1899-   )
       Without Halos.   Philadelphia: Westminster, 1947.   172pp.

The daughter of a minister describes the social expectations and "unmistakable" atmosphere of the parsonage, a
world bounded by the church and church people; she provides
humorous anecdotes of her father's work and of their happy
family life, but she also includes some serious observations
on parishioners' apathy and misguided mission work.

435   COCHRAN, JACQUELINE
       The Stars at Noon, with Floyd Odlum. Boston: Little,
       Brown, 1954.   274pp.

       An aviation pioneer and holder of several propeller and
       jet speed records, she describes a Southern childhood in
       which poverty, lack of education, and hard work generate
       a fierce independence; she begins flying in 1932 and racing
       in 1934, "determined to travel with the wind and the stars";
       with a passion for information and for contacts with people,
       she also runs a successful cosmetics business; during World
       War I she organizes and trains women pilots.

436   COENS, SISTER MARY XAVIER
       GI Nun, as told to Robert C. Healey. New York: P. J.
       Kenedy, 1967.   186pp.

       The director of a Catholic college theater troupe de-
       scribes their 1964 U. S. O. tour which includes fifty-one
       performances amid Time magazine coverage; she is proud
       of the young women she accompanies and pleased with their
       organizational triumphs, and she is dedicated to serve the
       G. I. ; her good-humored account also explores some common
       misconceptions of the religious life and some parallels be-
       tween the convent and the army.

437   COFFEE, DOROTHY (pseud.)
       see AUER, FRANCES LEVENIA

438   COHEN, RUTH KOLKO
       A Boy's Quiet Voice. New York: Greenberg, 1957.   115pp.

       This is a mother's story of her fourteen-year-old son's
       death of bone cancer, from the initial shock of an amputa-
       tion to his final weeks; sustained by family solidarity, her
       Jewish religion, and her son's spirit and courage, she finds
       quiet acceptance.

439   COLBY, CONSTANCE TABER (1927-   )
       A Skunk in the House.   Philadelphia: Lippincott, 1973.
       144pp.

       She describes her attempts "to integrate a wild creature
       into our family pattern"; moving between a Connecticut sum-
       mer home and a Manhattan apartment, she learns the ani-
       mal's behavior patterns and must make major adjustments
       of her own; she closes with the disappearance of the skunk,
       and she is sorry, but grateful for what she's learned.

440 COLE, MARGARET ROSSA (1887-)
Grandma Takes a Freighter; The Story of an Atlantic Cross-
ing. New York: Exposition, 1950. 104pp.

She travels to fulfill a "gypsy urge" in 1949 as the only
passenger amid forty-eight male crew members; her diary
entries describe a warm friendship with the gallant captain,
pranks of crew members, and sightseeing visits to ports in
Germany before landing in Ireland; she writes with laughter
and a light touch.

441 COLE, MARIA ELLINGTON (1926-)
Nat King Cole: An Intimate Biography, with Louie Robinson.
New York: Morrow, 1971. 184pp.

Raised in an upper-class New England family, she fulfills
a childhood ambition to become a singer; she marries fellow
singer Nat King Cole in 1948 and tells of their seventeen
years of married life with five children, struggling against
racial discrimination, managing the family's financial affairs,
seeing her husband through his terminal illness.

442 COLEMAN, ANN RANEY THOMAS (1810-1897)
Victorian Lady on the Texas Frontier: The Journal of Ann
Raney Coleman, ed. C. Richard King. Norman, Okla.:
University of Oklahoma Press, 1971. 206pp.

A proud and assertive woman, born in England, she endures the dangerous voyage to Texas with her mother and
sister to rejoin her father; her parents die; she accepts a
suitor and settles into plantation life, but war forces them
to flee to Louisiana; her two sons die and she is widowed in
1847; she marries an unjust man and divorces him in 1855,
supporting herself and her daughter.

443 COMSTOCK, ANNA BOTSFORD (1854-1930)   NAW
The Comstocks of Cornell: John Henry Comstock and Anna
Botsford Comstock; An Autobiography, ed. Glenn W. Herrick
and Ruby Green Smith. Ithaca, N.Y.: Comstock Publishing
Associates, 1953. 286pp.

She combines an autobiography with a biography of her
husband; she recalls her rural New York childhood, characterized by a love of learning; she enters Cornell in 1874
and tells of her social life and intellectual growth; she marries an entomologist in 1878 and begins to do wood engravings
for his books; she becomes the first woman professor at
Cornell in 1898 and writes nature study books for children
and teachers.

444   COMSTOCK, CLARA MABEL HAGGARD (1903-)
       When the World Was Ten Miles Wide.   Chicago: Adams
       Press, 1973.   107pp.

       A writer and columnist tells of a bygone era in an infor-
       mal account of her childhood in Arkansas; she describes her
       small town, her home, her extended family, and she includes
       brief chapters on spring cleaning, camp meetings, school,
       holidays, and family gatherings.

445   CONE, VIRGINIA S.
       Africa--A World in Progress; An American Family in West
       Africa.   New York: Exposition, 1960.   99pp.

       A professor, married to a professor, describes her stay
       in Ghana in 1958-1959 with her three children; she notes
       "the problems, adjustments, and frustrations" as well as
       the "new experiences, joys, and real fun"; she enjoys the
       warmth and courtesy of the people, the daily challenge of
       food preparation and of teaching adult classes and training
       salespeople.

446   CONNOLLY, MARIE MOORE (1895?-)
       Europe: '86--'14--'52.   New York: Pageant Press, 1958.
       97pp.

       Following her mother's account (see Moore, Kate A.),
       she writes of travels in Europe with her mother in 1914,
       noting that suffragist activity closes some tourist attractions
       and indicating the onset of World War I; after twenty-two
       years of marriage, she is suddenly widowed in 1946 and
       takes a brief vacation to the British Isles.

447   CONNOLLY, OLGA FIKOTOVA (1933-)
       The Rings of Destiny.   New York: McKay, 1968.   311pp.

       A Czechoslovakian discus thrower in the 1956 Olympics,
       she meets and marries a U. S. hammer thrower; she tells
       of the early political harassment of her family in Czecho-
       slovakia; she describes her athletic training, the excitement
       of competition, her gold medal, and the progress of her
       romance; she notes her difficulties in obtaining governmental
       permission to marry, but love triumphs.

448   COOK, ANNA MARIA GREEN (1844-1936)
       The Journal of a Milledgeville Girl, 1861-1867, ed. James
       C. Bonner.   Athens: University of Georgia Press, 1964.
       131pp.

In irregular journal entries, she touches on secession, fear of her own religious backsliding, close family ties, last year as a schoolgirl, the progress of the Civil War, the Yankee occupation; acknowledging her "undisciplined and chaotic mind," she harbors "schemes for mental improvement," but with a strong romantic streak she focuses on a series of infatuations; she later chronicles a sister's romance and finds true love with her own engagement.

449   COOK, BEATRICE GRAY
More Fish to Fry. New York: Morrow, 1951. 280pp.

In this breezy sequel to Till Fish Us Do Part, she tells of summers at her family's island home near Seattle; she enjoys the outdoor life and close family ties, the drama of her son's first king salmon, friendly neighbors, and their purchase of a farm.

450   Till Fish Us Do Part; The Confessions of a Fisherman's Wife. New York: Morrow, 1949. 249pp.

Married to a doctor, a "fishin' fool," she tells how she must learn fishing in self defense; her two sons also become avid fishermen, and she learns to appreciate the beautiful vistas and the excitement of the catch as her family life centers on fishing; she suffers only occasional bouts of peevishness in this humorous account.

451   COOKE, LYNNE
My Startled Childhood. San Antonio: Naylor, 1957. 77pp.

Focusing on her childhood, she provides brief portraits of her grandparents, aunts, uncles, and then describes the hasty marriage of her parents; her mother and father first endure the rigors of pioneer life and later run a large store; she enjoys the excitement of "running untamed," camping by wagon, parties and a "candy-breaking"; she closes with her entering boarding school and the first steps toward growing up.

452   COOPER, CATHERINE (pseud.)
see STROUD, MYRTLE REDMAN (1887-   )

453   COOPER, MIRIAM (1891-   )
Dark Lady of the Silents: My Life in Early Hollywood, with Bonnie Herndon. Indianapolis: Bobbs-Merrill, 1973. 256pp.

She has leading roles in D. W. Griffith's The Birth of a Nation and Intolerance; married to director Raoul Walsh,

she reluctantly continues to star in his films; she tells of
her two adopted sons; she later divorces; there is little discussion of her life after the 1930's.

454   CORBEN, MULAIKA
       Not to Mention the Kangaroos.   New York: Crowell, 1955.
       241pp.

       She marries a British physicist while he is a student in
the U.S. and they settle in Australia; she is delighted by
Australian slang, accepts being "the foreigner" with good
humor, and is amused by cultural differences, taking the
opportunity to correct misconceptions about the U.S.; she
teaches and raises three children; her entertaining narrative
closes with the family's return to the U.S.

455   CORNISH, NELLIE CENTENNIAL (1876-1956)
       Miss Aunt Nellie: The Autobiography of Nellie C. Cornish,
       ed. Ellen Van Volkenburg Browne and Edward Nordhoff
       Beck.   Seattle: University of Washington Press, 1964.
       283pp.

       She recounts her childhood in the Midwest, a move to
Oregon, her early studies on the piano; she begins teaching
piano at 14, and supports herself teaching after her mother's
death; she moves to Seattle in 1900, and in 1914 founds a
school for education in the arts which undergoes rapid expansion; she retires in 1939.

456   COSKE, LON (pseud.)
       see McCLOSKEY, EUNICE MILDRED (1906-   )

457   COTTON, ELLA EARLS
       A Spark for My People: The Sociological Autobiography of
       a Negro Teacher.   New York: Exposition, 1954.   288pp.

       An elementary school teacher who devotes herself to im-
proved race relations, she tells of her childhood without
"race consciousness" as the daughter of a white father and
a black mother; proud of her ancestral ties and strengthened
by community support for her college education, she marries
a fellow teacher and works primarily in Alabama, campaigning against racial prejudice and for a strong black community; she is happy in her work, marriage, and motherhood.

458   COUDERT, JO
       GoWell: The Story of a House.   New York: Stein and Day,
       1974.   275pp.

Highly articulate, she becomes "passionately involved" in the life of a New York village home whose purchase and renovation she shares with a friend; with a clear eye for detail, she describes the sleazy dignity of the former owner, the inarticulate pride of the carpenter, the deadening dealings with lawyers and bankers, her own creative ingenuity through a series of "demolition Saturdays" until the rehabilitation is complete and she can enjoy both city and country life.

459   COX, CARRIE MILLER
       Getting Around Somehow; Memories of World Travel.   New
       York: Exposition, 1965.   189pp.

She describes various trips to Mexico, Guatemala, the Pacific Northwest, Europe, South America, the Middle East, the South Pacific, Africa, and eastern Europe between 1948 and 1964; traveling with tour groups, she presents routine descriptions of sightseeing.

460   COX, EUGENIA M. (1886-   )
       From the Ground Up; The True Story of a Polio Victim.
       New York: Exposition, 1960.   61pp.

She is stricken by polio at three and grows up surrounded by afflictions and deaths in the family; she becomes a teacher, shouldering financial responsibility for her family; misunderstandings blight her search for happiness; she closes her third-person account darkly after a heart attack forces her retirement.

461   COXE, EMILY BADHAM
       Mother of the Maid, with Frances Warfield.   New York:
       Holt, Rinehart and Winston, 1960.   223pp.

A South Carolina mother of five writes a lively, humorous account of her pursuit of the "Maid of Cotton" title for her sometimes reluctant collegiate daughter; she vicariously satisfies her own thwarted beauty contest career by maternal plotting, tireless spending, and elaborate string-pulling to steer her daughter through the local and state competitions, all the while "beaming that smug, pride-of-ownership beam"; the loss of the contest brings a return to normality.

462   CRAIG, ELEANOR
       P. S. Your Not Listening: A Year with Five Disturbed Children.   New York: Richard W. Baron, 1972.   215pp.

A teacher and mother of four school-age children describes her "pilot class for the socially and emotionally

maladjusted"; her vivid description of the students' bizarre
behavior and the chaos of her school life is a sharp contrast with her family life; small improvements compete
with disappointing setbacks, and yet throughout she maintains patience, tolerance, and a kind of affection for her
students.

463   CRAIG, LILLIAN K.
       The Singing Hills. New York: Crowell, 1951. 242pp.

       In the early 1930's, she is a schoolteacher among "moun-
tain people who make moonshine liquor"; she describes their
living conditions, customs, storytelling, and vivid characters; although she is once threatened when the people think
she is a revenue officer, she finds them generally receptive
and loving; she takes a young boy home to her family to
further his education; her narrative is "telescoped" for effect.

464   CRAIN, CLARA MOORE (1905-)
       We Shall Rise. New York: Pageant Press, 1955. 68pp.

       An intensely religious Baptist missionary nurse tells of
tragedies during her childhood, an unhappy marriage and
divorce, and her entry into the Army Nurse Corps in 1943;
later remarried, she takes seminary training and works in
a leprosarium, "serving God and humanity."

465   CRATER, STELLA WHEELER (1887-)
       The Empty Robe, with Oscar Fraley. Garden City, N.Y.:
       Doubleday, 1961. 210pp.

       She writes a bitter account of the effects on her life of
the mysterious disappearance in 1930 of her husband, Judge
Crater; she describes an extremely happy thirteen years of
marriage, during which she is nonetheless lonely and "the
perfect foil for his ambition"; she suffers physical and mental exhaustion, is suspected of murder, is hounded from her
home, and is fired from jobs during the course of thirty
years of conjecture.

466   CRAWFORD, DOROTHY PAINTER (1892-)
       Stay with It, Van; From the Diary of Mississippi's First
       Lady Mayor. New York: Exposition, 1958. 312pp.

       She describes her tomboy childhood pioneering in the
Oklahoma territory; after college, she marries in 1916,
teaches home economics and engages in church work, club
work, and other community activities; in 1942 she settles on

a Mississippi farm, managing it while her husband serves
as a state legislator and mayor; a women's struggle for a
community center in 1950 leads to her victorious campaign
with an all-woman slate; enjoying national publicity, she
continues work for municipal improvements, learning much
and describing "the day-by-day story" of her duties.

467   CRAWFORD, FLORENCE
       Girl of the Desert; The Life and Writings of One of the
       Most Extraordinary Women in America Today.   New York:
       Greenwich Book Publishers, 1961.   134pp.

       Her anecdotes focus on her hunting, trapping, and fishing
exploits first with her brothers and then with her husband;
she is delighted to impress men with her skill and courage
in "male" pursuits; in 1954 she is a member of an Arctic
expedition; the book's title refers to a short story which
opens her account.

468   CRAWFORD, JOAN (1908-1977)
       My Way of Life.   New York: Simon and Schuster, 1971.
       224pp.

       A movie star describes her fascination with her husband's
work as a Pepsi-Cola executive, work which she continues
after his death as a "good-will ambassador" for Pepsi; she
notes her recipe for a successful marriage, her ideas on
interior decorating, entertaining, working wives, fashion--
all illustrated with personal anecdotes.

469   A Portrait of Joan; The Autobiography of Joan Crawford,
       with Jane Kesner Ardmore.   Garden City, N.Y.:   Doubleday,
       1962.   239pp.

       She recounts a childhood marked by insecurity, work which
interferes with education, and a strong desire to dance; she
leaves home for Hollywood at 17, and stars in popular films
but fights for the chance to be a dramatic actress; she
leaves film temporarily to protest poor roles; she twice
marries actors; widowed in her fourth marriage, she has
strong domestic impulses; she adopts and raises four children with joy and devotion; account reveals her toughness,
drive, ambition, vitality.

470   CREHAN, FERN M.
       The Days Before Yesterday.   New York: Dodd, Mead, 1958.
       214pp.

       In a nostalgic account which focuses primarily on her
sixth year, she tells of settling on her grandparents' Ohio

fruit farm with her newly widowed father; adjusting with the help of her grandmother's subtle understanding, she enjoys the independence of outdoor farm life and the warm family life centered in the kitchen, rejecting an aunt who wishes to make a little lady of her.

471   CRISLER, LOIS
       Arctic Wild. New York: Harper, 1956. 301pp.

       In this account of a year and a half on the Arctic tundra to film wildlife with her husband, she describes her initial ignorance and "demands almost beyond my strength"; a keen observer of wildlife behavior, she notes the elation of witnessing a caribou migration, and the joy and fascination of rearing wolf cubs; her marvelous anecdotes reveal the subtleties and magic of communication and understanding with wild creatures; she closes with their decision to take the wolves to their Colorado home (see Captive Wild).

472   Captive Wild. New York: Harper & Row, 1968. 238pp.

       She tells of devoting seven years to raising orphan Alaskan wolf cubs on a Colorado farm; her detailed observations of rich social interaction of wolves are marred by anthropomorphism; she tells of the surviving female, successive litters of wolf-dogs, shifts in social structure among the animals; her own "human loneliness and work" are rewarded by intimate understanding; ultimately she feels forced to euthanize the animals.

473   CROMWELL, HELEN WORLEY (1881?-)
       Dirty Helen; An Autobiography, with Robert Dougherty. Los Angeles: Sherbourne Press, 1966. 286pp.

       She presents a slangy, slightly obscene account of her "career as a woman of pleasure"; she breaks permanently from her parents with her marriage in 1903 and retaliates for her husband's infidelity by becoming a prostitute; she has a platonic alliance with a bank robber, is "kept" by a lumber czar, runs a famous speakeasy, becomes a madam, makes a love match with a pimp and bootlegger, and caters to servicemen during World War II; riding high, she cultivates an image as a lover of luxury and rough language.

474   CROSBY, CARESSE JACOB (1892-1970)
       The Passionate Years. New York: Dial, 1953. 342pp.

       From a "crystal chandelier" background in New York cultured circles at the turn of the century, she marries in 1915

into "a bonded circle of Boston hierarchs," but soon rebels
against convention to pursue "hedonistic adventure," divorcing her first husband and marrying Harry Crosby; settling
in France, she relishes the unreality of the "fabulous twen-
ties," turns to writing poetry, and founds the Black Sun
Press in 1927, enjoying the acquaintance of numerous writers; she is grief-stricken at the suicide of her husband in
1929, but later remarries and settles in wartime Washington, D. C.; she asserts that "personal life is the individual's
only means of expression."

475   CROSBY, KATHRYN
        Bing and Other Things.   New York: Meredith, 1967.   214pp.

    She opens with a description of her youth, participation in
beauty contests, and her early Hollywood career; her romance with Bing Crosby is beset with difficulties and delays,
but they marry; she pursues a nursing degree and training
in elementary education; raising three children and caring
for her husband, she nevertheless continues her movie career.

476   CROSBY, MARY PHELPS JACOB
        see   CROSBY, CARESSE JACOB (1892-1970)

477   CROSBY, RUTH
        I Was a Summer Boarder.   Boston: Christopher, 1966.
        142pp.

    In evocative detail she illuminates the "slow, unchanging
pace" of an "old-fashioned country boarding house" in Maine
prior to World War I; she tells of the annual trip, other
boarders, her favorite places in the barn, by a brook, and
in the mountains; the proprietress's death in 1913 marks
both the end of the author's childhood and the end of an era.

478   CROWELL, MARNIE REED
        Greener Pastures.   New York: Funk & Wagnalls, 1973.
        241pp.

    Her account moves month by month from August to June;
wife of a biology professor with two young sons, she lives
on an upstate New York farm, writing with evocative detail
of their busy life as "nouveaux rurals" and of her quiet observations of seasonal activities, enjoying summer garden
bounty, savoring winter's satisfactions, responding to spring's
reawakening, she lives intimately with abundant nature.

479   CROWNINSHIELD, CLARA
       The Diary of Clara Crowninshield; A European Tour with
       Longfellow, 1835-1836, ed. Andrew Hilen.   Seattle: Uni-
       versity of Washington Press, 1956.   304pp.

       The illegitimate daughter of a wealthy New England mer-
       chant, she tours Europe as a student and companion to Mrs.
       Longfellow (see entry #1266); her spirited, detailed por-
       trayal of travel modes and accommodations at the time re-
       veals her good humor, although she occasionally bemoans
       her lack of "natural ties" with a family; she nurses Mrs.
       Longfellow during the latter's miscarriage, illness, and
       death; she remains with Longfellow, lodging with a German
       family for language study, continually resolving to achieve
       greater self-discipline; lack of a chaperone prevents her
       going to Italy with Longfellow, so she returns to the U.S.,
       sorrowfully lacking a family to whom to return.

480   CUERO, DELFINA (1900?-)
       The Autobiography of Delfina Cuero, a Diegueno Indian, as
       told to Florence C. Shipek.   Los Angeles: Dawson's Book
       Shop, 1968.   67pp.

       She describes her tribal customs and beliefs, ceremonies,
       typical food, children's games; her youth is marked by work
       "like a man" and moves to avoid white settlement; she mar-
       ries, bears children, is widowed and suffers hunger and
       hard times; her children also marry, hoping for security
       but finding hard work and suffering; her struggle to keep
       her family together is unsuccessful.

481   CULBERTSON, MANIE
       May I Speak?   Diary of a Crossover Teacher, ed. Sue Eakin.
       Gretna, La.:   Pelican Publishing Co., 1972.   156pp.

       A white teacher in Louisiana, she is among the first
       teachers to be assigned to a black school under court-or-
       dered integration in 1970; transferred against her will, she
       describes her initial extreme anxiety; genuinely surprised
       by the lower standards and poor facilities of the black
       schools, she meets the challenges, grateful for cooperative
       students and interested in the cultural differences she finds
       through what she comes to see as a valuable experience.

482   CULLMAN, MARGUERITE
       Ninety Dozen Glasses.   New York: Norton, 1960.   273pp.

       The wife of the Commissioner General for the 1958 Brus-
       sels World Exposition, she describes her high anticipation,
       settling into her routine of "pastry and protocol," the social

whirl among royalty and diplomats, maintaining a household
with her husband and young son; she leaves with a great
fondness for Belgium; an entertaining account.

483   Occupation: Angel. New York: Norton, 1963. 256pp.

With her husband, she is a financial backer of plays from
the late 1930's to the present, and she is a theater-owner;
she recounts her success judging manuscripts; she offers
flashbacks to a childhood of wealth followed by poverty, early newspaper work, a job in public relations for Bonwit
Teller, and marriage.

484   CUMMINGS, EVANGELINE HAAS (1886-)
       Breakfast at Haas Park; The Story of an American Family.
       New York: Greenwich Book Publishers, 1959. 32pp.

Opening with a brief family history, she describes her
domestic activities in a Michigan family of sixteen children;
her random memories include school days, her high school
graduation in 1906, her teaching, and her marriage in 1913.

485   CURWELL, LAURA E.
       Whither Shall I Wander? An Autobiography. New York:
       Vantage, 1958. 129pp.

A social worker, she tells of her childhood in a large
English family and of her ambitions which take her to Canada; she enlists in the U. S. Navy during World War I and
begins the welfare work which becomes her lifelong career;
she tells of her various assignments with the Veterans Administration and reflects on careers for single women.

486   CURZON, GRACE ELVINA TRILLA HINDS DUGGAN (1879-
       1958)
       Reminiscences. New York: Coward-McCann, 1955. 256pp.

The daughter of an American diplomat, she settles in Ar-
gentina with her family after growing up in the U. S. ; she
marries a diplomat in 1902, raises two sons, and enjoys a
prosperous life "glowing with happiness"; widowed in 1915,
she marries Lord Curzon in 1917, easily stepping into her
role amid the British aristocracy and royalty until she is
widowed again in 1925.

487   CUSHING, MARY FITCH WATKINS
       The Rainbow Bridge. New York: Putnam, 1954. 318pp.

She describes seven years, from 1911-1918, as friend, secretary, and "buffer" for the tempestuous Wagnerian opera singer Olive Fremstad; "in spite of some frayed illusions," she becomes a willing slave, indulging her love for opera and forming a profound attachment for her arrogant, flamboyant, disarming employer; her lively account displays a fine sense of the absurd.

488   CUSSLER, MARGARET
       Not by a Long Shot; Adventures of a Documentary Film Producer. New York: Exposition, 1951. 200pp.

       A sociologist and filmmaker, she describes her work in 1941 on a nutrition film set in North Carolina; she later works on informational films for Eastman Kodak and forms a documentary film company which produces a film on the Hopi Indians, a project she describes in detail.

489   CUSTER, ELIZABETH BACON (1842-1933)
       The Custer Story; The Life and Intimate Letters of General George A. Custer and His Wife, Elizabeth, ed. Marguerite Merington. New York: Devin-Adair, 1950. 339pp.

       The letters are published with connecting text; she meets Custer in 1862 and they exchange love letters; although she trembles at the responsibility of marriage, she marries in 1864; her charming letters describe her pleasure and pride in her husband's reputation and her anxiety during his absences; she tells of "grand fun" being with him on army duty, "never happier than when sleeping in a tent" on the frontier; she is widowed in 1876.

490   CUTHRELL, FAITH BALDWIN (1893-1978)
       Evening Star. New York: Holt, Rinehart and Winston, 1966. 191pp.

       She is a writer and novelist; this book is written when she is over seventy, an account covering one year and organized by months; her random reflections are filled with the love of nature and much domestic detail.

491   Face Toward the Spring. New York: Rinehart, 1956. 203pp.

       A novelist, she finds the writing for Christian Herald magazine leads to a shift in her level of consciousness in the mid-1950's, and she turns to reflective, autobiographical essays; she explores the "climate of the heart," noting the ever-present promise of spring; she describes the creation of a novel, kinds of communication, the "spiritual remedy" of relaxation, major changes after her husband's death; sustained by her religious faith, she suggests that solutions are to be found within.

492   Harvest of Hope.   New York: Holt, Rinehart and Winston, 1962.   148pp.

A prolific writer and poet, she reflects at sixty-eight on her times of joy and sorrow during the period of a year; quietly, she savors the meaning of the new year, change and her response to change, and the necessary multiplicity of a writer's personality; with sharp images and vivid memories, she explores love, hope, trust, understanding, and sharing.

493   Living by Faith.   New York: Holt, Rinehart and Winston, 1964.   152pp.

In another volume written "after the manner of an almanac," she explores the spiritual meanings of various holidays, cherishing the traditions that surround each; in her beloved house, associations and reflections are inspired by favorite objects, memories, and daily tasks, for she values the details of living, finding opportunities for creativity everywhere; she is thankful for "a lifetime spent with words."

494   Many Windows; Seasons of the Heart.   New York: Rinehart, 1958.   219pp.

She presents a series of reflective, autobiographical essays inspired by the aspects of the various months, from one December to the next; she appreciates the "special beauty and compensations" of each season, treating natural phenomena such as growth, storms, decay with a metaphorical cast of mind; she takes stock of her spiritual, emotional, and creative accomplishments, offering glimpses of her past as they illuminate her present introspection.

495   Testament of Trust.   New York: Holt, Rinehart and Winston, 1960.   223pp.

A novelist and prolific writer presents a series of reflective, autobiographical essays organized around a one-year cycle of months; she cultivates a thankful heart, taking the time to dwell on "past loveliness"; using metaphorical architectural devices drawn largely from the home, she discusses her religious values, books she has loved, time, love, beauty, "quietude and trust," all in an intimate tone; some chapters were previously published in magazine form.

496   DACHE, LILLY (1906?-)
       Talking Through My Hats, ed. Dorothy Roe Lewis.   New
       York: Coward-McCann, 1946.   265pp.

       Born in France, she studies millinery there, then emi-
       grates to the U. S. in 1924 at eighteen; thrilled by New York
       City, she works, buys her own shop, and is quickly success-
       ful in the exuberant 1920's; she describes serving famous
       customers; she marries in 1931 and is a devoted wife as
       well as a famous creator of hats.

497   DAGGS, ELISA
       Doorways to the World; Revealing Glimpses of People and
       Places in Word Vignettes and Photographs.   Garden City,
       N. Y. : Doubleday, 1960.   319pp.

       She offers many detailed descriptions and fragmentary
       impressions of the usual as well as unusual sights on a
       four-month flight around the world; she visits acquaintances
       in remote places.

498   DAHL, BORGHILD MARGARETHE (1890-)
       Finding My Way. New York: Dutton, 1962.   121pp.

       An author and teacher, she describes her adjustment to
       blindness; she wishes to maintain her independence and to
       continue to live alone; she describes details of her first days
       and weeks alone, including food preparation, household tasks;
       she conquers fear and overcomes isolation, returns to writ-
       ing, and travels to promote her first book.

499   DALLENBACH, PAULINE WHITE (1926-)
       Dear Friends. . . .   Zarenpath, N. J. : Pillar of Fire, 1953.
       114pp.

       The granddaughter of Alma White (see companion vol-
       ume) describes in diary-like entries her work in England
       with her husband and parents for the Pillar of Fire
       evangelical church headquarters; the account consists of
       random impressions.

500   DALRYMPLE, JEAN
       From the Last Row.   Clifton, N. J. :   James T. White,
       1975.   301pp.

       Her memoirs delineate twenty-five years of work with
       opera, ballet, and theater at New York City Center begin-
       ning in 1943; portraying herself as a background figure, she
       notes struggles over policy, gives portraits of the artists
       with whom she works, describes season-by-season perform-
       ances, and tells of averting financial and artistic crises.

501   September Child: The Story of Jean Dalrymple, by Herself.
       New York: Dodd, Mead, 1963.   318pp.

       After little formal education, she takes a business course,
       and gets a secretarial job at 16; her love for theater leads
       to acting in a touring company; she shifts to public relations
       and theatrical production; she enjoys friendships among the
       stars; she is the director of City Center Light Opera and
       Drama Companies; a bubbly account.

502   DALY, IDA (1901-   )
       Adventure in a Wheelchair; Pioneering for the Handicapped,
       with Hazel Flagler Begeman.   Philadelphia: Whitmore,
       1973.   77pp.

       A quadriplegic due to muscular dystrophy, she describes
       her pursuit of education and her "passion" for painting; after
       her marriage in 1944, she travels extensively, organizes a
       Seattle center for the handicapped, produces a newsletter,
       campaigns for accessible apartments; when she is widowed,
       she continues her active life of service to others, writing
       and speaking to promote mobility and independence for the
       handicapped.

503   DALY, MARIA LYDIG (1824-1894)
       Diary of a Union Lady, 1861-1865, ed. Harold Earl Ham-
       mond.   New York: Funk & Wagnalls, 1962.   396pp.

       An uninhibited Union supporter and wife of a prominent
       judge, she provides an anecdotal account full of lively por-
       traits, sharp wit, and stinging criticism; strangely enough,
       she admires Lee, and initially Davis, as well as Grant,
       reserving her barbed comments for President and Mrs. Lin-
       coln and the "demoniacal spirit" of Southern woman; ap-
       palled by "this dreadful, unnatural war," she follows its
       military and political progress closely.

504   DALY, MAUREEN
       see   McGIVERN, MAUREEN DALY (1927-   )

505   DANA, ETHEL NATHALIE SMITH (1878-   )
Young in New York: A Memoir of a Victorian Girlhood.
Garden City, N.Y.:   Doubleday, 1963.   205pp.

The daughter of a prosperous minister and a dynamic
mother describes the warmth and security of her family life;
she spends summers close to nature in Connecticut; she tells
of her first glimpses of "the life of the mind" at school,
away from parochial home atmosphere; in a period of intellectual change, she begins to question social custom; "un-
feminine and therefore a problem," she chooses music over
college, studies piano in Munich in 1902; her social life runs
in musical circles; she marries in 1911 into a privileged,
literary family.

506   DANDRIDGE, DOROTHY (1924-1965)
Everything and Nothing: The Dorothy Dandridge Tragedy,
with Earl Conrad.   New York: Abelard-Schuman, 1970.
215pp.

A popular black singer and movie actress, she tells of
her mother's high ambitions for her and she begins traveling
to and performing in black churches at three; after a disturbing failed first marriage and the ordeal of her daughter's
retardation, she achieves her first professional success, but
then endures the collapse of a second marriage, bankruptcy,
and career problems; she explores the psychological distortions of success, and her racial ambivalence between the
black and white worlds; the account is reconstructed from
tape recordings.

507   DANFORTH, SISTER MARIA DEL REY
see   MARIA DEL REY, SISTER

508   DANIEL, DOROTHY
Circle 'Round the Square; Pictures from an Iowa Childhood.
New York: Wilfred Funk, 1959.   248pp.

Her account opens in 1914, but thereafter time is indefin-
ite; she alludes to the "random life" of her parents; the book
focuses on the warm family life spent with her grandparents;
she includes vignettes of Indianola and its inhabitants.

509   DANIELS, AMY ESTHER (1882-   )
Amy and Her Long Island; An Account of Constructive Work
in a Rewarding Community.   New York: William-Frederick,
1950.   56pp.

She takes a job as an organizer of women's study groups
in the fine arts, groups that also promote poise and leader-

ship skills; she travels among a number of Long Island towns, a talented organizer; she writes in the third person.

510   DANIELS, BEBE VIRGINIA (1901-1971)
        Life with the Lyons; The Autobiography of Bebe Daniels and Ben Lyon. London: Odhams Press, 1953. 266pp.

        Narratives written by Daniels and by her husband Lyon alternate; she describes her early career in film, acting with her mother; she marries in 1930; her career later shifts from film to radio comedy; she lives and entertains in England during World War II.

511   DARLINGTON, JENNIE (1925-)
        My Antarctic Honeymoon: A Year at the Bottom of the World, as told to Jane McIlvaine. Garden City, N.Y.: Doubleday, 1956. 284pp.

        In an articulate and perceptive account, she tells of her hasty marriage to a compelling explorer and of the emotional strain of his preparations for a polar research expedition in 1947; accompanying him to Chile, unusual circumstances result in her invitation to become one of the first women to live in Antarctica; her initial uncertainty, lacking a clear role, gives way to her full participation in daily routines, attempting to remain "inconspicuous," to ask no favors, especially when she is pregnant near the end of the year, and to gain "an education in ethics and human relations" when the expedition is plagued by accidents and tension; she feels grateful for the uniquely intense marital closeness forced by Spartan living conditions on the base.

512   DARNTON, ELEANOR CHOATE
        The Children Grew. New York: Crown, 1954. 199pp.

        After her husband's death in World War II, she becomes a reporter and in 1946 organizes a Women's National News Service; later she works for H. E. W.; at the same time, she carefully builds and nurtures a warm relationship with her two young sons, offering vignettes of motherhood; she writes in the third person.

513   DAVENPORT, ELOISE
        I Can't Forget. New York: Carlton Press, 1960. 236pp.

        Reluctant, but persuaded to enter a mental health clinic, she gradually reveals the marital stress and personality traits leading to her breakdown; engaging in mutually supportive discussions with other patients, she tries to heed doctors' advice to express her feelings more freely, but she is indignant when psychiatrists ignore her physical pain and illness; ultimately she finds she must recover from the negative effects of poor clinic treatment.

514   DAVENPORT, MARCIA GLUCK (1903-   )
       Too Strong for Fantasy.   New York: Scribner, 1967.
       483pp.

A novelist and music critic, she provides a rich, articulate, and sensitive account of the forces in her life, the strongest of which is her love for her mother, the opera singer Alma Gluck; she is also devoted to music, books, work, and Prague; she holds a deep affection for Toscanini and a deep love for Czechoslovakia's Jan Masaryk; the book is marked by a tone of restrained but intense emotion.

515   DAVIDSON, FLORA MARION (1879-   )
       Hidden Highway; Experiences on the Northwest Frontier of
       India.   New York: Revell, 1948.   191pp.

A missionary in the area between India and Afghanistan, she writes in the third person with an outward focus on the people among whom she lives; she describes the frustrations, isolation, dangers, and hardships, as well as the joy of friendships and "glimpses of glory."

516   DAVIDSON, JAQUIE (1938-   )
       I Am a Housewife!--A Housewife Is the Most Important Per-
       son in the World.   New York: Guild Books, 1972.   108pp.

A proud "wife, mother and homemaker" writes to combat the threat posed by women's liberation and the Equal Rights Amendment; having lived with poverty, rape, and divorce, she finds that her life is transformed by "Fascinating Womanhood," an organization for which she becomes a lecturer; in 1970 she organizes "Happiness of Womanhood" to gain media exposure for her anti-ERA stand and her arguments for home and family.

517   DAVIES, MARION (1897-1961)
       The Times We Had: Life with William Randolph Hearst, ed.
       Pamela Pfau and Kenneth S. Marx.   Indianapolis: Bobbs-
       Merrill, 1975.   276pp.

An actress and mistress of Hearst, she prepared tapes from 1951 to 1961 from which this narrative is constructed; the daughter of a prominent New York family, she takes her first stage job at 13, although she coolly assesses her lack

of talent; she is 16 when Hearst begins his gentle pursuit;
in a naïve style, she tells of other movie stars, her travels,
the parties and social life at San Simeon, the "companionship and devoted love" of Hearst.

518   DAVIS, ADELLE (1904-1974)
       Exploring Inner Space; Personal Experiences Under LSD-25.
       New York: Harcourt, Brace & World, 1961. 216pp.

       A writer, she reports in vivid detail immediately after
each of five experiences with the drug as part of a scientific
experiment beginning in 1959; she undergoes highly intensified emotions and sensations, from terror to religious "self-
less love"; she explores the meaning and symbolism of each
experience and feels her perceptions and emotions are permanently altered.

519   DAVIS, ALICE PAULINE (1920-   )
       Bayou Boats.   New York: New Voices Publishing Co. , 1950.
       143pp.

       In an anecdotal account written in strong vernacular with
much dialogue, she describes her work during World War II
in a Texas shipyard office; she notes the daily routine, fellow workers, boy friends, and closes with her marriage to
a soldier.

520   DAVIS, ANGELA (1944-   )
       Angela Davis: An Autobiography.   New York: Random
       House, 1974.   400pp.

       Offered as a political autobiography, her account opens
with several months underground and her capture in 1970;
she shifts to a chronological discussion of her childhood
amid Birmingham racism, and her later study of philosophy
at Brandeis and in Paris and Frankfurt; membership in the
Communist Party threatens her UCLA teaching job, but involvement in work to free political prisoners takes prece-
dence, leads eventually to charges against her of kidnapping,
murder, and conspiracy; her trial (and book) ends with ac-
quittal.

521   DAVIS, BETTE (1908-   )
       The Lonely Life: An Autobiography.   New York: Putnam,
       1962.   254pp.

       This is a strong, articulate account, including her de-
scription of a childhood marked by her father's desertion and
her mother's lifelong support of the author's career as an

actress; after stock company experience on the East Coast, she moves to Hollywood, where her film career peaks in 1939; she wins two Academy Awards; she is married four times in her search for a family life.

522   DAVIS, HARRIET IDE EAGER
World on My Doorstep; A Venture in International Living. New York: Simon and Schuster, 1947. 274pp.

An editor and writer, she presents an articulate and perceptive chronicle of the "slow and halting growth" of her knowledge of foreign affairs through her marriage to an idealistic international specialist; accompanying her husband to Geneva in 1931 for the Disarmament Conference, she is initially preoccupied with her home and two young sons; gradually she learns about the League of Nations, the prelude to the Spanish Civil War, the rise of Hitler, diplomatic and political maneuvering, and she becomes convinced that women's patriotism and pacifism could have a beneficial effect on world events; she closes with an exhortation to women to gain political knowledge and hence increased power.

523   DAVIS, JULIA
Legacy of Love.   New York: Harcourt, Brace & World, 1961.   237pp.

A novelist, historian, and author of children's books presents a sensitive portrayal of her childhood and youth; motherless, educated by a grandmother who is a model of strength and intellectual aspiration, and raised by her father and two aunts of "unforgettable influence," she is surrounded by a diverse, loving clan; when her father serves as ambassador to England during World War I, she leads an active "sub-embassy" social life; after they return to the U.S., she remains close to her father, a distinguished lawyer.

524   DAVIS, LORRIE
Letting Down My Hair: Two Years with the Love Rock Tribe--from Dawning to Downing of Aquarius, with Rachel Gallagher.   New York: Arthur Fields, 1973.   279pp.

In an account written largely in the present tense, a black actress describes her joining the cast of Hair in 1968, the unorthodox rehearsals "in a crazy house," the "evangelical" anti-Establishment fervor; the "crack in the dream" for both cast and audience is caused by the issue of nudity; she tells of the tension and improvisation of the Broadway opening and of later problems with sex, drugs, racial rifts, and constant cast turnover; she is shaken, finally glad to leave.

525   DAVIS, MABLE EIGHMY
        A Kansas Schoolma'am (1898-1951).   Chicago: Adams
        Press, 1960.   153pp.

        She enters the teaching profession after high school gradu-
        ation and offers numerous tales about her students in west-
        ern Kansas through the years; a "born reformer," she notes
        "dirty politics" in some job assignments and occasional nicks
        in her vanity and dignity; she tells little about her two mar-
        riages and her children.

526   DAVIS, MARY ELIZABETH MORAGNE
        see MORAGNE, MARY ELIZABETH (1815-1903)

527   DAVIS, VARINA ANNE HOWELL (1826-1906)   NAW
        Jefferson Davis: Private Letters, 1823-1889, ed. Hudson
        Strode.   New York: Harcourt, Brace & World, 1966.
        580pp.

        Calling her husband "the one absorbing love of my whole
        life," nevertheless she dislikes his activities in "politics or
        soldiering," willing to be sharply critical as well as senti-
        mental and emotional in her letters; separated from her hus-
        band often during the Civil War, she agonizes over his
        health after his imprisonment, offers him cheering news of
        their children, and graciously notes the kindness of sym-
        pathizers; after unremitting effort, she helps to secure his
        release in 1867; her letters afterwards contain constantly
        renewed expressions of her love; an intense, courageous
        woman, she endures the deaths of four of her six children
        and a nervous breakdown in 1876, yet sees her husband
        through the publication of the history of the confederacy in
        1880.

528   DAWSON, HELENE (pseud.)
        On a Quiet Street; Memories of an Unhappy Marriage.   New
        York: Exposition, 1963.   44pp.

        She describes troubles behind the façade of a marriage of
        two professional people with four well-behaved children; her
        husband's alcoholism, violence, and threats frighten her and
        damage her children's emotions; she is anxious, worried
        about debts, and bitter about betrayals by lawyers and rela-
        tives.

529   DAY, DOROTHY (1897-1981)
        The Long Loneliness: The Autobiography of Dorothy Day.
        New York: Harper, 1952.   288pp.

After twenty-five years of insecurity and floundering, she finds her vocation with the Catholic Worker Movement; consistent with her early love for "the masses," she is a journalist for New York socialist newspapers and is jailed for suffrage activities but inwardly stricken by feelings of self-preservation during a hunger strike; she describes country domesticity and the birth of a daughter in a common-law marriage, but she breaks with her husband over her religious commitment; choosing poverty, she writes for The Catholic Worker from 1933 until her death; she notes that autobiography is similar to religious confession.

530   DAY, EFFIE BRELAND
       Birds of Paradise. New York: Theo. Gaus' Sons, 1949.
       129pp.

       A writer enjoys a partial return to pioneer days by gardening and raising chickens in the 1940's; saying "they are mine and I am theirs," she finds her devotion to the chickens "regenerating," and she tells of lessons she learned from observing and knowing them.

531   DAY, HELEN CALDWELL (1926-   )
       Color, Ebony. New York: Sheed and Ward, 1951. 182pp.

       A black writer tells of her childhood struggles with poverty and racial prejudice in Texas; her religious searching culminates in her conversion to Catholicism and after a brief marriage and the birth of her son, she works for The Catholic Worker; her nurses' training is interrupted by tuberculosis, and she spends nineteen months in a sanitarium where she begins to write.

532   Not Without Tears. New York: Sheed and Ward, 1954.
       270pp.

       In this sequel to Color, Ebony, she tells of her efforts to organize the Blessed Martin House in Memphis as an interracial center for child care and religious study for the poor; she seeks to end segregation in southern Catholic churches; she combines faith and love with great personal sacrifice in order to solve daily problems and crises, living according to her beliefs.

533   DAY, LARAINE (1920-   )
       Day with the Giants, ed. Kyle Crichton. Garden City, N.Y.:
       Doubleday, 1952.   219pp.

       A former movie actress, she describes her life as a

"baseball wife," married to Leo Durocher, manager of the New York Giants; in numerous lively anecdotes she tells of her initial ignorance about baseball, her charming husband, her coping with dramatic moments caused by games, and her relatively quiet life apart from baseball.

534   DEAN, AGNES
       We Bought a Restaurant.   New York: Pageant, 1956.   69pp.

During World War II, she and her husband and their adult son move from the family farm and open a restaurant on a whim; initially a novice, she learns to cook and develops a tough business sense; she tells of various customers and of her determination to provide good service.

535   DEAN, EDITH M. (1913-)
       But Half the Universe.   San Antonio: Naylor, 1976.   232pp.

She tells of the early years of her marriage when she struggles with unemployment, debts, and futility during the depression of the 1930's; small advances are checked by multiple setbacks, but she finally finds nursing and secretarial work for herself and a "suitable job" for her handicapped husband, establishing a home and raising a nephew; hers is a story of satisfactions after great pain.

536   DEAN, LILLIAN
       Once Is a Habit!   New York: Pageant, 1962.   125pp.

In a series of humorous sketches of daily life, she writes about surprise visitors who rattle her composure, the annual chaos of trimming the Christmas tree, her faux pas as a photographer, the family's pet dogs and cat, her "clunker" car, and fishing.

537   This Is Our Land.   New York: Vantage, 1950.   221pp.

She writes a humorous, anecdotal account of "a pleasant and soul satisfying auto journey" from California to Washington, D. C. and back; traveling with her husband, she enjoys the lifting of wartime travel restrictions, and they savor visits with their parents and their grandchild; they delight in each other's company.

538   DEAN, MAUREEN (1945-)
       "Mo": A Woman's View of Watergate, with Hays Gorey.
       New York: Simon and Schuster, 1975.   286pp.

A young widow, she first meets John Dean in 1970 in
Washington, D. C.; she tells of the euphoria of their wedding
in 1972 followed by the gradual revelation of the unthinkable
as the shadow of Watergate quickly grows; naïve and insulated
from the "world of power" and the public mood, she resents
the loss of privacy as reality breaks in and disillusionment
and insecurity follow; she pleads on her husband's behalf,
closing with his release from prison.

539   DEANE, MARTHA (pseud.)
       see   McBRIDE, MARY MARGARET (1899-   )

540   de ANGELI, MARGUERITE LOFFT (1889-   )
       Butter at the Old Price.   Garden City, N. Y.:   Doubleday,
       1971.   258pp.

       She writes of her childhood in a small Michigan town; her
       promising singing career is willingly abandoned for marriage
       and motherhood; in 1922 she begins as an illustrator for
       books and magazines; by 1936 she settles into her career
       as a writer and illustrator of children's books; warm family
       ties throughout.

541   DECKER, MARY BELL
       The World We Saw; With Town Hall.   New York: Richard R.
       Smith, 1950.   281pp.

       She presents the impressions of "an inquiring plain citi-
       zen" as she participates in a "Round the World" tour with
       the Town Meeting forum in the summer of 1949; a perceptive
       observer, she notes the still-visible effects of World War II
       in Europe, the Middle East, and the Far East, comments
       on her meetings with each country's leading politicians, re-
       produces some of her "indelible picture-memories," and
       demonstrates a deep interest in the common people; she re-
       turns heartened by tokens of international understanding.

542   DECKER, SUNNY
       An Empty Spoon.   New York: Harper & Row, 1969.   115pp.

       A teacher from 1966 to 1968 in a Philadelphia ghetto high
       school, she describes the contrast between her upper-class
       background and her students' daily struggles; she learns
       much during her first year, and goes on to become intense-
       ly involved with the students, leaving only due to her preg-
       nancy.

543   DeFORE, PENNY
       With All My Love.   Englewood Cliffs, N. J. :   Prentice-Hall,
       1965.   175pp.

          Written with teen bounce and slang, her account describes
       her year in Korea at 18; she arrives to care for orphans
       after having been inspired by a film of her father's and her
       own natural gift of play; romance gives way to reality of
       confrontations with the orphanage director, so she shifts to
       more satisfying work with crippled children; she closes with
       her resolve to continue her education.

544   De FOREST, ELSIE DAVIS
       Out of My Cabin.   Boston: Christopher, 1956.   180pp.

          She describes a sojourn in the Ozarks begun in poverty
       and low spirits during the depression; she lives with her
       husband and mother in a simple cabin with the "bare essen-
       tials" as she provides their sole support by teaching; sup-
       ported by her religious faith, she learns tolerance as she
       grows in devotion to her students, her church, and her
       community.

545   De FREES, MADELINE
       The Springs of Silence.   New York: Prentice-Hall, 1953.
       173pp.

          Through her perceptions, she evokes "the essence of a
       way of life" as a teaching nun; her childhood desire to be-
       come a nun is fulfilled as she embraces the discipline of
       convent routine, learning composure, simplicity, and love
       in her struggle for "holy perseverance."

546   DeHAVILLAND, OLIVIA
       Every Frenchman Has One.   New York: Random House,
       1961.   202pp.

          An actress and film star describes her first meeting with
       her French husband-to-be and their married life in Paris;
       she writes in a light tone about Parisian social life, "the
       cure," fashion, a hairdresser, servants, breasts, and the
       French language.

547   De HUECK, CATHERINE (1900-)
       Friendship House.   New York: Sheed and Ward, 1946.
       157pp.

          She tells of having been driven out of her native Russia
       at the time of the revolution, fleeing first to Canada where

she finds "a life's vocation" in the Catholic Action movement, founding the first Friendship House in 1930 in Toron-
to; she then settles in the U. S., in Harlem, and lives
among the poor, serving them through a community center;
Catholic Action is for her a necessary ideological opponent
to communism.

548   My Russian Yesterdays. Milwaukee: Bruce, 1951. 132pp.

She writes a nostalgic account of close, loving family life
in St. Petersburg; she learns domestic tasks such as baking,
cleaning, cooking, and weaving, seeing such work as "a
hallowed occupation"; she reflects on education, music, marriage, death, and the importance of religious faith in everyday life.

549   DE LAVAN, ELIZABETH GARNSEY (1898?-)
       Upstate Family. New York: Vantage, 1972. 143pp.

She opens with a family history, reconstructed from her
father's stories, clippings, and diaries; she describes her
childhood, first in Seneca Falls, then for three years in
Oklahoma Territory in an "informal rugged household"; her
family returns in 1909 to New York and she recounts anecdotes of gypsies, Chautauqua, a meeting with Teddy Roosevelt, the first family auto in 1915, church activities, rustic
summers on a lake, and numerous colorful relatives.

550   del REY, SISTER MARIA
       see MARIA del REY, SISTER

551   Del VILLAR, MARY
       Where the Strange Roads Go Down, with Fred Del Villar.
       New York: Macmillan, 1953. 244pp.

She and her husband, poor but adventurous freelance journalists, describe a three-month hike in western Mexico in
1951; open and observant, she tells of the hospitality of the
poor, travel with two donkeys, hunger and illness, mountain
and desert countryside; she closes with a sense of toughness
and personal satisfaction.

552   DeMILLE, AGNES GEORGE (1905-)
       And Promenade Home. Boston: Little, Brown, 1958.
       301pp.

This account focuses on the first unsettled years of her
marriage during World War II and on her choreography for

successful musicals; she gives a detailed description of the
preparations for Oklahoma!; she rides the crest of success
with Carousel; she relates a dreary sketch of domesticity
before her husband goes overseas and the agony of waiting
out the war; in addition she reflects on transformations of
choreographic style, on women and dance, on the economic
state of choreography.

553   Dance to the Piper.   Boston: Little, Brown, 1951.   342pp.

She describes herself as a "spoiled egocentric wealthy
girl"; she offers fine portraits of her parents--her adored
father a playwright, her mother a woman of fierce moral
purpose and strong will; inspired by Pavlova, she begins
dance training at fourteen although her parents try to tem-
per her mania for work; she auditions and gives recitals in
New York, persisting despite her failures as a dancer and
choreographer; deeply influenced by Martha Graham, she
lives on her "own strength" in London and evolves a style
based on folk dance and American cultural roots; she finds
her first successes with Rodeo in 1942 and Oklahoma!; this
is an extremely articulate, perceptive account.

554   Lizzie Borden: A Dance of Death.   Boston: Little, Brown,
1968.   302pp.

An extremely articulate writer and distinguished choreographer, she tells of her early fascination with the Lizzie
Borden story and of her investigations which lay the factual
foundation for her translation of the legend into a dance triumph in 1948; she presents a brilliant examination of the
creative process involving her own emotions and skills as
well as the interplay of tensions and personalities as the
American Ballet Theatre prepares the piece; she is eloquent
in her horror over the conditions under which dancers work
and in her passionate support for the life of dance.

555   Speak to Me, Dance with Me.   Boston: Little, Brown, 1973.
404pp.

The highly articulate narrative focuses on her life and
work in London in the mid-1930's and consists of long letters to her mother interspersed with additional commentary;
she gives a detailed description of her studies, performances, years of exhilarating and grinding work, years of
sweat and poverty; she paints marvelous portraits of colleagues in dance; she enjoys social ties with Single-Taxers
(for her mother is the daughter of Henry George); called to
work on a movie for uncle Cecil, she later quits in a fury;
she relates her struggles to find a style; she offers a moving

account of her long intimate relationship with a dying young
poet, and of their travels in the western U. S.

556   DEMING, BARBARA (1917-)
       Prison Notes. New York: Grossman, 1966. 185pp.

       Jailed in Georgia in 1964 for participating in a Peace
       Walk to protest nuclear testing, she discusses the actual
       details as well as the symbolism of her arrest and impris-
       onment, recalls other imprisonments for protests; she tells
       of her belief in the power of noncooperation and nonviolent
       action, and of her fears about reasons for a fast which she
       later breaks; she celebrates the solidarity of other jailed
       protestors.

557   DENDEL, ESTHER WARNER
       see WARNER, ESTHER SIETMANN (1910-)

558   DENSEN-GERBER, JUDIANNE (1934-)
       Walk in My Shoes: An Odyssey into Womanlife.   New York:
       Saturday Review Press/Dutton, 1976. 289pp.

       A lawyer and psychiatrist, she discusses her own "middle-
       age identity crisis," describing her approach to career, mar-
       riage, and motherhood; struggling against all woman's op-
       pressions, she celebrates the variety of female experience;
       she notes her role models and states "plurality is the rich-
       ness of my essence"; a strongly affirmative account.

559   We Mainline Dreams; The Odyssey House Story.   Garden
       City, N. Y.: Doubleday, 1973. 421pp.

       A psychiatrist and lawyer, her life, identity, and career
       are inextricably bound up with her aggressive efforts on be-
       half of young drug addicts; a strong woman with a family
       heritage of pride and pressure to achieve, she works with
       the full support of her husband and three children; she de-
       scribes the dynamics of her interracial program at Odyssey
       House, her confrontations with political and legal barriers,
       and her experiences with "the female addict" and child ad-
       vocacy.

560   de PIERREFEU, ELSA TUDOR
       Unity in the Spirit. Rindge, N. H.: Richard R. Smith,
       1955. 167pp.

       A poet and short story writer, she undertakes a "self-
       imposed mission" in 1925 to convince world political and

religious leaders of the power of prayer to end war and
unite mankind; she seeks "unity in the spirit" among all
faiths, traveling extensively, writing letters, and holding
personal interviews in her unremitting effort to present and
argue for her ideas.

561   De PREE, GLADIS LENORE (1933-   )
        The Spring Wind. New York: Harper & Row, 1970.   112pp.

At the request of Chinese Church leaders, she and her
husband and children move to Hong Kong where she works
with dressmakers in a Family Center; anxious for involvement and acceptance, she moves from the foreign enclave
to a Chinese area and builds trusting relationships among
the people; she feels learning the language is "all-important"
and is "inspired and humbled" in her work.

562   de RACHEWILTZ, MARY (1925-   )
        Discretions. Boston: Little, Brown, 1971.   312pp.

The daughter of poet Ezra Pound and violinist Olga Rudge,
she is raised by a Tyrolean peasant family, only later making the uneasy, gradual connection with her parents' "house
of elegance," the emotional ambiguity of her "several realities ... playing in counterpoint"; in her parents' shadow
she absorbs history, music, art, languages, and grows up
steeped in the Cantos; during the war she returns to the
security of the countryside; she maintains a transcendent
respect for her father in spite of his imprisonment, and at-
temps to plead his case in the U.S. in 1953; upon his release, she desires to create for him a final happiness.

563   D'ESSEN, LORRAIN
        Kangaroos in the Kitchen; The Story of Animal Talent Scouts.
        New York: McKay, 1959.   306pp.

In a lively, anecdotal account she describes her "singular
success" as a professional supplier of animals for advertising and show business; when her husband's illness requires
her financial support, she uses her lifelong affinity for animals to create a unique career; her common sense and determination enable her to cope with unusual jobs, bizarre
requests, and a wide variety of animal personalities.

564   DESSLER, JULIA SHAPIRO
        Eyes on the Goal.   New York: Vantage, 1954.   54pp.

After experiencing Russian anti-Semitism and pogroms
which begin in 1905, she attempts to emigrate in 1914 from

Lithuania to the U.S., but is blocked by the outbreak of
World War I; she finally leaves in 1921, marries, and
raises two sons in the U.S.; during World War II, she is
horrified by the Nazi persecution of Jews and concerned
about her family.

565   DETZER, DOROTHY (1900-)
Appointment on the Hill. New York: Holt, 1948. 262pp.

She recounts twenty years' zealous work in the peace
movement, beginning with her association with Hull House
and Quaker relief work in Europe and Russia after World
War I; she serves as a lobbyist on Capitol Hill for the
Women's International League for Peace and Freedom, campaigning passionately for disarmament and against U.S. im-
perialism.

566   DEUTSCH, HELENE (1884-)
Confrontations with Myself: An Epilogue. New York: Norton, 1973. 217pp.

A psychoanalyst, she examines the recurrent emotional
patterns of her "stormy and turbulent life," acknowledging
both the free play of memory and the inevitable accompanying psychological distortion; born a Polish Jew, she tells of
her devotion to her scholarly father, her drive for a university education, medical studies, her marriage, the complex-
ities of combining motherhood and the professional life, her
major publications between 1925 and 1945; her family provides the emotional center to her life while Freud constitutes
the intellectual center; she settles in the U.S. in 1934.

567   DEVI, NILA
see WOODY, REGINA LLEWELLYN JONES (1894-)

568   de VIVI, ANNE
Indrani and I. New York: Red Dust, 1965. 127pp.

Settling in India to study dancing and Sanskrit and "determined to like it," she tells of the unique atmosphere of her
university; friendships take her into several Indian homes
which she describes in sharp and vivid detail; amid the detail and surrounded by perceptions of custom, caste, and
family tensions and balances, her portrait of an "arresting,
compelling" friend emerges.

569   DEWEY, MAYBELLE JONES (1888-)
Push the Button; The Chronicle of a Professor's Wife. At-
lanta, Ga.: Tupper and Love, 1951. 180pp.

She describes a joyful southern childhood, school days, and her "stretch of happiness" at college; after working as a society editor for her home town newspaper, she marries a professor; she tells of the "domestic, religious, intellectual, social" aspects of her career as a professor's wife; she describes later travels in Europe with her husband's boys' glee club; she offers other random anecdotes.

570   DICK, CLARIBEL FEATHERNGILL
How Long the Night.   Philadelphia: Judson, 1955.   117pp.

She writes "the true story of my hospital experience as the result of an automobile accident"; concerned for her three children but comforted by her family, she occupies her time with recollections; her religious convictions remain strong.

571   DICKERSON, NANCY
Among Those Present: A Reporter's View of Twenty-five Years in Washington.   New York: Random House, 1976. 238pp.

In an account full of anecdotes of politics and personalities, she tells of her first staff job in 1951 with the Senate Foreign Relations Committee; then she becomes the "first woman CBS television-news correspondent," later shifting to NBC; struggling with sexism as she covers political conventions and events during the Kennedy, Johnson, and Nixon administrations, she notes some advances in women's rights; she also describes her marriage and the Washington social whirl.

572   DICKINSON, EMILY (1830-1886)   NAW
Emily Dickinson, Selected Letters, ed. Thomas H. Johnson. Cambridge, Mass.:   Belknap Press, Harvard University Press, 1971.   364pp.

These letters are taken from the 1955 variorum, three-volume edition and they cover the years from 1842 to 1886; the contents range from charming domestic details to the intense and severely epigrammatic expressions of the early 1860's (the flood time of her poems) to her sensitive responses to death; most of the letters were written to a small circle, including T.W. Higginson.

573   Emily Dickinson's Letters to Dr. and Mrs. Josiah Gilbert Holland, ed. Theodora Van Wagenen Ward.   Cambridge: Harvard University Press, 1951.   252pp.

The collection includes ninety-three letters written to the Hollands between 1853 and 1886; her letters are characteristically witty, affectionate, and effusive; rather demanding as a friend, she writes "Belong to me!" and her eccentricities and condensation of expression increase through the years; as her identity as a poet grows, she encloses poems; as deaths of acquaintances and family members occur, she notes that "Blow has followed blow" and she explores the mysteries of the "Adventure of Death" in spite of her assertion that "we are mentally permanent."

574   The Letters of Emily Dickinson, ed. Thomas H. Johnson. Cambridge, Mass.: Belknap Press, Harvard University Press, 3 vols., 1958. 999pp.

These three volumes constitute the variorum edition; letters numbered 1-1049 cover the years 1842-1886; her letters are marked by "acute sensitivity," loneliness, and increasingly poetic, even enigmatic diction into the early 1860's; the letters are arranged chronologically; see comments for Johnson's Emily Dickinson, Selected Letters.

575   DIENSTAG, ELEANOR (1939-   )
       Whither Thou Goest: The Story of an Uprooted Wife. New York: Dutton, 1976. 187pp.

The double standard in marriage and career goals is explored by a journalist who ceases to write after having two sons; her husband's job forces a move from New York City to Rochester, precipitating a crisis with her feelings of isolation, culture shock, lack of control; the women's liberation movement causes further strains and she turns to a psychiatrist; she comes to feel acceptance and personal growth.

576   DILLARD, ANNIE (1945-   )
       Pilgrim at Tinker Creek. New York: Harper's Magazine Press, 1974. 271pp.

In an impressionistic account structured by the yearly cycle of months, she describes her home in the Blue Ridge Mountains; with close observations of nature, she reflects on the implications of natural events such as winter, insects, the renewal and wonder of spring, floods, predators, migration, and the appalling fecundity of nature.

577   DIMOCK, GLADYS GOUVERNEUR OGDEN
       A Home of Our Own. New York: Macmillan, 1963. 233pp.

She tells of eight years on a Vermont farm seeking free-

dom and independence with her husband; they depend on subsistence farming and the joint publication of several books
for a living, raise a son, and "invite our souls"; she describes their home and garden, their first winter, and their
growing satisfactions as they become deeply involved in farm
and community life; she reflects on "the Vermont character";
travels and work in Puerto Rico, Turkey, and England interrupt farming, as she balances professional life, householding,
and creative freedom.

578   di PRIMA, DIANE
        Memoirs of a Beatnik.   New York: Olympia Press, 1969.
        174pp.

        Painting a slangy, erotic portrait of beatnik subculture
in the New York City of the 1950's, she notes the details of
her own bisexual explorations, playing "aesthetic games" under the "rule of Cool" through life in various "pads," on the
streets, and in a summer country commune; she closes with
her first pregnancy, "a whole new adventure."

579   DIRKSEN, LOUELLA CARVER (1899-)
        The Honorable Mr. Marigold; My Life with Everett Dirksen,
        with Norma Lee Browning.   Garden City, N.Y.:   Doubleday,
        1972.   297pp.

        Stating that "he was my idol," the wife of the late Senator
from Illinois recalls numerous anecdotes of political life;
after a happy childhood, she marries in 1927 and manages
the family business accounts, personal finances, and after
her husband enters politics in 1929, campaign funds; initially
insecure in Washington, she learns to play "the best supporting role," speaking and campaigning for her husband and
totally dedicated to his career; although she admits to some
loneliness living in his shadow, nevertheless she writes "an
old-fashioned love story."

580   DIXON, JEANE
        My Life and Prophecies; Her Own Story as told to Rene
        Noorbergen.   New York: Morrow, 1969.   219pp.

        Famous for her predictions, she is deeply religious and
opens with a description of her marriage, home, and work
as a real estate broker; partly to dispel rumors, she tells
anecdotes about her psychic experiences, many of which involve politics and politicians and anti-communist warnings;
she discusses dreams, revelations, meditation, telepathy,
healing; she adds a list of predictions for the future, including the coming of the anti-Christ.

581   DJERASSI, NORMA LUNDHOLM
       Glimpses of China from a Galloping Horse (A Woman's Jour-
       nal). New York: Pergamon, 1974. 141pp.

       A poet and public school teacher, she presents "a vivid
       picture of everyday life in China in simple, nonjudgmental
       writing"; during a trip in 1973 she visits schools, labora-
       tories, homes, factories, stores, and museums; she ob-
       serves women's roles; her account is largely positive, al-
       though she is troubled by pressures for social conformity.

582   DODD, BELLA VISONO (1904-1969)
       School of Darkness. New York: P. J. Kenedy, 1954.
       264pp.

       She spends her early childhood in Italy, settling in the
       U. S. , she is involved in student politics at Hunter College
       and later teaches at Hunter; she earns a law degree; turn-
       ing to communism, she spends eight years as a Teachers'
       Union organizer and as an open leader of the CPUSA in 1943;
       post-war disillusionment sets in and she is expelled from
       the party; she turns to the Catholic Church.

583   DODGE, ANNE ATWOOD
       Recollections of Old Stonington. Stonington, Conn. : Pequot
       Press, 1966. 45pp.

       The account, a "merest hodge-podge of memories," was
       written in 1950 and includes impressions of village life in
       an age of simplicity and innocence, "country pleasures" and
       activities, the dignity of the village women, and the vitality
       of the past to village present.

584   DODGE, HELEN CARMICHAEL
       My Childhood in the Canadian Wilderness. New York: Van-
       tage, 1961. 77pp.

       In a rambling account, the daughter of a lumberman tells
       of her large family, "always on the move"; little schooling
       and the outdoor life produce in her a love of the wilderness
       and an urge for independence; going "out in the world," she
       works as a teacher and a housekeeper, closing the account
       with her engagement.

585   DOE, JANE (pseud.)
       Crazy. New York: Hawthorn, 1966. 224pp.

       A professional writer describes daily life in a state men-
       tal hospital; she tells of the financial strain, the job insecur-

ity, and a sanity hearing which leads to her incarceration;
she recounts long conversations with other patients, portraying their humor as well as despair; she meets a young poet
and carries on a brief love affair until he escapes from the
hospital; she notes patients' criticism of the hospital system
and closes with a plea for understanding.

586   DOLINGER, JANE
       The Jungle Is a Woman.   Chicago: Regnery, 1955.   225pp.

       Afflicted with an "insatiable curiosity," she answers an
       ad for an adventurous "girl Friday" and accompanies a tra-
       vel writer to Peru to study Indian tribes in the remote
       reaches of the Amazon; eager to learn about another culture,
       she embraces discomfort and hardship in "the most thrilling
       phase of my life," which includes her ceremonial adoption
       by a tribe after they capture her; her return to civilization
       is anti-climactic, and she marries her boss and joins him
       in another expedition.

587   DOLSON, HILDEGARDE
       Sorry to Be So Cheerful.   New York: Random House, 1955.
       207pp.

       Her account consists of chapters previously published as
       humorous stories in The New Yorker and elsewhere over a
       period of twenty years; she includes stories of her job as
       an advertising copywriter, a naïve encounter with commun-
       ism, tea with Emily Post, a Paris misadventure, flying
       lessons, and her myopia.

588   DONLAN, YOLANDE (1920-)
       Sand in My Mink.   London: Macgibbon & Kee, 1955.   144pp.

       A movie actress presents chatty anecdotes of "a broad
       abroad" beginning with tales of a rest cure in southern
       France following a movie lot accident; accompanied by her
       future husband and a friend, she enjoys a vacation interlude
       in Italy, film work in Spain, then a honeymoon in Hamburg,
       and travels in Morocco.

589   Third Time Lucky.   New York: Dial, 1976.   245pp.

       After a chaotic childhood spent alternately with her father,
       a Hollywood actor, and her mother, a French "frustrated
       opera star," and an eccentric aunt, she gets her first Holly-
       wood job as a dancing extra at sixteen, beginning her acting
       career in "utter confusion"; married, pregnant and unem-
       ployed, she rejects the roles of housewife and mother, and

joins the road company of "Born Yesterday," later acting in
post-war London and achieving the family's first real acting
success.

590   DORCY, SISTER MARY JEAN (1914-)
        Never the Golden City. New York: Sheed and Ward, 1962.
        213pp.

        An author and artist, she describes "an improbable jour-
        ney" to New Mexico in search of information, folklore, and
        evidence of early Spanish missions; hoping that the family
        of a friend, an Indian workman who is the grandson of
        Geronimo and a "powerful personality," will provide her
        with an entrance to Indian society, she is dismayed when
        the family members turn out to be dead or non-existent;
        amid the phantoms, she salvages from her quest a vision
        of local folk legend, illuminated by the stories of the work-
        man.

591   Shepherd's Tartan. New York: Sheed & Ward, 1953.
        179pp.

        A Dominican nun, teacher, author of children's books,
        and maker of silhouettes muses about her eighteen years of
        convent life in a series of random recollections; "in love
        with God," she is deeply serious about her religious voca-
        tion, yet she writes with humor.

592   DORSEY, ELAINE VENABLE
        So I Had Breast Cancer! And How Are You? New York:
        Exposition, 1972. 78pp.

        Writing about her mastectomies in 1962 and 1963, she
        describes the terror of her first discovery of cancer; she
        is sharply critical of the medical care she receives; she
        suffers pain and misery from both surgery and cobalt ther-
        apy and seeks psychiatric help; unemployed and bankrupt,
        she nevertheless overcomes her suffering and looks forward
        to a new life, bolstered by the "tremendous capacity of the
        human spirit."

593   DORTZBACH, DEBBIE
        Kidnapped, with Karl Dortzbach. New York: Harper &
        Row, 1975. 177pp.

        A missionary nurse in Ethiopia, she is captured by Erit-
        rean rebels in 1974 and held for twenty-six days; horrified
        by the murder of a companion, concerned for the safety of
        her unborn child, she is sustained throughout by her strong

religious faith; she is befriended by village women, grateful for small kindnesses, and she has sympathy and understanding for her captors; her chapters alternate with those of her husband.

594   DOSS, HELEN GRIGSBY (1915-   )
        The Family Nobody Wanted. Boston: Little,   Brown,   1954.
        267pp.

        With a light, humorous touch, she tells of the gradual growth of her adopted family, from her first son to her tenth, eleventh, and twelfth children; she and her husband, a minister, choose children from a variety of racially mixed backgrounds; she presents a story of love and coping.

595   DOUGHERTY, HELEN B.
        Athenai, I Loved You! New York: Vantage,   1960.   59pp.

        The wife of an Air Force officer and the mother of three children, she travels to Athens in 1954 to join her husband; she tells of the social whirl, seaside activities, adjusting to servants and Greek homemaking, marketing, and her ambivalence toward the American Women's Organization in Athens; she is grateful for her store of fond memories.

596   DOUGLASS, LILLIE BERNARD
        Cape Town to Cairo.   Caldwell, Idaho: Caxton,   1964.
        348pp.

        An adventurous grandmother describes a 1959 trip with her husband by travel trailer through Africa with a Caravan Club; she notes caravan logistics and struggles with rugged roads, telling of visits to native festivals, wild animal reserves, historical monuments, colorful villages, and magnificent scenic areas, culminating with the caravan's reception by Emperor Haile Selassie; her numerous contacts with natives, especially children, are friendly; her straightforward, detailed descriptions include brief historical and cultural comments.

597   DOWLING, COLETTE
        How to Love a Member of the Opposite Sex: A Memoir.
        New York: Coward, McCann & Geoghogan, 1976.   220pp.

        A journalist and divorcée writes in an attempt "to understand the past and find a new direction"; she tells of her Catholic upbringing, her early sexual experience and pregnancy leading to a hasty marriage; forced to choose between husband's and children's needs and beset by conflicting emo-

tions, she feels oppressed and limited; following a separation, she explores her sexuality in affairs, finding an open,
loving relationship.

598   DOWNING, MARY SAMUEL
       Creation. New York: Vantage, 1957. 67pp.

A psychic explains how the story of the creation of the
universe is revealed to her through automatic writing; first,
however, she briefly establishes her credentials by describing prior psychic experiences.

599   DRAGONETTE, JESSICA
       Faith Is a Song; The Odyssey of an American Artist.   New
       York: McKay, 1951. 322pp.

A concert singer, she tells of a childhood "close to no
one" in a convent orphanage; "extremely precocious," she
is encouraged by fine voice teachers and dedicates her career "humbly to give pleasure" to the widest possible audiences, including radio listeners in the 1920's; her self-
discipline and devotion to singing become "all-consuming"
and she marries only after much hesitation.

600   DRAKE, ALICE HUTCHINS
       Miss Hutchinson Steps Out, "Adventures of a Small Doll at
       Large." New York: Field-Doubleday, 1946. 76pp.

Accompanied in her childhood by a beloved doll acquired
in 1938 and named after Anne Hutchinson, she travels extensively with her family, meets interesting and prominent
people, and grows up under the "influence of the Arts"; she
evokes a child's imaginative responses overlaid with a woman's mature reflections on having learned certain lessons
and values.

601   DRAPKIN, FRITA ROTH
       Papa's Golden Land. New York: Comet, 1960. 182pp.

She tells of the chaos of immigration as she comes to the
U.S. from Hungary as a child; she settles in Michigan and
illustrates her Americanization in the midst of an extended
family with humorous anecdotes; her account closes with her
high school graduation and her mother's citizenship.

602   DREISER, HELEN PATGES
       My Life with Dreiser. Cleveland: World, 1951. 328pp.

She writes her "own personal reactions to such a vital force as he was"; she meets Dreiser in 1919, settling in California and enjoying three happy years in spite of the tension between her movie career and her home life with Dreiser; then, spiritually drained, she is driven to leave him in 1924, and although she sees him infrequently, she feels a "telepathic" closeness to him; married in 1944, she closes with his death in 1945.

603   DUFF, ANNIE
"Longer Flight"; A Family Grows Up with Books.   New York: Viking, 1955.   269pp.

Through a series of examples drawn from her family life, she illustrates and reflects upon the effects of books on her children; she describes the usefulness of literature in developing intelligence and imagination, the joys of plays, the possibilities for vicarious adventure, her views on "the classics," and her nostalgia for reading time she shared with her children.

604   DUFFEE, MARY GORDON (1844-1920)
Sketches of Alabama, Being an Account of the Journey from Tuscaloosa to Blount Springs Through Jefferson County on the Old Stage Roads.   University, Ala.:   University of Alabama Press, 1970.   96pp.

Now substantially edited, these sketches by a writer and poet were originally published as fifty-nine articles between 1885 and 1887; her four-day journey is illuminated by descriptions of the people she meets, the countryside and flowers, the towns through which she passes, and the industry she sees; discussing local schools, hospitality, and conditions of slavery, she adds much historical material on each locale.

605   DUFFY, GLADYS
Warden's Wife, with Blaise Whitehead Lane.   New York: Appleton-Century-Crofts, 1959.   346pp.

The daughter of a sensitive, reform-minded prison guard, she is raised in San Quentin and recounts a childhood of happiness troubled occasionally by brief glimpses of prison conditions; she attends college, teaches, then marries a childhood boyfriend in 1921, sharing with him youthful hopes and dreams of prison reforms; their roots remain deep in the San Quentin community; when her husband is appointed warden in 1940, his sweeping reforms fulfill some of their lifelong ambitions; she closes at the end of her twelve satisfying years as the warden's wife.

606 DUNAWAY, JANE ENGLISH (1879-)
     Letters from Doctor Jane. New York: Exposition, 1964.
     100pp.

     Cast in the form of letters to a nephew studying medi-
     cine, her account consists of anecdotes of her personal ex-
     periences with individual mental patients beginning with her
     acceptance in 1922 of a position in a midwestern state men-
     tal hospital.

607 DUNBAR, MARY CONWAY SHIELDS (1845-)
     My Mother Used to Say; A Natchez Belle of the Sixties, by
     Elizabeth Dunbar Murray. Boston: Christopher, 1959.
     224pp.

     These stories are recorded by her daughter "just as
     though my mother were telling them"; born on a Mississippi
     plantation, she recalls a beloved black mammy; her mem-
     ories of happy and prosperous days include a trip to Louis-
     ville, a fancy dress ball in 1860, "Christmas on the planta-
     tion"; the war intrudes in 1861 and her mother, "an ardent
     Southerner," is banished to the plantation for insulting the
     Union flag; their Natchez home is destroyed and must be
     rebuilt in 1865; she notes the terror of yellow fever in 1867,
     her own illness and recovery; she marries in 1869.

608 DUNCAN, IRMA (1897?-1977)
     Duncan Dancer; An Autobiography. Middletown, Conn. :
     Wesleyan University Press, 1965. 352pp.

     In 1905 she is separated from her mother and enters Isa-
     dora Duncan's Berlin dance school; she idolizes Isadora (see
     entry #609) and recognizes her spiritual force but suffers
     some unhappy times with bad teachers; she is torn later
     when caught in the competition between Isadora and her sis-
     ter; she serves as a teacher to Isadora's daughter before
     the latter's death; she is a member of the "Duncan Dancers"
     tour in the U. S. , performing with Isadora, then accompany-
     ing her to Russia in 1921, remaining in Moscow to teach
     dance; she closes with the shock of Isadora's death.

609 DUNCAN, ISADORA (1878-1927)   NAW
     "Your Isadora," The Love Story of Isadora Duncan and Gor-
     don Craig, ed. Francis Steegmuller. New York: Random
     House, New York Public Library, 1974. 399pp.

     Passionate and effusive from their first meeting in 1904,
     the famous dancer writes free-form, rambling, euphoric
     letters to her lover; she masks her anxiety during her preg-
     nancy and the birth of their daughter; gradually estranged

from Craig by "brutalizing" financial concerns, illness, and
breakdown, her letters become muted after a final rebuff in
1907, and their final exchange comes after the deaths of her
children in 1913; the editor provides connecting narrative.

610   DUNFORD, KATHERINE (1920-   )
       The Journal of an Ordinary Pilgrim.   Philadelphia: West-
       minster, 1954.   133pp.

       "An ordinary housewife" in Connecticut keeps a journal
       from 1951 to 1953 which describes her search for a satisfy-
       ing Protestant religious foundation for herself and for her
       children; her life is gradually illuminated by religious cer-
       tainty.

611   DUNHAM, KATHERINE (1910-   )
       Island Possessed.   Garden City, N.Y.:   Doubleday, 1969.
       280pp.

       An anthropologist and dancer describes a series of visits
       to Haiti beginning in 1936 and continuing until 1962; there,
       "embroiled in the sorcery and sociopolitics of Africa," she
       observes voodoo rituals, participates in an initiation cere-
       mony dance, performs professionally, joins carnival festiv-
       ities, notes Haitian political events; her response to Haitian
       culture remains ambivalent, producing an inner "struggle be-
       tween science and art."

612   Katherine Dunham's Journey to Accompong.   New York:
       Holt, 1946.   162pp.

       The prominent dancer tells of one month of anthropologi-
       cal field work in a remote Jamaican village in the 1930's
       while she was a University of Chicago undergraduate; her
       daily diary entries chronicle the excitement of the songs,
       stories, magic rites, and dances she observes; she departs
       reluctantly.

613   A Touch of Innocence.   New York: Harcourt, Brace, 1959.
       312pp.

       Written in the third person with an intense, introspective
       style, the account tells the story of a vanished world;
       she describes her childhood fears and melancholia; after the
       lingering death of her mother, she moves from suburbs to
       Chicago, experiences the humiliation of racist discrimination;
       growing conflicts mark her father's second marriage, until
       her revered older brother and herself are estranged from
       their father; feelings of vague guilt, psychological pain,
       gradual loss of emotional innocence are profoundly explored.

614   DUNLAP, JANE (pseud.)
       see DAVIS, ADELLE (1904-1974)

615   DUNNING, MARY PARKER
       Mrs. Marco Polo Remembers.   Boston: Houghton Mifflin,
       1968.   203pp.

       Married to a "modern Marco Polo" in 1908, she recounts
       her travels, drawing on letters from 1908 to 1956; her wed-
       ding trip takes her to the Far East, the Middle East, and
       southern Europe; later travels include Africa, Australia, and
       the Far East; she writes with much description of local his-
       tory and customs.

616   DWYER, MABEL
       No Tomorrow.   Detroit, Mich. :   Harlo Press, 1964.   128pp.

       In a book written in memory of her daughter who dies in
       1961 of leukemia at twenty-four, a mother recalls the young
       woman's "exemplary life"; she opens with an account of her
       daughter's last days; she then recalls the unrecognized onset
       of the disease; she closes with a mother's fond memories of
       her daughter's childhood, illuminated by warmth and vivacity.

617   DYKEMAN, WILMA (1920-   )
       Look to This Day.   New York: Holt, Rinehart and Winston,
       1968.   342pp.

       A novelist and journalist, she recounts the satisfactions
       of "the simple life" with two sons in the Great Smoky Moun-
       tains; she writes numerous brief but reflective vignettes,
       each with a moral, on family life, nature, travels in the
       U. S. and in Europe; rejecting "pernicious anemia of the
       spirit, " she is offended by "human sloth, selfishness, and
       indifference. "

618   EATON, EVELYN SYBIL MARY (1902-   )
      Every Month Was May.   New York: Harper & Brothers,
      1946.   241pp.

      A Canadian-born novelist, she presents a light-hearted
      narrative of her stay in Europe in the 1920's and 1930's;
      choosing a secretarial career for its independence, she
      marries, bears a daughter, and divorces, settling in France
      to work as a social secretary, a Paramount script girl, and
      a writer; she leaves the "light, sane joy" of France shortly
      before the outbreak of World War II.

619   The North Star Is Nearer.   New York: Farrar, Straus,
      1949.   232pp.

      Each chapter is a vignette suffused with quiet, wry hu-
      mor; raised in Canada by British parents, she finds herself
      caught "between two worlds," a feeling intensified when she
      settles as an adult in Paris for "harsh, sad, formative and
      rich" years; she describes French village life, a translation
      job, a visit to her mother's English estate, and her emigra-
      tion to the U. S. where she becomes a citizen.

620   The Trees and Fields Went the Other Way.   New York:
      Harcourt Brace Jovanovich, 1974.   342pp.

      A novelist and poet, she describes her search for a
      spiritual home among the Indians, her distant ancestors; in
      England with her Canadian parents during World War I, she
      compares her restricted, "dull, Edwardian childhood" with
      the hypothetical freedom of an Indian childhood; drawn to
      France as a young woman, she experiences "love, child-
      birth, marriage, divorce," before returning to North Amer-
      ica during World War II, then serving as a foreign war
      correspondent; later she joins her Indian past in the western
      U. S. , growing "strong in the desert"; her narrative includes
      long diary entries.

621   EBENER, CHARLOTTE
      No Facilities for Women.   New York: Knopf, 1955.   283pp.

A reporter, she gains a "political education" traveling in Russian-occupied Manchuria in 1946 with a group of foreign correspondents to report on the Russia-China conflict; later she travels with the French Foreign Legion in Cambodia and Viet Nam, then covers post-war Czechoslovakia and other points in eastern Europe, then goes to Palestine in 1947; married, she accompanies her husband to the South Seas, the Middle East, north Africa, and the Far East as she produces free-lance articles; throughout she is a keen political observer.

622   EBERHART, BETH
       A Crew of Two.   Garden City, N. Y. :   Doubleday, 1961.
       286pp.

       With the last of her three children grown, she bows to her husband's dreams of the wandering life aboard an Alas- kan fishing boat; she keeps a chronicle of her reluctant first season, beginning with misadventures on their maiden voyage and continuing with mistakes, good luck, bad luck, hard- ships, and danger; she paints nature scenes, selling some to outdoor magazines; she overcomes her fears and frustra- tions to continue the adventure.

623   EDEY, MARION ARMSTRONG
       Early in the Morning.   New York: Harper, 1954.   236pp.

       She comes from a distinguished family of writers and artists; entering into the spirit and perceptions of a child- hood in the 1890's, she provides fine descriptions of her country home on the Hudson, an atmosphere of freedom and intimacy with Nature, and her own "addiction to outdoor pursuits"; she writes in the third person.

624   EDWARDS, ANNE (1927-   )
       The Inn and Us, with Stephen Citron.   New York: Random
       House, 1976.   181pp.

       A novelist and film script writer and the mother of two college-aged children, she settles in a Stockbridge, Massa- chusetts luxury inn to live with her lover, an innkeeper and musician; straightforward about her unmarried status, she finds her involvement with the inn exhilarating but eventually the difficulties of mixing a home with business lead to their decision to sell; she writes two of the book's five sections.

625   EDWARDS, CHARLOTTE
       Heaven in the Home.   New York: Hawthorn, 1959.   246pp.

A writer, she presents a series of essays in which personal experiences trigger reflections and exhortations of
great feeling; she focuses on marriage, motherhood, and
the lessons learned from the innocence of children, and inner consciousness.

626   EDWARDS, LETA MARGUERITE
       Holi-Daze on the Farm; A Sequel to Sauce for the Geese.
       New York: Exposition, 1952.   127pp.

       This is a light account of "enjoyable living" on the farm
       with her parents and sisters and the hired help; her domes-
       tic anecdotes follow a one-year cycle, from "a typical New
       Year's Day," to other holidays, spring butchering, summer
       vacation, school days, and Christmas.

627   Sauce for the Geese; The Story of a Nebraska Farm.   New
       York: Exposition, 1949.   125pp.

       The daughter of pioneers, she describes the "strenuous
       days" of her childhood, enumerating the daily house and field
       tasks on her family's dairy farm; she has immense awe and
       affection for her energetic parents and, although she plans
       an "escape" through a secretarial career, she is grateful
       for her rural heritage of strong values.

628   EDWARDS, MARY LOUISE
       Love Me, Puerto Rico.   Hato Rey, Puerto Rico: Barton
       House, 1962.   173pp.

       In very short chapters on a wide variety of aspects of
       Puerto Rican life, she tells of her "paradise days," having
       accompanied her husband there; she describes the landscape,
       culture, and customs of the island.

629   ELDRIDGE, RETHA HAZEL
       From the Rising of the Sun.   Washington, D. C.:   Review
       and Herald Publishing Association, 1963.   252pp.

       A Seventh-day Adventist missionary, she serves for
       twenty-five years in Japan with her husband beginning in
       1937; during World War II she is interned in the Philippines,
       but she returns to Japan in 1946; writing with quiet fervor,
       she tells of conversions among the Japanese, and of her
       work with a Bible school and a religious radio station.

630   ELFMAN, BLOSSOM
       The Girls of Huntington House.   Boston: Houghton Mifflin,
       1972.   212pp.

An English teacher tells of "an unusual teaching year" in a maternity home for unwed mothers; naïve and enthusiastic, she is fascinated and frustrated by her students' apathy; she is gradually caught up in the plights of individual students, learning some of "the verities of the human heart."

631   ELKIN, JUDITH LAIKIN (1928-   )
       Krishna Smiled: Assignment in Southeast Asia.   Detroit:
       Wayne State University Press, 1972.   251pp.

       A U. S. Foreign Service Officer, she travels for two years beginning in 1952, acquiring published material for U. S. libraries in a "great scavenger hunt"; she describes in numerous anecdotes her encounters with people, her keen observations, and her experiences as the only woman to travel alone in remote Afghanistan, recording as well her innermost impressions; she also includes reflections on a Foreign Service career during the McCarthy era.

632   ELLIOT, ELISABETH (1926-   )
       The Savage My Kinsman.   New York: Harper, 1961.   159pp.

       A missionary, widowed when her husband is murdered by Auca tribesmen in Ecuador in 1956, she feels called to seek out the tribe and live among them; her first contact with two Auca women paves the way to her later settlement with her young daughter in their village for nearly a year; she is accepted, living in the most primitive conditions and working on the Auca language; she reflects on her own culture and that of the Aucas.

633   These Strange Ashes.   New York: Harper & Row, 1975.
       132pp.

       A novelist, author of religious books, and biographer of her husband, she tells of her first year in 1952 as a missionary among the Indians of the Ecuador forest; going for adventure as well as for spiritual reasons, she finds the work doesn't meet her naïve expectations of sacrifice and service; her inability to save a woman in childbirth, the murder of her native informant, and the theft of her year's language work leave her feeling bewildered and undone, but she retains her faith, leaving to accept a marriage proposal.

634   ELMORE, ELLAINE
       The Sunrise of the Soul; An Autobiographical and Historical
       Dissertation on Psychic Phenomena and Divine Law.   New
       York: Exposition, 1959.   103pp.

       Describing her "life search for the Truth," she tells of

years of study on spiritualism, communications with her deceased mother and brother, and personal experiences that
confirm the reality of the spirit world, all of which explain
why she is a spiritualist.

635   EMERSON, ELLEN LOUISA TUCKER (1809?-1831)
       One First Love; The Letters of Ellen Louisa Tucker to
       Ralph Waldo Emerson, ed. Edith W. Gregg.   Cambridge,
       Mass.:   Harvard University Press, 1962.   208pp.

       From the first blushing love letters of a seventeen-year-
       old to a rhymed journal of a trip to Philadelphia after her
       marriage, this collection covers the years from 1828 to
       1831; in her marvelous early letters, she is spirited and
       effusive, offering mock apologies for her style and for "these
       obscure labyrinths"; news and emotion tumble on together,
       sometimes punctuated only with spaces and dashes and fre-
       quently embellished with literary allusion and quotation; this
       collection also includes her poems.

636   EMERSON, GLORIA
       Winners and Losers: Battles, Retreats, Gains, Losses and
       Ruins from a Long War.   New York: Random House, 1976.
       406pp.

       A war correspondent for The New York Times finds her-
       self profoundly moved and disturbed by her experiences cov-
       ering the war in Southeast Asia; she holds discussions and
       interviews with a variety of Vietnamese and Americans--
       soldiers, officers, protestors, deserters, wounded, prison-
       ers of war, journalists--both during and after the war; her
       account shifts from the past to the present, from Vietnam
       to the U.S., exploring the cumulative effect of persistent
       memories and revelations.

637   EMERY, EMMA WILSON (1885-)
       Aunt Puss and Others; Old Days in the Piney Woods.   Aus-
       tin, Texas: Encino Press, 1969.   101pp.

       Each chapter consists of random personal reminiscences;
       her portraits of relatives describe her mother, father, and
       an aunt--"Aunt Puss"; these family anecdotes from a child-
       hood spent in Texas and Louisiana are written with a good
       ear for local diction.

638   EMMERSON, IRMA LEE
       The Woods Were Full of Men, with Jean Muir.   New York:
       McKay, 1963.   242pp.

Convinced that she's "impractical and unsuccessful," she
goes to an Oregon logging camp as a cook to recover from
a lost love; her initial dismay turns to pride in her ability
and in a growing sense of belonging as she learns of the
loggers' life; she tells of personality conflicts, tragedy,
fire, sabotage; she ends with her love and marriage to a
logger; she writes a lively account brimming with vivid detail.

639   ENGLE, ADA M.
       It Happened at 1001.   New York: Vantage, 1959.   80pp.

       She and her husband run a Philadelphia hardware store
and she provides brief portraits of their immigrant, working
class customers and a celebration of "the old order of joy
and hard work"; she also recalls her several childhood
homes with nostalgia, grateful for a heritage that includes
the love of nature; widowed, she later finds contentment in
a seaside home, still close to nature.

640   ENTERS, ANGNA (1907-   )
       Artist's Life.   New York: Coward-McCann, 1958.   447pp.

       She describes a passionately creative life of "unending
exploration"; her theatrical tours as a mime artist, present-
ing compositions on contemporary world political and social
themes, alternate with pilgrimages to Europe for cultural
revitalization; her later work as a novelist and playwright
in Hollywood is frustrating and brings on a nervous collapse
in 1945; she presents mime in London and Paris in 1950,
then in Berlin in 1951, noting her sharp impressions of
postwar conditions; several performing tours to London continue until 1956; she reflects on her various artistic crafts
and her commitment to the personal expression of images;
the account includes passages from First Person Plural
(1937).

641   ERDMAN, LOULA GRACE
       Life Was Simpler Then.   New York: Dodd, Mead, 1963.
       186pp.

       In a series of chapters organized by a one-year cycle of
seasons, she writes about the "innocent days" of her Missouri childhood; close family ties are evident in her anecdotes of colorful hired hands, the central telephone exchange,
housecleaning rituals, Sunday observances, family reunions,
Chautauqua, joyful school days, and winter visiting; she is
the author of several books.

642   A Time to Write. New York: Dodd, Mead, 1969. 247pp.

A novelist, she describes her first story's genesis during
the depression; a teacher by profession, with an M. A. in
creative writing, she continues to write, noting the creation
and selling of various short stories and books; winning a
publisher's prize, she enjoys a flurry of fame.

643   ERWIN, CAROL (1898?-)
The Orderly Disorderly House, with Floyd Miller. Garden
City, N. Y. : Doubleday, 1960. 284pp.

A madam, proud of her shrewd business sense and her
fierce independence, she tells in a tough, slangy style of
her poverty-stricken childhood in Oklahoma; her "rebellious
spirit" leads her to run away from home at fourteen, and
her naïvete soon fades during several years as a hobo and
then as a madam; although she marries in 1929, her rest-
lessness takes her to many cities in which she runs sport-
ing houses and private gambling clubs; she retains her early
sympathy with outlaws and prostitutes, thriving on challenge
and even conflict.

644   ESPY, HILDA COLE
Look Both Ways. Philadelphia: Lippincott, 1962. 191pp.

Writing with humor, warmth, and nostalgia, she describes
the inevitable fragmentation of her family as her children
leave home; she offers a mother's view of her children's
gentle rebellions, keeping the home as a haven for them before they taste the lonely independence of adulthood; ridding
her files of outdated ideas for fiction writing symbolizes
her move into new life patterns and growth as an editor for
a women's magazine.

645   Quiet, Yelled Mrs. Rabbit. Philadelphia: Lippincott, 1958.
251pp.

A former press agent describes with delightful sensitivity
her life as a suburban housewife, exploiting her "capacity
for adventure" by raising five children; she notes the mix-
ture of joy and drudgery, the confrontations of children's
culture and adults' culture, and the obligations imposed by
a "children first" generation; she provides amusing anecdotes
of her fiercely competitive twins, family pets, brushes with
danger, and her children's religious experiments, all this
and more providing her with golden moments.

646   ETHRIDGE, WILLIE SNOW
Going to Jerusalem. New York: Vanguard, 1950. 313pp.

In 1948 she accompanies her husband, a U. S. representative on the U. N. Conciliation Commission, to the Middle East; freely confessing her initial ignorance, she includes notes on historical background as she learns; she meets a wide variety of people, both Jews and Arabs, whose views reveal the roots of unresolved political tension.

647   I Just Happen to Have Some Pictures.... New York: Vanguard, 1964. 191pp.

In a series of humorous anecdotes, a doting grandmother of twelve describes with exhausted adoration her grandchildren's intelligence, spirit, and imagination, providing lively portraits of each child with peripheral glimpses of their parents.

648   It's Greek to Me. New York: Vanguard, 1948. 297pp.

She joins her husband, a member of the U. N. Balkan Commission, in Greece; she enjoys a series of genial hosts as she is introduced to Athens society, diplomats, and royalty, but her travels also reveal numerous wartime tragedies and some efforts to alleviate suffering; feeling privileged to have gone, she returns with compassion for the people of postwar Europe.

649   Russian Duet; The Story of a Journey. New York: Simon and Schuster, 1959. 313pp.

An author, journalist, and lecturer, she accompanies a Russian-born friend to the Soviet Union to assist in the ultimately unsuccessful search for her friend's family; with a sharp eye for telling detail and great skill in portraying people, she describes their visits to Leningrad and Moscow, to museums, a collective farm, a village, a circus, a wedding, a public bath; her narrative includes both the foreigner's and the native's view of post-war changes.

650   Side by Each. New York: Vanguard, 1973. 180pp.

In a pleasant, literate account, she tells of her husband's retirement from journalism and publishing and of their purchase of "the Land" in the wooded countryside near two of their children's families; engrossed in building a new home, landscaping, and gardening, she describes the pattern of her days, enjoying the fellowship of family and friends.

651   There's Yeast in the Middle East! New York: Vanguard, 1962. 309pp.

Accompanying her husband on a trip to the Middle East to evaluate the Ford Foundation's work, she assists him with women's projects; escorted by Foundation and local officials, she travels extensively, meeting people from royalty to isolated villagers; she offers descriptive anecdotes with a smattering of history, closing with a sense of the area's irresistible urge to development and modernization.

652   You Can't Hardly Get There from Here.   New York: Vanguard, 1965.   175pp.

A series of humorous anecdotes of her "sallyings-forth" as a public speaker include near-misses and mishaps on tight train connections, visits to a married daughter, a trip to Greece in 1947, and numerous speaking engagements.

653   EVANS, DALE
        See ROGERS, DALE EVANS (1912-)

654   EVANS, EVA KNOX (1905-)
        Nothing Is Dripping on Us.   Boston: Little, Brown, 1954.
        308pp.

A writer of children's books, she meets a Russian baron who is an engineer in Washington, D. C. and enters a marriage full of surprises; in 1945 they pioneer in primitive Alaska, then move to New Hampshire where they find a ramshackle house and idyllic piece of land and "struggle to make a living" with a mail-order business selling hand-made items; slightly exotic stories from her husband's youth in Russia and Mongolia add flavor to this delightful narrative.

655   EVERS, MYRLIE BEASLEY (1933-)
        For Us, The Living, with William Peters.   Garden City,
        N. Y. : Doubleday, 1967.   378pp.

Emphasizing the life and work of her husband, black civil rights leader Medgar Evers, she contrasts her protected youth in a family dedicated to education to his courageous stand against racism; as her husband's work for the NAACP in Mississippi intensifies, she resents not having a normal family life with children and is frightened but proud of his activities; she cites the harassment and fear, the rising tension in 1963 as numerous blacks are murdered and their own home is fire-bombed; finally she describes the chaos of her husband's assassination, her acceptance of a public role in the civil rights movement; her account includes much detailed history of the movement in Mississippi.

656   EVERT, GERTRUDE S. (1885-   )
       My 28 Years as an Army Nurse.   New York: Exposition,
       1959.   84pp.

       A retired major in the Army Nurse Corps, she tells of
    joining the army in 1918 with her sister, to serve during the
    war and the flu epidemic; she describes her duties and re-
    sponsibilities as well as recreation and sightseeing on vari-
    ous assignments, first in Texas, then in the Philippines,
    taking vacation time in Japan and China in 1923; she later
    works in U. S. posts, proud of her profession.

657   EWING, RUTH GRIMES
       Our Life with the Garos of Assam, India.   Philadelphia:
       Dorrance, 1971.   197pp.

       She and her husband are eager Baptist missionaries who
    settle in India in 1921 soon after their marriage; her ac-
    count, reconstructed from letters she wrote home, focuses
    on the first seven years of their assignment; she describes
    the countryside, the people, and the "pattern of living" she
    establishes which combines intensive language study and
    mission tasks among the villagers.

658 FAETH, MARY LILLIAN PLANK (1870-)
Kansas in the 80's; Being Some Recollections of Life on Its
Western Frontier. New York: Procyon Press, 1947. 32pp.

After her marriage in 1887, she moves from Iowa to
Kansas and tells with enthusiasm of her husband's hardware
store, her homemaking, "real cowboys," and her social life.

659 FALKENBURG, JINX (EUGENIA) (1919-)
Jinx. New York: Duell, Sloan and Pearce, 1951. 273pp.

In a lively, enthusiastic style, she describes a peripatetic
childhood spent in Spain, the U.S., and Chile, during which
she becomes an accomplished swimmer and tennis player;
her family moves to Hollywood, where she finds small parts
in movies and becomes a model; she entertains overseas
during World War II; she marries a journalist and they work
as a team on radio and television in the late 1940's.

660 FALLIS, EDWINA HUME (1876-)
When Denver and I Were Young. Denver: Big Mountain
Press, 1956. 198pp.

These are her random recollections of old family stories,
customs, and activities; she tells of growing up with her
grandparents, aunts, uncles, mother, and sister; she includes much domestic detail and descriptions of neighbors
and the neighborhood; the account ends with her graduation
from grammar school.

661 FARMER, FRANCES (1914-1970)
Will There Really Be a Morning? New York: Putnam,
1972. 318pp.

The first half of her account is told through flashbacks
from a seven-year commitment to a state mental hospital;
her background includes a hostile, unstable mother, an in-
effective father, and two failed marriages; she breaks down
under the pressures as a Hollywood actress; she describes
the horrors, corruption, and degradation at the hospital; after her release, she finds television and theater work in the

Midwest; her first close friendship helps her through drinking problems and the prospect of terminal cancer.

662   FARRINGTON, CHISIE
       see   FARRINGTON, SARA HOUSTON CHISHOLM

663   FARRINGTON, SARA HOUSTON CHISHOLM
       Women Can Fish.   New York: Coward-McCann, 1951.
       238pp.

       An expert who holds several world records tells first of her marriage in 1934 to an avid sport fisherman; through the years they travel for both salt-water and fresh-water fishing to the Atlantic, the Pacific, South America, Hawaii, and Australia and she provides anecdotes of notable catches; during World War II they tour the armed forces with films and lectures on their experiences in sport fishing.

664   FARROW, TIERA (1881-   )
       Lawyer in Petticoats.   New York: Vantage, 1953.   214pp.

       Raised in a large family in a small Kansas town, she is soon conscious of the limitations on girls' aspirations; she works first as a stenographer, but her feminism gives her the courage to go to law school, where fellow students are supportive; she graduates in 1903; she serves two terms as city treasurer, then opens a law office in Kansas City with another woman; she recounts various legal cases, a brief marriage, and time out for B. A. and M. A. degrees in the 1920's; she offers classes to laywomen, serves as temporary judge, and works in legal aid during the depression and World War II.

665   FELPS, JETTIE IRVING (1889-   )
       East, West, Then North in U. S.   Boston: Forum, 1960.
       143pp.

       A novelist and religious essayist, she writes a rambling account of travel and sightseeing with her husband and son in 1929, of a trip west after earning her M. A. degree, and of a trip to New England in 1950 after her husband's death; she also recounts world travels as "a Christian welfare worker. "

666   FERBER, EDNA (1885-1968)   NAWM
       A Kind of Magic.   Garden City, N. Y. :   Doubleday, 1963.
       335pp.

This is an articulate and perceptive continuation of A
Peculiar Treasure, opening with her writing of the first
volume of the autobiography, at the same time that she
builds her stone house on a Connecticut hilltop; she includes
sections on writing as a craft and an obsession, on her intense devotion to America as a source of her regional novels, on World War II, and on women.

667   FERMI, LAURA
       Atoms in the Family: My Life with Enrico Fermi.   Chicago:
       University of Chicago Press, 1954.   267pp.

       Born in Italy, she marries the noted Italian physicist
       Fermi in 1928 and describes his scientific pursuits and
       achievements and her own "inevitable inferiority complex";
       in 1938 they use a trip to accept the Nobel Prize as an oc-
       casion to leave fascist Italy and settle in the U.S.; she de-
       scribes her Americanization and "the secret life on the
       mesa" at Los Alamos during her husband's work with the
       atom bomb.

668   FERNEA, ELIZABETH WARNOCK
       Guests of the Sheik.   Garden City, N.Y.:   Doubleday, 1965.
       333pp.

       Married to a social anthropologist, she describes "the
       first two years of my married life," from 1956 to 1958, as
       the first western woman in an Iraq village; abiding by local
       customs, she is gradually accepted by the women and offers
       a sensitive portrayal of the women's subculture; a clear
       record of her observations and reactions, from her early
       misgivings to later understanding.

669   A Street in Marrakech.   Garden City, N.Y.:   Doubleday,
       1975.   382pp.

       With much lively detail, she describes her year in 1971-
       1972 spent with her husband and three children; they make
       their home in the old "traditional city," finding themselves
       "strange and alien, in a strange and alien world"; her daily
       pattern is built around relationships with her landlady and
       her maid, local shopping customs, the children's French
       school, her neighbors and the neighborhood with "its own
       logic, its own structure"; friendships slowly grow under her
       open approach and she leaves with great affection for the
       people.

670   A View of the Nile.   Garden City, N.Y.:   Doubleday, 1970.
       320pp.

In this personal chronicle of the years from 1959 to 1965
she describes domestic life in Cairo and is realistic and
open about her adjustments to a different culture; joining her
husband in a Nubian village, she establishes a household with
her three young children; relations with village women are
difficult, but social isolation fades with her involvement in
a local wedding.

671   FERRIS, LOUANNE (pseud.) (1925-   )
        I'm Done Crying, as told to Beth Day.   New York: M.
        Evans, 1969.   275pp.

        A black woman describes her work as a kitchen aide, a
        nurse's aide, and then a nurse in a city ghetto hospital; in
        a recital of horrors, corruption, and neglect, she makes
        only brief allusions to her own husband and children.

672   FIELDING, JANICE (pseud.)
        The Bitter Truth of It.   New York: Exposition, 1963.   64pp.

        This is a highly emotional, bitter account of the years
        following a hysterectomy, performed on her without medical
        necessity and without her informed consent; she feels that
        the physical mutilation leads to her mental unbalance and
        she resents the attitudes of doctors toward their female pa-
        tients.

673   FINLETTER, GRETCHEN DAMROSCH
        From the Top of the Stairs.   Boston: Little, Brown, 1946.
        252pp.

        The daughter of conductor Walter Damrosch and an ardent
        suffragist mother describes her childhood amid musicians
        and artists in a household of charming chaos and vitality;
        she is plied with elocution, music, and dancing lessons, and
        summer pursuits of culture and knowledge; her account is
        filled with warm humor and wry observations.

674   FIRTH, GRACE
        Living the Natural Life.   New York: Simon and Schuster,
        1974.   192pp.

        In this anecdotal account, recipes and advice are freely
        mixed with recollections of life in Virginia where she "grew
        up brining and smoking"; an avid gardener, she finds can-
        ning "a deeply satisfying ritual," and she delights in "pre-
        serving the earth's gifts."

675   FISCHER, BERTHA MARK
       see FISCHER, MARKOOSHA

676   FISCHER, MARKOOSHA
       Reunion in Moscow; A Russian Revisits Her Country.   New
       York: Harper & Row, 1962.   240pp.

       Having fled her native Russia in 1939, she returns in
       1960 and finds that her positive first impressions override
       her suspicion and anxiety; she visits former friends, re-
       news old family ties, and sees places that recall fond mem-
       ories; she observes the press, religion, books, theatre, and
       culture in contemporary Russian life, noting particularly the
       activities of Russian women and the existence of a ravaged
       older generation; nevertheless, she leaves with a sense of
       the lack of mutual understanding.

677   FISHER, FLORENCE
       The Search for Anna Fisher.   New York: Arthur Fields,
       1973.   270pp.

       An adopted child, she recounts the highly dramatic search
       for her natural parents in a personal quest for continuity
       and identity; her childhood curiosity strains the relationship
       with her adoptive parents; initial efforts are blocked by doc-
       tors, hospitals, lawyers, and her adoptive father; after twen-
       ty-eight years, her second husband supports further efforts,
       and she is aided by her experience as a legal secretary; in
       an emotional reunion she meets her mother in 1970, and
       later also meets her father; her search includes working to
       organize adoptees and promoting legislation.

678   FISHER, FLORRIE (1920-)
       The Lonely Trip Back, as told to Jean Davis and Todd Per-
       sons.   Garden City, N.Y.: Doubleday, 1971.   212pp.

       She tells a grim story of twenty-three years as a drug
       addict; the middle-class daughter of Jewish immigrants, she
       rejects her conventional upbringing, turns to drugs after a
       brief unsuccessful marriage; she then becomes a prostitute
       to pay for her drug habit; she describes numerous arrests
       and jail terms and tells of horrifying prison conditions; aided
       by Synanon, she finally breaks from drugs, using her exper-
       iences to speak to young people about the horrors of addic-
       tion.

679   FISHER, MARY FRANCES KENNEDY (1908-)
       Among Friends.   New York: Knopf, 1971.   306pp.

A gastronomical writer, she focuses in this narrative on
her loving, secure childhood, the daughter of a newspaperman and non-Quaker in the Quaker enclave of Whittier,
Calif.; writing with rare sensitivity, she reveals family relationships, dynamics, tensions, and tells of relatives and
local characters whose lives touch hers; a compulsive reader, she is also interested as a child in food and cooking.

680   Map of Another Town; A Memoir of Provence.   Boston:
       Little, Brown, 1964. 273pp.

       She writes a superb narrative "of a place and therefore
of myself" during several extended stays with her two daughters over a seven-year period; evocative vignettes of her
"visible and invisible life" there illuminate the architecture
and spirit of the village main street, community cafe life,
the mysterious power of a gypsy, her French landlady, the
"raw wounds of war" which remain, the gaiety and tawdri-
ness of the carnival; always an "outlander," she learns much
during her "strangely permanent impermanence."

681   FISHER, WELTHY HONSINGER (1880-)
       To Light a Candle. New York: McGraw-Hill, 1962. 279pp.

       A teacher and author, she goes as a missionary teacher
to China in 1906; she is idealistic and headstrong, with
strong beliefs in education for women, and she deeply admires much in Chinese culture; she does YWCA work in
Europe during World War I, then writes, lectures, and
travels; at 44 she marries and settles in India to aid her
husband's missionary work, returning later as a widow to
aid the literacy effort; at 80 she is honored by the U.N.

682   FITZGERALD, EILEEN
       Expo Summer. Garden City, N.Y.: Doubleday, 1969.
       168pp.

       A student at McGill University, she describes her job in
a souvenir shop at the 1967 Exposition in Montreal and her
association with members of a rock band there.

683   FITZGERALD, EMILY McCORKLE (1850-1912)
       An Army Doctor's Wife on the Frontier; Letters from Alaska
       and the Far West, 1874-1878, ed. Abe Laufe. Pittsburgh:
       University of Pittsburgh Press, 1962. 352pp.

       In long, descriptive, and outspoken letters to her mother
and sister, she first tells of ports and people on the way to
Sitka, an untrustworthy black nursemaid for her daughter,

shortages of goods, social isolation, disgusting Indians; later
she tells of anxiety and fear in an Idaho army fort during
Indian wars, again beset by servant troubles.

684   FITZGERALD, TAMSIN (1950-)
        Tamsin, ed. Richard A. Condon.   New York: Dial, 1973.
        180pp.

        Arrested in 1969 at the age of 18 with her boyfriend for
        attempted hijacking, she writes letters from Alderson Fed-
        eral Penitentiary; edited to form a narrative with poetry, the
        account reveals her attempts to keep her inner self and love
        inviolate from the effects of prison life.

685   FITZ-GIBBON, BERNICE
        Macy's, Gimbels and Me; How to Earn $90,000 a Year in
        Retail Advertising.   New York: Simon & Schuster, 1967.
        380pp.

        She moves from teaching and reporting to advertising,
        strikes it rich, and combines her autobiography with advice;
        she works for Marshall Field's, Wanamaker's, and Macy's
        until 1935, is then the advertising director at Wanamaker's
        and Gimbels, and then opens her own agency in 1954; some
        of her anecdotal material appeared previously in magazines.

686   FLACK, NANNETTE
        Singing Can Be Ecstasy, as told to Leila Sherman.   New
        York: Exposition, 1965.   64pp.

        After offering suggestions for young singers, she recalls
        random incidents from her career beginning at the age of
        eighteen as the leading soprano in light opera at the New
        York Hippodrome; her anecdotes reveal a lively sense of
        humor.

687   FLEET, DOROTHY MITCHELL
        Our Flight to Destiny.   New York: Vantage, 1964.   193pp.

        The wife of an aviation pioneer and wealthy businessman,
        she tells of meeting him first in 1929, the man destined to
        change, and "create, my whole future"; under the powerful
        spell of his dominant personality, she becomes his secretary,
        then his wife, willingly taking second place to his business
        interests; she raises three children, entertains a great deal
        in aviation circles, provides a background to his career,
        which she describes in some detail.

688   FLEISCHMAN, DORIS ELSA (1891-)
       A Wife Is Many Women. New York: Crown, 1955. 209pp.

       Married in 1922, she compares being a wife to being an
       "executive amateur"; she writes on housekeeping, public re-
       lations, financial management, parenting, medical care,
       shopping, cooking, and economic and intellectual partnership
       with her husband to present examples from "the daily lives
       of women" based on her personal experiences.

689   FLEITMANN, LIDA LOUISE
       see BLOODGOOD, LIDA FLEITMANN (1894-)

690   FLEMING, FANNIE BELLE
       see STARR, BLAZE (pseud.)

691   FLEMING, JO (pseud.)
       His Affair. New York: M. Evans, 1976. 194pp.

       After twenty-six years of marriage, she tells of the shock
       and pain of discovering her husband's infidelity; writing about
       her emotions--insecurity, frenzy, anger, despair--aids her
       catharsis and search for understanding of this "meaningful
       event" in her marriage; she emerges as a different person,
       proud of having survived and learned to love unconditionally;
       she writes in the present tense and in diary form.

692   FLETCHER, GRACE NIES
       I Was Born Tomorrow. New York: Dutton, 1961. 253pp.

       She tells the "triumphant story" of her husband's terminal
       illness, his death forcing her to a reexamination of her faith
       and values; anecdotes and reminiscences illuminate her inner
       explorations, in which she acknowledges that her family and
       religious faith are of the utmost importance; she closes in
       agony and grief over his death, but her feelings are tem-
       pered by an acceptance of rebirth and renewal.

693   In My Father's House. New York: McGraw-Hill, 1955.
       235pp.

       She describes growing up in an era of high ideals and
       strong religious faith, the daughter of a Methodist minister
       whose calling sets the tone for their family life; her parents'
       marriage is an old-fashioned joyful love story, shadowed in
       its final years by her mother's long illness and her father's
       breakdown under the burden; she presents the flavor of her
       childhood by implication.

694 Preacher's Kids. New York: Dutton, 1958. 255pp.

She presents her narrative as a gift to her father in thanks for a rich heritage of music, laughter, compassion, and family solidarity centered in the "Puritan parsonage" of her childhood; as an adolescent she chafes at the restrictions of propriety and wages a "private war of independence" to establish her own values as an adult; but her father's legacy sustains her in times of crisis and sorrow.

695 The Whole World's in His Hand. New York: Dutton, 1962. 219pp.

After attending meetings of the World Council of Churches in India, she extends her travels to include Nepal, Hong Kong, and Japan; she expresses a deep personal anger and agony over the poverty and hunger she encounters in India, and in Japan she feels great shame for the effects of the atom bomb; a "mere woman-in-the-pew," she feels an intense desire to make a difference in the world, to live Christianity in her daily life.

696 FLETCHER, INGLIS CLARK (1888-1969)
Pay, Pack, and Follow; The Story of My Life. New York: Holt, 1959. 308pp.

A prolific writer, she describes the "education of a novelist," beginning with her happy, imaginative childhood, a time of flourishing in the wholesome, democratic atmosphere of midwestern "village life"; married, she embraces the "great adventure" of western mining camp living with her husband, enthusiastically following him from place to place, just as he later enthusiastically follows her when she settles temporarily in various locations to do extensive research for a series of historical novels.

697 FLETCHER, MRS. JOHN GOULD
see SIMON, CHARLIE MAY HOGUE (1897-)

698 FLORIAN, SISTER M.
see REICHERT, FLORIAN, SISTER (1900-)

699 FLYNN, ELIZABETH GURLEY (1890-1964) NAWM
The Alderson Story; My Life as a Political Prisoner. New York: International Publishers, 1963. 223pp.

A prominent member of the American Communist Party, she describes her arrest in 1951 and trial under the Smith

Act; jailed in 1955, she spends over two years in the women's federal prison; proud of being a "political prisoner," she is concerned about dehumanizing prison conditions, offers her personal experiences in and political analysis of the prison system.

700   I Speak My Own Piece: Autobiography of "The Rebel Girl."
       New York: Masses & Mainstream, 1955.   326pp.

       Born in New England of Irish immigrant parents, she describes her politically radical forbears and her own early political awareness; she begins public speaking at fifteen, joining the IWW at sixteen; she engages in speaking and organizing tours to support strikers, laborers, free speech, and post-World War I amnesty; she marries in 1908 but separates in 1910; she is a founding member of the American Civil Liberties Union in 1920 and a prominent member of the Communist Party; she discusses radical politics in the U.S. in detail and offers many portraits of activists; she writes in a vehement, positive style.

701   FOOTE, MARY HALLOCK (1847-1938)
       A Victorian Gentlewoman in the Far West; The Reminiscences of Mary Hallock Foote, ed. Rodman W. Paul. San Marino, Cal.: Huntington Library, 1972.   416pp.

       A novelist and illustrator, she describes her Quaker childhood on a Hudson River farm, influenced by the dominant women in her family; trained as an artist and then married to an engineer in 1876, she settles in various western mining towns, drawing and writing local color stories often to keep the family financially afloat; she presents a candid and ambivalent exploration of the west's attractions and deprivations, its beauty and dangers.

702   FORSTER, MINNIE JANE WYATT (1875-)
       He Led Me Through the Wilderness.   Wichita: Preston Printing Co., 1947.   189 pp.

       She describes her rural Missouri childhood, learning household skills but gaining little formal education; she marries at eighteen and becomes the mother of four; she and her sons work their Oklahoma farm while her husband travels and invents; financial success and failure alternate in this rambling account.

703   Was the Hill Barren?   The Story of an American Family.
       New York: Exposition, 1953.   173pp.

       Widowed after fifty years of marriage, she looks back on

years of hardship; she homesteads with four children in
Oklahoma, maintaining the farm with strength and competence
during her husband's frequent absences, carrying out his
plans; financial difficulties and her husband's westering urge
dash her desires to establish a permanent home; she enjoys
sudden prosperity in later life and raises three grandchildren.

704   FORTEN, CHARLOTTE L. (1838-1914)   NAW
The Journal of Charlotte L. Forten, 1854-1864, ed. Ray
Allen Billington. New York: Dryden, 1953. 248pp.

A young black woman of Philadelphia, she tells of her
quest for self-improvement and excellence as she begins her
teaching career in New England; she is intensely conscious
of racial prejudice and she remarks on anti-slavery activities; in 1862 she teaches in a black school for former
slaves in South Carolina; she provides sensitive descriptions
of living conditions and of the people around her.

705   FOSTER, ADDA C.
Reminiscences of Life. New York: Comet, 1960. 178pp.

In a dismal tale made up of "little homey anecdotes," she
describes herself as the "black sheep" of a large family;
she broods about a sister's death, childhood illnesses, fears,
friendlessness; an unfortunate marriage is marred further by
the death of her first baby, by troubles with her other children, and by poverty; she interprets dreams with a religious
cast, but finds life "harder to bear each day."

706   FOSTER, DOROTHY F.
The Noisesome Day, The Stilly Night; An Autobiography:
Fact and Fancy. New York: Exposition, 1973. 93pp.

An artist recounts the experiences of a year in loosely
woven fragments; she engages in some delving into the past,
as her "thoughts flit from here to there."

707   FOWELL, EDITH ANNE
Mama Was a Drummer. New York: Vantage, 1956. 66pp.

Writing to encourage older women in careers and to show
"what happens behind the scenes in the retail stores," she
describes how her musical education as a child develops the
confidence which, added to her enthusiasm and sense of humor, enables her to triumph over the handicaps of age and
lack of experience; when her husband's death brings an end
to well-ordered domesticity, she responds to the challenge

of department store work, later becoming a "drummer," a traveling saleslady for a large company.

708   FOX, LYDIA MANTLE (1861-   )
        Eighty Plus; 1861 to 1945.   Boston: Christopher, 1950.
        330pp.

        She presents "scraps of memories" beginning with random
recollections of her childhood in an extended family; she dis-
likes teaching and so she opens a secretarial office in Washington, D. C. in the 1890's, becoming the first public stenographer in the capitol city where she works for prominent
businessmen, politicians, and newspapermen; she travels
around the world from 1913 to 1915; later bedfast, she
nevertheless keeps working as a notary public.

709   FRANKAU, PAMELA (1908-1967)
        Pen to Paper; A Novelist's Notebook.   Garden City, N. Y. :
        Doubleday, 1962.   237pp.

        The prolific novelist reflects on "a gift and the service
of it," opening with a delicate portrayal of the genesis of
an idea and her subsequent disciplined work on a "rough" and
a "smooth" draft; she discusses her aims and values as a
writer, emphasizing the need to preserve integrity and "inner
silence" amid her involvement with life; English-born, she
later settles in the U. S. , coping with "Transatlantic schizo-
phrenia" as the two cultures are equally part of her identity;
she notes an autobiography, I Find Four People, written in
1935 (see companion volume).

710   FRANKEN, ROSE (1898-   )
        When All Is Said and Done; An Autobiography.   Garden City,
        N. Y. : Doubleday, 1963.   397pp.

        A prolific novelist and playwright tells of a childhood ex-
ceptionally close to her mother, then of an abrupt marriage
at seventeen; she begins to write partly to fulfill her husband's belief in her abilities, partly to allay her anxiety over
what proves to be his terminal illness; left with two sons to
support, she writes film scripts in California, finding "rebirth" in a second marriage to a fellow writer; she describes
the rich, productive years on their New England farm, noting "my natural destiny and incontestable privilege to write
like a woman and function like a woman."

711   FRANKFORT, ELLEN (1936?-   )
        The Classrooms of Miss Ellen Frankfort.   Englewood Cliffs,
        N. J. : Prentice-Hall, 1970.   215pp.

In a light and anecdotal account, this "bright young female" with a Barnard philosophy degree enters teaching by
default; her first job is as an English teacher at Yeshiva
girls' school, where the students evade her "missionary
soul"; her second job is amid an eccentric faculty in an
upper-class private school; her third job is among self-
centered children at a private progressive school.

712   The Voice: Life at The Village Voice.   New York: Morrow, 1976.   272pp.

A regular contributor to The Village Voice, she evokes
the bohemian, radical chic atmosphere of the years from
1970 to 1974; her female colleagues serve as a mirror for
herself, as she provides portraits of her fellow writers,
and discusses staff upheavals, salary disputes, sexism on
the job, and her "distrust of radical male leaders."

713   FREEMAN, LUCY
Farewell to Fear.   New York: Putnam, 1969.   379pp.

Author and reporter for The New York Times, she discusses her second psychoanalysis, begun with a woman analyst after the depression of a second divorce and career
setbacks; she tells in detail of her dreams, anger, terror,
love, sexuality, relationships with both parents, emotions
upon the death of her father; at the death of her analyst,
the book becomes partially a memorial; she closes with her
return to New York.

714   Fight Against Fears.   New York: Crown, 1951.   332pp.

A reporter, she describes her five years of psychoanalysis, undertaken with great trust in her compassionate analyst, years which become a period of "continuous discovery"
of self as the sources of her psychic pain, anxiety, guilt,
and anger are explored; in this detailed reconstruction of the
analysis, she reveals the intricacies of memory as layers of
the past emerge; she feels she gains patience, understanding,
and acceptance.

715   FREMONT, JESSIE ANN BENTON (1824-1902)   NAW
Mother Lode Narratives, ed. Shirley Sargent.   Ashland:
Lewis Osborne, 1970.   156pp.

This account consists of eight delightful passages from
Far West Sketches (1890) embellished with previously unpub-
lished letters from 1858 to 1860; with a flair for telling
dramatic incidents, she describes the outdoor life, mining

conflicts, and threats against herself and her children, planning and building her "ultra-civilized" house, colorful neighbors, a local ball, the terror of her son's temporary disappearance, and her intense love of nature.

716   FRIEDAN, BETTY (1921-)
It Changed My Life; Writings on the Women's Movement.
New York: Random House, 1976. 388pp.

The book is a collection of essays written between 1963
and 1975 and includes an autobiographical narrative (pp.
187-254), "Betty Friedan's Notebook: Struggling for Personal Truth," covering the years between 1971 and 1973;
uneasy with the direction taken by the feminist movement,
seeking human liberation in her public and private lives,
she travels to support feminist groups in Holland, Brazil,
and Italy; she reflects on marriage and divorce, on human
love, on a woman's turning fifty.

717   FRIEDMAN, MARCIA
The Story of Josh. New York: Praeger, 1974. 281pp.

She recounts her anguish during her son's last year as
he is stricken with a cancer in the brain at the age of 21;
her experiences with the medical profession and the family
trauma are explored in depth; her account is interspersed
with transcriptions of her son's tape recordings, made during his last months.

718   FRISBIE, FLORENCE (JOHNNY) (1933-)
Miss Ulysses from Puka-Puka; The Autobiography of a South
Sea Trader's Daughter, ed. and trans. Robert Dean Frisbie.
New York: Macmillan, 1948. 241pp.

Her lively story is written when she is thirteen and trans-
lated by her father, an American trader married to her
Polynesian mother; she describes the daily life of an "atoll
child"; her mother's dying wish is that she be raised "like
white children," so she is sent to a school on Fiji and keeps
a journal to learn English; her father keeps the family together, settling on American Samoa after World War II.

719   FRIST, BETTY
No Wings in the Manse: Life and Laughter Under the
Preacher's Roof. Westwood, N.J.: Revell, 1956. 159pp.

One of seven children in an enthusiastically Southern family, she describes their "madcap, slap-happy lives" carried
out under her preacher father's idiosyncratic application

of rules, religious ritual, and culture; she marries a minister, to her father's specifications and delight; while she
appreciates the seriousness of her role and her husband's
calling, she keeps a light, human touch in her anecdotes of
their parishioners and her domestic life.

720   FRIST, ELIZABETH FERRAN
       see FRIST, BETTY

721   FROLICH, BEA
       How Clear Was My Vodka; The True Story of an American
       Model's Experiences in the Soviet Union.   New York: Ex-
       position, 1963.   154pp.

       A model and fashion designer accompanies her Russian-
born father-in-law who is seeking a visa for a prospective
wife from the U.S.S.R.; she goes along ostensibly to investigate Russian fashion, but finding none, spends her time
sightseeing with Intourist guides and coping with bureaucrats;
intrigued by the people she meets, she records her humorous
impressions.

722   FROST, LESLEY (1899-)
       New Hampshire's Child; The Derry Journals of Lesley Frost.
       Albany, N.Y.:   State University of New York Press, 1969.
       (no pagination)

       This is a facsimile edition of her childhood notebooks
from 1905 to 1909 by the daughter of poet Robert Frost; noting the great spiritual force of her mother, she says "life on the
Derry farm was to be a long and passionate borning"; her
parents encourage close observation of and open response to
nature and her entries are conversational, perceptive, and
nicely shaped; she comments on poetry, writes poems and
fantasies, and tells of stories she has been told about historical events and figures; the journals provide a uniquely
intimate glimpse of a child raised in a simple but intense
family life.

723   FRYER, KATHARINE HOMER (1907-)
       Kathy; A Mother's Inspiring True Story of Her Daughter's
       Fight to Regain Health.   New York: Dutton, 1956.   224pp.

       The mother of five teen-age girls tells of her initial mild
concern for a daughter's listlessness and irritability; a psychiatrist's diagnosis of her daughter's anorexia nervosa
raises fear and maternal guilt; told she is a "dominant mother," she engages in bewildered self-examination and helpless-
ly watches with mounting horror as her daughter's condition

deteriorates; taking her emaciated daughter to the Florida
sun, she finds new hope with a new doctor who finds a simple physical ailment and effects a dramatic cure through
thyroid treatments; her relief and joy are strangely unmixed
with bitterness.

724   FULDHEIM, DOROTHY
       A Thousand Friends.   Garden City, N. Y.:   Doubleday, 1974.
       183pp.

       In a jumble of vignettes, she recalls twenty-seven years
       of experience as a television interviewer and commentator;
       she describes her routine, minor irritations, threats, a
       brief love, and various men and women she has interviewed;
       she is critical of youth culture, yet offers pro-student re-
       flections on the events at Kent State; in 1967 she covers the
       Arab-Israeli war.

725   I Laughed, I Cried, I Loved; A News Analyst's Love Affair
       with the World.   Cleveland: World, 1966.   204pp.

       A lecturer, television interviewer, and editorialist, she
       describes first her "childhood of cold and hunger, and the
       humiliation that poverty brings"; she begins her travels in
       the mid-1930's, writing on Mussolini, Hitler, and the Spanish
       Civil War; she interviews refugees from the Chinese Revolu-
       tion in 1955, travels to Israel in 1956, and to Egypt in 1959;
       also in 1959 she reports on Eisenhower's trip around the
       world; throughout she provides anecdotes of her meetings
       with prominent world figures.

726   FULLER, JAN (pseud.)
       Space: The Scrapbook of My Divorce.   New York: Arthur
       Fields, 1973.   (no pagination)

       The book consists of diary excerpts covering the first
       three months after her divorce, a time of consolidation be-
       fore the establishment of a "new life"; after initial numb-
       ness, she explores her reawakened feelings, acquiring
       strength and independence, caring for her two young chil-
       dren, working through anger to wholeness and joy.

727   FULTON, EILEEN
       How My World Turns, as told to Brett Bolton.   New York:
       Taplinger, 1970.   208pp.

       This light account by a minister's daughter describes her
       early love of acting; she moves to New York and finds act-
       ing jobs; her marriage fails; she finally lands steady work

in a television soap opera As The World Turns, in addition
to other stage and singing jobs.

728   FURMAN, BESS (1894-1969)   NAWM
       Washington By-Line; The Personal History of a Newspaper-
       woman.   New York: Knopf, 1949.   348pp.

       She begins her career as a reporter in Omaha covering
the 1928 presidential campaign, then moves to "fictionesque"
Washington, D. C. to work for the A. P. , writing feature
stories of interest to women and covering political events
during the New Deal years; later she is a free-lance writer,
and still later, a correspondent for the Washington bureau
of The New York Times, privileged to be one who can
"write history as it happens. "

729   FURNESS, THELMA, LADY (1905-)
       Double Exposure; A Twin Autobiography.   New York: Mc-
       Kay, 1958.   369pp.

       The sister of Gloria Morgan Vanderbilt (see entry #2044),
she describes her childhood as a "chaotic family game of
transatlantic musical chairs"; her hasty marriage to a romantic ne'er-do-well is brief and is followed by a "blissfully
happy" but also brief marriage to a British duke, her entry
to high society; at the close of her account, she is a partner
with her sister in the perfume business.

730 GABLE, KATHLEEN WILLIAMS
Clark Gable; A Personal Portrait.   Englewood Cliffs, N. J. :
Prentice-Hall, 1961.   153pp.

Her story is a celebration of her "great love" for Gable,
married to him for five years of happiness, simplicity, and
an intensely close family life; a model with two children
from previous marriages, she marries Gable in 1955, completely devoted to pleasing him; she relates the shock of his
sudden death and the birth of their son a few months later;
she finds continuing support in the joy of her children.

731 GABOR, EVA
Orchids and Salami.   Garden City, N. Y. :   Doubleday, 1954.
219pp.

Born in Budapest, she comes to the U. S. with her first
husband to settle in Hollywood; she describes her first acting jobs, her second marriage, her move to New York for
work in theatre and television; she comments on her glamorous public image; this is the breezy, witty account of a highly ambitious woman.

732 GABOR, JOLIE
Jolie Gabor, as told to Cindy Adams.   New York: Mason/
Charter, 1975.   315pp.

A passionate, outspoken, flamboyant, and phenomenally
energetic Hungarian and the mother of Zsa Zsa (see entry
#733) and Eva (see entry #731) describes her childhood
need for love and attention; in a delightfully idiosyncratic
style, she tells of her "two enormous love affairs" and
three marriages; her ambition for a glamorous life is transferred to her three daughters whose careers she creates;
she escapes Europe during World War II and settles in the
U. S. , maintaining a life of wealth, publicity, and glamour.

733 GABOR, ZSA ZSA
Zsa Zsa Gabor, My Story, with Gerold Frank.   Cleveland:
World, 1960.   308pp.

The famous Hungarian-born film star opens her account
with a description of her childhood in a tempestuous, emotional household; she wins a beauty contest and earns her
first musical comedy role at 15; bored by life in Turkey as
the wife of a Turkish diplomat, she emigrates to the U. S.
in 1941, where her beauty opens Hollywood's doors; married
to Conrad Hilton, she tries to be "one-hundred-per-cent
American"; a third marriage to an actor leads to clashing
theatrical egos; she becomes "a one-woman business" and
remains devoted to her career.

734   GABRIELSON, CATHERINE
       The Story of Gabrielle.   Cleveland: World, 1956.   118pp.

The mother of a creative, energetic nine-year-old describes the swift onset of her daughter's cancer; she stays
in the hospital to nurse her daughter through her final days,
recounted in detail; she tells of her daughter's serenity and
understanding throughout "the most luminous weeks of my
life. "

735   GALE, GLORIA (1923-)
       Calendar Model.   New York: Frederick Fell, 1957.   254pp.

Proudly asserting that she is "femininity and sexuality
personified," she describes the serendipitous development of
her career as a nude model after she is cast out of her
home when she is sixteen; aided by numerous artists and
photographers and molded by a Pygmalion-like five-year affair with an older man, she maintains her dignity throughout,
closing her account with serious theatrical aspirations.

736   GALINSKY, ELLEN
       Beginnings; A Young Mother's Personal Account of Two Pre-
       mature Births.   Boston: Houghton Mifflin, 1976.   147pp.

A teacher and educational filmmaker, she explores her
inner feelings and thoughts during her first pregnancy; "un-
initiated" and uncertain, she struggles with dependence when
she is bedridden and is distressed by doctors' and hospitals'
practices which keep her uninformed and separated from her
premature son; as a parent, she must combat myths about
premature children and curb her overprotective impulses;
with her second pregnancy, she is more informed, assertive,
and confident about her needs as a parent, but the death of
the second infant brings anger and grief.

737   GALLAGHER, MARY BARELLI
       My Life with Jacqueline Kennedy, ed. Frances Spatz Leigh-
       ton.   New York: McKay, 1969.   396pp.

Working as a secretary first for Senator Kennedy, then
for Jackie's mother, then for Jackie, she is privy to intimate glimpses of their lives; her own family life is dominated by loyal service to the Kennedys, and she tells of her
activities on the White House staff from 1961 to 1963, maintaining a frenzied pace and working to exhaustion; close to
the tragedies of an infant's death and the President's assassination, she feels empty when her employment is terminated,
yet she remains grateful for the years of association with
the Kennedys.

738   GAMBLE, LILLIAN M. (1900-)
      Mor's New Land. New York: Exposition, 1951. 118pp.

      She focuses her childhood tale on her mother, a Norwegian
immigrant and "a powerful woman, morally and physically";
although her irresponsible father drinks and is often absent,
her mother's dreams of opportunity in America set the background for optimism, and she has a happy home life with
her mother in Minneapolis.

739   GANT, SOPHIA
      "One of Those"; The Progress of a Mongoloid Child.   New
      York: Pageant, 1957. 88pp.

      The mother of a twenty-year-old Down's Syndrome son,
her sixth child and born when she was past forty, writes of
her determination to raise and educate him against the advice of medical authorities; sustained by her religion through
years of hard work, sacrifice, and commitment, she takes
him through eight grades using school texts and teaches him
French, violin, and piano, depending on discipline and repetition; she encourages his independence and is proud of his
accomplishments.

740   GARDEN, MARY (1874-1967)   NAWM
      Mary Garden's Story, by Mary Garden and Louis Biancolli.
      New York: Simon and Schuster, 1951. 302pp.

      The famous opera singer describes her thirty-one years
on the stage; she tells of studying in Paris, then of her
Paris debut in 1900; her New York debut follows in 1907,
and her Chicago debut in 1910; loved and pursued by many
men, she insists that singing remains her passion and she
describes losing herself in her roles; she retires in 1934,
later turning to lecture tours; she sees herself as a simple person and writes in a correspondingly direct, conversational way.

741   GARDNER, DOROTHY WILLIAMS (1904-)
      Fun on a Freighter. New York: Vantage, 1957. 184pp.

At fifty, she makes a quick decision with her husband to take a dream trip by freighter; "heathens," they find their fellow passengers are missionaries; her diary entries note rough weather, her first sightseeing in Japan, her experiences with danger and cold in Korea, her accommodations in a Taipeh house of prostitution, and sightseeing in Hong Kong, Bangkok, and Singapore; she focuses on details of people and adventures.

742   GARDNER, ELVA BABCOCK
Lure of India.   Mountain View, Cal. :   Pacific Press, 1946.
143pp.

In a series of disconnected stories, the author tells of over ten years as a teacher with her husband in a mission school in India; she observes the market, the caste system, local mythology, and the area's natural beauty; she displays a warm tolerance for cultural differences and makes friends among her neighbors.

743   GARDNER, JEANNE FRANCIS (1930-)
A Grain of Mustard, as told to Beatrice Moore.   New York: Trident Press, 1969.   189pp.

A clairvoyant, she describes her childhood characterized by deep devotion to her mother and grandmother; at her mother's death in 1961, she continues her mother's prophetic and visionary activities, including the task of building a "Cathedral of Prayer"; in spite of a skeptical husband and her own impaired health, she pursues faith healing and the transcription of songs dictated by "the Voice."

744   GASSAWAY, FRANCES J.
The Robin's Nest.   New York: Vantage, 1958.   100pp.

Her random domestic reminiscences cover the pleasant, unpleasant, and comic events in twenty years as a "Navy wife"; she establishes homes at successive posts and raises foster children as well as her own; she enjoys the travel that her husband's career requires.

745   GASSMAN, McDILL McCOWN
Daddy Was an Undertaker.   New York: Vantage, 1952.
249pp.

This journalist tells of an Alabama childhood in the public eye and perceived as "different" due to her father's profession; her humorous and touching anecdotes center on her father's career, hardships during the depression, and the

dramatic incident in which he saves her life; she idolizes
her father, closing the account with his death.

746   GAUCHAT, DOROTHY
       All God's Children. New York: Hawthorn Books, 1976.
       180pp.

       She and her husband establish a "hospitality house" to
       care for handicapped foster children in addition to six of
       their own; their foster children's disabilities include blind-
       ness, cerebral palsy, hydrocephalus, while one daughter has
       epilepsy, another suffers a mental breakdown, and their last
       child has Down's Syndrome; they make a powerful case for
       greater sensitivity from the medical profession and more
       humane laws governing foster care and adoption.

747   GAZAWAY, RENA
       The Longest Mile. Garden City, N. Y.: Doubleday, 1969.
       348pp.

       In a devastating study of "enforced deprivation," she de-
       scribes a two-year study begun in 1960 of "the modern
       mountaineer in his own setting" in Kentucky; rescued by
       education from the poverty of her own childhood, she re-
       turns to live among the wretched, isolated residents of a
       hollow; her affection for the people builds "a whole new way
       of life for me"; her attempts to educate a local boy and in-
       troduce him to the outside world are unsuccessful, and she
       is forced into an intense examination of her own values; she
       closes with suggestions for social change.

748   GEBHARD, ANNA LAURA MUNRO (1914-   )
       Parsonage Doorway. New York: Abingdon-Cokesbury, 1950.
       144pp.

       The wife of a Minnesota parson and mother of four chil-
       dren tells of their relationships with parishioners; she de-
       scribes her children's growth and development, visitors,
       gardening, housekeeping, and a family life close to church
       activities.

749   Rural Parish!; A Year from the Journal of Anna Laura Geb-
       hard. New York: Abingdon-Cokesbury, 1947. 121pp.

       Her diary entries chronicle her first year as a minister's
       wife in rural Minnesota; she describes the parishioners, the
       Ladies' Aid Society, her work with youth groups, her service
       among the poor, the old, and the ill; joining her husband in
       shared tasks and shared joy, she helps build a sense of
       community.

750   GEE, MARY WILSON (1874-   )
       Yes, Ma'am, Miss Gee, with LeGette Blythe.   Charlotte,
       N. C. :   Heritage House, 1957.   220pp.

       A dedicated, lifelong Latin teacher, she describes the
       ways in which her life and the life of Converse College are
       intimately intertwined; a member of the first graduating
       class in 1893, she tells of the typical undergraduate routine,
       pointing out contrasts with later college life; her health is
       threatened after her first "challenging work-crammed years,"
       so she chaperones summer students in Europe from 1904 to
       1914; she describes the demands and rewards as Dean; with
       deep affection for her "eight thousand daughters," she main-
       tains a high moral tone and traditional values.

751   GEHRIG, ELEANOR TWITCHELL (1905-   )
       My Luke and I, with Joseph Durso.   New York: Crowell,
       1976.   229pp.

       The wife of New York Yankee baseball star Lou Gehrig
       tells of her Chicago background in sports and social circles
       and tells of her husband's background before their marriage
       in 1933; she describes their mutual accommodations to each
       other's activities and their gypsy life during the baseball
       season; in 1939, anxious over his failing health, she alone
       learns the full diagnosis of his terminal illness and for two
       years she maintains her "head of household" role, a happy
       front to protect him until his death in 1941.

752   GELD, ELLEN BROMFIELD (1932-   )
       The Heritage: A Daughter's Memories of Louis Bromfield.
       New York: Harper, 1962.   204pp.

       A writer and farmer, she produces a nostalgic account of
       a childhood filled with laughter, immense energy, and the
       "deep enjoyment" of close ties to the land; her father is a
       "vital character" surrounded by colorful people, and her
       mother is a haven of tranquillity; raised in a French village
       until she is six, she settles on an Ohio farm with her fam-
       ily and shares the dream of self-sufficient, cooperative farm-
       ing; she writes with understanding of her mother's loneliness
       amidst the ceaseless activity; after her mother's death, the
       family disperses; she settles with her husband on a Brazilian
       farm, carrying on with her father's agricultural legacy.

753   Strangers in the Valley.   New York: Dodd, Mead, 1957.
       237pp.

       In a sensitive and articulate account, the daughter of Louis
       Bromfield describes how she "learned a love of earth and a

delight in nature" on her family farm; later married to an
agronomist, they naïvely see a frontier paradise in Brazil's
fertile land; she gives the details of rehabilitating a large
estate, adding affectionate portraits of the local people; she
tells of her deep pleasure in her father's visit to their farm.

754   GENTRY, WINALEE
       One More River to Cross.   Philadelphia: Westminster,
       1955.   237pp.

       In an account full of enthusiasm and optimism, she tells
       the story of her marriage and her wholehearted support of
       her husband in his career as a pipeline builder; the child of
       divorced parents, she resolves to make a lasting marriage,
       and works through years of hardship and hazard to her final
       success, intensely proud of her husband.

755   GEOFFREY, THEODATE (pseud.)
       see WAYMAN, DOROTHY GODFREY (1893-   )

756   GERKEN, MABEL R.
       Ladies in Pants; A Home Front Diary.   New York: Exposi-
       tion, 1949.   96pp.

       When she is nearly fifty years old, she becomes a worker
       in an aircraft factory during World War II; she describes the
       years from 1943 to 1945 as "the darkest, most strenuous,
       nerve-wracking time of my life"; her diary entries record
       "the humorous, simple, homey things, " as she learns me-
       chanical skills and gets to know her fellow workers; she has
       much praise for women's contribution to the war effort.

757   GEVA, TAMARA
       Split Seconds; A Remembrance.   New York: Harper & Row,
       1972.   358pp.

       A dancer, she presents a highly emotional narrative of an
       enchanted Russian childhood with her beautiful mother, a mu-
       sic hall singer, and her wealthy father, who only later mar-
       ries her mother; financially pressed after the revolution of
       1917 yet obsessed with dance, she studies with her beloved
       governess' support; the death of her governess and her rejection
       of her mother throws her into a fierce self-sufficiency at an
       early age; she dances with the Moscow Theatre School, works
       with Balanchine, then marries him; they join the Diaghilev
       company, but later, separated from Balanchine, she joins a
       U. S. dance company and achieves professional fulfillment.

758   GIBSON, ALTHEA (1927-)
       I Always Wanted to Be Somebody, ed. Edward E. Fitzgerald.
       New York: Harper, 1958. 176pp.

       A black tennis champion, never "a racially conscious per-
       son," describes her childhood as the "wildest tomboy," in-
       volved in fights, truancy; fiercely independent, she quits
       school, and turns to the action and competition of tennis;
       sponsored by two doctors, she is given tennis training, home
       discipline, and the chance to finish her education; initially
       barred from tournaments, she proves herself on tours, win-
       ning Wimbledon and Forest Hills in 1957 and 1958.

759   So Much to Live For, with Richard Curtis. New York:
       Putnam, 1968. 160pp.

       A world champion amateur tennis player in 1958, she re-
       tires and pursues singing, movie, and business ventures,
       seeking financial security but finding no clear future for her-
       self; she discovers some racial barriers to a professional
       tennis career, and is disillusioned; she becomes a golfer,
       joining the professional tour in 1963; in 1964 she marries,
       looking forward to other pursuits after her efforts in sports.

760   GILBERT, FABIOLA CABEZA DE BACA (1895-)
       We Fed Them Cactus. Albuquerque: University of New
       Mexico Press, 1954. 186pp.

       The daughter of landowners in New Mexico, she presents
       stories from her childhood, many of them tales of a ranch
       cook that evoke the past, Hispanic customs, and Catholic
       religious practices; her summers on the hacienda become a
       permanent residence after she finishes her schooling; she
       describes a year of teaching, devoted to the rural children;
       she combines reminiscence with local history.

761   GILBERT, VIRGINIA JOHNSON
       Virginia Reel. Philadelphia: Lippincott, 1950. 254pp.

       She offers a humorous account of warm family life; her
       energetic mother, widowed during the depression, gives
       piano lessons and raises three daughters; the narrator gives
       dancing lessons to help the family finances and unsuccess-
       fully bids for chorus line jobs; she marries a playwright in
       1941; her account closes with the marriages of her two sis-
       ters.

762   GILDERSLEEVE, VIRGINIA CROCHERON (1877-1965) NAWM
       Many a Good Crusade; Memoirs of Virginia Crocheron Gild-
       ersleeve. New York: Macmillan, 1954. 434pp.

"A teacher always," she presents a highly articulate account beginning with her New York City childhood, the kind-
ling of her educational fervor at a fine preparatory school,
and her studies at Barnard College where she later serves
as Dean for thirty-six years, striving to expand educational
opportunities for women; she tells of close friendships with
women of achievement through her involvement with national
and international organizations.

763   GILES, JANICE HOLT
       The Kinta Years: An Oklahoma Childhood.   Boston: Hough-
       ton Mifflin, 1973. 337pp.

       The author describes her childhood from ages four to ten
in a small Oklahoma town; she devotes a section to family
history and a section to local Choctaw history; she includes
much daily domestic detail; she closes with her move from
Kinta; the events take place during the first decade of the
20th century.

764   GILLESPIE, JANET WICKS (1914?-)
       Bedlam in the Back Seat.   New York: Crowell, 1960.
       244pp.

       In a wry chronicle of the tribulations of European travel,
this wife and mother of four resists pressures to "do" Europe and establishes instead temporary roots at each stop,
settling into comfortable disarray; she describes the frights
of winter Alpine driving, two months in a friendly Italian
convent, an idyllic month near Oxford, and a visit to their
ancestral home in Scotland; she is particularly shrewd portraying the dynamics of family relations in the "life of a
journey."

765   A Joyful Noise.   New York: Harper & Row, 1971.   271pp.

       In this charming story of the magic of her family's sum-
mer home, the daughter of an unconventional minister describes lively birthday celebrations, gardening, birdwatching,
boating, and other "tribal excursions"; including sensitive
portraits of her Victorian grandmother and a retarded uncle,
she evokes a rich family life which gradually changes as the
children grow up; she closes with brief reflections of her
own children's and grandchildren's summers there.

766   With a Merry Heart.   New York: Harper & Row, 1976.
       231pp.

       The daughter of a Massachusetts minister tells of a joy-
ous childhood in the heart of a large, loving family; the

domestic "slow and dreamy pace" proceeds with seasonal
rhythms from Thanksgiving to Christmas to timeless vacations at their summer home; at fifteen, she perceives the
end of childhood, although she treasures the continuity established by each return to her summer home.

767   GILLMORE, MARGALO
       Four Flights Up. Boston: Houghton Mifflin, 1964. 171pp.

       The daughter of an actor, she is given to self-dramatizing;
       each chapter in the account is a separate vignette; various
       sections focus on a mystical, impecunious aunt, a family
       dinner with George Arliss, acting school, her first small
       parts, and her first major success in the theatre; she writes
       with a warm, gently ironic style.

768   GIOVANNI, NIKKI (1943-)
       Gemini: An Extended Autobiographical Statement on My First
       Twenty-Five Years of Being a Black Poet.   Indianapolis:
       Bobbs-Merrill, 1971. 149pp.

       Her impressionistic glimpses of childhood portray a fight-
       er, "a revolutionist," proud of her powerful father and "in-
       tellectual, aristocratic" mother; after a slangy account of
       her move "toward Black Power," she describes the birth of
       her son and the necessity to break from psychological de-
       pendency on her parents; reflects on Angela Davis (see entry
       #520) and politics, on Lena Horne (see entry #985), on
       black poetry, on black women who "measure ourselves by
       ourselves."

769   GISH, LILLIAN (1896-)
       Lillian Gish; The Movies, Mr. Griffith, and Me, with Ann
       Pinchot. Englewood Cliffs, N.J.: Prentice-Hall, 1969.
       388pp.

       The famous movie and theatre actress tells of a childhood
       among adults, when she and her sister begin acting as chil-
       dren in touring stock companies; her mother, "the most pro-
       found influence in my life," provides security and love; she
       has fond memories of the adored Griffith and the intense
       solidarity working with his film company; a woman of integ-
       rity and shrewd dramatic instincts, she deliberately rejects
       marriage in favor of her acting career and remains ex-
       tremely close to her mother and sister.

770   GLASGOW, ELLEN ANDERSON GHOLSON (1873-1945)   NAW
       Letters of Ellen Glasgow, ed. Blair Rouse. New York:
       Harcourt, Brace, 1958. 384pp.

The well-known novelist is represented by selected correspondence from 1897 to 1945; intensely dedicated, she vows
to "become a great novelist or none at all" and "to do justly
and fairly by my work"; she writes to her publisher, to fellow writers with graceful responses to their work, to re-
viewers concerning her own work; she sometimes writes
novels to escape too much introspection, too much living;
discouraged by the state of American literature, she is
nevertheless confident and proud of her own work.

771   The Woman Within. New York: Harcourt, Brace, 1954.
       307pp.

       In a personal narrative written in "great suffering of
mind and body," she attempts a "completely honest portrayal
of an interior world," having found her vocation as a writer
at seven; intensely emotional, given to brooding and nervous
headaches, she struggles with despair after her beloved
mother's breakdown and later death; two long love relationships and her ultimate recognition as a fine American novelist do little to lighten the "air of tragedy" that hangs over
her life, her terror of encroaching deafness, or the shadow
of literary isolation under which she writes; and she reacts
by producing a "protective ironic coloring."

772   GLENZ, MARIAN
       The B. S. Counter; Life in Alaska. New York: Exposition,
       1971. 271pp.

       She offers "some of our plain tales" from a childhood of
hard work and freedom; she helps in the family's general
store, where work and social life are combined and on the
family scow when her father is a fish-buyer; she writes of
customers and characters, gardening and trapping, outings
and entertainments.

773   GLESSNER, CHLOE HOLT
       Far Above Rubies. San Antonio: Naylor, 1965. 140pp.

       Writing in the third person, she describes pioneer life
in the Oklahoma Territory just after the turn of the century;
a dugout home, a close family life, and a dedication to the
importance of education form the basis for the "solid ethical
foundation" which is her heritage; she provides a portrait
of her courageous mother who copes with isolation, childbirth,
illness, cyclones, and prairie fire, the embodiment of pioneer spirit and ideals.

774   GLUCK, GEMMA LA GUARDIA (1881-1962)
       My Story, ed. S. L. Shneiderman. New York: McKay, 1961.
       116pp.

          The sister of New York Mayor La Guardia, she tells of
       her childhood on various army posts, then in Italy, but most
       of her account focuses on events during World War II; the
       wife of a Hungarian Jew and a grandmother by that time,
       she is arrested in 1944 and haled to Ravensbruck; she de-
       scribes the horrors of the concentration camp as well as
       the comradeship and affection among women prisoners; she
       is later transferred to Berlin and freed when Berlin falls,
       after which she works with American occupation forces; af-
       ter a fruitless search for her husband, in 1947 she settles
       in the U. S.

775   GODFREY, JEAN AND KATHY GODFREY
       Genius in the Family. New York: Putnam, 1962. 256pp.

          This is a family story of "love and creative imagination,"
       written in homage to their mother, a singer, composer, pi-
       anist, and amateur actress; through financial ups and downs,
       their mother maintains an unconventional manner, ingenious
       methods for keeping the creditors at bay, energy for family
       theatricals, and the conviction of her children's talents
       (their brother is Arthur Godfrey); an account full of lively
       anecdotes.

776   GODFREY, KATHY
       see GODFREY, JEAN

777   GOIN, OLIVE BOWN
       World Outside My Door. New York: Macmillan, 1955.
       184pp.

          A naturalist and wife of a herpetologist, she keeps a jour-
       nal beginning in 1946 of creatures patiently observed in her
       own Florida yard; in between household tasks, she watches
       frogs, lizards, snakes, turtles, birds, and small mammals,
       fascinated by "back-yard biology."

778   GOLDBERG, DOROTHY KURGANS
       A Private View of a Public Life. New York: Charterhouse,
       1975. 266pp.

          She provides a view of the 1960's from her position as
       the wife of Secretary of Labor, Supreme Court Justice, and
       Ambassador to the U. N. Arthur Goldberg; she recounts the
       pros and cons of her "consort status"; an artist, she tempo-

rarily shifts her attention to volunteer projects and is an
active aide to her husband.

779 GOLDBERG, RUTH L. POLHEMUS
     I Saw Israel; An American Reports.   New York: Exposition,
     1955. 217pp.

     She travels with her retired husband as part of a working
     tour to Israel; a keen observer, she attends classes and lec-
     tures, tours important sites, visits a kibbutz, and meets
     many people who offer her warm hospitality.

780 Ring-Around-the-World. New York: Pageant, 1963. 314pp.

     A member of a study group, she travels for over three
     months with her husband and keeps a diary of her observa-
     tions of the sights and people in Alaska, Japan, the Philip-
     pines, Cambodia, Thailand, India, Israel, Turkey, Greece,
     Italy, France, Spain, and Portugal; open and receptive, she
     believes in human brotherhood.

781 GOLDEN, GERTRUDE
     Red Moon Called Me; Memoirs of a Schoolteacher in the
     Government Indian Service, ed. Cecil Dryden.   San Antonio:
     Naylor, 1954. 211pp.

     Beginning in 1901, she serves in various teaching posts
     among Indian tribes in Oregon, Arizona, Oklahoma, and
     Montana; she enjoys the challenge of working with new peo-
     ple and loves her pupils; she presents lively descriptions of
     the colleagues and students with whom she works and com-
     ments frankly on conflicts among teachers and administrators.

782 GOLDMAN, EMMA (1869-1940)   NAW
     Nowhere at Home; Letters from Exile of Emma Goldman and
     Alexander Berkman, ed. Richard and Anna Maria Drinnon.
     New York: Schocken Books, 1975. 282pp.

     Organized by topic, her remarkable letters demonstrate
     her ceaseless, passionate commitment to the political ideals
     of revolutionary anarchism; deported in 1919, she struggles
     after the "tragedy" of her experiences in Russia in 1920 and
     1921 to expose the "bolshevik lie" to western radical organi-
     zations; she is buoyed by the devotion of those who remain
     friends, never losing hope in spite of discouraging political
     conditions; her correspondence with Berkman is an intense,
     extended discussion of the nature of revolution, of the rela-
     tions between men and women, of anarchism and "revolu-
     tionary ethics."

783   GOODSELL, JANE
       I've Only Got Two Hands and I'm Busy Wringing Them.
       Garden City, N.Y.: Doubleday, 1966. 161pp.

       In a humorous account of a typical housewife's "search
       for identity," she feels pushed and pulled by advicemongers;
       she examines the trivial dilemmas of the "Modern Woman,"
       among them her husband's foibles and her children's phases;
       some chapters were previously published in magazines.

784   GOODSPEED, BERNICE I.
       Criada. Mexico: American Book & Printing, 1950. 381pp.

       A playwright and novelist, she first goes to Mexico in
       1930 to travel and to write; she tells of a succession of
       "criadas," serving maids, and the insights they bring to her
       about Mexican Indian culture; some of her portraits reveal
       friendship and esteem, some illustrate her baffled attempts
       to explore veiled personalities.

785   GOODWIN, RUBY BERKLEY (1903-   )
       It's Good to Be Black. Garden City, N.Y.: Doubleday,
       1953. 256pp.

       A black poet, fiction writer, children's author, and civic
       leader writes of "life as I have lived it," denying racial
       stereotypes in her evocation of family and town; the daughter
       of an Illinois coal miner, she grows up with great respect
       for black men's strength through her father's and grand-
       father's examples; only in adulthood is her secure world
       broken by the knowledge of racism, but those consequences
       are counteracted by her great pride in her family history.

786   GOOSTRAY, STELLA (1886-1969)
       Memoirs: Half a Century in Nursing. Boston: Boston Uni-
       versity, Mugar Memorial Library, 1969. 182pp.

       Writing her memoirs at eighty, she describes her close
       associations with "important movements in nursing"; a
       graduate of the Boston Children's Hospital School of Nursing
       in 1920, she becomes a distinguished teacher, publishes sev-
       eral chemistry texts, serves as a strong nursing school di-
       rector, works with a professional nursing journal, and is in-
       volved with international nursing organizations; she maintains
       a lifelong dedication to the establishment of professional
       standards and a keen interest in the history of nursing.

787   GORDON, RUTH (1896-   )
       My Side; The Autobiography of Ruth Gordon. New York:
       Harper & Row, 1976. 502pp.

An actress tells of her early days in show business, breaking into the theatre at nineteen, coping with the rigors of touring and the anxiety of waiting for roles; always looking for "someone to show me how," she finds a protector and guide in her actor husband until his death; her impressionistic style provides staccato glimpses of the past, not always chronologically arranged, and of her roles and acquaintances among theatre and film people; she describes a life of "endeavor, hope, fear, triumph, despair, getting it right."

788   Myself Among Others. New York: Atheneum, 1971. 389pp.

An actress on the stage and screen since 1915, she writes a lively, impressionistic, anecdotal, non-chronological account, peopled with her friends from film and theatre.

789   GORNICK, VIVIAN
       In Search of Ali Mahmoud: An American Woman in Egypt.
       New York: Saturday Review Press, 1973. 343pp.

A journalist, she meets an Egyptian physicist in 1969, is drawn to him despite Jewish-Arab differences, and travels to Egypt to immerse herself in the web of his family relationships; she presents vivid portraits of individuals of "bizarre contrasts"; in spite of loneliness, she moves away from the Egyptian family ties, although her experiences there create echoes from her childhood; she is dogged by the political ramifications of her being Jewish, and feels drained of emotional energy spent in this intense retrospection.

790   GOTKIN, JANET (1943-)
       Too Much Anger, Too Many Tears; A Personal Triumph
       Over Psychiatry, with Paul Gotkin. New York: Quadrangle/
       New York Times, 1975. 395pp.

Glimpses of her youth establish a background of family tension, fear, intense despair, encounters with hated school counselors; she distrusts psychoanalysis, and is hospitalized in 1962 after slashing her wrists; she feels humiliated, fakes cooperation, and continues attempting suicide; in a second hospital, she is betrayed by her doctors and subjected to shock treatment; only in 1971 does she regain control over her life and experience a rebirth; written in a spirit of "bitterness and irreverence," her account on pages 3-10, 27-214, and 375-390 is interspersed with her husband's commentary.

791   GOULD, BEATRICE BLACKMAR
       American Story; Memories and Reflections of Bruce Gould

and Beatrice Blackmar Gould.   New York: Harper & Row,
1968.   330pp.

   She and her husband are joint editors of the Ladies' Home
Journal from 1935 to 1962 in a "tempestuous'' partnership;
she tells of her Iowa childhood, college, stints as a teacher
and a reporter and, after her marriage, a short story writer; in this vivacious narrative she describes her principles
and values, consistently maintained, as an editor; her shrewd
assessment of the magazine audience and her acceptance of
controversial topics contribute to her success; she vows that
"this marriage has been life's greatest gift"; she and her
husband write alternate chapters.

792   GOWAN, STELLA B.   (1872-   )
       Wildwood: A Story of Pioneer Life.   New York: Vantage,
       1959.   155pp.

   She offers a "memory of pioneer childhood," and harmoni-
ous family life centered on her father, a doctor and dream-
er, and her mother, beautiful and cheerful; the family goes
west in 1853, seeking gold; she describes in detail her everyday life of "home, friends, and decent living"; her education
is furthered both in and out of school and she becomes a
teacher even before she attains legal age.

793   GRAF, NELLY
       No Vacancy.   Denver: Alan Swallow, 1951.   256pp.

   She and her husband invest in a Colorado tourist court
and, in a light vein, she proceeds to tell of her trials and
tribulations, learning the business and coping with a variety
of guests; she finally sells out.

794   GRAHAM, ELINOR MISH
       Maine Charm String.   New York: Macmillan, 1946.   231pp.

   A former actress, she leads a home-centered life on a
peninsula in Casco Bay; she offers a subtle evocation of
Maine atmosphere, as her collection of strings of antique
buttons, each a "charm string," provides ways into her
neighbors' lives and ways for her to establish herself local-
ly; she meets "some very remarkable characters," portrayed
with sensitivity in this account.

795   My Window Looks Down East.   New York: Macmillan, 1951.
       218pp.

   A former actress, she settles in Maine with her husband
and daughter and is much taken by the "simple, unaffected

brotherhood" of her neighbors; she wishes to "catch the essence" of Maine life, and her reflections on nature and people and values reveal a great deal of insight and sensitivity.

796   GRAHAM, SHEILAH (1908?-)
       Beloved Infidel; The Education of a Woman, with Gerold
       Frank. New York: Holt, 1958. 338pp.

       Growing up in the fierce competition of a London orphanage, she dreams of romance and wealth; an employer gently polishes her manners, and when she marries him, she turns to drama and writing to relieve her boredom; her acquaintances in England are of the "finest society"; coming to the U.S. in 1933, she is known in Hollywood as a brash, tactless columnist; she tells of her four years as F. Scott Fitzgerald's mistress, her studies with him of literature and history, her despair at his drinking, and their anguished, tortuous relationship which ends with his death.

797   Confessions of a Hollywood Columnist. New York: Morrow,
       1969. 309pp.

       She gossips about the "spoiled unique society," "the Faustian nightmare" of Hollywood in alleged attempts to "understand" the celebrities, including Streisand, Grant, Tracy and Hepburn, Sinatra, Andrews, Brando, Sellers, Monroe, Elizabeth Taylor, Loren, and the Fonda family.

798   The Rest of the Story. New York: Coward-McCann, 1964.
       317pp.

       In a sequel to Beloved Infidel, she tells of her return to England as a war correspondent after Fitzgerald's death in 1941; marrying a British military official and bearing a daughter, she finds motherhood an intense experience; later, divorced and with two children, she pursues success in Hollywood, finding "two careers--as a columnist and as a private citizen"; she describes the writing, then the filming, of Beloved Infidel and closes with reflections on parenthood.

799   A State of Heat. New York: Grosset & Dunlap, 1972.
       244pp.

       Proud of having achieved success, money, fame, and all she has desired in sex and love, she tells of a life "drenched in experience"; she learns early to use sex to her advantage; the best years of her life are given to a long affair with F. Scott Fitzgerald (see entry #796); after numerous affairs, three marriages, two children, and a career as a Hollywood

columnist, she focuses on houses and gourmet food for her
satisfactions.

800   GRAHAM, VIRGINIA (1912-   )
        There Goes What's Her Name; The Continuing Saga of Vir-
        ginia Graham, with Jean Libman Block.   Englewood Cliffs,
        N. J.:   Prentice-Hall, 1965.   246pp.

        Always bold and adventurous, she capitalizes on her "gift
        of gab" and ultimately becomes a television personality; after
        marriage and motherhood, she works in radio, does volun-
        teer work during World War II, organizes for Cerebral Palsy
        in 1948, and serves as a beauty show emcee; in spite of her
        own cancer and her husband's breakdown, she rebuilds his
        business, participates in numerous telethons from 1952 to
        1962, has a daily radio program from 1956, then hosts a
        television interview program; her account is full of humor
        and energy.

801   GRANGER, KATHLEEN BUEHR (1902-   )
        The Hills of Home: A Vermont Idyll.   New York: Van-
        guard, 1966.   192pp.

        A professional artist and her husband leave Chicago during
        World War II for the country, determined to offer their chil-
        dren the outdoor life; she gives up painting in her absorption
        with farm activities and "small adventures"; their quest for
        self-sufficiency entails endless hard work, but their dogged
        determination gives way to deep contentment and the love of
        the "land we had earned."

802   GRANT, JANE COLE (1892?-1972)
        Ross, The New Yorker, and Me.   New York: Reynal, 1968.
        264pp.

        She opens with brief notes on her Kansas childhood, then
        her move to New York to study singing, where she instead
        becomes a reporter for The New York Times; she goes to
        France during World War I as an entertainer for the YMCA;
        she is pursued by Harold Ross, with whom she founds The
        New Yorker; she is married to Ross from 1920 to 1929; her
        account includes a biographical sketch of Ross and anecdotes
        of Ross and Woollcott.

803   GRANT, JULIA DENT (1826-1902)   NAW
        The Personal Memoirs of Julia Dent Grant (Mrs. Ulysses S.
        Grant), ed. John Y. Simon.   New York: Putnam, 1975.
        346pp.

She notes that in her childhood "life seemed one long
summer of sunshine, flowers, and smiles" on a plantation
near St. Louis; after seven years at boarding school, and
still a shy innocent, she is courted by Grant; delighted by
housekeeping and motherhood, her happiness is temporarily
marred by a two-year absence of her husband; at the onset
of the Civil War, she affirms her faith in Grant's military
skill; settling in Washington, D. C. , she describes post-war
political events, culminating in Grant's election as President;
she has "eight happy years" in the White House, enjoying
social events; she tells of their world tour in 1877 and of a
"triumphant journey" across the U. S. ; reiterating her abid-
ing love and respect for Grant, she closes with his death.

804   GRAY, BETTY A.
       Beyond the Serengeti Plains; Adventures of an Anthropologist's
       Wife in the East African Hinterland.   New York: Vantage,
       1971.   197pp.

       Of British parentage, she travels to Tanganyika for six
months after her marriage in 1955 to an American anthropologist; learning "anthropological diplomacy," she has access to women's activities, and to indirect information about
female circumcision rites, closed to her husband; she observes a harvest festival and a religious festival, joins in
women's agricultural work, and finds her perceptions sharp-
ened through her experiences and friendships; written with
sensitivity, the book is based on journals.

805   GREEN, ANNE (1899-1975?)
       With Much Love.   New York: Harper, 1948.   276pp.

       A writer, she describes "a perfect childhood" as the
daughter of American expatriates in Paris at the turn of the
century; the youngest in a large family, she focuses on certain siblings among the "American children" and the "French
children" and on her parents, delightfully and extravagantly
in love; she writes in a slightly exaggerated but witty style
in the third person.

806   GREEN, BETTY (pseud.)
       see PEPPER, NANCY

807   GREENAWAY, M. EMILY
       All Wool but the Buttons: Memories of Family Life in Up-
       state New York.   New York: Exposition, 1956.   157pp.

       In recollections focusing on her childhood, she tells of
her early unhappy memories of her father but also of her

later "doglike devotion" to him, desiring to be tough, strong,
and brave for his approval; she provides spirited family anecdotes and delightful portraits of her parents; noting their
idiosyncrasies, she describes her mother's money-making
schemes, relaxed religion, and amused admiration for her
husband.

808   GREENBURGER, INGRID (1913-   )
       A Private Treason; A German Memoir.   Boston: Little,
       Brown, 1973.   308pp.

       With the rise of Nazi power, her conscience forces her
       to leave her native Germany and she flees first to Vienna,
       then to a Dalmatian island, then to France in 1939; through
       flashbacks she creates a fine evocation of her childhood, in-
       cluding her studies in an Isadora Duncan (see entry # 609)
       school near Berlin; during the German occupation of France,
       she aids in hiding Jews, forging papers, helping the resist-
       ance; she closes this articulate narrative with the death of
       her French lover but includes a brief epilogue set in New
       England.

809   GREENE, GAEL
       Don't Come Back Without It.   New York: Simon and Schus-
       ter, 1960.   214pp.

       A reporter describes stories covered and uncovered in a
       series of humorous anecdotes; after a footloose summer in
       Europe at 17, she becomes a guest editor of Mademoiselle
       in 1955, going on to the New York Post and stories of Elvis,
       dance studios, reducing spas, fortune tellers, and hypnotism.

810   GREENE, MARGARET MORTON QUINCY (1806-?)
       The Articulate Sisters; Passages from Journals and Letters
       of the Daughters of President Josiah Quincy of Harvard Uni-
       versity, ed. M. A. DeWolfe Howe.   Cambridge, Mass. :
       Harvard University Press, 1946.   249pp.

       Her journal and letters cover the years from 1824 to 1828
       and are found on pages 51-145; she gives vivid details of the
       amusements and pleasures at a crowded resort hotel, of La-
       fayette's visit to a Harvard commencement, of a party at her
       country home in Quincy, of general domestic clamor; she
       later writes reflections on slavery from Charleston after her
       marriage in 1826; she also writes keen observations from
       Cuba, pitying "the women of this island. "

811   GREENMAN, FRANCES CRANMER
       Higher Than the Sky.   New York: Harper, 1954.   305pp.

A portrait painter, she describes with wry humor the
"close triumvirate" of her family, her elegant suffragist
mother who lectures and her idealistic father who teaches;
she studies art in Washington, then in Europe; she marries,
and her portraits of her daughter launch her career although
she feels that portrait commissions are limiting; she suffers
a breakdown before the birth of her second child, sees
prosperity fade after the 1929 crash, separates from her
husband, and later rejoins her parents, continuing her career and writing on art.

812   GREENWOOD, AMY
      Rolling North. New York: Crowell, 1955.   218pp.

A Philadelphian with a yen to pioneer, she follows the
lure of adventure and opportunity to homestead in Alaska
with her husband and three young sons in 1950; they pull a
trailer home cross-country in winter, a two-month saga of
uncertainty and breakdowns, relieved by their meeting many
interesting people along the way; the account ends with their
arrival in Alaska.

813   GREGG, ELINOR D.
      The Indians and the Nurse.   Norman: University of Okla-
      homa Press, 1965.   173pp.

She is a nurse with the Indian Service in South Dakota after seeing World War I duty in France; with no organized
program and inadequate government support, she must create her own position and her relations with the Indians, for
whom she holds respect and affection; happiest under pioneer
conditions, she works with boarding school children and
teaches women's groups; in 1924 she takes a supervisory job
in Washington, D. C. and recruits other nurses, but finds
little sympathy for "the uplifters"; she notes the expansion
of the federal bureaucracy in the 1930's.

814   GRIFFIN, MARY ANNAROSE, SISTER
      The Courage to Choose: An American Nun's Story.   Boston:
      Little, Brown, 1975.   214pp.

A Chicago-born woman recounts the impact of her Catholic education, her decision to become a nun in 1939, and
her convent life; her "independent soul" is a "fatal flaw" and
she later reassesses her place as a nun in the light of her
work as a teacher in a black Mississippi college, her activism against the war in Viet Nam, and the influence of the
women's liberation movement during her tenure as dean at
Mundelein College; she describes leaving the convent and dis-
carding the habit; she returns to secular life after thirty-one

years as a nun; she writes with warm humor, grace, and
sensitivity.

815   GRIFFITH, CORINNE
       Eggs I Have Known.   New York: Farrar, Straus and Cuda-
       hy, 1955.   230pp.

       A movie star, author, and real-estate agent, she com-
       bines recipes and reminiscences following her vow to gather
       recipes whenever she travels; from the 1930's to the 1950's
       she visits famous restaurants and meets prominent people
       all over the world, unabashedly dropping names as she de-
       scribes her culinary acquisitions.

816   I'm Lucky--At Cards.   New York: Frederick Fell, 1974.
       101pp.

       In a rambling, lightweight, and impersonal account, she
       tells of an ill-starred movie career, a brief marriage, her
       enjoyment of sports, and her travels.

817   My Life with the Redskins.   New York: A. S. Barnes, 1947.
       238pp.

       In 1936 she marries a wealthy businessman and president
       of the Boston Redskins football team; her anecdotes cover
       the years from 1937 to 1947, and she chronicles the team's
       progress, their move to Washington, D. C. , and politics and
       flamboyance that constitute the "inside story. "

818   Papa's Delicate Condition.   Boston: Houghton Mifflin, 1952.
       178pp.

       Her beloved father is a "man of large small-town affairs, "
       whose genial intoxication and extravagant, impulsive nature
       often pit him against his wife's sense of propriety and the
       morality of the small Texas town aristocracy; the author
       finds herself aligned with her father in benevolent opposition
       to her mother and sister in the family's saga of separation
       and reconciliation.

819   This You Won't Believe!   New York: Frederick Fell, 1972.
       115pp.

       In a lightweight, disorganized sequel to Truth Is Stranger
       (1964), she writes of fellow Hollywood celebrities, of a visit to
       the White House in 1971, of her speculations in real estate.

820   GRISSOM, IRENE WELCH (1873-)
       We Harness a River.   Caldwell, Idaho: Caxton, 1946.
       155pp.

       A poet and novelist, she focuses on her Colorado child-
       hood in a large happy family headed by her pioneering par-
       ents; she tells of her love of books and early attempts at
       poetry; her autobiography, previously published in serial
       form, covers pages 73-155; her book includes verse.

821   GROSSINGER, TANIA (1937-)
       Growing Up at Grossinger's.   New York: McKay, 1975.
       213pp.

       A distant relative of the owners of the famous New York
       resort hotel, she moves to the hotel at eight when her wid-
       owed mother becomes its social hostess; she describes the
       summer atmosphere and routine, her friendships and mis-
       chief-making with members of the huge staff, and acquaint-
       ances with numerous celebrities; growing up with little mat-
       ernal guidance, she copes with an adolescent search for
       identity, college at fifteen, and resentful rebellion against
       her hotel "home"; with no models for permanence, she
       abandons a brief marriage and works temporarily in public
       relations; after the deaths of her mother and a close friend,
       and a ten-year absence, she finds she can return to Gros-
       singer's with understanding and affection.

822   GROST, AUDREY
       Genius in Residence.   Englewood Cliffs, N. J. :   Prentice-
       Hall, 1970.   224pp.

       The mother of a phenomenally gifted child provides a
       lively account of his birth and early months marked by much
       parental attention and communication; his reading feats and
       comparisons with two younger siblings suggest high intelli-
       gence, but she struggles unsuccessfully with school author-
       ities for recognition; finally discovering the extent of his in-
       telligence when he's 9, she is careful to nurture university
       contacts but downplay the national attention he receives.

823   GROVE, MARGIE RITCHLEY (1911-)
       Papa Passes.   New York: Greenwich Book, 1956.   85pp.

       With a keen eye for human foibles, she presents a lively
       portrayal of her family life in a small midwestern town, a
       life centered on her exuberant card-playing father; she grows
       up with her sisters and brothers amid household clutter and
       mild parental eccentricities; her memories of childhood are
       cast in humorous anecdotes and darken only when she closes
       with her father's decline and death.

824   GRUBER, RUTH (1911-   )
       Israel on the Seventh Day.   New York: Hill and Wang,
       1968.   214pp.

       A magazine writer and correspondent for the New York
       Herald Tribune in Israel tells what she "saw, felt, and
       learned" in twenty years closely observing the growth of a
       nation; she covers major political events, interviews lead-
       ers, and travels extensively; born a Jew, she nevertheless
       feels that she only truly becomes a Jew through her experi-
       ences in Israel.

825   GUFFY, OSSIE (1931-   )
       Ossie; The Autobiography of a Black Woman, as told to
       Caryl Ledner.   New York: Norton, 1971.   224pp.

       Insisting that she is "average," she writes to explain
       what it is to be black, female, and the mother of nine chil-
       dren; she appreciates the strength of her mother and grand-
       mother, and the lessons in self-respect taught by her minis-
       ter grandfather; she recounts problems with men, an un-
       stable marriage, welfare assistance, subsistence jobs; in
       1964 she becomes a community organizer with a poverty pro-
       gram, intensely concerned about poor black people.

826   GUGGENHEIM, PEGGY (1898-   )
       Confessions of an Art Addict.   New York: Macmillan, 1960.
       176pp.

       This is a condensed version of the 1946 edition with some
       brief additions.

827   Out of This Century; The Informal Memoirs of Peggy Guggen-
       heim.   New York: Dial, 1946.   365pp.

       A prominent art collector opens with recollections of her
       "excessively unhappy" childhood in a wealthy family; in 1919
       she comes into her own fortune and the independence it
       brings; her work in a book shop acquaints her with artistic
       and literary figures, and when she later settles in Europe,
       she feels "liberated" from her bourgeois upbringing; she
       presides over a gallery of modern art in France before
       World War II and a gallery-home in Venice after the war,
       and describes protégés, eccentric artists, exhibits, and pur-
       chases.

828   GUILD, CAROLINE
       Rainbow in Tahiti.   Garden City, N.Y.:   Doubleday, 1948.
       253pp.

A Boston couple with a small child settles, with romantic expectations, in Tahiti; the wife is a prizewinning cultivator of tropical plants, but as an "incipient naturalist," she must also learn to establish a home, manage servants, observe the local social customs, raise chickens, and keep exotic birds; with the influx of tourists and the approach of World War II, they leave in 1940 after seventeen years; her account is gently humorous.

829   GULLEY, MARY LOU (1924-   )
       My Mystery Castle.   Culver City, Cal.:   Murray & Gee,
       1952.   295pp.

She idolizes her father, "a bum and an artist," a fairy tale figure absent from her childhood; at his death, she and her mother settle in the eccentric home he had built in Arizona; she is the administratrix of his estate and agrees to live for a stipulated two years in the desert "Castle"; she tells of primitive conditions, a growing tourist business, and her deep love for the desert, and she describes her gradual understanding of her father.

830   HABERSHAM, JOSEPHINE CLAY (1821-1893)
Ebb Tide; As Seen Through the Diary of Josephine Clay
Habersham, 1863, by Spencer Bidwell King, Jr. Athens,
Ga. : University of Georgia Press, 1958. 129pp.

An upper-class mother of twelve recounts family notes
and war news from her summer home; she displays anxious
concern for the safety of her soldier sons, her emotions
follow the advances and reverses of Confederate forces; a
lover of fine literature, she supervises her children's studies; she describes deep affection for her husband; her family
returns to Savannah at summer's end.

831   HACKET, MRS. JOHN T.
see WARFIELD, FRANCES (1901-)

832   HACKETT, MARIE G. (1923-)
The Cliff's Edge. New York: McGraw-Hill, 1954.
245pp.

She describes living with a husband whose mental illness
makes her fear for the safety of herself and her three children; she is forced into heavy responsibilities and hard decisions, racked by loneliness, and alternately hopeful and
hopeless; further difficulties include factional disputes among
the doctors, insensitive social workers, a son's illness, and
financial pressures.

833   HADLEY, LEILA ELIOTT-BURTON
Give Me the World. New York: Simon and Schuster, 1958.
343pp.

Well-travelled as a child, she escapes the routine of a
public relations career by taking her six-year-old son on
a one and one-half year tour of the Far East; she offers
vivid descriptions of ports of call, and is eventually accepted
as a partner by the crew of an American schooner; after her
son's return to the U.S. , she continues in the Mediterranean
with the schooner, finally marrying one of the crew after her
own return to New York.

834   HAHN, EMILY (1905-)
       Africa to Me: Person to Person.   Garden City, N.Y.:
       Doubleday, 1964.   277pp.

       A writer and journalist, intrigued by the tale of a Dutch
       female traveller murdered in Africa in 1869, travels to Af-
       rica in 1960; in her two years of extensive travels she in-
       terviews government officials, notes racial problems--partic-
       ularly Mau Mau activity--visits with friends, and offers
       some historical background.

835   England to Me.   Garden City, N.Y.:   Doubleday, 1949.
       271pp.

       Leaving postwar China, she arrives in England in 1946
       with her British husband and their daughter; they reclaim a
       deteriorated family home and she presents a wry view of
       English village life, of her ambiguous relationships with
       "family retainers," of subtle changes after the war, of
       democratic ideals versus aristocratic pressures; she creates
       perceptive portraits of the people around her; she closes
       with her return to the U.S.; some chapters were previously
       published in The New Yorker.

836   Hong Kong Holiday.   Garden City, N.Y.:   Doubleday, 1946.
       305pp.

       A journalist produces a companion-piece to China to Me,
       focusing on human relationships and illuminating moments in
       this vivid portrayal of life under the Japanese occupation of
       Hong Kong during World War II; she closes with her repatri-
       ation to the U.S.; much of the account was first published in
       The New Yorker.

837   The Tiger House Party; The Last Days of the Maharajas.
       Garden City, N.Y.:   Doubleday, 1958.   164pp.

       A journalist and prolific writer, she travels to India to
       explore the phenomenon of princes within a modern social
       structure; as the house guest of a prince, "complete with
       tiger-shooting" with the male guests, she describes the so-
       cial life, her developing friendship with the prince, and her
       meeting with his wife, still in purdah; the account was orig-
       inally published in altered form in The New Yorker.

838   Times and Places.   New York: Crowell, 1970.   304pp.

       Her chapters originally appeared in The New Yorker as
       articles between 1937 and 1970; after growing up in a "ma-

triarchy," the daughter of a "free-thinking female," she defiantly takes her degree in mining engineering, in 1926 the first woman to do so; she tells of a job with a mining company, work as a Fred Harvey guide, a half-hearted suicide attempt in depression-era New York, research in the British Museum Reading Room, and travels in the Congo, Japan, and China which are treated at greater length in several books.

839   HALE, NANCY (1908-)
        The Life in the Studio.   Boston: Little, Brown, 1969.
        209pp.

        The daughter of two Boston artists, her memories are triggered by clearing out their studios after their deaths; she tells of her mother's portrait painting and of her mother's personal solitude, innocence, ingenuity, and stylishness; she describes a maiden aunt, also an artist; her perspective on her parents' lives shifts with the sensitive, subtle alterations wrought by her own growth and maturity.

840   A New England Girlhood.   Boston: Little, Brown, 1958.
        232pp.

        An artist and writer, she presents "reverberations from childhood," fine vignettes in which present events or impressions are linked to or suffused with the layers of past experience; the daughter of cosmopolitan Boston artists, she recalls visits to the seashore, school days, adjustments after a move to Virginia, dancing school, romance as a debutante; she is a descendant of Lucy Larcom (see companion volume); some chapters were previously published in magazine form.

841   HALE, YVONNE TILLY (1894-)
        Laugh and Cry.   New York: Exposition, 1965.   64pp.

        In a rambling account, she describes her Louisiana childhood, "an empty life," marked by poverty and neglect in spite of her widowed father's medical practice; she becomes a teacher, marries, has three children, and tells anecdotes of her family, giving trivial and important incidents equal weight.

842   HALL, ENNEN REAVES (1890?-)
        One Saint and Seven Sinners.   New York: Crowell, 1959.
        243pp.

        In this delightful portrait of a frontier missionary family's life in the Oklahoma Territory, she focuses on her childhood and a way of life now gone; in lively anecdotes, she describes her easy-going father, her mother's rebellions and sharp tongue, the humiliations that accompany charity for the minister's family, and the five children who chafe under the parishioners' scrutiny.

843   HALL, EVA LITCHFIELD (1902-)
Above Adversity; Memories at Home and Abroad of Eva Litchfield Hall. New York: Exposition, 1966. 91pp.

Having lost her mother at twelve and having become fully independent at eighteen, her deep desire for an education leads to college and a teaching career; married in 1926, she suffers in 1936 the double tragedy of a child's death and her husband's death; she raises the remaining son alone, building a "new life" through teaching and traveling extensively; she closes with her second marriage to a fellow travel enthusiast.

844   Sampling Asia. Brooklyn, N.Y.: Theo. Gaus' Sons, 1974. 163pp.

She is a social studies teacher, world traveler, and lecturer who travels in Asia; her desire to see mainland China is thwarted, but elsewhere she is able to visit with and observe the people; she includes much detail and background material on each place visited.

845   This I Cannot Forget; Global Adventures. New York: Carlton Press, 1965. 98pp.

A teacher and lecturer, she provides anecdotes from her travels in Finland, Czechoslovakia, the Soviet Union, Syria, India, Japan, South Africa, Nigeria, New Zealand, and Brazil; she sometimes combines travel with study, enjoying her contacts with people of other cultures.

846   HALL, HELEN
Unfinished Business: In Neighborhood and Nation. New York: Macmillan, 1971. 366pp.

She describes how her youthful perceptions lead to social work training and settlement house work; she is chief administrator at the Henry Street Settlement from 1933 to 1967, a "second-generation" activist; she marries Paul Kellogg in 1935; she discusses the struggle with unemployment and archaic public relief measures during the depression; she relates anecdotes from personal experience with neighborhood incidents, and tells of community studies, com-

munity action projects, daily settlement work; she discusses
shifts in crisis areas, from unemployment to gang warfare
to drug abuse; the account demonstrates her vast experience
as writer and organizer.

847   HALL, LUCILLE HATHAWAY (1883?-)
       Memories of Old Alturas County, Idaho.   Denver: Big
       Mountain Press, 1956. 72pp.

       She grows up in a home at a stagecoach station on the
       emigrant trail; she describes those who pass through:
       "sporting girls," outlaws, and pioneers; her mother raises
       her "for a farm hand"; she homesteads with her son in
       1914 after leaving her husband.

848   HALL, MABEL WILSON (1893-)
       Upper Beaver Creek; Pioneer Life in Colorado.   New York:
       Exposition, 1972. 159pp.

       She writes to preserve a description of pioneer life for
       posterity, opening with local history to set the scene; she
       settles in Colorado in 1903 and tells of her family life, in-
       cluding the terrible shock of her father's proposal of incest;
       she becomes a teacher, columnist, and poet and marries in
       1916; she presents the domestic details of ranch life and her
       concerns in raising and educating four children; finally find-
       ing forgiveness for her father and reverence for her mother,
       she achieves a serene old age.

849   HALL, MINTA (1878-)
       Do You Remember? Memories of a Schoolteacher.   New
       York: Exposition, 1956. 44pp.

       Memories of "some outstanding incidents" from her years
       of teaching brighten her life after she is struck by blindness;
       she offers random, often amusing, anecdotes which demon-
       strate her creativity and her affection for children.

850   HALL, PAMELA
       Heads You Lose. New York: Hawthorn Books, 1971. 148pp.

       She writes of her personal experiences in the "teen-age
       drug world," including slangy excerpts from letters and
       diaries; she describes her first experiments with alcohol
       and drugs which lead to frequent use, her numerous con-
       flicts with her mother over drugs, and the trauma of com-
       mitment to a European clinic; finally scared away from
       drugs, she is disturbed by her friends who remain caught
       in the drug life and she recognizes peer pressure, loneli-

ness, insecurity, and boredom as factors in her own addiction.

851   HALLINAN, VIVIAN MOORE
      My Wild Irish Rogues.   Garden City, N. Y. :   Doubleday,
      1952.   255pp.

      Determined to have a large family since she is the "only
      child of a broken family," the adventurous author snares a
      lawyer who defends unpopular clients and causes, marries
      him, and rears six sons, "my primitives"; an unconventional
      mother, she encourages camping and athletics and, at the
      same time, manages an apartment house business in San
      Francisco during the depression.

852   HALSELL, GRACE
      Bessie Yellowhair.   New York: Morrow, 1973.   213pp.

      A journalist and author, she passes as Indian, lives on a
      Navajo reservation, and then takes a job as a domestic; she
      writes at length of differing cultures and values, of her
      shock at whites' systematic assault on Indian identity.

853   Soul Sister.   New York: World, 1969.   211pp.

      A free-lance reporter, she takes Black Like Me as a
      challenge and in 1968 becomes "a woman turned black by
      medication and the sun"; she describes her intense emotional responses to experiences in the Harlem ghetto, to the
      degradation and depression of domestic work in the South,
      and to the protection offered her by the black community;
      she notes the heavy psychological costs of her experiment.

854   HALSEY, MARGARET (1910-)
      Color Blind; A White Woman Looks at the Negro.   New
      York: Simon and Schuster, 1946.   163pp.

      She offers her experiences and reflections after working
      at an interracial servicemen's canteen in New York during
      World War II; in a gentle, chiding tone, she describes race
      relations and "how it seemed to me."

855   HAMERSTROM, FRANCES (1907-)
      An Eagle to the Sky.   Ames, Iowa: Iowa State University
      Press, 1970.   142pp.

      A wildlife biologist and falconer, she values "coming to
      understand a wild animal as a companion" as she cares for

a golden eagle in 1966; she offers detailed observations of
the bird's behavior and her own adjustments to its require-
ments; she hunts with a second eagle but later releases the
bird into the wild.

856   HAMILTON, ESTHER YERGER
       Ambassador in Bonds! East Stroudsburg, Pa.: Pinebrook
       Book Club, 1946. 264pp.

       A Baptist missionary in the Philippines beginning in 1933,
       she endures separation from her fiancé and internment in a
       concentration camp from 1941 to 1945; the hunger, crowding,
       and monotony are relieved by her optimism supported by her
       strong religious faith; she notes spiritual parallels to war-
       time conditions; she describes the turmoil of liberation, her
       return to the U.S., and her marriage.

857   HAMILTON, MARGUERITE
       Borrowed Angel. Garden City, N.Y.: Hanover House,
       1958. 287pp.

       A widow tells the story of the last two years of her life
       with her daughter, a victim of lymphohemangioma; both
       Catholic converts, they remain in indomitable good spirits
       despite financial pressures and the daughter's progressive
       deterioration; their dreams of a pilgrimage to Lourdes be-
       come a reality when contributions follow their television ap-
       pearances, and they gracefully accept the hospitality and
       kindness of hundreds; the mother's narrative is strangely
       self-denigrating while she extols her daughter's saintly
       character; because her child "was everything to me--my
       very life itself," her daughter's death at fourteen leaves a
       terrible emptiness.

858   Red Shoes for Nancy. Philadelphia: Lippincott, 1955.
       224pp.

       Widowed just before her daughter's birth, she courageous-
       ly faces the child's affliction with lymphohemangioma; she is
       buoyed by her daughter's sunny disposition in spite of the
       deformity and years of surgery and pain, and with pride she
       notes her daughter's growing independence; she and her
       daughter make a joint decision to convert to Catholicism;
       she is touched by the kindness of friends and strangers and
       by community support and generosity.

859   HAMILTON, VIRGINIA
       Everybody Duck; Or, Family Plan to Buenos Aires, with
       Virginia Taylor Klose. New York: McGraw-Hill, 1962.
       207pp.

A Long Island wife and mother of four teen-aged daughters
writes of her adventurous family travels in an adapted am-
phibious landing craft from World War II with three young
men along as crew members; driving through the southern
and western U. S., they continue through Mexico and Central
America, maintaining a relaxed outlook and pace, coping
with occasional dangers, illness, and mechanical breakdowns,
but enthusiastically embracing the months of adventure.

860   HAMILTON-MERRITT, JANE
        A Meditator's Diary; A Western Woman's Unique Experience
        in Thailand Temples.   New York: Harper & Row, 1976.
        154pp.

        A writer, teacher, former war correspondent in Southeast
        Asia, and holder of a Ph. D. in Asian Studies, she attempts
        to describe the inner world of meditation, "this journey to
        eliminate the self"; in Theravada Buddhism, she slowly
        learns serenity, detachment, and timelessness and is reluc-
        tant to leave the fragile harmony she achieves in residence
        at the temple, although she continues meditation after her
        return to the U. S.

861   HAMMOND, SUSAN S.
        Landfalls Remembered.   New York: Barnes, 1963.   285pp.

        The wife of a naval officer, she and her husband are dis-
        tinguished yacht sailors; she describes cruises on the Medi-
        terranean in 1959 and 1960 and four cruises in the 1930's
        which include sightseeing at various ports of call; in 1939
        they join the Harvard expedition, a "crowning experience,"
        retracing the route of Columbus to the Azores and arriving
        in Spain at the close of the Spanish Civil War.

862   HANDY, WILLOWDEAN CHATTERSON
        Forever the Land of Man; An Account of a Visit to the Mar-
        quesas Islands.   New York: Dodd, Mead, 1965.   233pp.

        The wife of an ethnologist, she is a volunteer member of
        her husband's expedition in 1920-1921, accompanying him to
        study women's culture, provide illustrations, and collect
        string figures; she provides lively anecdotes of the "hearty
        females" and the economic reasons for their promiscuity and
        multiple mates; she travels, sketching elaborate tattoo de-
        signs; faced with cultural differences, she notes the effects
        of missionaries and traders, recoils at the natives' open
        sexuality, and admires the "delicate art of gift giving."

863   HANES, MARY (1940-   )
       Lovechild: A Self-Portrait.   Philadelphia: Lippincott, 1972.
       251pp.

          A journalist describes her experiences as the unmarried
       mother of a four-year-old son, exploring her ambivalence
       toward her son and her fears of being a "bad mother"; she
       discusses her ignorance, shy delight, and fantasies of new
       motherhood as she copes as best she can with poverty, ill-
       ness, job worries, day-care arrangements, and her difficul-
       ties accepting the love of a man.

864   HANEY, GERMAINE
       No Reservations; A Personal Narrative by a Woman Who
       Traveled Alone in European Countries Without Reservations.
       Minneapolis: T. S. Denison, 1958. 311pp.

          A weekly columnist and sometime lecturer, she travels
       in Ireland, England, France, Switzerland, Italy, and Spain;
       she is primarily interested in observing and describing the
       people she meets, including a lecherous Welshman, Parisian
       prostitutes, jazz musicians, sinister Venetians, the Pope,
       and Spanish wolves; she balances the sense of being needed
       by her family with the wonder of being alone and free.

865   HANFF, HELENE
       The Duchess of Bloomsbury Street.   Philadelphia: Lippin-
       cott, 1973.   137pp.

          She describes her pilgrimage to London in 1971 after the
       success of 84, Charing Cross Road (see below); met by
       friends and her publisher, she enjoys her celebrity status,
       autograph parties, interviews, passionate sightseeing; she is
       much impressed by the friendliness, hospitality, and thought-
       fulness of those she meets, and chortles "it's all here, ev-
       erything's here."

866   84, Charing Cross Road.   New York: Grossman, 1970.
       97pp.

          A struggling playwright with an interest in rare books
       strikes up a spirited correspondence, reproduced here, with
       a London bookseller in 1949; her delightfully "outrageous
       letters" elicit stiff, proper British replies at first, but the
       exchange warms as she writes to a secretary as well and
       sends food parcels to alleviate postwar shortages; her dream
       of visiting England and "my bookshop" is repeatedly delayed
       and she is shocked to hear of her correspondent's death in
       1968.

867 Underfoot in Show Business. New York: Harper & Row,
     1962. 188pp.

     The daughter of "passionate theatregoers," and herself a
novice playwright, she tells of studies with the Theatre
Guild, writing under Theresa Helburn (see entry #917); she
endures "a fair gamut of garrets" in New York, writes for
television in 1952, writes for magazines, and describes her
friendships with theater people.

868 HANFORD, KATHERINE BURNS
     The Gods of Soldier Mountain; A Story of Pioneer Life in
     Idaho. New York: Exposition, 1955. 233pp.

     Married in 1906, she is excited by the pioneering oppor-
tunities of a homestead and the chance to be a "prairie
amazon woman"; unfortunately, she "lived in hopes while
dying of facts"; she must endure loneliness, an injury due
to an explosion, the birth of her first son assisted only by
a superstitious midwife, financial catastrophe, hardships
raising five children, and her own serious illness; in 1918
she leaves the homestead, bound for Boise.

869 HANNUM, ALBERTA PIERSON (1906-)
     Look Back with Love; A Recollection of the Blue Ridge.
     New York: Vanguard, 1969. 205pp.

     In a largely impersonal yet intimate account, she takes
"a different look at the Appalachian people"; she delights in
the mountain idiom and offers sensitive perceptions of their
hunting, weaving, herb-gathering, and myth-making; her
story includes much historical information.

870 HANSBERRY, LORRAINE (1930-1965)   NAWM
     To Be Young, Gifted and Black; Lorraine Hansberry in Her
     Own Words, adapted by Robert Nemiroff. Englewood Cliffs,
     N.J.: Prentice-Hall, 1969. 266pp.

     The collection by the black playwright consists of auto-
biographical fragments, diary excerpts, letters, and dramatic vignettes written "to put down the stuff of my life"; she
grows up in Chicago, of the middle class but antagonistic
to the "symbols of affluence"; after working on a black
newspaper in New York she turns to drama, full of passionate beliefs and anger, convinced of the urgent need for radical change to eliminate racism in America.

871 HANSEN, KAREN (pseud.)
     see MILLBERG, KAREN SCHWENCKE

872   HANSON, IRENE
        The Wheelbarrow and the Comrade, with Bernard Palmer.
        Chicago: Moody Press, 1973. 187pp.

        She recounts twenty-five years of missionary work, her
        "real life," in China's interior; she possesses cultural in-
        sights due to her unique position as an adopted member of
        a Chinese family; she undertakes evangelical work with two
        Chinese women, enduring much primitive travel but pleased
        by conversions; during World War II she is repatriated but
        returns to China after the war, only to face increasing anti-
        Christian harassment by communists which leads to her de-
        portation; she remains active in the U.S., speaking on be-
        half of the church in China.

873   HARBERT, MARY ANN (1945-   )
        Captivity; How I Survived 44 Months as a Prisoner of the
        Red Chinese, as told to Charles Einstein. New York:
        Delacorte, 1973. 319pp.

        An adventurous, self-reliant college graduate, trained for
        prison rehabilitation work, she joins an old family friend for
        sailing out of Hong Kong in 1968; captured and taken to the
        Peoples Republic of China, separated from her companion,
        she is subjected to tiring, surrealistic, but sometimes amus-
        ing interrogations; she studies the sayings of Mao, and de-
        scribes her relations with interpreters and guards, but with-
        holds acquiescence; hospitalized for illness, she is released
        in 1971 and returns home to her family.

874   HARD, MARGARET STEEL
        A Memory of Vermont; Our Life in the Johnny Appleseed
        Bookshop, 1930-1965. New York: Harcourt, Brace &
        World, 1967. 242pp.

        A delightful account of the establishment of a family book-
        store, the idea of her collegiate daughter; the store is fed
        by family publishing ventures, among them a Vermont travel
        book written with her husband; the store is enlivened by
        visits of literary figures, and she enjoys the friendship of
        Sarah Cleghorn (see companion volume); their total devotion
        to books brings "emancipation" from the family drugstore.

875   HARDIN, ELIZABETH PENDLETON (1839-1895)
        The Private War of Lizzie Hardin; A Kentucky Confederate
        Girl's Diary of the Civil War in Kentucky, Virginia, Ten-
        nessee, Alabama, and Georgia, ed. G. Glenn Clift. Frank-
        fort, Ky.: Kentucky Historical Society, 1963. 306pp.

        Fiercely anti-Yankee, she tells of her emotional defiance
        when the "long-dreaded" Civil War breaks out; she and her

mother and sister are arrested for protesting her grandfather's arrest and cheering secessionist guerrillas; she repeatedly refuses to pledge allegiance to the Union and makes a
dramatic escape through Yankee lines; she describes desolation, lawlessness, and bitter hatred at the war's end and exhibits herself the "supreme disdain of the conquered."

876   HARDING, BERTITA LEONARZ
       Mosaic in the Fountain.   Philadelphia: Lippincott, 1949.
       320pp.

       A writer of Hungarian parentage tells of her cosmopolitan
       childhood in Germany and Mexico in numerous vivid family
       anecdotes and stories of irregular schooling, Mexican civil
       unrest, and her own "alarming lack of emotional balance";
       World War I and political events in Mexico prevent her re-
       turn to Europe, and she finds herself on the threshold of a
       new life in the U. S.

877   HARDISON, IRENE (1917-)
       A Nightingale in the Jungle.   Philadelphia: Dorrance, 1954.
       133pp.

       She is a nurse from California who joins the army at the
       outbreak of World War II; she describes difficult conditions
       in India and in Burma and years of grueling work amid the
       horrors of wounded soldiers; she marries a U. S. soldier in
       1944 in the midst of the jungle war; she returns to the U. S.
       in 1945 and is eventually reunited with her husband.

878   HARDY, MARTHA
       Tatoosh.   New York: Macmillan, 1946.   239pp.

       A "dude school-teacher," she spends one summer as the
       first woman Forest Service fire lookout in the Cascade
       Mountains during the wartime "man-power shortage"; her
       small apprehensions are magnified by the isolation of the
       post, but she needs to prove herself worthy; she loves the
       woods and animals and gradually establishes a sense of home
       there; she describes the drama of a forest fire.

879   HARLOW, NORA
       Sharing the Children; Village Child Rearing Within the City.
       New York: Harper & Row, 1975.   154pp.

       When her daughter is born in 1965, she feels burdened
       with loneliness and heavy responsibility; she organizes neigh-
       borhood mothers to provide a co-operative day care center;
       she tells of adjustments to their different styles of parenting,

of their efforts at community organizing, of their confrontations with authorities in an attempt to find space, of their
attempts to involve fathers--all of which build a strong sense
of community.

880   HARMAN, JEANNE PERKINS
       The Love Junk.   New York: Appleton-Century-Crofts, 1951.
       312pp.

       A former editor from the staff of Life magazine, she
       marries and, with her husband, converts a barge into a
       houseboat in the Virgin Islands; she tells of their growing
       sightseeing business and writes entertaining anecdotes of
       neighbors, servants, and tourists in this light view of the
       idyllic life.

881   Such Is Life.   New York: Crowell, 1956.   210pp.

       A staff member of Life magazine for seven years, she
       describes her beginnings as a green Smith graduate, her
       first story, later interviews with prominent and interesting
       people, her stint as a Hollywood reporter, the "struggle
       against Communist infiltrators" in journalism circles, and
       the "peculiar campus atmosphere" of Life.

882   HARMON, CHARLOTTE
       Broadway in a Barn, with Rosemary Taylor.   New York:
       Crowell, 1957.   242pp.

       In a lighthearted account, she describes becoming a the-
       atrical producer with her husband and founding a Connecticut
       summer stock company in 1946; after restoring a hotel and
       a theater, she tells of the vicissitudes of coddling the stars,
       chaperoning the apprentices, placating the natives' "New
       England reserve"; in addition, she becomes a director and
       playwright; when her husband's health fails, she continues
       to produce alone.

883   HARRIMAN, MARGARET CASE
       Blessed Are the Debonair.   New York: Rinehart, 1956.
       254pp.

       In a lighthearted but articulate account, the daughter of
       Frank Case describes her youth as "a motherless hotel
       child" at the Algonquin; secure in a close, understanding
       relationship with her father, she enjoys the attention of the
       Algonquin's clientele and tells delightful anecdotes about
       them; after two years in France, she works on Vanity Fair
       and The New Yorker, surrounded by the bright and cele-

brated; her two marriages are made difficult by the closed
club of the Case family; after poverty-stricken domesticity
during the depression, she returns to magazine writing; she
closes with her father's death in 1946.

884   HARRINGTON, MARY RHODA SHINN (1869-1957)
       Adventuring With God, as told to Vivian W. Perry.   North
       Hollywood, Cal.:   Vivian W. Perry, 1962.   129pp.

       A Methodist with a Quaker background, she marries in
       1888 and joins her husband in missionary work, settling in
       Chile and later in Bolivia with her young children, teaching
       in and directing a school there; widowed in 1907, she mar-
       ries her late husband's brother and together they pursue
       their educational work in Chile; after their retirement in
       California, they continue in religious education and she re-
       mains active teaching "Americanization" classes for the
       Spanish-speaking.

885   HARRIS, BERNICE KELLY (1894-1973)
       Southern Savory.   Chapel Hill: University of North Carolina
       Press, 1964.   256pp.

       In brief vignettes, she provides portraits of "certain kin-
       folks," neighbors, a teacher who is the object of a school-
       girl crush; her married life is happy but marred by her
       husband's refusal to have children, and she begins writing
       newspaper articles and novels, initially "stunned by the ac-
       claim" given her writing; she conducts interviews for the
       Federal Writers' Project, speaks, and attends writers' con-
       ferences; after her husband's stroke, her "life was defined
       by my invalid's needs" until 1950.

886   HARRIS, MAE EVANS
       You Can Alcan.   Middleburg, Va.:   Denlinger's, 1960.
       96pp.

       She recounts three trips from Washington, D.C. to Alaska
       in 1950, 1951, and 1955 via the Alcan highway; traveling with
       her husband and two children, she enjoys the family adven-
       ture and the awesome scenery as they learn the hard way
       about variable road conditions.

887   HARRIS, RADIE
       Radie's World.   New York: Putnam, 1975.   288pp.

       A Hollywood columnist and radio interviewer opens with
       brief glimpses of her secure childhood, her loss of a leg
       at fourteen, her determination to avoid pity, and her first

job as a reporter; later she tells of a thirty-year love affair with a New York producer; but most of her gossipy account is a rushing stream of anecdotes about her friendships
and acquaintances among numerous movie and theater celebrities.

888   HART, DORIS
        Tennis With Hart.   Philadelphia: Lippincott, 1955.   192pp.

        A noted tennis player describes a childhood knee infection
        that mobilizes her family in a rehabilitation effort so suc-
        cessful that she enters her first tournament in 1936; touring
        regularly with strong family support, she plays exhibitions
        for the USO in 1945, and wins championships in Europe,
        Australia, and South Africa; she wins Wimbledon in 1951 and
        Forest Hills in 1954; tennis is her "whole life."

889   HART, MARION RICE (1891-)
        I Fly as I Please.   New York: Vanguard, 1953.   247pp.

        Licensed as a pilot in 1946, she relates her adventures
        in seven years of flying; she cherishes her "freedom in the
        air," experimenting with cross-country travels, transcon-
        tinental races, gliders, and flights to Alaska and the Carib-
        bean Circuit.

890   HART, SARA LIEBENSTEIN (1869-)
        The Pleasure Is Mine; An Autobiography.   Chicago: Valen-
        tine-Newman, 1947.   288pp.

        A prominent Chicago social reformer, she tells of her
        rather conventional childhood, although she is a willful
        "tomboy"; deeply influenced by Jane Addams (see companion
        volume), she becomes active in the National Council of Jew-
        ish Women after her marriage and motherhood; widowed in
        1901, she becomes heavily involved in social service, juve-
        nile justice, and child welfare in Chicago, continuing to work
        with great zeal and joy even after her second marriage to a
        wealthy businessman; she includes appreciative portraits of
        fellow social reformers.

891   HARTMAN, MAY WEISSER (1900-)
        I Gave My Heart.   New York: Citadel, 1960.   350pp.

        The daughter of Russian Jewish immigrants tells of her
        first job at 14 in a neighborhood orphanage; a fine organizer
        with energy and enthusiasm, she becomes superintendent of
        the Israel Orphan Asylum at 23, and tells of years of fund-
        raising and hard work; she marries the founder of the asy-

lum, a philanthropic judge, in 1928; they devote their lives
to work for orphans; widowed with two children, she assumes
even greater responsibilities.

892   HASLEY, LUCILLE CHARLOTTE HARDMAN
       Saints and Snapdragons. New York: Sheed & Ward, 1958.
       214pp.

       In a series of humorous personal essays, she writes of
family togetherness, of America's tastes in music and reading, of her correspondence with Catholic writer Frank Sheed,
of emotional crises, of random school memories, and of
advocates of positive thinking.

893   HASSELBLAD, MARVA (1937?-)
       Lucky-Lucky, with Dorothy Brandon. New York: M. Evans,
       1966. 220pp.

       The daughter of a missionary doctor fulfills a lifelong
dream of service when she goes to Vietnam in 1962 as a
nurse; her initial romantic expectations give way to the
realities of insufficient medical facilities, long hours, frequent deaths, and insecurity as war incidents threaten to
come closer; her anecdotes of numerous patients reveal a
deep sympathy for the Vietnamese people and "tremendous
satisfaction" in her work among the villagers; emerging
"wiser and tougher," she departs with mixed feelings of
sorrow and hope.

894   HASTINGS, HELEN KING (1903?-)
       A Little Widow Is a Dangerous Thing, with Jean Muir. New
       York: Putnam, 1959. 255pp.

       Widowed at forty-three, she decides to maintain the fam-
ily cattle business alone on a Florida "flatwoods" farm while
her son attends college; having "worked like hell all my
life," she continues with gusto, coping with the dangers of
widowhood, acknowledging her ambivalence toward a flamboyant suitor, and finally passing responsibility on to her
son when he marries and she can feel that her "job was
done."

895   HATFIELD, INGE
       Life with the Real McCoy. New York: Vantage, 1965.
       125pp.

       She enters the U.S. as a German immigrant in 1956; she
becomes deeply committed to a jobless, insecure suitor with
a drinking problem and marries him, providing strong emo-

tional support and a stable home to help him re-establish
himself as an editor until his death in 1964; she strives to
become a "perfect American."

896   HATHAWAY, KATHARINE BUTLER (1890-1942)
        The Journals and Letters of the Little Locksmith.   New
        York: Coward-McCann, 1946.   395pp.

        A writer and artist who endures life with a deformed
body, she is revealed as a woman of intricate, introspective, often dark moods and intense emotional hunger; she
studies and works in Paris, weathering the "terrible disappointment" of a shattered love; she later marries and leads
"a very retired cozy life" in Paris and then in New England,
suffering further emotional crises as her health deteriorates.

897   HATLER, GRACE
        Land of the Lighthouse, as told to Dorothy Molan.   Valley
        Forge, Pa.:   Judson Press, 1966.   110pp.

        An American Baptist missionary teacher in El Salvador,
she sees herself as an enthusiastic part of the challenging
missionary effort; she tells of "persons and needs and min-
istries" in anecdotes that focus on her Bible School students.

898   HAVEMEYER, LOUISINE WALDRONE ELDER (1855-1929)
                                                        NAW
        Sixteen to Sixty: Memoirs of a Collector.   New York: priv.
        pr. for the family of Mrs. H. O. Havemeyer and The Met-
        ropolitan Museum of Art, 1961.   267pp.

        A prominent art collector describes her Sunday musicales
for distinguished guests, her travels abroad for acquiring
art objects, her acquaintances among painters and fellow
collectors; she enjoys discussing the acquisition of certain
works, often depending on the advice and friendship of painter and collector Mary Cassatt.

899   HAVOC, JUNE
        Early Havoc.   New York: Simon and Schuster, 1959.   313pp.

        An actress on stage and television, and the sister of Gypsy
Rose Lee (see entry #1209), she recalls her childhood in
vaudeville, part of a family act run by her ruthless, ambitious mother; she alternates childhood memories with
scenes from a grueling, degrading dance marathon; alienated,
she escapes her mother at 13 by marrying and touring during
the last dying days of vaudeville.

900   HAWKES, ADELINE HEIN
       The Broom Behind the Door.   Boston: Meador, 1949.
       361pp.

       After memories of a brief happy family life, she offers
       a child's perspective on her mother's death and on her anxi-
       ety living with a dour, dishonest, and violent housekeeper;
       forced to live with intimidation, fear, and poverty, she is
       finally united with her guardian, Pauline Durant, a founder
       of Wellesley College; she feels grateful yet uneasy and
       struggles to overcome social ignorance and lack of educa-
       tion; she closes the book with the final illness of her guardi-
       an; the account is an odd mixture of present and past tense.

901   HAWKINS, CORA FREAR (1887-)
       Buggies, Blizzards, and Babies.   Ames, Iowa: Iowa State
       University Press, 1971.   191pp.

       The daughter of an Iowa country doctor weaves a family
       tale of her father's rural patients and her mother's "dedica-
       tion as a doctor's wife"; as a child, she is fascinated by
       her father's profession and she notes his strong influence on
       her life when she later pursues scientific studies and teaches
       school; she cares for her father during his terminal illness.

902   HAYES, CATHERINE
       The Ape in Our House.   New York: Harper, 1951.   246pp.

       In 1947 she and her psychologist husband adopt an infant
       chimpanzee, determined to raise it like a human child and
       observe the results; her "Viki stories" chronicle the chimp's
       progress in motor development, social responses, imitation,
       and "speech."

903   HAYES, HELEN (1900-)
       A Gift of Joy, with Lewis Funke.   New York: M. Evans,
       1965.   254pp.

       Her account is a blend of "reminiscence and quotation,"
       organized thematically; she writes chapters on her beloved
       husband, fame, her dedication to walking, her personal at-
       tachment to Shakespeare, her favorite scenes, gardening,
       religious faith, childrearing, the fruits of solitude, age,
       work, acting as "giving of self"; she reveals a love of artic-
       ulate and sensitive expression.

904   On Reflection: An Autobiography, with Sandford Dody.   New
       York: M. Evans, 1968.   253pp.

Her book is presented as an offering to her grandchildren; the "First Lady of the Theatre" describes her mother's total dedication to Hayes' stage career; she describes her warm relationships with her early stage colleagues, her quick success, her fierce commitment to professionalism; she reflects a great deal on her marriage to a husband who was at the same time a boy and a genius; she writes at length about her two children and about the death of her daughter at 19; it is an articulate, sensitive account.

905   HAYMES, NORA EDDINGTON FLYNN (1924-)
Errol and Me, as told to Cy Rice. New York: New American Library, 1960. 176pp.

The second wife of actor Errol Flynn tells briefly of her childhood; naïve and unpretentious, unwittingly procured for Flynn, she meets him at 19 and becomes his secretary, attracted by luxury, glamour, and culture; although she loves him, she consents to an affair only after she's raped; lonely, unhappy, and pregnant, she secures a marriage but lives with their two children apart from Flynn, troubled by his drugs and drinking and angered by his other women; she tells of happiness marred by the horror of beatings and of her two suicide attempts; finally divorcing Flynn in 1949, she marries a singer; she closes with Flynn's death in 1959.

906   HAYWARD, HELEN HARRY
The Other Foot. New York: Vantage, 1951. 122pp.

The daughter of a "fiery" Methodist minister, she tells of a childhood in a preacher's family, completely centered on her father; she describes "the lean ministerial years," dreary revival meetings, various parishioners, and rigid restrictions.

907   HAZELTON, NIKA STANDEN
Reminiscence and Ravioli. New York: Morrow, 1946. 148pp.

She describes the dedication of her rotund Italian relatives to good food and drink; her childhood summers are spent in a small village near Rome and her affectionate memories center on an aunt who is a fine cook and an uncle who is an appreciative diner; the account includes recipes.

908   HEAD, EDITH
The Dress Doctor, with Jane Kesner Ardmore. Boston: Little, Brown, 1959. 249pp.

The chief fashion designer of Paramount Pictures tells of her youth in mining camps, her college years, her job as a French teacher, her marriage and widowhood; delighted by Hollywood's flamboyance and convinced of the power of clothes, she learns much from the women and men she dresses for films, night clubs, television, and opera and recounts details of her work with celebrities; she becomes the first woman and the first without a European background to attain her position, winning several Oscars.

909   HEALY, MARY LANIGAN
      Spots and Wrinkles.   Garden City, N.Y.:   McMullen Books, 1957.   159pp.

      In brief random family sketches originally published as newspaper columns, a mother of nine describes the daily "morning madness," school activities, her teen-agers' energy, neighborhood events, her hopes for her children's futures; the Catholic Church is an integral part of her family's daily life.

910   HEATHER
      Heather: Confessions of a Witch, as told to Hans Holzer. New York: Mason & Lipscomb, 1975.   226pp.

      After a youth marked by puzzling incidents, unusual sexual powers, and extra-sensory perceptions, she accepts an invitation to explore witchcraft in New York City; fascinated, she studies the lore and quickly becomes a leader after her initiation, finding security in the coven; she uses her occult powers to attract and keep a man, but using her power for evil brings its own problems; her account is ostensibly straightforward but she does not resist the temptation to sensationalize.

911   HECKMAN, HAZEL
      Island in the Sound.   Seattle: University of Washington Press, 1967.   284pp.

      She settles on a Puget Sound island in 1950 with her husband and son, "summer people" who stay; their lives are enriched by their "admirable interdependence" with neighbors, and her charming anecdotes of the island community are colored by sensitivity and warmth; responding to the appeal of this "classless simplicity of living," she works on an island history.

912   Island Year.   Seattle: University of Washington Press, 1972. 255pp.

A "week-ender," she focuses on nature on a Washington island; she describes her explorations and observations, noting the "dependable rhythm of natural succession" as well as the "creeping destruction" wrought by the developers.

913   HEDGEMAN, ANNA ARNOLD (1899-)
       The Trumpet Sounds: A Memoir of Negro Leadership.   New
       York: Holt, Rinehart, & Winston, 1964.   202pp.

Reared in Minnesota in a family that stresses religion and education, she is the "first Negro student" at Hamline College; teaching at Rust College in 1922, she sees the "horror of educational denial"; she works in several YWCA posts, fighting northern racism; she holds a government position in 1944 and is the first black and the first woman to serve on a New York City mayor's cabinet in 1954; she is an editor and columnist for a New York black newspaper, travels to Ghana to meet with black women, and is an organizer for the 1963 March on Washington, continuing the struggles against racism and sexism.

914   HEGE, RUTH (1905?-)
       We Two Alone.   New York: Nelson, 1965.   192pp.

A Baptist missionary and lecturer since 1932, she tells of her four-day ordeal after being wounded and captured by Congo terrorists in 1964; she recalls her friendship with a fellow missionary who is killed in the attack, and their work among the villagers at the mission station; she is hidden and protected by loyal village friends and finally makes a dramatic escape by U.N. helicopter.

915   HEGEMANN, ELIZABETH COMPTON (1897-1962)
       Navajo Trading Days.   Albuquerque: University of New
       Mexico Press, 1963.   388pp.

First married to a western Park Ranger, she lives on the rim of the Grand Canyon, savoring old pioneer styles, building friendships among the Indians, learning Navajo weaving; covering the period from 1925 to 1939, she includes descriptions of native homes and customs, the local terrain and history; in 1929, she and a later husband take over a trading post, and she tells of Navajo customers and friends; sympathetic and receptive, she admires the intimate relationship between the land and the native Americans.

916   HEINER, MARIE HAYS (1907-)
       Hearing Is Believing.   Cleveland: World, 1949.   126pp.

She describes her sudden loss of hearing at nineteen; at
first embarrassed and reluctant to admit her handicap, she
searches in the U. S. and in Europe for a cure; she realis-
tically notes the need for more assistance for the deaf and
works for national organization; she becomes a wife and
mother and offers encouragement to others.

917   HELBURN, THERESA (1887-1959)   NAWM
A Wayward Quest; The Autobiography of Theresa Helburn.
Boston: Little, Brown, 1960. 344pp.

A bright child, she loves theatre and begins her career
as playwright and poet; she writes of her stay in Europe,
meeting Duncan (see entry #609), and Stein; at 28, her future is still uncertain; she becomes drama critic for the
Nation; in 1919 she is an organizer of the Theatre Guild and
describes 40 years as its Executive Director; she tells of its
peak in the 1920's, successes, failures, the battle against
censorship, and the later World War II successes of Oklahoma! and Carousel.

918   HELLMAN, LILLIAN (1905-)
Pentimento: A Book of Portraits.   Boston: Little, Brown,
1973. 297pp.

She offers a series of superb, evocative, stunning portraits on family ambience, adolescent ecstasy and pain, lifelong love and loyalty for a childhood friend, the theatre, the
ambiguity of a turtle's survival; "I wanted to see what there
was there for me once, what is there for me now."

919   Scoundrel Time.   Boston: Little, Brown, 1976. 155pp.

This is a memoir of the 1950's; her account is centered
on her appearance before the House Un-American Activities
Committee, and the pain of liberals' and intellectuals' inadequate response to the witch hunts and blacklists of the 1950's;
hers is an act of personal and cultural memory.

920   An Unfinished Woman: A Memoir.   Boston: Little, Brown,
1969. 280pp.

A noted playwright and author writes a fine, sensitive account with chapters on her parents, rebellious college years,
aimless time married and reading manuscripts in Hollywood;
she includes diary excerpts for stays in Spain (1937), Moscow (1944) and Europe (1967); she describes the good years
on her farm with Dashiell Hammett; she explores her com-

plex relationships with two black women, her childhood nurse
and her housekeeper.

921   HELM, EDITH BENHAM
       The Captains and the Kings.   New York: Putnam, 1954.
       307pp.

       A White House social secretary for twenty-five years, she
       grows up amid the glamour of Newport society and an educa-
       tion in Paris; she works at several embassies before serving
       Mrs. Wilson at the White House in 1915, aiding President
       Wilson at the Paris Peace Conference in 1919, working for
       Eleanor Roosevelt (see entry #1738), and working for Bess
       Truman; in addition to writing numerous "inside" stories,
       she provides a tangential view of politically prominent figures
       and major historical events.

922   HELMERICKS, CONSTANCE (1918-   )
       Australian Adventure.   Englewood Cliffs, N.J.:   Prentice-
       Hall, 1971.   357pp.

       With her two mechanically adept teen-age daughters, she
       spends a year "in the great Outback" traveling with a Jeep
       and tent; she describes in detail the flora, fauna, and desert
       conditions of Australia and the Tasmanian jungle where they
       hike; as they meet local people and other adventurers, she
       notes that it is "such a masculine Society"; she feels she
       and her daughters learn much.

923   Down the Wild River North.   Boston: Little, Brown, 1968.
       501pp.

       A homemaker, breadwinner, and mother of twelve- and
       fifteen-year-old daughters, she plans a canoe expedition to
       the Arctic Ocean to revitalize her life; relishing "the chance
       to be young out in nature," she projects a fine sense of the
       glories and dangers of the wilderness; she provides mar-
       velous portraits of people along the river and a sensitive
       examination of her relationship with her daughters, their
       courage and growth after two summers on the river; noting
       that her girls "would now always belong to two worlds," she
       reflects on their shared times of "tremendous happiness."

924   The Flight of the Arctic Tern, with Harmon Helmericks.
       Boston: Little, Brown, 1952.   321pp.

       She and her husband explore the Canadian and Alaskan
       Arctic by seaplane, collecting mammal specimens and pro-
       ducing films for later lecture tours; their base is a log cabin

home on an Alaskan lake; they stay a winter season to make
a documentary about Eskimo life, and establish close friendships among the villagers; she reflects on the place of hu-
mans in the wilderness, enjoying "a life of much danger but
of much living."

925   We Live in the Arctic, with Harmon Helmericks.   Boston:
      Little, Brown, 1947.   329pp.

      "Amateur explorers," she and her husband canoe northern
      rivers to the Arctic Ocean; they spend a year with no other
      human contact, building a cabin for winter, enjoying the
      satisfactions of hard physical work, learning survival tech-
      niques as the need for food looms large; her account closes
      with the spring breakup of the ice.

926   HEMINGWAY, MARY WELSH (1908-)
      How It Was.   New York: Knopf, 1976.   537pp.

      After the freedom of an outdoor childhood in northern
      Minnesota, she becomes a reporter, delightfully brash in
      her encounters with Lord Beaverbrook in London, serious
      in her coverage of the 1938 Munich Conference, vivid in
      her descriptions of the Blitz; in 1944 she meets Hemingway,
      who soon becomes "the most important part of me"; his
      fourth wife, she is exuberant, witty, "aggressive, impatient
      and unsympathetic to feminine niceties"; she describes their
      outdoor life in Idaho, their love of the sea when living in
      Cuba, their travels in Africa, embracing the negative as
      well as the positive in her marriage; after Hemingway's
      suicide, she served as his literary executor.

927   HENDERSON, GLENNA
      My Name Is Legion.   Minneapolis: Bethany Fellowship,
      1972.   128pp.

      The author recounts her personal struggles following the
      revelation in 1968 that she's possessed by "a demon spirit";
      she acknowledges that unbalanced emotional states and un-
      focused religious feelings characterize her youth and her
      years as a wife and mother of six; she describes in detail
      numerous harrowing sessions with her minister to exorcise
      a variety of demons who speak with different personalities;
      her final victory is marked by renewed physical and emo-
      tional health and by religious security as her life is "utter-
      ly changed."

928   HENDERSON, NANCY
      Out of the Curtained World.   Garden City, N.Y.: Double-
      day, 1972.   276pp.

"Marked for the convent" at an early age, she enters as
a postulate eager for education and the opportunity for missionary service; she describes the myriad adjustments to
convent routine and outlook; she experiences a gradual build-
up of tension, doubts about her vocation, stress in relationships among sisters, and she feels her desire to learn is
inconsistent with the attitude of her order; after six years,
she leaves.

929   HENLEY, NETTIE McCORMICK (1874-   )
       The Home Place. New York: Vantage, 1955. 182pp.

       Writing in a simple, straightforward style, she recalls
her life, "pretty close to average," in rural North Carolina
for the benefit of her children and grandchildren; she tells
of the love and security in her family home, of quilting
parties, of shared field work and other farm tasks, of the
family's religious beliefs and practices, of children's games,
of school, of musical pastimes.

930   HENRICHSEN, MARGARET KIMBALL (1900-   )
       Seven Steeples. Boston: Houghton Mifflin, 1953. 238pp.

       After her husband's death, she decides to enter the minis-
try and takes a position as pastor for two back-country
Maine churches; she describes her gradual acceptance by
the taciturn parishioners and the slow but warm encouragement as relationships grow; she tells of her love for the
countryside, learning to cope with the winters, her terror
of a forest fire, her joy in study and pastoral care.

931   HENRY, MARY ROBLEE
       A Farmhouse in Provence. New York: Knopf, 1969. 196pp.

       American-born but educated in Europe, she is a Vogue
editor who marries a French diplomat and is "transplanted
by marriage to a new ecology"; she describes the challenge
of restoring a ruin, establishing a subtle understanding of
the land, the village, the local history, and the people; telling of hospitality centered on food and neighbors, she rejoices with them in the first grape harvest and the rebirth
of the land.

932   HERSEY, JEAN (1902-   )
       Change in the Wind, with Robert Hersey. New York: Scrib-
       ner, 1972. 248pp.

       An author of gardening books, she writes a quiet and sen-
sitive account of her move from Connecticut to North Carolina

at her husband's retirement; delights of gardening and family visits at their new home are temporarily destroyed by fire, but she emphasizes the positive aspects of their rebuilding; writing with a relish for flexibility, inner change, and growth, she describes her intense joy in daily living; she and her husband write alternate chapters.

933   A Sense of Seasons. New York: Dodd, Mead, 1964. 307pp.

In a quiet, reflective account suffused with love, she describes a twelve-month cycle on her Connecticut land, "a miraculous segment of time"; from the dreams and preparations of January, to the joyful awareness of each present moment with visiting grandchildren, to the pleasures of summer gardening, and finally to the next return indoors, she savors and shares the domestic details of each season.

934   The Shape of a Year. New York: Scribner, 1967. 242pp.

A writer and gardener, she prepares a month-by-month chronicle of a new year, focusing on the quality of life, the rich meaning in events; she is an acute observer of nature, welcomes "intimate contact with the earth," enjoys the magic in certain moments of insight, and compares the "alternating tension and relaxation" of nature and of human affairs; her account is suffused with deep happiness and contentment.

935   These Rich Years; A Journal of Retirement, with Robert Hersey. New York: Scribner, 1969. 270pp.

Writing three years after her husband's retirement, she reflects on retirement's implications both for her and for them; she discovers new rewards in masculine and feminine roles, in becoming reacquainted with male company, and in restructuring her day to cherish private time; setting new goals, she finds joy in simple daily tasks, enjoys entertaining and travel and gardening, and devotes herself to continued "inner growing"; her chapters, alternating with those of her husband, reveal an articulate, perceptive woman who welcomes self-discovery.

936   HEWINS, CAROLINE MARIA (1846-1926)
        Caroline M. Hewins, Her Book. Boston: Horn Book, 1954.
        107pp.

A pioneer children's librarian offers random memories of her childhood in a Massachusetts village; she teaches for a time; "A Mid-Century Child and Her Books" contains recollections of favorite books and her gradual acquisition of a personal library.

937   HEWITT, ALBA ASHBY
       Riding the Rockies. New York: Vantage, 1957. 231pp.

       Told in 1922 that she might live only a year, she finds
       that rugged trail riding and pack trips on horseback in the
       mountains provide her with a sense of renewal and exhilar-
       ation; recounting numerous trips in vivid detail, she de-
       scribes her female companions, deer hunting, the challenge
       and magnificence of the mountains; after "a busy business
       life" and an interim without riding, she returns to the
       mountains after widowhood and financial reverses to find
       "time and calmness of spirit."

938   HICKS, ESTELLE BELL (1891-1971)
       The Golden Apples: Memoirs of a Retired Teacher.   New
       York: Exposition, 1959. 75pp.

       She writes of "the lighter strain of events" after her re-
       tirement in 1957 from public school teaching in Mobile, Ala-
       bama; she tells of miscellaneous incidents from her career
       as a science teacher in grades one through ten.

939   HICKS, JEAN JOHNSON
       Where Next, Lady Thuppence?   Philadelphia: Dorrance,
       1973. 251pp.

       This is the story of two married women who share vaca-
       tion adventures without their husbands beginning in 1956; in
       an exclamatory style, the author writes of their travels in
       northern Michigan, Canada, Wisconsin, the southwestern
       U.S., the west coast, Florida, and Jamaica, from resort
       life to fishing expeditions.

940   HIGBY, MARY JANE
       Tune in Tomorrow, or, How I Found the Right to Happiness
       with Our Gal Sunday, Stella Dallas, John's Other Wife, and
       Other Sudsy Radio Serials. New York: Cowles, 1968.
       226pp.

       In "semiautobiographical form," a daytime serial star
       during the 1930's, 1940's, and 1950's writes a lively, anec-
       dotal account of her auditions, various roles, and hard work;
       she includes material on the history of radio.

941   HIGGINS, MARGUERITE (1920-1966)   NAWM
       News Is a Singular Thing. Garden City, N.Y.: Doubleday,
       1955. 256pp.

       This Pulitzer Prize winning foreign affairs correspondent
       enters journalism in 1941; she is sent to Paris in 1944 and

covers the liberation of Buchenwald and of Dachau; in post-
war Czechoslovakia, she describes political terror and total-
itarianism; she covers the Soviet blockade, the Berlin air-
lift, and the Korean War; a strong anticommunist, she
emerges as competitive and ambitious.

942   Our Vietnam Nightmare.   New York: Harper & Row, 1965.
      314pp.

      An author and foreign correspondent for the New York
      Herald Tribune, she goes to Vietnam in 1963 to describe
      the "American myth and Vietnamese realities"; she travels
      extensively, interviews people in the countryside, speaks
      with Madame Nhu; adding historical material, she offers her
      political observations and opinions of the "muddle" of U.S.
      policy based on her strong anti-Communist beliefs and the
      cultural misunderstandings she perceives.

943   Red Plush and Black Bread.   Garden City, N.Y.:   Double-
      day, 1955.   256pp.

      This is a "reporter's report" of a ten-week journey in
      Russia, including Soviet Asia and Siberia; skilled at detailed
      observation and sensitive to the politics of post-Stalin Russia
      and post-war communism, she gains interviews with a bal-
      lerina, a poet, and an athlete, evaluates living standards,
      and attempts to speak with ordinary citizens to break through
      "Russian secretiveness"; sixteen brief arrests prove to be
      educational.

944   War in Korea; The Report of a Woman Combat Correspond-
      ent.   Garden City, N.Y.:   Doubleday, 1951.   223pp.

      A reporter for the New York Herald Tribune, she spends
      nearly six months at the front in 1950, part of a "personal
      crusade" to prove the abilities of woman journalists; she
      must sometimes struggle to communicate her reports to the
      U.S. and is once briefly banished from the front because she
      is a woman; she observes the political influences on the war
      and closes with an anticommunist exhortation for prepared-
      ness.

945   HIGHT, GLADYS
      African Tempo.   New York: Exposition, 1951.   132pp.

      A dancer and teacher travels to Africa in 1948 to study
      native dance for six months; traveling alone throughout the
      continent, she attends dances and ceremonies and enjoys the
      hospitality of the people, although she is troubled by segre-

gation and racial tension in South Africa; she is fascinated
by "the mystery that is Africa."

946   HILDEGARDE
        see SELL, HILDEGARD LORETTA (1906?-)

947   HILDRETH, EDITH WARDELL
        Between Bay and Ocean.   New York: Vantage, 1960.   92pp.

    In an unfocused and largely impersonal account written in
the third person, she tells of living in Puerto Rico from
1906 to 1921 as the wife of a missionary doctor, raising
three children and organizing maternal care services; she
later settles on Long Island, teaches Sunday School and attends international Bible School conferences; a widow and
grandmother at the close, she maintains a strong sense of
family tradition.

948   HILF, MARY ASIA (1874-)
        No Time for Tears, as told to Barbara Bourns.   New York:
        Yoseloff, 1964.   271pp.

    "A simple woman" writes of her joy and sorrow, her
prosperity and hard times; born in Russia and raised according to strong Jewish tradition, she travels to Warsaw at fifteen to learn millinery, opening a business in her home town
at sixteen; the family joins her successful brother in Milwaukee in 1897, and after her marriage, she enjoys prosperity working as a milliner in her husband's store and serving
others in civic and charitable organizations; the depression
brings financial reverses and when she is widowed, she must
support herself, her widowed daughter, and her grandson,
yet she continues to be concerned about the welfare of others.

949   HILL, PATRICIA (1921-)
        The Pit and the Century Plant.   New York: Harper, 1955.
        276pp.

    A model in Paris, she decides to purchase an abandoned
French farmhouse; as she clears the underbrush and works
to renovate the house, she gradually comes to know a neighbor woman's family, and her reflective vignettes explore her
daily encounters with and intimate knowledge of the villagers;
reproaching herself upon her return to the U.S., she goes
back to France, looking forward to the pleasure of a future
there.

950   HILLES, HELEN TRAIN
       Farm Wanted. New York: Julian Messner, 1951. 236pp.

       "The most urban person alive," she describes her fam-
       ily's purchase of a summer home in the country; she offers
       humorous anecdotes of learning by mistakes, "one of the
       most satisfying of struggles," renovating a house, raising
       children, gardening, and keeping livestock.

951   HINCKLEY, ANITA W. (1884-)
       Wickford Memories. Boston: Branden Press, 1972. 118pp.

       She opens with family history, then tells of her childhood
       in a small Rhode Island village; in nostalgic anecdotes, she
       writes of her neighbors, the family farm, "a land of plen-
       ty," and of a European grand tour during which she is
       courted by a Russian grand duke who is unfortunately not
       free to marry her; she describes "the source of my happi-
       ness" in her marriage and motherhood.

952   HINDMAN, JUANITA LEWIS
       Postpioneers. Fort Worth, Tex.: Branch-Smith, 1973.
       173pp.

       In a disorganized account, she offers reminiscences of
       her Texas childhood; after college and schoolteaching, she
       marries a cowboy and raises her children in the Southwest
       that she loves; her brief anecdotes center on her pioneer
       life.

953   HIRSCH, ABBY
       The Great Carmen Miranda Look-alike Contest & Other
       Bold-faced Lies, with Dale Burg. New York: St. Martin's,
       1974. 224pp.

       A Manhattan press agent writes a flippant, anecdotal ac-
       count of her career, replete with frenzied activity and bi-
       zarre characters; she serves Jacqueline Susann and other
       authors, and provides publicity for television, radio, and
       film clients; in addition, she works on several political
       campaigns.

954   HIRSCH, SHULA
       An American Housewife in Israel. New York: Citadel,
       1962. 128pp.

       A teacher of Jewish history tells with much enthusiasm
       of her "exciting trip to Israel" during the summer of 1961
       with her family; she describes "keeping house in Tel Aviv,"

her extensive traveling, people she meets, and a visit to a
kibbutz; the account contains a wide variety of random observations.

955   HOBART, ALICE TISDALE NOURSE (1882-1967)
       Gusty's Child. New York: Longmans, Green, 1959. 343pp.

       A novelist, she presents highly articulate reflections on
"a long journey in one short lifetime"; having grown up in
a close family "sufficient unto ourselves," she loses both
parents in her youth, and after three years at the University
of Chicago, in 1909 she joins her sister, a missionary teacher in China; after travels in Russia, she too teaches in
China, then marries an American businessman there in 1914;
she courageously accepts living in frontier conditions, turning to writing to record vivid experiences and to satisfy an
inner need, a "habit of reflection" bred by isolation; driven
from China by political turmoil, they settle in the U.S.;
she describes the genesis of each of her best-selling novels;
she achieves a delicate balance between self-assertion as a
writer and adjustments to domesticity in different cultures.

956   HOBBS, ANNE (1908?-)
       Tisha: The Story of a Young Teacher in the Alaska Wilder-
       ness, as told to Robert Specht. New York: St. Martin's,
       1976. 358pp.

       This is a charming story of her trip to a remote mining
town in 1927; impressed with the "bigness" and "rawness"
of the countryside, she is shocked at anti-Indian racism and
at conditions of Indian life; courageously she withstands community pressure when she falls in love with a half-breed;
she adopts two Indian children after a dramatic winter chase
to rescue them; the account closes with marriage in her future.

957   HOBBS, LISA
       I Saw Red China. New York: McGraw-Hill, 1966. 217pp.

       A journalist, in 1965 she becomes the first woman from
a U.S. newspaper (the San Francisco Examiner) to enter the
People's Republic of China since the 1949 revolution; entering illegally as an Australian tourist, she visits factories,
communes, cultural events, archaeological sites, and she
presents numerous images of contemporary China; attempting
a balanced view, she is much impressed by the people's
dignity and warmth and leaves convinced of the necessity for
peace and mutual understanding.

958   India, India. New York: McGraw-Hill, 1967. 216pp.

A journalist, she travels to India with high expectations,
searching for the "fire of the Indian spirit"; she interviews
a filmmaker, a missionary, educators, and officials and
takes special notes of the Indian woman's role and status;
to her dismay, she finds apathy, corruption, and despair
and vividly describes profound human misery and degradation, in marked contrast to what she had found in China
(see I Saw Red China).

959   Running Towards Life. New York: McGraw-Hill, 1971.
147pp.

An Australian-born journalist tells of "one full year of
ambivalence, probing, introspection" in 1967 when she and
her American husband and her two sons settle in a Vancouv-
er Island summer home; removed from urban pressure, she
restructures her time and struggles to find herself; appalled
by the tensions upon her return to city life, she moves permanently to the wilderness; she continues writing, exhilirated
by the constant learning required by the country.

960   HOBROCK, PEG MASTERS
Asafetida: That Was My Bag. Philadelphia: Dorrance,
1973. 44pp.

In a series of very brief sketches, she recalls typical
characteristics of her youth in the first decades of the century; she includes short descriptions of clothing, schedules,
the parlor, food, and entertainments.

961   HOBSON, MARY QUINN (1856?-)
Though Long the Trail, by Mabel Hobson Draper. New
York: Rinehart, 1946. 313pp.

The narrator's story of her pioneer experiences on the
Oregon trail is told by her daughter; she describes the
preparations for the trip, and then its dangers, accidents,
and monotony; after her mother's death and the family's
breakup, she asserts her independence and marries in 1881;
she homesteads in Kansas, New Mexico, and Missouri, enduring hardships, worries, and the deaths of two infants before finding a permanent home.

962   HOFFMAN, HELEN
We Lead a Double Life, by Ruth and Helen Hoffman. Philadelphia: Lippincott, 1947. 264pp.

This light and humorous account written by twins is full
of family anecdotes and the details of living as twins; as
high school students, they begin writing for magazines, then
turn to drawing, working in advertising and for greeting-
card companies; ambitiously they plan for art school, spend
a year at the University of Minnesota, study in Paris; they
return to New York during the depression, work for awhile,
then return to Paris for more study; everything they do, they
do as one.

963   HOFFMAN, MALVINA CORNELL (1885-1966)   NAWM
       Yesterday Is Tomorrow; A Personal History.   New York:
       Crown, 1965.   378pp.

       A distinguished sculptor, she describes her emergence as
an artist, driven by an intense emotional life and a "thirst
to learn"; accompanied by her widowed mother, she travels
and studies in Europe, learning much through her association
with Rodin from 1910 to 1917; she tells of her enriching
friendships with numerous musicians and artists; she suffers
personal tragedies and physical breakdowns which interrupt
her work; she describes the creation of individual pieces of
sculpture explaining "this inner passion to express something."

964   HOFFMAN, RUTH
       see HOFFMAN, HELEN

965   HOHOFF, TAY
       Cats and Other People.   Garden City, N.Y.:   Doubleday,
       1973.   252pp.

       A literary editor, she writes a delightful, nostalgic, sen-
sitively anthropomorphic account ostensibly organized around
the series of cats in her life; "these stories of the tyrants
I have known"; she offers a charming portrait of her extended Quaker household, and reveals much about her own
sensibilities as the cats mediate or accompany her experiences with other people.

966   HOLIDAY, BILLIE (1915?-1959)   NAWM
       Lady Sings the Blues, with William Dufty.   Garden City,
       N.Y.:   Doubleday, 1956.   250pp.

       A popular black singer describes her life of struggle and
accomplishment; working first at six, she is raped at ten,
spends time in a Catholic institution, is a maid at thirteen
with her mother; when she becomes a prostitute, she is
jailed several times and threatened by a pimp; she begins

singing jazz in Harlem, suffers discrimination when she
tours the South with a white band; she becomes a drug addict, spends a year in a federal penitentiary, but after her
release performs in Carnegie Hall; after a European tour,
she continues to struggle with her addiction to drugs.

967   HOLLAND, ELLEN MORLAND BOWIE
       Gay as a Grig; Memories of a North Texas Girlhood.   Aus-
       tin: University of Texas Press, 1963. 161pp.

       She opens with a family history, describing a line of
strong-willed Texas women from 1855; she has pleasant
memories and anecdotes from her childhood, and she tells of
a family year in England in 1902 as well as finishing school
in Washington, D. C. just before World War I; she stands in
awe of changes in technology and culture.

968   HOLLINGER, CAROL
       Mai Pen Rai Means Never Mind.   Boston: Houghton Mifflin,
       1965. 237pp.

       A dry, humorous account by a university teacher and the
wife of a Foreign Service officer in Thailand; noting her
distaste for the American colony, she sheds suburbia and
makes a smooth adjustment to Thai perspective, accepting
her servants as "part of the family," growing to love her
Thai students and friends; she discounts the experts' advice
about Eastern culture and becomes thoroughly charmed by
the East.

969   HOLMES, JULIA ANNA ARCHIBALD (1838-1887)
       A Bloomer Girl on Pike's Peak, 1858, ed. by Agnes Wright
       Spring. Denver, Col. : Denver Public Library, Western
       History Department, 1949. 66pp.

       The "first white woman to climb Pike's Peak," she ac-
companies her husband on the ascent which involves several
days of hiking and camping; the letters describing the ascent
were originally published in a women's dress reform journal,
for she is a feminist who wears the Bloomer costume since
it gives her "freedom to roam."

970   HOLMES, MARION C.
       Six in a Ford. Portland, Maine: Falmouth Publishing
       House, 1951. 141pp.

       In this "simple, direct narrative of a family trip" of six
months, she tells of their travels from New England to California via Mexico and their return through Canada; with her

professor husband and four children, she describes incidents,
sights, and people.

971   HOLMES, MARJORIE (1910-   )
        As Tall as My Heart; A Mother's Measure of Love.   Mc-
        Lean, Va. : EPM Publications, 1974.   120pp.

        She offers a series of reflections on motherhood focused
        on her own experiences; she notes particularly tender mo-
        ments shared with her children, coping with crises large
        and small, and her fond appreciation of each child's unique
        identity.

972   How Can I Find You, God?   Garden City, N. Y. :   Doubleday,
        1975.   202pp.

        An author of children's books and of numerous books on
        religious topics, she illustrates "some of the paths that have
        helped me find God again" in a series of meditations; she
        tells of people who infuse her life with meaning, of the
        "amazing experience" of birth, of death's reverberations, of
        the aid and influences of books, of the values in work of all
        kinds, of nature's lessons, of the role of the church and
        worship and prayer, of the benefits in personal suffering,
        and of the peace and rapture that come with her experiences
        of the "holy spirit. "

973   You and I and Yesterday.   New York: Morrow, 1973.
        191pp.

        A prolific author and magazine columnist, she writes with
        nostalgia of her childhood in a small Iowa town in the 1920's,
        "a time of being safe, being sheltered, being loved"; she de-
        scribes "abundant summers, " children's games, the kitchen
        as the emotional center of the family, alluring movies, the
        magic of a swing, laundry day, the thrill of the first family
        car, fellowship around the supper table, and the appeal of
        Chautauqua.

974   HOLMES, SARAH KATHERINE STONE (1841-1907)
        Brokenburn; The Journal of Kate Stone, 1861-1868, ed. John
        Q. Anderson.   Baton Rouge: Louisiana State University
        Press, 1955.   400pp.

        Well-educated, intensely patriotic, and possessing a sense
        of humor, she lives with her widowed mother on a prosperous
        Louisiana plantation, noting some "moral guilt" about the
        "natural" state of slavery; her brothers and uncle depart for
        Confederate service while she remains at home, visiting,

noting the health of family members and slaves, sewing for
soldiers, marking the war's progress; terrorized when the
fighting approaches, she flees with her mother to Texas
where they are refugees for over two years; commenting on
the bitterness and degradation of defeat and the sorrow of
three brothers' deaths, she nevertheless returns, optimistic
that "we might be happy yet."

975   HOMANS, ABIGAIL ADAMS (1879?-)
       Education by Uncles. Boston: Houghton Mifflin, 1966.
       149pp.

       In a charming memoir, the great, great granddaughter of
Abigail Adams (see entry #6) recounts her childhood in
Quincy and Boston; she offers a perceptive portrait of her
father, noting his breakdown and death after financial panic
in 1893; she then begins a long relationship, marked by her
"starry-eyed veneration," with her uncle Henry Adams; she
also enjoys an intimate association with her uncle Brooks
Adams, immersed in French studies but lightened by summers in the English countryside; after her Boston "Coming
out," she marries in 1907; she closes with the deaths of both
uncles, having illuminated their lives as well as her own by
her marvelous portraits.

976   HOMMELL, PAULINE
       Class Dismissed. New York: Vantage, 1962. 144pp.

       Having been a teacher for over forty years, serving in
one-room schools as well as large urban schools, she
presents brief random anecdotes that reveal her great love
of children, her delight in unpredictable, humorous events,
and her thankfulness for the "rich joys of fulfillment" in the
teaching profession.

977   HOOKER, MILDRED PHELPS STOKES (1881?-)
       Camp Chronicles. Blue Mountain Lake, N.Y.: Adirondack
       Museum, 1964. 60pp.

       In an account first written in 1952, she portrays the rich
social life full of outdoor activities maintained at an Adirondack cabin complex used by family and friends; she describes
her seventy years there, though her random anecdotes are
largely from childhood and tell of prominent guests as well
as her family's "firm stand against evening clothes."

978   HOOTON, BARBARA C.
       Guestward Ho! as told to Patrick Dennis. New York: Van-
       guard, 1956. 270pp.

A New Yorker, she is transplanted to New Mexico in 1953 when her husband buys a dude ranch; her gloomy predictions based on their inexperience and her lack of enthusiasm give way to a reality of learning through trial and error; she presents humorous anecdotes about "the servant problem" and various guests; she later rejects an opportunity to return to New York in order to remain in New Mexico.

979   HOOVER, HELEN (1910-)
       The Gift of the Deer. London: Heinemann, 1966. 228pp.

Grateful for the gifts of observation and understanding, she notes "to have the trust of any deer is a joy"; she feeds the first injured deer at her Minnesota wilderness home, and as others come with trust over the years, she notes the details of their behavior, altering some of her previously urban values in the process.

980   A Place in the Woods. New York: Knopf, 1969. 292pp.

Originally a metallurgist, she acquires a vacation home in the northern Minnesota woods as a retreat from Chicago; at 44, she decides to abandon the city and tells of her first winter, learning to adjust to the woods; she begins to write articles and books on nature and wildlife and enjoys days "rich with living."

981   The Years of the Forest. New York: Knopf, 1973. 318pp.

A free-lance writer and author of children's books as well as a dedicated conservationist, she describes sixteen years of wilderness living in northern Minnesota beginning in 1954; she provides details of daily domesticity, of her close observations of flora and fauna, of satisfying time spent writing; the gradual encroachment of people threatens the wilderness and her way of life, yet in an epilogue she notes that after a four-year search elsewhere, she returns to her beloved Minnesota woods.

982   HOPPER, HEDDA (1885-1966)   NAWM
       From Under My Hat. Garden City, N. Y.: Doubleday, 1952.
       311pp.

A famous Hollywood columnist, she writes an anecdotal, breezy account; acting provides an early escape from her family, and she offers a lively picture of early Hollywood with numerous bits of gossip about celebrities; never a star herself, she tries real estate, the "beauty business," and then writing.

983   The Whole Truth and Nothing But, with James Brough.
       Garden City, N. Y. : Doubleday, 1963. 331pp.

       An actress and journalist, she presents a gossip-filled
       account of her acquaintances among the Hollywood stars;
       those who receive more extended mention include Elizabeth
       Taylor (see entry #1973), Grace Kelly, Marilyn Monroe (see
       entry #1455), Frank Sinatra, fellow columnist and rival Lou-
       ella Parsons (see entry #1570), Judy Garland, Lucille Ball,
       Mary Martin (see entry #1390), James Dean, Marion Davies
       (see entry #517), and Mario Lanza.

984   HORN, JANE (pseud.)
       The Honeybee's Conclusion.   Philadelphia: Dorrance, 1966.
       144pp.

       This narrative by an alcoholic is written in the third per-
       son and is marked by her disorganized personality; her child-
       hood is lonely, insecure, and troubled by religious tension;
       married at eighteen, she searches obsessively for "the key
       to health"; she mourns her mother's death, begins drinking,
       is shot by her drunken husband, fights off a rapist, and suf-
       fers poverty and degradation; finally divorced, she struggles
       with Beelzebub and becomes more and more muddled, ending
       nevertheless on an upbeat note with the completion of the
       book manuscript.

985   HORNE, LENA (1917-   )
       In Person: Lena Horne, as told to Helen Arstein and Carl-
       ton Moss. New York: Greenberg, 1950. 249pp.

       She feels a strong desire to go on the stage, despite her
       grandmother's insistence on an education; managed and pro-
       tected by her mother, a former actress and dancer, she be-
       gins her career at sixteen; she marries in 1936 but her de-
       sire for a secure home life conflicts with her husband's
       political ambitions; she recounts years of hard work, painful
       struggles with racial discrimination, loneliness, but she
       gradually gains pride in her work as a singer and actress
       and overcomes her inability to relate to whites; her account
       ends with a remarriage and success as an entertainer.

986   Lena, with Richard Schickel. Garden City, N. Y. : Double-
       day, 1965. 300pp.

       A black singer and actress, she tells of her childhood
       alienation from both black and white worlds; raised partly
       by her strong clubwoman grandmother and partly by her
       peripatetic mother, she spends her childhood among adults;
       in the early 1930's she begins singing in nightclubs; she

marries, has two children, then divorces; she describes the
frustration of racial stereotypes and discrimination, but she
is unwilling to be a "symbol of Negro aspirations" in film;
she remarries in 1946, and finally settles in New York after
years of touring.

987   HORWITZ, SIMI
       South of the Navel.   New York: Crowell, 1973.   194pp.

       Her narration is a slightly fictionalized account of two
years in a university theater arts school in the late 1960's;
she offers a student's-eye view of counter-culture as establishment and the tyranny of "the movement"; her tale is told
with wry distance and a good ear for hip slang.

988   HOTCHKISS, CHRISTINE OPPELN-BRONIKOWSKA
       Home to Poland.   New York: Farrar, Straus and Cudahy,
       1958.   247pp.

       Married to an American and the mother of a young daugh-
ter, she is sent as a writer for the Reader's Digest to her
native Poland in 1957 after an eighteen-year absence; her
observations of the present are illuminated by contrasts with
the recent past of Soviet domination and the distant past of
her childhood; an emotional return to her childhood home
triggers memories of a childhood whose prosperity and security are broken by the events leading to World War II.

989   HOUSER, HARRIET HENTZ
       Hentz: Of Things Not Seen.   New York: Macmillan, 1955.
       235pp.

       She writes of much human bravery and beauty amid suf-
fering after her seventeen-year-old son becomes a quadri-
plegic following an accident in 1951; she tells of small triumphs, hope, and resilience after their rejection of the doctors' prognosis; she struggles to reestablish a normal home
life and some independence.

990   HOUSTON, JEANNE WAKATSUKI (1934?-)
       Farewell to Manzanar, with James D. Houston.   Boston:
       Houghton Mifflin, 1973.   177pp.

       In a sensitive, touching account of "Japanese American
experience during and after the World War II internment,"
she writes of her family's three years in a U.S. concentration camp, forced there when she is seven; beleaguered by
chaotic camp conditions, poor food, overcrowding, and humiliation, the family disintegrates, and she writes with rare

understanding and compassion of her parents' pain; in a hostile post-war world, she dreams of acceptance, but finds rejection; writing her story after a return to Manzanar thirty years later provides a partial resolution.

991   HOUSTON, RUBY R. (1908-)
       I Was Afraid to Be Happy.   New York: Carlton Press,
       1967.   48pp.

       A black woman, she tells an unrelieved tale of poverty and woe; growing up without a mother and blind in one eye, she faces numerous childhood fears; she marries with misgivings, divorces and remarries, raises seven children through poverty and ill health and widowhood; a third marriage becomes "another mistake," as she learns to distrust men.

992   HOWAR, BARBARA
       Laughing All the Way.   New York: Stein and Day, 1973.
       298pp.

       In this outspoken account she describes the strong influence of her mother, her childhood in the South, her Catholic education, a Washington finishing school, and her debut; a job as a legislative secretary leads to an active social life, and she works close to the Kennedy and Johnson families; later she is ostracized; divorced, she turns to television commentary to support herself and her children; her wit is sharp throughout.

993   HOWARD, JANE (1935?-)
       A Different Woman.   New York: Dutton, 1973.   413pp.

       A journalist describes a "watershed time" in her life, impelled by an assignment for Life on feminism and by the death of her mother; she begins her quest in 1971, exploring "what it meant to be a woman"; she travels extensively to interview "surviving woman" and engages in intimate self-scrutiny, discussing her sheltered origins, her close relationships with her mother and sister, relationships with men, and thoughts on childbearing, abortion, and divorce.

994   HOWE, MARVINE
       The Prince and I.   New York: John Day, 1955.   252pp.

       A journalist describes her "fairy-tale existence in Morocco"; beginning in 1950, she serves as a governess, works in Moroccan radio, enjoys a close friendship with the Crown Prince; she investigates and reports on the French-Morroccan conflict, finding it difficult to remain neutral in the midst of strong anti-colonial sentiment; she is open and receptive to the people and their culture.

995   HOWLAND, BETTE
W-3. New York: Viking, 1974. 206pp.

After a "massive overdose of sleeping pills," she becomes part of the "subculture" of the Intensive Care Unit; her piece-meal recollections recreate conditions which led to her suicide attempt; she describes the "community" of fellow patients in the psychiatric ward with horrifying clarity; she closes with her release.

996   HOYT, JO WASSON
For the Love of Mike, with Frank Graham, Jr. New York: Random House, 1966. 210pp.

The wife of a Foreign Service Officer, she tells of her organizational triumphs making adjustments to homemaking and the rearing of four children in Pakistan, Morocco, and the Congo; she tells of her evacuation from the Congo in a 1962 revolution and of unbearable tension for the three months that her husband is held hostage by rebel forces; reunited with him, she notes her intense pride in his dedication.

997   HUEY, LYNDA
A Running Start; An Athlete, A Woman. New York: Quadrangle/New York Times, 1976. 240pp.

A sprinter and later a physical education professor, she describes the problems "reconciling the female-athlete dichotomy"; she is frustrated by weak women's programs in college and so trains with men's teams; she tells of personal turmoil in her relations with activist black athletes and of later radical political activity as a teacher at Oberlin; she sees sex and sports as forms of physical exhilaration and demonstrates an intense awareness of the link between self and body.

998   HUFF, RUTH SCOTT
The High Seize. Philadelphia: Dorrance, 1955. 273pp.

In an unpretentious and enthusiastic account, she describes thirty years of planning for retirement voyages with her husband; "like children," they enjoy their first trip by freighter to South America and to Europe; she displays a love of life and laughter.

999   HUGHES, ADELLA PRENTISS (1869-1950)   NAW
      Music Is My Life.   Cleveland: World, 1947.   319pp.

      An accomplished pianist and the descendant of settlers of
      Cleveland, she becomes a founder and manager of the Cleve-
      land Symphony Orchestra; she begins as a "budding impres-
      ario," proud of the artists she brings to Cleveland, and she
      includes many anecdotes of concerts and performers; her
      campaign for a new concert hall succeeds in 1931 and in
      addition, she helps found a settlement music school; she
      combines her passion for music with strong organizational
      abilities in "a joyous crusade to make music permanent and
      vital" to the people of her city.

1000 HUGHES, LORA WOOD (1873-   )
      No Time for Tears.   Boston: Houghton Mifflin, 1946.
      305pp.

      She recounts her childhood on a Kansas homestead, then
      her move to California and difficulties during the depression
      of the 1890's; she fulfills her early desire to be a nurse,
      then marries but her daughter dies in infancy and her hus-
      band deserts her; she nurses in Honolulu during a typhoid
      epidemic and takes private cases in Montana and Canada;
      she relates some cases at length; she cares for her father
      and mother in their final illnesses, then has a heart attack
      but remains full of spirit and vitality.

1001 HULME, KATHRYN CAVARLY (1900-   )
      Look a Lion in the Eye; On Safari Through Africa.   Boston:
      Little, Brown, 1974.   223pp.

      She tells of the deep "impact of Africa" on her after a
      one-month safari in Kenya and Tanzania; she feels almost
      stupefied by the wealth of vivid impressions, noting the
      mystery of observing lions, enjoying native dancers, experi-
      encing atavistic fear in the African night, and marveling at
      the Olduvai Gorge and Ngorongoro; having traveled "with
      love and total attention," she is profoundly moved.

1002 Undiscovered Country; A Spiritual Adventure.   Boston: Lit-
      tle, Brown, 1966.   306pp.

      A highly articulate writer, she spends her youth in the
      world of books and is later attracted to writers' circles in
      Paris in the mid-1930's; interested in explorations of the
      buried self, she meets the famous mystic Gurdjieff and joins
      a group for whom he is "our common center of gravity"; his
      disciple for seventeen years, she later converts to Catholi-
      cism; in 1945, she works with UNRRA in France, "a torch

carrier for the international idea," describing her emotionally taxing work with displaced persons; she returns to the
U. S. and to her writing.

1003   The Wild Place.   Boston: Little, Brown, 1953.   275pp.

In 1945 she serves as the director of a Displaced Persons
camp in Germany, leading an international team sponsored
by the United Nations; with vivid detail, she describes the
individual horrors of thousands of Polish refugees; working
amid much tension and pressure, morale problems, and
U. S. military blunders, with no respite, she finds "all life
reduced to the stark simplicity of the supply line"; she reluctantly accompanies repatriates into Poland in 1946; the
account is sensitive and moving.

1004   HUMPHREY, DORIS (1895-1958)   NAWM
Doris Humphrey: An Artist First; An Autobiography, ed.
Selma Jeanne Cohen.   Middletown, Conn.:   Wesleyan Univer-
sity Press, 1972.   305pp.

A pioneer of dance in America, she writes of her lonely
childhood in a hotel managed by her parents; inspired by
dance classes and teachers, she studies, then teaches for
five stifling years when she must help to support her family;
she joins the Denishawn dancers, then tours with her own
group in vaudeville and concert dancing; she rejoins the
Denishawn company for a tour of the Orient; engaging in "new
experiments in movement," she is distressed to have to
break with Denishawn; her autobiography, on pages 3-65, is
cut short by her death.

1005   HUMULA, ANNA J. F.
Echoing Memories.   Boston: Christopher, 1963.   110pp.

Born in Moravia, she describes her happy youth prior to
1914 marked by a deep love of nature; after the tense early
days of World War I, she endures hardship, begging in the
countryside for food, caught in the influenza epidemic; in
1919, peace brings joyful celebration, followed by her marriage and emigration to the U. S. with her husband; her often
impersonal account is rather disjointed.

1006   HUNGERFORD, KATHERINE L.
Early Hollywood Crazy Quilt.   Washington, D. C.:   Stewart
Printing, 1949.   85pp.

She uses a trip to Hollywood in 1922 as an opportunity to
meet and photograph film stars; she enjoys brief friendships

with actors and actresses, and later uses her photos and experiences as material for lectures in the East.

1007   HUNT, CONNIE MOORE (1918-   )
Daddy Was a Deacon. Nashville: Broadman, 1961.   170pp.

Her father's death precipitates recollections of her Oklahoma childhood filled "with music and joy"; she describes her father as a man dedicated to his business and devoted to the education of his children; her memories range over a typical family Sunday, delightful school days, church activities, family holidays and vacations; sometimes rebellious against the strict Baptist codes and standards of her parents, she is later grateful when she meets congenial companions at Wheaton College, is courted, and happily marries.

1008   HUNT, ELSIE DENEAN
The Ship of Peace. New York: Pageant, 1957.   178pp.

A covered wagon she and her businessman husband build in 1947, a project to improve her husband's health, produces an "amazing metamorphosis in our lives"; she learns "to live in the present" with great simplicity, absorbing Nature's lessons and the "healing quality of the hills"; her greatest satisfaction comes from seeing a loving relationship grow between her husband and their adopted son.

1009   HUNTER, FRANCES GARDNER (1916-   )
My Love Affair with Charles. Glendale, Cal.: G/L Publications, 1971.   197pp.

A lecturer and writer on religious topics tells of the dramatic meeting in 1969 with the man who is to become her husband; she feels that her hectic traveling and speaking schedule will prohibit love and marriage, but after a three-month exchange of intense, exclamatory letters, she accepts marriage; her letters are filled with a joyful, active Christianity that is the entire focus of her daily life.

1010   HUNTER, RODELLO (1920-   )
A Daughter of Zion. New York: Knopf, 1972.   285pp.

As a writer she feels compelled to explore her doubts and dilemmas having been raised with the "powerful indoctrinations" of a Mormon child amid family zealots; she presents a loving portrait of her grandfather whose wisdom and influence are belatedly understood; after his death, she eases her sorrow by immersing herself in rewarding church work; from these personal experiences flow candid reflections on the strengths and weaknesses of women's role in the Mormon Church.

1011   A House of Many Rooms; A Family Memoir.   London: Heinemann, 1965.   215pp.

She presents a moving portrait of her large Mormon family whose children include "nine owned and five borrowed"; her father is a preacher and her mother a superb domestic manager; the growth of the family requires periodic additions to the home and generates what become wonderful old family stories in this narrative, a chronicle of entertainments, chores, delights, crises, and heartbreak as well as a celebration of the years before "time had separated us."

1012   Wyoming Wife.   New York: Knopf, 1969.   330pp.

A writer and editor of an outdoor magazine, she marries a wildlife expert and learns to live the life about which she had only written; with humor, she tells of learning outdoor skills, hunting and camping trips, her neighbors in their remote village, a grandson's visit, and her favorite recipes; she adds thoughts on the women pioneers of Wyoming.

1013   HUNTER, RUTH
Barefoot Girl on Broadway; The Story of the Original Ellie May of "Tobacco Road."   New York: Exposition, 1965. 115pp.

An actress, she tells of the early casting and rehearsals of Tobacco Road, and describes relationships with her colleagues; the play opens in 1933 to poor reviews, but its gradual success brings new actors to various parts over the years; she quits as Ellie May after five years.

1014   HUNTINGTON, ANNIE OAKES (1875-1940)
Testament of Happiness: Letters of Annie Oakes Huntington, ed. by Nancy Byrd Turner.   Portland, Me.:   Anthoensen Press, 1947.   235pp.

She writes marvelous letters covering the period from 1885 to 1940, beginning with observations from her childhood years in China, through life in Boston in the 1890's, to householding in rural New England with a close woman friend; her letters describe landscape studies, authorship of two books on trees, and devotion to her friend of over forty years; an early bout with nervous exhaustion is followed by years as a semi-invalid, but her letters are vivacious, affectionate, and playful.

1015   HURLBUT, GLADYS
       Next Week East Lynne!   New York: Dutton, 1950.   254pp.

       After graduating from the American Academy of Dramatic
       Arts in 1918, she gains her first stock company experience
       --an hilarious disaster; her account continues with humorous
       "backstage anecdotes" from years of touring with stock com-
       panies; she tells of leading men, learning roles, "juveniles,"
       much joy and satisfaction; after a fifteen-year break from
       acting, she returns to the stage in Life with Mother.

1016   HURST, FANNIE (1889-1968)   NAWM
       Anatomy of Me: A Wonderer in Search of Herself.   Garden
       City, N. Y. :   Doubleday, 1958.   367pp.

       A novelist and short story writer, she presents fine por-
       traits of her reserved father and her overpowering mother
       and describes growing up in a joyless middle class home in
       the middle west; her secretive inner life and desires to
       escape mediocrity lead her to a university education and in-
       tellectual awakening; her "fascination with the human scene"
       draws her to a variety of people; although married, she and
       her husband live separately; she comments on the unreality
       of her literary success, her constant dissatisfaction with the
       quality of her writing, and her distance from contemporary
       trends in this introspective and analytical narrative.

1017   HUSE, MABEL HALE
       The Old Home.   Boston: Meador Publishing, 1957.   69pp.

       She opens with a family history, tracing her roots in
       America to the late seventeenth century; amid close family
       ties, the legacy of three aunts is particularly strong and
       this legacy includes religion, temperance, painting, and po-
       etry; she mentions her conversion, Bible training, and mar-
       riage to a minister.

1018   HUTCHENS, ALICE SAVIAH (1892-)
       The Gift of Little Things.   Caldwell, Idaho: Caxton, 1968.
       152pp.

       She recounts her childhood in Minnesota with her grand-
       parents, then the move west with her parents; she teaches
       school, describing the local families; she marries and tells
       of hardships and happiness in homesteading; the most detail
       is devoted to her early years, farming, gardening, house-
       holding; a nostalgic portrayal of the serenity of their rural
       northwest setting.

1019 IGLAUER, EDITH
Denison's Ice Road. New York: Dutton, 1974. 237pp.

A free-lance writer goes to the Canadian Northwest Ter-
ritories on assignment for The New Yorker; she relates her
winter travels with an ice road builder and construction
crew, enduring the cold and the dangers of thin lake ice
and learning to be unobtrusive.

1020 ILEANA, PRINCESS OF ROMANIA (1909?-)
I Live Again. New York: Rinehart, 1951. 374pp.

The daughter of a Romanian king, she tells of her devotion to the duties of royalty and service to the people of her
native land; married in 1931 to an Austrian archduke, she
bears six children yet continues her humanitarian efforts
during the Nazi regime and the ensuing horrors of World
War II, aiding in hospital and refugee work; driven from
her beloved Romania in 1948 by political conditions, she
severs her emotional and cultural ties only for her children's sake, searching for a new life in the U.S.

1021 ILIFF, FLORA GREGG
People of the Blue Water; My Adventures Among the Walapai
and Havasupai Indians. New York: Harper, 1954. 271pp.

In a book reconstructed from letters written to her mother,
she tells of the challenge of pioneering and of teaching Indians in a remote Arizona school in 1900; a woman of quick
sympathy, she is eager to explore the harmony and beauty
of Indian culture and build friendships; she is a superintendent at a second school, serves as a magistrate to settle
local disputes, and, married to a fellow teacher, continues
as a dedicated teacher in the "greatest adventure of my life."

1022 INGRAM, GLADYS LITTLE
Traveling an Uncharted Road. Philadelphia: Dorrance,
1970. 109pp.

A chiropractor describes her "fifty-five years of personal
service to mankind"; she comes to chiropractic through her

own illness and her search for a career beyond narrow definitions of woman's sphere, earning her degree in 1915; writing partly to correct misconceptions about chiropractic, she
describes various cases and tells of years of harassment by
doctors; she lectures on behalf of chiropractic, works with a
national professional organization, and joins in women's club
activities.

1023   INMAN, DEE
       Don't Fence Me In; Life of a Teacher in a Navajo School
       Hogan. New York: Exposition, 1955. 167pp.

       A "sour-dough schoolmarm" describes her pioneer work
       as an Indian Service teacher in excerpts from her diary;
       fascinated by Navajo culture and her desert surroundings,
       she loves the children and enjoys "an experience out of this
       world"; she closes with her sudden transfer to another school.

1024   IREDALE, EDITH PEARL BRUBAKER (1885?-)
       A Promise Fulfilled. Elgin, Ill.: Brethren Press, 1962.
       208pp.

       A teacher, writer, and professional storyteller, she re-
       counts her fourteenth year in which she promises her father
       to keep a one-year journal of her family life; one of twelve
       children, she offers a lively, detailed chronicle which in-
       cludes vignettes of country school, hog butchering, seasonal
       tasks and entertainments, a lecherous hired hand, her
       brothers' departure for college, and a sister's marriage;
       her portrait of a close family is illuminated by a special
       affection for her father.

1025   ISAAC, BETTY
       A Breast for Life. New York: Exposition, 1974. 110pp.

       The mother of five young daughters describes the torment
       of discovering a cancerous breast tumor; in 1970 she first
       refuses mastectomy but is convinced by her husband and
       doctors to undergo surgery; she discusses her apprehensions,
       her overcompensating attempts at bravery, her problems
       with drug withdrawal and depression; she seeks psychiatric
       help for a mental breakdown, and closes the account as her
       recovery begins.

1026   ISABELL, SHARON (1942-)
       Yesterday's Lessons. Oakland, Cal.: Women's Press Col-
       lective, 1974. 206pp.

       Her childhood is marred by poverty and numerous minor
       clashes with the authorities over her fights, smoking, shop-

lifting, and vandalism; she joins the army in 1960 but is lonely and confused by her early sexual experiences; she finds some camaraderie in softball, some temporary love in a lesbian relationship, but at twenty-four feels despair, as if she is "dead inside"; at the close of this slangy, almost illiterate account, she finds her freedom, a hollow satisfaction.

1027   IVES, HILDA LIBBY (1886-   )
        All in One Day; Experiences and Insights.   Portland, Me.:
        Bond Wheelwright, 1955.   155pp.

A minister, she writes memories of a happy childhood but notes that religion is not a significant part of her life until she is past thirty, a wife, and mother; the death of her husband precipitates a "spiritual pilgrimage" and she feels called for missionary work in rural Maine; apprehensive and unprepared, she settles there for thirteen years, struggling against "the sin of male superiority in the church"; in 1938 she visits Palestine for a church conference, and after World War II she serves with the American Friends Service Committee; her account is reflective.

1028 JACK, EULA O.
Hey, Teach. Philadelphia: Dorrance, 1972. 103pp.

A former college teacher responds to the teacher shortage
in secondary schools during World War II and finds chaos,
frustration, and a surprising education in youth's ways; seeking not only to teach but to influence her students, she nevertheless maintains her sense of humor.

1029 JACKSON, HARRISENE BAILEY (1941-)
There's Nothing I Own That I Want. Englewood Cliffs, N.J.:
Prentice-Hall, 1974. 168pp.

At six she witnesses her mother's murder; she tells of a
childhood of ghetto poverty; pregnant at 16, she reluctantly
marries, helps her husband through college; she tells of five
children, an abortion, a second failed marriage, confrontations with social workers, doctors, the welfare system, the
pain of her oldest daughter's mental illness; the account is written in a direct, vernacular style, full of rage and strength.

1030 JACKSON, LILLIE M. COOPER (1886-)
Fanning the Embers. Boston: Christopher, 1966. 154pp.

In a rambling narrative, she tells of her West Virginia
childhood marked by hard times and the departure of her
father; she heads west, rejects a suitor at gunpoint, runs a
ferry, does farm work, and forges a "new life" working for
a rancher and "doing for others"; later left with two children to support, she does housework, child care, and nursing, continuing her lifelong pattern of hard work.

1031 JACKSON, MAHALIA (1911-1972)   NAWM
Movin' on Up, with Evan McLeod Wylie. New York: Hawthorn, 1966. 212pp.

A famous black gospel singer, she describes her childhood
in New Orleans, characterized by a strong religious upbringing and her recognition of the "real jubilation" of church
singing; the Chicago of 1928 represents the "open door" of
opportunity, as she notes "the depression became responsible

for my whole career"; her sense of mission leads her to
reject blues and classical music, and her recordings allow
her to break into television and American and European
tours; having suffered from racial discrimination, she works
for civil rights.

1032   JACKSON, SHIRLEY HARDIE (1916-1965)   NAWM
        Life Among the Savages. New York: Farrar, Straus and
        Young, 1953. 241pp.

        In a delightfully wry examination of family life, the noted
        writer describes the eccentricities of her ramshackle Ver-
        mont home, the inevitable fraying caused by living "in the
        society of small children," the saga of household helpers;
        her renditions of family conversations are marvelously dis-
        jointed, comprehensible only to the participants.

1033   Raising Demons. New York: Farrar, Straus and Cudahy,
        1957. 310pp.

        In self-contained chapters, she explores the numerous
        small harassments of family life, from cooking, to Little
        League, to family vacations, to her adjustments when all of
        her four children are in school, to her position as a faculty
        wife; she finds humor and vitality in daily events, and her
        children emerge with delightful personalities.

1034   JACOBS, MARGARET BRANCH MOORE (1901-   )
        The Secret of a Happy Life. Rock Island, Ill.: Augustana,
        1952. 112pp.

        A writer of religious works, she offers random inspira-
        tional recollections and reflections; anecdotes from a happy
        childhood are used to illustrate various religious lessons.

1035   JAMES, ALICE (1848-1892)   NAW
        The Diary of Alice James, ed. Leon Edel. New York:
        Dodd, Mead, 1964. 241pp.

        Stranded permanently in England due to her deteriorating
        health, she writes between 1889 and 1891 to "lose a little of
        the sense of loneliness and desolation which abides with me";
        her perceptions of human nature from examples within her
        "microscopic field" are sharp, particularly when dissecting
        the English class structure in the company of her brother
        Henry or her beloved companion Katherine Loring; alive to
        subtlety and wit, her immense mental vitality is tragically
        at odds with her physical and emotional "surrender"; a keen
        observer of her own invalid state, she is as fascinated by
        her dying, noting that "imperishable experience survives."

1036 JARAMILLO, CLEOFAS M.
Romance of a Little Village Girl. San Antonio: Naylor,
1955. 200pp.

She tells of her Spanish heritage, growing up in New
Mexico the daughter of a prosperous farmer and merchant;
she describes feast days and Catholic religious festivals
amid a loving family; married in 1898, she suffers the deaths
of her first two infants, then the illness and death of her
husband which leaves her plagued by debts with a small
daughter to support; the final blow is the brutal murder of
her daughter; she turns to work in Spanish folklore; the
book is a sequel to Shadows of the Past (see companion
volume).

1037 JAROS, ELIZABETH C.
Sunshine and Shadow. New York: New Voices, 1950. 143pp.

She writes in a spirited, flowery style, responding to her
son's request to tell of her past, and she reviews the "res-
onant years" which fulfill her childhood vow to care first for
others; she is a governess in Cuba, is a teacher in Virginia
and in Idaho, accompanies two students to Europe for travel
and education, serves as a housemother at a New York Jewish girls' school, and spends three enriching and adventurous
years as a Red Cross volunteer in Europe during World War
I; she later returns to the U.S. and marries.

1038 JARRETT, KAY
Sex Is a Private Affair. Garden City, N.Y.: Doubleday,
1966. 234pp.

Noting that an escort service is "polite prostitution," she
goes on to describe her fifteen years as head of a Chicago
escort service; she writes about police corruption, her
"girls," male customers, and sexuality in tough, slangy
style; having gone through four husbands and several busi-
nesses, she remains unsatisfied, still "in search of my
identity."

1039 JEBB, CAROLINE LANE REYNOLDS (1840-1930)
With Dearest Love to All; The Life and Letters of Lady Jebb,
by Mary Reed Bobbitt. Chicago: Regnery, 1960. 277pp.

Her highly articulate, spirited letters and journal cover
the years from 1858 to 1924; married to a naval officer, she
enjoys her "belleship" and its "pleasant taste of power"; losing a young son and widowed at twenty-eight, she settles in
England and fends off suitors until her marriage to an English scholar in 1874; focusing on her social life, she tells

of "ever increasing happiness" in the academic world; in
1902, she is again widowed.

1040   JEFFCOAT, GLADYS NEILL
        God's Wayside Beauty.   New York: Vantage, 1958.   61pp.

        Her fond childhood memories include an "old-fashioned
    country home"; her recollections of visits to various churches
    in the South and her spiritual enjoyment of nature are em-
    bedded in religious reflections; the account includes some
    poems.

1041   JEFFERIES, SUSAN HERRING
        Papa Wore No Halo.   Winston Salem, N. C. :   John F. Blair,
        1963.   457pp.

        This is a lively yet nostalgic narrative by the daughter of
    a Southern Baptist missionary in China at the turn of the
    century; "together we coped with Boxers, racial and reli-
    gious mores, fleas, bandits, scarlet fever, kites, wheel-
    barrows, visiting celebrities, beggars, and civil wars";
    writing of herself in the third person, she sadly notes the
    ultimate scattering of the family, including her return to the
    U. S. for college, and the death of her father.

1042   JEFFERS, JO JOHNSON (1931-   )
        Ranch Wife.   Garden City, N. Y. :   Doubleday, 1964.   273pp.

        Raised in Minnesota with an enormous appetite for experi-
    ence and dreaming of the cowboy life, she must reconcile
    her studies of literature and her desire for freedom with
    her marriage in 1956 to an older Arizona rancher; with can-
    dor and realism, she tells of her affection for anachronistic
    old cattlemen, her love of nature, her hardening under the
    rigors of ranch work, and her acceptance of the lean years;
    she finds peace and a sense of profound belonging on the
    ranch.

1043   JEFFERSON, LARA (pseud.)
        These Are My Sisters; An "Insandectomy. "   Tulsa, Ok. :
        Vickers, 1947.   238pp.

        Written by a patient in a state mental hospital, the account
    describes her insanity as "a naked--and a lonely thing"; the
    chaos of the ward, doctors' insistence that she "learn to
    think differently, " and her own emotions and violence cause
    her to appeal for changes in treatment; she is fiercely deter-
    mined to recover and shows some improvement by the end
    of the book.

1044   JENKINS, MINNIE BRAITHWAITE
        Girl from Williamsburg.   Richmond, Va.:   Dietz Press,
        1951.   343pp.

        She asserts her independent spirit by going west against
        her mother's wishes and teaching at the turn of the century
        in a remote pioneer Indian school in Arizona; she describes
        in detail her experiences with frontier hospitality, the charm-
        ing children, her exhaustion from overwork, a hostile school
        matron, and an epidemic; she establishes open, comfortable
        friendships with Indian residents; she closes when she leaves
        teaching for marriage.

1045   JENKINS, SUE PERRIGO
        Memories of Ebeeme; The Delights of Nature and Living at
        a Summer Camp in Maine.   New York: Exposition, 1959.
        43pp.

        She writes with a deep appreciation of nature, gained in
        twenty-five years of family summer vacations in the Maine
        woods; exploring the locale, learning about the many "things
        of beauty and interest," she then describes the landscape and
        the flora and fauna.

1046   JENKS, KATHLEEN (1940-   )
        Journey of a Dream Animal: A Human Search for Personal
        Identity.   New York: Julian Press, 1975.   246pp.

        She writes of "the beginnings of a journey into the inner
        world of dreams" during painful years from 1963 to 1967;
        she tells of her unhappy childhood, marked by a desire to
        die, a temporary religious conversion, and vaguely exotic
        yearnings; while she is depressed by a stultifying job and
        an unresolved love affair, she keeps a notebook of her vivid
        dreams, guided in her solitary explorations by Jung, evolving
        a private set of symbols and interpretations through the
        years; reaching a turning point in 1967, she enjoys solitude
        in Wales, turns to novel writing, and returns to Catholicism
        in her "god-hunt."

1047   JENSEN, MARGARET ADELIA ROUNDS (1889-   )
        Looking Back, with Leila Williams.   Denver: Big Mountain
        Press, 1966.   59pp.

        She writes a rambling account of her childhood recollec-
        tions of the Oklahoma Territory, where her large family
        moves frequently from farm to farm; she marries in 1912
        and raises five children on a Montana farm, enjoying "a
        wonderful life."

1048   JESSOP, MARY
        Bubbles in My Soul; The Story of a Woman's Life.   New
        York: Exposition, 1953.   241pp.

        Written in perpetual chatter style, the account describes
        a life of "bing, bang, bang, every minute"; she discusses
        the men in her life: her first husband whom she divorces,
        her second husband who dies after twenty years, and a third
        husband who closes the account; her jobs in journalism and
        movies are unstressed background in this unfocused book.

1049   JESSUP, CLAUDIA
        Supergirls: The Autobiography of an Outrageous Business,
        with Genie Chipps, ed. Betty Baer Krieger.   New York:
        Harper & Row, 1972.   182pp.

        Two women with ideas and the ambition "to be women
        starting a business" launch their offer to do "anything as
        long as it is legal and in good taste"; most of the book con-
        sists of anecdotes of their many highly unusual jobs; they
        make shrewd use of media attention, their own public rela-
        tions work, and their rapidly growing business skills.

1050   JEWETT, SARAH ORNE (1849-1909)   NAW
        Sarah Orne Jewett Letters, ed. Richard Cary.   Waterville,
        Me. :   Colby College Press, 1956.   117pp.

        Her letters, written between 1869 and 1908, reveal an
        unpretentious woman of spirit, warmth, and affection; her
        notes to editors reflect her initial graceful modesty and then
        her growing confidence in her abilities as a writer; she re-
        flects on her reading and her own literary values and prac-
        tices; she writes of daily domestic detail to family members
        and friends.

1051   JIGGETTS, J. IDA
        Israel to Me: A Negro Social Worker Inside Israel.   New
        York: Bloch Publishing, 1957.   274pp.

        A black social worker writes to promote international and
        intercultural understanding; traveling to Israel in 1950 and
        1953, she goes with a study group, engaged in research for
        her Ph. D. ; she reflects on race and on her personal response
        to Israel; she notes her observations of the places she visits
        and of the people she meets, especially those involved with
        education and women's activities.

1052   JOHNSON, CLAUDIA ALTA TAYLOR
        see JOHNSON, LADY BIRD

1053 JOHNSON, EDITH E.
Leaves from a Doctor's Diary.   Palo Alto, Cal.:   Pacific
Books, 1954.   279pp.

A California doctor keeps a diary from 1927 to 1954 and
provides hundreds of brief anecdotes of her patients; because
she works a great deal with the underprivileged, she notes
the effects of economic deprivation on people; her stories
reveal her strong humanitarian concern.

1054 JOHNSON, JOHNILE CURRY
Sunspur.   New York: Pageant, 1954.   117pp.

She opens with a description of her childhood in a small
Texas town; during her mother's illness, she is sent to live
with grandparents in Louisiana and she provides vignettes of
the domestic routine there; upon the return of her parents,
she pleads to remain with her grandparents.

1055 JOHNSON, JOSEPHINE WINSLOW (1910-)
The Inland Island.   New York: Simon and Schuster, 1969.
159pp.

Moving through the year from January to December, she
describes her "need to record and cherish" the world of
nature with minute attention; describing "layers of life,"
she compares nature's way with humankind's "world of war
and waste"; she experiences a deep personal horror of the
Vietnam War, and calls for "a new world"; her own over-
grown land provides an "island of sanity" and serves as an
inspiration for her sensitive and poetic reflections.

1056 Seven Houses; A Memoir of Time and Places.   New York:
Simon and Schuster, 1973.   157pp.

In a delicate, evocative account, she tells first of the
dignity, grace, and intellect associated with her mother's
family home; her own childhood homes provide "shelters on
a long slow traveling"; summer vacation homes constitute a
separate world; married and the mother of two children, she
enjoys a rich family life, later enhanced by the natural surroundings of a country home.

1057 JOHNSON, LADY BIRD
A White House Diary.   New York: Holt, Rinehart and Winston, 1970.   806pp.

Thrust into public view as First Lady after the assassination of President Kennedy in 1963, she adjusts to "the caul-

dron of activity that has become our life"; a keen observer,
always warm and open, she travels on official business often
and studies seriously to prepare herself for political duties
and work in support of the arts and national beautification,
sincerely grateful for the opportunity to accomplish much as
First Lady; throughout she maintains a tender pride in her
husband's achievements and a concern for his endurance,
while she provides a family life for her two daughters; she
makes the transition to private life in 1969; her account is
reconstructed from tapes begun in 1963.

1058   JOHNSON, MARGARET
       18, No Time to Waste.   Grand Rapids, Mich.:   Zondervan,
       1971.   117pp.

       A magazine writer and the mother of five, she describes
her family life, exploring her maternal feelings during the
sometimes stormy years of her second daughter's adolescence; shortly after the "years of misunderstanding" give
way to close friendship and mutual respect, her daughter is
killed in an accident; she finds peace through her strong religious faith, noting the impact of the death on her family
and friends.

1059   JOHNSON, OSA HELEN LEIGHTY (1894-1953)
       Last Adventure: The Martin Johnsons in Borneo, ed. Pascal
       James Imperato.   New York: Morrow, 1965.   233pp.

       She and her husband explore and photograph in the jungle
interior of North Borneo in the 1930's during a two-year expedition; she is the first white woman in the territory; they
build headquarters, and she describes local people, the cli-
mate, insects, and dangerous animals; earlier volumes
chronicle other adventures (see companion volume).

1060   JOHNSON, VIRGINIA WIESEL
       Lady in Arms.   Boston: Houghton Mifflin, 1967.   181pp.

       Married to a retired senior army officer, she recounts
"twenty-five years as an army wife"; an eager newlywed,
she learns the exigencies and perils of her role as a wife
and camp follower on a wide variety of posts, each with certain social obligations; she describes the changes in her role
as World War II brings modernization.

1061   The Long, Long Trail.   Boston: Houghton Mifflin, 1966.
       184pp.

       "Part of the great migration" from the depression dust-
bowl, her parents open a Rocky Mountain dude ranch in the

pioneer spirit; she fondly describes local characters and an
old hired hand; during World War II she returns to the ranch
with her own children; a yet later return brings sadness at
the invasions of modern life.

1062   JOHNSTON, DORIS RUBENS
       Bread and Rice.   New York: Thurston Macauley, 1947.
       235pp.

       A correspondent who feels her destiny lies in the Far
East, she tells something of her background and marriage;
in the Philippines during World War II, she and her husband
are forced to hide for over a year in the mountains where
they establish strong bonds with Filipino friends; captured
by the Japanese in 1943 and imprisoned with other American
internees for nearly a year, she endures fear and hunger;
her narrative closes with her liberation.

1063   JOHNSTON, FRAN (1926?-)
       Please Don't Strike That Match; A Young Mother in Today's
       World Faces the Fires of Adversity.   Grand Rapids, Mich.:
       Zondervan, 1970.   133pp.

       She and her husband serve as Evangelical missionaries in
France; she chronicles a series of family crises as she
"shatters" a leg and turns her hospital stays into opportunities to proselytize, she nears a nervous breakdown due to
tension between her parental and missionary roles, and she
fears cancer; in addition, her children have various medical
problems; she feels the family's sufferings are alleviated by
their religious faith.

1064   JOHNSTON, JILL
       Gullibles Travels.   New York: Links, 1974.   283pp.

       A writer, "evolving some new personae," presents her
collage of thoughts, experiences, and recollections, charac-
terizing her life as one of "risk and speed"; in a headlong
style, she discusses cars, a wilderness lake, travels, feminism, lesbianism, arrests, dreams, politics, and sexual
politics, "carrying everything along with me jilly nilly fact
legend gossip glory and gore"; the account is drawn from a
series of articles originally published in The Village Voice.

1065   JOHNSTONE, MARGARET BLAIR (1913-)
       When God Says "No": Faith's Starting Point.   New York:
       Simon and Schuster, 1954.   311pp.

       Having been trained as a teacher, educated at the Chicago
Theological Seminary, and employed in settlement house

work, she enters the ministry, later combining her profession with marriage and motherhood; she describes nineteen years as a Congregational minister, serving in a big city, in a mountain community, and in a New England town; she finds she must combat sexism.

1066 JONES, ANN (1938-)
Uncle Tom's Campus. New York: Praeger, 1973. 225pp.

Without missionary zeal, she takes a job teaching remedial classes at a small black Southern college because it is her only job offer; she finds the college a plantation-like closed system, "a school for servility," with a rigid hierarchy that stifles initiative and promotes racism.

1067 JONES, CANDY
More Than Beauty; A Behind-the-Scenes Look at the Modeling World. New York: Harper & Row, 1970. 175pp.

A writer of fashion books and founder of a modeling school, she tells anecdotes of her own career in New York, her social life, her eventual boredom with celebrities and millionaires; during World War II she tours with the U.S.O.; she describes modeling as "a profession full of the bizarre."

1068 JONES, CLARA J. (1900-)
Above the Tumult in China. Minneapolis: Augsburg, 1948. 182pp.

Her account is drawn from a diary of seven years in China as an Evangelical Lutheran missionary; she opens with the drama of the Japanese invasion and her flight into the mountains; she describes the general living conditions of the Chinese people, changes in some of the old customs, "the liberation of the women of China," and her health work; she closes with her return to the U.S.

1069 JONES, EDNA LAMBERTH
Harps in the Willows. New York: Pageant, 1965. 97pp.

In a series of charming vignettes, she pays warm tribute to the school teachers in her happy childhood; she is profoundly influenced first by a beloved black nurse, learning of love, beauty, and inner peace; she comes away with many valuable lessons and a deep love of learning.

1070 JONES, MARY SHARPE (1808-1869)
Yankees A'Coming; One Month's Experience During the Inva-

sion of Liberty County, Georgia, 1864-1865, with Mary
Jones Mallard. Tuscaloosa, Ala.: Confederate Publishing
Co., 1959. 102pp.

A mother and daughter's joint journal of the Civil War
describes in detail Yankee raiders following Sherman's
march to the sea; their home is plundered by successive
groups of soldiers; women alone with small children are
fearful, endure insults and threats; she describes their anxiety as her daughter bears her third child in the midst of
terror; she tells of "the great mercy of nights" without the
enemy's presence.

1071 JONES, RACHEL (pseud.)
      see BAKER, TRUDY (pseud.)

1072 JONES, VIOLET DRUCK
      "Hooray! PE Today!" Memoirs of a Physical Education
      Teacher. New York: Pageant, 1959. 126pp.

      An elementary teacher describes one school year in anec-
      dotes of her students, their sweetness, and their funny say-
      ings.

1073 JORDAN, GRACE EDGINTON
      Home Below Hell's Canyon. Lincoln, Neb.: University of
      Nebraska Press, 1954. 243pp.

      She tells of her domestic life beginning in 1933 on an
      Idaho sheep ranch with three young children; her household
      activities include cooking for hired hands, coping with ill-
      nesses and injuries, caring for the animals, but her family
      is able to avoid the worst effects of the depression.

1074 JORGENSEN, CHRISTINE (1926-)
      Christine Jorgensen; A Personal Autobiography. New York:
      Eriksson, 1967. 332pp.

      A nightclub and theatre performer, she is a transsexual
      whose medical conversion in 1950 caused international con-
      troversy; in spite of a close family, she suffers isolation
      and unhappiness as a boy and endures mental turmoil after
      being drafted by the army in 1945; secretly undergoing treat-
      ment to become a female in Denmark, she finds confidence
      and survives the publicity nightmare with personal courage
      and dignity; her sincere account avoids sensationalism.

1075 JUDSON, PHOEBE NEWTON GOODELL (1832-1926)
      A Pioneer's Search for an Ideal Home; A Book of Personal

Memoirs.   Tacoma,   Wash.:   Washington State Historical Society, 1966.   207pp.

She recounts "the homely, everyday incidents of a plain
woman," and "the romance of frontier life beyond the con-
fines of civilization"; she tells of the strenuous overland
journey west in 1853, including dangerous river crossings,
the birth of her son, the difficult descent from the Rockies;
she loves the sublime Oregon terrain; she notes details of
domestic establishment and farm drudgery; forced to flee to
a fort during Indian wars in 1855 and 1856, she later moves
from Olympia to remote wilderness; she establishes close
ties with the local Indians; she is active in politics from
1883 to 1887 and is widowed in 1899.

1076   "JULIE"
        My Nights and Days.   New York: Putnam, 1974.   256pp.

Her description of five years as a prostitute begins with
a discussion of her unhappy family life as a child; she tells
of events leading to her decision to become a prostitute; her
account goes on to include stories about various clients, her
temporary depressions, much travel; she closes with her decision to leave prostitution.

1077   K., MRS.
The Couple: A Sexual Profile by Mr. and Mrs. K, as told
to Monte Ghertler and Alfred Palca.   New York: Coward,
McCann & Geoghegan, 1971.   181pp.

She and her husband tape their recollections of two weeks
as "patients at the Reproductive Biology Research Foundation
of Masters and Johnson in 1970" in order to encourage others with similar sexual problems; in brief chapters alternating with those of her husband, she gradually reveals the details of her first marriage and the development of problems
with her second husband; she notes their progress as she
moves through stages of anger, depression, trust, and love.

1078   KAEHELE, EDNA
Living with Cancer.   Garden City, N.Y.:   Doubleday, 1952.
160pp.

In 1946 this mother of four is stricken with cancer and
given six months to live; existing under this "overwhelming
shadow," she frankly discusses her emotional and physical
suffering, but a powerful "life instinct" sustains her courage
and will for six years during her "slow progress back to
life"; she offers advice based on her own mistakes and successes.

1079   KAHN, FRIDA (1905-)
Generation in Turmoil.   Great Neck, N.Y.:   Channel Press,
1960.   224pp.

She presents her experience as typical during a unique
period of revolution, war, and emigration and portrays a
lifelong struggle to protect her inner life from the intrusion
of cataclysmic public events; the daughter of a wealthy Jewish Ukranian industrialist, she flees post-revolutionary Russia in 1920; she settles in Germany, becomes an accomplished
musician, and marries a composer, enjoying a rich intellectual and artistic life between 1925 and 1932, deeply devoted to
her husband and his work; in 1933 they flee to France, only
to be driven out again in 1940 when, after a harrowing escape, they arrive in the U.S.; her account is extremely perceptive and articulate.

1080   KAMB, ELEANOR WILLIAMS
        We Kept Mother Single.   New York: Dodd, Mead, 1951.
        245pp.

        A divorced mother writes from her youngest daughter's
        point of view, describing the family upheaval when her hus-
        band leaves in the midst of the depression; she copes with
        spirit, eagerness, and imagination, asserting her independ-
        ence in spite of persistent suitors and finally landing a
        "dream job" in New York City.

1081   KAMPEN, IRENE
        Are You Carrying Any Gold or Living Relatives?   Garden
        City, N.Y.:   Doubleday, 1970.   164pp.

        She writes a light, humorous tale of adventures and mis-
        haps, having been railroaded into a trip to Russia by a Rus-
        sian friend; she travels by car, by train, by ship, and at
        each destination she has amusing confrontations with In-
        tourist.

1082   Due to Lack of Interest, Tomorrow Has Been Cancelled.
        Garden City, N.Y.:   Doubleday, 1969.   168pp.

        In a light, humorous vein, she tells of her return, after
        a twenty-five year hiatus, as an undergraduate to the Uni-
        versity of Wisconsin during the years of protest; she en-
        counters various campus types among the students, admin-
        istrators, and faculty; she closes with a look at an alumni
        class reunion.

1083   Europe Without George.   New York: Norton, 1965.   166pp.

        This is a humorous account of a divorcée's six weeks in
        Europe with her Amazonian eighteen-year-old daughter; ex-
        aggerating for effect, she describes misadventures in rainy
        England, on a French beach, and with lecherous Italians,
        romantic Parisians, and her fellow tourists.

1084   Last Year at Sugarbush.   New York: Norton, 1966.   158pp.

        She humorously describes the pitfalls and pratfalls on and
        off the ski slopes as she chaperones her daughter and her
        daughter's boyfriend, at the same time finding opportunities
        for lessons with suave ski instructors.

1085   Life Without George.   Garden City, N.Y.:   Doubleday, 1961.
        191pp.

In a humorous tale of the hazards of life after divorce, she writes of sharing a house with another divorcée and their two children, of domesticity punctuated by mechanical crises without a man around the house, of her work as a journalist, of visits to a marriage counselor, of local politics, local theatricals, and finances; she reflects on the married state.

1086   Nobody Calls at This Hour Just to Say Hello.   Garden City, N. Y. : Doubleday, 1975. 135pp.

She writes random humorous anecdotes describing her Jewish mother, always expecting the worst, her daughter, a genetics professor, her term at a summer camp, inadvertently associating with communists, her neighbor's "Perfect Child. "

1087   KANDARIAN, BELLE A.
Fifty Years in Fresno; The Life Story of Belle A. Kandarian.
New York: Exposition, 1963. 87pp.

In a rambling, inarticulate account she tells of her marriage and of her initially happy family life, raising three children; after farming and real estate reverses, her husband fades from the family, and she endures years of poverty and hard work in a cannery; later she nurses her husband through his final illness, recounting his visions of angels; as an amateur spiritualist, she "gives messages" herself.

1088   KANE, ALISON (1919?-)
Worst Foot Forward. Boston: Christopher, 1965. 209pp.

Relentlessly optimistic, she seeks a cure for arthritis; after being stricken in 1940, she attempts to regain her health living in Arizona with an eccentric family, "a clutch of oddballs"; temporary remission enables her to earn a degree, begin teaching, and get married, but arthritis returns; she tries numerous orthodox and unorthodox methods, all recounted in detail in this slangy, breezy narrative.

1089   KANE, FAN
Suitcase Diplomats. New York: Carlton Press, 1962.
98pp.

A widowed grandmother describes her adventures traveling in the Far East with her two grandchildren, noting "the innocent diplomacy of youth," and delighting in the opportunities they have to promote international friendship and understanding; while traveling, she visits facilities for victims

of cerebral palsy, connected in an unspecified way with her
work in the U.S.

1090   KANE, PAULA
        Sex Objects in the Sky; A Personal Account of the Stewardess
        Rebellion. Chicago: Follett, 1974. 159pp.

        In an earnest, polemical account, she describes her ca-
        reer as a stewardess from 1968 to 1973; criticizing the
        "stewardess fantasy" and the "glamour myth," she discusses
        the evolution of her attitudes from romantic idealism to dis-
        illusionment and rebellion; the feminist movement of the
        1970's and the inevitable pressures for increasing profes-
        sionalism deeply influence her career and her most profound
        sense of identity.

1091   KATZENSTEIN, CAROLINE
        Lifting the Curtain; The State and National Woman Suffrage
        Campaigns in Pennsylvania as I Saw Them.   Philadelphia:
        Dorrance, 1955.   376pp.

        A woman's suffrage leader, "in a strategic position at a
        critical time," she tells of her work as the Executive Secre-
        tary of the Pennsylvania Woman Suffrage Association from
        1910 to 1912 and her work with the National Woman's Party
        from 1916 to 1920; with much detailed material of historical
        interest as well as descriptions of her personal experiences
        working closely with Alice Paul and Anna Howard Shaw, she
        discusses the drama leading to the suffrage amendment in
        1920.

1092   KAUCHER, DOROTHY JUANITA (1892-   )
        Armchair in the Sky; Ocean Flights with Air Pioneers.   New
        York: Exposition, 1954. 144pp.

        An adventurer who thrills to this "new frontier of the
        world," she tells of the wondrous flying clippers in a 1937
        Pacific flight, of an Amazon flight in 1938, of a flight to the
        Isle of Man in 1939; her second-person narrative gives her
        impressions of new sights, new experiences, new destina-
        tions.

1093   On Your Left the Milky Way.   Boston: Christopher, 1952.
        308pp.

        Writing in an impressionistic, inflated style, she notes
        her "great awakening" in 1924, a dedication to adventure
        through flying; the narrative chronicles her presence on many
        historic flights including transcontinental flights in 1931,

1933, and 1934; in 1937 her dream of a Pacific flight is
realized on one of the great China Clippers; she celebrates
America's pioneering heritage in the sky.

1094   Wings Over Wake.   San Francisco: John Howell, 1947.
       158pp.

       "A lady sitter-in-the-sky" with an intense love of avia-
       tion, she begins flying in 1930; this account describes a
       1937 flight across the Pacific, going via Hawaii and Midway
       to Guam and China; the outbreak of the Sino-Japanese War
       forces her return to the U.S.; her experiences are overlaid
       with romance, the pioneer spirit, and patriotic fervor.

1095   KAUSE, SELMA
       Mahalo, nui, nui, Aloha.   Tucson, Ariz.:   Post Printing,
       1966.   341pp.

       A teacher, she writes an extremely disorganized account
       with chapters on her parents, her brothers, church activi-
       ties, religious work in Hawaii, travels in Russia and Ger-
       many in 1932; she incorporates the texts of some religious
       skits.

1096   KAVANAUGH, ETHEL (1901-)
       Wilderness Homesteaders.   Caldwell, Id.:   Caxton, 1950.
       303pp.

       She discusses her "joys and struggles" on an Alaskan
       homestead, pioneering with her adult daughter; they endure
       mishaps and frustrations, but glory in their natural sur-
       roundings, growing strong and self-sufficient through physical
       labor; she backpacks supplies, raises a log cabin, clears a
       road, drives a team of horses, and dreams of the future in
       "the loveliest spot in the world."

1097   KAVINOKY, BERNICE (1916?-1966?)
       Voyage and Return.   New York: Norton, 1966.   72pp.

       A teacher and writer, she writes of her experience with
       breast cancer to clarify her own feeling and thinking; hers
       is a sensitive chronicle of inner states, from the initial
       shock to the "high drama" of the first few weeks after sur-
       gery to a daily routine shadowed by vulnerability and fear.

1098   KEAYS, ELIZABETH PARKE (1830-1922)
       The Saga of "Auntie" Stone and Her Cabin ... with the Over-
       land Diary of Elizabeth Parke Keays, by Nolie Mumey.
       Boulder, Colo.:   Johnson Publishing, 1964.   128pp.

The diary is found on pages 51-93 and recounts the trip
of a widow with her 1-year-old son in 1866 to Fort Collins,
Colorado in a party of seven; she absorbs each new experience, admires the beautiful scenery, points out the flowers,
notes inflated prices; enjoying "every inch of the way," she
is happy to settle with an aunt and earn her living.

1099   KEIFFER, ELIZABETH (1923-)
        Year in the Sun. Indianapolis: Bobbs-Merrill, 1956.
        275pp.

        A journalist, she writes of a year in Mexico with her
        painter husband and infant son; describing in amusing detail
        the delights and frustrations of their small town home, she
        tells of various little domestic adventures, endless cultural
        faux pas, making friends, and a succession of maids with
        maddening Mexican insouciance; later she tours several
        Unesco educational projects; she realizes that her percep-
        tions gradually have become more "Mexican," and when
        they decide to return to the U.S., she bids Mexico a tear-
        ful farewell.

1100   KEITH, AGNES NEWTON (1901-)
        Bare Feet in the Palace. Boston: Little, Brown, 1955.
        370pp.

        A writer, she joins her husband in the Philippines and
        establishes a household, although her domesticity is unset-
        tled due to the pervasive political instability and the striking
        contrast between extravagant wealth and horrible poverty;
        raising a son, she becomes acquainted with the children of
        the barrio, local fiestas, servants; when she returns to the
        U.S., she notes "how American I am in my ways."

1101   Children of Allah. Boston: Little, Brown, 1965. 467pp.

        A one-year stay in Libya in 1955 extends to nine years
        as she settles there with her son and her husband, a U.N.
        forestry expert; she finds life there both "basic and gay,"
        as they travel extensively and gradually form a "Libyan
        identification"; she presents a detailed discussion of women's
        lives, customs, and traditions, noting vast changes during
        the nine years under consideration; she finds their departure
        painful.

1102   Three Came Home. Boston: Little, Brown, 1947. 317pp.

        She writes a moving, sensitive narrative which evokes the
        horrors of war and serves to remind her son of the power

of sustaining love; married to a British forester in Borneo,
she is caught in the Japanese occupation and, separated
from her husband, is interned with her child; she presents
a vivid description of the filth, hunger, heavy labor, illness, and beatings that constitute camp life, closing with
her liberation and return to the U. S.

1103   White Man Returns.   Boston: Little, Brown, 1951.   310pp.

She opens with her return to her former home in Borneo
and her reunion with her husband after liberation from a
Japanese concentration camp (see Three Came Home); amid
the ghosts of wartime memories, she raises her son, renews close ties with native friends, and lives in "scented,
sensual, primitive beauty"; she describes a household characterized by humanity, trust, understanding, and affection.

1104   KEITLEN, TOMI (1923?-)
       Farewell to Fear, with Norman M. Lobsenz.   New York:
       Bernard Geis, 1960.   286pp.

She celebrates a triumph of "the human spirit" over her
blindness; after going blind, she refuses to accept the segregation of the handicapped, conquers her own fear and
self-pity, and is bolstered after her divorce by an understanding daughter; aided by a guide dog, she returns to her
work with the Anti-Defamation League, accepts the challenges of travelling, lecturing, skiing in the Swiss Alps, and
serving as a business partner for fitness expert Bonnie
Prudden.

1105   KELLER, HELEN ADAMS (1880-1968)   NAWM
       Teacher: Anne Sullivan Macy.   Garden City, N. Y. :   Double-
       day, 1955.   247pp.

She presents a moving "Tribute by the Foster-child of
Her Mind," written partly to correct the youthful insensitivity of her earlier books by her more mature perceptions of
the subtleties of their unique relationship; she is grateful for
her teacher's insistence on a life among the non-handicapped
and a life of service to others; distressed to recall her un-
civilized "Phantom" childhood, she notes her gradual recognition of Macy as a distinct, proud, driven personality;
keenly aware of Macy's bent toward self-sacrifice, she works
in later life to provide for her; stricken by her teacher's
death, she nevertheless resolves to lecture, write, and travel, working always on behalf of others.

1106 KELLNER, ESTHER
The Devil and Aunt Serena.   Indianapolis: Bobbs-Merrill,
1968.   207pp.

Raised in a small Midwest town by her grandparents and
a fiercely moral great aunt, she recalls childhood in "an
orderly, familiar world" with a series of warm, perceptive
vignettes; she tells of her two younger, feminine and well-
behaved sisters, of long underwear season, of "boughten
music" and catalog purchases, of visiting city folks, of a
revered country doctor, of Christmas and Santa Claus.

1107 Out of the Woods.   Garden City, N.Y.:   Doubleday, 1964.
228pp.

A naturalist and author of books on religion, she opens
with a sensitive portrait of an Indiana backwoodsman who
teaches her animal ways, Indian hunting, and a deep appreciation of nature's beauty; later when she is married, she
raises orphaned wild creatures, gaining an unparalleled
knowledge of squirrel behavior over a period of five years.

1108 KELLY, MARY ELIZABETH
Adventures of an Exchange Teacher.   New York: Vantage,
1954.   205pp.

A teacher from South Dakota, "a pioneer in the field of
exchange teaching," spends a year in England from 1939 to
1940; receptive to a new school environment, she teaches in
several kinds of schools and at different grade levels; she
notes ominous signs of approaching war and, before depart-
ing, helps to prepare the evacuation of children to the countryside; her account was written in 1943.

1109 KELLY, MARY ELLEN (1922-)
But with the Dawn, Rejoicing.   Milwaukee: Bruce, 1959.
182pp.

In a straightforward, open account that reveals courage
and pride, she tells of her life defined by rheumatoid arthritis; living with constant pain and almost totally immobilized
by eighteen, she nevertheless forms many deep and lasting
friendships; her need for self-expression leads to her organizing a Catholic sodality for invalids, publishing a national
newsletter, and writing for Catholic magazines; her extensive
travels, made possible by her devoted parents and friends,
culminate in a pilgrimage to Fatima, Lourdes, and Rome.

1110 KELSEY, ANNA MARIETTA (1863-)
Through the Years; Reminiscences of Pioneer Days on the
Texas Border. San Antonio: Naylor, 1952. 179pp.

She opens with a family history; adopted in 1865, she
learns the household arts from her mother and tells of their
prosperous ranch life in rambling anecdotes; after her parents' deaths, she manages the family business, is active in
women's club work, and builds a church as a memorial to
her parents in 1948.

1111 KEMBLE, FRANCES ANNE (1809-1893)   NAW
Fanny, The American Kemble: Her Journals and Unpub-
lished Letters, ed. Fanny Kemble Wister. Tallahassee:
South Pass Press, 1972. 227pp.

The account consists of selections from Records of a Girlhood, her American journals (see companion volume), and
new letters; writing with wit, she admits being an independent, "unmanageable" child; her stage career, to which she
has a lifelong aversion, is begun out of duty to aid her parents financially and is met with immediate public adulation;
touring the U.S. with her father in 1833 and 1834, she is
often sharply critical of Americans and American culture,
yet inexplicably, she enters a disastrous marriage to an
American slave-holder which ends in a hostile divorce and
the loss of her children; she returns to the stage as reader
of classics to support herself, then turns to writing her superb autobiographical narratives.

1112 KEMPKEN, MINNIE L. (1906-)
Aloha Malihini; Vacation in Romantic Hawaii. New York:
Exposition, 1960. 93pp.

A schoolteacher describes her trip in 1958 as part of a
university study tour; she makes friends among the tour
members, and attends classes, shops, and sees the local
sights; she adds notes on Hawaiian customs and traditions.

1113 KENMORE, CAROLYN
Mannequin; My Life as a Model. New York: Bartholomew
House, 1969. 313pp.

In a light account, this red-haired model offers glimpses
of her childhood and anecdotes of various jobs with various
photographers; initially "giddy and green and innocent," she
begins by modeling for commercials and magazine ads, fending off lecherous employers.

1114   KENNEDY, FLORYNCE R. (1916-)
        Color Me Flo: My Hard Life and Good Times.   Englewood
        Cliffs, N.J.:   Prentice-Hall, 1976.   169pp.

        A slangy, tough, opinionated, feminist lawyer tells of
        growing up "very poor, very proud, and a Negro"; she
        graduates from Columbia Law School but becomes disen-
        chanted with the legal system; she reflects on contemporary
        society, politics, racism, sexuality, oppression; she works
        for social change, speaking widely and engaging in radical
        politics and demonstrations with feminist colleagues.

1115   KENNEDY, MARGUERITE WALLACE
        My Home on the Range.   Boston: Little, Brown, 1951.
        341pp.

        When her family settles on an Arizona desert homestead,
        she teaches in a country school, enjoying the colorful local
        characters and lively social activities; she marries a cattle
        rancher, adjusting to an "already established household,"
        learning the management and business aspects of ranching,
        cooking for her family, hired hands, and guests; drought
        forces the sale of the ranch, and the death of her mother-
        in-law marks the "end of an era," the loss of a way of life.

1116   KENNEDY, ROSE FITZGERALD (1890-)
        Times to Remember.   Garden City, N.Y.:   Doubleday, 1974.
        536pp.

        A vigorous, indomitable woman, she wishes to present "a
        faithful portrait and history of our family" although she
        chooses to "reminisce selectively," emphasizing the good
        times; raised in an extremely close, energetic, political
        family, she marries in 1914 and forms a strong partnership
        with her husband, "the architect of our lives"; she views the
        rearing of her nine children to the ideals of service and ex-
        cellence as a professional commitment; facing the multiple
        tragedies of a retarded daughter, the deaths of her eldest
        son and eldest daughter, the assassinations of two of her
        politically prominent sons, and the death of her husband, she
        nevertheless continues to face the future with undiminished
        devotion to activity and growth.

1117   KENT, ADALINE (1900-1957)
        Autobiography from the Notebooks and Sculpture of Adaline
        Kent, ed. Jermayne MacAgy, Alice C. Kent, and Robert B.
        Howard.   Houston, Texas: Gulf Printing, 1958.   82pp.

        The book consists of a series of reflections on art, ex-
        perience, and expression, interspersed with photographs of

her sculpture and drawings, revealing a depth of intensity
and introspection; "These are the expressions of experience
--emotional and physical--as such they are autobiography--
the record of personal adventure."

1118   KENT, LOUISE ANDREWS (1886-1969)
       Mrs. Appleyard and I. Boston: Houghton Mifflin, 1968.
       414pp.

       A prolific author of books for adults and children, she
       writes at eighty of her literary persona, "I wish I could tell
       Mrs. Appleyard and me apart"; her genial, articulate nar-
       rative describes Mrs. Appleyard's genesis in the early days
       of her marriage; when her children are young, she writes
       children's books, her first Mrs. Appleyard book appearing
       in 1941; her favorite family stories are scattered throughout.

1119   The Summer Kitchen (Mrs. Appleyard's, Of Course), with
       Elizabeth Kent Gay. Boston: Houghton Mifflin, 1957.
       234pp.

       A Vermont author of children's books and cookbooks pre-
       sents a tale of good food and good company; she delights in
       the seasonal variations of nature and nature's produce and
       in the domestic pleasures of sharing meals; writing of her-
       self in the third person, she describes with great affection
       and satisfaction the preparations for parties, dinners, and
       picnics for family and friends; she includes recipes.

1120   KERN, JANET (1924-   )
       Yesterday's Child. Philadelphia: Lippincott, 1960. 239pp.

       Born and raised between the wars, she presents herself
       as typical, a member of a unique generation; she grows up
       in Chicago, the ordinary daughter of colorful parents, a
       Jewish immigrant doctor and a non-religious mother, and
       depression times touch her only lightly; she attends Catholic
       and public schools, and her adolescent questions include
       "what is it to be Jewish?" as the rise of Hitler brings her
       Jewish heritage to consciousness.

1121   KERR, JEAN COLLINS (1923-   )
       Penny Candy. Garden City, N.Y.: Doubleday, 1970. 186pp.

       She presents short, wry essays on fashion, conversing
       with babies, houseplants, company menus, Christmas toys,
       her experiences as "a part-time playwright," marriage and
       rearing six children, futile attempts to read uplifting books,
       and her amusing but successful attempts to introduce her

children to poetry; her chapters were previously published
in magazine form.

1122   Please Don't Eat the Daisies.   Garden City, N. Y. :   Double-
        day, 1957.   192pp.

   In a series of wry essays, she tells of her marriage to
a professor and drama critic, her own attempts as a playwright, her four sons, her eccentric house, her acquaintance
with various theatrical producers, dogs she has known, and
a hospital stay; some chapters were previously published in
magazine form.

1123   The Snake Has All the Lines.   Garden City, N. Y. :   Double-
        day, 1960.   168pp.

   In a series of humorous autobiographical vignettes she
tells of taking her children to the beach, writing protest
letters, being a reluctant airline passenger, learning "how
to talk like a man," taming her children's manners, attending plays, and performing as an adolescent "Queen of the
May"; the chapters were previously published in magazine
form.

1124   KEYES, FRANCES PARKINSON WHEELER (1885-1970)
        All Flags Flying; Reminiscences of Frances Parkinson Keyes.
        New York: McGraw-Hill, 1972.   655pp.

   She explores a series of significant changes in her life,
beginning with her marriage, an enchanting "revelation" followed by the glorious fulfillment of motherhood; she learns
fortitude by living throughout her life with a severe physical
handicap; writing, her "secret vice," becomes her lifework as
well as a way to ease financial strain; at the same time, she
accepts the heavy social obligations of a governor's, then a
senator's wife; she travels extensively to cover national and
international events for magazine articles; a superb writer,
she is a model of vigor.

1125   The Cost of a Best Seller.   New York: Julian Messner,
        1950.   126pp.

   She offers a frank discussion of her initial secret writing
in an attic retreat when the family finances run low, the
physical strain of writing, and of the difficulties and expenses
in research for a novel's background; although she feels the
achievement of a best seller is small compensation, she sees
writing as a form of fellowship, keeping her "in touch with
the human family."

1126   Roses in December.   Garden City, N.Y.:   Doubleday, 1960.
        335pp.

        Highly articulate and a phenomenally prolific writer, she
tells of her childhood, enabled to become a "semi-Bostonian"
by her charming, beautiful mother's third marriage; she acquires a genteel education, enjoying "small social triumphs,"
but her mother discourages her desire to write and publish;
at fifteen, she is under the wing of her future husband; a
breakdown and ill-fated engagement interrupt her schooling;
her narrative closes with her marriage to Keyes; for other
autobiographical works, see companion volume.

1127   KEYTON, CLARA Z.
        Destiny Beckons.   Banning, Cal.:   Deeble Press, 1964.
        136pp.

        In a pedestrian account, she describes the world of her
rural Missouri youth, as "the home, the school, and the
church"; she teaches, graduates from college in 1914, is a
travelling bookseller, and marries in 1920; widowed in 1940,
she travels, then remarries in 1943, enjoying satisfying but
difficult garden and orchard work and traveling in the U.S.
and England.

1128   Tourist Camp Pioneering Experiences.   Chicago: Adams
        Press, 1960.   152pp.

        In 1925 she and her husband wish to go into business for
themselves; establishing a tourist camp, she tells of steady
improvements from tents to modern cottages over the years;
she provides numerous anecdotes of tourist customers, successes as well as difficulties during the depression, satisfaction as well as hard work; widowed in 1940, she writes her
account between 1940 and 1942.

1129   KIEFER, MARCY
        Retire and Be Gay---Florida, U.S.A.   New York: Vantage,
        1960.   60pp.

        In this light account of a middle-aged couple's retirement
in Florida, she and her husband overcome their initial difficulties finding income property; they buy a tourist home,
and she tells of their remodeling work, experiences with
tourists, relationships with local residents; she closes noting
their decision to return north and abandon retirement.

1130   KILBORN, JOAN S.
        Over the Horizon; Vignettes of a Voyager.   Portland, Me.:
        Dirigo Press, 1950.   150pp.

An enthusiastic traveller, she tells of numerous trips and
sightseeing in New England, England, Scandinavia, the western U. S., Egypt, the Middle East, Greece, South America,
and Mexico; although most of the dates are unspecified, some
trips take place before World War I.

1131 KILGORE, HERMINA GERTRUDE (1912?-)
Rough Road in the Rockies. Denver: Big Mountain Press,
1961. 135pp.

Married during the depression, she describes her economic struggles on a Colorado fox farm; "adjusted to insecurity," she writes for magazines, raises two sons, and
endures years of deprivation before final financial collapse
in 1947; she graduates from college at forty, teaches, earns
an M. A. in 1954, proud of her education and her new career.

1132 KILLILEA, MARIE LYONS
Karen. New York: Prentice-Hall, 1952. 314pp.

This is a mother's story of her dedication to the development and independence of a daughter born in 1940 with cerebral palsy; she rejects doctors' diagnoses of a hopelessly
handicapped, mentally deficient child, and devotes herself
with great courage and stamina to physical therapy and intellectual stimulation for her daughter; beginning in 1946,
she works in New York to organize other families with CP
children; her chronicle of eight years is full of hope.

1133 With Love from Karen. Englewood Cliffs, N. J.: Prentice-
Hall, 1963. 371pp.

She writes in response to the voluminous correspondence
which followed Karen (1952); she serves as "wife, mother,
physiotherapist, occupational therapist, nurse, teacher, and
now psychologist" as her children mature and seek wider
horizons; she portrays a daily life of joy and courage under
the loving influence of a close family life, and her pain
when two of her children marry and leave home; she remains deeply concerned over Karen's difficult decisions af-
fecting dependence versus freedom.

1134 KILMER, PAT
Dough, Ray and Me: The Adventures of a Family Who Gave
Up Social Security for Home on the Range. New York:
William Sloane, 1957. 318pp.

In a humorous account, "Mr. and Mrs. Average City
Dweller" strike out for self-employment and settle in a

small New Mexico town to open a family bakery; savoring her independence, nevertheless she must adjust to a simple lifestyle, living from day to day on a tight budget; as she becomes involved in the life of the community, she notes the interdependence of the people; after a period of demoralization, they begin to exploit the bakery's potential with creative ideas; her triumph comes when the bakery provides a comfortable living.

1135   KIM, AGNES DAVIS
        I Married a Korean.   New York: John Day, 1953.   246pp.

        She marries a Korean Christian minister in 1934, taking a "pioneer step in interracial relationships"; settling in Korea, she fights prejudice and accepts hardships in the spirit of her frontier forbears; she establishes a place for herself in community work and leadership; after study in the U. S. during World War II, she returns to Korea to find changes in Korean customs and values and distressingly offensive American occupational forces; she closes on a reflective note, with great praise for her mother-in-law.

1136   KIMBALL, GUSSIE (1901?-)
        Gitele.   New York: Vantage, 1960.   355pp.

        The narrative focuses on her three "families"; that of her childhood in New York as the daughter of Polish Jewish immigrants, that of her adulthood when she is a wife and mother, and that of her work with charitable causes; she is uneducated but writes with warmth and candor about her sorrows and difficulties.

1137   KIMBROUGH, EMILY (1899-)
        And a Right Good Crew.   New York: Harper, 1958.   273pp.

        An irrepressible traveller and prolific writer tells of two weeks on English canals, a return engagement after the trip described in Water, Water Everywhere; the first week she tours with a friend and a hired "lad," enjoying her contacts with "barge people" and villagers along the way; for the second week of beauty and tranquillity, she joins three more friends, whose personalities and endearing foibles make this an entertaining account, as always.

1138   Better Than Oceans.   New York: Harper & Row, 1976.
        231pp.

        She recounts two river voyages, the first in 1974 in France, virtually repeating a trip taken in 1968 (see Floating

Island) and combining her present observations with her
memories of the past trip; she enjoys the small dramas of
village sightseeing and slowly unfolding landscapes; the
second voyage is along the East River and the Hudson River
with a small group of congenial friends, offering new perspectives on New York City.

1139   Floating Island. New York: Harper & Row, 1968. 243pp.

She offers this articulate, breezy account of a trip on a
French barge with a group of congenial friends; after gay
preparations, they get underway and maintain a leisurely
pace, scattering at village stops for sightseeing, visiting
vineyards; they achieve a kind of distant intimacy with crew
members.

1140   Forty Plus and Fancy Free. New York: Harper, 1954.
        240pp.

Traveling in Europe in 1953 with three friends, all of
them grandmothers, she enjoys Paris in the spring, a trip
on the Orient Express to Italy, an audience with the Pope;
she closes with her arrival in London where she is assigned
to cover the coronation of Queen Elizabeth II for CBS radio;
her narrative is, as usual, entertaining.

1141   The Innocents from Indiana. New York: Harper, 1950.
        229pp.

She describes the upheaval of a move from Muncie to
Chicago when she's eleven as "an American incident"; witty
anecdotes portray the artificiality of hotel and apartment life;
she keeps a wry eye on her brother's social, cultural, and
financial pastimes; mocked in a private girls' school as "the
Hoosier hayseed," she slowly learns "the social customs of
people who lived in cities," establishes a few hesitant friendships, and finishes high school.

1142   Now and Then. New York: Harper & Row, 1972. 176pp.

She writes vignettes, some humorous and some touching,
about being the mother of twin daughters, stories of her
children recalling stories of her childhood; her daughters'
mumps recall her childhood brush with diphtheria; she recounts the death of an infant sister, an afternoon of innocent
drunkenness with her Senator grandfather, examples of life's
"improbabilities," other family lore; she has "the most
thrilling time of my life" in 1915 as a theatrical heroine.

1143 Pleasure by the Busload. New York: Harper, 1961.
      276pp.

      She writes this chronicle of travel in Portugal with four
      friends "to share the pleasure my companions and I had
      from landscape and people"; with characteristic gentle, wry
      humor she portrays both her friends and the objects of their
      sightseeing.

1144 So Near and Yet So Far. New York: Harper, 1955. 241pp.

      She sets out with six former college friends to "explore
      the Cajun country"; her delightful, spirited anecdotes portray
      a conspicuous group of middle-aged women, each with her
      own sightseeing foibles, in old New Orleans; she manages
      to include much local color.

1145 Through Charley's Door. New York: Harper, 1952. 273pp.

      Charley, a doorman, opens the way into a world of adver-
      tising and journalism; in the early 1920's she finds herself a
      naïve young fashion copywriter with Marshall Field's in Chi-
      cago, and her entertaining anecdotes describe her learning
      the ropes; she is promoted to editor of a Field's magazine,
      then becomes the fashion editor of the Ladies Home Journal.

1146 Time Enough. New York: Harper & Row, 1974. 216pp.

      She offers another delightful travel memoir; with congenial
      friends, she cruises the River Shannon in Ireland in 1972;
      together with portraits of her friends' personalities and styles
      of travel, her account includes charming anecdotes of sight-
      seeing, relaxation, and her own fondness for people and
      landscapes.

1147 Water, Water Everywhere. New York: Harper, 1956.
      308pp.

      A prolific magazine and travel writer, she is inspired by
      her childhood studies to see Greece; with characteristic wry
      humor she describes sightseeing there in 1955 with three
      friends; they return to the U. S. via England.

1148 KING, BILLIE JEAN (1943-)
      Billie Jean, with Kim Chapin. New York: Harper & Row,
      1974. 208pp.

      Writing in a chatty, colloquial style, the famous tennis

star tells of her youthful competitive spirit and dedication to become "the best tennis player ever"; she marries in 1965, and her husband supports her pursuit of excellence; eager and intense, she becomes "a tough, aggressive professional," leading a revolution in women's tennis; she comments with insight on the rigors of competition.

1149   KING, CAROLINE BLANCHE CAMPION
        This Was Ever in My Dream.   Caldwell, Idaho: Caxton,
        1947.   297pp.

A zealous gardener, she describes the combination of a Pennsylvania acre of land and her desire for "orderly romance"; over a number of years and with a succession of gardeners, she gradually shapes the garden, notes her "failures and triumphs," and tells anecdotes of various individual trees, shrubs, and flowers; she is deeply pleased with her garden planted with "memories and dreams."

1150   KING, CORETTA SCOTT (1927-)
        My Life with Martin Luther King, Jr.   New York: Holt,
        Rinehart and Winston, 1969.   372pp.

The widow of civil rights leader Martin Luther King tells of her rural childhood in a family that emphasizes self-respect and educational achievement; she is educated at Antioch College and the New England Conservatory of Music, then marries in 1953 and dedicates her own life to that of a leader with a sense of destiny; she describes the drama of the Montgomery bus boycott, bombings, threats, arrests, tragedies of friends' murders, as she joins her husband's work for the civil rights movement; she provides a moving account of her husband's assassination and its aftermath.

1151   KINGSTON, MAXINE HONG (1940-)
        The Woman Warrior; Memoirs of a Girlhood Among Ghosts.
        New York: Knopf, 1976.   209pp.

Attempting to "name the unspeakable," to integrate her Chinese immigrant parents' culture and the American culture in which she grows up, she speculates about ancestors to give herself roots; she is caught in the contradiction between her mother's fable of an avenging swordswoman and restrictive demands to be a submissive female; with intensity and sensitivity, she evokes the difficulties of distinguishing the implications of her mother's experiences, of distinguishing truth from legend, of distinguishing one culture from another.

1152   KINNEY, JEAN BROWN
       Start with an Empty Nest.   New York: Harcourt, Brace &
       World, 1968. 276pp.

       With breathless vitality, this New York advertising execu-
       tive, with two daughters grown and gone, recounts her search
       for a husband and the idyllic country life; she describes her
       hectic career, the arrival of her first grandchild, the pro-
       gress of a romance, and she closes with her marriage,
       complete with country home.

1153   KINSEY, NINA (pseud.)
       Nineteen Years with an Alcoholic.   New York: Vantage,
       1954. 208pp.

       Within months after her marriage, she recognizes her
       husband's severe drinking problem, and her life settles into
       a pattern of fights and reconciliations; in spite of his beat-
       ings, broken promises, and other women, she remains hope-
       ful and feels in 1951 that her marriage has reached an op-
       timistic turning point.

1154   KIRBAN, DIANE (1956?-)
       Stranger in Tomorrow's Land; A Pictorial Commentary on
       the Holy Land.   Huntingdon Valley, Pa. : Salem Kirban,
       1970. 96pp.

       Her account is a travel journal recounting a trip to the
       Holy Land with her father, sister (see Kirban, Doreen), and
       several others; her sightseeing recalls many related Biblical
       passages with which she embellishes her journal.

1155   KIRBAN, DOREEN (1953?-)
       Stranger in Tomorrow's Land; A Pictorial Commentary on
       the Holy Land.   Huntingdon Valley, Pa. : Salem Kirban,
       1970. 96pp.

       Her account is a travel journal recounting a trip to the
       Holy Land with her father, sister (see entry #1154), and
       several others; visiting sites with scriptural associations,
       she is moved to rather mature religious reflection in addi-
       tion to straightforward description; Biblical quotations abound.

1156   KISTNER, RITA CUSTADO
       South Sea Adventure Cruise.   New York: Vantage, 1960.
       119pp.

       She describes a trip by yacht in 1956 to various South Sea
       islands; with her husband, the captain, and sixteen others,
       she enjoys sailing and meeting the island people.

1157   KITT, EARTHA MAE (1928-   )
       Alone with Me.   Chicago: Regnery, 1976.   276pp.

       A famous black singer, dancer, and actress tells of her
       unhappy, poverty-stricken youth, rejected by her family,
       merely tolerated in a foster home, kept reluctantly by an
       aunt in New York City; she is drawn to acting and music
       and attends a performing arts high school, then joins Kath-
       erine Dunham (see entry #611) and her company for train-
       ing and performance; in Paris, she becomes a star, but
       only after years of "professional exile" does she succeed in
       the U.S.; intense and driven, she feels a split between her
       public persona and her private self.

1158   Thursday's Child.   New York: Duell, Sloan and Pearce,
       1956.   250pp.

       A famous singer, dancer, and actress opens her account
       with painful scenes from her poverty-stricken childhood, re-
       jected as a "yalla gal" by her mother; she joins an aunt in
       New York City and soon begins dancing with Katherine Dun-
       ham (see entry #611); she performs in Mexico, Hollywood,
       and Europe, finally leaving the Dunham troupe for cabaret
       work in Paris; overwork brings breakdowns and she never
       conquers a sense of pervasive loneliness, but she gradually
       finds her own style and achieves stardom in New York.

1159   KITT, EDITH STRATTON (1878-   )
       Pioneering in Arizona; The Reminiscences of Emerson Oliver
       Stratton & Edith Stratton Kitt, ed. John Alexander Carroll.
       Tucson: Arizona Pioneers' Historical Society, 1964.   178pp.

       Born in the Arizona territory, she recalls childhood ranch
       activities, Indian scares in the early 1880's, attending school
       in Tucson during the winters, becoming a teacher; she mar-
       ries in 1903, and is "frightened and awkward" in her new
       social position; she is active in womens' clubs and works for
       twenty-two years with the Arizona Pioneers' Historical Soci-
       ety; her reminiscences are on pages 111-164.

1160   KJOME, JUNE C.
       Back of Beyond: Bush Nurse in South Africa.   Minneapolis:
       Augsburg, 1963.   237pp.

       Presenting her personal experiences as typical, she writes
       of her service in a small mission hospital among the Zulus
       beginning in 1945; necessity forces her to master many
       skills, including midwifery; she travels into remote areas,
       struggling constantly against native superstitions and the in-
       fluence of native medicine men; on furlough in 1952, she
       lectures in the U.S., then returns to Africa.

1161 KLABAN, HELEN (1941?-)
Hey, I'm Alive! with Beth Day.   New York: McGraw-Hill,
1963.   206pp.

This is a straightforward account of her ordeal of forty-
nine days before her rescue after a Yukon plane crash in
1962; both she and the pilot sustain injuries and are forced
to cope with bitter cold and little food; with her feet crippled
and frozen, she reads, keeps a journal, and gingerly establishes a friendship with the pilot; when he leaves to seek
help, she notes her dreams, fears, and fantasies; her rescue generates massive press coverage, and she experiences
a sense of love, independence, and rebirth.

1162 KLASNER, LILY CASEY (1862-1946)
My Girlhood Among Outlaws, ed. Eve Ball.   Tucson, Ariz.:
University of Arizona Press, 1972.   336pp.

She tells of her pioneer home following her family's move
to New Mexico in 1866, describing domestic and farm tasks,
an Indian raid, insect plagues, epidemics, economic struggles, the murder of her father, harassment by members of
local warring factions, and "other tragedies and shooting
scrapes"; she takes her first teaching job in 1882.

1163 KLASS, ROSANNE
Land of the High Flags; A Travel-Memoir of Afghanistan.
New York: Random House, 1964.   319pp.

The first and only woman to serve as an English teacher
at a provincial boys' school in Afghanistan from 1951 to
1954, she is a keen observer and offers much detailed description of the landscape, local customs, and domestic ar-
rangements; she forms a deep attachment to the school and
her students, leaving them with an emotional farewell.

1164 KLASS, SHEILA SOLOMON
Everyone in This House Makes Babies.   Garden City, N.Y.:
Doubleday, 1964.   174pp.

A novelist, accompanying her husband, an anthropologist,
to Trinidad in 1957, she settles in a village and learns much
about local customs, food, householding, and women's lives;
she describes her pregnancy and the birth of a daughter
there; her humorous anecdotes portray warm and open friendships with neighbors, and she closes with the ceremony at
their departure.

1165 KLEIN, GERDA WEISSMANN (1924-)
All But My Life.   New York: Hill and Wang, 1957.   246pp.

A Polish Jew, she writes a moving narrative of the years from 1939 to 1945; prevented from fleeing before the German invasion by her father's illness, she bids "farewell to my childhood," first suffering in the ghetto, then separated from her family and interned in a concentration camp; with great inner strength and courage, she endures the "infamous death march to Czechoslovakia" in 1945 and backbreaking camp labor; at liberation, she is among the few survivors; she comes to love an American soldier, and her account closes just before their marriage.

1166 KLEIN, ROCHELLE (1899-)
The Girl Who Never Played. New York: Comet, 1957. 54pp.

After a childhood marked by poverty, she marries a wealthy egotist and endures years of unhappiness; convulsive attacks caused by a brain tumor begin after her grief over an adult daughter's death; she becomes reclusive yet cares for her husband in his long terminal illness; after her own surgery and rehabilitation attempts, she finds it hard to accept being handicapped; her narrative is disconnected.

1167 KLIGMAN, RUTH
Love Affair; A Memoir of Jackson Pollack. New York: Morrow, 1974. 220pp.

A model and an art student, her work in a New York gallery leads to her meeting with painter Jackson Pollack; they immediately become intense lovers, their relationship full of drama and unspoken meaning; she "loved making him happy" and enjoys a summer idyll in his home, yet she feels deeply threatened by his inner torment; "totally annihilated" by his personality; Pollack dies in an auto accident, remaining "the ultimate mystery, my deep love, my archetypal lover and father."

1168 KLOSE, VIRGINIA TAYLOR (1911-)
Call Me Mother. New York: Dodd, Mead, 1956. 243pp.

Having attended college seeking an education and a husband, she gets both and proceeds to raise six children, noting "a certain untamed quality" to her family; her humorous anecdotes describe the pitfalls of traveling with children, living the rustic life, hosting inevitable houseguests, working as an interviewer on radio and television, and reaching happy middle age.

281   Kohut

1169 KOHUT, REBEKAH BETTELHEIM (1864-1951)   NAWM
      More Yesterdays: An Autobiography (1925-49): A Sequel
      to My Portion. New York: Bloch Publishing, 1950. 209pp.

         A lecturer, social worker, and ardent Zionist describes
      a life of service at both civic and national levels; she tells
      of finding anti-Semitism in Poland in 1926, of an "endless
      chain" of committee work, of spiritual support as the daugh-
      ter and wife and mother of rabbis, of her vicarious joy in
      the scholarly pursuits of her husband and son, of her work
      on the National Council of Jewish Women; she reflects on
      "the quality of Jewishness"; her recollections are not pre-
      sented in chronological order.

1170 KOKENES, VIOLETA CONSTANTINE
      On Wings of Faith. New York: Random House, 1960.
      244pp.

         She and her pilot husband and five-year-old son are the
      first family to fly their 19,000 mile tour around South Amer-
      ica; planning the trip as a good-will mission, she describes
      their preparations and the excitement and dangers of the
      trip over ocean and jungle; an extremely close family with
      strong religious faith, they plan other good-will tours upon
      their return to Florida, but the book ends with the tragedy
      of her husband's and son's deaths in a plane crash which
      she survives.

1171 KONSTANTINU, EUGENIE CLARK
      see CLARK, EUGENIE

1172 KOREN, ELSE ELISABETH HYSING (1832-1918)
      The Diary of Elisabeth Koren, 1853-1855, trans. and ed. by
      David T. Nelson. Northfield, Minn. : Norwegian-American
      Historical Association, 1955. 381pp.

         She marries a minister in 1853 and emigrates from Nor-
      way to the U.S. ; with a fine eye for detail, she describes
      her shipboard activities and companions and her travels
      overland from New York to Iowa; she is welcomed and
      housed by a close-knit Norwegian community; she keeps a
      diary for her traveling husband to read when he returns;
      she recounts the joy of finally settling into the parsonage;
      her diary, a warm, responsive account, ends just before
      the birth of a daughter.

1173 KRAEMER, HEDDY
      More Time Than Money; A Retired Couple Travel Around

the World for Twenty Months on Freight Ships.   Brooklyn,
N.Y.:   Theo. Gaus' Sons, 1963.   169pp.

She writes of a journey begun in 1960; she and her husband use the trip as an introduction to retirement and to explore the possibilities of permanently settling abroad; she
provides travel advice and straightforward descriptions of the
accommodations, sights, and people of thirty countries; she
returns to the U.S., although she is distressed by some aspects of modern American society.

1174   KRAMER, HELEN MARY (1892-   )
       When We Were There.   Rockford, Ill.:   Bellevue Books,
       1954.   246pp.

She recounts her "memorable journey to Rome" in the
Holy Year of 1950; traveling with a tour group, she visits
European shrines and notes religious associations with vari-
ous sightseeing stops; she gains an audience with the Pope.

1175   KRAUCH, VELMA
       Three Stacks and You're Out; A Light-Hearted Account of
       the Last Great Voyage of the R.M.S. Queen Mary Around
       Cape Horn.   Los Angeles: VanLee Enterprise, 1971.
       191pp.

In an anecdotal account, she tells of the ship's last thirty-
nine day voyage in 1967; it is the first cruise for her and
her husband, and she enjoys of the 1930's elegance of the ship,
sightseeing at various ports, entertainment and activities on
board; she describes the extravagant welcome the ship re-
ceives in California, its permanent place of retirement.

1176   KRUGER, JUDITH
       My Fight for Sanity.   Philadelphia: Chilton, 1959.   244pp.

A writer and amateur actress, she tells of her mental
breakdown after the birth of her son, overwhelmed by the
responsibilities of motherhood; she provides a vivid evocation of her terror and irrational responses, of shock treatments, of her struggle to be docile, of emotionally grueling
psychotherapy after her release from a mental hospital.

1177   KRUMREY, KATE WARNER (1894-   )
       Saga of Sawlog.   Denver: Big Mountain Press, 1965.   417pp.

A teacher and newspaper columnist, she opens her account with a detailed family history illuminated by much
local history of the rural Kansas area in which she grows

up; writing of herself in the third person, she describes
pioneer living in rich detail, noting the daily pattern of
domestic and farm tasks, their neighbors, their home,
school days, holidays, and entertainment during "the good
years" of the early twentieth century; her recollections become more random after she leaves home, including anecdotes of her World War I clerical work in Washington,
D. C. and her married life.

1178   KUSHNER, ROSE
       Breast Cancer: A Personal History and an Investigative
       Report. New York: Harcourt Brace Jovanovich, 1975.
       400pp.

       Discovering a lump in her breast in 1974, she immediate-
       ly searches for information, finding instead "a breast-cancer
       controversy" over methods of treatment; insisting on her
       right to informed consent, she interviews doctors and spe-
       cialists, chooses a surgeon for herself, and notes the physi-
       cal and psychological after-effects of surgery; she closes
       with a call for further research.

1179   KUYKENDALL, LUCY ROUNTREE
       P. S. to Pecos. Houston, Texas: Anson Jones, 1946.
       260pp.

       This is a "tale of army life in a small west Texas town";
       the author is an officer's wife and tells of the "gypsy life,"
       the dirt and grit of settling in Pecos; her housework suffers
       when she begins to write the book; the account closes with
       the demise of the base after three years.

1180   LaBASTILLE, ANNE
         Woodswoman.   New York: Dutton, 1976.   277pp.

      A writer, lecturer, photographer, and ecological consult-
ant, she describes her move to simplicity, self-sufficiency,
and personal liberation after a divorce; she lives alone in
the Adirondacks, builds a log cabin herself, and becomes
one of the few licensed female Adirondack guides; entering
a "new emotional era," she finds love but cannot give up
her wilderness independence; after ten years as a "woods-
woman," she takes a job in Washington, D. C. and finds intellectual stimulation mixed with culture shock.

1181   LACKEY, CLEATICE INGOLD
         Preacher's Kid's Dad; A True Story.   New York: Greenwich
         Book Publishers, 1958.   94pp.

      Telling of "a happy, normal, everyday family," she opens
with the story of her father's youth; the extended portrait of
her father, a preacher and teacher, illuminates her family
life, described in anecdotes enlivened with a sense of humor; her father's example constitutes her "greatest heritage."

1182   La FARGE, PHYLLIS
         Keeping Going.   New York: Harcourt Brace Jovanovich,
         Inc. , 1971.   180pp.

      She presents a collection of reflective personal essays
written over a six-year period; she notes a restoration of
the intensity of living after her children are born and their
humanity unfolds; she offers vignettes evoking her relationship to her austere, vehement mother; she also discusses
her sense of place, her marriage, and her emotions.

1183   LAKE, LOUISE
         Each Day a Bonus: Twenty-Five Courageous Years in a
         Wheelchair.   Salt Lake City: Deseret, 1971.   212pp.

      Stricken with polio in 1945, she struggles with courage,
determination, and self-discipline to maintain her independence and a positive self-image; she is supported by her

religious faith and by close ties with her daughter after her
husband leaves her; she engages in Mormon youth work,
campaigns for a rehabilitation center, becomes a center
staff member, and is the first woman to be named "out-
standing handicapped American" in 1957; she also travels
in the U. S. and South America.

1184   LAKE, VERONICA (1917?-1973)
        Veronica, with Donald Bain. New York: Citadel, 1969.
        281pp.

        Stating that "Veronica Lake is a Hollywood creation,"
        she describes the invention of her image and her breaking
        into films in 1940; she marries, suffers the deaths of a
        daughter and son, and divorces; "a bit of a misfit in the
        Hollywood of the Forties," she tries single life and a second
        tempestuous marriage; in 1952 she leaves Hollywood for tele-
        vision and the theatre, then falls on hard times and struggles
        with a drinking problem.

1185   LAMAR, DOLLY BLOUNT (1867-   )
        When All Is Said and Done. Athens: University of Georgia
        Press, 1952. 286pp.

        Steeped in politics as the daughter of a southern congress-
        man, she describes her childhood in reconstruction Georgia,
        her intense loyalty to the South, and her term as a "rebel
        at Wellesley"; she marries in 1896, enjoys a social life
        among prominent people in Washington, D. C. , works with
        the United Daughters of the Confederacy, and works against
        woman suffrage.

1186   LAMAR, EUGENIA DOROTHY BLOUNT
        see LAMAR, DOLLY BLOUNT (1867-   )

1187   LAMARR, HEDY (1915-   )
        Ecstasy and Me; My Life as a Woman. New York: Barthol-
        omew House, 1966. 318pp.

        A disorganized account by a movie actress, the "last
        product of Hollywood's unbelievable pre-war star system";
        born in Vienna and made famous by a movie banned in the
        U. S. , she tells of her first U. S. movie contract, and later
        films, both successful and unsuccessful; she describes her
        six marriages and divorces and numerous other sexual rela-
        tionships; she describes the joy of motherhood, the curse of
        beauty.

1188 LAMPORT, FELICIA (1916-)
Ermine on Sunday see Mink on Weekdays

1189 Mink on Weekdays. Boston: Houghton Mifflin, 1950.
309pp.
The daughter of a wealthy Jewish "Captain of Industry" in
New York writes a delightful, humorous tale of growing up
over-privileged; she produces a strong portrait of her mother, a general constantly marshalling her forces, combining
the attributes of a "duchess" and a "fishwife"; her childhood
is a round of governesses, shopping, extravagant parties,
world tours, and European finishing schools.

1190 LANCASTER, EVELYN (pseud.) (1927-)
The Final Face of Eve, with James Poling. New York:
McGraw-Hill, 1958. 290pp.

A victim of "multiple personality," she tells of the emergence in 1954 of her final integrated personality; she recalls
incidents in the lives of the so-called Eve White, Eve Black,
and Jane, including a failed marriage, blackouts, fear of insanity; her first contact with a psychiatrist is in 1951 and
marks the delicate task of revealing each personality; she
closes as a fourth personality in a potentially happy marriage.

1191 LANDVATER, DOROTHY (1927-)
David; A Mother's Story of Her Son's Recovery from a Coma
and Brain Damage. Englewood Cliffs, N.J.: Prentice-Hall,
1976. 157pp.

A professional lecturer, she describes three years of unwavering devotion and relentless hard work after her seventeen-year-old son is injured in an auto accident; rejecting
hysteria, she faces both the initial crisis and later years of
therapy with fierce determination; at least temporarily, her
son's recovery becomes her career, his success, her success.

1192 LANE, LEE (1919-)
I Gathered the Bright Days; A Courageous Woman's Story of
Her Family, Struggles, and Triumphs, with Suzanne Gleaves.
New York: Dial, 1973. 280pp.

A nurse presents a chronicle of twenty-seven years of
family life; she marries a doctor in 1941, and raises their
eight children in addition to keeping a pre-school to contribute to the family finances, later returning to her nursing

career; supported by a sense of partnership with her husband, she endures the problems of a Down's Syndrome child, the death of her youngest child, the drug addiction and suicide attempt of a daughter, the wounding of a son in Viet Nam, and finally her husband's death.

1193   LANE, ROSE WILDER (1886-1968)
        The Lady and the Tycoon; Letters of Rose Wilder Lane and
        Jasper Crane, ed. Roger Lea MacBride. Caldwell, Id.:
        Caxton, 1973. 401pp.

        She is a novelist, a journalist, and the daughter of Laura Ingalls Wilder (see entry #2131) and carries on an extensive correspondence with businessman Crane on political and economic issues from 1946 to 1966; the holder of strong views fiercely defended, she argues at length for individual rights and against government regulation; her comments reflect wide and serious reading in political and economic works; she discusses religion, moral principles, human nature, education, and the good society as well.

1194   LANG, LUCY FOX ROBINS
        Tomorrow Is Beautiful. New York: Macmillan, 1948.
        303pp.

        A Russian Jew, she emigrates to the U.S. as a child, lives in poverty in New York and Chicago, and begins to work before she's ten; drawn into anarchist circles in Chicago, she marries a radical; she is inspired by Emma Goldman (see entry #782) and begins a long involvement with labor organizing; she works for amnesty after World War II; she enjoys a close association with both Gompers and Debs and works with the AFL; after a second marriage, she travels to Europe and Russia; a later trip to Scandinavia helps to relieve her near-suicidal breakdown.

1195   LANGHORNE, ORRA HENDERSON MOORE GRAY (1841-1904)
        Southern Sketches from Virginia, 1881-1901, ed. Charles E.
        Wynes. Charlottesville: University Press of Virginia, 1964.
        145pp.

        These are heavily edited selections from her contributions to a Negro monthly newspaper; a prolific writer, she is an abolitionist and suffragist, discussing the advances in "property and education" for blacks; she illustrates many of her points through personal experiences.

1196   LANGSETH-CHRISTENSEN, LILLIAN
        Voyage Gastronomique; A Culinary Autobiography. New York:
        Hawthorn, 1973. 358pp.

Deeply influenced by her Austrian gourmet father, she
recalls a childhood spent in perpetual travel between New
York and "food trips" all over Europe; her account is liber-
ally sprinkled with the names of exotic dishes; she becomes
a set and costume designer with the Metropolitan Opera, a
mural painter, and finally drawing on her father's heritage,
a food writer; she continues with her double life in the
U. S. and Europe, raising children, pursuing an artistic
profession, and cherishing fine food; her delightful autobiography is on pages 3-193 and is followed by recipes.

1197   La ROE, ELSE KIENLE (1900-   )
Woman Surgeon; The Autobiography of Else K. La Roe, M. D.
New York: Dial, 1957. 373pp.

Born in Germany and "born to be a surgeon," she throws
herself passionately into grueling medical studies, financed
by her grandmother against her father's wishes, beginning
in 1918; she opens a private sanatorium, supported by a
banker to whom she is married until political conflict over
the rise of National Socialism causes divorce; she flees to
the U. S., where she again practices general medicine and
reconstructive surgery, continuing a life of "work and love."

1198   LASKY, BESSIE MONA GARNESS (1890-   )
Candle in the Sun.   Los Angeles: DeVorss, 1957.   316pp.

Although she is the wife of Hollywood's Jesse Lasky and
enjoys the acquaintance of numerous movie celebrities, she
finds her "life's work" in painting; she combines a life of
luxury with a life of studying and learning in art; later she
tells of experiences with spiritualism and a project to paint
religious missions.

1199   LASSER, TERESE
Reach to Recovery, with William Kendall Clarke.   New York:
Simon and Schuster, 1972.   158pp.

The nationwide Reach to Recovery volunteer program
grows out of her own needs and efforts following her mastectomy in 1952; she learns much also from her initial visits
to others and creates a booklet and kit to aid women after
surgery; a woman of vast energy and initiative, she meets
with some welcome and some opposition from doctors; she
suggests exercise and emphasis on a woman's femininity to
aid recovery.

1200   LAUNE, SEIGNIORA RUSSELL
Sand in My Eyes.   Philadelphia: Lippincott, 1956.   256pp.

When she is fifteen, she settles in Texas with her family,
inexperienced in rural ways; she teaches, then marries a
lawyer in 1896 and they settle in Nebraska, then in the Oklahoma Territory; she offers lively anecdotes of householding, raising three children, working with women's clubs for
civic progress, and doing volunteer work during World War
I; she closes with her husband's sudden death in 1928.

1201   LAW, VIRGINIA W.
       Appointment Congo.   Chicago: Rand McNally, 1966.   289pp.

       Married in 1942, she accepts her husband's religious vo-
cation and they become lay missionaries and teachers in the
Congo in 1950; while raising three children, she teaches
women's classes and does hospital work; she survives sleeping sickness; after their second furlough to the U.S., her
husband is killed by rebels during Congo civil unrest.

1202   LAWRENCE, MARY CHIPMAN (1827-1906)
       The Captain's Best Mate; The Journal of Mary Chipman
       Lawrence on the Whaler Addison, 1856-1860, ed. Stanton
       Garner.   Providence: Brown University Press, 1966.
       311pp.

       Based on the Sandwich Islands, she describes a series of
seven voyages undertaken with her husband and young daughter during the height of the American whaling industry; she
becomes "quite a sailor," noting the daily weather conditions, their success accumulating barrels of oil, their contacts with other whalers which feed their hunger for news
and company, her busy social life when ashore, her daughter's shipboard activities; she reveals her strong New England religious background as well as occasional flashes of
insight and humor.

1203   LAWRENSON, HELEN BROWN NORDEN (1907-   )
       Stranger at the Party: A Memoir.   New York: Random
       House, 1975.   244pp.

       She is a reporter, magazine writer, and managing editor
of Vanity Fair from 1932 to 1936; she describes a life that
combines "Park Avenue and the waterfront," political conservatism and radicalism; the daughter of a flirtatious mother and a weak father, she was raised by her grandmother;
the account includes chapters on Clare Boothe Luce, Bernard
Baruch, and her husband, maritime union organizer Jack
Lawrenson.

1204   LAZARRE, JANE
       The Mother Knot.   New York: McGraw-Hill, 1976.   188pp.

She explores her own experiences and emotions as a
mother of two young children, her motherhood complicated
by an interracial marriage; discussing her ambivalence in
the face of the myth and the reality of motherhood, she
writes with honesty of her isolation, fear, resentment, and
loss of "selfhood"; she also describes her relationships with
her mother, with other women, and with her husband.

1205   LAZARUS, EMMA (1849-1887)
        The Letters of Emma Lazarus, 1868-1885, ed. Morris U.
        Schappes. New York: New York Public Library, 1949.
        68pp.

This collection of seventy-eight letters opens with several
to Emerson, thanking him for his encouragement, although
in 1874 she writes a baffled, bitter letter expressing her
disappointment when he excludes her from a poetry anthol-
ogy; she corresponds with Henry George to express her sympathy for his views, with Emerson's daughter, and with various editors, revealing her increasing interest in and contribution to Jewish culture.

1206   LEAH
        Leah. Old Tappan, N.J.: Revell, 1973. 90pp.

In a personal narrative of drug abuse, theft, and prostitution, she tells in impressionistic fragments of her sordid life,
numerous arrests and trials, and final assignment to a religious rehabilitation program; initially distrustful, she finds
salvation and rejects her old way of life.

1207   LeCONTE, EMMA FLORENCE (1848?-)
        When the World Ended: The Diary of Emma LeConte, ed.
        Earl Schenck Miers. New York: Oxford, 1957. 124pp.

This passionate account of the last months of the Civil
War is written when she is seventeen, her youth clouded by
the "stern realities of life" in wartime; berating the Union
soldiers as "fiends incarnate," she notes the "violent excitement" of attacks, pillage and destruction during the Yankee
occupation, the unwelcome news of the armistice when she
suggests that women should have been called to swell the
ranks of Confederate troops; "rebellious and bitter" at the
fall of the Confederacy, she tires of keeping a journal and
wishes to "lose herself" in her studies.

1208   LEE, FLORIDE CLEMSON (1842-)
        A Rebel Came Home, eds. Charles M. McGee, Jr. and
        Ernest M. Lander, Jr. Columbia, S.C.: University of
        South Carolina Press, 1961. 153pp.

In a diary covering the Civil War years from 1863 to
1866, she tells of her travels to Baltimore and to Niagara
Falls, of her brother's fighting and being taken prisoner,
of her hope for peace; she notes that singing and riding are
her "two passions"; she travels to Philadelphia to visit relatives, then travels to South Carolina, fearing the approach
of Union troops; as the war ends, she notes the wartime
deaths of some acquaintances, the return of her brother,
and the resumption of social life.

1209   LEE, GYPSY ROSE (1914?-1970)   NAWM
       Gypsy: A Memoir. New York: Harper, 1957. 337pp.

       She and her dainty younger sister (see entry #899) enter
show business as children, managed by their charming,
shrewd, and ruthless mother; she relates wry anecdotes
about life and characters on the vaudeville circuit; she is
jealous of her sister's roles; when vaudeville fades, she
opens in burlesque and becomes "a star without any talent";
she plays in Billy Minsky's troupe and the Ziegfeld Follies,
becoming a strip-tease star with a flair for publicity; a
highly colorful account.

1210   LEE, HELEN BOURNE JOY (1896-)
       Traveling with Gran'ma; Camping Around the World. Phila-
       delphia: Dorrance, 1952. 205pp.

       At fifty-five, she covers 20,000 miles in nearly a year
in Europe, the Middle East, and India; accompanied by her
Swiss journalist "godson," she feeds her vast curiosity with
sights, stories, and history; she visits the Braidwoods (see
entry #260) at an Iraqi archaeological dig.

1211   LEE, MABEL BARBEE (1886-)
       And Suddenly It's Evening: A Fragment of Life.   Garden
       City, N.Y.: Doubleday, 1963. 201pp.

       Confessing to "a certain excitement about life and an urge
for learning," she accepts the position as Dean of Women at
Colorado College in 1922 to support herself and her daughter; she appreciates the social upheaval among undergraduates
and seriously searches for understanding; she studies social
work, lectures, and writes on education; she later resigns
as dean at Radcliffe to make a home for her daughter at
Bennington, in "an endless adventure in learning"; she closes
with the publication of her reminiscences of childhood at
Cripple Creek.

1212   The Gardens in My Life; An Intimate Memoir.   Garden City,
       N.Y.: Doubleday, 1970. 144pp.

Rejoicing in "the healing power that lies in tilling the
soil and planting seeds," she explains her first gardening
as a child in Cripple Creek; her gardens brighten mining
camp life in Oregon (see The Rainbow Years); widowed at
thirty-four, she becomes the Dean of Women at Colorado
College, then the director of admissions at Bennington in
1932; she discusses her daughter's upbringing and her own
growth in understanding through the years.

1213   The Rainbow Years; A Happy Interlude.   Garden City, N.Y.:
        Doubleday, 1966.   175pp.

In a charming memoir, this teacher writes of the "rich,
rewarding years in eastern Oregon" from 1911 to 1918; she
joins her mining engineer husband, alive to the spirit of the
mining camp, and she enjoys nature, gardening, and community activities and celebrations, adding civilized touches;
she begins to keep a journal, publishes her first story, and
tells of the birth of a daughter; leaving camp with her husband, she is later widowed in the 1918 flu epidemic; when
she returns to the camp in 1964, she realizes that the past
has been obliterated and only memories remain.

1214   LEE, REBA (pseud.) (1930-   )
        I Passed for White, as told to Mary Hastings Bradley.   New
        York: Longmans, Green, 1955.   274pp.

She notes her first awareness of shades of skin color and
the social implications thereof in her own family; she later
learns she has a white father; first taken for white in a new
high school, then ostracized as a black, she quits school and
passes for white in a secretarial job but feels she must flee
to New York to avoid exposure; she marries a wealthy white
man but is caught in a web of subterfuge and tension mounts
as she fears her child will appear black; the child is still-
born; she quits pretending and returns to her family in Chicago.

1215   LEEK, SYBIL
        Diary of a Witch.   Englewood Cliffs, N.J.:   Prentice-Hall,
        1968.   187pp.

Born in England, she carries on the "family tradition of
witchcraft"; with little formal education, she learns the oc-
cult from her grandmother, and copes with prejudice against
her; widowed at eighteen, she becomes a priestess, and recounts her extrasensory perceptions and healing activities;
after much publicity she is forced from her antique business
and settles in the U.S. where she becomes a New York
celebrity.

1216   LeGALLIENNE, EVA (1899-)
        With a Quiet Heart.   New York: Viking, 1953.   311pp.

        The prominent actress writes of a second phase of her
        life in which her interest shifts from action to experience;
        she describes her serious injuries in a home explosion and
        her agony and courage in recovery; she returns to the Civic
        Repertory Theatre in 1932, but the company is forced by the
        depression to disband; she continues to act and direct, dedi-
        cated particularly to repertory theatre; she discusses vari-
        ous successful roles and extended tours; her career is pur-
        sued with "ruthless singleness of purpose."

1217   LEGENDRE, GERTRUDE S. (1901-)
        The Sands Ceased to Run.   New York: William-Frederick,
        1947.   245pp.

        She describes her six-month internment in a German
        prison camp during World War II; in 1941 she joined the
        Red Cross Motor Corps, worked in Washington, D.C., and
        then worked in London with the O.S.S., "exhilarated" by
        danger; she is captured "sightseeing" near the front in
        France; held in several prisons, she describes guards and
        fellow prisoners; a German assists her escape in Switzer-
        land.

1218   LEIMBACH, PATRICIA PENTON
        A Thread of Blue Denim.   Englewood Cliffs, N.J.:   Pren-
        tice-Hall, 1974.   241pp.

        In a series of short personal essays originally published
        as newspaper and farm journal articles, she describes "what
        it is to be a country wife"; she treasures the values of rural
        living, finding an "abundant and joyous" life perfect for rais-
        ing children; alternately pensive and rhapsodic, she muses on
        herself, her husband, her children, the land, and the world.

1219   LEINSTER, RAFAELLE KENNEDY FitzGERALD
        The Duchess from Brooklyn; Rafaelle, Duchess of Leinster.
        New York: John Day, 1973.   198pp.

        The daughter of possessive, divorced parents, she grows
        up with loneliness; enchanted with and taken up by British
        high society, she reluctantly marries an Englishman in 1932
        but soon chafes under the restrictions of British propriety
        and divorces; she marries a duke who is romantic, imprac-
        tical and bankrupt; plagued by financial crises, they flee
        from house to house, eventually divorcing; she begins a more
        independent life.

1220   LEITCH, MARY SINTON LEWIS (1876-   )
        Himself and I; Our Sea Saga.   New York: Fine Editions
        Press, 1950.   246pp.

        Her "blood runs salty" in spite of a bookish background
        as the daughter of a scholar; after an education at Smith cut
        short by deafness, she travels abroad frequently and does
        literary work in New York; she marries a Scotch ship cap-
        tain in 1907 and describes their "wanderings," the source
        of her poetry and travel articles; she closes with their shift
        in 1909 to a "life ashore."

1221   L'ENGLE, MADELEINE (1918-   )
        A Circle of Quiet.   New York: Farrar, Straus and Giroux,
        1972.   245pp.

        In this reflective work, she explores "the precarious tri-
        angle of wife-mother-writer"; in her thirties she raises
        small children, obeys the compulsion to write, and later
        teaches writing; she discusses her "icons" and a summer of
        ontological revelation; analyzing identity, reality, and art,
        she feels the moral responsibility and deep seriousness of
        the writer's task.

1222   The Summer of the Great-Grandmother.   New York: Far-
        rar, Straus and Giroux, 1974.   245pp.

        A writer tells of the summer during which her mother
        descends into senility and then death; the implications of her
        mother's decline affect her deeply and she reflects on their
        reversal of roles, on death, on her feelings of false guilt,
        on her mother's creative life, and on the "enormous debt
        of gratitude" she owes her mother; she is particularly dis-
        tressed by her mother's loss of memory, for as a writer
        she cherishes and depends on her own memory.

1223   LENIHAN, MINA WARD
        Betwixt the Here and There.   Philadelphia: Dorrance, 1953.
        339pp.

        A musician from New Zealand, she marries a retired
        U.S. army officer and travels across the United States sight-
        seeing and visiting her husband's grown children; she tells
        of the impact on her life of World War II and celebrates its
        close; she spends twelve years in the U.S.

1224   LENSKI, LOIS (1893-1974)
        Journey into Childhood; The Autobiography of Lois Lenski.
        Philadelphia: Lippincott, 1972.   208pp.

A writer and illustrator of children's books tells of her "beloved childhood home" in the midwest; an intensely shy child, she turns to books and to observation of the events around her; she attends college from 1911 to 1915, continuing her art studies in New York; refusing a teaching career, she begins illustrating children's books, marrying in 1921; her creative work sustains her other duties as "stepmother and homemaker"; she moves gradually into writing historical and regional books for which she is well-known.

1225   LeROY, ULDENE RUDD
       Six on an Island: Childhood Memories from Lake Huron.
       New York: Exposition, 1956.   78pp.

       The daughter of an island caretaker and member of "a pretty self-sufficient family," she describes an outdoor life full of mischief and activity; when "summer neighbors" depart, a very different set of winter activities begins; she notes inevitable changes over the years but fond memories of the past remain.

1226   Le SHAN, EDA J. (1923?-)
       In Search of Myself--And Other Children.   New York: M.
       Evans, 1976.   167pp.

       An author explores her own childhood after years of research on the nature of childhood; she opens with her grandmother's diary from 1855; seeing herself as a small child through her mother's notes and letters, she recognizes details of her mother's personality and its influence on her own; she has fond memories of a childhood marked by a "zest for life," although later she suffers from inferiority and anxiety and spends years in psychotherapy; she deepens her understanding of childhood by the analysis of her own.

1227   LESLIE, SARAH (SARABETH) SATTERTHWAITE (1864-)
       Morningshore Joins the 37th.   New York: Exposition, 1947.
       64pp.

       Initially "lyric days" are overshadowed by her son's enlistment during World War I; her acreage is used as a military camp and she serves in the Red Cross; the beauty of her country home "sanctuary" is marred by fears for her son; she closes with an armistice celebration and reunion with her son.

1228   LESTER, CAROL E.
       To Make a Duck Happy.   New York: Harper & Row, 1969.
       148pp.

Living in an ark with her son in Sausalito, California, she is first given a baby duck; she describes its behavior and personality and its impact on her family life; in addition to anecdotes of six years of duck-raising, she offers advice to others who wish to keep ducks.

1229   LES TINA, DOROTHY
        Icicles on the Roof.   New York: Abelard-Schuman, 1961.
        181pp.

A former WAC, she makes her home on the Alaskan tundra with her husband, an Army bush pilot; to relieve the isolation of her first month, she raises baby lemmings and gets to know the characters among the local women; she makes a home from a quonset hut, teaches Eskimo students, visits Eskimo settlements, and becomes "a part of the active life of the village," realizing her deep affection for Alaska upon her departure.

1230   LEVERTOV, DENISE (1923-   )
        The Poet in the World.   New York: New Directions, 1973.
        275pp.

Gathering her highly articulate "scattered prose writings," she reveals a thoughtful, passionate espousal of her views; she discusses the integration of her craft and her values, the inextricable ties between "the meditative and the active," her political commitment during the Vietnam war years, and the influence of teaching on her understanding; she includes essays on her responses to other contemporary writers.

1231   LEVIT, ROSE (pseud.)
        Ellen; A Short Life Long Remembered.   San Francisco:
        Chronicle Books, 1974.   156pp.

Reeling from a divorce and torn by her older daughter's rebellion and rejection, she must bear her younger daughter's terminal illness with cancer; after a suicide attempt, she achieves a strong emotional commitment to life in spite of the alternations of hope and despair; she develops a close, intense relationship with her ill daughter, convinced of the "overwhelming importance" of recording her experience.

1232   LEVY, HARRIET LANE (1867-1950)
        920 O'Farrell Street.   Garden City, N. Y.:   Doubleday, 1947.
        273pp.

She presents a fine evocation of growing up in the "Jewish merchant class" in San Francisco, with lively portraits of her neighbors including Alice B. Toklas (see entry #2006); she describes the special associations held by each room of her home; she closes after the earthquake and fire of 1906, when the family separates after her father's death and her sisters' marriages.

1233   LEWIS, ELEANOR FRANCES (1882-)
       Beads of Jade. New York: Vantage, 1958. 258pp.

The daughter of pioneer missionaries in a remote province of China, she tells of her constant fascination with the Chinese people and customs; in 1895 she returns to the U. S. by way of India, France, and England, keeping a journal of the long journey home at the end of her "celestial childhood"; her account is articulate and charming.

1234   LEWIS, FAYE CASHATT (1896-)
       Nothing to Make a Shadow. Ames, Iowa: Iowa State University Press, 1971. 155pp.

This doctor and writer describes her "homesteading days in South Dakota," where she finds great happiness amid hard work; she describes the quietness of the virgin prairie, a wide variety of neighbors, family diversions, inevitable family friction, country school, and the visits of Chautauqua; her account closes with her return after fifty years.

1235   Patients, Doctors, and Families. Garden City, N. Y.: Doubleday, 1967. 240pp.

A doctor in a general practice with her husband in a small Iowa town describes the rewards of satisfying work and of family life as the mother of three; anecdotes of her patients reveal her quick sympathy and warm concern for her patients' total well-being.

1236   LEWIS, GRACE HEGGER
       With Love from Gracie; Sinclair Lewis: 1912-1925. New York: Harcourt, Brace, 1951. 335pp.

After a genteel childhood, she becomes a minor editor at Vogue; she marries Sinclair Lewis in 1914, drawn to him by love, laughter, and romantic idealization; she delights in their "working partnership" and their early wandering, a life of freedom tinged with rootlessness and irresponsibility; she lives intimately with the Main Street manuscript until its 1920 publication; during Lewis's years of success, she enjoys some stimulating encounters with literary figures; noting that their peripatetic life causes repeated separations from

their son, she is sorrowful when their marriage fails, for
she is "woven permanently into the pattern of his life"; her
narrative is quiet, poignant, and perceptive.

1237   LEWIS, OMA BARNES
        I Love Vermont--But....; Life in the Green Mountains.
        New York: Exposition, 1956. 123pp.

        In 1940 she and her adult sons locate a summer home in
        Vermont; she copes with the "constant challenge" of restora-
        tion and improvement; she describes the strong character of
        a neighbor woman, a local workman with Vermont quirks,
        her encounters with poisonous snakes, and her attempts to
        wrest a garden from the wildlife.

1238   LIBMAN, LILLIAN
        And Music at the Close: Stravinsky's Last Years; A Per-
        sonal Memoir. New York: Norton, 1972. 400pp.

        Her professional association with Stravinsky begins in
        1959 when she acts as his personal manager and press rep-
        resentative, but she later becomes a privileged companion
        of the family until Stravinsky's death in 1971; in vivid detail,
        she tells of the complexities of her work, negotiating con-
        tracts and accompanying the "Maestro" on tours; the line
        between professional and domestic devotion blurs as she
        willingly dedicates herself to small personal services, ab-
        sorbed by his genius; with delicacy and sensitivity, she ex-
        plores the subtle relationships among Stravinsky, his wife,
        his children, Robert Craft, and herself; she closes with a
        chronicle of the infinite sadness of his physical decline.

1239   LIDDELL, VIOLA GOODE (1901-   )
        With a Southern Accent. Norman, Okla.: University of
        Oklahoma Press, 1948. 261pp.

        In a nostalgic account written for her children, she offers
        a fond description of her home in a small Alabama village;
        her large extended family includes a passive and gentle
        mother, a proud and adventurous father, and a social milieu
        which changes greatly between the first and last children;
        her father enjoys offering his children the advantages of the
        "shiny new world" of the early 20th century; her account
        ends with her father's death in the financial crash of 1921.

1240   LIFTON, BETTY JEAN
        Twice Born: Memoirs of an Adopted Daughter. New York:
        McGraw-Hill, 1975. 281pp.

A journalist and children's author, she undertakes a "psychological journey into the past" in her quest for contact with her biological parents; after her marriage, a sojourn in Japan and acquaintance with its strong ancestral traditions colors her search; her "detective work" among the records and work with Florence Fisher's adoptee organization (see entry #677) lead ultimately to a link with her mother after an initial rebuff and ties with a friend of her deceased father, so that she can give her own children their extended past, "a mythic tale."

1241   LILLY, DORIS
       How to Meet a Millionaire.   New York: Putnam, 1951.
       182pp.

       Flippant and vaguely illiterate, she follows a desire to become a Hollywood starlet, attempting to exploit her contacts among domestic and foreign millionaires; the social whirl, "a gigantic fraud," includes Chicago crooks, Mexican bandits, Texas ranchers, and Parisian playboys.

1242   LINCOLN, EVELYN
       My Twelve Years with John F. Kennedy.   New York: Mc-
       Kay, 1965.   371pp.

       The personal secretary to Kennedy through his Senate and Presidential years, she demonstrates her total dedication and her sense of pride and accomplishment; her ambition is expressed by attaching herself to an ambitious man; stricken with an ulcer and a spinal tumor, she fights to regain her health in order to regain her job; she notes the frenetic activity of the campaigns, the excitement of working in the White House, the pleasure of meeting prominent people; she closes with the assassination.

1243   LIND, MIRIAM SEIBER
       "No Crying He Makes...."   Scottsdale, Pa.:   Herald Press,
       1972.   93pp.

       A poet and writer, already the mother of six, she becomes the foster mother of a brain-damaged infant; she writes candidly of the "feelings stirred up by personal involvement," a mixture of pain, anger, and love; she teaches discipline, learns patience, and has faith in slow progress; her own mother is a maternal model against which she measures herself.

1244   LINDAL, AMALIA
       Ripples from Iceland.   New York: Norton, 1962.   239pp.

In a candid, perceptive account, she tells of her marriage to an Icelandic man and of settling in Iceland in 1949; painfully aware of "being foreign," her early feelings of isolation are mitigated by growing knowledge and affection; she provides a "housewife's point of view," describing her adjustments to food, housing, and clothing customs and to the raising of four children; at the same time, she seeks intellectual companionship in a "man's country," eventually writing for The Christian Science Monitor.

1245   LINDBERGH, ANNE MORROW (1906-   )
        Bring Me a Unicorn: Diaries and Letters of Anne Morrow
        Lindbergh, 1922-1928.   New York: Harcourt Brace Jovano-
        vich, 1972.   259pp.

        A writer, she keeps extensive diaries in her family's tradition of sharing experiences in writing; her adolescent diaries are sentimental but sincere, noting her college years and family travels that constitute part of her education; in Mexico in 1927 as the U. S. ambassador's daughter, she meets the hero Lindbergh, and she is drawn to the revelation of flying, exalted as Lindbergh's presence shatters her quiet, shy world.

1246   Earth Shine.   New York: Harcourt, Brace & World, 1969.
        73pp.

        The book consists of two long essays, originally published in magazine form; at Cape Canaveral for the 1968 launching of Apollo 8, she notes the dramatic juxtaposition of massive technology with a wildlife refuge nearby and of modern space-flight with the early years of aviation; she spends a month on an East African safari with her husband to view wildlife, struck by the "intensity and variety of life itself."

1247   The Flower and the Nettle: Diaries and Letters of Anne
        Morrow Lindbergh, 1936-1939.   New York: Harcourt Brace
        Jovanovich, 1976.   605pp.

        She enjoys a period in England of absorption in her sons, "private peace and happiness" and freedom from public images, yet underneath she remains insecure and fearful; emotionally a pacifist, she tells the truth of their travels in Hitler's Germany for U. S. intelligence; in 1938 she again enjoys a period of "intense housekeeping," noting with warmth a wealth of domestic detail; settling in Paris in 1939, she comments on her sense of exile and impending war; as the volume closes, she is bound for the U. S. and uncertainty.

1248   Gift from the Sea. New York: Pantheon, 1955. 128pp.

In this quiet, reflective book, she writes "to think out
my own particular pattern of living"; each chapter is generated by certain features of seashells she examines; as a
writer, wife, mother, and citizen, she is keenly aware of
the dangers of fragmentation and the need for an inner core
of simplicity and peace; she values being alone and being
"centered," continual growth, and balance.

1249   Hour of Gold, Hour of Lead: Diaries and Letters of Anne
       Morrow Lindbergh, 1929-1932. New York: Harcourt Brace
       Jovanovich, 1973. 340pp.

She finds her love of Lindbergh a "great liberating force"
which gives her "confidence, strength, and almost a new
character," and the freedom of flying leads her from introspection to action; she notes the "abnormality" of her courtship, hounded by the press, culminating in a secret wedding
in 1929; their early years are spent in constant travel for
the cause of aviation; in 1932 she tells of the unreality and
horror when her firstborn son is kidnapped; her intense grief
is softened by the birth of her second son, although the
memory of her loss is constant.

1250   Locked Rooms and Open Doors: Diaries and Letters of Anne
       Morrow Lindbergh, 1933-1935. New York: Harcourt Brace
       Jovanovich, 1974. 352pp.

In 1933 she describes an "interim between two lives" as
she makes a slow recovery from her grief and joins in a
six-month exploratory flight around the Atlantic; fleeing continued publicity, she goes to England seeking asylum and a
normal life for her son; in 1935 she offers her first book to
the public (see companion volume) with trepidation; she
achieves new insights into herself and her family as she
prepares a biography of her father.

1251   LINDHEIM, IRMA LEVY (1886-)
       Parallel Quest; A Search of a Person and a People.   New
       York: T. Yoseloff, 1962. 458pp.

She describes a lengthy "individual quest for identity";
born into a middle-class Jewish family in New York, she
defies parental domination when she marries; with her husband's success, assimilation causes her Jewish identity to
fade; then she describes the exaltation of her conversion to
Zionism and work with Henrietta Szold (see companion volume); she lectures and studies Jewish history; after her first
trip to Palestine, she organizes U.S. Jewish women, is national

president of Hadassah; her dream is fulfilled as she settles
in Palestine and is accepted in 1933 as a kibbutz member.

1252   LINDSAY, ANNA FISHER (1896-   )
        With Deep Grown Roots.   New York: Vantage, 1959.   129pp.

She writes of her loss of identity and terrible loneliness
after widowhood follows forty years of marriage; she is
buoyed by the care and support of her three children and
her grandchildren and recounts her daily activities, quiet
reflections, travels, and visiting, "blessed by love" of family and friends.

1253   LINSTEAD, JOAN
        My 21 Years with Cancer.   New York: Exposition, 1963.
        62pp.

In her search for relief, she turns not only to doctors
but to a nutritionist, a chiropractor, and a cancer clinic for
treatment; she undergoes several major and minor operations
and X-ray therapy to treat recurrences of the disease; her
faith and courage sustain her as she vigorously pursues a career and plans for the future.

1254   LINY LU (pseud.)
        see BOOZER, CELINA LuZANNE

1255   LIPPITT, MARION ALMY
        I Married a New Englander.   Los Angeles: Ward Ritchie,
        1947.   75pp.

A Philadelphian, she marries a senator's son in 1914 and
raises five children; her narrative includes brief portraits
of her father-in-law, her husband, and an Indian hired man,
as well as tales of rural summers, of a move to California,
and of her children's sayings.

1256   LIVINGSTONE, BELLE (1875-1957)
        Belle Out of Order.   New York: Holt, 1959.   341pp.

In this sequel to Belle of Bohemia, she describes her rebellion against convent school and her growing passion for a
theatrical career, reveling in "the Bohemia of stage life";
fortunately made a wealthy widow as a young woman, she
becomes a socialite in London, Paris, Cairo, Monte Carlo,
travelling around the world on her wits; in a series of marriages, she swings from luxury to financial ruin; always
flamboyant, she gains international notoriety by running a

prohibition speakeasy, getting caught up in a "mad Volstead-
ian maelstrom," continuing a life of adventure and reckless-
ness.

1257 LOCKE, ELIZABETH N.
Turn of the Century. New York: Vantage, 1967. 151pp.

In a diffuse account, she presents anecdotes from her
close family life in New England; she attends teacher's college but is forced to drop out to raise younger siblings, although later she is able to pursue an education in art; she
provides numerous examples of the deep influence of her
family background on her later life, for she feels misunderstood, thwarted, and slightly eccentric.

1258 LOCKERBIE, JEANETTE W.
The Image of Joy. Old Tappan, N.J.: Revell, 1974. 125pp.

Each chapter contains a lesson in Christian living, learned
through examples drawn from her personal experiences.

1259 LOCKERBIE, JEANNIE
On Duty in Bangladesh. Grand Rapids, Mich.: Zondervan,
1973. 191pp.

A Baptist missionary nurse sympathetic to the birth of
Bangladesh tells of being caught in the political turmoil in
1971; remaining at the mission as long as possible, she
cares for wounded and supports her Bengali friends; she
flees temporarily to Burma, but returns in spite of continuing danger, working with the Red Cross after the war is
over; she writes with great sadness of the poverty and dis-
ruption there.

1260 LOCKWOOD, GERTRUDE M. (1925?-)
The Keg & I. New York: Pageant, 1955. 224pp.

Her teetotaler parents become depression bootleggers in
Seattle in the 1930's to earn a living; she and her bumptious
brothers join the family enterprise, warming to "the excitement and challenge of an unorthodox pursuit"; her light, humorous anecdotes also portray a variety of customers.

1261 LOCKWOOD, MYNA
A Mouse Is Miracle Enough. New York: Farrar, Straus &
Giroux, 1965. 184pp.

Describing herself as a fiercely independent but "lone,
aging widow," she tells how her self-sufficiency is broken

by the gift of a caged mouse; naming the mouse bestows a
personality on it, and the animal's presence leads to contacts with her apartment neighbors; her seclusion ends and
she comes back into the world of people and friendship.

1262   LOGAN, MILLA ZENOVICH (1904?-)
       Bring Along Laughter. New York: Random House, 1947.
       247pp.

       She comes from a large Serbian family in San Francisco
       and cherishes a "deep nostalgia for a world that was warm,
       abundant and spicy"; her marvelous collection of relatives
       display distinct, eccentric personalities in these detailed
       anecdotes of family customs; only in grade school does she
       begin to "discover 'Amerika.'"

1263   Cousins and Commissars; An Intimate Visit to Tito's Yugo-
       slavia. New York: Scribner, 1949. 222pp.

       The daughter of Yugoslavian parents who settle in the
       U.S., she makes a "sentimental pilgrimage" in 1948 to the
       family village in Yugoslavia; as an American, she is eagerly
       questioned and engaged in long conversations; sensitive to the
       patriotism, humor, and fierce spirit of the Yugoslavians, she
       achieves a quick intimacy with the people, and describes an
       emotional reunion with her relatives.

1264   LONE DOG, LOUISE
       Strange Journey; The Vision Life of a Psychic Indian Woman,
       ed. Vinson Brown. Healdsburg, Cal.: Naturegraph Pub-
       lishers, 1964. 68pp.

       Of Mohawk and Delaware ancestry, she is taught by her
       father and mother "the old ways" including the study of na-
       ture and its "spiritual teachings"; when she has psychic ex-
       periences, her family understands and does not suppress
       them; hostile to false spiritualism, she describes some of
       her visions and predictions.

1265   LONG, MARY ALVES (1864-)
       High Time to Tell It. Durham, N. Car.: Duke University
       Press, 1950. 314pp.

       The daughter of a prominent North Carolina lawyer and
       the youngest in a large, loving, extended family, she pre-
       sents fine portraits of a beloved grandmother, a cherished
       "aunty," an influential older sister; vignettes of work and
       play all have a strong domestic center; in 1882 her family
       settles in Minneapolis, a "strange new world" and she pur-

sues undergraduate and graduate degrees and a teaching career.

1266   LONGFELLOW, FANNY APPLETON (1817-1861)
        Mrs. Longfellow: Selected Letters and Journals of Fanny
        Appleton Longfellow, ed. Edward Wagenknecht. New York:
        Longmans, Green, 1956. 255pp.

        Keenly observant and extremely articulate, she exhibits
        her boundless love for American poet Henry W. Longfellow
        after their marriage in 1843; she finds being the mother of
        five children deeply satisfying and remarks "we so dearly
        delight in our own fireside"; yet her concerns range from
        international and national politics, including the issue of
        slavery, to a sensational local murder, and she presents
        "vivid glimpses" of New England literary figures.

1267   LOOS, ANITA (1893-   )
        A Girl Like I. New York: Viking, 1966. 275pp.

        She describes her childhood in San Francisco, basking in
        the adulation of a raffish father; she enjoys some early work
        as an actress, then is a film script writer for D.W. Griffith; she is the author of Gentlemen Prefer Blondes; hers is
        a lively account, populated by characters.

1268   Kiss Hollywood Good-By. New York: Viking, 1974. 213pp.

        In her sequel to A Girl Like I, she tells of her second
        career writing movie scripts starting in 1931 and remaining
        with MGM for eighteen years; in a light-hearted style, she
        recounts anecdotes of studio celebrities and of her own bittersweet marriage.

1269   Twice Over Lightly; New York Then and Now, with Helen
        Hayes. New York: Harcourt Brace Jovanovich, 1972. 343pp.

        She writes a breezy enthusiastic account of an adventurous
        year of personal visits, observations, and interviews in New
        York City with her friend Helen Hayes (see entry #903);
        guided by humble citizens as well as by civic leaders, they
        explore out-of-the-way places in an effort to get to know
        their own city.

1270   LORD, CAROLINE M.
        Diary of a Village Library. Somersworth: New Hampshire
        Publishing Co., 1971. 269pp.

In this charming account, a librarian covers the period
from 1943 to 1960, describing her delight in introducing
books and people to each other; her library serves as a
community center and she serves as town clerk and treasur-
er as well as librarian during World War II; she notes the
varied interests of the people and enjoys offering "a little
enticement" to the readers.

1271   LORENZ, SARAH E. (pseud.)
        And Always Tomorrow.   New York: Holt, Rinehart and
        Winston, 1963.   250pp.

        The mother of an emotionally disturbed son presents a
        chronicle of her seven-year search for a cure; she relent-
        lessly examines her fears, her feelings of guilt, the finan-
        cial strain, the chaos of competing medical theories, and
        her family's anxiety and discord over ways to proceed; she
        gains some insights into mental illness and is left with a
        degree of quiet hope.

1272   LOTHROP, ELEANOR BACKMAN
        Throw Me a Bone; What Happens When You Marry an Archae-
        ologist.   New York: McGraw-Hill, 1948.   234pp.

        In this humorous account, she describes her honeymoon
        on an archaeological trip that features primitive facilities
        at the Chilean digging site and the thrill of her "first skele-
        ton"; she goes on to recount a second trip to Guatemala
        where they maintain uneasy relations with the natives, and
        a third trip to Panama; she notes the qualifications required
        of an "archaeological wife. "

1273   LOTHROP, ELSA MARVEL
        I Married Four Children.   New York: Pageant, 1954.
        220pp.

        A nurse, she marries an army officer with four children
        when she is only twenty-three; with warmth and good humor,
        she learns the roles of army wife and mother simultaneously;
        she bears two children of her own, and chronicles the lives
        of all six through their college years and marriages, main-
        taining close family ties; she notes the effects of World War
        II on her family, including the death of her eldest son.

1274   LOUCHHEIM, KATIE SCOFIELD (1903-)
        By the Political Sea.   Garden City, N.Y.:   Doubleday, 1970.
        293pp.

        An ambitious political activist, having learned accommoda-
        tion in a childhood among tempestuous adults, she works with

the New Deal in Washington, D. C. and with Democratic Party politics; "liberated" by World War II, she shifts from volunteer to professional political work, becoming a press officer for U. N. N. R. A. , then serving with the Democratic National Committee for seven years, working to involve women in party politics, then serving in the State Department to provide leadership to international women's organizations; she presents numerous anecdotes of her acquaintances with prominent political figures.

1275   LOUCKS, JENNIE ERICKSON (1893-   )
        Oklahoma Was Young and So Was I.   San Antonio: Naylor,
        1964.   166pp.

        Opening with the story of her Finnish immigrant parents, she continues with random anecdotes of her family life, including descriptions of friends, neighbors, and school days which bring her the delights of books and music; she studies music in college, graduating in 1915 and going on to teach in high school and college; she marries in 1917, her "happy days" interrupted by World War I, during which she does volunteer work; she closes with her post-war reunion with her husband.

1276   LOUD, PAT
        Pat Loud, A Woman's Story, with Nora Johnson.   New York:
        Coward, McCann and Geoghegan, 1974.   223pp.

        She relates her personal experiences with the filming of the television series "An American Family" and the sometimes devastating effects of the filming of the members of her family; she goes on to reflect on marriage, motherhood, divorce, and women's roles.

1277   LOW, EDITH McLEAN
        No Rank to Speak Of; Adventures of an Air Force Wife.
        New York: Exposition, 1965.   64pp.

        She describes her twelve years as a "military wife, " the mother of three, and a participant in Wives' Club activities, coping with frequent moves and daily frustrations with patience and a sense of humor; she finds it "a wonderful way of living. "

1278   LOWE, PATRICIA TRACY
        The Cruel Stepmother.   Englewood Cliffs, N. J. :   Prentice-
        Hall, 1970.   260pp.

        After twenty years of step-parenthood, she offers a sensitive "hodgepodge of experience and advice"; she explores

the delicate adjustments, the intense feelings, and the self-
consciousness inherent in the new family structure, and
notes special pressures because she feels the mother "sets
the tone" for family spirits.

1279 LOWRY, ANNIE
Karnee; A Paiute Narrative, by Lalla Scott. Reno, Nev.:
University of Nevada Press, 1966. 149pp.

In an account transcribed in 1936 for the WPA, she tells
first of her Indian mother and Anglo father; boarding with a
white family, she attends school, but later she rebels
against her father's plans and remains loyal to her mother
and Indian ways; she marries reluctantly and tells of her
role as an Indian wife and mother as she struggles against
poverty to support her children.

1280 LOWTHER, WINIFRED E. (1882-)
The Old Beach Road. San Antonio: Naylor, 1973. 91pp.

She offers "a child's earliest awareness, recollections,
and impressions"; random memories evoke a youth of great
freedom and love, including times of hardship as well as
prosperity along the "Old Beach Road" on the Texas coast.

1281 LUBCHENCO, PORTIA McKNIGHT
Doctor Portia, Her First Fifty Years in Medicine, as told
to Anna C. Petteys. Denver: Golden Bell Press, 1964.
315pp.

The first female graduate of the North Carolina Medical
College in 1912, she marries a Russian agronomist and
settles in Russia where she bears three children and practices medicine, observing contrasts in social class, women's
roles, and political questions; caught by World War I and
the revolution, they flee in 1917 through Siberia and China
to the U.S.; she settles in Colorado where she establishes
a practice; she is proud to provide her five children with a
fine heritage of two cultures; in 1954 she is named Colorado
Mother of the Year.

1282 LUBOLD, JOYCE KISSOCK
This Half of the Apple Is Mine. Garden City, N.Y.: Doubleday, 1965. 204pp.

In a humorous account of "the life of the very married,"
she describes homemaking with four children in the 1950's
in a New York City housing development; throwing up her
hands in mock despair for not living up to media prescrip-

tions for sexy living, she copes with "Being Transferred," money problems, pets, community causes, and other occupational diseases and pitfalls.

1283   LUECKE, JESSIE RAYNE
Trailer Travails; Adventures in Cross-Country Travel. New York: Exposition, 1954. 68pp.

Traveling with her husband to recover her health, she visits far-flung family members, children, and grandchildren, and enjoys a life without commitments; her stories include a "trailer park initiation," minor accidents, and amusing incidents.

1284   LUMPKIN, KATHARINE DuPRE (1897-   )
The Making of a Southerner. New York: Knopf, 1946. 248pp.

Writing with sensitivity and understanding, she tells of her youth, the third generation on a Georgia plantation, and her heritage of a simple, abundant life bolstered by a devout religious faith; steeped in the history of slavery, the Civil War, and reconstruction, she "inherits a Lost Cause";- her broader experiences during college, the years of World War I, and a two-year interlude in New York City challenge her preconceptions about race and she comes to accept the necessity for change.

1285   LUND, DORIS HEROLD
Eric. Philadelphia: Lippincott, 1974. 345pp.

A free-lance writer, she provides a detailed chronology of her seventeen-year-old son's leukemia and of her own reactions, adjustments, and emotions; she must learn to allow him his courage and freedom and to accept the challenge of remaining an outsider to the intense drama of dying; she is left with her attempts to understand both his and her experiences.

1286   LUQUER, ELOISE PAYNE (1862-1947)
Old Bedford Days; Recollections of Eloise Payne Luquer. Bedford Village, New York: priv. pr., 1953. 39pp.

A botanist and artist, she presents random recollections of her childhood as the daughter of an Episcopal rector; she describes the people of her village as well.

1287   LUSSIER, BETTY (1921-   )
Amid My Alien Corn. Philadelphia: Lippincott, 1957. 288pp.

Having worked a Maryland farm with her father, ferried
airplanes for the R. A. F. , and worked for the American
O. S. S. during World War II, she marries a prosperous
Catalan businessman but soon tires of Madrid social life;
she takes up the challenge of farming in Spanish Morocco,
living there with her four young sons and gaining the support and friendship of the workers, alongside whom she
works daily; she creates a school and better housing for
them but is rejected by managers because she brings changes
to the lives of the poor; "born a farmer," she forges deep
emotional ties to the land.

1288   LUSTER, GERTRUDE
        Well, for the Love of Greg.   San Antonio: Naylor, 1962.
        102pp.

        In a lightweight account, she tells of traveling to Arizona
        in 1951 with her daughter and grandsons for the health of
        one of the boys; she describes her strenuous travels with
        the mischievous children and the difficulties of entertaining
        them in a small cottage for long, monotonous days; she
        closes with their return home.

1289   LUTHER, EDNA ETTA (1887-)
        Fear I Have Known.   Philadelphia: Dorrance, 1973.   37pp.

        In this saga of unhappiness, the author describes her
        childhood of hard work and isolation in rural New York; at
        sixteen she marries a thief and drunkard and soon goes
        through the misery and shame of divorce; her second mar-
        riage, marked by illness and hardship, also ends in divorce,
        freeing her for a third marriage of strife; she loses all faith
        in people.

1290   LYNIP, G. LOUISE
        On Good Ground; Missionary Stories from the Philippines.
        Grand Rapids, Mich. :   Eerdmans, 1946.   149pp.

        A Baptist missionary nurse in a place of great natural
        beauty offers "a presentation of the Bukidnon people" with
        "sin-darkened hearts"; forced to live in the forest for two
        years during World War II, she continues her ministry and
        cares for children; she later escapes to Australia; her nar-
        rative is told in the third person.

1291   LYNN, LORETTA WEBB
        Loretta Lynn, Coal Miner's Daughter, with George Vecsey.
        Chicago: Regnery, 1976.   204pp.

A country music star, she describes growing up with
poverty and hunger in Appalachia during the depression;
married at thirteen and a mother at fourteen, she notes
that her husband is responsible for her singing career; her
work at the Grand Ole Opry constitutes "the education of a
country singer" and she writes songs from her own experience; regretting her lack of time for her six children and
her grandchildren, she nevertheless appreciates the atten-
tions of her fans; she writes in a vernacular style.

1292   LYON, JEAN (1902-)
       Just Half a World Away; My Search for the New India.   New
       York: Crowell, 1954.   373pp.

       A journalist, she is widowed after extensive work and
       residence in China and takes a free-lance assignment which
       leads to a three-year stay in India; her travels to urban
       centers as well as to remote villages bring her contacts
       with royalty, landlords, fellow journalists, holy men, refu-
       gees, educators, a poet, and the degraded poor; she absorbs
       everything, providing subtle and highly detailed descriptions;
       she closes with reflections on international understanding.

1293   LYON, MARGUERITE (1892-)
       Hurrah for Arkansas!   From Razorbacks to Diamonds.   In-
       dianapolis: Bobbs-Merrill, 1947.   296pp.

       With her husband, "the Jedge," she moves to Arkansas
       and writes an enthusiastic account with much local descrip-
       tion of extensive travels throughout the state.

1294   LYON, PHYLLIS
       see   MARTIN, DEL and PHYLLIS LYON

1295   LYTHGOE, GERTRUDE C.
       The Bahama Queen; The Autobiography of Gertrude "Cleo"
       Lythgoe.   New York: Exposition, 1964.   167pp.

       A well-known bootlegger during Prohibition days, she
       writes to counteract press sensationalism and damage to her
       reputation; after some recollections of her youth, she de-
       scribes her secretarial work before the end of World War I;
       entering the spirits export business, she encounters an un-
       trustworthy partner, prejudice against women, bitter com-
       petition, and personal danger; she is arrested on false
       charges but finally acquitted and released.

1296   MABIE, JANET
        Heaven on Earth.   New York: Harper, 1951.   242pp.

        A journalist and magazine writer, she presents an under-
        stated narrative of her childhood summers in Northfield,
        Massachusetts, as the adopted daughter of a prominent, dis-
        tant but admirable, minister in the early 1900's; she pro-
        vides a child's perspective on revivals and ministers and
        missionaries, among them Dwight Moody; life seems sus-
        pended during Boston winters, while her real existence cen-
        ters on vibrant summers full of "high-minded influences. "

1297   MABUCE, ETHEL LINDY (1886-   )
        I Always Wore My Topi; The Burma Letters of Ethel Ma-
        buce, 1916-1921, ed. Lucille Griffith.   University, Ala. :
        University of Alabama Press, 1974.   336pp.

        The account consists of long descriptive letters written
        home to her family by a Methodist Episcopal missionary;
        she prepares for the "foreign field," then writes of new
        sights, of learning the language, of World War I; she com-
        ments on the food, housekeeping, weather, her missionary
        activities, travels, Burmese customs, her adventures, "such
        full days"; the letters close with her return to the U. S.

1298   McBRIDE, MARY MARGARET (1899-1976)
        A Long Way from Missouri.   New York: Putnam, 1959.
        254pp.

        She begins her career as an ambitious young newspaper
        reporter in the east; she escapes the "sob-sister ghetto" to
        more serious interviews with celebrities, articles on the
        nonsensical events of the 1920's; successful magazine work
        and free-lancing come to an end with the depression and she
        lives in poverty from 1930 to 1934, suffering a nervous
        breakdown in 1931; this account ends with the opening of
        what is to be a highly successful radio career.

1299   Out of the Air.   Garden City, N. Y. :   Doubleday, 1960.
        384pp.

Radio "was my miracle," she notes, providing her with a
third career for twenty years; she begins as a folksy grand-
mother-type but moves into interviewing; she offers lively
portraits of both colleagues and interviewees and writes
fondly of her "radio family"; noting that "popularity was a
heady business," she participates in World War II fund raising with a "sense of dedication" and reports on politicians
and political events; she includes some excerpts from broad-
cast interviews.

1300   McBRYDE, BETH (pseud.)
       see JAROS, ELIZABETH C.

1301   McBURNEY, LARESSA COX (1883-   )
       A Doctor Called Charlie.   San Antonio, Tex.:   Naylor,
       1966.   204pp.

       After writing in the third person of her childhood in sen-
       timental chapters interspersed with biographical information
       about her husband's youth, she tells of her college years,
       their rocky courtship, and their marriage in 1908; they
       settle in Oklahoma, where she raises her younger brother
       and sister, fulfills her role as the wife of a pioneer doctor,
       and engages in Red Cross work during World War I; while
       most of the book is on their early married years, she
       closes with her husband's terminal illness in 1955.

1302   McCALL, LENORE
       Between Us and the Dark.   Philadelphia: Lippincott, 1947.
       303pp.

       She recounts over four years of mental illness in the
       1930's; she provides a detailed mental landscape of deep
       fear, horror, sleeplessness, and suicidal impulses; she de-
       scribes the difficulties her husband and three children have
       adjusting to her illness; she tells of treatment in two hos-
       pitals that includes heavy sedation and insulin shock treat-
       ment; she writes with much insight into her own condition.

1303   McCAMMON, DOROTHY SNAPP (1923-   )
       We Tried to Stay.   Scottdale, Pa.:   Herald Press, 1953.
       208pp.

       An "evangelistic" Mennonite missionary with her husband
       in China reconstructs her account from letters and articles
       written between 1947 and 1951, "epoch-making years" during
       the revolution; she accepts the challenge of learning the
       Chinese language and culture, settling on a mission station,
       establishing a children's Bible school, and assisting in a

modest medical clinic; increasingly discouraged in his missionary activities, her husband is arrested and deported,
and she is later deported as well, just after the birth of
her first child; she feels a oneness with the Chinese, "a
lovable people."

1304   McCARTHY, ABIGAIL QUIGLEY (1915?-)
        Private Faces, Public Places. Garden City, N.Y.: Double-
        day, 1972. 448pp.

        Her 24-year marriage to Eugene McCarthy is the central
        focus of the account; she describes her enthusiasm and dedi-
        cation in her first teaching job in 1936; she meets McCarthy
        in 1938 and provides a delicate portrayal of their years of
        courtship, idealism, religious probing; married in 1945, their
        plans for a Christian rural community are not fulfilled; their
        political activity begins in Minnesota in the late 1940's; she
        tells of years as wife of Representative, then Senator; she
        reflects on the vocation of "political wife"; her account
        closes with painful memories of the 1968 campaign and the
        Chicago convention.

1305   McCARTHY, MARY (1912-)
        Memories of a Catholic Girlhood. New York: Harcourt,
        Brace, 1957. 245pp.

        First addressing the reader, she analyzes the traditional
        dilemmas of writing autobiography, exacerbated in her case
        by the shattered "collective memory of a family" since she
        is orphaned; attempting to reconstruct her past, she pre-
        sents a series of brilliant, closely focused essays which re-
        veal an aggressively Catholic grandmother, a strangely
        mean-spirited aunt and uncle who are guardians, a tolerant
        Protestant grandfather, the intellectual romanticism of con-
        vent school, and a haunting portrait of her Jewish grand-
        mother; each episode is followed by an analysis of "dubious
        points" which raise fundamental questions about identity and
        truth.

1306   McCARTHY, MARY EUNICE
        Meet Kitty. New York: Crowell, 1957. 186pp.

        The youngest in a family of thirteen children, she offers
        recollections that focus on her Irish mother, a dramatic,
        merry, and shrewd woman who raises the children single-
        handedly and with great flair; she describes her youth in
        San Francisco, her stint as a cub reporter, her work in
        Hollywood, and her activity in the 1928 political campaign;
        after her mother's death in 1940, she realizes that her
        mother touched the lives of many and lives on in their
        memories.

1307   McCARTNEY, HAZEL SEVERSON
       In the Gray Rain. New York: Harper, 1957. 246pp.

       A missionary teacher tells of her post-war return to
       Japan with her husband; she enjoys reunions with friends,
       including former students, a teacher, and a seamstress, "a
       tiny silken mother"; her delicate vignettes illuminate the
       grace, dignity, and strength of the Japanese people whom
       she knows; she closes with another return in 1955.

1308   McCLANAHAN, ALICE M.
       Her Father's Partner; The Story of a Lady Lawyer. New
       York: Vantage, 1958. 122pp.

       Especially close to her lawyer father from childhood, she
       is strongly encouraged by him to pursue legal training and
       graduates in 1914; she neither seeks nor receives special
       treatment as a woman but does encounter obstacles due to
       sexism in the profession; she becomes her father's partner
       in Chicago in 1920, specializing in child custody cases.

1309   McCLOSKEY, EUNICE MILDRED (1906-)
       Potpourri; An Autobiography. Philadelphia: Dorrance,
       1966. 157pp.

       In this sequel to So Dear to My Heart, the poet, novelist,
       and painter provides portraits and vignettes of neighbors and
       acquaintances that reveal her deep interest in and enjoyment
       of people; she writes with an eye for significant detail; she
       also tells of her family and her commitment to marriage.

1310   So Dear to My Heart. Boston: Bruce Humphries, 1964.
       228pp.

       A poet and novelist, she writes with nostalgia for the
       "dreamy, awkward, temperamental child" she was; the
       daughter of a wise, capable mother and a mercurial father,
       she loves adult company in her large extended family; books,
       a vivid imagination, a strong interest in people, a fascina-
       tion with local history, and a bent for storytelling all feed
       her later career as a writer; she evokes the poignancy of
       growing up; she rejects her first passionate love in favor of
       poetry but later marries, achieving happiness and a satisfy-
       ing career.

1311   McCOLLUM, VASHTI CROMWELL
       One Woman's Fight. Garden City, N.Y.: Doubleday, 1951.
       221pp.

       She describes her "fight against religious instruction in

the public schools" from 1945 to 1948, campaigning as a result of her son's school experience; as the public is aroused
and polarized, she is both praised and persecuted; she is
harassed and her son is beaten; after losing early court battles in Illinois, she refuses to capitulate and carries the
issue to the Supreme Court.

1312   McCONNELL, PAULINE
       George Washington's Horse Slept Here.   New York: Crowell,
       1956.   218pp.

       She tells of her family's purchase in 1950 of a barn in a
       Long Island village; she describes how the family, including
       six children, shares renovation work, transforms the barn
       into a home, and enjoys "the magic of an enchanted land."

1313   McCONNELL, ROBERTA
       Never Marry a Ranger.   New York: Prentice-Hall, 1950.
       261pp.

       She describes her varied roles as a ranger's wife in the
       western mountains; householding in primitive conditions, she
       advises cattlemen, sheepherders, and tourists, copes with
       storms and forest fires, and raises two children, "wondrous-
       ly happy" in the outdoors; nevertheless she finds the Forest
       Service "a man's business."

1314   McCORMACK, LILY FOLEY (1887?-)
       I Hear You Calling Me.   Milwaukee: Bruce, 1949.   201pp.

       A talented Irish singer, she first comes to the U.S. to
       sing at the St. Louis World's Fair at sixteen; she marries
       an Irish tenor in 1906, and she abandons public singing,
       devoting herself to his career; they settle in the U.S. in
       1914 and find success and prosperity; her account, focused
       on her husband's career, closes in 1945 when she is widowed.

1315   McCOY, MARIE BELL
       Journey Out of Darkness.   New York: McKay, 1963.   205pp.

       Suddenly stricken with blindness but supported by a happy,
       enduring marriage, she works through her rebellion against
       helplessness and learns household and shopping skills and
       other coping techniques; sometimes discouraged by the in-
       sensitivity of others, she nevertheless finds emotional and
       spiritual compensations by writing, attaining "the luminous
       high country of fulfillment and peace."

1316   McCRARY, EUGENIA ("JINX") FALKENBURG
       see   FALKENBURG, JINX (EUGENIA)

1317   McCULLY, ETHEL WALBRIDGE
       Grandma Raised the Roof.   New York: Crowell, 1954.
       211pp.

       She recounts "three years of creative effort" when she
       buys land in the Virgin Islands for the "ideal retirement
       spot"; wintering there and coping with both good and bad
       luck, she clears the land and supervises the building of a
       house and planting of a citrus grove, noting that "manual
       labor agreed with me."

1318   MacDONALD, BETTY BARD (1908-1958)
       Anybody Can Do Anything.   Philadelphia: Lippincott, 1950.
       256pp.

       A prolific writer, her account opens with family anecdotes
       to illustrate that "anybody can do anything, especially Betty";
       having left her husband during the depression in 1931, she
       describes years of poverty and fun in the "warmth and loyal-
       ty and laughter of a big family"; she tells of being pushed by
       a sister, hunting for brief jobs, free entertainment, working
       in government positions, all with characteristic wry humor.

1319   Onions in the Stew.   Philadelphia: Lippincott, 1955.   256pp.

       A writer, she describes living for twelve years on an
       island in Puget Sound; her account consists of witty domes-
       tic anecdotes about househunting, moving, storms, garden-
       ing, neighbors, writing, guests, and her adolescent daugh-
       ters.

1320   The Plague and I.   Philadelphia: Lippincott, 1948.   254pp.

       To set the stage for what follows, her account opens with
       a description of her father's health regimen for his children;
       later married and still later divorced, the author lives with
       her mother, sisters, and daughters, when she discovers she
       has tuberculosis; she tells of sanatorium life, other patients,
       staff, and her attempts to adjust to the routine.

1321   Who, Me?   The Autobiography of Betty MacDonald.   Phila-
       delphia: Lippincott, 1959.   352pp.

       Selections from The Egg and I (1945), The Plague and I
       (1948), Anybody Can Do Anything (1950), and Onions in the

Stew (1955) are placed in chronological order to provide an autobiographical narrative in one volume.

1322 MacDONALD, ELIZABETH P.
Undercover Girl. New York: Macmillan, 1947. 305pp.

A newspaper reporter, she joins the O. S. S. in 1943 in the "Morale Operations" branch which produces subversive propaganda; sometimes gently spoofing her work with other imaginative amateurs, she tells of training in Washington, D. C. and assignments in India and China; in China at the end of World War II, she assists in freeing U. S. prisoners of war but returns home in 1945 when the revolution intensifies.

1323 MacDONALD, SUSANNE RIKE
The Backward Look; Memoirs of Susanne Rike MacDonald.
New York: Exposition, 1957. 62pp.

A poet, she describes her childhood home and her mother, a woman of "rare intelligence"; after a lively adolescence, she studies voice in Paris and London; she teaches voice, marries a doctor, travels; during World War I she writes "propaganda pieces" for a local newspaper.

1324 McDOWALL, SUE ELLEN PRIDE (1877-)
Cotton and Jasmine; A Southern Mosaic. New York: Vantage, 1956. 131pp.

She describes her Arkansas childhood in vignettes that focus on her close family life and her plantation home, "a haven of blissful happiness" where she gains a "deep appreciation" of religion and nature; at thirteen she moves to town, pursues her education, and enjoys simple diversions; she closes with her courtship and marriage in 1899, noting the deaths of three of her four children in a brief epilogue.

1325 McEWEN, INEZ PUCKETT
So This Is Ranching! Caldwell, Id.: Caxton, 1948. 270pp.

A former journalist and teacher, she presents a down-to-earth picture of a "slice of rural living" along Idaho's Snake River; she and her husband are initially ignorant city "dudes," but they develop strong ties to the land; her narrative is sprinkled with passages from Walt Whitman.

1326 MacFARLAND, ANNE (pseud.)
see MacDONALD, SUSANNE RIKE

1327 McGARR, MARGARET AIKENS
And Lo, The Star.   New York: Pageant, 1953.   116pp.

Once mentally ill but unjustly institutionalized, she writes
to assist others with mental illness; her disjointed explana-
tion of the events leading to her commitment is full of por-
tents and Biblical support for her interpretation of those
events; after her "rebirth" into the "free world," she is
aided by friends, returns to her work as an art teacher,
and helps others similarly afflicted.

1328 McGARVEY, LOIS (1885-1959)
Along Alaska Trails.   New York: Vantage, 1960.   200pp.

In 1911 she sets out for the Alaskan gold camps, adventurous, independent, and "truly an eager-beaver"; she works
in grocery stores, cooks, then marries a railroadman in
1913; still ambitious, she races cars, is a railroad agent,
traps, and drives a dog team; from 1921 to 1931 she owns
a successful fur business, and from 1941 to 1949 she runs
a boarding house, later moving into real estate; she writes
entertaining anecdotes of a wide variety of colorful people.

1329 McGEHEE, FLORENCE
Please Excuse Johnny.   New York: Macmillan, 1952.
242pp.

She takes a job in attendance enforcement and becomes a
"hookey cop"; she describes the poverty and conditions that
keep some children from school and her attempts to inter-
vene in difficult family situations.

1330 Sailors Kiss Everybody.   New York: Macmillan, 1955.
224pp.

In this re-creation of a Victorian childhood in Oakland,
California, she portrays an exuberant extended family full
of colorful figures and dominated by her grandmother; incidents described include the San Francisco earthquake of
1906; she writes with gentle humor and nostalgia, closing
with the death of her grandmother, the heart of the family.

1331 McGINLEY, PHYLLIS (1905-1978)
The Province of the Heart; Essays.   New York: Viking,
1959.   181pp.

A poet, she presents a series of autobiographical essays,
reflecting on "the honor of being a woman," "premature"
social life among children, her "heresy" of holding to notions

of right and wrong, her admiration for the new generation, the privilege of solitude and privacy, the consolations of a bad education, and marriage; she notes that her writing career is not at the center of her life.

1332   Sixpence in Her Shoe. New York: Macmillan, 1964. 281pp.

A poet, essayist, and children's author, she writes "for, by, and about the American housewife," offering "a kind of autobiography" which draws on her personal experiences to illuminate woman's role; she focuses on her home and family and the "antique sisterhood" of housewives; much of the material was previously published in the Ladies Home Journal.

1333   McGINNIS, MABEL (1916-)
        Life with George; Ups and Downs Down on the Farm.   New
        York: Exposition, 1959.   170pp.

A city girl with "rustic aspirations," she weds a farmer and tells in humorous anecdotes of their life as chicken farmers, beset by constant financial strain and hard work; she raises four sons and several foster children, runs the farm when her husband is hospitalized, recovers herself from a serious illness, yet throughout all it is a tale of happiness.

1334   McGOVERN, ELEANOR (1921-)
        Uphill; A Personal Story, with Mary Finch Hoyt.   Boston:
        Houghton Mifflin, 1974.   234pp.

In this thoughtful and perceptive account, she first tells of her childhood in rural South Dakota and of her close relationship with a twin sister; defying her father, she marries in 1943, and as her husband is a flier, a minister, a professor, and a politician, each of his careers entails different roles and demands for her; raising five children, she also contributes time and energy to her husband's campaigns, remaining "unabashedly idealistic" about family and politics; she notes that their lives are transformed by the 1968 Democratic convention; during the 1972 presidential campaign, an "extraordinary learning experience," she struggles with the ambiguity of her role, then moves on to "new beginnings."

1335   McGOWAN, HELEN (1911-)
        Motor City Madam.   New York: Pageant, 1964.   197pp.

Known as Helen "Rocking Chair" McGowan, this Detroit madam describes her "learning fast" when her parents reject her after a shotgun marriage at fifteen; maintaining her respectability, "a matter of money," she tells of her activities over a period of thirty years with the whiskey racket, Al Capone, pimps, policemen, jail, and "her girls"; enjoying a long and unique career, she reflects on her personal values.

1336 MACHETANZ, SARA
The Howl of the Malemute: The Story of an Alaskan Winter.
New York: Sloane, 1961. 204pp.

A writer, she marries a documentary filmmaker in Alaska; they settle in a remote Eskimo village to collaborate on a film of the life of a sled dog; she tells of the birth of the puppies, their sod-banked cabin, the drama of the first blizzard, filming in the bitter cold, the danger of spring breakup, and her pride in the dogs' performance; she gains insights into Eskimo culture through many friendships, and suffers a sense of loss when she must leave on completion of the film.

1337 MacIVER, JOYCE (pseud.)
The Frog Pond. New York: Braziller, 1961. 412pp.

A journalist and writer in New York provides a seven-year fragment of an autobiography covering the years from 1942 to 1949; paralyzed by passivity, she is raped several times and possessed by "the Thing" or a "Devilman"; she gradually reveals her childhood fears and notes a series of sometimes bizarre relationships with psychiatrists in her quest for "the cure"; she closes with a final, almost accidental "cure."

1338 McIVERS, PATRICIA TAYLERT
Good Night, Mr. Christopher. New York: Sheed and Ward, 1974. 127pp.

A mother tells of her family's saga during the course of her youngest son's terminal illness in 1968; bitter about two years of unnecessary pain and fruitless searching for competent doctors, she describes the family's adjustment as they keep the secret of a malignant brain tumor from the son; against her husband's wishes, she seeks the help of a faith healer; she closes with her son's final rapid deterioration.

1339 MACKAY, MARGARET MACKPRANG (1907-)
I Live in a Suitcase. London: Faber and Faber, 1953. 224pp.

A novelist, she presents chronologically and geographically random sketches of her travels in twenty-four countries; having lived in California, China, and Hawaii, she does much of her traveling from her England home alone after she is widowed; her short vignettes reveal images and flavors, sometimes with a touch of humor for she enjoys people with a hint of eccentricity.

1340   McKELVIE, MARTHA GROVES
       The Empty Sleeve.   Philadelphia: Dorrance, 1961.   99pp.

Using her childhood memories of a visit to Zerelda James (the mother of Frank and Jesse), she weaves a tale of the James family and her own, comparing Mrs. James and the "female rebels" of her family; she focuses on recollections of her grandmother and the self-sufficient pioneer life in Missouri.

1341   The Journey.   Philadelphia: Dorrance, 1962.   207pp.

After recalling her childhood, marked by poverty and loneliness, she tells of her marriage at sixteen to a "Nebraska V. I. P.," later governor of the state; conservatory educated, she teaches music and works for support of the arts; in a parade of acquaintances, she describes numerous friendships with political figures including Roosevelt, Taft, Hoover, and tells of hosting Coolidge at a Black Hills hideaway; widowed after fifty-three years of marriage, she returns home to seek her roots.

1342   McKENNEY, RUTH (1911-1972)
       Far, Far from Home.   New York: Harper, 1954.   210pp.

She presents a lighthearted, entertaining narrative of her family's "adventures in Belgium" from 1947 to 1949; their various adjustments are exasperating and amusing, from their "heroic efforts" to learn French, to coping with a succession of servants, to her teenaged son's attempts at cross-cultural dating, to their attempts to produce an authentic Thanksgiving dinner; they gratefully return to their New York City apartment; the account first appeared in Holiday magazine.

1343   The Loud Red Patrick.   New York: Harcourt, Brace, 1947.
       161pp.

Her Irish grandfather, "the hero of the various stories in this book," is an outrageously flamboyant freethinker and Irish patriot; her anecdotes illuminate her strong family feeling and fascination with her grandfather.

1344   Love Story. New York: Harcourt, Brace, 1950. 303pp.

    A personal radical, she marries a scientific radical, an
editor of The New Masses, in 1937, the beginning of a marriage of two fiery characters; she writes humorous articles
for The New Yorker to keep them financially afloat, then
publishes a book on her eccentric sister (see companion volume) as well as a book on the CIO; in 1945 she has a financially successful but "wretchedly unhappy" year writing
for films in Hollywood and flees back to her country home
where she enjoys a "rich and varied" life, raising her step-
son, her nephew, and her daughter in a strong, united family; her narrative is witty yet moving.

1345   MACKENSON, KATHERYN M.
    Christmas Forever. Boston: Christopher, 1966. 95pp.

    Her chapters consist of her annual Christmas letters,
some frenzied, some quiet, from 1947 to 1965; a nurse
married to a doctor, she chronicles the arrival of each of
her five daughters, news of the growing accomplishments of
each, and domestic activities which are centered about the
Christmas celebration.

1346   MACKENZIE, GERTRUDE
    My Love Affair with the State of Maine, with Ruth Goode.
New York: Simon and Schuster, 1955. 311pp.

    She flees from the world of New York public relations
and advertising and buys a store and guest house on the
Maine coast with a woman friend; she presents a humorous
and lively account of their harried preparations, mistakes,
tender relations with the natives, coping with winter in
Maine; her account ends with a disastrous forest fire and
the first steps in community rebuilding.

1347   MacKENZIE, RACHEL
    Risk. New York: Viking, 1970. 59pp.

    A victim of congestive heart failure, she discusses the
feelings and questions she has throughout diagnostic procedures; after open heart surgery, she writes her impressions
of the intensive care unit, as she comprehends snatches of
conversation, copes with pain and complications; she closes
the third person narrative with her hospital release.

1348   McKIBBIN, ALMA ESTELLE BAKER (1871-)
    Step by Step; An Autobiographical Sketch. Washington, D. C.:
Review and Herald Publishing Association, 1964. 96pp.

A writer of Bible textbooks for children and a church
school teacher, she tells of her strong religious faith in an
account sprinkled with Biblical quotations; having experienced
salvation at a camp meeting and avoided the secular pressures of town and school, she endures through the poor
health of her husband, the death of an infant, and her own
poor health yet cares for and supports family members
through the years.

1349   MacLAINE, SHIRLEY (1934-   )
        "Don't Fall Off the Mountain." New York: Norton, 1970.
        270pp.

Born into a "middle-class Virginia family," she takes up
dancing, which leads to career in show business; she goes
to New York at 18, and gets chorus line work and unsuccessful film roles; her husband's deep ties to Japan require
separate residences; she and her daughter live alternately
there and in U.S.; loneliness and poor films are followed by
success, and adjustments to "fame, affluence, and power";
a quest for inner understanding takes her to civil rights
work in the South, travels in Africa and India.

1350   You Can Get There from Here. New York: Norton, 1975.
        249pp.

After an unsuccessful television series and work for the
McGovern campaign, she visits China with a group of American women; she discusses frankly her culture-shock and reevaluation of her basic values; the account ends on a note
of re-dedication to entertainment.

1351   MacLEOD, LILY
        Return to Life. Philadelphia: Lippincott, 1950. 128pp.

She describes her shock at a diagnosis of cervical cancer
but finds the "strength of knowing the truth"; she shares her
burden with her adult daughter and with her mother, exploring her own emotional responses to the illness and its treatment; she is determined to return to her magazine work.

1352   McMANUS, VIRGINIA
        Not for Love. New York: Putnam, 1960. 288pp.

An idealistic Chicago school teacher, she becomes "eman-
cipated" when prostitution provides guilt-free, detached,
businesslike opportunities for easy money; she loses her job
and alienates her family, her life degenerating into a parade
of men; arrested and jailed, she feels she no longer has "a

way of life" and upon her release turns to writing the autobiography to provide focus and direction for herself.

1353   MacMILLAN, MIRIAM LOOK
        Green Seas and White Ice.   New York: Dodd, Mead, 1948.
        287pp.

        After her marriage to an Arctic explorer, she desires to
        share in her husband's voyages, feeding her own "profound
        and inborn" love of the sea; she works for an Eskimo vil-
        lage school, then joins an Arctic expedition, accepted by the
        crew as a fellow member; her vivid anecdotes of storms
        and icebergs portray a dangerous adventure; the onset of
        World War II prevents further voyages.

1354   McNEAL, VIOLET (1888?-)
        Four White Horses and a Brass Band.   Garden City, N. Y. :
        Doubleday, 1947.   267pp.

        A child starved for attention, she leaves her Minnesota
        home in 1904 to join "the fabulous world of medicine shows";
        ensnared by an opium-dealing quack doctor, she creates her
        own successful medicine pitch using the tricks of the trade;
        the thrill of riches and a reputation fades with the growing
        misery of a brutal husband, drug addiction, divorce; she
        closes optimistically, having achieved a cure and a good
        marriage.

1355   McPHERSON, AIMEE SEMPLE (1890-1944)   NAW
        The Story of My Life.   Waco, Tex. :   Word Books, 1973.
        255pp.

        The famous evangelist left an incomplete manuscript at
        the time of her death, from which this account is recon-
        structed; a 1907 revival meeting settles her adolescent reli-
        gious doubts and marks a turning point as she acknowledges
        her desire to be a preacher; widowed in the Chinese mission
        field, she returns to the U. S. , remarries, and holds numer-
        ous revivals across the nation; she builds a temple in 1923;
        in 1926 she must vindicate her claim of having been kid-
        napped; having devoted her life to evangelical service, "only
        a woman, " she feels she could have done more if she'd been
        a man.

1356   MADELEVA, SISTER MARY (MARY EVALINE WOLFF)
        see WOLFF, SISTER MARY MADELEVA (MARY EVALINE)
        (1887-1964)

1357   MAGEE, GRACE SPENCER
        Ten Angels in a Pontiac; A Family Chronicle of a Cross-
        Country Trip. New York: Exposition, 1965. 124pp.

        A doctor's wife and the mother of ten children tells of a
        one-month trip during the summer of 1960; her spirited ac-
        count includes descriptions of scenery along the way as well
        as transcriptions of family chatter; details illustrate her role
        as keeper of the peace among the different personalities
        within her family.

1358   MAGRUDER, GAIL (1938-)
        A Gift of Love. Philadelphia: A. J. Holman, 1976. 160pp.

        She tells of her husband's political activities culminating
        in his job as an aide to President Nixon; her early misgiv-
        ings are intensified as her family life suffers under the
        strains of Washington obligations; when her husband is im-
        plicated in the Watergate scandal, she sees her marriage
        damaged and her home "violated" by the press; after the
        tension of the Watergate trial, she lives with humiliation and
        fear while her husband is in prison, but she is sustained by
        new friendships and renewed religious faith; she emerges
        without bitterness into a permanently altered life, working
        with her husband for a Christian service organization.

1359   MAIULLO, MINERVA
        A Tapestry of Memories. South Brunswick: A. S. Barnes,
        1972. 335pp.

        She is an opera and concert singer from Detroit who
        makes her debut in 1925 but later chooses marriage and
        motherhood over her career; with her familial and artistic
        roots in Italy, she later travels and lives in Europe, hold-
        ing salons in her home; her fragmentary recollections of
        places and people are held together by the twin themes of
        love and music.

1360   MAKANOWITZKY, BARBARA NORMAN
        Requiem for a Spanish Village. New York: Stein and Day,
        1972. 192pp.

        A free-lance writer and author of cookbooks moves in
        1961 with her husband, a concert violinist, from Paris to a
        house in a village in northeastern Spain; they value the
        "timelessness" of the old house, for they seek "peace and
        stability," but the inevitable changes brought by moderniza-
        tion over a decade erode traditions and the village becomes
        "a ruin on a hill"; writing with profound sadness, she
        chronicles the changes through sensitive portraits of her
        neighbors.

1361   MALL, E. JANE (1920-)
       How Am I Doing, God?   St. Louis: Concordia, 1973.
       160pp.

       Addressing other women, she writes about the Christian
       spirit and about "taking pride in being a woman"; she de-
       scribes important lessons she has learned through living--
       lessons in how to express her love, how to forgive, how to
       be a mother, how to be effective in her church work, how
       to be a friend; when she is widowed, she must learn how to
       create a new life with her three children.

1362   P. S. I Love You.   St Louis: Concordia, 1961.   166pp.

       A writer and minister's wife, she writes an anecdotal ac-
       count of the "many children we loved and cared for and lost"
       as a foster parent; later she adopts first a Japanese and two
       German children, then three others, searching for ways to
       understand and aid their adjustment; in a life hectic "but
       never boring," her writing is temporarily halted for child-
       rearing as she builds a family, but these years later pro-
       vide the subject matter for her books.

1363   MALLARD, MARY JONES
       see   JONES, MARY SHARPE (1808-1869)

1364   MALONE, DOROTHY
       How Mama Could Cook!   New York: A. A. Wyn, 1946.
       178pp.

       She extols the beauty, charm, and courage of her mother, "a
       feminist to her soul"; her reminiscences are organized by cook-
       ing categories and triggered by certain foods and recipes.

1365   MANDEL, URSULA GREENSHAW (1898-)
       I Live My Life; The Autobiography of Ursula Greenshaw
       Mandel, M. D.   New York: Exposition, 1965.   647pp.

       After witnessing the "psychological disintegration" of her
       family by the time she has graduated from Vassar and medi-
       cal school, and having suffered "adverse experiences" in two
       failed marriages and a suicide attempt, she develops a cer-
       tain gentle defiance and self-sufficiency; she achieves serenity
       and maturity in her middle years and focuses her energy on
       her successful medical practice.

1366   MANDER, ANICA VESEL (1934-)
       Blood Ties; A Woman's History, with Sarika Finci Hofbauer.
       New York: Random House, 1976.   297pp.

Integrating her Yugoslavian maternal grandmother's story
with her own, she explores "my roots ... my female line-
age"; her memories begin with her Jewish family's flight
from the Germans in 1941; her adolescence is spent in Italy
and she tells of her school days, friendships, sexual experiences; she notes the continuing tension between her mother
and her grandmother over religious practices; when her family settles in the U.S., her acculturation is hastened by the
movies and by junior college life; she discusses her growth
in intellect, experience, and independence.

1367   MANN, EDNA
        Flight from Fear.   New York: Pageant, 1964.   127pp.

She writes a straightforward account of living in France
at the outbreak of World War II; concerned for her five-
year-old grandson's safety, she seeks a refuge beyond Paris,
traveling from village to city and back to prepare a secure
home; she is haunted by the scenes of refugees, constant
uncertainty, and the final German occupation; after a reunion
in Paris with her husband and daughter, they decide to return to the U.S., reaching their ship in Lisbon after delay
and difficulty.

1368   MANN, STELLA TERRILL
        Beyond the Darkness; Three Reasons Why I Believe We Live
        After Death.   New York: Dodd, Mead, 1965.   178pp.

The author of several books on religious topics offers her
"report on personal experiences" that lead her to explore the
possibilities of an afterlife; she tells of voices and visions
that came to her before and after her husband's death in
1961 from automobile accident injuries.

1369   MANNES, MARYA (1904-   )
        Out of My Time.   Garden City, N.Y.:   Doubleday, 1971.
        251pp.

In a subtle, introspective account drawn from diaries,
notes, and letters, she tells of her "extraordinary family";
a tomboy, she is surrounded by the music of her violinist
father and pianist mother and the atmosphere of summers in
Europe; after her school years, she studies sculpture in
England, then turns to writing as a vocation, fighting for the
freedom to be herself, "obsessed with curiosity and driven
by visions," a "spiritual hermaphrodite," sustained by a
fierce independence and ambition; she writes for Vogue, enjoys years of beauty and luxury married to an artist in Italy
--one of three marriages--experiences ambivalent motherhood, and pursues her free-lance writing and criticism.

1370   MANNIX, JULE
       Married to Adventure.   New York: Simon and Schuster,
       1954.   276pp.

       A former actress describes twelve years of marriage
       filled with adventure; in 1939 she helps her husband prepare
       a film and lecture on hunting iguanas with trained eagles in
       Mexico; they are accused of spying there during World War
       II; while raising a child, she searches for vampire bats in
       Mexican caves, tames and hunts with a cheetah in the west-
       ern U.S., and films wild animals in Africa; her activities
       serve as the bases for lectures and magazine articles.

1371   MARBLE, ALICE (1913-   )
       The Road to Wimbledon.   New York: Scribner, 1946.
       167pp.

       A famous tennis player tells of her active, sports-cen-
       tered California childhood as "the tomboy of the neighbor-
       hood"; she initially wants to be a physical education teacher
       but finds she enjoys the fierce competition of tennis, enter-
       ing national competition in 1931; in 1939, after rigorous
       training, she wins the Wimbledon singles crown; later she
       is stricken with pleurisy and struggles for "victory over ill-
       ness"; she closes with her fiancé's death in World War II.

1372   MARGOLIES, MARJORIE
       They Came to Stay, with Ruth Gruber.   New York: Coward,
       McCann & Geoghegan, 1975.   352pp.

       A television journalist tells of her love for children and
       a compulsion to adopt an oriental orphan; she finds numerous
       obstacles as a potential single parent, but her parents pro-
       vide assistance and emotional support; she learns much from
       her first Korean daughter and participates in publicity on be-
       half of other hard-to-place children; her research for a pro-
       gram on Vietnam war orphans leads to an emotional search
       for a second daughter, whose adjustment to a new family
       proves to be a harrowing experience; she maintains an in-
       tense yet realistic approach to combining a career with sin-
       gle motherhood.

1373   MARIA DEL REY, SISTER
       In and Out the Andes; Mission Trails from Yucatan to Chile.
       New York: Scribner, 1954.   281pp.

       A Maryknoll sister describes eight months of travel in
       Bolivia, Chile, Peru, Panama, Nicaragua, and Yucatan,
       visiting Maryknoll medical and teaching missions; full of ad-
       miration for her colleagues, she writes with vigor, enthusi-
       asm, and a sense of humor.

1374   Pacific Hopscotch. New York: Scribner, 1951. 181pp.

A Maryknoll sister, she travels to China, the Philippines,
Guam, Palau, Japan, Korea, and Hawaii, visiting missionary
schools and bringing support, optimism, and encouragement;
in China she describes in vivid detail primitive conditions
that test her endurance and strength and there she notes the
growth of Catholic missions in spite of communist opposition;
everywhere she demonstrates her affection for the people she
meets.

1375   Safari by Jet; Through Africa and Asia. New York: Scribner, 1962. 308pp.

A Maryknoll sister tells of eight months touring with the
Mother General to visit Maryknoll missions in Tanganyika,
Ceylon, the Philippines, Hong Kong, Taiwan, Korea, Japan,
and several Pacific islands; a keen and enthusiastic observer,
she provides anecdotes of dedicated priests and nuns and of
devoted Christian natives, portraying the life of the people
and the flavor of each location; she writes with a sense of
strong international sisterhood.

1376   MARION, FRANCES (1888-1973)   NAWM
Off with Their Heads! A Serio-Comic Tale of Hollywood.
New York: Macmillan, 1972. 356pp.

Originally an advertising artist, she is drawn to Hollywood at twenty-four by an intense desire to "get into the
picture business"; she makes her career as a screenwriter,
often assigned to produce vehicles for successive rising
stars; she exhibits great admiration for many of her colleagues, sharp criticism of others in an account drawn from
extensive diaries that constitutes a lively history of Hollywood and "the fun and fury of our anamorphic life."

1377   MARRIOTT, ALICE LEE (1910-)
Greener Fields; Experiences Among the American Indians.
New York: Crowell, 1953. 274pp.

An ethnologist, she tells how her work as an Oklahoma
librarian leads to her passionate interest in Indian culture
and to graduate studies; her first field work among Oregon
Indians results in close rapport and friendship with her first
translator and her touching adoption by the Indian family;
from 1936 to 1943 she works with the Indian Arts and Crafts
Board to organize native artisans; she is moved when her
several books about them are accepted by the Indians; each
chapter in this account is a perceptive, articulate vignette.

1378   The Valley Below.   Norman, Okla.:   University of Oklahoma
       Press, 1949.   243pp.

       An ethnologist describes her valley home in New Mexico
       with a fine eye for detail, telling of her adobe house, her
       cats, irrigation gardening, pottery collecting, and the local
       social life, marked by a "strong community feeling"; she
       develops a deep fondness for the valley, its people, and its
       way of life.

1379   MARSHALL, CATHERINE WOOD (1914-   )
       Beyond Our Selves.   New York: McGraw-Hill, 1961.   266pp.

       In this story of a spiritual pilgrimage, she tells first of
       her childhood, her marriage (see A Man Called Peter), and
       her struggle in 1943 with tuberculosis; her discovery of the
       "gospel of healing" and full religious commitment create a
       turning point in her illness; she describes the subsequent
       presence of God in her daily life.

1380   A Man Called Peter; The Story of Peter Marshall.   New
       York: McGraw-Hill, 1951.   354pp.

       She presents a biography of her husband as well as the
       story of their marriage; drawn to the Scotch clergyman by
       his compelling sermons, she marries in 1936; her initial
       concerns about the heavy demands as the wife of a prominent
       Washington, D. C. minister are allayed by her sense of privi-
       lege sharing his life and career; their marriage is charac-
       terized by intense love, honesty, strong religious bonds,
       and deepening harmony; at her husband's sudden death, she
       is sustained by her religious faith, achieving "a quiet mind
       and a steady heart."

1381   To Live Again.   New York: McGraw-Hill, 1957.   335pp.

       The wife of a famous minister, she opens her perceptive
       account with the death of her husband in 1949; supported by
       her religious faith and concern for her son, and refusing to
       "give in to poverty," she begins the "pure joy" of editing
       her husband's sermons; caught in the tension between femin-
       inity and career and the difficulties of a "manless house-
       hold," she nevertheless continues writing with a biography of
       her husband which becomes a bestseller in 1952; moved by
       readers' responses to the book, she enjoys an intimate in-
       volvement with its film version; her work is sustained by a
       "continuing sense of destiny."

1382   MARSHALL, KATHERINE TUPPER (1882-)
        Together; Annals of an Army Wife.   New York: Tupper
        and Love, 1946.   292pp.

        A widow with three children, she marries General George
        C. Marshall in 1930 and offers a "homespun account of our
        years together"; her anecdotes focus on the social role of an
        army wife and on her husband's accomplishments, particular-
        ly during World War II; she joins soldiers' aid work, main-
        taining her home as "a sanctuary for my husband. "

1383   MARSHALL, RUTH TERRY
        Land of Mabuhay.   Philadelphia: Dorrance, 1965.   123pp.

        The wife of a serviceman stationed in the Philippines
        tells of her voyage across the Pacific to join her husband
        in 1949; she describes homemaking with a native housekeep-
        er and a native driver and "garrison living" as civil unrest
        leads to uneasiness among the Americans; when she has
        cancer, she returns to the U. S. for surgery and a slow con-
        valescence, continuing affectionate ties with friends in the
        Philippines.

1384   MARTIN, ANNA
        Around and About Alaska.   New York: Vantage, 1959.
        94pp.

        A missionary teacher in Alaska for over twenty-five
        years, she writes "to inspire other women to venture north, "
        either accompanied or alone; the account largely ignores her
        career and focuses on her vacation travels as she seeks
        new scenes, new experiences, and new adventures; she in-
        cludes some diary excerpts.

1385   MARTIN, BETTY PARKER (pseud.) (1908-)
        Miracle at Carville, ed. Evelyn Wells.   Garden City, N. Y. :
        Doubleday, 1950.   302pp.

        When she discovers at nineteen that she has leprosy, she
        is troubled by fear and ignorance of the disease; she enters
        the national leprosarium at Carville, "an unreal world" iso-
        lated from her former life, and builds a network of new
        friends as she becomes involved in "Carville's human prob-
        lems"; she masters her fear of marriage to a fellow patient
        and her fear of being stigmatized on the "outside"; her mira-
        cle comes with sulfa drug therapy in the early 1940's; she
        and her husband, both cured, devote themselves to a cam-
        paign against prejudice and misinformation.

1386   No One Must Ever Know, ed. Evelyn Wells.   Garden City,
       N. Y. : Doubleday, 1959.   231pp.

       In this sequel to Miracle at Carville, this victim of Han-
       sen's disease compares the security and friendship she'd
       found after twenty years in a leprosarium with the secrecy
       and uncertainty she finds on the "outside"; naïve and trust-
       ing, handicapped by physical weakness and inexperience, she
       fears exposure and cannot fully function in society or enjoy
       the success of her first book; after ten years of struggling
       with poverty and isolation, she and her husband fulfill their
       dream of a home; she finds the slow lifting of the stigma of
       leprosy heartening.

1387   MARTIN, DEL (1921-)
       Lesbian/Woman, with Phyllis Lyon.   San Francisco: Glide
       Publications, 1972.   283pp.

       Among the founders of the Daughters of Bilitis in 1955,
       they offer their personal experience with identity crises in
       their roles as children, mothers, and lesbian women; in a
       straightforward manner, they describe their own marriage
       of nineteen years, and offer an historical, legal, and social
       background for lesbian women, issuing a call for liberation.

1388   MARTIN, MARTHA (pseud.)
       Home on the Bear's Domain.   New York: Macmillan, 1954.
       246pp.

       She describes her love of the wilderness and of a "life
       close to nature"; she settles in Alaska with her husband, a
       prospector and miner; she loves children, so after the death
       of an infant daughter, she raises "stray urchins," including
       two Yugoslavian children; she tells of a family life of hard
       physical labor and "pedagogy in the wilderness," extremely
       close to her Serbian daughters; loneliness sets in as the
       children grow up and leave home; calamities force her to
       abandon her wilderness home; she draws this account from
       diaries covering forty years.

1389   O Rugged Land of Gold.   New York: Macmillan, 1952.
       223pp.

       Wife of a prospector, she is trapped alone in their iso-
       lated cabin during a winter storm and landslide; pregnant
       and coping with a broken arm, she makes two unsuccessful
       attempts to escape but winter conditions make it impossible;
       fortunately she has enough supplies to survive the winter and
       prepare for the birth of her daughter; memories weave in

and out of her daily existence, aiding her sanity; in the
spring, she and her child are first found by local Indians.

1390   MARTIN, MARY (1913-   )
        My Heart Belongs. New York: Morrow, 1976. 320pp.

        A star of stage and screen, she describes her joyful
        Texas tomboy childhood of singing and dancing; at sixteen
        she plays at marriage and motherhood, but as she studies
        and teaches dance, she realizes her attraction to show busi-
        ness; once in Hollywood, she breaks into film and her ca-
        reer is shaped and guided by her second husband, a pro-
        ducer to whom she is deeply devoted; describing the "very
        hard work and endless discipline" of Broadway, she recounts
        lively anecdotes about her experiences in South Pacific,
        Peter Pan, and The Sound of Music; she later enjoys two
        uninterrupted years with her husband on their Brazilian farm
        and delights in her son, daughter, and grandchildren; her
        account is warm and effervescent.

1391   MARTIN, MILDRED ALBERT
        The Martins of Gunbarrel. Caldwell, Id.: Caxton, 1959.
        280pp.

        Although she is originally a city dweller, her summer job
        as a Yellowstone waitress leads to a sudden marriage to a
        wrangler in 1923 and the rigors of learning the ways of
        wilderness housekeeping; she describes the hardships and
        satisfactions of their first winter, then their purchase of a
        Wyoming dude ranch; she tells of hired help, her hunger for
        female companionship, summer dudes, the birth of a son,
        the development of her own self-sufficiency; she focuses her
        delightful account on the first two years of her marriage.

1392   MARTIN, WANDA (1908-   )
        Woman in Two Worlds; A Personal Story of Psychological
        Experience. Norwalk, Conn.: Silvermine Publishers, 1966.
        171pp.

        Married and the mother of two, she tells of mental dis-
        turbances from 1946 to 1959; she experiences mysterious
        psychic events and wide mood swings but finds equilibrium
        after reading on mystical and religious topics; with meno-
        pause comes another inner crisis although she maintains a
        controlled external life; only after years of torment does she
        reveal the trauma of living in "two worlds" to her husband;
        engaged in an intense "intellectual journey," she reflects on
        "woman's main task on earth. "

1393 MARYANNA, SISTER
With Love and Laughter: Reflections of a Dominican Nun.
Garden City, N.Y.: Hanover House, 1960. 213pp.

She describes her 30 years as a Catholic nun, proud of
the achievements and contributions of her sisters; she tells
of the "true family spirit" of her order, the maternal role
of the teaching sister, fond memories of students; she pursues her own education and writing career which includes
writing poems, stories, and books for children; she tells of
a trip to Europe to visit holy sites.

1394 MARY FRANCIS, SISTER (1921-)
A Right to Be Merry. London: Sheed & Ward, 1957.
212pp.

She writes to correct common misunderstandings of the
cloistered nun's poverty, penance, contemplation, and en-
closure, describing her own "full, joyous, beautiful life";
she tells of her appointment to found a new monastery of the
Order of Poor Clares in New Mexico in 1948; examining typical monastery routine, she praises the simple life that combines contemplation with a sense of humor.

1395 MARY JEREMY, SISTER (1907-)
All the Days of My Life. Indianapolis: Bobbs-Merrill,
1959. 191pp.

In a lively and spirited account, she tells of her unflag-
ging devotion to the convent community and to her teaching
career; she brings ambition and enthusiasm to her high
school and orphanage assignments as well as to her pursuit
of a Ph.D. in chemistry at the University of Illinois, after
which she engages in deeply satisfying college teaching and
professional activities.

1396 MASON, LUCY RANDOLPH (1882-1959)   NAWM
To Win These Rights; A Personal Story of the CIO in the
South. New York: Harper, 1952. 206pp.

Having inherited from her parents and distinguished
Southern forbears a "strong sense of social responsibility,"
she is drawn to civil rights and union causes, working for
the YWCA, the National Consumer's League, and the CIO;
she is a salaried organizer for the CIO beginning in 1937,
serving among southern textile workers; she writes with admiration of fellow union leaders, seeing the union movement
in the South at the forefront of the drive for democracy.

1397   MASSING, HEDE
       This Deception.   New York: Duell, Sloan and Pearce, 1951.
       335pp.

       After an unhappy childhood in Vienna, she marries com-
       munist revolutionary Gerhard Eisler and becomes an actress
       in Berlin, immersed in radical politics in the early 1920's;
       she emigrates and becomes a U. S. citizen in 1927, then
       serves as a Soviet agent in the early 1930's, recruiting oth-
       ers; in 1937, however, she renounces communism and later
       testifies in the Alger Hiss trial; she writes to help herself
       discover the truth.

1398   MASTERSON, JENNY GOVE (pseud.) (1868-   )
       Letters from Jenny, ed. Gordon W. Allport.   New York:
       Harcourt, Brace & World, 1965.   223pp.

       A middle-aged mother writes to a friend of her adult son
       from 1926 to 1937, recounting her tortured relationship to
       her son; in intense, open, and expressive terms, she tells
       a tale of sacrifice, frustration, poverty, and loneliness,
       feeling her "whole life has been wasted"; after her son dies
       in 1929, she continues in "a sort of living death"; the letters
       are found on pages 7-146.

1399   MASTERTON, ELSIE
       Nothing Whatever to Do, with John Masterton.   New York:
       Crown, 1956.   277pp.

       In a lively style, she relates how she and her husband
       attempt to create a ski resort on a Vermont mountain in
       1949; as city novices, they learn quickly that they must
       abandon winter for summer guests; offering the simplicity
       and relaxation of their home to their guests, they flourish;
       while raising three daughters and establishing a blueberry
       jam business, she becomes a cook with a regional reputa-
       tion.

1400   Off My Toes!   Boston: Little, Brown, 1961.   298pp.

       In this sequel to the above entry, she describes the ef-
       fects on their resort business of the earlier book's publica-
       tion; after noting some of the inexorable changes in Vermont
       mountain country, she recounts the saga of installing a new
       bathroom, coping with local workmen's customs; her neigh-
       bors provide care and support during her husband's illness;
       she tells of a painful attempt to run a Florida restaurant in
       the winter season; she describes the rise of her blueberry
       jam mail order business and her school board duties, as
       well as her guests and hired help; she closes with her ex-
       periences with breast cancer.

1401   MATHER, JULIETTE (1896-   )
       Taiwan As I Saw It.   Nashville: Broadman, 1965.   128pp.

       After thirty-five years of missionary work in the Far
       East, she tells in a largely impersonal account of the land-
       scape, government, and customs of the Chinese people in
       Taiwan; although she shares their anti-communist views,
       she contrasts their religious beliefs with her own Christian-
       ity.

1402   MATHER, MELISSA
       Rough Road Home.   Philadelphia: Lippincott, 1958.   256pp.

       The mother of four children including a developmentally
       disabled son finds herself suddenly widowed in 1950; preg-
       nant with her fifth child, she moves to an isolated Vermont
       farm, to immerse herself in renovation work and gardening
       and make the psychological transition to a simplified, self-
       sufficient country life; she later marries, finding pride and
       deep contentment in the establishment of a successful dairy
       farm and the legacy of a "true childhood" for her children.

1403   MATHEWSON, ALICE CLARKE
       Ali-Mat Takes Off.   Raleigh, N. C. :   Forest Hills Distri-
       butors, 1956.   152pp.

       An energetic woman travels extensively, sometimes with
       tour groups and sometimes alone, after her children are
       grown; she focuses on typical tourist attractions, visiting
       Europe, North Africa, Alaska, the Caribbean, and Mexico.

1404   Ali-Mat Takes Off Again.   Raleigh, N. C. :   Forest Hills
       Distributors, 1957.   47pp.

       She recounts her travels to Hawaii, Japan, and Hong
       Kong, and then returns to New York by way of Oregon,
       describing the sights in each location.

1405   MATHEWSON, DONNA
       Bananas Have No Bones.   New York: Comet Press Books,
       1960.   212pp.

       Obeying the "call of the open road," she travels with a
       friend in Mexico, for her a land of enchantment and ex-
       tremes; she describes explorations and adventures from the
       capital city to plantations to small villages, enjoying the
       landscape, sights, people, and customs of Mexico.

1406   Down Mexico Way.   New York: Comet Press Books, 1956.
        213pp.

        An enthusiastic tourist who travels in Mexico, she pro-
        vides lively descriptions of her friendly encounters with peo-
        ple and of her sightseeing in numerous cities and villages.

1407   MATTHEWS, RUTH LOIS
        Come Abroad with Me; On Vacation Tour Through Europe.
        New York: Exposition, 1955.   138pp.

        She fulfills a lifelong dream and travels through Europe
        alone in 1953; beginning with Queen Elizabeth's coronation,
        she continues to all of the usual places, offering her super-
        ficial "impressions and reactions."

1408   MAUS, CYNTHIA PEARL (1878-   )
        Time to Remember; The Memoirs of Cynthia Pearl Maus,
        Lit. D.   New York: Exposition, 1964.   278pp.

        The author of books on youth and religion and an opinion-
        ated, energetic writer provides "a joysome autobiography,"
        dividing the book into eight decades; her pioneer childhood
        is characterized by a Christian home life; influenced by a
        fine teacher, she herself becomes a teacher, pursues a
        doctorate, and is a reader and entertainer on the Chautauqua
        and Lyceum circuits; she undertakes national field work in
        religious education; retiring at fifty-three in economic inde-
        pendence, she continues to travel and write.

1409   MAXWELL, ELSA (1883-1963)
        The Celebrity Circus.   New York: Appleton-Century, 1963.
        214pp.

        Acknowledging that she is plain and fat, she reveals her
        deliberate and highly successful campaign to become a dyna-
        mic, witty conversationalist and much sought-after hostess;
        she offers numerous anecdotes of her friends and acquaint-
        ances among the world's celebrities; she enjoys being fea-
        tured on television talk shows.

1410   R. S. V. P.:   Elsa Maxwell's Own Story.   Boston: Little,
        Brown, 1954.   326pp.

        The world famous hostess tells a little of her early life
        in which music serves as her "meal ticket and chief social
        grace"; her gay and energetic account is a steady stream of
        anecdotes illustrating her acquaintance with famous artists,
        celebrities, and politicians; with "contempt for snobs" and
        bores, she delights in capturing social lions.

1411   MAXWELL, NICOLE
       Witch Doctor's Apprentice.   Boston: Houghton Mifflin, 1961.
       353pp.

       A former medical student, she travels alone for ten
       months in 1958-1959 in the jungles of South America to col-
       lect medicinal herbs; courageous in the face of dangers, she
       contacts local Indians, gaining their confidence and learning
       their tribal customs, practicing medicine when she can help;
       each specimen she obtains represents new experience and
       friendship; she closes with her dramatic search for contra-
       ceptive plants.

1412   MAYNARD, JOYCE (1953-)
       Looking Back: A Chronicle of Growing Up Old in the Sixties.
       Garden City, N.Y.: Doubleday, 1973. 160pp.

       In a series of essays, she explores the "aged, weary
       quality" of her generation; she discusses her deadening ele-
       mentary school experiences, the uncomfortable dawning of
       sexuality, the tyranny of popularity and good looks, the
       "tranquilizing sameness" of television, fads and the "junk
       era," awkward parties, the abandonment of language, and
       the "hopelessness of the virgin's situation."

1413   MEAD, MARGARET (1901-1978)
       Blackberry Winter: My Earlier Years. New York: Mor-
       row, 1972. 305pp.

       A prominent anthropologist, she feels she is raised "two
       generations ahead of my time"; she closely analyzes her ties
       with her academic father, combining deep respect with shrewd
       criticism, but her grandmother emerges as the "most deci-
       sive influence" on her identity; the worlds of the intellect
       and books are central to her life, as is her intense commit-
       ment to anthropological fieldwork and writing, and her life
       and work are "closely interwoven"; her lifelong love of chil-
       dren is fulfilled when she has a daughter and embellished
       later by the perspectives gained by being a grandmother; her
       account is extremely articulate and perceptive.

1414   MECOM, JANE FRANKLIN (1712-1794)
       The Letters of Benjamin Franklin & Jane Mecom, ed. Carl
       van Doren. Princeton: Princeton University Press, 1950.
       380pp.

       The younger sister of Benjamin Franklin writes with high-
       ly idiosyncratic spelling primarily to her brother and his
       wife between 1751 and 1794; she notes how "unfourtunate a
       famely" is hers, for nearly all of her eleven children died

young, suffered poor health, or were unstable, yet she is optimistic and thankful for her "blessings"; "Politics & Riligous contryverces" form a background for what are primarily domestic communications; she is grateful for Franklin's continuing financial support and expresses her touching hope that they can achieve a greater closeness in their old age; at Franklin's death in 1790, she notes her great pride and pleasure in his prominence and accomplishments.

1415   MEGQUIER, MARY JANE COLE
        Apron Full of Gold; The Letters of Mary Jane Megquier
        from San Francisco, 1849-1856, ed. Robert Glass Cleland.
        San Marino, Cal. : Huntington Library, 1949.   99pp.

        She writes of three visits to San Francisco, during which she runs a boarding house, seeking financial stability for herself and her children; at first she finds "not one redeeming trait" of California life, sharply criticizing the uncouth hordes and the difficulties leading an ordinary life under extraordinary conditions; however, her desire for independence leads to a final permanent settlement there.

1416   MEHDEVI, ANNE SINCLAIR
        From Pillar to Post.   New York: Knopf, 1956.   273pp.

        Married to a Persian businessman in 1945, she establishes nineteen different homes and learns six languages in the next eleven years; her first son is born in Mexico and she is caught between her maid's superstitions and child-rearing advice from a government pamphlet; when she first introduces her two sons to their Kansas grandparents, she must interpret cultural differences; she presents a touching portrait of her husband's old Persian uncle in Vienna; she keeps house in Majorca, concerned over her children's fragmentary formal education; she finally settles in Persia.

1417   Persia Revisited.   New York: Knopf, 1964.   271pp.

        The wife of an Iranian diplomat, she writes of their return, hoping for reconciliation, to the extended household of her father-in-law; she offers a remarkable portrait of the domineering, regal patriarch as well as sharply perceptive portraits of other colorful family members; drawn into a vastly different family life, characterized by "the ubiquitous influence of women," she notes that her family embodies in miniature the traits and trends in modern Iran; the death of her father-in-law marks the end of an era.

1418   Persian Adventure.   New York: Knopf, 1953.   272pp.

A Kansas newspaperwoman marries an Iranian diplomat,
and after living in slightly exotic poverty in New York and
entertaining her "highly colored fancies of Iran, " she visits
Iran with her husband and three children; she feels a "polite
confinement" and some loneliness and alienation in her Iranian family dominated by her tyrannical father-in-law; she
notes contradictions in Persian life and customs and discusses her ambivalence toward Iranian culture.

1419   MELIN, MARGARET
       Modern Pioneering in Alaska.   New York: Pageant, 1954.
       78pp.

With her husband and two children, an Illinois housewife
travels ten thousand miles north to the end of the Alcan
highway in Alaska in 1952; the family station wagon is rigged
for camping; she recounts their adventures on the road.

1420   MERAS, PHYLLIS
       First Spring: A Martha's Vineyard Journal.   Riverside,
       Conn. :   Chatham Press, 1972.   143pp.

A journalist, she writes about "the order of the seasons
and of conversations and notable events" in order to portray
an endangered way of life; she renews her senses and absorbs nature lore on long exploratory walks, noting contrasts
with her previous urban life; she interviews local natives as
well as some prominent residents; parts of her account first
appeared in the Vineyard Gazette.

1421   MERIWETHER, ELIZABETH AVERY (1824-   )
       Recollections of 92 Years, 1824-1916.   Nashville, Tenn. :
       Tennessee Historical Commission, 1958.   249pp.

Her account is written to allay the loneliness of old age;
she is "one of the first women in the South publicly to advo-
cate Woman suffrage"; she votes illegally in 1876; she describes ante-bellum days in Tennessee; married at twenty-
five, she frees the family slaves, is a refugee during the
Civil War, sells a story to avoid starvation, describes the
horrors of reconstruction, and recounts her husband's activities in the Ku Klux Klan; she writes for a newspaper in
1872, works for woman suffrage and temperance, speaks in
New England for suffrage, writes a novel; the bulk of the
account is vivid Civil War memories.

1422   MERMAN, ETHEL
        Who Could Ask for Anything More, as told to Pete Martin.
        Garden City, N.Y.: Doubleday, 1955.   252pp.

        The popular singer describes her early ambitions to go
        on the stage and to use the gift of her voice; she begins as
        a nightclub entertainer, becomes a celebrity, and performs
        in a series of hit Broadway shows; outspoken, assertive,
        and thoroughly professional, she describes various roles
        and colleagues in this anecdotal account.

1423   MERRILL, MARGARET BECKER
        Bears in My Kitchen.   New York: McGraw-Hill, 1956.
        249pp.

        Married in 1930 to a U.S. Forest Ranger, she is trans-
        formed from a city girl into a ranger's wife; during her
        first winter, she faces danger when she must evacuate her
        injured husband in a mountain blizzard; over the years she
        learns much about nature and wildlife, offering anecdotes
        about amusing and unexpected incidents at their posts in
        several parks, about threats posed by bears and snow and
        forest fires, and about her appreciation of nature's beauty.

1424   MESTA, PERLE SKIRVIN (1889-1975)   NAWM
        Perle; My Story, with Robert Cahn.   New York: McGraw-
        Hill, 1960.   251pp.

        A famous Washington, D.C. hostess and Ambassador to
        Luxembourg, she describes her youth as the daughter of an
        Oklahoma oil and hotel magnate; marrying a wealthy busi-
        nessman at seventeen, she channels her energy into work-
        ers' welfare at her husband's plant and into Washington so-
        cial life; as a widow she is active in Republican Party poli-
        tics and works with the National Woman's Party beginning
        in 1938; she does canteen work during World War II and
        later organizes Truman's inaugural ball; in 1949 she is ap-
        pointed Ambassador and is serious and dedicated to the task;
        later she continues to travel, entertain, and work for wom-
        en's rights and passage of the ERA.

1425   MEYER, AGNES ELIZABETH ERNST (1887-1970)   NAWM
        Out of These Roots: The Autobiography of an American
        Woman.   Boston: Little, Brown, 1953.   385pp.

        A writer and translator tells of her "delightfully demo-
        cratic" childhood in a rural community; she struggles through
        a painful, rebellious youth; she finds the adjustment to the
        responsibilities of marriage and motherhood difficult, yet at
        the same time she begins her long career of public service
        in Washington, D.C., engaging in Republican political activ-

ities, promoting recreation and the arts, reporting on the
British war effort during World War II, campaigning after
the war for health care and education and community involvement, always dedicated to social justice.

1426   MEYER: ANNIE NATHAN (1867-1951)   NAWM
       It's Been Fun: An Autobiography. New York: Henry Schu-
       man, 1951. 302pp.

       A novelist, playwright, reviewer, author of a book on
women's work, and founder of Barnard College, she tells
of her "tempestuous" childhood and unstable family life; she
is a sister of Maud Nathan (see companion volume); she
marries a doctor who supports her ambitions as a writer
and as a leader in women's education, and her account includes fine portraits of her husband and of her daughter;
she notes that she has "never been a specialist."

1427   MEYER, EDITH PATTERSON
       For Goodness' Sake! Growing Up in a New England Par-
       sonage. Nashville: Abingdon, 1973. 176pp.

       A librarian and writer, she tells of her childhood as the
youngest of five lively children, trained in thrift, discipline,
and love; she describes the family Sabbath routine, her passion for reading, vacations on Martha's Vineyard, attending
camp meetings, and a social life centered around the
church; she feels her family life has provided her with a
"liberal education."

1428   MICHAL, MIRA (1914-   )
       Nobody Told Me How; A Diplomatic Entertainment.   Phila-
       delphia: Lippincott, 1962. 184pp.

       A journalist, she opens with her London marriage in 1946
to the Polish ambassador to the Court of St. James and of
the subsequent social obligations of a diplomat's wife; raising
two sons with the aid of a British nanny, she recounts wry
tales of seven years in London, followed by three years in
Poland where she continues writing humorous feature columns; settling in New York in 1956 while her husband is
with the U.N., she casts a sardonic but affectionate eye on
American customs and international "New Experiences."

1429   MICHEL, TRUDI (1921-   )
       Inside Tin Pan Alley. New York: Frederick Fell, 1948.
       172pp.

       A young woman with an off-beat sense of humor, she
finds marriage and motherhood near Central Park West un-

fulfilling; she writes a song, describing its creation and
existence in terms of "pregnancy," "infancy," "growing
pains," and "the ingrate child"; the daughter and niece of
show people, she knows how to publicize it and herself ag-
gressively but finally decides it is not worth the struggle
to break into the recording business.

1430   MICKELSEN, MARY BIKKIE
        The Northern Light; An American Looks at Finland and
        Scandinavia.   New York: Exposition, 1955.   537pp.

        Traveling with her minister husband, she attends Luth-
        eran Church conventions and is able to meet people and
        make intimate contacts due to her religious affiliation; she
        tells of her experiences and impressions in great detail in
        an observant, straightforward narrative.

1431   MILETO, CECILE (1940?-1980)
        Louie's Widow: One Woman's Vengeance Against the Under-
        world, with Dave Fisher.   Chicago: Playboy Press, 1975.
        309pp.

        In a particularly sordid account, she tells of her disas-
        trous marriage at fifteen, bearing five children in quick
        succession; she seeks escape in drugs and boyfriends, and
        when she is dazzled by Mileto, a thief and con artist and
        the ruling passion of her life, she joins him in a life of
        "fun and love," luxury and travel; she becomes his partner
        in crime, transporting drugs for him; his invincibility fails
        and he is imprisoned; unhinged, she turns to drugs in des-
        pair; she is jailed time and again, alienated from her chil-
        dren and horrified when they all turn to drugs; reconcilia-
        tions with her husband fail as he rejects her for her addic-
        tion; when he is brutally murdered, she testifies against
        those responsible, her "vengeance," but the government's
        protective custody is not enough to establish a new life, free
        of fear.

1432   MILLAY, EDNA ST. VINCENT (1892-1950)   NAW
        Letters of Edna St. Vincent Millay, ed. Allan Ross Mac-
        dougall.   New York: Harper, 1952.   384pp.

        A distinguished poet, her letters cover the period from
        1900 to 1950; her early correspondence is with publishers
        and fellow poets, witty, vivacious, and full of charming
        candor in her comments on poems by herself and others;
        she notes her studies and writing at Vassar, then several
        "small" nervous breakdowns after her return home; she
        writes many long, affectionate letters to her family, and
        love letters to a fellow poet; letters after her marriage in

1923 describe lecture tours, travels, and life in their country home.

1433   MILLBERG, KAREN SCHWENCKE
        Flight Against the Wind.   New York: Odyssey Press, 1947.
        182pp.

        She emigrates from Denmark in the 1920's to make a new
        life for herself and her teen-aged son; she first works as a
        seamstress, then with an interior decorating firm; optimistic
        and determined in spite of the depression, she builds a
        prosperous business through integrity and hard work; she
        takes great pride in buying a farm, her "place of peace,"
        rejecting the opportunity to become involved in a large and
        impersonal business.

1434   MILLER, ANN (1923-)
        Miller's High Life, with Norma Lee Browning.   Garden
        City, N.Y.: Doubleday, 1972.   283pp.

        A Hollywood movie star and dancer "born to dance," she
        vows at 11 to support her mother; attending to her "school-
        work by day ... glamour world at night," she enjoys "too
        much and too soon," acting in her first Broadway show at
        fifteen and then in a series of "B" films; in her chatty
        style, she notes various psychic experiences, and she tells
        of the men in her life, including three brief marriages to
        millionaires; she returns to her career, concentrating on
        theatre and television.

1435   MILLER, MADELAINE HEMINGWAY (1904-)
        Ernie: Hemingway's Sister "Sunny" Remembers.   New York:
        Crown, 1975.   149pp.

        The younger sister of the famous writer recalls their
        close, spirited family life in Oak Park, Illinois and open-air
        summers spent in northern Michigan; a "tomboy," she bears
        an intense affection for her brother, later typing a manu-
        script for him, traveling to Europe where he solicitously
        shows her around, and still later naming her son after him;
        she maintains close ties with him through letters and is
        deeply shaken by his death in 1961; she writes partly to
        correct some popular misinformation about her family.

1436   MILLER, MARION FREED (1920-)
        I Was a Spy.   Indianapolis: Bobbs-Merrill, 1960.   224pp.

        Strongly patriotic, she joins the Communist Party in 1950
        as an undercover agent for the F.B.I.; for five years

"workaday espionage" gives meaning to her life, in spite of her social isolation, the deterioration of her health, the negative repercussions for her children; anecdotes of various communist characters strengthen her beliefs in the dangers of communism; her testimony in 1955 results in vituperation from her friends and an end to her spying.

1437 MILLER, MARTHA GRAY KING
      Land of My Ancestors. New York: Vantage, 1959. 117pp.

      She travels in Scotland and England with her mother, husband, and daughter in the 1920's, recounting her impressions in a series of letters to friends; she visits not only tourist attractions but also close relatives, and the countryside comes alive with her memories of family history and her mother's literary anecdotes; she gains a deeper understanding and love for her ancestral land.

1438 MILLER, MARY BRITTON (1883-1975)
      Under Gemini; a Memoir, by Isabel Bolton. New York:
      Harcourt, Brace & World, 1966. 128pp.

      A writer, she provides a sensitive evocation of her New England childhood with a twin sister, "my other self"; orphaned, she and her siblings are first reared by a grandmother, then by an eccentric guardian; an illness constitutes a unique experience not shared by her twin, with whom she is ordinarily "one and indivisible," exploiting twinhood; at fourteen, boarding school and a break with her guardian mark the end of childhood.

1439 MILLER, MAXINE ADAMS
      Bright Blue Beads; An American Family in Persia. Caldwell, Id. : Caxton, 1961. 329pp.

      She recounts her stay in Iran from 1957 to 1959 with her professor husband and two teen-aged children; she makes a good-humored adjustment to local customs and describes in entertaining detail her housekeeping, holidays and ceremonial occasions, travels, friendships, attendance at a Moslem wedding, and observations of women's roles.

1440 MILLETT, KATE (1934-)
      Flying. New York: Knopf, 1974. 546pp.

      In a highly detailed, documentary style, she covers events in the year after Sexual Politics was published; she recounts tensions generated by her fame within the women's movement, and her struggles to produce a film; the intimate joys and

frustrations in her sexual relations with her husband and
with several women are explored; the account is singularly
intense and exhaustive.

1441   MILLS, NETTIE ELIZABETH WEST (1880-   )
       The Lady Driller; The Autobiography of N. Elizabeth Mills.
       New York: Exposition, 1955. 176pp.

       Having boarded other students to pay her way through
       secretarial school, run a hotel, and operated a restaurant,
       she invests in oil and natural gas businesses in the 1930's,
       becoming the only woman drilling contractor and operator
       in the U. S., a fact which leads to some publicity; a shrewd
       businesswoman, her account is nevertheless pedestrian.

1442   MITCHELL, ELEANOR SWANN
       Postscript to Seven Homes.   Francestown, N. H. :   Marshall
       Jones, 1960. 217pp.

       An imaginative tomboy as a child and later the wife of an
       American diplomat, she provides anecdotal diary entries
       from 1957, "one year of my life" as a "Southerner in New
       England"; she is a Sunday school teacher, a sponsor for a
       Hungarian refugee family, a lecturer; she notes national and
       international events, reflects on her children and grandchil-
       dren, and comments on her reading, visiting museums, and
       attending others' lectures.

1443   Seven Homes Had I; Experiences of a Foreign Service Wife.
       New York: Exposition, 1955. 172pp.

       Born in the 1890's and reared in Virginia, she grows up
       in a large family, full of admiration for the "shining exam-
       ple" of her mother; married to a Foreign Service officer,
       she finds each assignment stimulating and rewarding, as she
       establishes homes and raises her three children on posts in
       Mexico, Canada, Belgium, and Spain, before her husband's
       retirement to Massachusetts.

1444   MITCHELL, LUCY SPRAGUE (1878-1967)   NAWM
       Two Lives: The Story of Wesley Clair Mitchell and Myself.
       New York: Simon and Schuster, 1953. 575pp.

       She presents a sensitive narrative of forty-eight years as
       an educator and writer; her Chicago childhood is darkened
       by family tragedy and breakup, and she grows up a shy
       child who reads much and writes in secret; at Radcliffe, she
       enters a "new world" of freedom and independence; she
       serves as professor and dean of women at Berkeley from

1906 to 1912, then marries and begins her work with the
New York Bank Street College of Education and research on
children's language; the mother of four, she sees her marriage as a symbol of new human relationships, integrating
professional and personal commitments.

1445   MITCHELL, MARGARET (1900-1949)
Margaret Mitchell's Gone with the Wind Letters, 1936-1949,
ed. Richard Harwell. New York: Macmillan, 1976. 441pp.

In long, articulate, vibrant letters, she reveals her "passionate desire for personal privacy"; she thanks numerous
critics for their favorable reviews but bitterly resents the
unpleasant shock of fame and the public's "siege"; noting
that "life has been awful since I sold the movie rights," she
describes the continuing furor as the film proceeds and the
"final tidal wave" of the film's première; she is troubled
by fights over plagiarism and international copyrights;
throughout her struggles, she maintains a "very proud and
very humble" attitude, and modestly delights in praise.

1446   MITCHELL, SUZANNE (pseud.)
My Own Woman: The Diary of an Analysis. New York:
Horizon Press, 1973. 269pp.

Married and the mother of two grown children, she
struggles "to establish my own identity"; her diary entries
begin in 1964 and reveal marital troubles, worries over a
delinquent daughter's loneliness; she works through a romantic attachment to her first analyst and the pain of a long
separation and divorce; after making major adjustments,
she enters a career in social work and finds "the freedom
to grow."

1447   MOATS, ALICE-LEONE
A Violent Innocence. New York: Duell, Sloan and Pearce,
1951. 312pp.

A skilled storyteller, she is raised in Mexico with much
freedom and independence by her American parents and given
an unorthodox education by tutors; she lives daily with the
tragic and comic sides of the Mexican revolution as it swirls
about her; in 1914 she returns from a visit to the U.S. into
the midst of the U.S. occupation of Veracruz, then is a
refugee in New Orleans, then returns to the chaos of Mexico; in 1918 she is sent to an American boarding school for
a traditional education to be followed by a tour of Europe in
1921, marking the formal end of her childhood.

1448   MOCK, JERRIE (1926?-)
        Three-Eight Charlie.   Philadelphia: Lippincott, 1970.
        288pp.

        Feeling like "an explorer" and buoyed by the support of
        her husband and three children, in 1964 she becomes the
        first woman to complete a solo flight around the world; her
        initial tension and sense of unreality fade as she handles
        the dangers of bad weather and mechanical malfunctions,
        holds press conferences at each stop, writes daily press
        dispatches, copes with red tape and restrictions; she re-
        ceives a tumultuous welcome on her return and receives
        from President Johnson the highest civil aviation award.

1449   MOELLER, ELSIE S.
        Pack a Bag; A Merry-Go-Round of Places, Transportation
        and Clothes.   New York: Exposition, 1955.   284pp.

        A master of adjustment with good humor, she provides
        a spirited travel account full of lively anecdotes; she tells
        of a Key West speakeasy, a happy cruise along the Maine
        coast, summers on Martha's Vineyard, train trips in New
        York and Texas, living in Latin American army posts with
        her officer husband, and work in San Francisco and Provi-
        dence shipyards during World War II.

1450   MOELLER, HELEN
        Tornado; My Experience with Mental Illness.   Westwood,
        N.J.:   Revell, 1967.   109pp.

        An Iowa farm wife describes her illness as "one of the
        most rewarding experiences of my life," for it brings her
        to a deeper recognition of her religious faith; after twenty
        years of marriage and the rearing of six children, she is
        suddenly stricken and hospitalized in 1963 and struggles
        through two years of depression; a job and the love of her
        family aid her recovery.

1451   MOENNICH, MARTHA L.
        Europe Behind the Iron Curtain.   Grand Rapids, Mich.:
        Zondervan, 1948.   153pp.

        She writes her impressions after nearly five months of
        travel in fifteen countries shortly after World War II; she
        visits concentration camps and displaced persons camps,
        and she participates in revival meetings; she sees commun-
        ism and atheism as twin threats and calls for a widespread
        religious revival in Europe.

1452   From Nation to Nation.   Grand Rapids, Mich.: Zondervan,
        1954.   153pp.

        On this her eighth missionary journey, she visits mission
        stations in Europe, Africa, the Middle East, India, and
        Hawaii; she notes the difficulties and satisfactions of the
        missionary effort.

1953   On the China Road.   Grand Rapids, Mich.: Zondervan,
        1947.   150pp.

        A missionary in China for ten years, she tells of con-
        verts to Christianity, her attempts to halt the "trafficking
        in human lives" in Shanghai, her visits to a Korean mis-
        sion for lepers, her acquaintance with cases of deliverance
        from "demon-possession."

1454   MOLLENKOTT, VIRGINIA RAMEY (1932-   )
        In Search of Balance.   Waco, Tex.: Word Books, 1969.
        151pp.

        An English professor with a background in evangelical
        Christianity, she shares her "continuing stages of self-
        examination," exploring the nature of choice, moral action,
        and human responsibility; searching for truth among para-
        doxes, she quotes extensively from literature and the Bible.

1455   MONROE, MARILYN (1926-1962)   NAWM
        My Story.   New York: Stein and Day, 1974.   143pp.

        The movie star tells of her insecure childhood marked by
        her mother's breakdown and a succession of foster homes,
        loneliness, and daydreams; a passionless siren at thirteen,
        she marries at sixteen but soon divorces; she describes her
        loneliness among the "phonies and failures" of Hollywood,
        bit parts, and parties; after an intense and brief love, her
        movie career brings her fame and riches, but she grows
        "depressed and finally desperate," desiring to become an
        accomplished actress and not simply a sex symbol; the un-
        polished account ends abruptly soon after her marriage to
        Joe DiMaggio.

1456   MONTGOMERY, RUTH SHICK (1912-   )
        Hail to the Chiefs; My Life and Times with Six Presidents.
        New York: Coward-McCann, 1970.   320pp.

        A newspaper reporter and shrewd political reporter whose
        career begins in the "wartime Washington" of 1944 describes
        her travels with various Presidential campaigns, travels

around the world, and interviews with heads of state; she is the recipient of honorary degrees and several journalism awards and serves as the president of the Women's National Press Club in 1950; herself a Republican, she states, "I have loved life."

1457   A Search for the Truth. New York: Morrow, 1967. 284pp.

A political columnist, she maintains a vigorous career while carrying on her spiritual quest, a "search for the deeper meaning of life"; her experiences with mediums begin in 1956 and her training as a reporter causes initial skepticism, but as she collects what she considers irrefutable evidence, her own psychic powers increase; spirit "guides" communicate "lessons" through automatic writing and lead to her religious reawakening; she includes numerous anecdotes of friends who experience psychic events.

1458   MONTI, CARLOTTA
        W. C. Fields & Me, with Cy Rice. Englewood Cliffs, N. J.: Prentice-Hall, 1971. 227pp.

The mistress of W. C. Fields for fourteen years, she tells of her first meeting with him in 1932; she recounts numerous anecdotes, with quotations from Fields' humor; her love and tolerance survive his perversity and jealousy and alcoholism; she describes his final days.

1459   MONYPENY, AGNES MABEL
        Bibbie, the Sunflower from Plymouth; Education in Nebraska and Kansas, 1889-1961. New York: Exposition, 1963. 116pp.

Writing of herself as "Bibbie" in the third person, she describes her dedication as a teacher to education, good citizenship, and "moral soundness"; she discusses the changes in educational emphasis through the five decades of her career, pointing out interactions of home, school, and society, and noting her work with troubled students.

1460   MOODY, ANN (1940-   )
        Coming of Age in Mississippi. New York: Dial, 1968. 348pp.

Her perceptive narrative is divided into sections on childhood, high school, college, and the civil rights movement; raised in poverty, she gets an early taste of agricultural and domestic work and experiences her first clear realization of racism at seven; a bright student but a loner, she is anxious and tense in her knowledge of racial incidents which include beatings and murders; in college she joins the NAACP and then works for SNCC and CORE, civil rights activities that give meaning to her life in spite of constant threats and fear.

1461   MOON, CHRISTINE COOPER (1902-   )
Dear Christy....   New York: Exposition, 1955.   127pp.

She writes of her childhood in the early 1900's in the form of letters to a granddaughter; in random recollections she tells of her grandparents, domestic activities on the family farm, a one-room school, the first family car; she stresses the differences between her own childhood and that of her granddaughter.

1462   MOORE, COLLEEN (1902-   )
Silent Star.   Garden City, N.Y.:   Doubleday, 1968.   262pp.

Growing up in a happy, loving, and secure atmosphere, she fulfills her childhood dream of becoming an actress; an uncle pulls strings and at fifteen she enters the "fairytale world" of Hollywood; she learns much from silent films with D. W. Griffith and westerns with Tom Mix and tells numerous stories of films and colleagues; married in 1921, she is disillusioned being the dependent "child wife" and divorces in 1929; after sixty films, both silent and sound, she becomes a "private" person, devoting much time to her elaborate and famous doll house and to a happy marriage.

1463   MOORE, JENNY (1923-   )
The People on Second Street.   New York: Morrow, 1968.
218pp.

This minister's wife and mother of nine describes their eight years in an urban Episcopal rectory; her naïve enthusiasm for change confronts a "dying church," their "first experience of race," a "very fragile community," and many disappointments with "the snail's pace of reform"; destitution becomes familiar as she describes the people with whom they live and work in a vivid, touching, and unsentimental account.

1464   MOORE, KATE A. (-1914)
Europe: '86--'14--'52.   New York: Pageant, 1958.   97pp.

In an account subtitled "Trials and Triumphs of a Summer Vacation," she writes of a fulfillment of a childhood dream; enjoying a "gradual widening of my mind," she recounts her

personal impressions of the prominent sights in London,
Paris, Ireland, and Scotland; her portion of the book covers
pages 11 to 58 and her daughter's portion follows (see Connolly, Marie Moore).

1465   MOORE, MARTHA EDITH BANNISTER (1910-   )
        Unmasked; The Story of My Life on Both Sides of the Race
        Barrier. New York: Exposition, 1964. 106pp.

        In a rambling account, a black woman who sometimes
        passes for white describes her experiences with discrimina-
        tion due to sex, race, and political affiliation; after a com-
        fortable childhood, she is married at seventeen but soon
        divorced; she holds a succession of jobs and does U. S. O.
        work during World War II, engaging in Republican Party
        politics and running for elective office in Pittsburgh.

1466   MOORE, NANCY (1807-1889)
        The Journal of Eldress Nancy, Kept at the South Union,
        Kentucky, Shaker Colony, August 15, 1861-September 4,
        1864, ed. Mary Julia Neal. Nashville: Parthenon Press,
        1963. 256pp.

        A Shaker pacifist keeps a diary to chronicle "this unna-
        tural war" when the community is overrun by the military
        forces of both sides; with disarming hospitality, she offers
        food and lodging to soldiers but expresses her views which
        include sympathy for the union and the oddly inconsistent
        approval of violence done to "rebels"; throughout she notes
        rumors and direct and indirect reports of the war's prog-
        ress.

1467   MOORE, OLGA
        I'll Meet You in the Lobby. Philadelphia: Lippincott, 1949.
        250pp.

        A Washington, D. C. lobbyist describes her background as
        a secretary, reporter, and student lobbyist in the Wyoming
        state legislature; after her marriage to a professor, she
        lobbies for a law school; in 1941 the sudden deaths of her
        mother, father, and husband lead to a more professional ca-
        reer in lobbying, with an interim spent as a reporter for the
        government in the O. W. I.

1468   MOORE, VIRGINIA (1903-   )
        The Whole World, Stranger. New York: Macmillan, 1957.
        352pp.

        She travels around the world to Japan, Southeast Asia,
        India, Pakistan, the Middle East, and Greece with her sis-

ter; seeking "new experiences ... a larger life" and a feel
for other people, she describes in vivid detail sights that
"interpret a people," from breathtaking beauty to horrifying
degradation; her vignettes, sometimes moving, reveal subtle
changes in herself wrought by her desire to touch the heart
of a country.

1469   MOORE, VIRGINIA BLANCK
        Seeing Eye Wife. Philadelphia: Chilton, 1960. 177pp.

        A sighted woman tells of fifteen years as the wife of a
blind man; she is badly scarred by burns as a child and
grows up hating to be labeled "handicapped"; after excelling
in college, she works for a state commission for the blind
and meets her future husband; with common sense and good
humor, she describes her adjustments to marriage and
parenthood, establishing a closely knit family; she is proud
to keep house, confident in her husband's capabilities as a
breadwinner.

1470   MOORMAN, FAY (1887-)
        My Heart Turns Back: Childhood Memories of Rural Vir-
        ginia in the Nineties. New York: Exposition, 1964. 124pp.

        In a series of anecdotes told with rich detail and fond
nostalgia, she evokes a picture of her close family life
marked by tolerance, companionship, and intimacy with nature; she notes the intertwined history of black and white
people in the neighborhood; her mother's strong religious
faith constitutes the family foundation and she offers a fine
portrait of her mother.

1471   MORAGNE, MARY ELIZABETH (1815-1903)
        The Neglected Thread; A Journal from the Calhoun Communi-
        ty, 1836-1842, ed. Delle Mullen Craven. Columbia, S. C.:
        University of South Carolina Press, 1951. 256pp.

        In an account liberally sprinkled with literary quotations,
she writes of "this easy and matter of fact age," of almost
non-stop visiting, parties, lectures, plays, and concerts;
her lively, detailed descriptions of people and places are
colored by a sensitive romanticism as well as a sense of
humor; in 1838 she becomes "an authoress," but later under
the influence of religion and her growing affection for a minister, she resolves to stop writing; the manuscript ends
abruptly.

1472   MORGAN, GERALDINE (1927-)
        Shadows in the Sunshine. Philadelphia: Dorrance, 1973.
        92pp.

She opens with her marriage in 1943; her religious conversion follows a serious illness, and she is baptized in
1951; through years of hardship and further family illness,
she and her husband evangelize, "a great responsibility,"
serving churches in Oregon and in Hawaii; her account is
drawn from a diary and is followed by some of her husband's sermons.

1473   MORGAN, KAY SUMMERSBY (1909?-1975)
       Past Forgetting; My Love Affair with Dwight D. Eisenhower.
       New York: Simon and Schuster, 1976. 251pp.

       A British subject and former model, she volunteers as a
       driver in London during World War II and is assigned to
       General Eisenhower in 1942; she becomes completely ab-
       sorbed in her work as driver, staff aide, and confidante,
       and in the closed world of war, with her attention and emo-
       tion closely focused, she comes to love Eisenhower; when
       he must break off the relationship at war's end, she has no
       regrets, understanding the prior and greater claims on the
       General by his country; profoundly discreet, she does not
       write about it until he is dead and she is dying.

1474   MORGAN, LUCY (1889-   )
       Gift from the Hills; Miss Lucy Morgan's Story of Her Unique
       Penland School, with LeGette Blythe. Indianapolis: Bobbs-
       Merrill, 1958. 314pp.

       Determined to preserve the handicraft skills, particularly
       weaving, of the mountain people of North Carolina, she and
       her brother establish a school and settle there permanently;
       she treasures her friendships while learning much about
       marketing and financing; she stresses the school's importance
       to the financial affairs of the local women and its overall
       social and artistic value, noting that "its growth has been
       my growth, its people my people."

1475   MORGAN, MANIE KENDLEY (1848-1938)
       The New Stars; Life and Labor in Old Missouri, arr. by
       Jennie A. Morgan, ed. Louis Filler. N. p. : Antioch Press,
       1949. 301pp.

       In an oral account produced when she was eighty-eight
       and transcribed by her daughter, she recalls memories of
       her family life, rich in detail and strong in the evocation of
       family values; she tells of her father's death and her moth-
       er's coping with financial strain; she describes the impact
       of the Civil War in terms of domestic adjustments and fam-
       ily fears for safety and economic well-being; she notes her
       mother's concern for education, yet she avoids an arranged

marriage by secretly wedding another man; the period covered is from her childhood through the end of the Civil War.

1476   MORSE, THERESA A.
       Future à la Carte. New York: McKay, 1955. 167pp.

       After twenty-nine prosperous years, she and her husband
       abandon the pressures of New York City life and move to
       Martha's Vineyard where they convert a house into guest
       rooms; working in joyous partnership, they find excitement
       and "deep contentment" during their first season.

1477   MORTON, LENA BEATRICE (1902-   )
       My First Sixty Years; Passion for Wisdom. New York:
       Philosophical Library, 1965. 175pp.

       A black English professor and a "lover of mankind" de-
       scribes her protected childhood in rural Kentucky, influenced
       by her mother and grandparents and by a "thirst for knowl-
       edge"; she attains her Ph. D. in 1947 and later studies at
       Oxford and Harvard; she reflects on her experiences with
       racial prejudice and on her forty years of pedagogy; her
       book includes some poems and the texts of speeches.

1478   MOSBY, ALINE
       The View from No. 13 People's Street. New York: Random
       House, 1962. 308pp.

       She describes her "experiences as a woman reporter in
       Moscow" for the UPI from 1959 to 1962; her "fresh discov-
       eries" of the first six months include descriptions of her
       surroundings, of housekeeping "adventures," of the Soviet
       people, of fellow foreign correspondents, of working under
       censorship; she notes the impact of more open relations
       with the U. S. in 1959; she finds Russia "intriguing, com-
       plex, and confusing."

1479   MOSES, ANNA MARY ROBERTSON (1860-1961)   NAWM
       Grandma Moses: My Life's History, ed. Otto Kallir. New
       York: Harper, 1952. 140pp.

       The famous painter provides simple, random recollections
       of her childhood in rural New York; after her marriage in
       1887, she bears ten children, five of whom survive; her
       domestic routine changes after her children are grown and
       she is widowed in 1927; her painting, a "very pleasant hob-
       by," is encouraged by a New York art collector, and even
       after she is honored by President Truman in 1949, she takes
       celebrity in stride.

1480   MOSLEY, JEAN BELL (1913-   )
       The Mockingbird Piano.   Philadelphia: Westminster Press,
       1953.   192pp.

       Her charming vignettes of family activities "in the Val-
       ley" in rural Missouri celebrate the simple life; each chap-
       ter illustrates a lesson and her insights into the together-
       ness of maple syrup season, the extended family's colorful
       relatives, nature's annual spring renewal, the gift of music
       in an old piano.

1481   Wide Meadows.   Caldwell, Id. :   Caxton, 1960.   236pp.

       She recounts her childhood in an extended family and de-
       scribes outdoor activities on the family farm as well as
       domestic impressions; noting that "the kitchen was the hub
       of our lives," she writes much about family personalities
       and relationships; each chapter is a self-contained vignette
       and much of her narrative is taken from previously published
       magazine articles.

1482   MOUNTAIN WOLF WOMAN (1884-1960)
       Mountain Wolf Woman; Sister of Crashing Thunder; The Auto-
       biography of a Winnebago Indian, ed. Nancie Oestreich Lurie.
       Ann Arbor: University of Michigan Press, 1961.   142pp.

       She relates her story to an anthropologist who is a niece
       by adoption; she tells of her family's customs, seasonal
       activities, and migrations in Wisconsin; after a brief educa-
       tion she is forced into an arranged marriage; later initiated
       into a medicine lodge, she has a second marriage of her
       own choice, raises eight children and a grandchild; her con-
       version to a peyote cult is highly significant, yet she also
       becomes a Christian; she emerges as a strong-willed wom-
       an, saddened by many of the changes brought by time.

1483   MOURA, JONI AND JACKIE SUTHERLAND
       Tender Loving Care; The Uninhibited Memoirs of Two Air
       Force Nurses.   New York: Bartholomew House, 1969.
       374pp.

       Their lightweight account of "the male world of the mili-
       tary" includes titillating anecdotes of basic training in Texas,
       lecherous male officers and doctors, and a series of virtue's
       narrow escapes.

1484   MOXLEY, VERNA
       Wind 'Til Sundown.   Caldwell, Id. :   Caxton, 1954.   223pp.

She leaves Detroit with her husband and three children to
become a modern pioneer on a South Dakota ranch; the
promise of new beginnings is tempered by the hardships of
primitive conditions, isolation, illness, poverty, and bad
weather; determined to remain on the land, she looks to the
future.

1485   MUELLER, AMELIA
       There Have to Be Six; A True Story About Pioneering in the
       Midwest.   Scottdale, Pa.:   Herald Press, 1966.   255pp.

She writes "the story of a way of life that no longer ex-
ists," focusing on her childhood as the daughter of German
Mennonite immigrants who farm in Kansas and Texas; her
entire family endures years of struggle with the land, years
of poverty and hardship; she offers an abundance of domestic
detail; her education is cut short by the depression, when
she must teach school; she closes with the scattering of her
family members.

1486   MUIR, FLORABEL (1890?-1970)
       Headline Happy.   New York: Holt, 1950.   248pp.

An aggressive newspaper reporter organizes her slangy
account as a series of tales of scoops, big stories, trickery,
and luck.

1487   MUNDIS, HESTER
       No He's Not a Monkey, He's an Ape and He's My Son.   New
       York: Crown, 1976.   154pp.

In a humorous account of a cherished experience, she describes her wildly irrational decision to buy a baby chimpan-
zee and raise it with her husband and son in a Manhattan
apartment; with radical shifts in routine, she soon drops
her "romantic anthropomorphism" and copes maternally with
the reality of destruction and training; she reluctantly gives
the chimp up to a zoo when her pregnancy requires it.

1488   MURIE, MARGARET E. (1902?-)
       Two in the Far North.   New York: Knopf, 1962.   438pp.

A nature writer and the wife of a game biologist, she
tells in rich detail of her pampered childhood in Fairbanks,
protected from the isolation and wilderness by the social
bulwark created by the settlement women; after two years
at Reed College, she marries, becoming a "field assistant"
and relishing the unspoiled beauty of northern Alaska as they
travel, camp, and study wildlife under rugged conditions; in

1926 she travels with an infant son into the Arctic, enjoying challenge and adventure with her husband; they return to the North thirty years later to continue studies, still strong conservationists.

1489   Wapiti Wilderness, with Olaus Murie. New York: Knopf, 1966. 302pp.

In this celebration of the free, relaxed atmosphere of the wilderness, she and her husband each contribute chapters; married to an outdoorsman and naturalist with a staunch Norwegian mother, she settles in Wyoming in 1927 and describes childrearing in the wilderness and among wild creatures; in 1943 World War II breaks into their routine and she works as a housekeeper on a dude ranch; after some years of town life, she returns to her beloved wilderness ranch.

1490   MURPHY, GRACE EMLINE BARSTOW
        Your Deafness Is Not You; New Design for Deafness. New York: Harper, 1954. 238pp.

Open and willing to discuss the pain of her disability, a hearing loss that increases to total deafness by her adulthood, she describes her determination "to face life foursquare"; after a year-long tour of Europe and debut, she marries a naturalist and raises three children, sharing a "full and varied life" that includes public speaking, work in civic organizations, enjoyment of concerts and plays; always she strives to "minimize the isolation" that deafness can cause.

1491   MURPHY, PATRICIA (1911?-)
        Glow of Candlelight: The Story of Patricia Murphy. Englewood Cliffs, N.J.: Prentice-Hall, 1961. 260pp.

Bown in Newfoundland, she grows up in a fishing village; she moves to New York in 1929, and shifts from restaurant work to owning her own business; she expands from modest meals in Brooklyn to a fancy tea room in Manhattan; through instinct and hard work, she succeeds on a large scale and helps to support her family in Canada; her second husband becomes a business partner; they expand to single large restaurant-garden-gift shop complex; continued hard work helps her over grief after her husband's death; the autobiography is followed by sections on gardening and cooking.

1492   MURRAY, PAULI (1910-)
        Proud Shoes: The Story of an American Family. New York: Harper, 1956. 276pp.

Raised by her grandparents, she provides vibrant portraits of her deeply religious grandmother, who lives out the
tensions of her ambiguous position as the daughter of a slave
and a white aristocrat, and of her soldier grandfather, who
keeps alive his memories of the Civil War; illuminated by
an intense family pride, her account tells of her childhood
with a legacy of tenacity and independence in a world of
"unbelievable contradictions"; she closes with the death of
her grandfather in 1919.

1493   NADLER, SUSAN (1947-)
       The Butterfly Convention.   New York: Dial, 1976.   181pp.

      In a slangy, heavily ironic narrative of her "hideous
memories" of three months in a Mexican hospital detention
cell, she reveals her own deep moral confusion; arrested for
drug abuse, she slowly acknowledges a reality of uncertainty, ill health, and fear; having rebelled against her parents'
values, she is nevertheless touched by her father's support
and assistance gaining her release; after much self-deception
and degradation, she is forced to take responsibility for her
actions.

1494   NAPEAR, PEGGY
       Brain Child: A Mother's Diary.   New York: Harper &
Row, 1974.   503pp.

      A fascinating story of her stamina and total dedication is
contained in her detailed diary entries describing her brain-
injured daughter's training and education from 1964 to 1972;
she discusses the often disappointing contacts with doctors
and other professionals, her own self-education and intense
work with her daughter; she notes with joy the emergence
of her child's personality and identity.

1495   NATHAN, BEATRICE STEPHENS (1895?-)
       Tales of a Teacher.   Chicago: Regnery, 1956.   302pp.

      First certified in California in 1915, she begins her ca-
reer in a remote country school, describing it in lively detail; through her later varied experiences which continue after
her marriage, she evokes a bygone era in education; having
found great joy in her "calling," she is sad to record the
decline in a teacher's prestige and sense of accomplishment
and she closes with proposals for educational reform.

1496   NEAL, EMILY GARDINER
       A Reporter Finds God Through Spiritual Healing.   New York:
Morehouse-Gorham, 1956.   192pp.

      Initially skeptical of faith healing, she mounts a detailed

investigation in several churches; she comes to accept the
evidence but for a time remains emotionally unprepared to
believe religious explanations; ultimately she takes "an ag-
nostic's journey into faith. "

1497   NEEDHAM, JANE BOYLE
        Looking Up, as told to Rosemary Drachman Taylor.   New
        York: Putnam, 1959.   191pp.

        A polio patient for nine years and the mother of three,
        she recalls her shock and despair when she is first stricken
        with polio in 1949; confined to an iron lung, she describes
        her misery in a county custodial care hospital; she fights
        for permission to leave, and struggles for child custody
        when her husband divorces her; a Catholic, she experiences
        a religious revival and dedicates her efforts to helping oth-
        ers regain courage and cheer; aided by her parents and
        nurses, she copes with tight finances and difficulties with
        her children's adjustment, but she closes on a positive note,
        planning for the future.

1498   NEELY, ANN ELIZA McCURDY STERLING (1860-)
        Just Me; An Autobiography of Ann E. Sterling Neely.   Phila-
        delphia: Dorrance, 1949.   165pp.

        She presents random anecdotes about her extended family,
        friends, and neighbors in Philadelphia; married in 1882, she
        pursues an active social life that includes women's clubs and
        the D. A. R. ; for twenty-one years she invites numerous
        prominent guests to share her summers on a Colorado ranch;
        widowed in 1935, she remarries and is widowed again in
        1941.

1499   NEF, ELINOR CASTLE (1894?-1953)
        Letters & Notes, Volume I, ed. John U. Nef.   Los Angeles:
        Ward Ritchie Press, 1953.   499pp.

        She writes essays to record "some of my observations"
        on living, reading, conversing, cherishing friendships; her
        letters date from the late 1930's and include some describ-
        ing summers in France with her husband; she reflects on
        American culture, noting a lack of tradition, a hurried
        superficiality, the value of American literature as a basis
        for a shared intellectual tradition; she writes with affection
        and understanding of the French culture and character; a
        strong sense of her moral, intellectual, and cultural values
        emerges; portions of the book were prepared by 1940 but
        compiled by her husband after her death.

1500   NEGRI, POLA (1899-)
        Memoirs of a Star.   Garden City, N.Y.:   Doubleday, 1970.
        453pp.

           Born in Poland, she is raised in poverty until a wealthy
        patron befriends her and her mother, supporting her early
        dance studies; tuberculosis forestalls a dance career, so
        she turns to acting, through discipline and intuition achiev-
        ing success on the stage at fourteen and in films at seven-
        teen; in Hollywood she is an idol by 1922; rejoicing in hard
        work, nevertheless she feels tensions between her career
        and love, searching after an affair with Chaplin for an
        "overwhelming passion" which she finds with Valentino; after
        the 1929 crash, she works in sound films and vaudeville,
        makes movies in Germany prior to 1939, then settles per-
        manently in the U.S.

1501   NELSON, BETTINA
        Venture by Cargo; Around the World by Way of South Africa.
        New York: Exposition, 1953. 211pp.

           Traveling alone on "blind impulse," she makes many
        friends along the way; she describes sightseeing and tours
        of national parks, a gold mine, and a farm in South Africa,
        "a land of promise and achievement."

1502   NELSON, ELSIE REDMAN
        Islands in My Life. New York: Vantage, 1964. 79pp.

           A teacher recalls her experiences on islands beginning
        with her birthplace, Manhattan; her husband, an Episcopal
        minister, is assigned to parishes on several islands, and
        their vacation travels include the islands of Mont St. Michel,
        Capri, Ceylon, and Bermuda.

1503   More Islands; A Sequel to Islands in My Life.   New York:
        Carlton Press, 1967. 60pp.

           In a rather impersonal account, she describes various
        holiday trips in the 1960's to Australia, Tahiti, Moorea,
        Fiji, the Bahamas, the Azores, Hawaii, England, and Scot-
        land; her observations are straightforward.

1504   NELSON, TERESA LEOPANDO LUCERO (1917-)
        White Cap and Prayer. New York: Vantage, 1955. 226pp.

           Drawn to nursing by a spirit of service and sacrifice,
        this Filipino woman tells of her rigorous training and her
        work during the Japanese occupation in World War II; widowed

with a young son to support, she studies in the U.S., settling here in 1950, marrying an American, and working as
a public health nurse; she writes partly as a religious inspiration to others.

1505   NESBITT, HENRIETTA
        see NESBITT, VICTORIA HENRIETTA KUGLER (1874-1963)

1506   NESBITT, VICTORIA HENRIETTA KUGLER (1874-1963)
        White House Diary.   Garden City, N.Y.:   Doubleday, 1948.
        314pp.

        F.D.R.'s housekeeper describes her small-town, "home-
        body" background; she first meets Eleanor Roosevelt through
        political activities, begins baking for her, and then is asked
        to serve with her husband at the White House; always un-
        pretentious, she tells of the heavy responsibilities, logistical
        complexities, and growing organizational skills required by
        the position; she closes with F.D.R.'s death.

1507   NESTOR, AGNES (1880-1948)   NAW
        Woman's Labor Leader.   Rockford, Ill.:   Bellevue Books,
        1954.   307pp.

        Beginning as a factory laborer at seventeen, she sees the
        need for union organizing which leads to a distinguished ca-
        reer; in 1904 she works with the Women's Trade Union
        League, and in 1906 she becomes an officer in the Interna-
        tional Glove Workers Union; she works with a Washington
        vocational education commission in 1914, supports women's
        suffrage, works with the American Labor Mission to Europe
        in 1918, campaigns against the Equal Rights Amendment in
        1922, earns an honorary law degree in 1929, and celebrates
        the victory of the eight-hour day in 1937.

1508   NEUGEBAUER, KATHERINE
        Russia as I Saw It; The Journal of a Tour in 1960.   New
        York: Exposition, 1961.   82pp.

        She and her husband, both of Russian ancestry, travel to
        Russia with a tourist group; they look for the brighter side
        and are pleasantly surprised by the accommodations and
        conditions they encounter; she describes sightseeing in Mos-
        cow, Leningrad, and Kiev, and notes visits with several
        relatives.

1509   NEVELSON, LOUISE BERLIAWSKY (1900-   )
        Dawns + Dusks; Taped Conversations with Diana MacKown.
        New York: Scribner, 1976.   190pp.

A sculptor, she is an artist in control of her destiny and completely absorbed by her work, never doubting her genius; she notes the artistic implications of the "totally female" experience; economic and artistic struggles and anger give her great strength; she discusses her aesthetic values, her work in many media, and her numerous exhibitions.

1510   NEWELL, HARRIETT CHASE (1881-)
       In Retrospect, An Autobiography.   Littleton, N. H. :   Courier
       Printing Co. , 1968.   165pp.

       She writes "random reminiscences" for her children and grandchildren, opening with a family history; a shy only child, she attends school in her New England village and graduates from a girls' academy in 1902; after travels, she marries in 1907, raises seven children, is a member of the D. A. R. , and is active in civic volunteer work; she is widowed in 1924; in 1966 she is named "Citizen of the Year" by her town for having written about local houses.

1511   NEWHALL, SUE MAYES
       The Devil in God's Old Man.   New York: Norton, 1969.
       253pp.

       She recounts her work as a lab technician at a Burmese frontier hospital with her doctor husband and three small sons from 1963 to 1969, "a time for introspection, re-dedication, and spiritual re-armament"; perceptive and open to Burmese culture, she nevertheless notes the primitive medical conditions and provides an ambivalent portrait of the autocratic founder of the hospital; she adopts Burmese twins and has mixed feelings about their final deportation as nationalization policies intensify.

1512   NEWLAND, CONSTANCE A. (pseud.)
       My Self and I.   New York: Coward-McCann, 1962.   288pp.

       In a pursuit of self-knowledge, this writer, widow, and mother of two, volunteers for an experiment in psychotherapy involving LSD; first skeptical about the unconscious, she discusses in vivid detail nine episodes under the drug; continually reinterpreting her fantasies, she discovers hidden leanings toward being "a murderess, a pervert, a cannibal, a sadist, and a masochist" but resolves several neurotic problems including sexual frigidity; she emerges "reconstituted as a human being. "

1513   NEWMAN, JUDITH STERNBERG
       In the Hell of Auschwitz; The Wartime Memories of Judith
       Sternberg Newman.   New York: Exposition, 1963.   136pp.

In a straightforward, chilling account of unrelieved horrors, a German Jewish woman recounts the fear and uncertainty which preceded her imprisonment; she witnesses daily
atrocities and the deaths of all of her family members and
her fiancé, enduring over two years of "constantly fighting
for survival"; a grueling evacuation claims more lives as
the Russian troops near; after liberation, she works in nursing and hospital administration in the Russian zone, marries
a "concentration-camp comrade," and emigrates to the U. S.
in 1947 to build a new life.

1514   NICHOLDS, ELIZABETH
        Thunder Hill. Garden City, N. Y.: Doubleday, 1953. 248pp.

She leaves New York City to settle on a Catskill farm
with her mother, an aunt, and a former student; having
tried and rejected beekeeping, sheep herding, raising hogs
and fowl, and cheese-making, the four "females on a farm"
learn to run a successful goat ranch, reaping the rewards
of a deeply satisfying way of life.

1515   NICHOLS, GEORGIA L.
        For Land's Sake. New York: New Voices Publishing Co.,
        1954. 56pp.

She leaves teaching to homestead for a sister in South
Dakota before World War I, carrying on the family pioneering tradition; writing in the third person, she describes a
ten-year investment in the land.

1516   NICHOLS, NINA BELLE SUITS HURST (1882-)
        Vinegar Pie: Being the story of a teacher who taught forty-
        five years in the public elementary schools of the United
        States of North America. San Antonio: Naylor, 1957.
        259pp.

A pioneer teacher in Oklahoma who begins her career in
1905, she produces a rambling, humorous account of her own
experiences as a student as well as later experiences as a
teacher, emphasizing the contrasts and dramatic changes in
schools and teaching methods over the years; she writes with
nostalgia, paying high tribute to pioneer women; she finds
teaching "a strenuous, challenging vocation."

1517   NICHOLS, RUTH ROLAND (1901-1960)   NAWM
        Wings for Life, ed. Dorothy Roe Lewis. Philadelphia: Lip-
        pincott, 1957. 317pp.

A pioneer woman pilot feels an immediate passion for flying after her first ride in 1919; a "society aviatrix," she

tours the nation in 1929 promoting aviation; in 1930 she sets
a transcontinental flight record and follows it in 1931 with
altitude and distance records; she survives several near-
fatal crashes through the years; her adventurous spirit joins
her humanitarian impulses when she organizes an air am-
bulance service in 1941 and works with UNICEF on behalf of
international understanding.

1518   NICHOLSON, MARTHA SNELL (1886-)
        His Banner Over Me. Chicago: Moody Press, 1953. 192pp.

        A poet writes of her "long years of illness and sorrow"
        after presenting a nostalgic account of her childhood in "an
        old-fashioned Christian home"; her frail health gives way to
        a long struggle with tuberculosis; after her marriage in 1919,
        she endures a spinal illness which leaves her an invalid; she
        finds solace in her writing and her religion.

1519   NICKERSON, ELINOR B.
        Kayaks to the Arctic. Berkeley, Cal.: Howell-North Books,
        1967. 197pp.

        A lifelong camping enthusiast, she describes a kayak trip
        up the Mackenzie River with her husband and three sons;
        humorous and dramatic anecdotes illustrate their experiences
        with mosquitoes, river squalls, the calm and beauty of na-
        ture, and the various people along the river; she takes spe-
        cial pride in her eldest son's manhood.

1520   NIN, ANAÏS (1903-1977)
        The Diary of Anaïs Nin, 1931-1934, ed. Gunther Stuhlmann.
        New York: Swallow Press, 1966. 368pp.

        The keeper of a massive, lifelong diary which constitutes
        her finest literary achievement, she tells of her life in Paris
        among fellow artists; writing with great delicacy about elusive
        qualities and intensely aware of her own "multiplicity of
        selves," she explores the subtleties of her relationships with
        Henry and June Miller, psychoanalysts Allendy and Rank,
        Artaud, and her father; she makes her literary debut with a
        book on D. H. Lawrence but is "at ease" only when writing
        for the journal; a vivid description of the birth of her still-
        born child closes the first volume.

1521   The Diary of Anaïs Nin, 1934-1939, ed. Gunther Stuhlmann.
        New York: Swallow Press, 1967. 357pp.

        After an interlude in New York City during which she joins
        psychoanalyst Otto Rank, she escapes absorption in his schol-

arly and clinical work by returning to Paris, strengthened in her identity as a writer; she takes on a "mother role" living in voluntary poverty while she cares for, nurtures, and supports numerous friends, including Miller; the onset of war means "the end of our romantic life" and she must follow her husband (excised from the diaries) back to the U. S.

1522   The Diary of Anaïs Nin, 1939-1944, ed. Gunther Stuhlmann. New York: Harcourt Brace Jovanovich, 1969. 327pp.

Repeating her childhood exile in New York, she finds the literary creation of "an inner and intimate world" both in the diaries and in her novels a way of establishing permanence in the face of chaos; the maternal in her is "devoured" by the demands of others, yet she continues to feed her treasured relationships; she contrasts the rhythm and drive of America with the reverie of Europe, cherishing the warmth, the sense of the past, the personal intimacy possible only in Europe; working with her own press, she struggles to establish herself as a writer through a new language of feminine consciousness.

1523   The Diary of Anaïs Nin, 1944-1947, ed. Gunther Stuhlmann. New York: Harcourt Brace Jovanovich, 1971. 235pp.

Living and then recording, interpreting, and clarifying through the medium of the diaries, she finds her first modest success as a writer in America; she continues to focus on the "subtleties of relationships" with others, always seeking harmony and distrusting polemics; she is drawn to youth and its orientation to the future; the depth of her personal revelation becomes "universal, mythical, symbolic. "

1524   The Diary of Anaïs Nin, 1947-1955, ed. Gunther Stuhlmann. New York: Harcourt Brace Jovanovich, 1974. 275pp.

She achieves a psychic divorce from the oppressiveness and cold superficiality of America, finding a place of "beauty and feeling," joy and completeness in Mexico and, to a lesser extent, in California; she faces the "enormous, stark harsh failure" of her books as she is mismanaged by publishers and misunderstood by critics; the death of her mother triggers her deepest exploration and analysis of her mother's maternal servitude and her own repetition of the pattern with her artistic "children. "

1525   The Diary of Anaïs Nin, 1955-1966, ed. Gunther Stuhlmann. New York: Harcourt Brace Jovanovich, 1976. 414pp.

Her recurring interludes of psychoanalysis lead to deeper exploration of the themes of intuition, neurosis, freedom, art, and the feminine; as each succeeding volume of the diaries is more richly peopled, she moves away from her earlier intense introspection; she gains sufficient emotional distance in her editing of the diaries to consent to their publication, commenting that "it is my thousand years of womanhood I am recording."

1526 NINABELLE (pseud.)
      see NICHOLS, NINA BELLE SUITS HURST (1882-   )

1527 NOBLE, CORA MOORE
      Memories. Boston: Christopher, 1964. 238pp.

      Writing in the third person, she takes a patronizing tone toward her childhood self as she recalls random memories of her beloved father and the importance of school and religious instruction in her life; certified as a teacher at sixteen, she develops self-reliance; after her marriage, she enjoys a career in county politics as a court clerk and tax commissioner from the 1920's to the 1960's, engaging in some fierce campaigns.

1528 NOONE, MARY (pseud.)
      Sweetheart, I Have Been to School. New York: Harcourt, Brace & World, 1961. 152pp.

      With a sense of humor, she tells the story of her mental breakdown and her voluntary hospitalization; during a slow convalescence, she tells of fellow patients, second-guessing the psychiatrists, and the absurdities of ideological diagnoses; resenting her father and her husband's proceeding with a divorce without consulting her, she returns home to begin a new, independent life, free of her old inhibitions.

1529 NORMAN, BARBARA
      see MAKANOWITZKY, BARBARA NORMAN

1530 NORRIS, KATHLEEN THOMPSON (1880-1966)   NAWM
      Family Gathering. Garden City, N.Y.: Doubleday, 1959. 327pp.

      A prolific author of novels, short stories, and articles, she tells of the "priceless possession" of a close, loving family life before the deaths of her parents when she is nineteen mark the end of her youth; with "abounding ambition," she establishes a home for her younger siblings, works as a reporter, then marries and settles in New York, combining domestic interests and literary pursuits and emerging from poverty into affluence; she presents a fine portrait of her beloved husband; she takes pride in her solid literary achievement.

1531   NOVAK, LILLIAN B.
        The Majesty of Jacob; A Mother's Story of Her Son.   New York: Exposition, 1961.   56pp.

In this story of her sixteen-year-old son's terminal illness with cancer, she describes her shock at each successive stage of the disease; she marvels at her son's unfailing good humor and is grateful for a supportive doctor; hope and despair alternate until his death.

1532   NUGENT, SISTER ROSAMOND
        Poor Little Millionaires.   New York: Pageant, 1959.   67pp.

A vivacious college dean writes four light-hearted chapters on four aspects of her life as a nun; praising the "communist" ideal of convent life, she tells of her community's establishment of a college, of teaching in a rural summer vacation school, of the nun's habit.

O

1533 OAKES, MAUD van CORTLANDT (1903-)
Beyond the Windy Place; Life in the Guatemalan Highlands.
New York: Farrar, Straus and Young, 1951. 338pp.

An ethnologist, she wishes to live and work in an isolated Indian village to study contemporary culture and ancient Mayan religion; she establishes a home, provides simple medical care, and patiently builds friendships with the natives, through whom she is then allowed to witness important ceremonies; she portrays the subtleties of the relationship between the Indians and "Ladinos"; she achieves deep happiness, having come to love the village and its people.

1534 O'BRIEN, PATRICIA
The Woman Alone. New York: Quadrangle/New York Times, 1973. 285pp.

To her own search for "personal wholeness" she adds her accounts of the experiences of other women alone; after growing up Catholic in the 1950's and docilely accepting marriage and motherhood, she attempts to combine family and a career in journalism; she comes to a recognition of the difficulties and ambiguities as well as the pleasures inherent in such a combination.

1535 O'DONOVAN-ROSSA
see COLE, MARGARET ROSSA (1887-)

1536 OFFENBERG, BERNICE
The Angel of Hell's Kitchen. New York: Bernard Geis, 1962. 277pp.

In this account of drama, adventure, and service during her ten years as a New York City social worker, she describes her introduction to the horrors and shocks presented by her "cases"; she is beaten, stabbed, ambushed by mobsters, and honored for her services; supported by legal officials and the welfare system, she is sometimes able to help others, especially the elderly; she breaks an engagement to continue her work, but later resigns after a bad beating and marries, continuing to aid others unofficially.

1537   OGILVIE, ELISABETH MAY (1917-   )
       My World Is an Island.   New York: McGraw-Hill, 1950.
       270pp.

       A writer, she fulfills a deep desire to write about an is-
       land off the Maine coast that contributes significantly in her
       childhood to her identity; as an adult, she moves to another
       Maine island and enjoys the adventure of renovating the
       house, getting to know the neighbors, gardening, caring for
       her pets, observing the local wildlife, offering simple hos-
       pitality to her guests including various editors, becoming
       skilled with a boat; she is at peace in "a sort of marriage"
       to the island.

1538   O'HARA, CONSTANCE MARIE (1907-   )
       Heaven Was Not Enough.   Philadelphia: Lippincott, 1955.
       381pp.

       In a narrative of lost and found faith, the only child of
       "one of the great Catholic families" of Philadelphia describes
       her cherished memories of the "absolute perfection" of
       Catholic ritual and of her convent education; she presents a
       loving portrait of a nun, "the greatest woman I have ever
       known"; a "modern" in the 1920's, her literary and theatri-
       cal successes come during a period of religious indifference;
       later a halt in her creative writing and serious illness trig-
       ger a spiritual reawakening and she closes her sensitive,
       articulate narrative on a hopeful note.

1539   O'HARA, MARY (pseud.)
       see STURE-VASA, MARY ALSOP (1885-1980)

1540   O'HARA, ROBIN
       Nobody Would Tell Me.   New York: Vantage, 1963.   162pp.

       In a book "dedicated to motherhood" yet illustrating years
       of domestic turmoil, she describes her earnest efforts to
       forestall her son's alienation, disloyalty, and betrayal after
       he is married; she suspects mental illness as the cause of
       her daughter-in-law's diabolical machinations; her painful
       account is offered ostensibly to aid other parents in similar
       straits.

1541   OLENDER, TERRYS T.
       For the Prosecution: Miss Deputy D. A.   Philadelphia: Chil-
       ton, 1961.   380pp.

       In a book dedicated to "those who must work twice as hard
       to get half as far," she details her struggles in her legal ca-

reer in an "airy informal manner" to demystify law; rejected as editor of the UCLA Law Review because she's female and repeatedly rejected by major law firms, she does political hack work for the D.A.'s office hoping for a patronage job; after months of humiliation, her dogged persistence results in a five-year stint as a Deputy District Attorney in Los Angeles, and she describes numerous trials, the excitement of courtroom drama and the interplay of wit and personalities between opposing lawyers.

1542   OLESON, THURINE (1866-)
       see XAN, ERNA OLESON (1898-)

1543   OLIVER, SUSAN LAWRENCE (1881-)
       Reminiscences of a Bostonian. Boston: Industrial School
       for Crippled Children, 1952.   88pp.

       "Just a rather commonplace old maid," she presents brief, random recollections of her childhood which include an afternoon with Julia Ward Howe (see companion volume), summers on Cape Cod, and domestic events.

1544   The Scrap Basket.   Boston: Bruce Humphries, 1955.   80pp.

       Her random reminiscences touch on her experiences in a small private sanitarium during World War I, her reflections on religion, her efforts at philanthropy, her anecdotes of Boston neighbors.

1545   O'NEAL, MARY T. (1887-)
       Those Damn Foreigners.   Hollywood, Cal.:   Minerva Printing & Publishing Co., 1971.   220pp.

       A native of Wales, she presents a straightforward account of courage and persistence; abandoned by her husband, she follows him to Colorado, insisting on support until she can establish a business; quickly pro-union in the mining camp, she plays a crucial role in a 1913 strike, and is invited to report on the Ludlow massacre to President Wilson in Washington, D.C. where she gains national attention speaking on mining conditions; in a storybook ending she marries for love and acquires the shop of which she has dreamed.

1546   O'NEILL-BARNA, ANNE
       Himself and I.   New York: Citadel, 1957.   313pp.

       The mother of four and married to an Irishman, she describes living in Ireland for five years beginning in 1951; she

produces an entertaining, lively account of a colorful locale
and charming people, including some droll characters among
her neighbors; she records her difficulties providing for her
children's education; she is taken aback by class distinctions
and rigid conservatism but loves the beauty of the countryside.

1547   ORIGO, IRIS CUTTING (1902-)
        Images and Shadows: Part of a Life.   New York: Harcourt
        Brace Jovanovich, 1970.   278pp.

        A writer, she recalls in this quiet, introspective narra-
        tive "three totally distinct periods" in her life: before 1914,
        between the wars, and the postwar years; a privileged child,
        she learns freedom within restraint from a beloved Irish
        grandfather, enjoys a legacy of independence from her father,
        learns the pleasures of travel, books, and beauty from her
        mother; through an early, intense exposure to art and culture
        in Italy, she becomes "too sophisticated"; after her marriage
        she lives "an entirely new kind of life," in the Italian coun-
        tryside, close to the land.

1548   O'SHEA, BETH
        A Long Way from Boston.   New York: McGraw-Hill, 1946.
        266pp.

        An adventurous Boston working girl and her friend drive
        to California and back in a Model-T Ford in the early 1920's;
        she takes a few temporary jobs along the way to make mon-
        ey, enjoys the variety of people she meets, falls in love
        three times, and never loses her enthusiasm.

1549   OTIS, CLARA PAINE
        Letters from Across the Sea to You from Clara Paine Otis.
        Chuo-Ku, Tokyo, Japan: the author, 1957.   212pp.

        She writes "to share my life in Japan" with American
        friends; she travels by cargo liner for over one year in
        1954 and 1955, describing sightseeing in various ports of
        call; she stays with her missionary sister in Japan, is a
        missionary teacher temporarily, and is charmed by the
        Japanese people and moved by her sense of fellowship with
        Japanese Christians.

1550   Sojourn in Lilliput; My Seven Years in Japan.   New York:
        Carlton Press, 1962.   240pp.

        After the death of her husband, she joins her sister as a
        missionary teacher in a social welfare center in Tokyo in

1954; she appreciates the Japanese "quietness of soul" and holds deep respect for Japanese values and customs; she teaches, travels, and develops a close friendship when she lives with her Japanese assistant; she closes with her sorrowful farewell to Japan.

1551   OVINGTON, MARY WHITE (1865-1951)   NAWM
The Walls Came Tumbling Down. New York: Harcourt, Brace, 1947. 307pp.

She serves as a Brooklyn settlement worker from 1896 until 1903, when "the Negro and his problems came into my life"; a socialist, she begins with an intensive investigation of economic problems; she describes her first trip to the South and her meetings with black leaders; she is among the founders of the NAACP in 1909, and organizes her account according to the organization's goals and activities during each president's tenure; she closes with a summary of advances toward racial equality.

1552   OWEN, JANET
Who Fought That War, Anyhow?: The Other Side of the Coin. N. p. : Janet Owen, 1976. 122pp.

She describes how she copes with a home and three children when her husband enlists in 1942; forced into unfamiliar tasks, she learns how to stoke a furnace and handle finances; she forges her family into a close unit and finds inner strength when her husband becomes a prisoner of war; after three years, the family is reunited.

1553   OWEN, MAGGIE (pseud.)
see WADELTON, MAGGIE JEANE MELODY (1896-)

1554   OWENS, LORENA (pseud.)
see OWENS, THELMA PHLEGAR (1905-)

1555   OWENS, THELMA PHLEGAR (1905-)
Daddy Was a Doctor. New York: Dutton, 1951. 221pp.

The daughter of an "individualistic and unorthodox" doctor in the Tennessee mountains, she returns home after her marriage and gains a new perspective on her parents and their chaotic ways; her father depends on his wife, who contributes inefficient common sense and office skills to their "joint informal practice of medicine"; eccentricities notwithstanding, they are loved by their patients.

1556   PABST, LETTIE LITTLE (1891-)
<u>Kansas Heritage.</u> New York: Vantage, 1956. 153pp.

With an emphasis on domestic detail, she tells of her hard life tempered by the "love, humor, and discipline" of her religious family; events are "seen through the eyes of a child and interpreted by the mind of experience."

1557   PADDLEFORD, CLEMENTINE (1900-)
<u>A Flower for My Mother.</u> New York: Holt, 1958. 64pp.

The well-known food editor offers a tribute to her mother in a series of vignettes of her childhood on a Kansas farm; her mother, a woman of fine understanding, loves simple pleasures, knows how to find "drama in trivial things," and delights in creating beauty; the account reveals an extremely close family life.

1558   PADOW, MOLLIE POTTER (1888-)
<u>A Saga of Eighty Years of Living.</u> Philadelphia: Dorrance, 1971. 228pp.

The daughter of Lithuanian Jewish immigrants, she is "a joiner, a fixer, a one-woman crusader"; she grows up familiar with New York City sweatshop labor in the garment industry and in 1912 she marries a Polish immigrant and becomes a devoted partner in her husband's garment business; they weather the depression, and later retire to Florida, where she is active in Jewish community affairs and humanitarian work; at eighty-one, she makes a dream trip to Israel; her account is enthusiastic and unpretentious.

1559   PAINTER, CHARLOTTE
<u>Confession from the Malaga Madhouse; A Christmas Diary.</u> New York: Dial, 1971. 212pp.

A writer relates her fragmented impressions from a mental hospital in Spain where she is recuperating from drug abuse; in flashbacks she tells of her friends, her son, and snatches of her past.

1560   Who Made the Lamb.   London: Michael Joseph, 1965.
       158pp.

       Her journal is an introspective exploration of "the mystery
       of new life" inspired by her own radiant pregnancy; her in-
       timate moods and musings focus on the nature of women,
       the "voluntary bondage" of motherhood which she embraces,
       the drama and rapture of birth; she includes sensitive por-
       traits of other women as their lives briefly cross hers.

1561   PALMER, FRANCES
       And Four to Grow On.   New York: Rinehart, 1958.   222pp.

       She provides a warm, joyous story of her four adopted
       children; numerous family anecdotes illustrate her own initial
       anxiety as a mother, gradually tempered by her growing love
       amid the pains of mutual adjustments; she closes with a plea
       for easing adoption procedures; portions of her account were
       previously published in magazine form.

1562   PAMPLIN, LILY MAY (1884-   )
       The Scamps of Bucksnort; Memories of a Nineteenth-Century
       Childhood in Rural Tennessee.   New York: Exposition, 1962.
       119pp.

       In a humorous, down-home style, she relates numerous
       family anecdotes, including tales of her colorful grandfathers
       and uncles and vivid stories of her neighbors; part of a
       closely knit community, she tells of activities and mischief
       that are centered around the family.

1563   PARK, CLARA CLAIBORNE
       The Siege.   New York: Harcourt, Brace & World, 1967.
       279pp.

       She recounts in detail the story of her assaults on the
       fortress of her eight-year-old daughter's autism; highly sen-
       sitive to her own responses as a mother, she notes her
       gradual realization of the abnormality of the child's passivity
       and detachment and provides a record of her intense efforts;
       noting the difficult family adjustments, her daughter's small
       accomplishments and discouraging setbacks, and her indigna-
       tion at the limited help available from professionals, she
       finds at last sympathetic and skillful aid in England.

1564   PARK, ETTA WOLCOTT (1863-1938)
       A Story for My Children, ed. Nettie W. Park.   New York:
       Vantage, 1968.   253pp.

She tells of "our thirty-eight year struggle for a home"; married in 1881 and ultimately the mother of fourteen children, she focuses her anecdotal account on the family's goal of owning a farm; working together they endure repeated moves, the difficulties of sharecropping, floods, drought, and poor crops, but by 1919 the goal is reached.

1565   PARK, MAUD MAY WOOD (1871-1955)   NAWM
Front Door Lobby, ed. Edna Lamprey Stantial.   Boston: Beacon, 1960.   278pp.

In a memoir which includes much valuable historical material, she recounts her experiences of the closing years of the women's suffrage campaign; working with Carrie Chapman Catt, she describes a drama of progress and setbacks, her lobbying efforts in Washington, the work of fellow suffragists, their heightened campaigns at the onset of World War I; she rejoices in the final "belated victory."

1566   PARKER, ELIZABETH KITTREDGE
Panama Canal Bride; A Story of Construction Days.   New York: Exposition, 1955.   90pp.

She travels to the Canal Zone in 1907 and is wed upon her arrival; her adjustment to tropical living includes housekeeping with a sense of humor, raising three children, absorbing some local culture; learning from her husband's work, she comments on the canal's construction; her account culminates in the 1914 inaugural boat trip through the canal.

1567   PARKS, LILLIAN ROGERS (1897-   )
My Thirty Years Backstairs at the White House, with Frances Spatz Leighton.   New York: Fleet, 1961.   346pp.

Herself the daughter of a White House maid and crippled by polio, she serves with pride as a White House maid and seamstress for thirty years; her anecdotes of First Ladies and other prominent personalities are loosely organized around the themes of "clothes problems," guests, First Families, the servants' point of view; she also tells stories from her mother's years as a maid.

1568   PARKS, NITA
How to Win a Fortune.   Los Angeles: American Book Institute, 1957.   126pp.

Married and the mother of four, she fills her household hours by entering contests, a profitable hobby that changes her life; she provides anecdotes of her studies and various successful methods, describing her use of daily personal experiences in her entries.

1569   PARSONS, FRANCES THEODORA SMITH DANA (1861-1962)
       Perchance Some Day. N. p.: Priv. pr., 1951. 360pp.

       She grows up "perfectly happy" in a large well-to-do family, enjoying a vigorous social life; a fervent amateur botanist, she publishes several books on wild flowers and ferns; her first husband is a naval officer, her second an advisor to New York Governor Theodore Roosevelt and later consul to Mexico; she is active in the women's suffrage movement and Republican women's groups; she notes her "long years of intimacy with the T. R. family"; her narrative is dense with descriptive detail.

1570   PARSONS, LOUELLA OETTINGER (1881-1972)   NAWM
       Tell It to Louella. New York: Putnam, 1961. 361pp.

       A Hollywood columnist, she follows her credo: "to report facts, with a fondness for my friends and a responsibility to my readers"; always happy to be "the first to know," she relates anecdotes from years as a journalist and offers personal glimpses of movie stars who are close friends; she takes time to attack her attackers.

1571   PARTON, MARGARET (1915-)
       Journey Through a Lighted Room: A Memoir. New York:
       Viking, 1973. 248pp.

       Out of "the deep well of the past," she recounts tales of her childhood with her radical journalist parents, the intellectual idealism of her college years, her job as a newspaperwoman with the New York Herald Tribune from 1943 to 1955; she tells of years spent in Japan and in India, where her son is born; later she writes for the Ladies Home Journal; she tells of caring for her mother in old age, and of the death of her son; a sensitive, sometimes wry but moving book.

1572   The Leaf and the Flame. New York: Knopf, 1959. 277pp.

       A foreign correspondent for the New York Herald Tribune, she produces this highly literate account of five years spent in India; written in diary form, it is sensitive and perceptive and contains lovely evocations of Indian culture.

1573   PATTERSON, BONNIE
       From Hell to Here. Boston: Christopher, 1963. 211pp.

An alcoholic tells of her years of struggle and degradation in "jails, hospitals, sanatoriums, state institutions,
psycho-wards, and therapy"; her troubles begin at fourteen
with a family breakup and heavy responsibilities as the oldest child; she masks loneliness and bitterness with drinking,
continuing through three unstable marriages; with the help
of A. A. , a supportive husband, a dedicated "mom," and renewed religious faith, she becomes the operator of a nursing
home and regains her self-respect and pride.

1574   PATTERSON, GRACE DANIEL (1896-)
        The Strawberry Apple Tree. San Antonio: Naylor, 1971.
        273pp.

        A Texas teacher and journalist writes after blindness
halts her teaching career; focusing on her childhood, she
describes her large, busy family of "proud landowners,"
adding much detail about her home and physical surroundings; she tells of family entertainments, an "enchanted orchard," seasonal activities, all of which, together with security and love, constitute a fine heritage.

1575   PATTERSON, HARRIET-LOUISE HOLLAND (1903-)
        Around the Mediterranean with My Bible. Philadelphia:
        Judson Press, 1948. 366pp.

        Traveling in the period between the wars, she makes a
complete circuit and describes numerous sites of religious
and secular significance in vivid, rich detail, infusing the
present with a strong sense of the past; she is alive to
scenic beauty and enjoys the crowded market places as well
as peaceful museums and monuments.

1576   PATTERSON, KATHERYN (1936-)
        No Time for Tears. Chicago: Johnson Publishing, 1965.
        109pp.

        A black woman describes her childhood plagued by epilep-
sy and insecurity; marrying at sixteen, she attempts suicide
during her first pregnancy; her second child is a hydrocephalic
son and she struggles to overcome her own shame and self-
pity to reach acceptance of his deformity; she engages in
special work with him, finds joy in his achievements, and
fights for his right to an education, concluding that her
"handicapped child is my blessing."

1577   PATTERSON, STELLA WALTHALL (1866-)
        Dear Mad'm. New York: Norton, 1956. 261pp.

Having vowed to stay a year in a cabin on her mountain claim, she experiences "an adventure of living alone at eighty"; she chronicles the growing mutual affection for and dependence on two young men who are neighbors; she gardens, improves the cabin, courageously shoots a cougar, and enjoys a delightful Christmas, deeply satisfied with her new life.

1578   PAUL, CHARLOTTE (1916-   )
       Minding Our Own Business.   New York: Random House,
       1955.   309pp.

       A novelist and journalist, she moves from the Chicago newspaper world with her husband and buys a weekly newspaper and printing business in a small Washington town; disabused of her naïve expectations, she adjusts to a heavy work schedule, welcomes civic involvement, and uses the locale in her free-lance writing; with an articulate defense of the satisfactions of the self-employed, she concludes her description of "five of the hardest and best years of our lives."

1579   PAUL, MARGARET
       Free to Love, with Jordan Paul.   Los Angeles: J. P.
       Tarcher, 1975.   145pp.

       A marriage counselor who works with her husband discusses with candor her own marriage and adjustment to motherhood; in short sections that alternate with those of her husband, she describes their mutual attempts to break patterns of manipulation and to work toward equity, "creating and sustaining intimacy in marriage"; she writes in a jargon-filled, popular style.

1580   PAULI, HERTHA ERNESTINE (1909-   )
       Break of Time.   New York: Hawthorn Books, 1972.   239pp.

       A writer and literary agent presents a vivid, dramatic narrative that opens with the rise of the Nazis and her chaotic escape from Vienna to Paris; after an idyllic interlude with a lover in the French countryside, she returns to Paris, again fleeing amid terror and chaos with the assistance of the French underground just before the fall of Paris; she arrives safely in the U. S. in 1940.

1581   PAWLOWICZ, SALA KAMINSKA
       I Will Survive, with Kevin Klose.   New York: Norton, 1962.
       286pp.

A Polish Jew, she describes her fierce struggle to maintain her humanity during the horrors of World War II; citing
atrocities committed against family members by the German
occupying forces, she tells of her misery and degradation
both before and after her internments which include a period
in Bergen-Belsen; after five years of terror, she is barely
able to comprehend liberation; in 1946 she marries a fellow
former prisoner who inspires her to improved health; in
1949, disturbed by continuing anti-Semitism in Germany,
they settle in the U. S.

1582　PAXTON, JUNE LeMERT (1882-　)
My Life on the Mojave.　New York:　Vantage, 1957.　168pp.

A poet, columnist, and feature writer, she first settles
in a California desert cabin in the early 1930's, seeking
physical and mental health; she tells of her daily routines,
of the joys of "the simple life," of her scattered neighbors,
and of writing for a local newspaper; she feels that the
pioneering challenges contribute to her recovery; portions
of her account were first published in magazines.

1583　PAYNE, ETTA (1902-　)
Home Was Never Like This.　New York:　Greenwich Book
Publishers, 1957.　184pp.

Subtitled "A Trailer's-Eye View of Europe Today," her
account describes her travels with the Wally Byam Trailer
Caravan in 1956; after a straightforward chronicle of typical
tourist sightseeing, she notes her increased appreciation after her return for life in the U. S.

1584　Land-Yachting to Central America; A Trailer's-Eye View of
Our Nearest Latin Neighbors.　New York:　Greenwich Book
Publishers, 1960.　150pp.

With her husband, she is a member of a Wally Byam
trailer caravan in 1958; for four months she travels in
Mexico, Guatemala, El Salvador, Honduras, Nicaragua,
Costa Rica, and Panama; she enjoys adventure and describes
the countryside, the people, and the history of the areas she
visits.

1585　PAYNE, MARY
I Cured My Cancer.　New York:　Vantage, 1954.　69pp.

She tells of her overwhelming fear when a tumor is diagnosed as cancer in 1941; her firm determination to be cured
carries her through years of treatment and leads to her

equally firm determination to become an X-ray technician to help others like herself.

1586   PEABODY, MARIAN LAWRENCE (1875-)
        To Be Young Was Very Heaven.   Boston: Houghton Mifflin,
        1967.   366pp.

        "Following in the steps of my forebears in keeping a jour-
        nal," she writes an account condensed from eighteen volumes
        of diaries; extracts from her diary entries are interspersed
        with connecting narrative; she is the daughter of a prominent
        Boston family and focuses much of her account on her social
        life, travels in Europe, acquaintances; she attends art
        school, tells of idyllic summers in Bar Harbor, does char-
        ity work in a boys' club; the account ends with her marriage
        in 1906.

1587   PEALE, RUTH STAFFORD (1906-)
        The Adventures of Being a Wife.   Englewood Cliffs, N.J.:
        Prentice-Hall, 1971.   266pp.

        The wife of minister Norman Vincent Peale writes an
        "upbeat" book about her own marriage; growing up with a
        strong sense of family solidarity, she stresses the import-
        ance of fun and partnership in a couple's work, study, tra-
        vel, and childrearing; her reflections and advice are illus-
        trated with anecdotes from her personal experience, "a rich
        and rewarding pilgrimage."

1588   PEARSON, VIRGINIA EDWARDS TAYLOR (1899-)
        Everything but Elephants.   New York: McGraw-Hill, 1947.
        211pp.

        The wife of a medical doctor, she spends the first two
        years of her married life in an oil camp in the jungles of
        Colombia; her consuming interest in new people and places
        eases her adjustment to tropical, rather basic housekeeping;
        she enjoys traveling and being of assistance to her husband,
        learning cultural tolerance and understanding.

1589   PECK, CHARLOTTE TREAT
        The Wife Who Went Along.   New York: Carlton Press,
        1964.   85pp.

        Married to a U.S. Army officer, she tells of her nursing
        service in 1917 at the American Ambulance Hospital in
        France; her acquaintances among patients and visitors range
        from royalty to humble soldiers; she tells of Paris air raids,
        of the armistice, and of her work for the return of American

soldiers to the U. S. ; her World War I activities constitute
her "greatest adventure. "

1590   PECK, CLARA TEMPLE BOARDMAN (1885-1950)
       Letters and Verses of Clara Boardman Peck, ed. Lawrence
       P. Peck. New York: Dodd, Mead, 1951. 432pp.

       From her first letter in 1910, she reveals her high spirit
       and impish sense of humor; in 1913 she travels in Europe
       and studies bookbinding in Paris, a craft she continues
       throughout her life; she finds her volunteer work in a French
       wartime hospital in 1915 strenuous and satisfying; she mar-
       ries in 1916 and letters to her husband reveal unflagging
       lighthearted romance, ebullience, and of course, character-
       istic whimsy; delighted by motherhood she later writes her
       two children letters of wry advice and fulsome praise; her
       letters are altogether charming.

1591   PEDEN, RACHEL
       The Land, The People. New York: Knopf, 1966. 332pp.

       A newspaper columnist, she turns to country topics, first
       recalling with nostalgia her childhood on a farm, enjoying a
       close and warm family life; throughout her later years "the
       land was healing, beautiful, full of adventure, beckoning";
       she writes of her experiences as a farm wife, noting that
       "the strength of the family farm is in ... sharing" and in
       "kinship with the earth. "

1592   Rural Free; A Farmwife's Almanac of Country Living. New
       York: Knopf, 1961. 382pp.

       Her account is drawn from columns written for two Indi-
       ana newspapers; in sections organized by a year's cycle of
       months, she writes graceful, delicate, intimate vignettes and
       impressions of the "small, remarkable surprises" of nature,
       the joys of the harvest, the deep satisfactions of raising
       children on the land, wildlife, and neighbors.

1593   Speak to the Earth; Pages from a Farmwife's Journal. New
       York: Knopf, 1974. 240pp.

       Taking her material from her Indiana newspaper farm
       column, she writes a series of brief vignettes; she presents
       portraits of her neighbors, people close to the land and
       possessing a unique vocabulary; she explores local folklore,
       and writes of nature's variety, reflecting that "the yearning
       for earth contact is inherent. "

1594   PELLEGRENO, ANN HOLTGREN
       World Flight: The Earhart Trail.   Ames, Iowa: Iowa State
       University Press, 1971.   225pp.

       An "individualist," she recalls her active and adventurous
       childhood to set the scene for her later challenge; learning
       to fly after her marriage, she decides to duplicate Amelia
       Earhart's (see companion volume) last flight of 1937 thirty
       years later; acquiring financial backing, she proceeds, ac-
       companied by a navigator, co-pilot, and mechanic; she re-
       lates anecdotes of routine stops, meeting people, and en-
       countering small difficulties, then dramatically describes
       her difficulty finding the island that Earhart missed; she
       enjoys a triumphant return.

1595   PELLET, BETTY
       see   PELLET, ELIZABETH EYRE

1596   PELLET, ELIZABETH EYRE
       "That Pellet Woman" with Alexander Klein.   New York:
       Stein and Day, 1965.   379pp.

       In a vibrant tale rich in adventure and experience, she
       recounts her "maverick ways"; she is an actress and a
       "Greenwich Village suffragette" before marrying a mining
       engineer in 1918; she tells of frontier homemaking in Colo-
       rado and the raw but colorful camp life as a partner in her
       husband's mine; she responds to the "goad of anti-feminine
       bias" by entering Democratic politics and serves 22 years
       in the Colorado state legislature; she reflects on women in
       politics.

1597   PEMBER, PHOEBE YATES (1823-1913)   NAW
       A Southern Woman's Story; Life in Confederate Richmond,
       ed. Bell Irvin Wiley.   Jackson, Tenn.:   McCowat-Mercer
       Press, 1959.   199pp.

       Widowed in 1861, she serves as the matron at Chimborazo
       Hospital from 1862 to 1865, noting the men's objections to
       "petticoat government" but assertively defending the propriety
       of women's nursing and administration which she finds deeply
       satisfying; she has affection and admiration for the common
       soldiers, sharing their increasing privations until her health
       breaks; she notes the "mad gaiety" just before the confeder-
       ate defeat; first published in 1879, her account is here aug-
       mented with nine long letters with a wealth of daily detail
       lightened by a sense of humor.

1598   PENZIK, IRENA
        Ashes to the Taste.   New York: University Publishers,
        1961.   378pp.

        She describes the "quiet horror of human relationships
        under Communism--a horror particularly dreadful to wom-
        en"; born a Polish Jew and raised in a politically conscious
        family, she settles in the U. S. in 1939, marrying an Amer-
        ican with whom she is active in communist political circles;
        but she becomes disillusioned by conditions in Poland, by
        views of her American comrades, by her husband's expul-
        sion from the party; fear of deportation during the McCarthy
        era leads to her fervent renunciation of communism.

1599   PEPPER, NANCY
        Ex-Prostitute Tells All.   New York: Vantage, 1960.   65pp.

        In a slangy, superficial account, she writes to expose the
        "truth" about prostitution; born in rural Kentucky and mar-
        ried at fourteen, she turns to prostitution after her infant
        dies and her husband leaves her; seeking money, clothes,
        and comfort, she finds instead work in a variety of houses
        from the coarse to the refined and a series of men who
        abandon her; later as a madam, she is a strict, shrewd
        businesswoman.

1600   PERENYI, ELEANOR SPENCER STONE (1918-   )
        More Was Lost.   Boston: Little, Brown, 1946.   278pp.

        She marries into the Hungarian "country noblesse," and
        settles on a "squalid and romantic" estate in Czechoslovakia,
        taking an intense interest in the people, the house, and the
        land; caught in the midst of Hungarian-Czechoslovakian con-
        flict and communist-fascist tension before and during World
        War II, she manages the estate when her husband is called
        for military duty; reluctantly she goes to the U. S. for the
        birth of her first child, a tragic departure that marks the
        end of her European life as well as the end of the narrative.

1601   PERKINS, FAITH
        My Fight with Arthritis.   New York: Random House, 1964.
        183pp.

        A reporter and radio journalist, she describes her first
        recognition of the symptoms of osteoarthritis; faced with the
        necessity to support her two sons, she is under severe
        stress, searches for the "right doctor"; after much reading
        and research, she learns the "hard way," trying quack doc-
        tors and unorthodox treatments; after ten years of coping with
        the disease, she is reconciled to living with pain.

1602   PERKINS, MARY (1912-   )
       Mind the Baby! New York: Sheed & Ward, 1949. 122pp.

       She describes the daily routine of Christian motherhood
with her two young sons, "fascinating and exasperating children"; she reflects on the miracle of new life and her visions of a glorious future; some chapters were previously
published in magazine form.

1603   PERKINS, SARA (1892-   )
       Red China Prisoner; My Years Behind Bamboo Bars. West-
       wood, N.J.: Revell, 1963. 127pp.

       A missionary nurse and teacher of nursing in China tells
of her first stay there in 1920, interned briefly during the
Japanese occupation; returning in 1946, she sees her training efforts curtailed by the communists in 1949; arrested,
she endures pain, illness, interrogations, and isolation but
is sustained by hymns, prayer and memorized scripture, a
"wonderful experience with God"; the account closes with her
release.

1604   PESOTTA, ROSE (1896-1965)   NAWM
       Days of Our Lives. Boston: Excelsior, 1958. 262pp.

       Russian-born, she comes to the U.S. as a teenager, and
finding work as a shirtwaist maker, she ultimately becomes
an organizer and national vice president of the International
Ladies Garment Workers' Union; her narrative focuses on
"the joy and happiness" of her childhood in the Ukraine and
her affectionate portrayal of her village and its people; she
grows up with a strong Jewish family tradition and a strong
sense of social justice.

1605   PETERSEN, MARJORIE
       Stornoway east and west. Princeton: Van Nostrand, 1966.
       189pp.

       After two years of preparation, she and her husband cross
the Atlantic on a thirty-three-foot sailboat and cruise in the
Mediterranean; she notes her growing appreciation of the
sea's beauty, drama, and danger, couching much of her
vivid narrative in technical sailing terms; she encounters
warm hospitality in many of their eighty-five ports of call.

1606   PETERSON, FLORA CULP
       Life and She. Boston: Christopher, 1960. 166pp.

       Writing in the third person, she describes her early life
on an Indiana farm in a Mennonite pioneer family, though

her childhood is marred by loneliness and religious agnosticism; after her marriage in 1908, she homesteads in Canada under primitive conditions; a religious conversion leads
to psychic experiences, and she discusses her experiences
with spiritualism and automatic writing.

1607   PETERSON, VIRGILIA (1904-1966)
        A Matter of Life and Death.   New York: Atheneum, 1961.
        334pp.

        A writer, translator, and lecturer, she presents a re-
lentlessly accusatory account addressed to her mother and
full of intense pain for the fear and limitations inflicted upon
her; she reflects on motherhood from her double perspective
as a daughter and mother, and on being an American from
her perspective as the wife of a Polish diplomat caught up
in the political events before and during World War II, who
finds herself in 1940 a refugee back in her native U.S.

1608   PETROVSKAYA, KYRA (1920?-)
        Kyra.   Englewood Cliffs, N.J.:   Prentice-Hall, 1959.   344pp.

        Russian-born and the romantic, rebellious daughter of a
prince who loses everything in the revolution, she is married at seventeen to a distinguished but unfaithful musician,
widowed at eighteen, and a survivor of the siege of Leningrad at twenty; an actress, and again widowed, she makes
films in Moscow and serves in a front-line theatre troupe
during the war; after the war, she divorces her doltish
third husband and marries an American diplomat, settling
in the U.S.; she emerges as a tough, colorful woman.

1609   PETZOLDT, PATRICIA (1914-)
        On Top of the World; My Adventures with My Mountain-
        Climbing Husband.   New York: Crowell, 1953.   248pp.

        She begins her married life in Wyoming characteristically
by skiing seventy miles over the Tetons to her first home;
she and her husband manage a dude ranch and she learns
mountain climbing; when her husband joins the first American expedition to climb K2 in the Himalayas, she travels to
India to meet him and to study with an Indian religious guru;
back in Wyoming, she becomes the first woman to climb the
north face of Grand Teton; after World War II, they settle
on a homestead near their beloved Tetons.

1610   PFISTER, LOUISE
        I Married a Psychiatrist, as told to Frances Spatz Leighton.
        New York: Citadel, 1961.   284pp.

In a light vein, she tells "the truth about the life of one psychiatrist's wife"; her first job as a nurse in a state mental hospital leads to a six-year courtship mixed with laughter and indoctrination; she relates anecdotes of various patients, of her husband's foibles, of her sons' childhood antics, and of their chaotic household; she stages a mock protest at providing secretarial support for her husband, but enjoys sharing in his work.

1611   PHELPS, ORRA ALMIRA PARKER (1867-)
       When I Was a Girl in the Martin Box. New York: Island
       Press, 1949. 157pp.

       Focusing on her childhood and youth, she describes her Connecticut home in great detail, allowing each room and its furnishings to trigger fond memories of her family and its activities; she tells of children's games, a visit to the 1876 Philadelphia Centennial exhibition, home remedies, school days, church functions; especially appealing are her colorful stories of people, from loving relatives to eccentric local characters.

1612   PHILIPSBORN, MARGERY L.
       Loathe Thy Neighbor. New York: Vantage, 1966. 56pp.

       She writes brief humorous chapters on a variety of domestic topics such as children's illnesses, neighbors, her honeymoon, the family car, and her role as a doctor's wife.

1613   PHILLIPS, CLAIRE
       Manila Espionage, with Myron B. Goldsmith.   Portland,
       Ore.: Binfords & Mort, 1947. 226pp.

       A nightclub singer, after a brief marriage she returns to Manila with her young daughter in 1941; she marries an army officer and they flee Manila during the war, going from village to village, caring for civilian wounded; she raids and destroys a Japanese ammunition dump; widowed and claiming to be Italian, she returns to her Manila nightclub to raise money and food under the code name "high-pockets" for guerrillas and prisoners, to gather information, and to help with an underground newspaper; arrested by the Japanese, she is imprisoned and tortured but is freed after the American invasion; this is a remarkable tale of drama and courage.

1614   PHILLIPS, KATHRYN SISSON (1879-)
       My Room in the World; A Memoir by Kathryn Sisson Phillips, as told to Keith Jennison. Nashville: Abingdon, 1964.
       157pp.

Writing at eighty-two, a world flight generates recollections of her past; she grows up in the rural midwest amid
the rich intellectual atmosphere of her family and the major
influences of church and school; she graduates from college
in 1901, turning to teaching after the deaths in quick succession of an infant, her mother, and her husband; she becomes
a leader in the Association of Deans of Women and remarries, takes an active role in her husband's foundation, continuing her involvement with wide-ranging interests after being widowed again in 1959.

1615   PHIPPS, JOYCE
       Death's Single Privacy; Grieving and Personal Growth.   New
       York: Seabury, 1974.   143pp.

       She recounts the sudden death of her husband and de-
scribes her responses, abilities and inabilities to "handle"
the situation; within a religious framework, she attempts to
integrate the experience of death into her own life and the
lives of her sons; she struggles with loneliness, changes in
her standard of living, the necessity for child care, and
anger at some social expectations, but grows in independence.

1616   PICKER, LORRAINE
       My Inward Journey.   Philadelphia: Westminster, 1957.
       187pp.

       She recounts her long struggle and recovery from bronchi-
al asthma, cured after six years in psychotherapy; exploring
her relationships with her mother and brother, she recog-
nizes the dark side of a "happy" childhood, revealing stress,
anger, and guilt which produce physical illness; her intellectual understanding precedes emotional upheaval and insights which transform her life as a wife and mother when
she achieves "self-assurance and maturity."

1617   PICKFORD, MARY (1893-   )
       Sunshine and Shadow.   Garden City, N.Y.:   Doubleday, 1955.
       382pp.

       The famous movie actress tells of her Toronto childhood,
devoted to her mother; she begins acting at five, moving to
New York for the theatrical opportunities; she starts to work
in films with D.W. Griffith in 1909, becoming a shrewd
businesswoman as her wealth increases, and she tells of her
various roles throughout her career; she presents a moving
description of her marriage to actor Douglas Fairbanks
which lasts from 1920 to 1936; afflicted by a fragile sense
of confidence in herself, she writes with modesty about a
deeply satisfying life.

1618   PICON, MOLLY (1898-)
        So Laugh a Little, as told to Eth Clifford Rosenberg.   New
        York: Julian Messner, 1962.   175pp.

        In this humorous account an actress and singer of the
        1930's describes her unusually close family, with a Russian
        immigrant grandmother and a mother who becomes an "ener-
        getic businesswoman" when abandoned by her husband; poor
        as a child, she begins her stage career at five; she marries
        a playwright and is active in the Yiddish theatre; her tale is
        full of amusing transcriptions of her grandmother's fractured
        English, a fine mix of logic and illogic.

1619   PIERCE, DEBORAH (1938-)
        I Prayed Myself Slim, as told to Frances Spatz Leighton.
        New York: Citadel, 1960.   128pp.

        Withdrawn and "humiliatingly fat," she tells of her com-
        mitment while she is a university student to diet with the
        help of prayer; she loses her inferiority complex as well as
        weight and enters beauty contests; after her marriage, she
        becomes a fashion model; she discusses her methods of diet-
        ing and includes sample prayers and menus.

1620   PIERREFEU, ELSA
        see de PIERREFEU, ELSA TUDOR

1621   PIKE, DIANE KENNEDY
        Life Is Victorious! How to Grow Through Grief; A Personal
        Experience.   New York: Simon and Schuster, 1976.   209pp.

        Widowed in 1969 (see Search), she wishes to share her
        experiences of the stages of grief, her detailed analysis of
        feelings, and her growth in self-awareness as she integrates
        four aspects of her own identity; after telling of her "perfect
        union" with Bishop James Pike, she describes the intensity
        of her shock at his death; a period of suffering and deep
        emotional pain follows; with the loving support of others,
        she recovers and rebuilds for the future with new spiritual
        commitment.

1622   Search: The Personal Story of a Wilderness Journey.   Gar-
        den City, N.Y.: Doubleday, 1970.   198pp.

        The widow of Bishop James Pike tells of their tragic trip
        into the desert near Jerusalem; lacking water and forced to
        abandon their car, her husband's strength fails and she leaves
        him to continue looking for help; she describes graphically her
        ten-hour struggle to an Arab camp, and days of intense anxi-

ety as a search party attempts to find her husband; she recalls their brief marriage; she experiences a vision of his
dying moments before his body is found and affirms his
spirit's immortality.

1623   PIKE, EUNICE V.
       Not Alone.   Chicago: Moody Press, 1964.   160pp.

A public health nurse and missionary with the Mazatec
Indians in Mexico writes of the years from 1936 to 1939;
working for the Wycliffe Bible Translators, she settles in a
village, studies the language, works with informants, teaches
literacy, and proselytizes with elementary translations of
scripture; under the constant scrutiny of the villagers, she
nevertheless becomes close to the people, describing local
personalities and customs.

1624   PILLET, NETTIE ETHEL LEIST (1877-)
       The Kingdom of My Soul.   New York: Comet Press, 1955.
       109pp.

Insisting she is "not remarkable in any way," she provides
random recollections, each of which generates religious reflections; she endures financial hardships in her forty-two
years of marriage, raises a daughter, adjusts to widowhood,
becomes a violinist, and writes on china painting when she
turns seriously to ceramics; she writes this account at the
age of seventy-eight.

1625   PINCKNEY, ELIZABETH LUCAS (1722?-1793)   NAW
       The Letterbook of Eliza Lucas Pinckney, 1739-1762, ed.
       Elise Pinckney.   Chapel Hill: University of North Carolina
       Press, 1972.   195pp.

At eighteen she manages three plantations, happy to be
thus useful to her father; her charming letters reveal a
gentle humor and widely varied interests and activities including music, reading, needlework, nature, and business;
she marries in 1744 and settles in England, returning to
South Carolina as a widow after 1757 to manage family business and property; her later letters notify friends of her
widowhood and grief and others to her sons warn them against
the temptations of "youthful passions."

1626   PITKIN, DOROTHY
       And Live Alone; The Story of a Year in New Hampshire.
       New York: Pantheon, 1957.   214pp.

In a reflective and intimate exploration of the life of a
single middle-aged woman, a "widow, with children grown,"

she enters a new stage of life with her move into an old
farmhouse; recollections of childhood, of her married life,
and of "these tempestuous widowed years" are woven into
the fabric of her new existence; her aloneness is tempered
by the "benediction" of the daily greeting from the train
engineer, the masculine touch lent by her handyman, neighbors in a nearby village; paying homage to Thoreau, she
enjoys the "healing companions" of nature and seasonal vari-
ations, feeding her desire to write as she transforms loneliness into "the gift of time."

1627   PLATH, SYLVIA (1932-1963)   NAWM
       Letters Home, by Sylvia Plath; Correspondence 1950-1963,
       sel. and ed. Aurelia Schober Plath. New York: Harper &
       Row, 1975.   502pp.

       The letters cover her years at Smith College, her growth
as a woman and as a writer and poet, the recovery from
her suicide attempt, her Fulbright year at Cambridge, the
extremity of her passion for her husband, the poet Ted
Hughes, her joyful motherhood, the shock of separation and
divorce; the letters testify to her intimate relationship with
her mother; the letters illuminate a life of deep reflection,
of unrestrained enthusiasm, of growing strength and pride,
and of final despair.

1628   PLUMMER, BEVERLY
       Give Every Day a Chance.   New York: Putnam, 1970.
       222pp.

       This is a mother's story of her third child, a daughter
born with osteogenesis imperfecta; determined to bring her
up as normally as possible, she describes frequent fractures
and numerous harrowing experiences with incompetent doctors and dehumanizing hospital procedures; she learns all
she can about the disease, and copes throughout with financial strain, the adjustments of other family members, the
anguish of uncertainty, and her daughter's physical and mental suffering; she relates her immense admiration for her
daughter's courage.

1629   POCHMANN, RUTH FOUTS (1903-   )
       Triple Ridge Farm.   New York: Morrow, 1968.   232pp.

       A writer and professor's wife describes the family's pur-
chase and renovation of a Wisconsin farm; she experiences
"deep spiritual content" as they restore the farm house, create a garden, construct a pool, reforest large areas with
thousands of tree seedlings, and build a fine wildlife habitat;
she notes with joy the farm's contribution to her daughter's

growth and maturity and later to her grandchildren's youth;
her activities feed inner resources and "a sense of our good
fortune" pervades the years.

1630   POLK, MARY (1900?-)
        The Way We Were.   Winston-Salem, N. C.:   John F. Blair,
        1962.   242pp.

        In a charming memoir, the daughter of a small town
        North Carolina lawyer describes her childhood in the early
        1900's; each chapter is a perceptive vignette, suffused with
        gentle humor; she provides a subtle portrayal of relations
        between black and white people, loving portraits of her par-
        ents, and an account of her education which includes a girls'
        finishing school and Columbia University, and her marriage
        which marks an end to years of "happiness and irresponsi-
        bility"; her father's death concludes a special relationship.

1631   POLLAK, BETTY RAUH
        Manhattan Transplant.   New York: Crowell, 1959.   198pp.

        In an entertaining, anecdotal account, the wife of the
        Antioch College business manager describes their sabbatical
        year with two young children in New York City; she estab-
        lishes the children in school, explores, adjusts to apartment
        life, welcomes houseguests, copes with the rigors of urban
        social activities, and leaves with a real fondness for at
        least some aspects of New York life.

1632   POLLARD, ELLEN H. (1895-)
        My Family Torn Asunder; A Woman's Intimate Chronicle.
        New York: Exposition, 1958.   157pp.

        The daughter of a Cree Indian father and a white mother,
        she is left with her Indian grandmother after her father's
        death; she endures hardship and cruelty as a bond-servant,
        traded from family to family; married and the mother of
        seven, she achieves some happiness before being driven
        away by her drunken husband; separated from her children
        for twenty-three years, she is finally reunited with them and
        a long-lost sister.

1633   POLYKOFF, SHIRLEY
        Does She ... Or Doesn't She?   And How She Did It.   Gar-
        den City, N. Y.:   Doubleday, 1975.   131pp.

        The daughter of Jewish immigrants and married with two
        daughters, she describes half a century in advertising; she
        recounts the creation of many famous slogans; she was se-

lected Advertising Woman of the Year in 1967; after retirement, she opens her own advertising agency; the account is
light and anecdotal.

1634   POPKIN, ZELDA (1898-)
        Open Every Door. New York: Dutton, 1956. 379pp.

A reporter and novelist, she recounts the "pastoral years"
of benign poverty in her Jewish family; newspaper work,
which she begins at sixteen, teaches her to be inquisitive
and assertive; in 1919 in New York City she marries, sharing business and domestic life, "modern and uninhibited,"
through twenty-five years of intense married companionship;
her travels to post-war Germany and to Israel teach her
that she cannot hate, in spite of the Jewish experience during
the war; she writes first as a sideline to marriage and motherhood, later as a way of fulfilling her "need to live completely."

1635   PORTER, REBECCA NEWMAN (1883-)
        Raisin Valley. New York: Vantage, 1953. 217pp.

Her San Francisco parents purchase a California raisin
ranch to benefit her mother's health and to give the children
the advantages of country life; she loves ranch life and has
rich memories of cutting and selling fruit, enjoying friends
and neighbors, enduring financial and agricultural setbacks,
and making steady improvements on the house and land; as
her sisters marry and leave, it marks the end of an era;
she hopes to impart a kind of "immortality" to her parents'
achievement by writing the book.

1636   POTTER, JOSEPHINE HUNTER
        No One Fell Overboard. New York: Wilfred Funk, 1953.
        312pp.

Her dream of adventure is fulfilled when, with her husband and four young children, she takes an eleven-month
voyage of six thousand miles along the east coast, through
the inland waterway, into the Gulf of Mexico, and up the
Mississippi and Ohio Rivers; she describes "glorious sails,"
growing skills, dangers, sightseeing, friendships in a
straightforward, enthusiastic narrative.

1637   POTTS, ABBIE FINDLAY (1884-1964)
        Letters Written to Winifred Comstock Bowman, 1923-1963.
        New York: Regency Press, 1975. 225pp.

A poet and scholar, she writes to a student during her
years as a Vassar English professor; with affection, intimacy

and much teacher's advice, she writes of her own reading
and research and examines her student's literary efforts with
loving care; a vivacious, delightful, rhapsodic correspondence
marked by her joy with words.

1638   POWDERMAKER, HORTENSE (1896-1970)   NAWM
        Stranger and Friend: The Way of an Anthropologist.   New
        York: Norton, 1966. 315pp.

        After describing factors in her past and personality that
lead to her profession, an anthropologist recounts four field
experiences; after studying with Malinowski in London in
1925, she works in New Guinea in 1929 and 1930; from 1932
to 1934 she works in rural Mississippi, examining "Negro
and white spheres"; in 1946 in Hollywood she exploits her "so-
ciological interest in movies"; and she studies mass media in
Northern Rhodesia in 1953 and 1954; she enjoys participating in
other cultures and "stepping in and out of my own society."

1639   POWERS, BARBARA MOORE (1934-)
        Spy Wife, with W. W. Diehl.   New York: Pyramid, 1965.
        188pp.

        The wife of the American pilot shot down over the
U. S. S. R. in 1960, she writes to correct false accusations
and attacks on her character; "a simple Southern girl," she
grows to resent her husband's secrecy and absences; she is
shocked by his disappearance and by later C. I. A. psychological and emotional cruelty to her; after attending the Moscow
trial, she is beset by an unsympathetic press, local gossip,
hostile family members; in despair, she attempts suicide
and endures bitter divorce proceedings; she closes with sharp
criticism of the C. I. A.

1640   PRATT, ALICE DAY (1872-)
        Three Frontiers.   New York: Vantage, 1955.   132pp.

        By family background and by nature "attuned" to frontier
life, this school teacher decides in 1911 to homestead alone
in Oregon, gaining title to the property by "proving up" the
land almost single-handedly; although forced to give it up
later during the depression, she cherishes having had "the
opportunity to use one's whole self completely."

1641   PRATT, MARSHA WHITNEY
        Sculptured in Faith.   New York: Exposition, 1965.   95pp.

        Lacking parental affection and later suffering her child's
and her own precarious health, she searches for religious

support, "for Christianity in its simplicity"; her faith produces healing and regeneration for both her child and herself; later, when her daughter is grown and her husband leaves and her father disowns her, her religious commitment remains unwavering; the account is sprinkled with Biblical citations.

1642   PRETTY-SHIELD
       Pretty-Shield, Medicine Woman of the Crows, by Frank B. Linderman. New York: John Day, 1972. 256pp.

       Originally published in 1932 as Red Mother, the account consists of answers to questions relayed through an interpreter; she describes remembering as "like looking for things in a bag"; much of her life is told within the framework of tribal custom; she tells of her parents, her own adventures, her marriage at sixteen, her children, her tribe's wars.

1643   PREVIN, DORY LANGAN
       Midnight Baby: An Autobiography. New York: Macmillan, 1976. 211pp.

       A composer, performer, and writer evokes the chaotic interior atmosphere of her disturbed childhood in flashbacks and poems; a bizarre relationship with her father gradually unfolds, his mental illness partly explained by his doubts about his paternity and shellshock from World War I; she, her fearful mother, and her infant sister are boarded up in their dining room for over four months by her father when he breaks down completely; she feels she doesn't exist and is terrified when she is finally released; her horrifying story is told in impressionistic, staccato style.

1644   PREWETT, VIRGINIA
       Beyond the Great Forest. New York: Dutton, 1953. 302pp.

       Disillusioned as a foreign correspondent in Latin America, she invests her life's savings and dreams in a Brazilian woodland homestead in 1947, exploring "the very nature of escape"; struggling with risks and the mistrust of her laborers, she is appalled by the heavy responsibility, yet her commitment to the land and its people marks a shift in a lifetime of vacillation; she marries and returns to New York in 1949, but subsequent economic catastrophe on the farm triggers her reflections on landowners, primitive farming methods, democracy, and nationalism.

1645   PRICE, EUGENIA (1916-)
        Burden Is Light!   The Autobiography of a Transformed Pa-
        gan Who Took God at His Word.   New York: Revell, 1955.
        221pp.

        She describes herself as a bright child of a prosperous
        family, close to both her parents; after an ambitious, ex-
        travagant youth, she struggles through a period of boredom,
        self-deception, and worry but finds a Christian re-birth at
        thirty-three; she details her conversion experience, her
        "witnessing for Jesus Christ," and her subsequent work in
        Christian radio and as a lecturer.

1646   PRICE, GLADYS BIBEE
        Tune on an Aspen Leaf.   New York: Vantage, 1952.   114pp.

        After years of urban living, she returns with her husband
        and young son to the Montana cattle ranch where she grew
        up; she helps build a log home, raises livestock, cherishes
        her friends and neighbors; the memories and spirit of her
        childhood illuminate her present, and she reflects on the
        simplicity of her "peaceful, contented life."

1647   PRICE, SOPHIE
        The Sacramento Story.   New York: Vantage, 1955.   80pp.

        Writing at eighty-two, this Sacramento native recreates
        images of the city's past as a background for her own ran-
        dom recollections of childhood and school days.

1648   PRIEST, IVY MAUDE BAKER (1905-1975)   NAWM
        Green Grows Ivy.   New York: McGraw-Hill, 1958.   270pp.

        A former Treasurer of the U.S., she discusses her two
        identities, "the public official and the wife-mother"; bolstered
        by her strong Mormon faith, she grows up in poverty in a
        Utah mining community, influenced by her mother's activities
        in local politics; on her own after a brief early marriage,
        she works and begins activities in Republican politics; a mar-
        riage in 1935 brings her great happiness, love, and security;
        she returns to politics after the death of a daughter, cam-
        paigning nationwide for Eisenhower and seeking women's
        votes; as Treasurer, she enjoys her family's support for
        duties that include public speaking and official socializing.

1649   PROUTY, AMY
        Mexico and I.   Philadelphia: Dorrance, 1951.   258pp.

        "Completely converted to Mexicana," and charmed by the
        Mexican people, she keeps a journal of her extensive travels

with friends and offers detailed and enthusiastic descriptions of places as well as of her own reactions and impressions.

1650   PROUTY, OLIVE HIGGINS (1882-1974)
        Pencil Shavings: Memoirs.   Cambridge, Mass.:   Riverside
        Press, 1961.   233pp.

A novelist, she writes partly to preserve her memories for her grandchildren; the pampered youngest child in her "New England family," she is torn by anxiety and unhappiness; she prefers writing to sightseeing on the family's tour of Europe in 1896, and her writing is further encouraged at Smith College where she enrolls in 1900; married in 1907 and the mother of four, she endures the tragic deaths of two children as well as her and her husband's breakdowns; she puts family life first even after the success of Stella Dallas, although she feels the tension between writing and her home life.

1651   PROXMIRE, ELLEN
        One Foot in Washington; The Perilous Life of a Senator's
        Wife.   Washington, D. C.:   Robert B.   Luce, 1963.   175pp.

In an account written near the end of her husband's first full term, she describes the "harried, challenging and thoroughly unpredictable life" she leads; the mother of five, she tells of the rigors of campaigning, the need for "patience and discipline" when controversy shatters her peace of mind, her activities in Democratic Party politics, her charity work, her social entertaining, and above all, the deep satisfaction of political life.

1652   PULLIAM, NINA
        I Traveled a Lonely Land; This Is Australia and These Are
        the Australians--As I Saw Them.   Indianapolis: Bobbs-
        Merrill, 1955.   400pp.

She fulfills a childhood wish to travel to Australia and offers an account combining impersonal description and historical information with her personal experiences of extensive sightseeing and of warm Australian hospitality.

1653   PULSIFER, SUSAN FARLEY NICHOLS
        A House in Time.   New York: Citadel, 1958.   220pp.

She presents quiet, gentle, nostalgic vignettes of her childhood on Washington Square in New York City in the 1890's; she describes her family home and the associations which this highly imaginative child holds with each room;

she offers a loving portrait of her parents and suggests that her own character is molded by her relationships with her four older sisters and brothers; after this fine evocation of atmosphere and place, she states "this house is myself. "

1654   PURTELL, THELMA C.
Can't Read, Can't Write, Can't Takl Too Good Either; How to Recognize and Overcome Dyslexia in Your Child.   New York: Walker, 1973. 280pp.

She discusses her family's eighteen years of struggle and adjustment, haunted by a son's problem diagnosed first as retardation, then as dyslexia; she is slow to interpret early danger signals, as are complacent doctors and teachers; she comes to a delayed realization of her own dyslexia and compensations she makes; she comments on her research into the disability.

1655   QUICK, DOROTHY (1900-   )
        Enchantment; A Little Girl's Friendship with Mark Twain.
        Norman: University of Oklahoma Press, 1961. 221pp.

        A writer and poet recalls her childhood meeting with
        Twain on a ship from England; in a charming illustration of
        Twain's grace with children, she finds him "a grand play-
        mate and storyteller"; she describes the thrill of a later
        week-long visit to Twain, his teaching her to write, other
        letters and visits characterized by "the simplicity that goes
        with true greatness"; she recounts her grief at his death.

1656   QUIN, SISTER ELEANOR
        Last on the Menu. Englewood Cliffs, N.J.: Prentice-Hall,
        1969. 182pp.

        In a humorous, exuberant narrative, a nun tells of her
        tomboy childhood; she enjoys the "social side" of college for
        a year, then holds numerous brief jobs; her general dissatis-
        faction leads to the decision to join a convent in 1951; she
        describes convent routine and the sisters' personalities; she
        fills speaking engagements for ten years, raising funds for a
        home for dependent children.

1657   QUINCY, ANNA CABOT LOWELL
        see WATERSTON, ANNA CABOT LOWELL QUINCY
        (1812-   )

1658   QUINCY, ELIZA SUSAN (1798-1884)
        The Articulate Sisters; Passages from Journals and Letters
        of the Daughters of President Josiah Quincy of Harvard Uni-
        versity, ed. M.A. DeWolfe Howe. Cambridge, Mass.:
        Harvard University Press, 1946. 249pp.

        Selections from her journal cover the years from 1814 to
        1821 and provide domestic details of numerous social occa-
        sions; her acquaintances through family connections include
        Webster, President Adams, President Monroe, and other
        prominent political and intellectual figures; she notes the
        death of Abigail Adams (see entry #6); her passages are on
        pages 11-44.

1659   QUINCY, MARGARET MORTON
       see GREENE, MARGARET MORTON QUINCY (1806-)

1660   QUINCY, MARIA SOPHIA (1805-)
       The Articulate Sisters; Passages from Journals and Letters
       of the Daughters of President Josiah Quincy of Harvard Uni-
       versity, ed. M. A. DeWolfe Howe.   Cambridge, Mass.:
       Harvard University Press, 1946.   249pp.

       Her journal of 1829 describes a journey by carriage from
       Cambridge to upstate New York, presenting details of travel
       conditions, of inns ("noisy enough certainly"), of a spa, of
       socializing along the way; she also tells of the 1929 Harvard
       commencement; her account is on pages 149-189.

1661   QUINN, BARBARA (1942-)
       Cookie.   New York: Bartholomew House, 1971.   256pp.

       In a slangy account, she describes her rebellious New
       York City childhood which leads to later sordid, self-destruc-
       tive episodes as she seeks "to experience everything"; prom-
       iscuity at twelve, marriage and motherhood at fifteen, mari-
       tal separation, abortion, a lesbian affair, drug abuse, theft,
       prostitution, a suicide attempt, arrests, and jail; after near-
       ly three years at Synanon, she reaches maturity, helping
       others by working in a New York drug abuse prevention
       program for youth.

1662   QUINN, SALLY
       We're Going to Make You a Star.   New York: Simon and
       Schuster, 1975.   256pp.

       A reporter for The Washington Post, she tells how she
       was selected to co-host the CBS morning news show; she
       accepts the job despite misgivings and lack of training; she
       recounts the subsequent personal attacks by the press; after
       a detailed account of her first disastrous broadcasts, she
       recognizes her ultimate failure and describes its effects on
       her personal life.

1663   RAITT, HELEN
      Exploring the Deep Pacific.   New York: Norton, 1956.
      272pp.

      She first plans only to meet her husband, an oceanograph-
er, for Christmas in the South Seas, but she is invited to
join the Capricorn Expedition in 1952-1953 for three months,
violating "American oceanographic tradition" by entering "a
man's world" on board; helping where she is needed, she
notes her work in the log, the drama and tension of experi-
mentation and exploration, the warm hospitality they find
on the islands; as the only woman on board, she feels a
special kind of loneliness but relishes her "lovely experience," "just happy to be part of the group," and anticipates
numerous cultural readjustments when she returns to her
four children and "normal" life.

1664   RAMA RAU, SANTHA (1923-   )
      East of Home.   New York: Harper, 1950.   303pp.

      A gifted observer, she describes her journey through
Japan, China, Indo-China, Siam, and Indonesia from 1947
to 1949; the daughter of an Indian ambassador, she feels her
own Asian identity is strengthened the more she learns of
the subtleties of other cultures; she studies theatre and
dance, gains interviews with political leaders during times
of unrest, and travels extensively in the countryside, establishing a quick rapport with people of every social level.

1665   Gifts of Passage: An Informal Autobiography.   New York:
      Harper, 1961.   223pp.

      She presents a "highly irregular self-exploratory essay"
focusing on occasions that "moved, impressed, instructed
or interested" her; she evokes the atmosphere of her grandmother's extended household in India, her sense of cultural
dislocation having lived six years of her youth in England
and having been educated at Wellesley, her cultural explorations in Asia where her father serves as a diplomat; she
marries an American in France, continuing to combine her
"nomadic existence" with a writing career, and continuing to
note the interplay of the modern and the traditional in her life.

1666   My Russian Journey.   New York: Harper, 1958.   300pp.

She describes a three-month stay accompanied by her
husband and young son in Leningrad and Moscow in 1957,
a trip undertaken to satisfy her curiosity; seeking both old
and new Russia, she enjoys some remarkable encounters
with artists, dancers, actors, and writers; she skillfully
evokes the atmosphere of monumental Leningrad and the
severity of Moscow; portions of her account were first published in Holiday magazine.

1667   This Is India.   New York: Harper, 1954.   155pp.

She writes on her native India, basing her descriptions
on her own travels and experiences; she wishes to introduce
India to Westerners, to lay to rest certain stereotypes, to
begin to probe the subtleties of Indian culture; much of the
account was previously published in Holiday magazine.

1668   View to the Southeast.   New York: Harper, 1957.   240pp.

She offers a "personal view" of the Philippines, Vietnam,
Cambodia, Laos, Thailand, Singapore, Indonesia, Bali, Burma, and Ceylon; traveling for over a year with her husband
and young son, she often settles in small villages to enjoy
closer contact with the people and to savor the culture; a
sensitive observer, she is much taken by the warmth of the
people and the beauty of the countryside.

1669   RANDALL, MARGARET (1936-   )
Part of the Solution: Portrait of a Revolutionary.   New
York: New Directions, 1973.   192pp.

In a series of poems, translations, and diary entries from
1970 and 1971, she paints her political self-portrait; attracted
by the passion, comradeship, and revolutionary zeal in Cuba,
she lives there, noting her children's communist awareness
as well as her own radical politics; she reflects on other
world events, including the U.S. invasion of Cambodia and
the death of George Jackson.

1670   RANKIN, HATTIE LOVE (1884-1960)
I Saw It Happen to China, 1913-1949.   Harrisburg, Pa. :
J. Horace McFarland, 1960.   235pp.

Her account is drawn from a diary of thirty-six years as
a medical missionary in China; after earning her M.D. in
1911, she settles in China, describing with fine detail her
work among the country people, discussing various medical

cases, and telling of her opportunities for travel and observation; she endures periods of civil unrest and war; she marries a fellow missionary in China in 1929; from 1943 to 1945 she is held in a Japanese concentration camp; an anti-communist during the revolution, she leaves with great sorrow in 1949, reaffirming her deep love for China.

1671 RASEY, MARIE I. GARN (1886?-)
It Takes Time; An Autobiography of the Teaching Profession.
New York: Harper, 1953. 204pp.

She writes of herself as a student and of herself as a teacher, for her vocation is chosen as a "protest against tyranny" of one of her own teachers; she recounts her intense studies in high school and college, her inspirations and experiences as a teacher; she earns a Ph.D., publishes books, and does research in educational psychology.

1672 RASMUSSEN, ANNE-MARIE (1938-)
There Was Once a Time. New York: Harcourt Brace Jovanovich, 1975. 237pp.

At eighteen she comes from her native Norway to the U.S., "the promised land," and is employed as a domestic in the Nelson Rockefeller home; unable to remain a servant while carrying on a secret romance with son Steven, she returns to Norway, is courted and married there to Rockefeller in 1959; she learns to fill her role as a Rockefeller, struggling for privacy and haunted by a need for affection and reassurances; troubled by marital tension, she engages in civic activities, campaigns for Nelson Rockefeller in 1968; after an unhappy divorce, she dedicates herself to raising her three children.

1673 REBEN, MARTHA (pseud.)
see REBENTISCH, MARTHA RUTH (1911-)

1674 REBENTISCH, MARTHA RUTH (1911-)
The Healing Woods. New York: Crowell, 1952. 250pp.

After three years in a tuberculosis sanatorium, she seeks a cure by living "a simple life" in the open in the Adirondacks accompanied by an old guide; her first return to the village reveals profound alterations in her perspective and behavior; the wilderness teaches her the joy of nature, fortitude, and self-reliance, while improving her health.

1675 A Sharing of Joy. New York: Harcourt, Brace & World, 1963. 183pp.

After a long illness, she retreats to the Adirondack woods to recover, renouncing comforts and "human companionship"; curious and patient, she is enthralled by the behavior of wild animals; she cares for geese, flying squirrels, a duck, a rabbit, a crow, a raccoon, a partridge, a robin, a bear, an owl, a nighthawk, a goat, and sparrows, often nursing injured animals back to health; she finds high adventure in her companionship with wildlife.

1676   The Way of the Wilderness: An Adventure in Self Discovery.
New York: Crowell, 1955.   276pp.

In this sequel to The Healing Woods, she continues her pursuit of health, independence, and peace through the solitude and simplicity of wilderness living, assisted by a wise old woodsman; winter weather and financial necessity force her to return to the village and work, but she is ill-suited to the indoor life; her joy in nature is multiplied when she falls in love, but when he dies in a sudden accident, her grief is overwhelming; she is devoted to writing of her woodland existence.

1677   REEDER, ELEANOR CHRISTINE
Ports O' Call; Intimate World Experiences and Sketches.
New York: Vantage, 1972.   77pp.

She and her husband travel around the world in six months aboard a cargo and passenger ship; she describes the places and people they visit; her sketches were originally written for local newspaper publication.

1678   REEDER, LUCILLE LOIS (1904-)
What Faith Can Do.   San Antonio, Tex.:   Naylor, 1966.
83pp.

She describes her happy childhood in rural Texas; in 1914 she contracts polio and is confined for the rest of her life to a wheelchair, but she cultivates self-reliance and service to others; she opens a mail order business to establish financial independence; after marriage, she adds homemaking to her business skills; after "twenty-five lovely years" she is widowed, is defrauded by a second husband, but finds happiness with a third.

1679   REICHERT, FLORIAN, SISTER (1900-)
Chamber Music.   New York: Pageant, 1958.   142pp.

She tells of her conversion to Catholicism at seventeen, cast out by her vehemently anti-Catholic parents; with enthusiasm and no regrets, she follows a "cherished dream," entering a convent; she describes daily convent life to dispel its mysteries and tells of her various assignments in elementary teaching and music in an account suffused with joy.

1680   REIS, CLAIRE RAPHAEL
        Composers, Conductors and Critics.   New York: Oxford,
        1955.   264pp.

        This is a personal account of her founding of the League of Composers and twenty-five years' effort from the 1920's to the 1940's to support contemporary music; a skillful and enthusiastic organizer, she describes performances, her associations with composers and musicians, and the constant struggle to overcome resistance to contemporary works; her account includes numerous anecdotes about prominent composers and musicians.

1681   REISS, JOHANNA (1932-)
        The Upstairs Room.   New York: Crowell, 1972.   196pp.

        A Jewish woman tells of her childhood in the Netherlands during World War II, describing her initial uncertainty and then the actual anti-Jewish discrimination after the German occupation of Holland in 1941; with her sister, she hides in an upstairs room, then later on a farm, constantly fearing discovery; the account closes as her sister escapes with false identification papers.

1682   RENAY, LIZ
        My Face for the World to See.   New York: Lyle Stuart,
        1971.   457pp.

        A high fashion model, pursuing a childhood dream of becoming a movie star to escape ugliness and poverty, describes "the never-ending procession of men" in her sometimes sordid past; a naïve rebel, she is a runaway bride at fifteen, but soon ends the first of her six marriages; she lives "the good life" with a wealthy cattleman, models, acts in nightclubs, enjoys luxury as a "mafia moll," but sees her movie career ruined by the notoriety of her connection with a gangland murder; she stages a comeback, looking for more "fun and frolic."

1683   RESNICK, ROSE (1916-)
        Sun and Shadow.   New York: Atheneum, 1975.   274pp.

        She describes growing up poor in New York in the 1920's, with a dictatorial father and docile mother; blinded by mea-

sles at two, she is educated with sighted children, studies
piano, attends summer camp, participates in drama and
dance; she attends Hunter College and the Manhattan Conservatory; barred from teaching, she studies piano in
France, then moves to the West Coast and plays in bars to
earn her living; she organizes a million-dollar project for
a blind children's camp but success is followed by betrayal
at the hands of administrators; hampered by social agencies,
she offers many criticisms of lack of opportunities for the
blind.

1684   RESNIK, MURIEL
        Life Without Father.   New York: Vanguard, 1955.   287pp.

        A divorcée and mother of two young rambunctious, out-
spoken sons writes an entertaining account of her earnest
dedication to their psychological well-being; she takes a wry
look at progressive education, describes her qualms about
the boys' summer camp, mentions a series of suitors, tells
of her "nesting" attempts, and finally settles in a New York
City apartment; she closes as her sons are "on the brink of
manhood. "

1685   REUTHER, RUTH E.
        The Wife of Four Hobbies.   New York: Pageant, 1956.
        81pp.

        She writes about her reactions to, adjustments to, and
mock frustrations because of her husband's hobbies in photography, art, magic, and the circus; caught up in his activities, she is one of the founders of a Texas community circus and is involved, together with her husband and daughter.

1686   REYNOLDS, BERTHA CAPEN (1885-   )
        An Uncharted Journey; Fifty Years of Growth in Social Work.
        New York: Citadel, 1963.   352pp.

        Combining "autobiography and limited history," she covers
the years roughly from 1914 to 1954; with a rural New England background and "a need to make sense of things and a
maverick mind," she enters social work after her graduation
from Smith College, partly to relieve her own nervous pros-
tration; after work in child welfare, she is a teacher and
administrator in Smith's School of Social Work; she works
in New York City clinics, engages in research and publication; in 1926 she enters psychoanalysis, and through the
1930's experiences personal growth and "liberation"; during
World War II, she works with the Merchant Marine and unions; she closes with her personal credo.

1687   REYNOLDS, DEBBIE
       see REYNOLDS, MARY FRANCES (1932-)

1688   REYNOLDS, FEZA M.
       My Trip Abroad. Boston: Christopher, 1961. 208pp.

       She fulfills a childhood dream by touring Holland, Ger-
       many, Switzerland, Italy, France, Belgium, and England;
       enumerating sights, she includes much impersonal historical
       and descriptive material.

1689   REYNOLDS, MARY FRANCES (1932-)
       If I Knew Then, with Bob Thomas. New York: Bernard
       Geis, 1962. 192pp.

       A movie, stage, and television actress produces a bouncy,
       but superficial combination of anecdotes and advice; after a
       depression childhood in El Paso, she moves to California
       and enters show business at sixteen; she reflects on her ca-
       reer, her religious beliefs, her discovery of "mature love"
       in motherhood and a second marriage.

1690   RHEA, MINI
       I Was Jacqueline Kennedy's Dressmaker, with Frances Spatz
       Leighton. New York: Fleet, 1962. 334pp.

       A custom dressmaker in Washington, D. C. , in business
       to support her two daughters, tells of her initial work for
       Mrs. Kennedy's mother, then of her growing acquaintance
       with Mrs. Kennedy; they collaborate on designing fashions,
       and she recounts anecdotes of various costumes.

1691   RHODES, HARRIE VERNETTE (1871-)
       In the One Spirit; The Autobiography of Harrie Vernette
       Rhodes, as told to Margueritte Harmon Bro. New York:
       Harper, 1951. 192pp.

       A self-professed psychic, she begins by telling of her
       childhood and the desire to help heal others which is gener-
       ated by her own fragile health; a musician and mother of
       five, she experiences a turning point in 1910, suddenly aware
       of healing powers; she accepts messages from her deceased
       father and other "helpers and teachers" from the spirit
       world.

1692   RHODES, LAURA
       Chastise Me with Scorpions, with Lucy Freeman. New York:
       Putnam, 1964. 283pp.

Unable to cope with marriage and new motherhood, she
enters a private psychiatric hospital and keeps a diary "of
my stricken self"; she establishes a circle of friends among
her fellow patients; her past emerges as she explores her
relationships with her parents and her husband; after struggling with intense anger and two suicide attempts, she is
able to resolve her conflicts and return home to a stronger
marriage.

1693   RICE, INEZ
        Valley Over the Hill.   San Antonio: Naylor, 1959.   266pp.

With a wealth of detail, she portrays her pioneer family
and the domestic duties and activities on their Arizona
homestead; she struggles with hardship, danger, illness, and
financial strains; she notes the impact on her family of national events such as World War I and prohibition; in 1921
the family must leave their ranch and face the challenge of
beginning again.

1694   RICH, LOUISE DICKENSON (1903-   )
        The Forest Years.   Philadelphia: Lippincott, 1963.   225pp.

This is a collection into a single work of We Took to the
Woods (1942) and My Neck of the Woods (1950); see entries
in companion volume.

1695   Happy the Land.   Philadelphia: Lippincott, 1946.   259pp.

She presents a "purely personal history" of her life in a
remote cabin in northern Maine after her husband's sudden
death; she writes with a fine sense of place, illuminated by
her deep love of nature and her appreciation of things "old
and precious"; in spite of the complications of living "the
simple life" with children, she feels she holds a "spiritual
lease" in the area.

1696   Innocence Under the Elms.   Philadelphia: Lippincott, 1955.
        285pp.

A prolific and perceptive writer, she finds that a visit to
the small Massachusetts town of her childhood after a twenty-
year absence triggers reminiscences of a certain way of life;
she presents a fine evocation of small town social life,
domestic frugality, the family's religious observations, her
parents' work as publishers of the local newspaper, her
"ruling passion" for books, her independent spirit, and above
all, the glowing "magic of youth."

1697 The Natural World of Louise Dickenson Rich. New York:
      Dodd, Mead, 1962. 195pp.

      A writer and New England "countrywoman," she recalls
      her childhood experiences of growth, tranquillity, security,
      renewal, and patience learned through her "true intimacy"
      with nature; her return to the wilderness after marriage is
      a homecoming (see We Took to the Woods); still later, wid-
      owed, she settles near the sea and absorbs its austerity and
      particular rewards in a life "reduced to fundamentals"; deep-
      ly reflective, her examination of outward things parallels
      inner explorations.

1698 Only Parent. Philadelphia: Lippincott, 1953. 223pp.

      Her early married life is characterized by a love of na-
      ture and of wildlife; when she is widowed with two young
      children, she finds it necessary to endure "my stint in civil-
      ization" for the children's education, and she compares city
      and country living; her anecdotes about parenting are wry
      and perceptive.

1699 The Peninsula. Philadelphia: Lippincott, 1958. 281pp.

      "Seeking simplicity and peace and room," she describes
      with quiet appreciation her intense emotional response to the
      landscape and quality of life on a sparsely inhabited Maine
      peninsula; she becomes acquainted with the local lobstermen
      and villagers, learning "what it means to live with the sea
      constantly" and delighting in the imaginative language of the
      peninsula; she welcomes the "return to yesterday," the per-
      manence of old customs and close family life.

1700 RICHMOND, BERNICE (pseud.)
      see ROBINSON, BERNICE NELKE (1899-)

1701 RICKETSON, ANNA HOLMES (1841-)
      Mrs. Ricketson's Whaling Journal, 1871-1874, ed. Philip F.
      Purrington. New Bedford: Old Dartmouth Historical Society,
      1958. 79pp.

      The book by a captain's wife is alternatively entitled "The
      Journal of Annie Holmes Ricketson on the Whaleship A.R.
      Tucker, 1871-1874"; with a sharp eye, she observes whaling
      activities, tolerating the grease and odor for the "clean
      money" earned; she is grief-stricken when her newborn in-
      fant dies on the voyage; she notes frequent "rugged" weather,
      meetings with other vessels, stops in foreign ports, and
      some contact with natives; she writes with a simple style
      and eccentric spelling.

1702 RICKETT, ADELE
Prisoners of Liberation, with Allyn Rickett. New York:
Cameron Associates, 1957. 288pp.

She and her husband write alternating sections on their
four years in a Chinese communist prison, focusing on
changes in their attitudes and beliefs; in 1948 her studies in
China begin, and she observes the early stages of the revolution; after her husband's arrest in 1951, she's held in her
home, interrogated and lectured for over a year; later held
in a prison, she describes the interplay of her cell-mates'
personalities, her examination of values, and her self-
criticism; when she is deported to the U.S., she is viewed
as having been brainwashed and, in the midst of the Mc-
Carthy era, she must reaffirm the community values she
learned in China.

1703 RIDDLE, ALMEDA (1898-)
A Singer and Her Songs: Almeda Riddle's Book of Ballads,
ed. Roger D. Abrahams. Baton Rouge: Louisiana State
University Press, 1970. 191pp.

The account is transcribed from taped conversations with
folk singer Granny Riddle; in a disconnected narrative, she
describes a family life rich in songs; she learns much from
her father, a singer and voice teacher, and she later collects ballads and songs from the Ozarks; texts and music
are included in this volume, and each song is discussed with
its personal associations.

1704 RINEHART, MARY ROBERTS (1876-1958)   NAWM
My Story: A New Edition and Seventeen New Years. New
York: Rinehart, 1948. 570pp.

A prolific novelist who enjoys "a career gone wild" after
having been "pitchforked into literary America," she tells of
difficulties with her writing and of editors with whom she
works; writing is the stable center of her life, while personal crises occur around it; the material new to this edition, written while recuperating from a heart attack, is on
pages 433 to 570.

1705 RINKER, ROSILAND
Within the Circle. Grand Rapids, Mich.: Zondervan, 1973.
120pp.

The author of books on prayer describes her "journey
through the wilderness of religious prejudice"; having passed
adolescent self-scrutiny, she experiences religious conversion
and serves as a missionary in rural China; while abroad,

she struggles with issues such as confession and personal
commitment, seeking a balance; she later returns to the
U. S. for a college education.

1706   RITCHIE, JEAN (1922-   )
        Singing Family of the Cumberlands.   New York: Oxford,
        1955.   282pp.

        Born the fourteenth child in her family,   she relates her
        own and others' family anecdotes; she describes both her
        fear of and respect for her father, the warmth of a family
        Christmas, her first love at fourteen, school; her account
        is written with much dialogue and a good ear for mountain
        slang; songs accompany every occasion and music is printed
        in the text, an intimate part of her family memories.

1707   RIVERS, CARYL (1937-   )
        Aphrodite at Mid-Century: Growing Up Catholic and Female
        in Post-War America.   Garden City, N. Y.:   Doubleday,
        1973.   283pp.

        Growing up in an "average American family," she tells of
        her early memories of World War II; her childhood includes
        life in parochial school, puberty rites, crushes on movie
        stars, the anti-communism of the 1950's; with an awareness
        of popular media prescriptions for women, she enters col-
        lege in 1955; a trip to Europe and graduate school mark her
        independence from her family; with marriage, she emerges
        from the protective Catholicism of her youth.

1708   RIVES, HALLIE ERMINIE
        Dome of Many Colored Glass, with Post Wheeler.   Garden
        City, N. Y.:   Doubleday, 1955.   878pp.

        Wife of a diplomat and herself a novelist and short story
        writer, she presents "colored beads ... strung on a string
        of reminiscence"; weathering a storm of publicity after her
        first two controversial novels, she marries and settles on
        posts in Japan, Russia, Rome, Stockholm, London, Para-
        guay, and Albania, continuing her writing career; she is
        sharply critical of the Foreign Service, accusing it of "ram-
        pant favoritism and nepotism, craft, falsehood, sycophancy,
        and chicanery"; she and her husband write alternate chapters.

1709   RIZZI, MARCIA SALO (1942?-   )
        Some Pictures from My Life: A Diary.   New York: Times
        Change Press, 1972.   64pp.

        The book consists of "an assemblage of diary entries,
        dreams, drawings and photographs"; she records her reflec-

tions on a brief marriage, art and politics, sexuality, feminism, risks, loneliness.

1710   ROBBINS, EDNA M.
Round the World Retirement; The Story of One Woman's
Joyful Trip at Sixty-five.   New York: Exposition, 1958.
89pp.

She writes to encourage others in retirement; she travels
alone in 1954 in Spain, Italy, Greece, Turkey, Egypt, India,
Southeast Asia, New Zealand, Hawaii, and Alaska, delighting
in the sights and discussing politics, economics, and religion
whenever possible with people she meets; having learned
much, she shares her impressions and opinions.

1711   ROBBINS, FLORENCE GREENHOE
Bout with Cancer.   Boston: Christopher, 1955.   112pp.

She writes to share a new way of living, thinking, and
feeling with others who have had cancer, since she learns
how to endure "two constant companions and enemies":   fear
and isolation; through "Mystical Christianity" and an unorthodox combination of diet, breathing, and meditation, she survives surgery and keeps a rigorous schedule which includes
work, marriage and parenting, and therapy.

1712   ROBERTS, EVELYN (1917-   )
His Darling Wife, Evelyn: The Autobiography of Mrs. Oral
Roberts.   New York: Damascus House, 1976.   273pp.

Relentlessly positive, the wife of the famous evangelist
tells of her marriage, when "his career became my career";
she is thrilled to be wed to a "world missionary" and, intensely proud of her four children, finds motherhood "the
highest calling"; she describes their years of financial and
religious struggle, the controversy about healing, and their
extensive crusades, although she remains throughout a rather
private person.

1713   ROBERTS, JOAN (1922-   )
Never Alone.   New York: McMullen Books, 1954.   204pp.

"Music-mad by nature," this musical comedy actress describes her childhood, supported by a family who believes in
her destiny as a performer; she undertakes rigorous training
in voice, drama, and dance, wishing to use her talent to
serve others; tragedy strikes when her beloved is killed in
World War II; yet she finds professional triumph in 1943
as the lead in Oklahoma!

1714   ROBERTS, KATHERINE
       And the Bravest of These.   Garden City, N. Y. :   Doubleday,
       1946.   311pp.

       A correspondent, she joins a post-war U. S.
       aid mission to Belgium "to find out what was happening in the lives of
       people"; she travels throughout the country noting extensive
       destruction and interviewing citizens and government officials
       about issues such as food, health, employment, and the re-
       building effort.

1715   ROBERTS, NANCY (1924-)
       David.   Richmond, Va. :   John Knox, 1968.   72pp.

       This is a mother's story of the first five years of raising
       her son who has Down's Syndrome; candidly, she describes
       her emotional response to his retardation, emphasizing the
       positive rewards of his personality and development.

1716   ROBINETTE, VIVIEN
       We Moved to California; A Travel Book.   New York: Ex-
       position, 1951.   104pp.

       A former Texan tells of her experiences and observations
       in 1948 in the "first flush of enthusiasm" for California; she
       settles in Los Angeles, sees the sights, makes friends, buys
       a house, and establishes roots.

1717   ROBINS, ELIZABETH (-1952)
       Raymond and I.   New York: Macmillan, 1956.   344pp.

       In a moving account, an English-born actress and writer
       tells of her extremely close relationship with her younger
       brother in Alaska; sent by a newspaper to record her "Nome
       experience," she portrays her brother's missionary work,
       the local corruption and intrigues, the chaos of Alaska at the
       turn of the century; each episode explores subtle psychologi-
       cal reverberations; idolizing her brother, she is intensely
       concerned about his mental and spiritual health and is agon-
       ized when she must leave "this Nome which had devoured
       me" without him; the manuscript was finished in 1934.

1718   ROBINS, MARGARET DREIER (1868-1945)   NAW
       Margaret Dreier Robins: Her Life, Letters, and Work, ed.
       Mary E. Dreier.   New York: Island Press Cooperative,
       1950.   278pp.

       A noted reformer, suffragist, and trade unionist writes
       long letters that explore the issues of democracy and educa-

tion in Chicago, of civil liberties and the struggle for truth
and against injustice, of wages and hours legislation, of
Hitler's deplorable rise; she joins her husband in reform
activities, participating in strikes, protest meetings, and
speeches at local and national levels; she is the sister-in-
law of Elizabeth Robins (see entry #1717); her sister includes biographical information and connecting text.

1719   ROBINSON, BERNICE NELKE (1899-)
        Our Island Lighthouse.   New York: Random House, 1947.
        275pp.

        She and her husband are New York City professional peo-
        ple, but they embark on an experiment in self-sufficiency for
        three summers between 1942 and 1944; she tells of her love
        of the sea, caring for the house and garden, affection for
        kind friends, contentment in the primeval atmosphere of
        wartime blackouts, and her family's first winter on the is-
        land; having met the challenge of the weather and the sea,
        she creates "a home with a deep meaning."

1720   ROBINSON, IONE (1910-)
        A Wall to Paint On.   New York: Dutton, 1946.   451pp.

        An artist, her account, suffused with a pervasive inno-
        cence, is drawn first from letters to her mother and then
        letters to her daughter, exploring "what world events were
        doing to me as a person and an artist"; serious and intense,
        she studies in New York, Paris, Italy, and finally Mexico,
        a source of "tremendous influence" where, in 1929, she
        works with Rivera on the National Palace frescos; drawn to
        radical politics by her concern for social justice, she lives
        in Spain during part of the civil war, despairing when wider
        war comes to Europe and she is forced to flee to the U.S.

1721   ROBINSON, JILL SCHARY
        Bed/Time/Story.   New York: Random House, 1974.   307pp.

        A writer, interviewer, and mother of two, she describes
        her intense relationship with her present husband; "our love
        story" is a tale of game playing, sexual experimentation,
        Esalen encounter groups, all mediated by drugs and alcohol.

1722   ROBINSON, MARY ANN (1935-)
        The Sparrows Are Looking Good.   Philadelphia: Dorrance,
        1973.   47pp.

        She tells of her search for God which dates from early
        childhood; her missionary training is cut short by poor

health in 1961 and she turns away from religion; after a
religious reawakening in 1971, she encounters religious
controversy on the job and experiences visions; her account
is sprinkled with Biblical quotations.

1723   ROBSON, ELIZABETH
       Seems but Yesterday.   Philadelphia: Dorrance, 1972.   54pp.

       In a series of vignettes, she tells of a rabbit in her gar-
       den, her desires to accumulate "a little learning," various
       small domestic tyrannies, her World War II victory garden,
       a maid who becomes part of the family, sending her son to
       prep school, travels in England, and pet dogs.

1724   ROCKEFELLER, ABBY GREENE ALDRICH (1874-1948)
                                                           NAW
       Abby Aldrich Rockefeller's Letters to Her Sister Lucy.
       New York: 1957.   328pp.

       The articulate, energetic wife of John D. Rockefeller, Jr.
       writes to her peripatetic sister during the years from 1919
       to 1948; she engages in a wide variety of philanthropic activ-
       ities, including work with the YWCA; her family ties are
       extremely close and she notes her children's health and
       progress; her interest in art, especially the art of the Far
       East, is stimulated by her sister's travels.

1725   RODLI, AGNES SYLVIA
       North of Heaven; A Teaching Ministry Among the Alaskan
       Indians.   Chicago: Moody Press, 1963.   189pp.

       In an account of three years in the Alaskan interior, she
       describes her first impressions of the village and villagers;
       sensitive to Indian culture, she learns much from her stu-
       dents, while organizing adult classes and other activities in
       addition to teaching children; she develops a deep fondness
       for the people and leaves with sorrow.

1726   RODRIGUE, ROSALIE
       Oh! For the Life of a Stewardess.   New York: Comet
       Press, 1953.   123pp.

       A stewardess of a cruise ship to Latin America describes
       her tasks and responsibilities and tells of various types of
       passengers; she combines a celebration of the joys of travel
       with a plea for tolerance and international understanding.

1727   RODZINSKI, HALINA (1904-   )
       Our Two Lives.   New York: Scribner, 1976.   403pp.

Polish-born and raised with a rich musical heritage, she
settles in the U. S. in 1933 and marries conductor Artur
Rodzinski; she delights in the "genteel socializing" of her
role but feels inadequate to the demands of his brilliance,
jealousy, rages, affairs, and hypochondria; living an intense
life of emotional extremes, she finds the cost of her love
and tolerance is near self-effacement but she has no regrets,
having learned the art of being an artist's wife; she writes
with sensitivity and perception.

1728   ROGERS, DALE EVANS (1912-   )
        My Spiritual Diary.   Westwood, N. J.: Revell, 1955.   144pp.

Western entertainer and wife of Roy Rogers, she writes
to "check on my soul's progression"; religion is a strong
force in her daily life, coloring her family relationships,
her career, and her evangelical activities in the U. S. and
in England; each brief entry closes with a prayer.

1729   The Woman at the Well.   Old Tappan, N. J.: Revell, 1970.
        191pp.

Writing an autobiography that is also her "Christian witness," she opens with a description of her childhood as a
"strong-willed little rebel"; married at fourteen and divorced
soon after with a son to support, she begins her radio and
singing career; in Hollywood singing westerns she meets
Roy Rogers and marries him; her grown son presses her
for a Christian commitment, and her religion becomes a
fundamental part of her strong family life; she bears tragedy
when a Down's Syndrome daughter dies at two, another daughter dies at twelve, and her son dies in the army; other
adopted children and thirteen grandchildren bring her joy.

1730   ROGERS, DOROTHY (1914-   )
        Jeopardy and a Jeep; Africa Conquered by Two Women Pro-
        fessors.   Rindge, N. H.: Richard R. Smith, 1957.   301pp.

A psychology professor, she succumbs to the "lure of the
unknown" in a 25, 000 mile adventure; she begins with the
challenge of the Sahara, learning much through danger, mistakes, and physical hardship, and scoffing at those who doubt
the capabilities of two women; describing dramatic pano-
ramas, she travels south through West Africa and north
through East Africa; she enjoys her contacts with native
people and observes varieties of black-white relations and
of the position of women; she closes with reflections on her
most vivid impressions.

1731 ROGERS, HOPE
      Time and the Human Robot.   N. p. :   Ink Spot Press, 1975.
      112pp.

      In this narrative of a mental breakdown, she describes
      her "terrifying aloneness" as her fears, deadened emotions,
      and acute hearing and strength render her "more animal than
      human"; painting and music therapy help her gradual recov-
      ery, but she must struggle to remain stable upon her return
      home to a husband and three small children; she bears two
      more children and slowly returns to full sensory perception.

1732 ROGERS, PAULA (pseud.)
      see LINDSAY, ANNA FISHER (1896-)

1733 ROISDAL, AGNES (pseud.)
      Defend My Mother. New York: Vantage, 1951. 226pp.

      The daughter of Norwegian immigrants, she tells in a
      third-person narrative of a New York childhood marred by
      parental dissension; in 1914 she is sent to a Norwegian farm
      to stay with relatives for two years; after her return her
      mother's death by drowning and her residence with her father
      and step-mother intensify her tension and ambivalence.

1734 ROLLIN, BETTY
      First, You Cry.   Philadelphia: Lippincott, 1976.   189pp.

      A magazine editor, television news correspondent, and
      writer, she describes with candor the shock of a diagnosis
      in 1974 of breast cancer that threatens her previously healthy,
      successful "golden life"; grateful for her mother's fighting
      spirit, she passes from an initial euphoria generated by the
      care and attention of others to a wry assessment of "my
      crazy time, " a series of emotional ups and downs; she
      struggles with ever-present fears of cancer's recurrence
      and death.

1735 ROMBERG, MARGARET
      Time Out of Mind; A Mosaic of Places and People.   San
      Antonio, Tex. : Naylor, 1964.   186pp.

      Her marriage is followed by far-flung adventures: she
      accompanies her professor husband to Hawaii in 1915 and
      attends the Queen's funeral; she travels and camps in the
      western U. S. ; she tours central Europe in 1925, observing
      the effects of the war; she tells of a summer stay with a
      Mexican family to escape the Texas heat; she travels without

her family to the Far East to sightsee and to attend a popu-
lation control convention in India.

1736   ROME, FLORENCE
        The Scarlett Letters.   New York: Random House, 1971.
        209pp.

        An advertising writer married to a composer, she joins
        her husband when he is invited to adapt Gone with the Wind
        as a musical for the Japanese theatre; using her letters
        home and some connecting narrative, she writes a humorous
        account of "my romance with Tokyo," cultural differences,
        rehearsals, and the drama of opening night.

1737   ROOSEVELT, ANNA ELEANOR
        see ROOSEVELT, ELEANOR (1884-1962)

1738   ROOSEVELT, ELEANOR (1884-1962)   NAWM
        The Autobiography of Eleanor Roosevelt.   New York: Harp-
        er, 1961.   454pp.

        The volume includes shortened versions of This Is My
        Story (see companion volume), This I Remember and On My
        Own (see below) and an additional section entitled "The
        Search for Understanding"; she discusses her continued
        strenuous traveling and lecturing on behalf of international
        communication, understanding, and peace; not particularly
        introspective, she notes that her personal objectives are
        her public objectives and that it is necessary "to grasp op-
        portunity for broader experience when it appears" for "life
        was meant to be lived."

1739   On My Own.   New York: Harper and Row, 1958.   241pp.

        Opening with a discussion of her adjustments after her
        husband's death in 1945, she describes her attendance as the
        only woman at the 1946 organizational meeting for the United
        Nations in London, beginning her long association with the
        U. N. and its Human Rights Commission; she engages in ex-
        tensive foreign travel, including trips to Germany, Japan,
        and Russia, and re-enters politics in 1956, campaigning for
        Stevenson.

1740   This I Remember.   New York: Harper, 1949.   387pp.

        Writing a second autobiographical volume in a detached
        controlled tone, the wife of President Franklin D. Roosevelt
        tells of ways in which the "personal life of the family" is

sacrificed to public interest; learning to be a keen political
observer for her husband early in his career, she rises to
the demands of her role as First Lady, establishing thrift,
common sense, and hospitality as key values at the White
House; she builds strong relations with the "women of the
press" and writes herself, valuing her financial independence
to pursue worthy projects; after her husband's death, she
reflects on her adjustments, contributions, and a few deep
friendships, commenting that she thinks she "lived those
years very impersonally."

1741 Your Teens and Mine, with Helen Josephine Ferris. Garden
      City, N.Y.: Doubleday, 1961. 189pp.

      Drawing on material from earlier autobiographies, she
      focuses on universal concerns of teenagers; anxious because
      she is not as beautiful as her mother, troubled by separa-
      tions from her drinking father, raised by her grandmother,
      she describes loneliness, attachment to books, suffering
      through social events, overcoming fears of all kinds, lack
      of self-confidence, learning how to think critically, learning
      tolerance through travel; she makes each point with a per-
      sonal anecdote.

1742 ROOSEVELT, ELEANOR BUTLER ALEXANDER (1888?-1960)
      Day Before Yesterday; The Reminiscences of Mrs. Theodore
      Roosevelt, Jr. Garden City, N.Y.: Doubleday, 1959.
      478pp.

      Of a socially prominent New York family, she marries
      the younger Roosevelt in 1910 and is soon caught up in his
      business and political career; during World War I, she aids
      the YMCA in France and cares for her wounded husband;
      she speaks publicly in her husband's New York campaigns;
      in the late 1920's she joins two Field Museum expeditions to
      Asia; she does civic volunteer work when her husband is
      governor in Puerto Rico and the Philippines; during World
      War II, she serves with the Red Cross in Europe; in addition
      to her public service, she is proud of her three children's
      accomplishments.

1743 ROOSEVELT, PATRICIA PEABODY
      I Love a Roosevelt. Garden City, N.Y.: Doubleday, 1967.
      387pp.

      A divorcée with four children, she becomes the fifth wife
      of Elliott Roosevelt in 1960, adjusting to her role in a prom-
      inent family with a combination of pride and insecurity; noting
      the "heroic stature" of Eleanor Roosevelt (see entry #1738),
      she describes the public and private aftereffects of her

mother-in-law's death; weathering financial scandal and debt and the death of an infant son, she later supports her husband's activities in Florida politics.

1744 ROSAMOND, SISTER M.
see NUGENT, SISTER ROSAMOND

1745 ROSE, ANNA PERROTT
see WRIGHT, ANNA MARIA ROSE (1890-1968)

1746 ROSENBERG, ETHEL GREENGLASS (1915-1953)   NAWM
The Rosenberg Letters. London: Dennis Dobson, 1953.
191pp.

Arrested on espionage charges in 1950, tried in 1951, and executed in 1953, she exchanges letters with her husband during their imprisonment; she expresses her intense, unwavering love and devotion to her husband, her agonized concern and "frenzied longing" for her two young sons, her disbelief over the "ever-narrowing circle of tightening time"; she writes little on external events as fruitless appeals proceed, except for a single moving letter to President Eisenhower; the powerful collection includes her last letter to her sons.

1747 ROSS, DOROTHY
Stranger to the Desert. New York: Wilfred Funk, 1959.
249pp.

Born and raised in England, her sudden marriage to an American cattle rancher finds her unprepared for motherhood and a homestead on the Texas range just after the turn of the century; she presents an amusing juxtaposition of cultures as she adjusts to camping, hunting, isolation, and monotonous housework; after eight years, she leaves to settle in California.

1748 ROSTENBERG, LEONA AND MADELEINE BETTINA STERN
Old and Rare: Thirty Years in the Book Business. New
York: Abner Schram, 1974. 234pp.

Writing alternate chapters with articulate warmth and humor, she tells of her graduate studies at Columbia in 1932-1933 and her studies in the history of printing in Strasbourg; Nazism in pre-war Strasbourg overrides her intellectual exhilaration there, and she returns to the U.S. to an apprenticeship in a rare book store, continuing to write for scholarly journals; she opens her own business with Stern (see entry

#1926) and describes her delight on acquisitions and sales, offering portraits of other booksellers, librarians, and scholars.

1749   ROTH, LILLIAN (1910-   )
        Beyond My Worth.   New York: Frederick Fell, 1958.
        317pp.

        Writing five years after the publication of her autobiography I'll Cry Tomorrow, she describes her struggles during a gradual comeback as an actress and nightclub performer; having conquered alcoholism with the aid of her supportive husband, she searches for religious faith and accepts the heavy responsibility of advising and assisting others in need; she reflects on the joys of entertaining and the rewards of "the full utilization of my talents."

1750   I'll Cry Tomorrow, with Mike Connolly and Gerold Frank.
        New York: Frederick Fell, 1954.   292pp.

        A Hollywood star writes to re-establish her integrity and dignity after sixteen years of alcoholism and despair; her parents' ambitions for her career as a child actress cause unhappiness, and she moves into several ill-considered marriages which inevitably fail as she descends into a sordid life of excessive drink, illness, and self-loathing; through A. A. and the love of a good husband, she finally finds support, hope and the courage to stage a career comeback.

1751   ROTHMAN, ESTHER P.
        The Angel Inside Went Sour.   New York: McKay, 1970.
        333pp.

        A teacher and psychologist writes a tough, compassionate narrative of her experiences in 1959 as principal of a New York City school for aggressive girls; after the shock of the first day, she struggles to establish mutual respect between the teachers and students, breaking through violence, obscenity, and confrontations; she also struggles to obtain needed assistance for the girls from legal, social, and educational authorities.

1752   ROWE, DOROTHY SNOWDEN
        At the End of the Pond; Historical Reminiscences of Weekapaug, R. I.   Stonington, Conn. :   Pequot Press, 1963.   64pp.

        Against a background of historical lore, she describes a summer resort which served as a place of "magic revitalization" for 63 years for her family and friends; her visits

there begin in 1899; she builds a house there in 1954; her
random recollections include tales of two hurricanes, social
pastimes, and favorite recipes.

1753   RUBENS, DORIS
        see JOHNSTON, DORIS RUBENS

1754   RUBINSTEIN, HELENA (1870-1965)   NAWM
        My Life for Beauty. New York: Simon and Schuster, 1966.
        251pp.

        Born in Poland, the famous cosmetician grows up in an
"intensely feminine household" in which beauty care is a
daily ritual; she establishes beauty salons first in Australia,
then in London, enjoying a rapidly expanding business; she
marries, becomes an "avid collector" of art, and flourishes
in New York and Paris social circles, although her success
costs her her first marriage; stating "I believe in hard
work," she rebuilds her European business after World War
II, continues to devote herself to her career; her account
concludes with reflections and tips on beauty.

1755   RUBY, EDNA R.
        Shorthand with Champagne. Cleveland: World, 1965. 246pp.

        In a chatty, anecdotal account, a public stenographer em-
ployed by a Beverly Hills luxury hotel describes her unpredictable, varied duties for numerous exciting and famous
clients; she relies on her genuine interest in people to see
her through some unusual situations.

1756   RUDOLPH, MARGUERITA (1908?-)
        The Great Hope. New York: John Day, 1948. 175pp.

        She writes of her childhood and youth in the Ukraine, pre-
senting a child's perspective on the Russian revolution and
its effect on her family's life; she touches on her new opportunities for schooling, dangers from anti-revolutionary bandits, her patriotic desires to be useful to the new Russia;
on an uncle's invitation she emigrates to the U.S. in 1923
but maintains close contact with family members who stay
behind; she writes in the third person.

1757   RUNBECK, MARGARET LEE (1905-1956)
        Miss Boo Is 16. Boston: Houghton Mifflin, 1956. 263pp.

        A prolific novelist and short story writer provides an en-
tertaining series of family anecdotes loosely clustered around

three topics: her teen-age daughter and the perils and
pleasures of adolescence, her own memories of a childhood
full of security and love and poverty enlivened by an imaginative mother, and her Japanese houseman and cook who is
both dignified and eccentric.

1758 RUSH, HELEN SHERKANOWSKI
      Rooms to Let, with Mary Sherkanowski.   Boston: Houghton
      Mifflin, 1952. 275pp.

      A former jeep driver, she and her sister become "over-
      worked landladies" in Boston for three years; her experi-
      ences with "funny, pathetic, wonderful" roomers provide
      anecdotes which offer glimpses into the variety of human
      nature.

1759 RUSKAY, SOPHIE
      Horsecars and Cobblestones.   New York: Beechhurst, 1948.
      240pp.

      Growing up in turn-of-the-century New York City, the
      daughter of Russian Jewish immigrants, she enjoys school
      days, street life, dancing and elocution lessons, summers
      in the Catskills, visits to the Yiddish Theater; her parents
      own and operate a garment-making shop, and her mother is
      a powerful figure in the family business, saving it from
      strikes and depression; the account closes with her youthful
      aspirations toward independence.

1760 RUSS, LAVINIA
      The Girl on the Floor Will Help You.   Garden City, N.Y.:
      Doubleday, 1969.   140pp.

      A buyer for children's books in Scribner's New York City
      bookstore recalls her own childhood joys with books; de-
      lighted by her life and career in New York, she lectures on
      children's literature, writes two books of her own, and cre-
      ates a television show on which children review children's
      books.

1761 A High Old Time, or How to Enjoy Being a Woman Over
      Sixty.   New York: Saturday Review Press, 1972.   141pp.

      In a series of anecdotes cast in the form of advice to
      others, she describes "defining and redefining" her role af-
      ter retirement; with grace and spirit, she discusses groom-
      ing and fashion, the pursuit of good health, altered relation-
      ships with her adult children and other young people, finan-
      cial adjustments, the use of leisure time, and inevitable re-
      flections on death.

1762   RUSSELL, BEATRICE
        Living in State. New York: McKay, 1959. 272pp.

        She marries an aspiring Foreign Service officer in 1947,
        settling in Ethiopia in 1951, learning her duties as a Foreign
        Service wife and coping with the heavy and exacting social
        schedule; in a sensible and straightforward manner, she tells
        of the "post-enchantment period," householding and raising
        children in difficult circumstances on later assignments in
        Tunisia and Lebanon; she closes with their home leave in
        the midst of Lebanon's 1957 civil unrest.

1763   RUSSELL, LUCY PHILLIPS (1862-   )
        A Rare Pattern. Chapel Hill: University of North Carolina
        Press, 1957. 185pp.

        Writing for her children and grandchildren, she presents
        the "plain and simple, intricate and complex" pattern of her
        life; raised in Chapel Hill in an educated, cultured family,
        she tells of the dislocations of reconstruction, the "lean
        years" from 1869 to 1875, providing portraits of her father
        and aunt, prominent scholars; she teaches school, then mar-
        ries a merchant in 1883, raises three children, and is active
        in women's clubs; her later years are darkened by her hus-
        band's long invalidism and death, and the deaths of many
        other close family members.

1764   RUTH, CLAIRE MERRITT
        The Babe and I, with Bill Slocum. Englewood Cliffs, N.J.:
        Prentice-Hall, 1959. 215pp.

        "In love with a legend," she writes to present the facts;
        when she first meets Babe Ruth in 1923, she is a mediocre
        actress, supporting her daughter and herself; after a long
        courtship, they marry in 1929, and her life revolves around
        caring for his needs and career; she notes his particular
        affinity for children, and describes her immense sorrow that
        there was no place for him in baseball after his playing days
        were over; she closes with his death in 1948.

1765   RUTHERFORD, BLANCHE SCOTT
        One Corner of Heaven. San Antonio, Tex.: Naylor, 1964.
        294pp.

        Writing to preserve Texas history, she portrays the daily
        life of a typical family in a closely knit community; her fam-
        ily settles in Texas in 1903, invited to establish a school;
        her home is a place of security, rest, and beauty, providing
        a focus together with the church and school, "meccas in the
        wilderness"; she serves as a teacher for thirty-one years,

describing times of hardships and loneliness; she closes noting various signs of progress.

1766   RUTLAND, EVA (1917-   )
       The Trouble with Being a Mama.   New York: Abingdon,
       1964.   143pp.

       Raised in a poor family during the depression but with a
       sense of "dignity and worth," a black woman describes the
       daily cares of motherhood; she discusses racial discrimination against her husband in the Air Force during World War
       II and her desire to keep her children free from prejudice;
       experiencing "integration qualms" in California, she nevertheless works with civic groups and imbues her children with
       pride in their black heritage.

1767   RUY BARBOSA, DIAN
       see   BARBOSA, DIAN RUY

1768   RYAN, MARGARET G.
       African Hayride.   New York: Rand McNally, 1956.   255pp.

       An adventurous, wealthy widow tells of her travels through
       twelve African countries with her driver and a custom-built
       car; she offers vivid descriptions of the rugged roads and
       desert terrain; stranded in a Sahara outpost for weeks, she
       endures sandstorms and hunger; later she visits an elephant
       training station, travels through Kenya during Mau Mau
       troubles, tours Angolan diamond mines (to which she is
       connected through her late husband), survives a bout with
       malaria, and meets the sultan of Zanzibar; her entertaining
       account reveals an unpretentious, gregarious woman who delights in her many friendly encounters with African people.

1769   ST. JOHNS, ADELA ROGERS
Final Verdict.   Garden City, N.Y.: Doubleday, 1962.
512pp.

    A writer whose father is a famous trial lawyer feels herself first and always "Earl Rogers' daughter" and she presents a subtle portrait of a remarkable relationship wherein they "lived and worked as one" from her childhood, combining her intuition and his legal genius; she learns deep lessons in human nature, both from legal cases and from her loss of innocence as she slowly comprehends her father's alcoholism; her final pain is having to commit him against his wishes, for she finds it difficult to forgive herself, even after the intense introspection of her book, "his story and mine."

1770   The Honeycomb. New York: Doubleday, 1969. 598pp.

    "One of the first woman reporters," she opens her rambling, anecdotal account with the debate on "Modern Woman"; settling in Hollywood to make a home for her children, she describes the town's magic and schizophrenia; among her various stories and scoops, she writes of the Hauptmann trial and the depression unemployed; she tells political anecdotes of her years in Washington, D.C. during the 1930's and 1940's; included are portraits of Anne Morrow Lindbergh (see entry #1245) and Wallis Simpson (see entry #2157).

1771   SALISBURY, CHARLOTTE Y.
Asian Diary. New York: Scribner, 1967. 158pp.

    A writer, she accompanies her journalist husband in 1966 to Cambodia, Thailand, Burma, India, Mongolia, Siberia, and Japan; she spends her time sightseeing and is receptive to new colors, foods, cultures, enjoying the special attention of host governments; frustrated and appalled by the U.S. role in Viet Nam, she calls for international understanding.

1772   China Diary. New York: Walker, 1973. 210pp.

    A journalist and keen observer writes of six weeks in

China in 1972; balancing praise and criticism, she describes her visits to a commune, the Great Wall, a school, a hospital, a factory, museums, and the ballet; she meets both common people and prominent leaders, dining once with Premier Chou En-lai; comparing cultures upon her return home, she is impressed with Chinese cleanliness, courtesy, and friendliness.

1773   Russian Diary. New York: Walker, 1974. 179pp.

A writer accompanying her husband to Moscow reveals her sensitivity to the quality of Russian life and her love of the people through much keen observation; she contrasts the daily life of the Russian housewife with her own; the novelty of new sights gives way to her perceptions of bureaucracy, restrictions, invasions of privacy, and she is angry and sorrowful at the personal repercussions of political repression.

1774   SALKMANN, VICTORIA (pseud.)
        There Is a Child for You. New York: Simon and Schuster,
        1972.   221pp.

In this exploration of the adoption process, she describes her husband, her three young biological children, herself, and her family's strengths and weaknesses in some detail; she discusses her motives for requesting a black or racially mixed child, motives which lead to highly self-conscious probing of her identity and values; when the infant's racial background is unclear, she is further confused and probes more deeply, finally discovering that her love and sense of motherhood is immediate and unambiguous.

1775   SAMOSSOUD, CLARA CLEMENS
        see CLEMENS, CLARA

1776   SAMPLE, ZOLA BELLIS (1900-   )
        The House with the Jillion Memories; The Story of a Pioneer
        Homestead in Oklahoma.   New York: Exposition, 1957.
        99pp.

The first half of the book is a description of pioneer days recorded as if by the family house; the second half is a series of letters to her aged mother, in which nostalgic memories of family activities are tinged with the bitterness of her realization that her mother didn't want children and with her own sorrow at remaining childless; she grieves that her mother refuses to live with her.

1777   SAMS, JESSIE BENNETT (1917-   )
        White Mother.   New York: McGraw-Hill, 1957.   241pp.

   The account opens with a description of her childhood
poverty; burdened with the care of a bedridden father, fearful and shy, she and her twin sister alternate work and
school under the watchful eye of a neighbor; a white woman
intervenes: "when Miss Rossie came into our lives, hunger
and fear went out"; they work, learn to trust, are introduced
to art, music, education; she gradually but painfully grows
independent from her sister, who marries at 15; she learns
eventually that Miss Rossie cannot control everything in the
world; she graduates from college to a life of self-sufficiency
and strength.

1778   SANDBERG, SARA
        Mama Made Minks.   Garden City, N.Y.: Doubleday, 1964.
        182pp.

   Sidelined by polio, she becomes an observer and recorder
of the drama of her "incredibly gay family" and her mother's
Harlem fur store; "practically raised in the store," she offers a lively portrait of her dynamic Austrian Jewish mother,
a woman of charming idiosyncrasies and "a howling success
as a businesswoman."

1779   My Sister Goldie.   Garden City, N.Y.: Doubleday, 1968.
        202pp.

   Each chapter of this wry, vivacious account is a vignette;
in the 1920's, her family moves from Jewish Harlem to
Riverside Drive; her outgoing mother is a furrier with a
colorful clientele and the store becomes her window on the
world; she is the brains while her sister is the beauty, and
her mother's matchmaking attempts are varied and intense
for her "nice Jewish girls"; after the 1929 crash, poverty
and despair surround them; she begins writing, turning suc-
cessfully to "Jewish stories"; the book ends with her sister's
parallel success, a triumphant wedding.

1780   SANDBURG, HELGA
        Sweet Music: A Book of Family Reminiscence and Song.
        New York: Dial, 1963.   180pp.

   In this charming memoir of childhood by the youngest
daughter of Carl Sandburg, "nostalgia is wound and fastened
about songs": family songs, folk songs, labor songs; her
rich family life is full of people, love, activity, nature, animals, and rural freedom; briefly married, she returns with
her two children after World War II to the Sandburg family

farm, absorbing regional songs with each move; later she leaves "the natural life" to live in Washington, D. C. and to travel in search of ancestral roots in Scandinavia; she writes books and composes songs.

1781   SANDERS, MARION K.
       The Lady and the Vote.   Boston: Houghton Mifflin, 1956.
       172pp.

       An editor in Washington for international periodicals, she resigns in 1952 to run for Congress as a Democrat in New York State; she takes a lively but wry look at "our strange political folkways," which include women's "political limbo"; knowledgeable about foreign affairs, she resents being limited to women's topics but is glad to be in politics in spite of the frustrations.

1782   SANDFORD, EMILY WHITE
       West Meets East; Our Home in North Africa.   New York:
       Vantage, 1958.   165pp.

       She and her artist husband live in Tunis half of each year for many years beginning in 1909; emphasizing their first visit, she notes her vivid impressions of the "exotic pageant," of the brilliant social whirl in diplomatic circles, of enduring friendships, of travels along the northern coast, of her private productions as a playwright, of the magic and romance of local color to which she is drawn; writing with nostalgia and a sense of humor, she hopes to preserve the spirit of Islamic culture.

1783   SANDOZ, MARI (1896-1966)   NAWM
       Sandhill Sundays and Other Recollections.   Lincoln: University of Nebraska Press, 1970.   165pp.

       In ten vivid chapters written between 1929 and 1965 and originally published elsewhere, she tells of hard work as a child on the family homestead; her uncle is murdered in 1908 in a homesteader-cattlemen conflict, and other dramatic incidents include her father's snakebite, a prairie fire, and a blizzard; she notes a sense of brotherhood with Indians; her first phonograph brings the power of music into her life; she offers a portrait of the frontierswoman; she closes with a description of her later "outpost in New York."

1784   SANFORD, AGNES MARY WHITE
       Sealed Orders.   Plainfield, N. J.:   Logos International, 1972.
       313pp.

The author of religious works, novels, and children's books, she describes her childhood in China as a missionary's daughter and her return to China after receiving an American education; married in 1923 to an Episcopal priest, she continues her teaching and healing in China until 1925; back in the U. S., she finds her creativity thwarted by domesticity, and only through a spiritual reawakening is she able to rediscover her destiny as a teacher, faith healer, writer, and artist.

1785   SANFORD, MARCELLINE HEMINGWAY (1898-)
        At the Hemingways; A Family Portrait.   Boston: Little,
        Brown, 1961.   241pp.

Written by an older sister of Ernest Hemingway, the account describes a warm, active family life; her charming father is a doctor and her talented mother is an opera singer, teacher, and painter; she relates family summers on a lake; most of her account covers the years when the older children were still close.

1786   SANFORD, MOLLIE DORSEY (1838-1915)
        Mollie; The Journal of Mollie Dorsey Sanford in Nebraska
        and Colorado Territories, 1857-1866.   Lincoln: University
        of Nebraska Press, 1959.   210pp.

In this delightful account, written "because I do not want to be forgotten," she tells of going to "a wild unsettled country" at eighteen; dismayed by her log house, she nevertheless shoulders family responsibilities and grows in independence as a dressmaker and schoolteacher; married at twenty-one, she settles in Colorado in 1860 and describes her domestic activities under primitive conditions, raising her children, managing during her husband's long absences.

1787   SANTAMARIA, FRANCES KARLEN
        Joshua: Firstborn.   New York: Dial, 1970.   194pp.

She learns she's pregnant just before she and her writer husband go abroad and settle in Greece; sensitive to her position as a foreigner, she helps dispel "one country's myth about another"; she finds a woman doctor who runs a natural childbirth clinic, describes her prenatal preparation and her strenuous birth experience; her initial apprehension yields to common sense and instinct as she combines Greek and American child-rearing practices; she "meddles" by offering advice to her Greek friends; she discusses the position of Greek women, then closes her account with her return to the U. S. with her son.

1788   SARGENT, WYN
        My Life with the Headhunters.   Garden City, N. Y. :   Double-
        day, 1974.   310pp.

        A journalist, she and her twelve-year-old son join an ex-
        pedition in 1968 to explore the jungles of central Borneo;
        she describes in vivid detail the remote villages, the cus-
        toms and rituals of the people, and the hunger, illness, and
        hardships of her travels; initiated into the Dyak tribe, she
        feels an intense desire to help their dying culture with edu-
        cational and medical assistance; she marries the tribal chief
        in 1973, but is forced to leave the people she loves.

1789   SARTON, MAY (1912-)
        I Knew a Phoenix; Sketches for an Autobiography.   New York:
        Rinehart, 1959.   222pp.

        A poet, novelist, and teacher, she opens her highly artic-
        ulate account with sensitive evocations of her father's Belgian
        past and her mother's Welsh past; after her early rich ex-
        periences in a "progressive" school, she spends three years
        as a theater apprentice, then goes to Paris in 1931, hoping
        to become an actress and relishing "poverty and freedom";
        later in London, turning toward writing, she enjoys Huxley's
        friendship and notes the beginnings of a "sense of vocation. "

1790   Journal of a Solitude, 1970-1971.   New York: Norton, 1973.
        208pp.

        A poet and novelist seeks time to think and to be, "to
        take up my 'real' life again at last," to "clarify, clarify";
        in her New England solitude, she attempts to resolve her
        inner rage and violence, to cope with boredom, panic, and
        depression, to accept the end of a love relationship; reflect-
        ing on poetry making and on the woman artist, she searches
        for "the poise of the soul when it is in true balance. "

1791   Plant Dreaming Deep.   New York: Norton, 1968.   189pp.

        She weaves together the threads of ancestry and of her
        own experiences in this exploration of "all this house is and
        holds for me," describing her life of solitude illuminated by
        the rich reverberations of writing, taking lecture tours, tra-
        veling, enjoying guests, and gardening passionately.

1792   A World of Light.   New York: Norton, 1976.   254pp.

        Suggesting that "we become what we have loved," she
        celebrates the deep friendships that enrich her life from age

twenty-six to forty-five; she chronicles her change and growth from a relationship with an older woman who releases the poet in her, to an unflawed friendship that opens "the heart of France" to her, to a childhood teacher who reveals a lesson in living and dying, to a "fiercely demanding" friendship with a Russian Jew, to her intimate friendships with Elizabeth Bowen and Louise Bogan (see entry #226); she writes, as always, with depth and charm.

1793 SAUNDERS, JERALDINE
The Love Boats. New York: Drake Publishers, 1974. 245pp.

In a breezy tale, this former model recounts her six years as the only woman cruise director; in anecdotes of "nautical naughtiness" among passengers, officers, and crew members of numerous cruises all over the world, she describes various "types" and her own ways of handling men.

1794 SAVAGE, MILDRED SPITZ (1919-)
The Lumberyard and Mrs. Barrie. New York: Holt, 1952. 243pp.

Married to a lumberyard owner who is impractical, easygoing, and nearly without business acumen, she steps in to rescue the business in 1950 with common sense and natural management skills, fending off creditors and competition as she learns from the ground up.

1795 SAVARY, GLADYS SLAUGHTER
Outside the Walls. New York: Vantage, 1954. 206pp.

She presents her reminiscences of the years during the Japanese occupation of the Philippines; she settles in Manila in 1939 and manages a restaurant, from which location during the occupation she helps internees with food, money, and messages, relying on a loyal Filipino staff; French by marriage, she avoids internment, although she takes major risks with her vehemently anti-Japanese stand; she describes the chaotic last days of the war and her refusal to return to the U.S., wishing instead to remain and rebuild her restaurant.

1796 SCHENCK, LUCY REISSIG
Seven, Eight--Shut the Gate! The Heartwarming Story of an American Family. New York: Greenwich Book Publishers, 1958. 86pp.

In an account written to give her youngest son a sense of his family roots, she recalls her childhood as one of eight

children of a German-speaking minister; she provides anecdotes of a resourceful mother and a spirited family life; after her family's dispersal, annual reunions prompt the collection of her memories into a book.

1797 SCHERMAN, BERNARDINE KIELTY
      Girl from Fitchburg. New York: Random House, 1964.
      189pp.

      A columnist and writer of books for young people, she
describes her New England childhood in a charming evocation
of middle-class innocence at the turn of the century; the New
York of 1908 presents a gilded vision to a college girl; after
the "spiritual experience" of working in a Jewish orphan asylum, she lives on the fringe of the Bohemian life among
writers and left-wing activists; after her marriage, she enjoys a wide range of acquaintances, a "completely satisfying" family life with two children, and the world of books
due to her husband's position as a founder of the Book-of-
the-Month Club.

1798 SCHERMAN, KATHARINE
      Spring on an Arctic Island. Boston: Little, Brown, 1956.
      331pp.

      She and her husband, amateur ornithologists, join a sci-
entific expedition in 1954 to an unexplored island for an
"adventure in ecology"; she learns the "slow, peaceful,
arctic ways" of the Eskimos whose culture she admires;
her personal record of the "primeval northerness" is sensitive and articulate.

1799 SCHIFF, JACQUI LEE
      All My Children, with Beth Day. Philadelphia: M. Evans,
      1970. 233pp.

      She and her husband are psychiatric social workers who
take as many as twenty disturbed, frequently schizophrenic
children into their home for "re-parenting"; with detailed
descriptions of the needs, violent behavior, and accomplishments of each child, she notes her own learning and use of
regression techniques and her acceptance of the vast responsibility, examining her own feelings as she proceeds.

1800 SCHNABEL, MARTHA (1926-)
      Officer Mama. San Antonio: Naylor, 1973. 100pp.

      Writing with intense pride, she describes her desire for
a law enforcement career; supported by her husband and

daughter, she completes her training in 1958 and becomes
the first woman undercover narcotics agent; she earns several awards for her work; an injury sustained in her work
forces her retirement.

1801   SCHNEIDER, FRIEDA JOHNETTA (1911-)
       My Devotional Diary.   Grand Rapids, Mich.:   Eerdmans,
       1959.   95pp.

       The author of numerous tracts and devotional works, a
       Ph. D., and an invalid since 1926, she continues to offer
       counsel and indirect assistance to others, especially the
       handicapped, by way of her writing; often struggling against
       pain and self-pity, she uses personal incidents to illustrate
       religious points in brief chapters.

1802   SCHNEIDERMAN, ROSE (1882-1972)   NAWM
       All for One, with Lucy Goldthwaite.   New York: Eriksson,
       1967.   264pp.

       Born in Russian Poland, she emigrates to the U.S. in
       1890 and is forced to enter the labor market at thirteen;
       her early work experiences lead to over fifty years in the
       labor movement, and she describes work for woman suffrage
       and her union struggles, traveling, educating, and organiz-
       ing; a close associate of Eleanor Roosevelt (see entry #1738),
       she works for the Women's Trade Union League, the Interna-
       tional Ladies' Garment Workers' Union, and the Labor Board
       of the National Recovery Act; she stresses the "spiritual
       side" of worker solidarity.

1803   SCHOLDER, VEDA
       Along Navajo Trails; An Account of the Intrepid Labor of
       Love by Veda Scholder Among the Navajos, as told to Violet
       May Cummings.   Washington, D. C.:   Review and Herald,
       1964.   189pp.

       A Seventh-Day Adventist and trained nurse tells of her
       missionary work during the 1950's, struggling against ignor-
       ance, superstition and dirt; each chapter focuses on a person
       in need; she finds a mixture of rewarding and discouraging
       responses as she raises an Indian infant, adopts a young boy
       for "taming and training," holds camp meetings, and offers
       health care.

1804   SCHROETER, ELIZABETH ARLENE
       From Here to the Pinnacles: Memories of Mennonite Life
       in the Ukraine and in America.   New York: Exposition,
       1956.   320pp.

Writing "to inspire others," she opens with recollections
from her youth in the Ukraine; her rebellious streak is tempered by a childhood pledge to be "a pious Mennonite"; from
a poor, hard working family, she has a fierce determination
to gain an education and is honored to study at a girls'
school until she is sixteen; when her money runs out, she
teaches, then emigrates to the U.S. at seventeen just before
World War I; after hard times she pursues university training through her triumphant Ph.D., sustained by "the rich
inner resources of the Mennonite life"; she writes in the
third person.

1805   SCHULTZ, EDNA MOORE
       They Said Kathy Was Retarded.   Chicago: Moody Press,
       1963.   128pp.

       A mother describes her anguish after the birth of a
daughter in 1951 when she is told that the child is a mongo-
loid with "no mind"; supported by her religious faith, she
copes with discouragement from doctors, and insensitivity
from others; working intensively with her daughter at home,
she finds joy in the child's progress and eventual ability to
enroll in school; the account closes with her daughter's
death from leukemia.

1806   SCHUSSLER, EDITH MAY (1894-)
       Doctors, Dynamite and Dogs.   Caldwell, Id.:   Caxton, 1956.
       189pp.

       In this "chronicle of real happenings on the last frontier,"
she describes strenuous times in Montana between 1907 and
1909; her husband is a doctor with the railroad builders and
she joins him to help in the primitive hospital, becoming
toughened to lawlessness and tragedy; she provides portraits
of local characters and she substitutes as "cook and flunky"
when needed; returning after her husband's death in 1949,
she finds she alone remains to tell the tale.

1807   SCHUYLER, PHILIPPA DUKE (1932-1967)
       Adventures in Black and White.   New York: Robert Speller,
       1960.   302pp.

       A talented composer and pianist and the daughter of a
racially mixed marriage, she describes her youth as a child
prodigy without regrets; drawing from diaries from 1950 to
1960, she tells of her concert travels "among black and
white people" in sixty countries of Europe, Asia, and Africa;
she maintains a "deep warmth of affection for all peoples."

1808   Good Men Die.   New York: Twin Circle Publishing Co.,
        1969.   256pp.

   This is a polemical, anti-communist account of her travels as a foreign correspondent and pianist in Viet Nam in
1966 and 1967; she describes the horrors of hospitals, notes
euphemistic military news releases, complains of harassment
and obstruction by U.S. officials, describes crime and corruption in Saigon, visits dangerous northern areas, is touched
by the plight of children in Viet Nam; she emphasizes her
great admiration for the Vietnamese people and culture; she
says little of her own occasional concerts.

1809   SCHWARTZ, FRANCIE (1944-   )
        Body Count.   San Francisco: Straight Arrow, 1972.   116pp.

   She writes a slangy, tough, cynical account of a series of
bodies, men with and without names, "that pass through my
life without touching my soul"; writing at twenty-seven, she
tells of incidents with drugs, psychiatrists, "depressing
game-ridden scenes."

1810   SCHWARTZ, HELENE E.
        Lawyering.   New York: Farrar, Straus and Giroux, 1976.
        308pp.

   A lawyer and professor, she describes the daily life of a
constitutional lawyer and the effect that being a woman has
had on her career; having earned her degree in 1965, she
chafes under restrictive work in a Wall Street firm, and
arrives at a "personal turning point" when she is compelled
to take a stand against sexism in the law team that handles
the Chicago Eight case from 1970 to 1972; she later works
with a legal collective on behalf of demonstrators during the
1972 Republican convention; she feels the personal impact of
professional women's solidarity.

1811   SCHWERIN, DORIS HALPERN
        Diary of a Pigeon Watcher.   New York: Morrow, 1976.
        288pp.

   A composer, she produces an intense, moving account of
her five-year wait to re-enter time after cancer surgery;
her attention shifts from herself to pigeons, which she describes with unabashed anthropomorphism, finding "coded
messages" in their instinctive behavior as parents and off-
spring; provided with "signals from my inner space," she
creates a profound portrait of her own parents and her relationship with them.

1812   SCOTT, ANN (pseud.)
        Woman with Arthritis; The True Story of a Recovery.   New
        York: Abelard-Schuman, 1957.   238pp.

        A business executive, writer, and lecturer, she describes
        her "unorthodox experiences in the development and cure of
        arthritis" through psychotherapy; she is convinced of the
        emotional origins of the disease in her struggle against
        "woman's role," her husband's affair, her mother's death,
        and her hysterectomy; she searches for a way to "live com-
        pletely as a woman. "

1813   SCOTT, TONI LEE (1933-   )
        A Kind of Loving, ed. Curt Gentry.   Cleveland: World,
        1970.   205pp.

        A professional singer from the age of fourteen, her child-
        hood is marked by the absence of both parents and years of
        minor troubles with the authorities; at nineteen, she is in a
        motorcycle accident and maintains a facade of toughness
        through months of hospitalization and two amputations; en-
        joying the Hollywood social whirl and singing on television
        and in nightclubs, she establishes a foundation to help the
        handicapped and is personally involved with amputees; she
        later suffers still more with an arm injury, a broken back,
        and throat cancer, but she maintains her courageous outlook.

1814   SCOTT-MAXWELL, FLORIDA PIER (1883-   )
        The Measure of My Days.   New York: Knopf, 1968.   150pp.

        A writer and Jungian psychologist offers her articulate
        notebook reflections of the "intense and varied experiences
        of old age"; she exclaims "my eighties are passionate," and
        discusses womanhood, religion, the "death of time," and the
        "weight of hope" for her children.

1815   SCOVEL, MYRA
        The Chinese Ginger Jars, with Nelle Keys Bell.   New York:
        Harper & Row, 1962.   189pp.

        A nurse, she accompanies her doctor husband to a mis-
        sionary post in China in 1930; after intensive language and
        culture study, she teaches her own five children over the
        years; she describes the Japanese occupation of their town
        in the late 1930's and her caring for her wounded husband
        as they remain prisoners in their home; after Pearl Harbor,
        they are interned but remain together; repatriated to the
        U. S. in 1943, she bears a sixth child; in 1946 she returns
        to China with her family and notes events during the revolu-
        tion; in 1951, after much harassment, they leave China.

1816   The Happiest Summer. New York: Harper & Row, 1971.
        117pp.

    A missionary and writer, she offers an intensely family
oriented account of "the high point of my motherhood"; of
her six grown children, five are married and have children
of their own, and the summer includes the marriage of her
last daughter and the birth of another grandchild; with all of
her children married, she feels she moves into "a new kind
of motherhood" in addition to her work on the manuscript
for a children's book.

1817   Richer by India. New York: Harper & Row, 1964. 151pp.

    After twenty-one years in China, she and her husband, a
medical missionary, settle with three of their six children
in the Punjab in 1953; candid about her initial misgivings,
she nevertheless undertakes intensive language study, organizes a medical library, welcomes visiting missionaries,
leads a student discussion group, and writes about her experiences for a church magazine; when she returns to the
U. S. in 1959, she finds she had struck deep roots in India;
her account is highly articulate.

1818   To Lay a Hearth. New York: Harper & Row, 1968. 148pp.

    After thirty years of missionary work in China and India
(see other works) with her husband, she settles permanently
in the U. S. in 1959; she is sensitive to her own ambivalence toward America and Americans, seeing new things with
a fresh and sometimes critical eye; in 1961 she welcomes
the challenge of a job in church journalism; she feels a
strong need to establish a permanent home, roots for her
four grown children and her first grandchildren.

1819   SCRIABINE, HELENE
        see SKRJABINA, ELENA

1820   SEAMANDS, RUTH (1916-   )
        Missionary Mama; the lighter side of the labors of those who
        serve the Lord in strange, exotic vineyards, revealed in de-
        lightfully realistic letters from India. New York: Greenwich
        Book Publishers, 1957. 128pp.

    Through letters written from 1936 to 1956 she traces her
courtship, service as a missionary in India from 1936 to
1940, from 1946 to 1953, and from 1954 to 1956; she tells
of housekeeping, typical daily activities, the births of four
daughters, and "loneliness, crises, and hard work."

1821   SEARGEANT, HELEN HUMPHREYS (1878-)
       House by the Buckeye Road.   San Antonio: Naylor, 1960.
       210pp.

          An Arizona pioneer in the early 20th century, she for-
       sakes city life for farm life when she marries; with mock
       grumbling, she describes her hard domestic and farm work,
       yet she pays nostalgic tribute to the home and the hard
       work and responsibility for which it stands; she includes
       anecdotes of farm workers and neighbors, of Arizona min-
       ing, and of some local history.

1822   San Antonio Nexapa.   New York: Vantage, 1952.   396pp.

          Led by her father, an inveterate pioneer, her family
       settles on a wilderness coffee plantation in Mexico in 1888;
       she throws herself into self-sufficient jungle life with energy
       and enthusiasm, enjoying contact with a neighboring Indian
       family, adventures in the nearby mountains, studies with her
       mother; her account, based on letters, closes with her de-
       parture for the U. S. in 1905.

1823   SEBASTIAN, FANNIE B.
       One of Ten.   Boston: Christopher, 1965.   185pp.

          A poet and novelist of unusual integrity, pride, and in-
       dustriousness, she tells of her large pioneer family in which
       religion and education are strong forces; later widowed twice,
       she teaches school, fully believing in the power of literature
       and the rewards of poetry; she writes in a flowery, oblique
       style.

1824   SEEMAN, ELIZABETH
       In the Arms of the Mountain; An Intimate Journal of the
       Great Smokies.   New York: Crown, 1961.   251pp.

          An artist and designer, "avid for firsthand experience,"
       she trades the city for a mountain farm with her husband;
       naïve but happy pioneers, their isolation is relieved by a
       large collection of animals; supporting her convalescent hus-
       band by her drawing, they enter difficult straits when her
       sight fails and they must try to make the farm self-sufficient;
       a hard winter brings despair and collapse, "our rout," but
       she stoically accepts all experiences.

1825   SEGAL, LORE GROSZMANN (1928?-)
       Other People's Houses.   New York: Harcourt, Brace &
       World, 1958.   312pp.

A writer, she presents a sensitive portrayal of her own geographical, economic, and psychological dislocation as a Viennese Jew during and after World War II; she is first sent to English camps with other Jewish children in 1938; reunited with her parents, she lives with several foster families while her mother struggles with exhausting domestic work and her father gradually collapses mentally and physically and dies; her three years of college in London are euphoric; then periods with her extended family, in the Dominican Republic (1948) and in the U.S. (1951) bring renewed benevolent interference and tensions as she is "surrounded by calamity."

1826   SEGAL, MARILYN M.
Run Away, Little Girl.   New York: Random House, 1966.
234pp.

Her fifth child, born prematurely, is handicapped by cerebral palsy, and she tells of her own mental and emotional adjustments as a mother; hopeful, yet realistic, she learns a great deal about the condition, and carries out a strenuous physical therapy program with energy, love, and imagination, involving her entire family and placing great value on the enriching experience.

1827   SEIBELS, FANNY MARKS (1884-   )
Wishes Are Horses; Montgomery, Alabama's First Lady of the Violin; An Autobiography.   New York: Exposition, 1958.
250pp.

Describing her life as "a dream of music," she tells of her idyllic childhood, her dedication to the violin and musical studies in New York and in Europe, and her concertizing during the early years of the century while maintaining an active social life; she marries in 1912, raises two sons, and continues to teach and perform.

1828   SEKAQUAPTEWA, HELEN (1898-   )
Me and Mine; The Life Story of Helen Sekaquaptewa, as told to Louise Udall.   Tucson: University of Arizona Press,
1969.   262pp.

A Hopi woman of Arizona describes her happy and secure childhood, marked by the tribal necessities of food, clothing, and shelter and by various tribal ceremonies; a split among tribal factions in 1906 leads to the disintegration of village life and she is forced to attend a white school; hostile at first, she is later eager and is gradually "weaned away from home"; she marries in 1919, "rich in love," and tells of her hard work raising ten children on an Idaho ranch.

1829   SELBY, HAZEL BARRINGTON
        Home to My Mountains.   Princeton, N. J. :   Van Nostrand,
        1962.   255pp.

        At sixty, she returns to the freedom of a pioneer home-
        stead in northern Idaho after a business and family interlude
        of forty years; she relives her rhapsodic introduction to the
        land as a young bride and rejoices in the present reclama-
        tion, surrounded by echoing memories; she writes with sen-
        sitivity of ten years building a home, meeting local charac-
        ters, working to establish a school and mail delivery; she
        reaps the rewards of age, balancing work, recreation, and
        mental stimulation.

1830   SELL, HILDEGARD LORETTA (1906?-)
        Over 50--So What! with Adele Whitely Fletcher.   New York:
        Devin-Adair, 1962.   184pp.

        In a bouncy, rambling account colored by nostalgia for
        her Wisconsin childhood, a famous supper-club entertainer
        tells of her strenuous career and of the public and private
        aspects of her life; afflicted with shyness, she overcomes
        insecurity by performing and living with a flair; an optimist,
        she willingly takes risks to make a name for herself; she
        is devoted to exercise, a good diet, and her beauty routine.

1831   SELVEY, VIRGINIA F.
        And My High Tower.   Garden City, N. Y. :   Doubleday, 1951.
        160pp.

        In 1945 she and her husband are troubled after twelve
        years of marriage and three children by discontent, finan-
        cial worries, and frustration; she describes the effect of
        her religious awakening on her daily family life; supporting
        her husband's decision to become a minister, she learns
        the role of a minister's wife, experiences spiritual growth,
        and finds happiness.

1832   SERMOLINO, MARIA
        Papa's Table d'Hôte.   Philadelphia: Lippincott, 1952.
        253pp.

        A journalist, she presents an entertaining, nostalgic ac-
        count of her childhood in the early decades of the twentieth
        century; her parents, Italian immigrants and owners of a
        Greenwich Village Italian restaurant, provide a marvelous
        heritage of unabashed gusto, hedonism, "love and laughter";
        she points out her own amusing confrontations with the cul-
        ture of American children; she closes with the death of her
        father, eulogizing him for having brought love, vitality, and
        gaiety to all.

1833   SETON, CELESTE ANDREWS
        Helen Gould Was My Mother-in-Law, as told to Clark An-
        drews.   New York: Crowell, 1953.   277pp.

        In 1933 she first meets her fiancé, one of four waifs
        adopted by Helen Gould Shepard, daughter of Jay Gould; she
        becomes acquainted with an atmosphere of extreme wealth,
        extreme conservatism, and extreme religiosity; after her
        marriage, she continues to visit various family estates,
        participating in slightly stilted but well-meaning forays into
        gardening, fancywork, and Bible study; her affection grows
        and she truly mourns the death of her mother-in-law.

1834   SETTLE, MARY LEE (1921?-)
        All the Brave Promises; Memories of Aircraft Woman 2nd
        Class 2146341.   New York: Delacorte, 1966.   176pp.

        A novelist, she volunteers for the women's auxiliary of
        the RAF in 1942 and goes to England full of innocence and
        romanticism; the only foreigner, she must forge a new
        identity in the "new world" of her comrades; vignettes de-
        scribe chilling incidents of fascism and tyranny, the subtle-
        ties of the English response to the war, her awareness of
        terror, the delicacy of maintaining morale; she produces an
        articulate, perceptive account of daily events behind the
        great historic event of war and their effects on the human
        spirit.

1835   SHAND, MARGARET CLARK (1851-1943)
        The Summit and Beyond, with Ora M. Shand.   Caldwell, Id.:
        Caxton, 1959.   326pp.

        In an account of thirty-eight years in the Yukon, she
        opens with her emigration from Scotland to the U.S. in 1889
        to marry a cousin and settle in San Francisco; she insists
        on accompanying her husband in search of Klondike gold in
        1897 and vividly portrays the chaos, danger, and grinding
        work of their early years, supporting her husband when he
        is stricken with snow-blindness; enjoying "unlimited strength,"
        she opens a roadhouse in 1900, and describes a stream of
        colorful characters who lodge there; when the roadhouse
        burns in 1918, she loses everything; her husband becomes
        terminally ill; for a time she runs the roadhouse alone, then
        decides to "go outside" and settle in California.

1836   SHAW, ANNA MOORE (1898-)
        A Pima Past.   Tucson: University of Arizona Press, 1974.
        263pp.

        Devoted to the presentation of traditional Pima culture,
        yet a devout Christian, able to take the best of two cultures,

she notes the "twofold learning" offered by her parents and
by schools; proud of her high school graduation and married
in 1920, she leaves the reservation and creates a happy
family life in Phoenix; with a strong belief in herself, she
becomes a civic leader, working for racial understanding;
after her children's education, she and her husband return
to the reservation and to a life close to nature; there she
publishes a book on Pima legends and continues her tireless
community work.

1837   SHEA, MARGARET HAMMEL (1910-)
        Tavern in the Town.   New York: Ives Washburn, 1948.
        215pp.

        The mother of two, she buys a country village restaurant
        in Maine in 1946 on impulse with a woman friend and her
        brother; the challenge of restoration and the exhilarating
        camaraderie of working with friends relieves an otherwise
        bleak post-war year, but she leaves the restaurant when it
        is finished, for the challenge is gone.

1838   SHEERIN, MARIA WILLIAMS
        The Parson Takes a Wife.   New York: Macmillan, 1948.
        204pp.

        In this warm, humane account a Virginia debutante mar-
        ries an Episcopal minister and tells of their work in parishes
        in Virginia, Texas, and Tennessee before and during the
        depression; with an emphasis on the social welfare of parish-
        ioners, she works against racism; she copes with "frequent
        uprootings" and childrearing as well in her varied roles; she
        finally settles in Washington, D. C.

1839   SHEKLOW, EDNA
        So Talently My Children.   Cleveland: World, 1966.   160pp.

        A playwright and advertising writer describes her child-
        hood in a New York Jewish family of thirteen during the de-
        pression years, "the prime of Mama's fighting condition";
        her mother emerges with an indomitable personality expressed
        in delightful, highly idiosyncratic English.

1840   SHEPARD, ELAINE
        Forgive Us Our Press Passes.   Englewood Cliffs, N. J.:
        Prentice-Hall, 1962.   301pp.

        A radio and television reporter describes her tomboy
        childhood and a brief fling as a movie actress; she estab-
        lishes her first important social contacts in Washington,

D. C. as the wife of a military man; after their separation, she wishes to become a foreign correspondent and exploits her contacts and good luck, learning much from other reporters; she covers American political conventions and recounts the excitement and adventure of her world travels and exclusive interviews with numerous political leaders, among them Castro.

1841 SHEPPARD, LILA
Dancing on the Desk Tops. Evanston, Ill.: Row, Peterson, 1960. 119pp.

An elementary school teacher uses anecdotes from her years of experience to illustrate observations and suggestions for the love and understanding of children; she describes various students and colleagues whom she has known.

1842 SHER, EVA GOLDSTEIN
Life with Farmer Goldstein. New York: Funk & Wagnalls, 1967. 247pp.

The daughter of Russian Jewish immigrants who settle in New Jersey to farm and deal in livestock, she describes the family pride and hard work as a lesson to the narrow-minded local people who fear "foreigners"; her lively portrayal of a spirited family life illuminates her parents' attempts to bridge the gap between the old and new worlds, Jewish and American customs.

1843 SHERMAN, JANE (1908-)
Soaring: The Diary and Letters of a Denishawn Dancer in the Far East, 1925-1926. Middletown, Conn.: Wesleyan University Press, 1976. 278pp.

Having trained from childhood at a New York City Denishawn school, she is asked to join the Far East tour; an ebullient teen-ager "learning heaps" in this association with Ruth St. Denis (see companion volume), she undertakes a grueling performance schedule interspersed with sightseeing and observations of native costuming and dance; at mid-tour she is "well, happy, fat, strong, and gay" but then becomes increasingly critical of the company and of the "artistic life"; in a brief afterward she notes the demise of the Denishawn spirit and her later association with Doris Humphrey (see entry #1004).

1844 SHERRY, MADAME (pseud.)
see BARNES, RUTH

1845   SHERWOOD, DEBBIE
        A Redhead in Red Square.   New York: Dodd, Mead, 1969.
        218pp.

        She writes a light, flippant account of a trip to Russia
        preceded by mock suspicions; she flirts with men, visits "a
        peasant's hut and a rich man's dasha," shops, copes with
        the eccentricities of Intourist; her reports of "one spine-
        tingling experience after another" are exaggerated for effect.

1846   SHICK, MAETE GORDON (1885-   )
        The Burden and the Trophy; An Autobiography, trans. Mary
        J. Reuben.   New York: Pageant, 1957.   209pp.

        Writing of her Lithuanian Jewish childhood and adoles-
        cence to provide cultural roots for her grandchildren, she
        then tells of her emigration to the U.S. in 1908 to be re-
        united with her husband; disappointed by their initial poverty,
        she takes the initiative and builds a successful dairy busi-
        ness while raising four children.

1847   SHIELDS, KARENA
        The Changing Wind.   New York: Crowell, 1959.   215pp.

        In an articulate, evocative account, she describes how her
        life is changed "profoundly and forever" when her father be-
        comes manager of an isolated jungle rubber plantation in
        Mexico; her education proceeds not only in the family library
        but also in the village and jungle, and in the melodrama and
        enchantment of plantation life; through encounters with a
        forest tribe and ancient Mayan culture, she discovers her
        own deepest identity; possessed by the jungle and the Indian
        tribe, her cultural separation is marked by a puberty ritual
        and she leaves the plantation, an end and a beginning.

1848   SHOR, JEAN BOWIE
        After You, Marco Polo.   New York: McGraw-Hill, 1955.
        294pp.

        Driven by wanderlust, she becomes the first woman to
        traverse part of Polo's route from Turkey to Pakistan; she
        provides marvelous anecdotes of royal hospitality, arrests
        by local police, border wars, and the drama of her hus-
        band's delirium in the desolate mountains; her vivid recol-
        lections include an account of her honeymoon trek across
        the Gobi desert after marrying in China, thrilling to
        danger and adventures; she is a writer for The National
        Geographic.

1849   SHORE, EVELYN BERGLUND (1917-   )
        Born on Snowshoes.   Boston: Houghton Mifflin, 1954.
        209pp.

        In an unpretentious narrative of a remarkable youth, she
        tells of growing up with her mother and two sisters in a
        cabin north of the Arctic Circle; from 1929 to 1941 she
        helps the family struggle to get out of debt, running a win-
        ter trapline, hunting bears and moose, fishing, caring for
        their dog team, making an annual supply trip to Civilization;
        finally tired of a trapper's life, she is married in 1941,
        ironically to a trapper.

1850   SHUMWAY, NINA PAUL
        Your Desert and Mine.   Los Angeles: Westernlore, 1960.
        322pp.

        In a memoir drawn partly from her diaries and contain-
        ing much local history, she tells of her family's pioneering
        in 1909 in California's Coachella Valley; initially dismayed,
        she soon grows to love "the desert's strange beauty"; taken
        from the valley by a premature marriage and a daughter's
        illness and death, she returns to resume an unusually close
        relationship with her mother and to share in the family's
        historic date cultivation; she begins writing, focusing on
        desert themes and her continuing explorations serve as a
        source for material; she herself pioneers on a desert home-
        stead, works through years of debt, marries again, and is
        widowed.

1851   SIBLEY, AGNES MARIE (1914-   )
        Exchange Teacher.   Caldwell, Id.:   Caxton, 1961.   230pp.

        A Missouri college teacher spends two years in England,
        enjoying a "multitude of impressions" from literary land-
        scapes, travels, and walks; she notes the warmth of her
        English colleagues and the enthusiasm of her English stu-
        dents; her sorrow at departing is softened by the satisfaction
        of lasting friendships.

1852   SIBLEY, CELESTINE
        A Place Called Sweet Apple.   Garden City, N.Y.:   Double-
        day, 1967.   240pp.

        A newspaper reporter and "content city dweller" in Atlan-
        ta, she is captivated in 1961 by an abandoned log cabin and
        enlists the help of her children and their college friends in
        its restoration; with the marriages of her two daughters, she
        decides to move permanently to the country; she describes
        her renovation work and notes the details of her first year
        living in the cabin, including recipes with her anecdotes.

1853 SIDDONS, ANNE RIVERS
      John Chancellor Makes Me Cry.   Garden City, N.Y.: Dou-
      bleday, 1975.   214pp.

      A journalist writes articulate, wry vignettes including
      those about her Christmas ritual and New Years' resolu-
      tions, an ice storm in Atlanta, animals, her teen years in
      the 1950's, a Princeton reunion, a visit by her husband's
      sons, her husband's unemployment, Maine, and parties; her
      account is roughly organized by the seasons of the year.

1854 SILLS, BEVERLY (1929-)
      Bubbles: A Self-Portrait.   Indianapolis: Bobbs-Merrill,
      1976.   240pp.

      Writing with buoyancy and vitality, the well-known soprano
      and opera star describes the influence of her mother's pas-
      sion for music and her own deep attachment to a vocal
      teacher; singing on radio as a child, she becomes "hooked"
      on opera, touring in light opera at sixteen; she notes the
      beginning of her operatic career in 1951, illuminated by
      "the joyful act of singing itself"; after marriage and the
      shock of her daughter's deafness and her son's mental re-
      tardation, she turns to opera as a refuge, to singing "as
      an act of giving"; she notes each stage of her career, in-
      cluding European tours and her Met debut in 1975.

1855 SIMKHOVITCH, MARY MELINDA KINGSBURY (1867-1951)
                                                          NAWM
      Here Is God's Plenty: Reflections on American Social Ad-
      vance.   New York: Harper, 1949.   184pp.

      A pioneer in social work and founder of Greenwich House
      in New York City, she believes in the "relatedness between
      our personal histories and our thoughts about life"; her chap-
      ters, in which autobiographical anecdotes are firmly con-
      sistent with her social views, are articulate personal reflec-
      tions on education, housing, recreation, the arts, welfare,
      community organization, politics, and religion.

1856 SIMON, CHARLIE MAY HOGUE (1897-)
      Johnswood.   New York: Dutton, 1953.   249pp.

      A highly articulate writer, she recounts "the full, rich
      life" she shared with her beloved late husband, the poet
      John Gould Fletcher; they began building their Arkansas home
      in 1941, enjoying the serenity of country life, the subtleties
      of nature; her perceptive and moving reflections are trig-
      gered by a suggestion to sell her home after Fletcher's death,
      but she remains with the consolation of memory.

1857   SINCLAIR, MARY CRAIG (1883?-1961)
        Southern Belle.   Phoenix, Ariz.:   Sinclair Press, 1957.
        407pp.

        She grows up in the quintessential romantic Old South,
        "an enchanted land," enjoying a secure, innocent childhood;
        the wider world of New York City introduces her to writers,
        intellectuals, and political radicals, and she is drawn to the
        zealous crusader Upton Sinclair; she marries in 1913 and
        becomes his close collaborator, noting that "his work was
        our life"; her anecdotes illuminate a multitude of acquaint-
        ances with literary and political figures.

1858   SIWUNDHLA, ALICE PRINCESS MSUMBA
        Alice Princess--An Autobiography.   Mountain View, Cal.:
        Pacific Press, 1965.   167pp.

        She tells of her childhood as an orphan in Nyasaland,
        determined to follow the ambitions of her older sister and
        rise above her village surroundings; with an ardent desire
        for education, she attends a mission school and rejects
        arranged marriages, only later marrying a fellow student
        in 1952; traveling to the U.S. in 1956 under missionary
        sponsorship, she earns two college degrees while raising
        three children; her story is one of courage and dedication
        to the intellect.

1859   My Two Worlds.   Mountain View, Cal.:   Pacific Press,
        1971.   198pp.

        African-born but educated in American mission schools
        and adopted by a white missionary family, she comes to the
        U.S. in 1956 after she is married and the mother of three;
        she attends college in Alabama, pursuing graduate work af-
        ter her B.A. and lecturing extensively to spread interna-
        tional and interracial love and understanding; at the same
        time she publishes her first autobiography (see above); with
        her strong interest in people and her warm and frank per-
        sonality, she cuts through prejudice.

1860   SKINNER, CORNELIA OTIS (1901-   )
        The Ape in Me.   Boston: Houghton Mifflin, 1959.   172pp.

        An actress and writer, she writes humorous vignettes
        including those on her unconscious imitation of others, her
        vague sense of history, her height, awkward departures,
        the vagaries of plane travel, stage fright, and her problems
        as one of the "manually tremulous"; some of the material
        was previously published in magazines.

1861   Bottoms Up! New York: Dodd, Mead, 1955. 208pp.

   The daughter of an actor and herself a fledgling actress
who turns to writing, she offers a series of delightful reminiscences of her early stage appearances, her stay in Paris
during which she wryly notes Franco-American cultural differences, her life as a "sports widow," and a hilarious ad-
dress to the American Gynecological Society; some chapters
originally appeared in The New Yorker.

1862   Family Circle. Boston: Houghton Mifflin, 1948. 310pp.

   Her account opens with the family backgrounds of first
her mother and then her father, both in the theatre, although her mother gives up her career to be a wife and
mother; the author offers a fine evocation of a child's perceptions; raised near Bryn Mawr, she describes her adolescent loves, petty defiance, resolution to become an actress despite her parents' assumptions that she won't; after
two undistinguished years in college and a year in Europe,
she makes her stage debut with her father.

1863   SKRJABINA, ELENA
        Siege and Survival: The Odyssey of a Leningrader, trans.
        Norman Luxenburg. Carbondale, Ill.: Southern Illinois
        University Press, 1971. 174pp.

   In a dramatic account of the 900-day siege of Leningrad,
a Russian-born professor opens with her ambivalence toward
the war due to her hatred of the Soviet regime and she is
torn between fleeing with her two sons and remaining with
her mother and nurse; with the "keenest anxiety" for the
children, she resists evacuation and life is reduced to the
search for food; responsible for her entire family, she begs
among the country peasants, sees a son grow weak, and
watches friends and neighbors starve to death; after the
death of her mother, she flees south by train, rejoicing in
the adequate food but caught in the chaos and anarchy as
Pyatigorsk falls to the Germans.

1864   SKUTT, MAYSIE (1908-   )
        World Safari; The Story of a Trip Around the World.   Pasa-
        dena, Cal.: Publication Press, 1954. 181pp.

   Accompanied by her husband, she travels for two months
by boat, train, and plane, visiting cities including Tokyo,
Manila, Hong Kong, Calcutta, Delhi, Beirut, Istanbul, Athens, and Paris; she describes people and sights.

1865   SLATER, LISA A. (1922?-)
        The Rape of Berlin.   Brooklyn: Pageant-Poseidon Ltd.,
        1972.   91pp.

        Born in Berlin, she volunteers as a teletypist for the
        German army at the onset of the war; fiercely anti-com-
        munist, she describes the horror, misery, and starvation
        of the Russian occupation of Berlin in 1944 in a strangely
        superficial account; she bears a child and loses her hus-
        band, thus forced to become self-reliant; she claims no
        knowledge of the holocaust.

1866   SLAUGHTER, LINDA WARFEL (1843-1920)
        Fortress to Farm; Or, Twenty-three Years on the Frontier,
        ed. Hazel Eastman.   New York: Exposition, 1972.   172pp.

        She writes a spirited account, part personal narrative
        and part local history, of the Dakota Territory in the
        1870's; married to an army surgeon, she tells of the "strange
        and peculiar charm" of army life in forts; in 1872 she settles
        in what becomes Bismarck observing the development of the
        town, the coming of the railroad that brings communication
        and growth; her account was first published in eastern news-
        papers in 1893 and 1894 to encourage settlement.

1867   SLAYDEN, ELLEN MAURY (1860-1926)
        Washington Wife: Journal of Ellen Maury Slayden from
        1897-1919.   New York: Harper & Row, 1963.   385pp.

        In a journal richly peopled with politicians and diplomats,
        the articulate wife of a Texas congressman offers lively,
        sharp observations of Washington social life; with her "pro-
        vincial eyes" opened and her "provincial prejudices" re-
        vised, she cuts through pretension with shrewd political ob-
        servations of several administrations; she comments on the
        Spanish-American War, relations with Mexico, World War
        I, the Women's Peace Party, woman's suffrage, and the flu
        epidemic of 1918.

1868   SLENCZYNSKA, RUTH (1925-)
        Forbidden Childhood, with Louis Biancolli.   Garden City,
        N.Y.:   Doubleday, 1957.   263pp.

        A concert pianist, she is the victim of the relentless am-
        bition and "fanatic perfectionism" of her father who trains
        her through violence; she studies in Philadelphia and Paris
        and makes her first U.S. concert tour at eight, never fully
        understanding "the grotesque pattern of abuse and exploita-
        tion I was trapped in" but only aware of her loneliness; a
        growing dread of the piano leads to a revolt and break with

her father at fourteen, and she plays only privately until eighteen, when the joy of music begins to return; after her marriage, she becomes a mature artist and her career gathers momentum.

1869   SLINEY, ELEANOR MATHEWS (1896?-)
        Forward Ho! New York: Vantage, 1960. 332pp.

Writing with nostalgia for a way of Army life that is fading, she offers her "impressions, thoughts and experiences" as an Army wife, having married a cavalry officer in 1915; she describes posts on the Mexican border, at West Point, in Washington, D. C. , in the Philippines, in Hawaii, and elsewhere in the U. S. ; in spite of many moves and adjustments, she notes the appeal and security of army hierarchy and discipline; on her own during World War II, she engages in volunteer work; after the war she joins her husband at the Presidio in San Francisco.

1870   SLOOP, MARY T. MARTIN (1873-1962)
        Miracle in the Hills, with LeGette Blythe.   New York:
        McGraw-Hill, 1953.   232pp.

A doctor in joint practice with her doctor husband, she settles among the mountain people in North Carolina in 1909, following her own pioneer and missionary impulses; dedicated to health care and education, she establishes a school system, campaigns against child marriage, campaigns for roads, organizes a school for native mountain weaving, and builds a hospital; she raises two children, both of whom also become doctors.

1871   SMALL, MARIE
        Four Fares to Juneau.   New York: McGraw-Hill, 1947.
        237pp.

Apprehensive about pioneering with two young children when unemployment prods her husband to settle in Alaska, she nevertheless endures a series of "minor and major disasters" including poverty, illness, and uncertainty, to build a wilderness home and enjoy pride in her "rocky route" and cherish Alaska's opportunities for "Freedom. "

1872   SMITH, BERTHA
        Go Home and Tell.   Nashville: Broadman, 1965.   154pp.

Assisted by old notes and letters, she writes of her forty-one years of missionary work in China beginning in 1917; making a covenant to sustain her "motherheart" with the

raising of spiritual children if she remains single, she
teaches in boarding schools, traveling and helping to establish country churches; she continues during the Japanese
occupation in 1937 and is interned and repatriated in 1941;
returning to post-war China, she finds her work hampered
by the communists and moves to a mission post in Formosa;
she retires at seventy.

1873   SMITH, CORINNA HAVEN PUTNAM LINDON (1876-   )
Interesting People; Eighty Years with the Great and Near-
Great.   Norman: University of Oklahoma Press, 1962.
456pp.

The articulate daughter of the distinguished publishing
Putnams, she marries a Boston artist and thus gains access
to the stimulating intellectual and artistic circles in Boston
as well as the New York literary world of her family; her
experiences in Egypt lead to her becoming a scholar of Islam; she campaigns vigorously for U.S. involvement in
World War I, contributing ten years of influential "unremitting work" in Europe during and after the war; she
demonstrates an extraordinary "sensitivity to history" as
well as personal commitment to civic improvement, working later in Indian affairs, public health, and the rehabilitation of female prisoners.

1874   SMITH, ELINOR GOULDING
Confessions of Mrs. Smith; Reckless Recollections, True &
Otherwise.   New York: Harcourt, Brace, 1958.   182pp.

She writes brief, humorous chapters on a wide variety of
domestic topics, with mock despair at her lack of skills,
her unappealing appearance, and the trials and tribulations
of a writer, wife, homemaker, and mother.

1875   SMITH, ELLA WILLIAMS
Tears and Laughter, in Virginia and Elsewhere.   Verona,
Va.:   McClure Press, 1972.   148pp.

She writes for her children, grandchildren, and great-
grandchildren; in a series of random recollections, she tells
of summers in the South, a New York finishing school, a
season in 1908 as a Richmond debutante, civic activities
after her marriage in 1914; she is the mother of five; during the depression, she devotes increased energy to civic
welfare and Red Cross work; in Europe on the eve of World
War II, she closes her account with the late 1930's.

1876   SMITH, ETHEL SABIN (1887-   )
A Furrow Deep and True.   New York: Norton, 1964.   224pp.

A teacher and writer describes "incidents and perspectives
from life on a Wisconsin farm in the 1890's"; she combines
straightforward recollection and description with thoughtful
perceptions of "the tapestry of values"; her memories focus
on the community's religious base, gypsy peddlers, hired
hands, the family doctor, the magic of older cousins, domestic tasks, "wasted years" in school, seasonal picnics,
other festive occasions, and the distance of world affairs;
she closes with reflections on time.

1877   Passports at Seventy.   New York: Norton, 1961.   240pp.

A writer involved with programs for the aging, she celebrates older people who are young in spirit as she travels
around the world for eight months on cargo ships; she offers
anecdotes of her fellow passengers, of extended stays in
Australia, Italy, and Greece, of her past travels, and of
her investigations into the treatment of the aging in other
countries.

1878   SMITH, FLORENCE BLAKE
        Cow Chips 'n' Cactus; The Homestead in Wyoming.   New
        York: Pageant, 1962.   118pp.

At twenty-one she is obsessed with the idea of homesteading, so she leaves her Chicago office job and settles on a
Wyoming claim; enchanted with her natural surroundings, she
works, reads, writes, enjoys her colorful but distant neighbors; she is intensely homesick for the West during working
winters in Chicago and ultimately settles in Wyoming permanently after marrying a neighboring rancher.

1879   SMITH, HANNAH MERRIAM
        For Heaven's Sake.   Boston: Little, Brown, 1949.   266pp.

The daughter of a "True Believer" fundamentalist preacher
writes with a warm sense of humor and understanding about
a childhood full of camp meetings, revivals, religious
schools, and family exhortations to let her "light shine" in
spite of peer pressure to ignore fundamentalist restrictions;
in 1931 at a Bible college she first fully realizes that truth
is not fixed and that she is free to choose a religious path
different from that of her father.

1880   SMITH, HANNAH WHITALL (1832-1911)   NAW
        Philadelphia Quaker: The Letters of Hannah Whitall Smith,
        ed. Logan Pearsall Smith.   New York: Harcourt, Brace,
        1950.   234pp.

The author of a popular religious work and of a spiritual

autobiography (see companion volume), she writes vivacious, witty letters to family and friends between 1847 and 1911; "a rather public character" due to her writing and preaching, she is never self-righteous but is devoted to a "plain simple common-sense faith" with a dash of worldliness, for she touches on suffrage, pacifism, unionism, agnosticism, art; absolutely charmed by being a mother and grandmother, she is delighted to grow old and longs cheerfully for the release of death.

1881   SMITH, ISABEL
       Wish I Might.   New York: Harper, 1955.   234pp.

Under treatment for tuberculosis for over twenty-one years, she has personal experience with three major medical approaches; she is forced to leave the nursing profession when she falls ill; sanatorium routine threatens her with stagnation, and she struggles to "recover my sense of participation in the world"; publicity follows a Life magazine article in 1937; she finds love, and when the advent of antibiotics provides a cure, marriage in 1949; in spite of financial difficulties and delicate health, she is determined to remain "outside."

1882   SMITH, KATE (1909-   )
       Upon My Lips a Song.   New York: Funk & Wagnalls, 1960.
       213pp.

She describes her early ambition to become a singer and dancer; the aspiring entertainer goes to New York in 1926 but is lonely, sensitive about her overweight, and hurt by comedians' insults in her first musical comedy; she begins a close, trusting relationship with her manager which sustains her career for twenty-six years; she moves into recording, radio and television; during World War II, she sells war bonds and broadcasts patriotic messages; unmarried, she reflects on the lives of single women.

1883   SMITH, LILLIAN EUGENIA (1897-1966)   NAWM
       The Journey.   Cleveland: World, 1954.   256pp.

An author, she undertakes an inward journey to explore the influence of memory and belief upon experience, "what I learned" and "how I learned it"; stories of her mother and grandmother constitute the family mythology; she describes the "tenderness and anxiety of childhood," examines the unity of faith and doubt, affirms the "delicate equilibrium" in life; she writes vignettes with great sensitivity to subtle nuances.

1884   Killers of the Dream.   New York: Norton, 1961.   253pp.

    A Southern white woman explores the personal meanings
of a segregated culture; from her childhood haunted by the
ghosts of "sin, sex, and segregation," she describes the
subtlety of the lessons learned about white woman's unten-
able position and about the dangers to the human spirit;
this edition is revised and enlarged since the first edition
in 1949.

1885   Memory of a Large Christmas.   New York: Norton, 1962.
83pp.

    A writer, she portrays with nostalgia the family activities
surrounding Christmas; disorder at the breakfast table, pecan
"tree-shaking day," and a hog-killing precede the celebration
that involves food, gifts, and visiting; her memories center
on the family kitchen, its associations, and her imperious
"Big Grandma."

1886   SMITH, NANCY COVERT (1935?-)
    Journey Out of Nowhere.   Waco, Texas: Word Books, 1973.
124pp.

    A writer, wife, and mother of four tells of her recovery
from mental illness; she reviews the roots of her breakdown
in years of frenzied activity and low self-esteem; she learns
to cope with depression, fear, indecision, and the "tremendous shock" of readjusting to home life after hospitalization;
aided by her realistic, supportive family, she writes of her
experiences for magazines, desiring to be of service to others with similar problems.

1887   SMITH, OLGA WRIGHT
    Gold on the Desert.   Albuquerque: University of New Mexico
Press, 1956.   249pp.

    She joins her civil engineer husband and prospector father-
in-law for a year in southwestern Arizona, searching for
copper and gold; initially she hates the hardship, loneliness,
heat, and fear of desert existence, but gradually she comes
to appreciate the desert's "awful vastness" and beauty and
to enjoy the excitement of mineral discoveries and to value
the experience in what becomes her "real home."

1888   SMITH, RUTH
    White Man's Burden; A Personal Testament.   New York:
Vanguard, 1946.   222pp.

Writing her "heart's testimony" with quiet conviction, she tells of her dedication to racial understanding and her decision to teach in an Alabama mission school for blacks; savoring the richness and vitality of relationships between teachers and students, she is nevertheless ashamed of "moral compromise" and the necessity to conform to some local standards; helpless when white teachers are dismissed, she is bitter toward her own white race and its prejudice.

1889   SMITH, SUSY
Confessions of a Psychic.   New York: Macmillan, 1971.
315pp.

She discusses her work in "spirit communication" since 1955; her background includes repeated childhood illnesses, marriage, divorce, and a variety of jobs; the death of her mother forces her independence; after her initial skepticism, spirit messages from her mother open the way to belief and she presents numerous anecdotes of communication and intervention by the spirit world; she is the author of other books on the subject.

1890   SMITH, VIRGINIA COX
Woman Alone Around the World.   New York: Exposition,
1955.   282pp.

On a voyage that fulfills her childhood dreams of travel, she visits Scandinavia, England, France, Switzerland, Austria, Italy, Greece, the Near East, and the Far East; her spirited account consists of letters recounting her sightseeing and adventures.

1891   SNORGRASS, WANDA
Not Left--Not Right--But Forward.   New York: Vantage,
1956.   109pp.

Following in her mother's and her grandmother's footsteps, she becomes a political crusader, first with the Democratic Party and then with the Republican Party; a dedicated, intensely patriotic volunteer, and an effective public speaker, she does much detailed, shrewd grass-roots organizing for the 1952 Eisenhower campaign.

1892   SNOW, CARMEL WHITE (1890-1961)
The World of Carmel Snow, with Mary Louise White Aswell.
New York: McGraw-Hill, 1962.   212pp.

An Irish immigrant, she enters the world of fashion through her mother's dressmaking establishment; she becomes the American editor of Vogue and later the editor of Harper's Bazaar; she writes in a straightforward style.

1893   SNOW, LOIS WHEELER
       A Death with Dignity: When the Chinese Came.   New York:
       Random, 1975.   148pp.

An actress and the wife of noted China writer Edgar Snow, she recalls the months in 1971 and 1972 when her husband is dying of cancer in their Switzerland home; their privileged access to Western medical care is unsatisfactory, and the arrival of a Chinese medical team with their humane attitudes toward illness, death, and family, provides her with "a profound experience in sharing"; her sensitive account is moving as she experiences terminal illness with mourning and understanding.

1894   SNYDER, GRACE McCANCE (1882-   )
       No Time on My Hands, as told to Nellie Snyder Yost.
       Caldwell, Id.:   Caxton, 1963.   541pp.

A widely known quilt-maker, she recalls her sod home on a Nebraska homestead in the 1880's; in rich detail, she describes her mother's homemaking efforts and the domestic and farm tasks shared by all; she tells of her tomboy activities, community entertainments, Swedish neighbors, haphazard schooling, drought, and epidemics; she becomes a teacher, tempering the loneliness with literary social gatherings; married in 1903, she raises her family in a sandhill sod home after the death of her first child; prominent events include the 1918 flu epidemic and dust storms in 1933; she is "blessed by having no time on my hands."

1895   SOELBERG, ETHEL MABUCE
       see MABUCE, ETHEL

1896   SOLOMON, BARBARA PROBST (1929?-   )
       Arriving Where We Started.   New York: Harper & Row,
       1972.   261pp.

A journalist, she writes with understanding of her younger self, a privileged New York City girl with working-class sympathies; in post-war Europe and fired by naïve optimism, she is a "revolutionary heroine" briefly for the Spanish republicans; accompanying her lover to Germany, she makes an emotional visit to a concentration camp site; later alienated from her family, troubled by the McCarthy years, and widowed, she returns to Spain to reflect on the shape of her personal experience.

1897   SOLOMON, HANNAH GREENEBAUM (1858-1942)   NAW
       Fabric of My Life.   New York: Bloch Publishing, 1946.
       263pp.

       A founder of the National Council of Jewish Women writes
       at the insistence of her children and grandchildren; raised
       in Chicago in a family with strong religious and cultural
       impulses, she notes her heritage of "civic obligation" which
       is reflected in her work with the Council, the Chicago Juve-
       nile Court, literary organizations, and other philanthropic
       activities; her life is devoted equally to her family and her
       work with the Council.

1898   SONE, MONICA ITOI (1919?-   )
       Nisei Daughter.   Boston: Little, Brown, 1953.   238pp.

       The daughter of Japanese hotel owners in Seattle, she
       describes her close family life and protected childhood,
       growing up with two cultural personalities; she is distressed
       by her first experience of racial discrimination, for she
       feels "elemental" loyalty to the U. S.; in 1941 her family is
       uprooted by the internment of Japanese-Americans, and she
       tells of life in an Idaho camp before she seeks independence
       in a job and a college education; she is not bitter, for she
       feels the experience helped to forge the two cultures within
       her into a single identity.

1899   SOREGI, PRISCILLA VARGA
       Come Back, My Son, Come Back.   New York: Comet
       Press, 1959.   43pp.

       Born in Hungary, she tells of her rural peasant back-
       ground before the family's emigration to the U. S. in 1904;
       her vivid recollections of traveling by ship with other immi-
       grants are followed by details of her overland journey by
       covered wagon to their Oklahoma homestead, where they are
       driven away "from our promised land" by cattlemen.

1900   SORENSEN, VIRGINIA EGGERSTEN (1912-   )
       Where Nothing Is Long Ago: Memories of a Mormon Child-
       hood.   New York: Harcourt, Brace & World, 1955.   213pp.

       In a series of skillfully-wrought vignettes, she tells of a
       neighbor's murder over water rights, a spirited white horse,
       a rejected second wife, her apostate grandmother, her in-
       tense love for a kitten, a brush with racial prejudice, her
       grandfather's love affair, and her own first love.

1901   SPARKMAN, IVO HALL
        A Glance at the East; Over the Senator's Shoulder.   Hunts-
        ville, Ala.: Strode, 1966. 176pp.

        The wife of the Alabama senator, she accompanies her
        husband on an official eighty-seven day trip around the
        world; her travels include Japan, Korea, Vietnam, Cam-
        bodia, Thailand, Malaya, Ceylon, India, Pakistan, Egypt,
        and Italy; she describes her visits to public institutions,
        social events with diplomats and heads of state, and sight-
        seeing, adding her own political comments, discussing the
        role of diplomats' wives, and issuing a call for increased
        international understanding.

1902   SPAUR, GRETIA HARRISON
        Pakistani Episode.   Philadelphia: Dorrance, 1972.   149pp.

        In 1955 she goes with her husband, a forester, to work
        for several years in Pakistan; in spite of the extremes of
        wealth and poverty, she enjoys observing the people and
        customs and offers a vivid description of her daily domes-
        tic life; she is gradually accepted by her neighbors and
        develops a sense of belonging which makes her reluctant
        to leave.

1903   SPELLETICH, CORNELIA ADELINE
        Chronicles of Cornelia; Stories from Childhood.   New York:
        Exposition, 1955.   82pp.

        Writing for her grandchildren, she produces a third-
        person narrative of her log-cabin childhood, a tale of simple
        pleasures focused on her parents, siblings, and grandpar-
        ents; the account consists of brief, random recollections.

1904   SPENCER, SUE W. (1908-   )
        African Creeks I Have Been Up.   New York: David McKay,
        1963.   212pp.

        In the form of letters to her college-age daughters in the
        U.S., she tells of four separate tours from 1956 to 1962
        accompanying her mining engineer husband and three sons;
        open, receptive, and eager to learn, she offers vivid de-
        scriptions of the people, customs, history, and daily rou-
        tine; she comes to feel "at home in Africa."

1905   SPINOLA, HELEN BULL CAMPBELL (1886?-   )
        Nothing but the Truth; The Reminiscences of Helen Spinola.
        London: Victor Gollancz, 1961.   222pp.

She offers lively, random recollections of her childhood before the turn of the century; stage-struck as a child, she later marries the son of actress Mrs. Patrick Campbell and tells sharp stories of her mother-in-law; she settles in London, is widowed before a divorce is final during World War I; she marries an Italian nobleman; her account covers the years through World War II.

1906   SPITZER, MARIAN
        I Took It Lying Down.   New York: Random, 1951.   247pp.

Having regarded herself as an "iron woman," vigorously pursuing a career as a Hollywood writer as well as marriage, motherhood, and a spirited social life, she is suddenly stopped by tuberculosis; struggling with her boredom and inner rage and the despair of several relapses, she slowly learns acquiescence and gains the rewards of unhurried reading, leisurely enjoyment of her family; she closes, noting her final reconciliation to the chronic nature of the disease.

1907   SPOONER, ELLA BROWN JACKSON (1880-)
        Way Back When; Ideas Wise and Otherwise and Memories
        About American Furniture.   New York: Exposition, 1953.
        118pp.

An authority on antique American furniture, she presents random childhood memories generated by and focused on certain old pieces of furniture; changes in and additions to the family furniture reflect changes in popular American styles; she goes on to describe various acquisitions.

1908   SPRIGGS, EDYTH ELIZABETH JONES (1887-)
        Legacy of Love.   Lincoln, Neb.:   Foundation Books, 1972.
        348pp.

A columnist focuses on her childhood, describing the difficulties and dangers of life on the trail across the Rockies to Oregon after her domineering father forces the family to abandon their security and head west in 1901; family illnesses and deaths follow, and her mother must support them when her father is crippled; at seventeen, a confrontation with her father thrusts her into independence, although she is sustained by the continuing love of her mother.

1909   SPRINGER, FRANCESCA
        The Redhead Takes a Holiday.   New York: Vantage, 1959.
        149pp.

She describes "some of the tribulations and a lot of the fun of motel life"; the mother of two small children, she is left with the motel in 1953 when her husband withdraws from their business partnership, and for six years she works with the "daily drama" of various guests.

1910 STACKHOUSE, MILDRED ORR
God's Plan for Russ; A Mother's Story of Her Gifted Son's Life. New York: Exposition, 1956. 98pp.

Her son's death at twenty-one provides a "spiritual awakening" for her as she explores his past; recalling a heavenly sign that he is "truly different," she comes to feel inadequate and guilty of not recognizing and understanding his intellectual, artistic, and musical gifts; suffering from depression herself, she misses the signs of his mental breakdown and she collapses after his sudden death, finding her only support in religious faith.

1911 STALVEY, LOIS MARK
The Education of a WASP. New York: William Morrow, 1970. 327pp.

She describes "what happened to one WASP family--my family--inside us and around us" in 1961 when she supports efforts to hire a black teacher; shocked by neighbors' reactions to a black homeowner, her family moves to an integrated neighborhood in Philadelphia and she tells of the subtle discrimination they find there; she struggles against stereotypes but feels fearful after the King assassination, and she closes on a note of reluctant despair over race relations.

1912 Getting Ready; The Education of a White Family in Inner City Schools. New York: William Morrow, 1974. 313pp.

In this perceptive account of how her children's education becomes her own eleven years of learning, she describes her initial naïve expectations when she settles in an integrated neighborhood; confronting her involuntary stereotypes and her liberalism, she finds herself struggling with teachers', parents', and children's prejudices; a volunteer teacher in 1969, her attempts to teach black history are unsuccessful and she is horrified at her black students' lack of preparation; she discovers that a year of private school offers no solutions for her children, and she remains caught between her hopes and Philadelphia reality.

1913   STAN, ANISOARA (1902?-)
        They Crossed Mountains and Oceans.   New York: William-
        Frederick, 1947.   386pp.

        Romanian-born, her country's liberation from Hungary in
        1918 feeds her intense patriotic fervor and her deep love
        and appreciation for Romanian folk art and crafts; in the
        early 1920's she begins years of travel in the U.S. with
        folk art to exhibit and lecture on and sell, hoping to aid
        the Romanian economy while increasing Romanian pride and
        fostering cultural understanding; she dreams of a living mu-
        seum of peasant folk art, taking her proposal to the White
        House and the U.N.; she writes in an unsettled mix of
        present and past tense.

1914   STANDEN, NIKA
        see HAZELTON, NIKA STANDEN

1915   STANFIELD, MATTIE COLE (1896?-)
        Sourwood Tonic and Sassafras Tea; Memories of Rural Life
        in Northern Alabama at the Turn of the Century.   New York:
        Exposition, 1963.   142pp.

        In this detailed domestic picture of a pioneer household,
        she describes the "rare sweetness" of her childhood recol-
        lections; a "tomboy" who prefers the outdoors to housework,
        she notes children's pastimes, hard work, family nights of
        music and reading, her school days and determination to be
        a teacher; she closes with the establishment of a permanent
        home.

1916   STANFORD, SALLY (1903-)
        The Lady of the House; The Autobiography of Sally Stanford.
        New York: Putnam, 1966.   255pp.

        This is a tough, slangy account of a high-class madam in
        San Francisco between the wars; she frankly describes her
        many marriages and her ambitions; she leaves the business
        of prostitution in 1949, opens a restaurant in Sausalito, and
        runs twice for the City Council.

1917   STANLEY, ILSE DAVIDSOHN
        The Unforgotten.   Boston: Beacon, 1957.   375pp.

        The fiercely independent daughter of a Berlin rabbi, she
        has ambitions to become an actress, director, and producer;
        she marries a violinist and, playing entrepreneur, launches
        his career, but the German political chaos of the early
        1930's accompanies the dissolution of her marriage; she

finally flees her beloved Germany, settling in the U.S. with
her son; after World War II, disturbed by the atmosphere
of hatred toward Germany and passionately idealistic, she
establishes an organization to promote international love and
understanding.

1918 STANWELL-FLETCHER, THEODORA MORRIS COPE (1906-)
      Driftwood Valley. Boston: Little, Brown, 1946. 384pp.

      A naturalist, she recounts two sojourns in northern Brit-
      ish Columbia, between 1937 and 1941 spent with her husband
      mapping, observing wildlife, and collecting plant and animal
      specimens for a Canadian museum; her narrative, drawn
      from diaries, tells of the wilderness life and of her love for
      the isolation and profound solitude which demand self-reliance
      and stamina for survival; she writes with rich detail.

1919 STARK, ELIZABETH WORTHINGTON PHILIP (1878-)
      Around the World in Three Years. New York: Vantage,
      1964. 44pp.

      A wealthy young woman travels to Japan in 1901 to study
      art for a year, combining her work with sightseeing and
      socializing in diplomatic circles; she then travels in India,
      Italy, Spain, France, and England, returning home in 1903.

1920 STARK, PHYLLIS
      I Chose a Parson. New York: Oxford University, 1956.
      240pp.

      Courted and engaged while she is a student at a small
      Minnesota church college, she marries an Episcopal rector
      and describes the church life, activities, and parishioners
      in several posts in Minnesota and South Dakota; they serve
      next at a Washington, D.C. cathedral, and she closes as
      her husband is consecrated a bishop; hers is a story of
      twenty-three years of Christian family life.

1921 STARR, BLAZE (pseud.)
      Blaze Starr; My Life, as told to Huey Perry. New York:
      Praeger, 1974. 210pp.

      Born Fannie Belle Fleming, a stripper recalls her "happy
      and contented" childhood in a large Appalachian family; at
      fourteen a "new and exciting world" is opened to her by a
      teacher and she is lured to Washington, D.C.; she begins a
      strip-tease act with misgivings, but success follows; her
      marriage and divorce precede her sincere love for Louisi-
      ana's Governor Long; at his death, she is troubled by theft,

a decline of her nightclub business, and disillusionment in love.

1922   STEICHEN, PAULA (1943-)
My Connemara.   New York: Harcourt, Brace & World, 1969.   178pp.

In a charming, highly evocative portrayal of the "wild, sweet way" of her childhood on the North Carolina goat farm of her grandfather Carl Sandburg, she writes of her intimate ties to the land and of her joyful family life, close to her grandmother, her aunts, and her mother, a woman of passionate and varied interests; her portraits of grandfatherly Sandburg and magical great uncle Edward Steichen reveal the roots of her "deep love for fantasy and language."

1923   STEIN, ANNE-MARIE (1943-)
Three Picassos Before Breakfast; Memoirs of an Art Forger's Wife, as told to George Carpozi, Jr.   New York: Hawthorn, 1973.   192pp.

She describes her "happy-tragic life," completely charmed and awed by a skilled art forger in 1964; she studies and becomes an expert critic of his work and participates with him in his brilliant hoax, years of luxury, and work in the highest art circles; when her husband's drug addiction and debts halt his career, she is left with three small children to support with a legitimate art dealership.

1924   STEINER, NANCY HUNTER (1933-)
A Closer Look at Ariel; A Memory of Sylvia Plath.   New York: Harper's Magazine, 1973.   83pp.

A roommate of poet Sylvia Plath at Smith College in 1954 and 1955, she describes their mutual interests, their involvement in the usual banalities of dorm life, as well as their introspective exchanges; she is delighted to follow Plath's lead; she sees Plath through a traumatic rape and the ensuing emotional crisis, but finds herself drained by Plath's "almost pathological dependence"; she withdraws and the friendship cools.

1925   STERN, CAROLYN
Reflections.   San Antonio: Naylor, 1960.   203pp.

A teacher and draftsman, she writes of a forty-nine day trip to Europe in 1959 which fulfills a lifelong dream; traveling with two friends, she describes the usual sights in England, Norway, Sweden, Denmark, Germany, Austria, Italy, Switzerland, France, and Holland.

1926 STERN, MADELEINE BETTINA (1912-   )
      Old and Rare: Thirty Years in the Book Business, with
      joint author Leona Rostenberg.   New York: Abner Schram,
      1974.   234pp.

      A scholar and biographer, she writes alternate chapters
      with Leona Rostenberg; she describes her early dedication
      to writing, studying for a Ph. D. in medieval English litera-
      ture, and her first literary biography of Margaret Fuller;
      joining Rostenberg in the book business, she travels in Eu-
      rope, recounting "the hunt and the quarry" and conveying a
      sense of continuing excitement.

1927 STERN, SUSAN HARRIS (1943-   )
      With the Weathermen: The Personal Journal of a Revolu-
      tionary Woman.   Garden City, N. Y. :   Doubleday, 1975.
      374pp.

      Covering the years from 1966 to 1972 in a grim chroni-
      cle, she tells of the appeal of the hippie lifestyle, of drugs
      and communal living; she joins the Students for a Demo-
      cratic Society, the Women's Liberation Movement, and is
      present during the 1968 Chicago demonstrations; mixing sex-
      ual adventure with politics, she becomes a zealot, denying
      her wealthy educated Jewish past and "intent on being as
      outrageous as possible"; following the 1969 "Days of Rage,"
      she goes underground to a life of "actions," vicious political
      criticism, self-flagellation, loneliness, and suicidal feelings;
      later arrested and jailed as one of the "Seattle 7," she be-
      gins writing.

1928 STEURT, MARJORIE RANKIN
      Broken Bits of Old China.   Nashville: Thomas Nelson, 1973.
      152pp.

      A Presbyterian missionary teacher, she first goes to
      China in 1912 to work in a girls' boarding school and super-
      vise country schools; through her extensive travels, she
      sees a China open to few foreigners; she proves to be good-
      humored, receptive, and eager to learn; her account focuses
      on her first seven-year period and emphasizes her contacts
      with the people; she writes to promote understanding of mod-
      ern China.

1929 STEVENSON, FANNY
      see STEVENSON, FRANCES VAN de GRIFT (1840-1914)

1930 STEVENSON, FRANCES VAN de GRIFT (1840-1914)
      Our Samoan Adventure, ed. Charles Neider.   New York:
      Harper, 1955.   264pp.

The American wife of Scotch writer Robert Louis Stevenson keeps a journal from 1890 to 1893 in which she is revealed as a keen observer with a lively sense of humor; she chronicles her "life in the bush," reluctantly serving as a maternal figure for their native helpers, gardening happily, noting local political intrigues, battling injuries and fevers of her own while caring for her husband's frail health; her diary ends just before his sudden death; her entries are interspersed with selections from Stevenson's letters.

1931   STEVENSON, JANET
        Woman Aboard.   New York: Crown, 1969.   312pp.

At fifty, this writer takes a six-month sea journey with her husband and two other men; she notes the weather, mistakes and crises, tensions among the crew members, her depression in the doldrums, and her elation at first landfall; she finds the Marquesas a dream world and offers anecdotes of the people there; after her return home, she is pleased with her strength and powers of endurance.

1932   STEVENSON, SARAH COLES (1789-1848)
        Victoria, Albert, and Mrs. Stevenson, ed. Edward Boykin.
        New York: Rinehart, 1957.   309pp.

The wife of the Minister at the Court of St. James writes long, detailed letters to her sisters and brothers between 1836 and 1841; she appreciates the warm hospitality shown her, but finds her health threatened by the heavy social obligations; never dazzled while among the powerful, she retains her Christian humility and a "republican" perspective on the aristocracy; she sends a vivid letter on Victoria's coronation and on her wedding; at the end she is eager to go home.

1933   STEWART, MARGARET ROSS EVANS (1874-   )
        From Dugout to Hilltop.   Culver City, Cal.:   Murray &
        Gee, 1951.   233pp.

A doctor, she grows up on a Nebraska homestead, helping her mother maintain the farm when wanderlust lures her father away; she marries a fellow medical student, graduating in 1900; later divorced, she studies at the Woman's Medical College of Pennsylvania, and establishes her first practice in California but remarries and works in public health and for the Veterans Administration in Washington, D. C.; her "greatest joy in life" is serving people.

1934   STEWART, ORA PATE (1910-   )
        I Talk About My Children.   San Antonio: Naylor, 1948.
        115pp.

        A writer and lecturer as well as an army wife, she is
        delighted by motherhood and presents disconnected anecdotes
        of her five children and their amusing sayings.

1935   STONE, KATE
        see HOLMES, SARAH KATHERINE STONE (1841-1907)

1936   STONEMAN, MARY E. (1885-   )
        Pioneering.   New York: Pageant, 1965.   97pp.

        She tells of pioneer life in the New Mexico Territory; she
        receives little schooling, since her family must all share
        the farm work; she takes on housekeeping at fourteen at her
        mother's death, then marries young to escape drudgery and
        she finds happiness in her nine children, in spite of a
        "blighted life" due to her husband's poverty and drunken-
        ness; she endures on the family homestead.

1937   STONER, ELSIE SHAW
        Vacation Daze, with Allen Stoner.   Raleigh, N.C.:   Capitol
        College Press, 1957.   118pp.

        In an account subtitled "Our Mexican Marriage and Other
        Travel Adventures," an insurance agent and businesswoman
        tells of her meeting and marrying a fellow agent while on a
        vacation tour of Mexico; in an exclamatory style, she notes
        their sightseeing, their second wedding at home in Ohio, and
        a later Pan American tour.

1938   STOUT, LUCILLE
        I Reclaimed My Child; The Story of a Family into Which a
        Retarded Child Was Born.   Philadelphia: Chilton, 1959.
        89pp.

        Deeply hurt by doctors' and friends' reactions to the birth
        of her Down's Syndrome child, she is persuaded to institu-
        tionalize the infant; tortured by secrecy, guilt, and shame,
        she later learns more about Down's Syndrome and comes to
        accept her daughter and the enrichment the child brings to
        her family life.

1939   STOUT, RUTH
        Company Coming; Six Decades of Hospitality, Do-it-yourself
        and Otherwise.   New York: Exposition, 1958.   155pp.

A columnist, lecturer, and gardener tells of the unending stream of guests on her Connecticut farm; recalling her childhood in a large, hospitable family, she transfers that sense of welcome to her "Poverty Hollow" farm as an experiment which begins during the depression; offering temporary communal living, she recounts her guests' various interpretations of the open invitation; her experiences trigger reflections on human nature, sharing, and an occasional "overdose of sociability."

1940 STRAINCHAMPS, ETHEL REED
      Don't Never Say Cain't. Garden City, N.Y.: Doubleday,
      1965. 168pp.

"Born a hillbilly" in the Ozarks, she chronicles her move from one culture to another, becoming a "female arriviste"; her voracious reading and intellectual daring propel her through work and school into teaching, although her progressive methods scandalize her colleagues and she leaves teaching after five years; a "thwarted female polemicist," she becomes a journalist and critic after her marriage and writes on dialects and English usage.

1941 STRAUS, DOROTHEA KUPPERMAN
      Palaces and Prisons. Boston: Houghton Mifflin, 1976.
      209pp.

A writer, she opens with a memoir of her brother whose "excessive nature" leads to dark mystery and muted pain and regret through the years until his decline and death; she describes a series of summer rentals, each evoking "another stage in growing up" and contrasting with the continuity of a summer farm she enjoys with her husband, son, and grandchildren; she presents portraits of Philip Rahv, Isaac B. Singer, and Edmund Wilson, each man placed in his literary and domestic milieu; she tells of ghost-ridden stays in Venice and Paris; chapters are framed by interludes cast in a dream state.

1942 Showcases. Boston: Houghton Mifflin, 1974. 200pp.

With faith in "capricious and evanescent" memory, she writes delicate vignettes, "searching for a fragment of the divine in the human scene"; she recalls various European crossings, her first love affair and its end, associations with the city of Paris which include memories from childhood, her courtship and honeymoon, and the death of her mother; she also recalls the birth of her first son, friendships gained through writing, memories of Rome and sitting for a portrait, and the days of her brother's terminal illness.

1943   Thresholds. Boston: Houghton Mifflin, 1971.   183pp.

Searching for "signs of herself" in the past, prior to her
birth, she relates her grandfather's and parents' reminiscences; she offers glimpses of her childhood in New York
City, the family Christmas ritual, frequent summers in
Europe, adults who figure in her childhood, adolescent hints
of sexuality, sharp images from her private school days;
the past is superimposed over the present in Central Park;
she closes with the decline and death of her father; her
writing produces an evocative threading of the past through
the present.

1944   STRONG, ANNA LOUISE (1885-1970)   NAWM
I Saw the New Poland. Boston: Little, Brown, 1946.
280pp.

Noting the lack of accurate information on Poland, she
goes there from Moscow, the only Western reporter in
Poland late in 1944; she describes "the ruined land" in vivid
detail, traveling extensively and arriving at the Warsaw front
as the first American; she talks with numerous people, from
peasants to political leaders, recounting their wartime experiences and their intense desire for democracy; she ends
on an optimistic note with the establishment of the provision-
al government in 1945.

1945   STRONG, JUNE
Journal of a Happy Woman. Nashville: Southern Publishing,
1973.   160pp.

The mother of six, including four adopted Oriental children, she writes of her pride in her home and family, of her
dedication to the Christian woman's role, of her strong religious faith as a Seventh-day Adventist, of her mission activities; her account is organized as a one-year cycle of months,
each with its seasonal associations with family activities.

1946   STROUD, MYRTLE REDMAN (1887-   )
The Land of Amanha: A Story of Brazil Today, the Coun-
try, the People, the Fiesta Spirit. New York: Greenwich
Book, 1958.   52pp.

These are "the letters of a much-of-the-time-homesick
girl to her loving mother"; she travels to South America,
settling in Brazil for over one year with her husband and
son, taking unsophisticated delight in new experiences; she
describes her householding and local customs and closes with
her return to the U.S.

1947   STRYKER, CHARLOTTE
        Time for Tapioca. New York: Crowell, 1951. 250pp.

    When she is fourteen, her family leaves Pennsylvania and
settles on a Javanese jungle tapioca plantation; living simply
and more slowly and absorbing the "customs of the country,"
she comes to recognize that the sojourn has a deep influence
on her life; in 1929, after two years, her father must admit
defeat, and the family returns to the U.S.

1948   STUHLDREHER, MARY A.
        Many a Saturday Afternoon. New York: David McKay,
        1964. 233pp.

    A journalist, she presents an amusing account of her
courtship and marriage in 1927 to a football coach; her
initial ignorance of sports gives way to her football education, a close family friendship with Knute Rockne, and
warm memories of players and coaches at Villanova and
Wisconsin; she feels the pain and bitterness of a final losing season and closes with her family's withdrawal from
football.

1949   STULL, RUTH O.
        Sand and Stars; Missionary Adventure on the Jungle Trail.
        New York: Revell, 1951. 189pp.

    A missionary nurse and teacher describes nearly a decade
of service with her minister husband among Peruvian Indians;
she portrays the people and their culture and her work to
earn their confidence; she raises two children in "this isolated post of glory"; her husband's health forces a return to
the U.S. where she travels and speaks on behalf of the mission, to which she returns after his death.

1950   STURE-VASA, MARY ALSOP (1885-1980)
        A Musical in the Making. Chevy Chase, Md.: Markane,
        1966. 260pp.

    An author, she dreams of combining her "two natural
gifts, writing and composing" in a musical; beginning in
1955, she follows her instincts yet learns much from a close
association with a composition teacher, and slowly grows in
confidence; she argues passionately on behalf of popular,
melodic music; her account is an intimate exploration of the
process of creating over a period of nine years.

1951   Novel-in-the-Making, by Mary O'Hara (pseud.). New York:
        David McKay, 1954. 244pp.

In a fascinating tale of the evolution of her creative
ideas, she describes the writing of The Son of Adam Wyn-
gate beginning in 1948; having "made the chaos," she shapes
the novel through introspection, inspiration, and editorial
hard work, committing herself to the agreeable "servitude"
of writing; as background, she tells briefly of her adventurous family, her time as a reader and scenario writer in
Hollywood, her married life on a Wyoming ranch where she
writes her famous trilogy.

1952   SUCCOP, MARGARET PHILLIPS (1914-)
        No Going Back: Odyssey of a Conversion.   Fresno, Cal. :
        Academy Guild, 1964.   100pp.

        A poet recounts her conversion to Catholicism, a "most
profound spiritual rebirth"; she refers only briefly to her
marriage and social and civic activities; beset by doubts
and troubled by an "inner poverty," she eventually finds
serenity and liberation with the help of a wise spiritual instructor despite the misunderstanding of family and friends.

1953   SUCKOW, RUTH (1892-1960)   NAWM
        A Memoir.   New York: Rinehart, 1952.   115pp.

        This narrative is the same as the memoir in Some Others
and Myself; Seven Stories and a Memoir, but it is here published separately.

1954   Some Others and Myself; Seven Stories and a Memoir.   New
        York: Rinehart, 1952.   281pp.

        A minister's daughter, the well-known writer presents a
testimony to the positive value of her father's "liberal spirit"
and "temperate" religion; she evokes the spirit of fresh beginning in the western Iowa church and community of her
childhood; she draws sensitive portraits of her father and
mother; she tells of her gradual withdrawal from the church,
exploring her own identity and freedom but later finding her
own religious path; her father's old age and death move her
deeply; her memoir covers pages 169 to 281.

1955   SULLIVAN, JUDY (1936-)
        Mama Doesn't Live Here Anymore.   New York: Arthur
        Fields, 1974.   243pp.

        Writing for other women in similar situations about "the
greatest risk of my life," she tells of leaving her husband
and daughter "to find my life"; raised with clear social expectations for feminine behavior, she marries at eighteen

with misgivings; small dissatisfactions, loneliness, and boredom grow to depression which requires psychiatric care; her
professional experience as a college teacher opens her perceptions to the appeals of independence, growth, and other
goals of the women's movement; she carefully prepares her
rejection of the wife and mother role and finds both pain
and freedom.

1956   SUMNER, CID RICKETTS (1890-1970)
        Traveler in the Wilderness.   New York: Harper and Broth-
        ers, 1957.   248pp.

        Believing that old age is the proper time for adventure
        and danger, a New England novelist in her sixties with no
        camping experience requests a place on a river expedition
        to film the canyons from Green River, Wyoming to the
        Grand Canyon; the only woman and determined to be self-
        reliant, she establishes a "quick understanding" and subtle
        friendships with the other expedition members; she observes
        nature as well as her companions and rises to the thrill of
        canyon vistas and running rapids; she reflects at length on
        the meaning of her experiences in this perceptive and articu-
        late account.

1957   A View from the Hill.   Englewood Cliffs, N. J. :   Prentice-
        Hall, 1957.   145pp.

        A fiction writer describes recovering herself from iner-
        tia; after marriage, motherhood, and divorce, she finds that
        age confers the privilege of quietude and self-knowledge; she
        renews her body through exercise, glories in friendships,
        strives for simplicity, sees the need for risks; she accepts
        the inevitability of death but insists on living fully until then.

1958   SUTHERLAND, JACKIE
        see   MOURA, JONI AND JACKIE SUTHERLAND

1959   SVENDSEN, GRO NILSDATTER (1841?-   )
        Frontier Mother; The Letters of Gro Svendsen, trans. and
        ed. by Pauline Farseth and Theodore C. Blegen.   Northfield,
        Minn. :   The Norwegian-American Historical Association,
        1950.   153pp.

        Written in a warm, intimate style, the account consists
        of letters written in the 1860's and 1870's to her parents in
        Norway; she emigrates to the U. S. in 1862 soon after her
        marriage and raises ten children, telling of the awesome
        responsibilities of motherhood; she describes the details of
        farm life, comparing life in Norway and America, although

she defends her decision to marry and emigrate; she teaches occasionally in a Norwegian school; she tells of her despair when her husband serves in the Civil War.

1960   TABER, GLADYS BAGG (1899-)
       Country Chronicle.   Philadelphia: Lippincott, 1974.   220pp.

    "A countrywoman and a writer," she opens with her dis-
covery and purchase of a Connecticut country home, where
she and a friend settle permanently when they are widowed,
providing a strong family life for their children; her reflective account follows a cycle of seasons, and she notes
the satisfactions of cooking, the appeal of the "New England
personality," the importance of friendships, the rhythm of
nature, rejoicing that "every day brings a new experience."

1961   Harvest of Yesterdays.   Philadelphia: Lippincott, 1976.
       224pp.

    A prolific writer, she presents a reminiscence of child-
hood and the "years before Stillmeadow" (see other works)
written with characteristic warmth; an only child, she provides a sensitive portrait of her parents, tells of growing
up in mining camps and in a small Wisconsin town; her education at Wellesley College opens the way to a teaching and
writing career which continues after her marriage and
motherhood; the serenity is broken by her husband's health
problems, when her writing must begin in earnest; she rebuilds security on a Connecticut farm with a close woman
friend and their three children.

1962   My Own Cape Cod.   Philadelphia: Lippincott, 1971.   251pp.

    In this meditative account, following the seasons from
spring to winter, she attempts to capture "the texture of
living" on Cape Cod as a summer resident; a writer and
conservationist, she tells of neighbors, bits of local history,
"the Cape way," nature, and the regrettable encroachments
of man.

1963   The Stillmeadow Calendar; A Countrywoman's Journal.   Phil-
       adelphia: Lippincott, 1967.   256pp.

    Structured by the yearly cycle from January to December,
her account focuses first on winter's time for guests, the

delights of grandchildren, and renewal through leisure;
spring brings cleaning, organization, and outdoor wandering;
summer offers the tranquillity and satisfactions of gardening; throughout she reflects on modern American culture,
"the secret of happy living," the "special reassurance" of
nature's patterns.

1964   Stillmeadow Daybook. Philadelphia: Lippincott, 1955.
       274pp.

    She looks back with great contentment and appreciation
on twenty years of delicate surprises, rich satisfactions,
and the intangible rewards of "country life" in Connecticut;
she shares her home with a close woman friend, their three
children grown, married, and gone; simple daily objects or
events trigger her reflections, and the present is infused
with the past as she savors "perfect moments."

1965   Stillmeadow Seasons. Philadelphia: Macrae Smith, 1950.
       256pp.

    Her Connecticut home on Stillmeadow Farm symbolizes
"the security we seek in a world highly unstable"; her wide-
ranging reflections follow a seasonal cycle beginning with
spring and reveal her capacity for intense wonder and enjoyment of nature and of her friends and neighbors.

1966   TALBOT, ROSE DEBORAH (1898?-)
       No Greater Challenge. New York: Vantage, 1955. 167pp.

    A spirited "doer" from childhood, her longing for inde-
pendence leads to an early marriage, but she is widowed in
1918; she remarries in 1920 and is a devoted mother to two
step-children, but the birth of her son causes years of tension and crises which involve her critical in-laws, her step-
children, and her own son; this tale of family anguish closes
optimistically, for she finally achieves a reconciliation with
all three adult children.

1967   TAMM, AUGUSTA
       By Dim and Flaring Lamps, transcribed by Katherine Boies
       McCallen. New York: Vantage, 1964. 143pp.

    A nurse, she tells of a life of hard work beginning in
childhood with the deaths of her parents; taken in by a
prosperous family, a serious illness leads to her determination at nineteen to become a nurse; she tells of various
patients, dramatic incidents, and her experiences in the
remote Cumberlands.

1968   TAPPING, MINNIE ELLINGSON (1867-1950)
        Eighty Years at the Gopher Hole; The Saga of a Minnesota
        Pioneer (1867-1947). New York: Exposition, 1958. 228pp.

        She opens with some family history, describing her par-
        ents' emigration from Norway; she then offers a detailed
        but random picture of her rural childhood, domestic tasks,
        games, pets, school days, religious activities; married in
        1901, she later gives up Minneapolis city life when she is
        widowed with two children and returns gladly to the country;
        with "glory in my strength," she keeps summer boarders,
        sells milk, and attends college in her middle age.

1969   TARRY, ELLEN (1906-   )
        The Third Door: The Autobiography of an American Negro
        Woman. New York: David McKay, 1955. 304pp.

        A black writer and journalist, she opens with random
        memories of a happy childhood in Birmingham; educated in
        a Catholic girls' school, she becomes a Catholic and works
        as a teacher, then a reporter, enduring hard times in New
        York during the depression; she serves in Harlem's Friend-
        ship House (see DeHueck, Catharine), then travels to gather
        folk tales, and publishes her first book in 1940, beginning
        her career as a children's author; during World War II, she
        works with the U.S.O. and later with Chicago's Friendship
        House; the pain of racial discrimination is sharpened when
        she raises a daughter.

1970   TATE, MARGUERITE GAYLORD (1898-   )
        Twelve Walked Away. New York: Harcourt Brace, 1948.
        150pp.

        She presents the frightening details of a plane crash on a
        winter flight over the Swiss Alps in an army plane piloted
        by her son; proud of her son's commanding courage, she
        attempts to match it, providing moral support and care for
        the injured; she endures cold, thirst, and hunger before
        their "epic" rescue by Swiss skiers.

1971   TAVES, ISABELLA
        Love Must Not Be Wasted; When Sorrow Comes, Take It
        Gently by the Hand. New York: Crowell, 1974. 214pp.

        A novelist and journalist becomes "an angry reporter" of
        the medical profession's treatment of her dying husband; she
        describes her own denial and withdrawal after his death,
        feeling particularly alone since she has no close family; she
        makes a career out of her needs, writing a book and a syn-
        dicated column, her own experiences embellished by the

experiences of others; she develops self-sufficiency and the ability to savor solitude.

1972   TAYLOR, EDITH VAIL
        Among Those Present.   Boston: Humphries, 1947.   62pp.

        In an anecdotal account she tells of her friendships with "distinguished personages," prominent artists and socialites in New York, and various presidents including Grant, Garfield, Hayes, Harrison, Cleveland, and Teddy Roosevelt.

1973   TAYLOR, ELIZABETH ROSEMOND (1932-)
        Elizabeth Taylor; An Informal Memoir.   New York: Harper & Row, 1965.   177pp.

        Writing in conversational style, the famous movie actress tries to deflate the myths surrounding her life; she enjoys an "idyllic childhood" in England before coming to the U. S. in 1939 to begin her film career with "National Velvet"; she describes her husbands, the cultured Wilding by whom she has two sons, the flamboyant Todd by whom she has a daughter, the emotional Burton to whom she is in ecstatic "proud subordination"; she sees luxury and wealth as superficial but is devoted to her children, valuing love and experience above all.

1974   Nibbles and Me.   New York: Duell, Sloan and Pearce, 1946.   77pp.

        Writing when she is thirteen, the actress presents a highly anthropomorphic account of her amusing experiences with an adored pet chipmunk; she writes with an eye for detail and an easy narrative flow unusual for a young author.

1975   TAYLOR, HELEN V.
        A Time to Recall; The Delights of a Maine Childhood.   New York: Norton, 1963.   224pp.

        In a delicate evocation of her tenth year, she tells of her family life amid grandparents, mother, sister, aunts, and uncles; the delights of her country summer home are portrayed in vignettes of a solitary day on the lake, the local mail coach, the village store, family hikes, long Sundays, July 4 celebrations, and the drama of a forest fire.

1976   TAYLOR, HELEN W.
        Don't Come Back Tomorrow.   New York: Pageant, 1952. 107pp.

She writes a lightweight, day-by-day account of her experiences as a patient at the Mayo Clinic, there for gall
bladder surgery; she describes hospital routine, her progress, and her concern for her family left at home.

1977 TAYLOR, KATHRINE KRESSMANN
Diary of Florence in Flood. New York: Simon and Schuster, 1967. 192pp.

She keeps a diary from November, 1966 to March, 1967,
opening with a dramatic account of the rising floodwaters;
in vivid detail, she notes "the extent of the tragedy of Florence," the desolation, the response of the people, and the
overwhelming artistic, property, and business losses; she
closes with hope as restoration begins.

1978 TAYLOR, ROSEMARY DRACHMAN
Harem Scare'm. New York: Crowell, 1951. 246pp.

This is a humorous account of her travels in Morocco in
1925 before returning to the U.S. to become a college dean;
an aspiring writer, she meets two American journalists in
Europe and, opting for adventure, joins them to cover a war
in Morocco, "stalking local color"; she attempts unsuccess-
fully to interview a sultan, but is successful in a visit to a
harem, a brothel, and the war front; she returns, using her
experiences as material for articles as well as for this
book.

1979 TEAL, MARION PEDERSEN (1912-   )
The Earth Is Ours. New York: Crowell, 1948. 205pp.

She and her husband, an agricultural economist, forsake
New York City to settle on his Illinois family farm in 1941;
a novice on the threshold of a year of "scientific farming,"
she describes colorful neighbors, her war on rats, the challenge of interior decorating, her efforts to raise chickens,
the satisfactions and concerns of planting and harvesting;
attic treasures provide links with the past; rising to the
demands for higher farm production during World War II,
they face the future with optimism, grateful for strong ties
to the land.

1980 TEAL, VALENTINE
It Was Not What I Expected. New York: Duell, Sloan and
Pearce, 1948. 255pp.

Having followed her grandmother's and Teddy Roosevelt's
exhortations on motherhood, she presents an entertaining ac-

count of rearing a large family with zest and by instinct;
she describes the inevitable collection of pets, her children's eccentric eating habits, her work as a Cub Scout
leader, and her relaxed housekeeping.

1981   TEILLARD, DOROTHY LAMON
        By These Things Have I Lived.   Harrogate, Tenn. :   Lincoln
        Memorial University Press, 1948.   176pp.

        Writing at the age of eighty-nine, she presents a brief
spiritual autobiography, followed by "inspirational gleanings"
from seventy-six years of notes; having travelled widely in
Europe, she marries, after a seventeen-year companionship,
a Frenchman who is "the spiritual force in my life."

1982   TEMPSKI, ARMINE von (1899-1943)
        Aloha; My Love to You; The Story of One Who Was Born in
        Paradise.   New York: Duell, Sloan and Pearce, 1946.
        235pp.

        A novelist and children's author, she writes a sequel to
Born in Paradise (see companion volume) in which she describes the "vehement beauty" of her beloved Hawaiian ranch
where she spends an enchanted childhood, the "tomboy daughter" of an adventurous widower; after her father's death, she
and her sister and brothers find a similar primal appeal of
nature in the Navajo desert; to keep her family intact, she
makes their Hawaiian home a guest ranch and begins her
writing career, interrupted yet fed by her restless traveling; she closes with her marriage to a kindred soul.

1983   TERASAKI, GWEN HAROLD (1907-   )
        Bridge to the Sun.   Chapel Hill: University of North Caro-
        lina Press, 1957.   260pp.

        She tells of her marriage in 1930 to a Japanese diplomat
and of her rapid education in Japanese culture and woman's
role therein; stationed in China for five years, then in Cuba,
then again in China, she and her husband are both distressed
by Japanese militarism and the onset of war; after Pearl
Harbor, she rejoins her husband in Japan, and describes the
strain of nursing her ill husband, raising a daughter, and
suffering slow starvation during the war, although she finds
little anti-American feeling against her; after Japanese sur-
render, she hopes for peace and reconciliation, closing her
moving account with her husband's death.

1984   THANE, ELSWYTH
        see   BEEBE, ELSWYTH THANE RICKER (1900-   )

1985   THAXTER, CELIA LAIGHTON (1835-1894)
        Sandpiper; The Life and Letters of Celia Thaxter, and Her
        Home on the Isles of Shoals, her family, friends & favorite
        poems, comp. by Rosamond Thaxter.   Francestown, N. H.:
        Jones, 1963.   287pp.

        A poet, her letters are embedded in connective text, com-
        piled by her granddaughter; she begins writing poems in 1861
        despite the heavy family burdens of her husband's ill health,
        a son's disabilities, her mother's illness, and family separ-
        ations; isolated from Boston cultural life yet maintaining
        friendships with other prominent literary figures, she notes
        the details of her island life close to nature.

1986   THOMAS, MARY PRYOR
        Follow the North Star.   Garden City, N. Y.:   Doubleday,
        1960.   165pp.

        She describes her youth in an adventurous family and the
        "constant travel" in the early years of her marriage to jour-
        nalist Lowell Thomas; she recounts filming in Alaska for an
        early television documentary, camping with her small daugh-
        ter and delighting in new sights and new people; she offers
        rich detail of "breathtaking" flights, the magnificent country-
        side, and the "rugged outdoor living" north of the Arctic
        Circle.

1987   Only in Alaska.   Garden City, N. Y.:   Doubleday, 1969.
        252pp.

        The wife of journalist Lowell Thomas tells of their estab-
        lishment in 1960 of a permanent home in Alaska with their
        two small children; she describes daily family life and her
        enjoyment of outdoor activities, family camping, travels in
        Alaska by car and plane; she also describes her experiences
        during and after the Anchorage earthquake in 1964 which
        destroyed her home.

1988   THOMAS, MONA BRUNS
        By Emily Possessed.   New York: Exposition, 1973.   165pp.

        An actress and lecturer describes her eight-year stint as
        a character in the television soap opera "Brighter Day"; by
        way of background, she tells of her childhood roles, her
        marriage to a fellow actor, and later retirement during
        which she transfers her acting ambitions to her son; all
        three family members join in television's early soap operas;
        a dedicated professional, she is deeply affected by the show's
        closing.

1989 THOMAS, MOTHER CATHERINE
      see CATHERINE THOMAS OF DIVINE PROVIDENCE,
      MOTHER

1990 THOMAS, TAY
      see THOMAS, MARY PRYOR

1991 THOMPSON, ARIADNE
      The Octagonal Heart. Indianapolis: Bobbs-Merrill, 1956.
      221pp.

      She writes of her enchanted childhood, suffused with
      Greek legends and classics, as the daughter of a Greek
      businessman and consul in St. Louis; she presents marvel-
      ously vibrant tales of passionate extended family gatherings,
      particularly during summers on a suburban estate; when the
      house is destroyed by fire, it marks the end of those "love-
      ly, lost days."

1992 THOMPSON, BETTY
      Turning World. New York: Friendship Press, 1960. 128pp.

      In this largely impersonal account, she describes her
      work as a World Council of Churches staff member in Eu-
      rope from 1955 to 1956 and her world travels in 1958, "wit-
      nessing together" with other dedicated religious workers.

1993 THOMPSON, ERA BELL (1907?-)
      Africa: Land of My Fathers. Garden City, N.Y.: Double-
      day, 1954. 281pp.

      A black journalist tells of a three-month trip in 1953 to
      see "what my own reaction would be to my African ances-
      tors"; traveling extensively, she meets with working people
      as well as royalty and heads of state, observing social sta-
      tus, economic conditions, health, education, and customs;
      with candor she describes racial prejudice in Rhodesia and
      South Africa; she returns, a loyal American but proud of
      her "black heritage."

1994 American Daughter. Chicago: University of Chicago Press,
      1946. 301pp.

      A black editor and journalist, she grows up in Iowa and
      North Dakota, coping with poverty and early responsibility
      when her mother dies; she begins writing in high school,
      later working for the Chicago Defender; gaining a "desolate
      freedom" with her father's death, she completes college in

Iowa, then, searching for links with her black heritage, she
works as a social worker and serves with the W. P. A.; she
struggles against both black racism and white racism.

1995   THOMPSON, GOLDIANNE GUYER (1880-   )
       Pioneer Living with Mema; The Autobiography of Goldianne
       (Guyer) Thompson.   Denver: Publishers Press, 1971.
       185pp.

       Writing at ninety-one, she offers random anecdotes of the
       extremely close family life of her childhood in Missouri and
       Texas; with admiration for the "honor and uprightness" of
       her parents, she learns to value education and music, inter-
       ests which remain strong after her marriage in 1898; she
       becomes the editor and publisher of a community newspaper
       and is honored for her contributions to journalism; later she
       works in a government printing office to support her ailing
       husband; she delights in her children, grandchildren, and
       great-grandchildren.

1996   THOMPSON, ISABEL ATKINSON
       When Washington and I Were Young.   New York: Exposition,
       1965.   50pp.

       The account is a series of disconnected memories from
       the turn of the century; she recalls childhood books, toys,
       games, penny-candy, travel, school, cooking, sewing, and
       other pastimes in this "folksy approach to old Washington."

1997   THOMPSON, JEAN (pseud.)
       The House of Tomorrow.   New York: Harper & Row, 1967.
       179pp.

       Describing her stay in a Salvation Army home for unwed
       mothers, she opens with her feelings of isolation, rebellion,
       and despair over her pregnancy; fleeing from her parents
       and rejecting marriage, she finds support, assistance, and
       acceptance at the home; she tells of the pain of making adop-
       tion arrangements and of her final parting from her son.

1998   THOMPSON, NORA BELLE (1898-   )
       Across These Waters.   Philadelphia: Dorrance, 1972.
       164pp.

       In an account drawn from letters written during years of
       extensive travel, she provides detailed observations of the
       Far East, the Middle East, and Africa; a journalist and
       scholar, she visits not only tourist sites but also orphanages,
       hospitals, and mission stations; among other things, she

studies in Japan, attends summer school in the U. S. S. R. in 1934, visits the South Sea islands in 1967, travels on the Nile in 1958, and stays in an African game reserve camp in 1961.

1999   From Here to There.   Philadelphia: Dorrance, 1974. 189pp.

She offers a travel account that covers the years from 1929 to 1967 and that is organized by country rather than by chronology; she lives in Paris as a student in 1929, 1933, and 1964; in 1950 she travels in Scandinavia, leads a tour in Germany, and visits Rome for the Holy Year; she travels in Spain in 1952, 1955, and 1964 both as a tour leader and as a student; and she stays in England in 1955 and 1967; throughout she describes architecture, landscapes, people, customs, concerts, and plays.

2000   Land of Eternal Spring (Guatemala).   Philadelphia: Dorrance, 1974.   172pp.

She recalls ten visits to Guatemala as well as numerous trips to Mexico, Central America, and South America; she stays a year in Guatemala in 1942 and tells of her household, travels, and friendships there; a second section of her book describes a decade of travel and research for her doctoral dissertation.

2001   THORESEN, LOUISE (1937?-)
It Gave Everybody Something to Do, with E. M. Nathanson. New York: Evans, 1974.   346pp.

Married to an extremely manipulative wealthy man, she is caught up in a sordid, bizarre series of self-destructive events which include her forced abandonment of her son, her participation in thefts, drug dealing, and gun-running, her repeated suffering from beatings, her abortion; incredibly, she notes some happy moments within the chaos, but finally she is driven to murder her husband and after the trial seeks to reestablish her life.

2002   THORNBURGH, ALLENE E.
Grandpa's Store; Vignettes of a North Carolina Girlhood. New York: Pageant, 1962.   86pp.

The granddaughter of a prosperous and prominent Raleigh businessman, she tells of her family heritage of honor and integrity; she provides a fine portrait of her grandfather, and evocative recollections of her grandmother's storeroom, a

northern governess, a country wedding, a family Christmas,
and State Fair time; nearly all of the essays were previously
published in The Christian Science Monitor.

2003   THYSELL, ELLEN RANDALL
        The Bride Grew Horns.   New York: Vantage, 1956.   151pp.

        In an account drawn from letters to her sister, she tells
        of a four-month "second honeymoon" in 1951, joining her
        businessman husband in Japan without their six children;
        "adopted" by a Japanese family, she participates in their
        daily life, learns about the customs and language of Japan.

2004   TILLICH, HANNAH
        From Place to Place; Travels with Paul Tillich, Travels
        Without Paul Tillich.   New York: Stein and Day, 1976.
        223pp.

        Written in a quiet, personal voice, her account describes
        her travels with a daughter and grandson in Europe and her
        reflections on the younger generations, referring to herself
        as "the old woman"; she also recounts her observations in
        Egypt and Israel in 1963, her enchantment with Japan in
        1960, her deep response to India and Southeast Asia in 1966,
        and her trips to the Caribbean in 1967, to Mexico in 1968,
        to Spain in 1971.

2005   TOBIN, AGNES (1894-1939)
        Agnes Tobin: Letters, Translations, Poems, with Some Ac-
        count of Her Life.   San Francisco: Howell, 1958.   120pp.

        Born in France and prominent in London literary circles,
        she develops a deep affection for the English writer and poet
        Alice Meynell; most of the letters are to Meynell from 1895
        to 1911; she is sharply observant and highly articulate, writ-
        ing of her translations, of deeply moving literature, of gifts
        and mementos, of her effusive praise for Meynell's writing.

2006   TOKLAS, ALICE BABETTE (1877-1967)   NAWM
        Staying on Alone: Letters of Alice B. Toklas, ed. Edward
        Burns.   New York: Liveright, 1973.   426pp.

        After her beloved Gertrude Stein's death in 1946, writing
        letters becomes her "work," and she is kept busy carrying
        out Stein's wishes on literary matters; often bored and ex-
        hausted by visitors, tormented by the financial necessity to
        publish her cookbook, she suffers the loss of Picasso's por-
        trait of Stein and eviction in 1963 from her Paris home; she
        says with poignancy, "I am nothing but the memory of her."

2007   What Is Remembered.   New York: Holt, Rinehart and Win-
        ston, 1963.   186pp.

        The lifelong companion of writer Gertrude Stein, she
        provides staccato glimpses of her childhood and youth in
        San Francisco; in 1907 she travels to Paris and meets Stein
        who captures and holds her "complete attention, as she did
        for all the many years I knew her until her death"; she
        chronicles their artistic and literary visitors in Paris, not-
        ing their travels in Spain and England, their work transport-
        ing supplies during World War I, their "great adventure" of
        an American lecture tour in 1934, their life in the French
        countryside during the German occupation, and Stein's final
        illness; she writes with touching, deep devotion.

2008   TOMLINSON, MONETTE WHALEY
        Crossroads Cameos; Character Sketches.   San Antonio, Tex. :
        Naylor, 1964.   104pp.

        She writes many brief vignettes of her childhood in a
        Texas town at the turn of the century, exploring "my exper-
        iences with these quaint and wonderful people. "

2009   TOMPKINS, LEONARA BROOKE (1911-   )
        My Lovely Days.   New York: Carlton, 1966.   136pp.

        In an unpretentious and lively narrative, the daughter of
        the Rajah of Sarawak describes her childhood in Britain and
        in Sarawak among adult artists and celebrities; she marries
        a wealthy older man and, although spoiled, "raw and
        gauche," she enjoys "wonderful years"; the sudden death of
        her husband during World War II causes feelings of weak-
        ness and vulnerability, although she serves as a volunteer
        war worker; at war's end, she marries an American colonel,
        living first in Germany, then settling in Vermont.

2010   TOOR, FRANCES (1890-1956)
        Three Worlds of Peru.   New York: Crown, 1949.   239pp.

        Long a resident in and student of Mexico, she describes
        her year in 1948 touring in Peru; based in Lima, her ex-
        tensive travels cover the coastal region, the jungle, and the
        Andes mountains; she meets people of all social strata; she
        provides much description of historical background and physi-
        cal setting.

2011   TOPP, MILDRED SPURRIER (1897-   )
        In the Pink.   Boston: Houghton Mifflin, 1950.   242pp.

In a series of delightful vignettes she portrays her family, friends, and neighbors in Greenwood, Mississippi just after the turn of the century; her narrative becomes an evocation of the community.

2012   Smile Please. Boston: Houghton Mifflin, 1948. 280pp.

She tells of her childhood home in a photographic studio when her mother becomes a photographer in 1904 to assert her independence and support her two daughters after having been deserted; her chapters portray small local dramas that involve her mother or herself, including a humorous glimpse of her salvation by revival at nine, her mother's gentle attacks on self-righteous Christian ladies, her own earnest but ill-fated attempts to do good.

2013   TORNABENE, LYN
       I Passed as a Teenager. New York: Simon and Schuster, 1967. 253pp.

A journalist passes at thirty-four for sixteen and attends a large urban high school "in the hope that I could restore some perspective to the way we have been looking at our burgeoning younger generation"; looking outward, she describes the clothes, makeup, slang, boys, and parties of her gang of girls; looking inward, she notes her reactions and the strange personal effects of the pose, including a "marked change in my attitude toward life."

2014   TORRE, MARIE
       Don't Quote Me. Garden City, N.Y.: Doubleday, 1965. 254pp.

A journalist, she writes a light account filled with "behind the headlines" anecdotes; she is once jailed briefly for protecting a source's identity; she recounts the television quiz-show scandals of the 1950's; she closes with her career as a television newscaster.

2015   TOWNE, M. CAROLA, SISTER (1897-)
       Keys and Pedals; An Autobiography. Philadelphia: Dorrance, 1972. 173pp.

Raised by an aunt and uncle, she becomes devoted to the piano, pursuing music studies at a conservatory after 1915; her positions as church organist lead her to investigate various religions and she enters a "new life" with her conversion to Catholicism; she becomes a postulant in 1919, and reaches her goal with the taking of final vows.

2016   TRAHEY, JANE (1923-   )
        Life with Mother Superior.   New York: Farrar, Straus,
        1962.   210pp.

        Her humorous account tells of four years at a Catholic
        girls' school as a boarding student; her first practical joke
        backfires, but she continues to rebel against rules and au-
        thority, to enjoy pranks, and to avoid classes.

2017   Pecked to Death by Goslings.   Englewood Cliffs, N.J.:
        Prentice-Hall, 1969.   168pp.

        In a humorous account filled with outrageous exaggeration,
        she describes her weekend flights from a New York City ad-
        vertising agency to the country; she buys a farm in rural
        Connecticut and renovates it through her own "coolie labor";
        later crowded out by "creeping suburbia" and her numerous
        guests, she moves into a neighboring house, unable to aban-
        don the lure of the country.

2018   TRAPP, MARIA AUGUSTA von (1907?-   )
        Around the Year with the Trapp Family.   New York: Pan-
        theon, 1955.   251pp.

        The mother of a world-famous musical family, she tells
        about the strong traditions from her Catholic religion and
        her Austrian heritage which are transplanted to the U.S.
        when she and her family emigrate in 1938; she describes
        her joyful preparations for and participation in the major
        religious celebrations, rich in family meaning and loving
        activities.

2019   A Family on Wheels; Further Adventures of the Trapp Fam-
        ily Singers, with Ruty T. Murdoch.   Philadelphia: Lippin-
        cott, 1959.   222pp.

        She writes of the family's world tours beginning in 1949,
        two years after her husband's death; they travel extensively
        in the U.S., then tour in South America, singing and sight-
        seeing; in 1950 they experience an emotional return to Aus-
        tria, having escaped before World War II; later travels in-
        clude Scandinavia, the Hawaiian Islands, and Australia, until
        their farewell concert in 1955; throughout she maintains a
        close, religious family life.

2020   Maria.   Carol Stream, Ill.:   Creation House, 1972.   203pp.

        In this sequel to her earlier autobiography, she reveals
        more about her unhappy, mischievous childhood, marked by

a distant, demanding father; her headstrong decision to enter
a convent leads to "two momentous years" in which she
learns discipline; her first real experience of love comes
as the stepmother of seven children; following a recapitula-
tion of her married life and years of concert tours, she describes a year of lay missionary work in the South Pacific
and her later lecturing and managing the family guest house
in Vermont; spirited and unpretentious, she presents a candid assessment of her problems, mistakes, and continual
growth, aided by her spiritual reawakening.

2021   The Story of the Trapp Family Singers, Yesterday, Today,
and Forever.   Philadelphia: Lippincott, 1949.   309pp.

She opens with the story of her tenure as governess in
the Trapp household in Austria and her marriage into the
family in 1927, becoming the joyful mother of seven step-
children and two of her own; in 1935 the Trapp Family
Singers are born after the financial crash destroys the family fortune; they flee the Nazis in 1938, settling in the
U. S., "learning new ways" as national concert tours allow
them to express a sense of mission through music; their
Vermont farm home establishes a deep attachment to the
land and to America as their "exile turned into glory"; she
closes with her husband's death in 1947.

2022   TRAUBEL, HELEN FRANCESCA (1899-1972)   NAWM
St. Louis Woman, in collaboration with Richard G. Hubler.
New York: Duell, Sloan and Pearce, 1959.   296pp.

Born in St. Louis, she describes a childhood of music,
happiness and security; with single-minded concentration
on her career as a singer, and proud to have been raised
and trained in the U. S., she becomes a Wagnerian soprano
with the Met in 1939; boredom moves her to try popular
songs, nightclub and television appearances beginning in
1953; she loves the response of new audiences; a disorgan-
ized, anecdotal, but lively and entertaining account.

2023   TRAUTMAN, KATHLEEN
Spies Behind the Pillars, Bandits at the Pass.   New York:
David McKay, 1972.   244pp.

In this humane account tinged with anti-establishment sen-
timents, the wife of an official with the U. S. Embassy in
Afghanistan describes householding with her husband and two
children in Kabul; observant, relaxed, and receptive, she
tells of her social faux pas, her experiences as an English
teacher, her friendships with her servants, her distress
over the "CIA and other disasters," and her discomfort as

"a member of the ruling class"; she closes with her husband's resignation from the foreign service and their return to the U. S.

2024   TRAVELL, JANET (1901-   )
Office Hours: Day and Night; The Autobiography of Janet Travell, M. D. New York: World, 1968. 496pp.

"The first woman to serve as Personal Physician to the President" during Kennedy's term, she describes her life of love, adventure, and achievement; following without hesitation in her father's footsteps, she pursues her medical vocation after studies at Wellesley and a European grand tour; she marries in 1929, engages in teaching and research as well as patient care, and raises two daughters; formally appointed as the President's doctor in 1961, she applies her knowledge of muscular pain and industrial seating; her account reveals a woman of vigor and imagination.

2025   TRAYNOR, EVELYN MARTIN KELLY (1892-   )
They Also Serve. New York: Vantage, 1965. 50pp.

This is the "life story of the travels of the wife of three Naval officers"; married first in 1913, she is widowed during World War I; she remarries in 1919 and enjoys extended stays in the Orient; widowed again, she does Red Cross work during World War II; after she is widowed a third time, she notes with gratitude her many years of happiness.

2026   TREVIÑO, ELIZABETH BORTON (1904-   )
My Heart Lies South: The Story of My Mexican Marriage. New York: Crowell, 1953. 248pp.

A journalist on assignment in Mexico, she marries there and is gradually drawn to her husband's family, traditions, and language; living in genteel poverty, housekeeping with servants who constitute a close part of a warm family life, entertaining in spite of social mishaps, enjoying an "enormous intimate club of pregnant ladies," she is completely charmed by life in Mexico and by woman's role there.

2027   TROBISCH, INGRID HULT
On Our Way Rejoicing! New York: Harper & Row, 1964. 254pp.

The daughter of a missionary, she is inspired after her father's death in Africa by her discovery of his journals, feeling a "call to action"; she finishes college and missionary training, then goes to Africa to teach; married in 1952 to a

fellow missionary, she continues work although her efforts
are thwarted by French administrators, African chiefs, and
native superstitions; she raises four children, maintaining
close ties with her family, all dedicated missionaries.

2028   TRUAX, SARAH
        A Woman of Parts; Memories of a Life on Stage.   New
        York: Longmans, Green, 1949.   247pp.

        Encouraged by an ambitious mother, she gains a strong
musical background, then begins drama school at thirteen
and joins a touring stock company, spending "winters on
the road ... summers in stock"; she marries, endures poverty and unemployment, divorces, remarries, vows to give
up the stage, but returns to amateur community theatre
work and to more stock company roles; she offers occasional reflections on the problems of combining motherhood
and career; she never attains her goal of starring in New
York.

2029   TRUMAN, MARGARET (1924-   )
        Souvenir: Margaret Truman's Own Story, with Margaret
        Cousins.   New York: McGraw-Hill, 1956.   265pp.

        In a warm, straightforward narrative, she tells of a
"completely happy" childhood, the daughter of Bess and
Harry Truman; her youth is split between homes in Washington and Independence; sincerely modest, she is nonetheless quick to appreciate the benefits accruing to her position; with parental support, she pursues a voice career,
finding snatches of family life in the interstices of public
obligations including grueling tours during the 1948 campaign; after her parents leave the White House in 1952, she
continues with a busy social life and singing career; throughout she maintains a strong sense of family privacy.

2030   TRUMAN, RUTH (1931-   )
        Underground Manual for Ministers' Wives.   Nashville: Ab-
        ingdon, 1974.   173pp.

        In an upbeat account, she offers advice to others based
on her own varied experiences as a minister's wife; she discusses social expectations, the relationships with a husband
and children, the necessity to establish one's own identity,
the associations with parishioners, financial cares, and the
ultimate joys and satisfactions of her role.

2031   TURK, MIDGE (1930-   )
        The Buried Life: A Nun's Journey.   New York: World,
        1971.   196pp.

She enters a convent in 1948 and describes her adjustments to convent routine and expectation; uncertainty marks
her years as a postulant and novice; she enters mission
work as a teacher and describes the burden of inadequate
professional training, added to tasks as a sister; she takes
her final vows in 1953; exhausted by her heavy schedule,
frustrated with male church hierarchy, shocked by horrors
of ghetto conditions at a slum school, her health breaks;
she leaves her order in 1966.

2032   TURLINGTON, CATHERINE ISABEL HACKETT
       Three to Make Ready.   New York: Vanguard, 1948.   303pp.

She presents a humorous series of small domestic episodes illustrating her pride and exasperation as the mother
of three teen-aged daughters; she notes the preparations for
a daughter's departure for college, teen parties, arrange-
ments with the family car, Christmas routine, spring gardening, the girls' summer jobs, and the family vacation.

2033   TURNBULL, AGNES SLIGH (1888-   )
       Out of My Heart.   Boston: Houghton Mifflin, 1958.   158pp.

A novelist and children's writer, she decides "to set down
a few of the most important lessons life has presented to
me"; in a series of quiet vignettes, she evokes scenes from
her childhood, illuminated by reflections on religion and
values.

2034   TURNBULL, GRACE HILL (1880?-   )
       Chips from My Chisel; An Autobiography.   Rindge, N.H.:
       Smith, 1953.   256pp.

A painter, sculptor, philosopher, and highly articulate
writer, she demonstrates a wide range of artistic and intellectual achievements; drawn to the common people as sub-
jects for her painting, she holds her first major exhibit in
1908; after study and work in Europe, she serves with the
Red Cross in France and Germany during and just after
World War I; in the 1920's she turns to sculpting; she publishes books on religion, philosophy, and social welfare; she
closes this account on a note of deep humility.

2035   TURNER, GLADYS VANDERBURG
       Hold Fast to Your Dream; The Story of Building a Life, a
       Home, and a Church.   New York: Exposition, 1962.   80pp.

Her random recollections include anecdotes of her childhood in an Indiana pioneer family, tales of difficult times

after her marriage, and stories of her work restoring a
community church; she is the author of newspaper and
magazine articles, and fulfills her childhood vow to write
a book.

2036   TURNOR, MAE CAESAR
        Memory Lane in My Southern World.   New York: Vantage,
        1968.   136pp.

In a narrative of random recollections, she tells of her
childhood experiences with discrimination, racial intolerance,
and "diabolical outrages" in Texas; later a touring singer
and a public school teacher in Oklahoma, she discusses the
support provided by her religious beliefs and the aspirations
of black people in spite of struggles with racism.

2037　ULRICH, SHARON
　　　　Elizabeth, with Anna W. M. Wolf.　Ann Arbor:　University
　　　　of Michigan Press, 1972.　122pp.

　　　　When her fifth child is born blind, she rejects the "mar-
　　　tyr" role and works intensely to develop her daughter's
　　　abilities; she participates in a project on babies blind from
　　　birth, treated as an equal by professionals and both learning
　　　from and teaching them; throughout she's realistic about the
　　　joys and discouragement that accompany her efforts.

2038　UNDERWOOD, AGNESS (1902-　)
　　　　Newspaperwoman.　New York:　Harper & Brothers, 1949.
　　　　297pp.

　　　　Her autobiography is told in a straight, spare, tough
　　　style; orphaned at five, shunted from relative to relative as
　　　a child, she is on her own by fifteen; she becomes a report-
　　　er for the Los Angeles Record and recounts numerous stories
　　　she covers; she later becomes the city editor for Hearst's
　　　Herald-Express.

2039　UNTERMEYER, JEAN STARR (1886-　)
　　　　Private Collection.　New York:　Knopf, 1965.　295pp.

　　　　A poet and translator, she feels "recurring nostalgia" for
　　　the idyllic land of her childhood; she is musically gifted and
　　　drawn to beauty, and after her marriage in 1907 she lives
　　　in a heady atmosphere of music and literature; after the
　　　shock of World War I, the death of her son, and the de-
　　　parture of her husband, she experiences a poetic renais-
　　　sance, providing miniature portraits of Teasdale, Millay,
　　　and Amy Lowell from her wide acquaintance; she lives in
　　　Europe from 1923 to 1925, makes her singing debut, and
　　　enjoys an intense "educative experience" with a German au-
　　　thor from whom she translates.

2040　UTINSKY, MARGARET (1900-　)
　　　　"Miss U."　San Antonio:　Naylor, 1948.　172pp.

　　　　Having refused evacuation to the U.S., she is present at

the Japanese occupation of Manila, hiding for several months, then posing as a Lithuanian; she builds an extensive underground network, smuggling money, food, and medicine into prison camps to aid Americans and collecting arms for guerrilla forces; captured and tortured by the Japanese, she flees into the hills, nursing guerrilla wounded until Manila's liberation by U.S. forces; her remarkable account reveals a tough, heroic woman.

2041   UTLEY, FREDA (1898-)
        Lost Illusion. Philadelphia: Fireside, 1948. 288pp.

Her narrative is a condensed and revised version of The Dream We Lost (see companion volume); born in England, she notes the profound influences of a happy childhood, a Continental education, and a socialist father, and she becomes a political romantic, a communist dedicated to social justice; married in 1928 to a Russian, she settles in Russia for six years, working as a researcher and fired by dreams of revolutionary progress; she describes her horror at the deterioration of political, social, and economic conditions but she is unable to speak out for fear of her husband's safety; with his arrest and disappearance in 1936, she flees with her son, able at last to follow her inner integrity and warn others.

2042   Odyssey of a Liberal; Memoirs. Washington, D.C.: Washington National Press, 1970. 319pp.

A writer, economist, and highly principled "ex-Communist anti-Communist," she presents a sequel to The Dreams We Lost; when she returns to England, having fled Russia in 1936, she finds her devastating knowledge of the communist terror in Russia poses a political and moral dilemma; she discusses writers Agnes Smedley, Edgar Snow, and Emily Hahn (see entry #834); she lives under continuing financial pressure to support her mother and son; in 1939 she settles in the U.S., finding it the closest to her political ideal and devoting herself to "alerting America to the Communist menace," deeply disappointed in the failure of her earlier memoir to have a political impact.

2043   VANDERBILT, CONSUELO
        see BALSAN, CONSUELO VANDERBILT (1877-)

2044   VANDERBILT, GLORIA MORGAN (1905-)
        Double Exposure; A Twin Autobiography.   New York: David
        McKay, 1958.   369pp.

        With her twin sister, Thelma Furness (see entry #729),
        she is raised with "enormous pride" in her family back-
        ground, the daughter of a diplomat and a "warped, obses-
        sive" mother; at seventeen she marries into the Vanderbilt
        family and, widowed three years later, finds herself caught
        in a long legal ordeal over the custody of her daughter
        Gloria; later, cut off from Vanderbilt financial support, her
        world of "splendor and extravagance" is shattered, and she
        is supported by her sister with whom she enters the per-
        fume business.

2045   VAN der VEER, JUDY
        My Valley in the Sky.   New York: Julian Messner, 1959.
        256pp.

        A writer, she describes her desire "to live in the coun-
        try and have lots of animals and write stories about them";
        she focuses on the small joys and quiet understandings of
        daily events, describing the personalities of her numerous
        animals, the beauty of the land, the seasons and the weath-
        er, and the renewal that comes with the rain.

2046   VANDEVORT, ELEANOR
        A Leopard Tamed; The Story of an African Pastor, His
        People and His Problems.   New York: Harper & Row,
        1968.   218pp.

        A college graduate, she goes to Africa as a missionary
        at twenty-four and spends thirteen years with the Nuer peo-
        ple in the Sudan; she marks the changes in her preconceived
        ideas, her growth in understanding, her acceptance of native
        culture; she is a friend and advisor to a young man with
        whom she collaborates on a Bible translation; in 1963 she
        and other American missionaries are evicted from the Sudan.

2047   VAN DOREN, DOROTHY GRAFFE (1896-   )
        The Country Wife. New York: Sloane, 1950. 246pp.

        A writer and prominent professor's wife, she tells of long
        summers on the family's Connecticut farm, from spring
        packing rituals to gardening, to traditional July Fourth cele-
        brations, to the enjoyment of weekend guests; during sabbati-
        cals, they remain in the country, savoring New England win-
        ters; she emphasizes the warm moments of close family life.

2048   The Professor and I.   New York: Appleton-Century-Crofts,
        1959.   246pp.

        A writer and the wife of a noted literature professor, she
        opens with the story of her son Charles' appearances on a
        television quiz show; but the book is largely a series of
        pleasant family anecdotes of their semi-retirement, dividing
        their time between New York and the country; taking quiet
        delight in small things, she tells of her New York house,
        family cats, travels, gardening, and bird watching.

2049   VAN DYKE, PHYLLIS (1905-   )
        So Close to Heaven. New York: Vantage, 1963. 46pp.

        A kindergarten teacher tells of her experiences from her
        first day in the classroom and describes what she learns
        through working with young children.

2050   VAN HOOSEN, BERTHA (1863-1952)   NAWM
        Petticoat Surgeon.   Chicago: Pellegrini & Cudahy, 1947.
        324pp.

        She is grateful for her rural heritage which gives her an
        intense interest in biology and "a kind of toughness"; she
        enters the University of Michigan in 1880, begins her medi-
        cal studies in 1885, and gains experience in hospital service;
        specializing in obstetrics and gynecology, she holds several
        teaching posts, and becomes the first woman professor of
        obstetrics at a co-educational medical school; she serves as
        the first president of an organization of women in medicine
        in 1917 and works to encourage the training of other women
        surgeons.

2051   VAN LEER, TWILA
        Life Is Just a Bowl of Kumquats. New York: Saturday Re-
        view Press, 1972.   133pp.

        A reporter and weekly columnist in Montana and a mother
        of nine children, she presents light, humorous reflections on

domestic topics; she acknowledges that "parenthood is hard," noting calamities of varying degrees of seriousness, everything complicated by the sheer size of her family.

2052   VAN NES, MARY FELTS
Into the Wind.   Philadelphia: Lippincott, 1957.   224pp.

Marriage and the raising of six children deflect her career as a concert pianist; her entire family loves sailing, and their seventy-foot schooner provides a fine heritage of adventure, experience, growth, and independence for her children; her numerous recollections focus on voyages, for the boat becomes a central "part of my emotional life."

2053   VAN NUYS, LAURA BOWER (1880-   )
The Family Band; From the Missouri to the Black Hills, 1881-1900.   Lincoln: University of Nebraska Press, 1961. 256pp.

The youngest of eight children in a close family, she describes how their pioneering in South Dakota is enlivened by musical activity; with the coming of the railroad, the family band becomes a semi-professional group, performing at church meetings and fairs; after recounting a typical year's events, lightened by much laughter, she tells of the family's final band concert in 1895.

2054   VEEVERS-CARTER, WENDY
Island Home.   New York: Random, 1970.   345pp.

After ten years of peripatetic marriage and still a devotée of travel and adventure, she opts for over three years of "life in the tropics" on an island off the east African coast with her British husband and two children; they establish a plantation, striving for self-sufficiency, and she discusses the subtleties of relationships with the foremen and laborers, presiding over births, illnesses, and deaths, attempting to understand another culture; she reflects on raising children in such a remote place, giving them a heritage of contentment.

2055   VESTER, BERTHA HEDGES SPAFFORD (1878-   )
Our Jerusalem; An American Family in the Holy City, 1881-1949.   Garden City, N.Y.:   Doubleday, 1950.   332pp.

Her parents seek peace and solace after a family tragedy and settle in Jerusalem in 1881, founding "the American Colony of Jerusalem"; in a "reverential and devout" home atmosphere, she grows up aware of her mother's work in nursing and maternal and child welfare and her father's

Bible teaching; following in their footsteps as an adult, she
directs a Moslem girls' school, provides humanitarian relief
for both sides during World War I, establishes a "Baby
Home" and works with the Red Cross after the war, demonstrating her lifelong dedication to the founding of a refuge
for all nationalities and creeds.

2056 VIERTEL, SALKA
The Kindness of Strangers. New York: Holt, Rinehart and
Winston, 1969. 338pp.

A Polish Jew, her early obsession with the theater is
discouraged by parents, but at the death of her fiancé she
studies acting in Vienna; she describes her grueling work in
German theater; marries a stage director in 1918, bears
three sons, continues to act; tells of theater in Berlin in
1920's; moves to Hollywood in 1928, works as a screenwriter, especially for Garbo films, but meets with much frustration; her marriage fails but she maintains close ties with her
husband; becomes U.S. citizen in 1939, tells of the German
refugee colony in California during World War II; she is
harassed in the 1950's by anti-communists.

2057 VIGNEC, ELSIE ESSMULLER
Children of Hope; Some Stories of the New York Foundling
Hospital. New York: Dodd, Mead, 1964. 213pp.

Fond of children, she volunteers her services at the
New York Foundling Hospital during World War II and "in
a single day my life changed"; she becomes a paid staff
member and breaks an engagement with a man who cannot
accept her devotion to her work; she is encouraged to seek
further education in college, continuing her strong attachment to the children; she later marries the home's medical
director; her emotional account is touching.

2058 VINING, ELIZABETH GRAY (1902-)
Quiet Pilgrimage. Philadelphia: Lippincott, 1970. 410pp.

A novelist and children's author, she tells of her happy
childhood and early recognition of her vocation; after attending Bryn Mawr, she returns home "to write" in 1923; in
1929 she enters an "old-fashioned marriage," but after four
idyllic years, her husband dies suddenly and she must draw
upon her religious strength as a Quaker; she cherishes her
experience as tutor to Japan's Crown Prince from 1946 to
1950, years which produce close friendships.

2059 Return to Japan. Philadelphia: Lippincott, 1960. 285pp.

She goes to an international P. E. N. congress in Japan in 1957 hoping to renew old friendships from her earlier stay; she is received with honor, enjoying touching reunions and traveling as a tourist as well; she returns in 1959 to attend the wedding of the Crown Prince, her former pupil.

2060 Windows for the Crown Prince.   Philadelphia: Lippincott, 1952.   320pp.

A Philadelphia Quaker, she is chosen to be the tutor to the Crown Prince of Japan just after World War II and spends four years there; she finds the imperial family generous and humane and they develop a deep respect and affection for each other; an imaginative teacher, she brings democratic ideals to imperial customs, rejoicing in her pupil's increasing confidence and maturity and welcoming her own absorption in Japanese culture.

2061 von MISES, MARGIT (1896?-)
      My Years with Ludwig von Mises.   New Rochelle, N. Y. :
      Arlington, 1976.   191pp.

Born in Germany, she pursues a theatrical career in spite of her mother's resistance; after her first marriage in 1917, she is torn between her career and motherhood and describes hardships during and after World War I; widowed at twenty-seven, she begins a "stormy relationship" with the prominent economist von Mises in 1925; fleeing from Vienna in 1937, they marry and she adjusts to his life and needs; in 1940 they settle in the U. S. and she dedicates her efforts to helping with his work; she closes with his death in 1973.

2062 von TEMPSKI, ARMINE
      see TEMPSKI, ARMINE von (1899-1943)

2063 von TRAPP, MARIA AUGUSTA
      see TRAPP, MARIA AUGUSTA von (1907?-)

2064 WADELTON, MAGGIE-OWEN
see WADELTON, MAGGIE JEANNE MELODY (1896-)

2065 WADELTON, MAGGIE JEANNE MELODY (1896-)
Gay, Wild and Free; From Captain's Wife to Colonel's Lady.
Indianapolis: Bobbs-Merrill, 1949. 312pp.

Married to an officer in 1917, she describes twenty-eight
years as an "army wife"; not overly fond of "precedent and
protocol," she gradually learns to relish army post life, describing in a humorous, arch vein characters and social
events on a series of posts.

2066 WAHLE, ANNE
Ordeal by Fire; An American Woman's Terror-Filled Trek
Through War-Torn Germany, as told to Roul Tunley. Cleve-
land: World, 1966. 152pp.

The wife of an Austrian diplomat posted in Dresden makes
an incredible escape after the fire-bombing of 1945; her six-
hundred-mile flight to a maid's Austrian village is a saga on
foot and by train in which she survives cold, hunger, and
numerous bombing raids; she reaches her haven only months
before the war's end.

2067 WAINER, NORA ROBERTS
Waterway Journey; The Voyage of Nora's Ark. New York:
Funk & Wagnalls, 1968. 247pp.

She and her husband fulfill their dreams of adventure on
the high seas by building a sailboat and traveling for three
months along the Atlantic Intracoastal Waterway; after two
years of preparation, they savor the "excitement, danger,
good times, strange ports" along the way; at journey's end,
they sell the boat, keeping only their experiences and memories.

2068 WAITZMANN, DOROTHEA
A Special Way of Victory, with Georgia Harkness. Richmond, Va.: Knox, 1964. 104pp.

Born with cerebral palsy and adopted by a single woman who later marries, she enjoys a singularly close and supportive family life and school career; she graduates from high school in the early 1930's and writes for local newspapers; she is forced to assume family responsibilities during her mother's and aunt's illnesses; after her mother's death, she vacillates between Catholicism and Methodism, focusing her writing on devotional material; she begins college at the age of forty-three, and is determined to be self-supporting.

2069   WALDRON, D'LYNN (1937?-)
Further Than at Home.   New York: Harper & Brothers, 1959.   183pp.

At twenty, she sets out to travel around the world and "to discover other peoples"; leaving by boat from the west coast, she begins to wander, look, and sketch in Japan, continuing across the Far East and the Middle East; her observations are detailed and straightforward.

2070   WALGREEN, MYRTLE R. NORTON (1879-)
Never a Dull Day, as told to Marguerite Harmon Bro. Chicago: Regnery, 1963.   334pp.

Raised in the midwest in a happy family, she recounts random memories; in Chicago, she takes secretarial training, marries Charles Walgreen and tells of the growth of their drug store business; an enthusiastic homemaker, she later works for civic causes, enjoys gardening, takes up nature photography, and works with 4-H; she tells of her acquaintances with prominent people.

2071   WALKER, ALVERA G.
My Genes from Daddy.   New York: Pageant, 1961.   35pp.

Opening with "I wish I were a man," she writes a rambling account primarily of her "hillbilly ancestors" and of a lively, close, extended family; she marries in 1930 and suffers the death of a long-awaited infant daughter.

2072   WALKER, GEORGIANA FREEMAN GHOLSON (1833-1904)
The Private Journal of Georgiana Gholson Walker, 1862-1865, with Selections from the Post-War Years, 1865-1876, ed. Dwight Franklin Henderson.   Tuscaloosa, Ala.:   Confederate, 1963.   148pp.

Determined to join her husband in Bermuda, she courageously runs a Yankee sea blockade with three young children and while pregnant with her fourth; she settles there amid a "confederate coterie," closely following the course of the war, whose human and economic costs she decries; crushed by the Confederate defeat, she lives in "exile" in England and returns sorrowfully to Virginia only in 1876.

2073   WALKER, MARGARET (1915-   )
How I Wrote Jubilee.   Chicago: Third World, 1972.   36pp.

A black poet and novelist describes the lifelong "organic growth" of her novel Jubilee (1966) whose genesis in her childhood leads to years of scholarship and research infused by the vibrant memory of her grandmother's tale of her great-grandmother's life in slavery; she persists, although her work is interrupted by marriage, motherhood, and graduate studies.

2074   WALL, KATHIE
Keeping Up with Kathie: A College Girl's Letters Home from England and the Continent.   New York: Exposition, 1963.   97pp.

A college student on a junior year abroad program in 1961-1962 writes enthusiastic, exclamatory letters home describing her schooling in a London convent, travels, and cultural activities; she absorbs all new experiences, grateful for the educational opportunity.

2075   WALL, MARTHA
Splinters from an African Log.   Chicago: Moody, 1960. 319pp.

A missionary nurse for twelve years in French West Africa, she describes joining a German Mennonite community at eighteen in defiance of her father; in 1939 she travels to Africa, learning nursing anew under difficult conditions, enjoys the "romance and novelty" and the camaraderie of mission personnel; she notes her initial revulsion at a leper settlement, her first contacts with the local women's culture, her struggles against Islam, her various patients; ill health cuts short her "magnificent career."

2076   WALLACE, ALLIE B. (1889?-   )
Frontier Life in Oklahoma.   Washington, D.C.:   Public Affairs Press, 1964.   136pp.

Her family homesteads in the Oklahoma Territory when she is five years old; she describes household tasks and general domestic conditions in great detail; she tells of her Indian acquaintances, religious practices, school, pastimes,

neighbors, seasonal activities; she credits pioneer life for
her own qualities of patience, simplicity, sincerity, and
love of nature; her account covers the years before her
marriage.

2077   WALLACE, CORNELIA (1939-   )
        C'nelia: An Intimate Self-Portrait.   Philadelphia: Holman/
        Lippincott, 1976.   240pp.

        She opens with a detailed account of the attempted assas-
        sination of her husband, Alabama Governor George Wallace,
        in 1972; she then recalls her own family ties with Alabama
        politics, growing up in the governor's mansion when her
        uncle was elected; she tells of a youthful romance, a luke-
        warm career as a singer, a job with a water-ski show, and
        a brief marriage that leaves her with two sons; marrying
        Wallace in 1971, she is devoted to him, setting aside her
        desires for a home life outside of politics, helping his re-
        covery and return to politics.

2078   WALLACE, ELIZABETH (1865-   )
        The Unending Journey.   Minneapolis: University of Minne-
        sota Press, 1952.   286pp.

        After a childhood spent in Colombia, she returns to the
        U.S. with her family and attends a female seminary, then
        Wellesley from 1882 to 1886; she teaches in Minneapolis;
        she joins the University of Chicago in 1892, relishing the
        excitement and comradeship of a new educational venture;
        she studies and teaches Latin-American history, Spanish,
        and French literature for thirty-four years, making numer-
        ous trips to France for further study; she is a friend of
        Mark Twain; she describes her work in France during World
        War I; after her retirement, she continues to travel, lec-
        ture, and study, a constantly learning and growing individual.

2079   WALLACE, MILDRED YOUNG
        We Three; Papa's Ladies.   San Antonio: Naylor, 1957.
        192pp.

        She produces a lively reminiscence of her particularly
        close family life with two sisters in a New York village; the
        family moves to a Mexican mining town for which she de-
        velops great fondness, and she tells delightful tales of her
        activities and amusements, as well as incidents during the
        Mexican revolution that touch her life; she is sent back to
        the U.S. for a high school education, a move that separates
        the three sisters; she closes with brief comments on her
        later marriage and motherhood.

2080   WALSTON, MARIE
        These Were My Hills.   Valley Forge: Judson, 1972.   128pp.

        She writes of family life in the Ozarks as a minister's
        daughter; she relates local anecdotes, describes her neigh-
        bors, and tells of her father's attempts to build a congrega-
        tion.

2081   WALTERMAN, EUNICE (1912-   )
        Don't Call Me Dad.   Kansas City, Kan.:   the author, 1950.
        195pp.

        Married and the mother of twins, she is shocked to dis-
        cover in 1943 that she was an adopted child; obsessed by the
        search for her biological parents, she has an emotional re-
        union with her mother but is rebuffed by her wealthy, power-
        ful father, Roosevelt's envoy to the Vatican; she suffers
        threats and intimidation but does achieve grim satisfaction
        in a melodramatic confrontation with him; her suit to estab-
        lish his paternity is unsuccessful in what she argues is a
        miscarriage of justice.

2082   WALTERS, BARBARA (1931-   )
        How to Talk with Practically Anybody About Practically Any-
        thing.   Garden City, N.Y.:   Doubleday, 1970.   195pp.

        A television journalist, she discusses in this combination
        of advice and anecdote her "techniques for drawing people
        out"; she recounts interviews with celebrities, tycoons,
        royalty, and other "difficult people."

2083   WALTERS, MADGE HARDIN SMITH
        Early Days and Indian Ways: The Journal of Madge Hardin
        Walters.   Los Angeles: Westernlore, 1956.   254pp.

        Her "interest and friendship" for Indians begins during
        her Wisconsin childhood; after an unhappy marriage and di-
        vorce during the early 1900's, she turns to writing to sup-
        port herself and her children; in 1922 she moves to Colorado
        and becomes absorbed by Indian life, dealing in Navajo rugs,
        pottery, and jewelry; she collects items, developing a fine
        appreciation for Indian craftsmanship and respect and admir-
        ation for Indian culture; portions of the book were written as
        early as 1940.

2084   WARD, ELIZABETH LESTER (1904-   )
        No Dudes Few Women; Life with a Navaho Range Rider.   Al-
        buquerque: University of New Mexico Press, 1951.   251pp.

Enduring the hardships and loneliness of pioneer life on a Navaho reservation with courage, a sense of humor, and increasing skill, she grows to love the land and the people; she notes Indians' hostility to some New Deal policies, some whites' racial prejudice, her own experiences with relief work, and the impact of World War II on the reservation; she leaves with deep contentment at having known Navaho culture.

2085   WARD, HARRIET SHERRILL (1803-1865)
        Prairie Schooner Lady; The Journal of Harriet Sherrill
        Ward, 1853.   Los Angeles: Westernlore, 1959.   180pp.

In April of 1853 she crosses the prairie with her daughter to settle with an adult son in California; she comments on various "miserable villages" in Iowa, and describes Nebraska's Platte River as "a miserable, unpleasant place indeed"; fearing the Indians and terrified by thunder and lightning storms, she nevertheless "becomes accustomed to privations," and gradually takes more pleasure in "our wandering Gypsy life."

2086   WARD, MAISIE (1899-   )
        To & Fro on the Earth: The Sequel to an Autobiography.
        New York: Sheed and Ward, 1973.   176pp.

A biographer, she is born in England but a later resident of the U. S.; in this largely impersonal sequel to Unfinished Business, she tells of her perspectives on the "confusion bordering on chaos of the tragic world"; she is active in the Catholic Worker movement and in efforts toward a nonviolent Christian revolution, reflecting on war and conscientious objectors; she travels in Australia and India and revisits England.

2087   Unfinished Business.   New York: Sheed and Ward, 1964.
        374pp.

Raised in a British family of "strong-minded characters," the daughter of a novelist mother and an editor and biographer father, both prominent in Catholic circles, she presents vivid recollections of an "unduly prolonged childhood"; as a young adult she pursues various "incoherent activities" including a Court presentation and volunteer nursing during World War I; after her marriage, she and her husband establish Sheed and Ward, a Catholic publishing house, and her full days are spent with her two children, home, publishing, and writing; she is deeply involved with the Catholic Worker movement, before and after her move to the U. S., and is an associate of Dorothy Day (see entry #529).

2088   WAREN, HELEN
        The Buried Are Screaming. New York: Beechhurst, 1948.
        186pp.

        A theatre and radio actress, she tours with the U. S. O.
        in 1944 and, a non-religious Jew herself, she becomes
        aware of the plight of the post-war Jews; in 1945 she goes
        to Germany, unprepared for the injustice and anti-Semitism
        of displaced-person camps and "the catastrophic horrors
        which I found'; she provides legal and illegal aid for Jews,
        facilitating their flight to Palestine via an underground net-
        work; returning to the U. S. , she carries her message to
        prominent Americans and to the public.

2089   WARFIELD, FRANCES (1901-   )
        Cotton in My Ears. New York: Viking, 1948.   152pp.

        She presents a child's perspective on her hearing prob-
        lems and her constant attempts to mask them; subterfuges,
        "narrow escapes," and defensive tactics continue in board-
        ing school and college; maintaining a career as a newspaper
        and magazine editor with small difficulties, she hopes for a
        cure; only when she lets down her defenses and accepts love
        and marriage can she finally acknowledge and accept her
        deafness.

2090   Keep Listening. New York: Viking, 1957.   158pp.

        A writer discusses her "personal revolution," struggling
        to admit and overcome her hearing loss; she probes its ef-
        fects on her childhood and youth; she studiously ignores her
        handicap until 1933 when she finally decides to learn lip-
        reading which leads to her active association with the New
        York League for the Hard of Hearing; after 1941 she uses a
        hearing aid, fighting to break old habits of inattention; she
        travels and lectures to bring deafness to public attention and
        also writes a semi-autobiographical novel about hearing dif-
        ficulties; her hearing is ultimately restored by surgery.

2091   WARNER, ESTHER SIETMANN (1910-   )
        The Crossing Fee; A Story of Life in Liberia.   Boston:
        Houghton Mifflin, 1968.   303pp.

        A collector of handicrafts, masks, textiles, and pottery,
        she describes the excitement of an expedition into remote
        areas; with her keen interest in people, she notes that "Af-
        rica helped form me"; when she returns with her husband
        twenty years later, she rejoins old friends and notes cultural
        changes; she feels that the Liberians know how to infuse
        meaning and "poetry in daily life"; and from them she learns
        joy.

2092   New Song in a Strange Land. Boston: Houghton Mifflin,
        1948.   302pp.

        A sculptor travels with her husband to Liberia to learn
        about "primitive carvings and native handicrafts"; in a
        charming, articulate account, she describes householding,
        traveling, and sculpting there, discovering a deep artistic
        kinship with an old woodcarver; she finds it painful to leave
        the "intrinsic fineness and the amazing culture" of the Lib-
        erians.

2093   Seven Days to Lomaland. Boston: Houghton Mifflin, 1954.
        269pp.

        In order to regain her position of trust among her Liber-
        ian acquaintances, she feels compelled to walk into the
        Liberian interior to witness a trial by ordeal to help clear
        the name of a friend; her "insatiable curiosity about every-
        thing native" is a further inducement for what emerges as a
        dramatic journey through which she achieves a sense of
        deeper understanding and intimacy with Liberian culture as
        well as with those individuals close to her.

2094   WASHINGTON, VIVIAN EDWARDS (1914-)
        Mount Ascutney. New York: Comet Press, 1958.   66pp.

        A black teacher and social worker, she notes that her
        "drive" and "aggressiveness" date from her childhood con-
        frontations with discrimination in a small Connecticut town;
        she loves academic work, learns much from domestic work,
        and enjoys summers of acceptance and hard work on a
        ranch; wishing to possess her black heritage, she attends
        Howard University, and later becomes the "first colored
        school social worker in Baltimore."

2095   WASIK, ANNE MARIE (1925-)
        Supposedly an Insomniac. New York: Vantage, 1962.   204pp.

        This is a dreary, rather inarticulate account of unending
        troubles; her childhood is beset by financial worries, par-
        ental restrictions, tensions due to her father's drinking, her
        mother's death followed by sibling squabbles and complaints;
        widowed soon after her marriage, she works as an aide in
        a mental institution; after her sister's mental illness, she
        too becomes a mental patient and suffers from punitive treat-
        ment, returning later to nursing work.

2096   WASON, BETTY (1912-)
        Ellen: A Mother's Story of Her Runaway Daughter.   New
        York: Reader's Digest Press, 1976.   216pp.

A writer and journalist, she tells of a reunion and partial reconciliation with her daughter after the latter's years
of behavioral problems, drug abuse, international wandering,
and subsistence commune living; discussing the background
of their relationship, she describes her feelings of maternal
guilt and helplessness, her initial inability to accept her
daughter's values, and the poignancy of her response to her
daughter's pregnancy and motherhood; seeking to understand,
she reads much and comes to accept some aspects of the
"hippie heritage."

2097   WATERMAN, SHERRY
       From Another Island; Adventures and Misadventures of an
       Airline Stewardess.   Philadelphia: Chilton, 1962,   206pp.

    She tells of her career from 1950 to 1959 on "the outer
edge of an inner circle" of flyers; writing of the routine
and the "accidental excitements" in numerous anecdotes, she
describes interesting colleagues, passengers, domestic and
international flights; she notes occasional fatigue and fear
but emphasizes the positive.

2098   WATERS, ETHEL (1900-   )
       His Eye Is on the Sparrow, with Charles Samuels.   Garden
       City, N.Y.: Doubleday, 1951.   278pp.

    The well-known black singer and actress recalls that she
never "was a child"; shunted among various relatives and
left to raise herself, she becomes street-wise and physically
tough, observing evils that later serve to bolster a strong
moral sense as well as a vast understanding; married at
thirteen but abused, she turns to vaudeville at seventeen,
touring in the South where her experiences reinforce her
solidarity with the downtrodden; always reserved, she demands respect as a performer; she finds emotional release
and complete fulfillment in her first dramatic stage role in
1939, portraying the anguished soul of a black woman.

2099   To Me It's Wonderful.   New York: Harper & Row, 1972.
       162pp.

    A singer and actress, she tells of feeling "alone and
troubled" in spite of professional success, having sought the
certainty of religious faith for fifty years; her problems are
intensified by permanently damaged health and severe overweight; at sixty-one she finds religious "clarification" and
intense "family" feelings with members of the Billy Graham
Crusade and she relinquishes fees to sing for religious revivals; through conversion she gains new perspectives on her
past, abandons her prejudices against whites, and is recon-

ciled with her mother; she writes in an open, conversational
style.

2100 WATERSTON, ANNA CABOT LOWELL QUINCY (1812-)
The Articulate Sisters; Passages from Journals and Letters
of the Daughters of President Josiah Quincy of Harvard University, ed. M. A. DeWolfe Howe.   Cambridge, Mass.:
Harvard University Press, 1946.   249pp.

The passages are taken from a journal written in 1833
and 1834 for her older sisters during their absence; aided
by an observant eye and ready laughter, she describes a
party with great wit; she tells of a series of plays featuring
actress Fanny Kemble (see entry #1111); her contribution is
on pages 194-244.

2101 WATSON, GEORGIA MITCHELL
So We Bought a Poet's Shrine; Incidents from Years Spent
in the First Home of Walt Whitman.   New York: Pageant,
1955.   116pp.

She and her husband purchase and renovate Whitman's
Long Island birthplace in 1917; as his poetry gains popularity, she opens a tea room; during the depression, they open
part of the home to the public but later become embroiled
in the controversial "Battle of the Birthplace" when others
wish to buy it.

2102 WAYMAN, DOROTHY GODFREY (1893-)
Bite the Bullet.   Milwaukee: Bruce, 1948.   229pp.

A reporter for the Boston Globe, editor of a country
weekly, novelist, essayist, and biographer writes to support herself and her three children when her marriage fails
in the early 1920's; she tells marvelous stories of her journalistic exploits, including a 1927 interview with Henry Ford,
interviewing coastguardmen and rumrunners during prohibition, discussing the Lindbergh kidnapping, being close to the
flow of history; she converts to Catholicism in 1939, the
"gift of faith" enabling her to carry heavy family and career
responsibilities, doing a "man's job."

2103 WAYNE, KYRA PETROVSKAYA
see PETROVSKAYA, KYRA (1920?-)

2104 WEAVER, ADELAIDE
Fairly Open House; Sketches from a Guest Ranch.   New
York: Exposition, 1953.   120pp.

She is a maid, tour guide, secretary, wife and mother at
a guest ranch in the mid-1940's; she describes times of high
drama and crisis as well as periods of relaxed enjoyment
with her numerous guests, writing with affection and nostalgia since she and her husband no longer run the ranch.

2105   WEBER, NANCY (1942-   )
        The Life Swap.   New York: Dial, 1974.   262pp.

        Acting on her recognition of the necessity to invent and
reinvent the self, this writer offers to swap lives for a
month to see "if people can get out of their skins"; she
trades with a Women's Studies academic, requiring total
commitment and agreements from friends, lovers, and a
husband; offering a daily journal of her old life and keeping
a highly detailed journal of her new life, she chronicles the
disintegration of the swap as accusations and anger build to
a climactic break; the fascinating if bizarre attempt brings
permanent changes to her life.

2106   WEBSTER, BARBARA
        The Green Year.   New York: Norton, 1956.   270pp.

        Following the cycle of the seasons from winter to fall,
a writer describes a year free of all obligations except those
to the land, the "priceless boon" of living close to nature;
her quiet, reflective vignettes focus on daily details and
friendships with her rural neighbors; the "green year" represents a state of mind and time for appreciation.

2107   WEBSTER, MARGARET (1905-1972)   NAWM
        Don't Put Your Daughter on the Stage.   New York: Knopf,
        1972.   379pp.

        In a highly articulate account, the daughter of British ac-
tors notes that she began her career as an actress but works
primarily as a director; known for her uncut production of
Hamlet, she directs much Shakespeare in the 1940's; she
argues and works for the establishment of experimental the-
atres and subsidized repertory companies; she directs several opera productions in New York City and undertakes ar-
duous lecture tours and one-woman shows in the 1950's and
1960's; she describes her experiences with the anti-com-
munism of the 1950's; she later teaches at several univer-
sities.

2108   WELLES, WINIFRED HALE (1893-1939)
        The Lost Landscape; Some Memories of a Family and a Town
        in Connecticut, 1659-1906.   New York: Holt, 1946.   299pp.

A poet from Norwich Town, Connecticut describes her New England childhood in a family whose life is closely bound to that of the community; she reconstructs her family history from "all the family tales and legends," evoking the family ambience with great sensitivity through people, associations, and attic keepsakes, all "a part of me myself."

2109   WELLS, IDA B.
see BARNETT, IDA B. WELLS (1869-1931)

2110   WENNER, KATE (1948-)
Shamba Letu. Boston: Houghton Mifflin, 1970.   256pp.

Fresh from Radcliffe, she spends a year on a communal farm in Tanzania in 1966-1967; she is involved in village meetings, hygiene for children, the establishment of a nursery school, a women's sewing class; she finds it a burden because of her youth to accept a position of authority; she senses a growing anti-Americanism fed by the war in Vietnam; organizing the women, she takes great pride with them in the village's accomplishments and she is grateful for what she learns about freedom and the spirit of community.

2111   WERTENBAKER, LAEL TUCKER (1909-)
Death of a Man. New York: Random, 1957.   181pp.

A journalist and author, she presents a fine portrait of a marriage rich in pleasure, profound trust, and high ideals; after her husband's cancer is diagnosed in 1954, they return to their home in France and find "emotional peace" based on "knowledge and acceptance" which carries them through the intense experience of death.

2112   WEST, JESSAMYN (1907-)
Hide and Seek: A Continuing Journey.   New York: Harcourt Brace Jovanovich, 1973.   310pp.

Noting that "solitude has always excited me," the novelist explores her recollections and dreams, "moments of seeing"; portraits of her parents emerge from a series of illustrative, non-chronological reminiscences; stressing the importance of place, she describes her travel trailer as a symbolic "Walden on Wheels" and she describes the reverberations of her experiences on the Colorado River and in the mountains and deserts of California.

2113   To See the Dream.   New York: Harcourt, Brace, 1957.
314pp.

A novelist, she tells of her lectures at university workshops and of her work in the "genuine gilded legend" of Hollywood on the movie script of her novel <u>Friendly Persuasion</u>; with enthusiasm and despair, she struggles to express her own vision in the film, developing a sense of communication with the actors and filmmakers; she presents her keen observations with a touch of humor.

2114   <u>The Woman Said Yes: Encounters with Life and Death: Memoirs.</u>   New York: Harcourt Brace Jovanovich, 1976. 180pp.

Sent home at the age of twenty-eight from a tuberculosis sanatorium to die and thus denied a future, she enters into her mother's past, ultimately to return to life and writing; later she supports her younger sister's choice of death; the book contains fine portraits of her mother and her sister and is an extremely moving account.

2115   WEST, MAE (1893-1980)
<u>Goodness Had Nothing to Do with It.</u>   Englewood Cliffs, N. J.:   Prentice-Hall, 1959.   271pp.

The famous Hollywood star of the 1930's describes her early determination, developing her personality and distinctive manner of speech deliberately; as a child she learns working in a stock company, becoming at eighteen a sex symbol on Broadway and in vaudeville; writing her own material is part of her shrewd creation of her self, and in 1926 she is tried and jailed for her play "Sex"; she writes and stars in "Diamond Lil," the beginning of sensational success in movies; not "the marrying kind," she lives "fully and in my way" with great style and pride, maintaining her image into old age.

2116   WESTCOTT, CYNTHIA (1898-   )
<u>Plant Doctoring Is Fun.</u>   Princeton, N. J.:   Van Nostrand, 1957.   280pp.

Having pursued botany at Wellesley and earned a Ph. D. from Cornell, she establishes a career in 1933 as a plant pathology consultant; she maintains a hectic schedule of writing, lecturing, and traveling to examine gardens, "desperately hard work," and encounters some discrimination as a woman scientist; during World War II she works on "victory gardens" and an azalea blight in the south; she writes both highly technical works and books for lay gardeners.

2117   WESTON, SHIRLEY TELFORD (1925-   )
        Confessions of a Girl Economist.   New York: Pageant,
        1963.   103pp.

        Briefly outlining her family background, she tells of the
        gradual formation of her ideas on economics; disenchanted
        with her college professors, she discovers Marxist thought
        and applies her own interpretation, seeking "to find an ideal
        economic system"; dedicated to study, she marries only when
        her research and writing are completed; the book includes
        her essays on economic change.

2118   WEXLER, SUSAN STANHOPE
        The Story of Sandy.   Indianapolis: Bobbs-Merrill, 1955.
        155pp.

        She and her husband love and care for their mentally
        handicapped three-year-old grandson; her earlier work with
        troubled children, love of reading, enjoyment of summer
        cabin living all provide sources of enrichment for the boy;
        awed by glimpses into a child's deepest emotional and psy-
        chological processes, she accepts uncertainty and risk with
        hope.

2119   WHARTON, MAY CRAVATH (1873-1959)
        Doctor Woman of the Cumberlands; The Autobiography of
        May Cravath Wharton, M.D.   Pleasant Hill, Tenn.:   Up-
        lands, 1953.   214pp.

        At forty-five she joins her husband in pioneer home medi-
        cal missionary work among the Tennessee mountain people;
        widowed after three years, she resolves to stay to help the
        people, opening a small hospital in 1921, building a tuber-
        culosis sanatorium in 1922, purchasing a farm to help pro-
        vide more nutritious food for her patients; her dreams con-
        tinue, and she works successfully for the establishment of a
        regional rural health care center in 1946, an achievement
        which brings her deep satisfaction.

2120   WHEATLEY, HARRIET VIRGINIA (1891-   )
        Lady Angler; Fishing, Hunting and Camping in Wilderness
        Areas of North America.   San Antonio: Naylor, 1952.
        192pp.

        She expresses her "gratitude and reverence for the great
        outdoors" in this account reconstructed from notes and jour-
        nals of eleven trips over a period of thirty-four years with
        her husband; her adventures cover much of Canada and the
        western U.S.

2121   WHEELER, GRACE DENISON (1858-   )
       Grace Wheeler's Memories.   Stonington, Conn.:   Pequot
       Press, 1948.   151pp.

       Writing at eighty-nine, she focuses on the Connecticut
       house where she was born, the fourth generation in the fam-
       ily home; her random recollections include memories of
       childhood and of her parents, sketches of friends and neigh-
       bors, tales of school days, stories of church activities,
       travels, and genealogical investigations; emphasizing the
       early years, she notes changes, not all for the better.

2122   WHIPPLE-HASLAM, MRS. LEE
       Early Days in California; Scenes and Events of the '50's as
       I Remember Them.   Jamestown, Cal.:   Mother Lode Mag-
       net, 1925.   34pp.

       Random recollections by a "typical pioneer" who argues
       that the histories of early California are "mostly exaggerated
       bunk" form the narrative; after crossing the plains in 1852,
       fearing Indians all the way, she finds a settlement without
       schools and so lawless that her father is murdered in 1856;
       she is acquainted with Mark Twain.

2123   WHITE, VIOLA CHITTENDEN (1890-   )
       Vermont Diary.   Boston: Branford, 1956.   145pp.

       She writes of twelve years "telescoped into one," organ-
       izing her diary-like entries by seasons; she finds happiness
       "amid the humble, the simple, the obscure"; noting colors,
       sounds, smells, she is alert to the fine details of daily
       events and describes nature with sensitivity; establishing a
       remarkable intimacy with the village and its environs, she
       embellishes her observations with literary quotations.

2124   WHITMAN, BERTHA YEREX
       A Tyro Takes a Trip.   Boston: Branden, 1971.   128pp.

       An architect, she writes "a day-to-day chronicle" of her
       trip alone around the world in 1965; she notes the sights
       and her impressions of them, particularly in Scandinavia;
       she leaves continuation of her chronicle to later books.

2125   WHITNEY, ELEANOR SEARLE
       Invitation to Joy; A Personal Story.   New York: Harper &
       Row, 1971.   195pp.

       Leading a life of luxury and pleasure, she feels neverthe-
       less a certain lack of depth and only achieves "genuine and

abundant joy" after a religious reawakening; in 1941 she
marries into the Whitney and Vanderbilt families and engages in philanthropy in the arts and in medicine, as well
as in political volunteer work; in 1957, moved by an evangelical crusade, her "new life" supports her through the
crisis of divorce and she takes to traveling extensively to
serve as a public witness on behalf of Christianity.

2126   WIDDEMER, MARGARET (1889-)
       Golden Friends I Had; Unrevised Memories of Margaret
       Widdemer. Garden City, N.Y.: Doubleday, 1964. 340pp.

       A poet and novelist, she tells of her childhood, "writing
       hard since the age of four"; she supports herself and her
       voracious reading by becoming a librarian and bookseller,
       becoming also part of "the Poetic Renaissance of America"
       in Greenwich Village; later a member of the MacDowell
       Colony, she presents the portraits of a fascinating parade
       of literary acquaintances from the 1920's to the 1960's.

2127   WIER, DELIGHT BOBILYA
       I Married a Farmer. Des Moines, Iowa: Wallace-Home-
       stead, 1973. 191pp.

       Her account consists of a series of columns published in
       the Prairie Farmer between 1955 and 1973; following season-
       al rhythms, she describes the cherished partnership and
       stability of farm life, the satisfactions and "underlying spirit-
       ual meaning" of domestic work, the privilege of "molding a
       future generation," and her deep attachment to the land.

2128   WIGODER, DEVORAH
       Hope Is My House. Englewood Cliffs, N.J.: Prentice-Hall,
       1966. 282pp.

       The tragic deaths of two brothers and her distress at
       racism and religious bigotry precipitate her questioning and
       gradual withdrawal from Catholicism; an actress, she is
       drawn to the Yiddish Theater and seeks religious education
       in Judaism, a "journey into Jewish consciousness" and reli-
       gious reawakening; a convert and married to an Irish Jewish
       scholar and rabbi, she settles in the new state of Israel,
       participating in communal life, working with Hadassah, speak-
       ing and fund-raising.

2129   WILDE, META CARPENTER
       A Loving Gentleman; The Love Story of William Faulkner
       and Meta Carpenter, with Orin Borsten. New York: Simon
       and Schuster, 1976. 334pp.

She describes a relationship that endures for nearly thirty
years, beginning with their first meeting in Hollywood when
she is a script girl; Faulkner is committed to writing,
haunted by debt and concerns for his beloved daughter and
his alcoholic wife, and tied closely to the Mississippi land;
sensing futility, she attempts to break with him and
establish an independent life, marrying twice, but separations are followed by reunions with Faulkner; their love
flourishes only in Hollywood, for she never intrudes on his
Mississippi life; she is devastated by his death in 1962.

2130   WILDENHAIN, MARGUERITE (1896-   )
        The Invisible Core; A Potter's Life and Thoughts.   Palo
        Alto, Cal.:   Pacific, 1973.   207pp.

An artist of great dedication and intensity, she offers "the
essence of my life," describing her childhood in France, her
art studies in Germany at the Bauhaus, and her emigration
to the U.S. in 1940; she establishes a community of crafts-
men at "Pond Farm" in California, placing great value on
artistic freedom and integrity; she strives "to make well the
simple things of everyday life."

2131   WILDER, LAURA INGALLS (1867-1957)   NAWM
        On the Way Home: The Diary of a Trip from South Dakota
        to Mansfield, Missouri, in 1894.   New York: Harper &
        Row, 1962.   101pp.

The well-known author describes a family trip forced by
economic depression; she tells of other emigrants, the countryside, the summer heat, the crop conditions; her daughter
finishes the account with a description of their first log
cabin.

2132   West from Home; Letters of Laura Ingalls Wilder to Almanzo
        Wilder--San Francisco 1915, ed. Roger Lea MacBride.   New
        York: Harper & Row, 1974.   124pp.

She travels to San Francisco to visit her daughter, Rose
Wilder Lane (see entry #1193) and to attend the Panama-
Pacific International Exposition; completely unpretentious,
she describes the countryside on the cross-country train
trip, then the "fairyland" of San Francisco and the overwhelming beauty of the exposition; she notes her daughter's
strenuous writing schedule, sandwiched in between numerous
visits to the exhibits and outlying areas of interest.

2133   WILEY, IRENA
        Around the Globe in Twenty Years.   New York: David Mc-
        Kay, 1962.   249pp.

Articulate and observant, she is a Polish-born sculptress and wife of an American diplomat who holds posts in Russia, Belgium, Austria, Estonia, Latvia, Colombia, Portugal, Iran, Panama, and Washington; she serves her diplomatic "apprenticeship" and describes in vivid detail the chaos of pre-war Austria, her poignant departure from occupied Latvia in 1940, the beauty of Colombia, the striking class distinctions in Panama; she emerges with a deep fondness for "peoples everywhere."

2134   WILKINS, MESANNIE
        The Last of the Saddle Tramps, with Mina Titus Sawyer.
        Englewood Cliffs, N.J.: Prentice-Hall, 1967.   215pp.

        Told by doctors at sixty-two that she has only a few years to live, and alone after the deaths of her mother and uncle, she undertakes a seventeen-month journey on horseback from Maine to California; traveling with $32 and a dog, she keeps a diary and describes the warm and hospitable people she meets along the way; followed by local reporters and television, she gains publicity and earns her way by selling postcards of herself; "born restless," she vastly enjoys her independence.

2135   WILLCOX, FAITH MELLEN
        In Morocco.   New York: Harcourt Brace Jovanovich, 1971.
        295pp.

        In a perceptive, highly articulate account, this "committed wanderer and wonderer" tells in rich, vivid detail of three visits to Morocco in 1965 and 1966; with her husband, she meets people from all walks of life, travels through the major cities as well as the countryside, and comments on the inevitable changes in the culture due to modernization and political tension; she finds Moroccan culture "rich in contradictions, ambiguous."

2136   WILLIAMS, ALICE CARY (1892-   )
        Thru the Turnstile; Tales of My Two Centuries.   Boston:
        Houghton Mifflin, 1976.   150pp.

        In this charming memoir, she provides vivid anecdotes of a "cluster of erudite friends" of her Boston family; her childhood home on Beacon Street is frequented by "Boston's literati," and Nantucket summers include visits by William James and Grover Cleveland.

2137   WILLIAMS, ANNABELLE RUCKER
        Operation Grease-Paint.   Hollywood, Cal.: House-Warven,
        1951.   240pp.

An actress offers a light-hearted diary account of "the
big event" of her life, a U.S.O. tour of the South Pacific
in 1945; she tells of island-hopping, living and performing
in sometimes primitive conditions; commenting on the visible
effects of the war, she returns to the U.S. with an altered
perspective.

2138 WILLIAMS, CELIA ANN
The Diary of a Teacher Along the Journey to Siberia. New
York: Exposition, 1972. 156pp.

A Missouri Latin teacher who holds deep affection for
students rails against the "injustices in our educational system" when she is fired; she describes her "daily humilia-
tions" at school, deterrents to learning, and the tyranny and
incompetence of administrators; she sues the school district,
and her bitter account includes formal correspondence as
well as her own diary entries and narrative.

2139 WILLIAMS, EDWINA DAKIN
Remember Me to Tom, as told to Lucy Freeman. New
York: Putnam, 1963. 255pp.

The mother of playwright Tennessee Williams recalls
painful memories of a lonely, isolated home life, horrified
by her daughter's mental illness and lobotomy, and fearful
of her husband, gaining her "freedom" only when she has
the courage to ask him to leave; she writes with great pride
of her son's achievement; she then recalls her own circum-
spect childhood and youth as the daughter of a Mississippi
minister and scholar.

2140 WILLIAMS, ELIZA AZELIA GRISWOLD
One Whaling Family, ed. Harold Williams. Boston: Houghton Mifflin, 1964. 401pp.

The captain's wife and only woman on board keeps a
diary, writing in a straightforward manner in the present
tense, on a three-year whaling voyage beginning in 1858;
she notes the weather each day, describes the people and
sights in various ports of call, observes the details of whaling, chronicles accidents and deaths on board, and enjoys
the rare opportunities to visit with other women; she bears
two children during the voyage.

2141 WILLIAMS, EVELYN LEWIS
In the Afterglow. New York: Vantage, 1950. 164pp.

One of eleven children, she tells of her childhood home in
rural Virginia and of a life of "simple pleasures"; nostalgia

colors her memories of her hospitable and understanding
mother and her easygoing father, of church activities, of
cozy evenings at home, and of her college days; the account
closes with the separation of the family when the children
are grown.

2142   WILLIAMS, KIM
        High Heels in the Andes.   New York: Crowell, 1959.
        194pp.

    In a humorous account, a "Manhattan secretary" married
to a mining engineer casts herself as the reluctant frontiers-
woman, roughing it for four years in Chile; nevertheless,
she enjoys the leisurely life in a Santiago suburb, going to
mining camps infrequently and joining her husband for skiing, fishing, and hunting.

2143   WILLIAMS, ROSE BERTHENIA CLAY (1910-   )
        Black and White Orange: An Autobiography.   New York:
        Vantage, 1961.   135pp.

    A black woman recalls her early years in an upright,
idealistic family; awareness of racial prejudice brings her
to "the stream of submission"; her career as a teacher is
unsettled by summers in New York aspiring to a career in
entertainment, but she eventually rejects the latter; she
provides anecdotes of her teaching and includes essays on
education and occasional poems.

2144   WILLIAMSON, ANNE A. (1868-   )
        Fifty Years in Starch.   Culver City, Cal.:   Murray & Gee,
        1948.   245pp.

    A nurse who is inspired by Clara Barton (see companion
volume) and settles on her profession after the death of her
fiancé, she works among the urban poor, cares for casual-
ties of the Spanish-American War in 1898, fights "skirmishes
with Army discipline," works and studies in Germany, and
works for the Red Cross in Europe during World War I; a
strong leader, she improves conditions for student nurses
and takes a prominent place in the California state nurses'
organization, struggling "to raise the standard of their profession."

2145   WILLIAMSON, MYRTLE
        One Out of Four; A Personal Experience with Cancer.   Rich-
        mond, Va.:   Knox, 1960.   77pp.

    A college professor, she writes to provide hope for other
cancer victims and to record her struggles and her gains;

she describes the shock of diagnosis and her fears after a
radical mastectomy; coping with the uncertainty of cure,
she uses sabbatical study time to provide a "new adventure," sustaining her spirits; death cuts short her account.

2146   WILSON, DOROTHY CLARKE
        Fly with Me to India. Nashville: Abingdon, 1954. 127pp.

        She is sent by the mission board of her church to India
for six months to gather material for a novel; she describes
with delight the "new world" she encounters as she travels
to many villages, mission hospitals, and schools; drawn to
the people, she expresses her hopes for a democratic India.

2147   WILSON, ELLEN AXSON (-1914)
        The Priceless Gift; The Love Letters of Woodrow Wilson
        and Ellen Axson Wilson, ed. Eleanor Wilson McAdoo. New
        York: McGraw-Hill, 1962. 324pp.

        Feeling her inspiration in the power of a great love, she
writes letters during her courtship which are modest and
tentative, quivering with unexpressed fervor; later letters
become touching, ardent, stating to Wilson after their marriage, "I glory in you"; her husband's rare absences call
forth letters full of intimate praise and utter devotion as
well as examples of a strong practical streak; the letters
continue in the same emotional vein in addition to comments
revealing her active interest in public issues through her
husband's years as president of Princeton, governor of New
Jersey, and President of the U.S.

2148   WILSON, EMMA PARKE (1899-)
        Under One Roof. New York: Funk, 1955. 238pp.

        In a delightful tale of the simple life in a Kentucky vil-
lage, she describes "a time and a place and some people";
the people include a gently domineering grandmother, a
country doctor grandfather, a tobacco-buyer father; some
of her spirited anecdotes reveal the drama of a Methodist
revival, the fear caused by lawless "Nightriders," the
bringing of Christmas goodwill to a neighboring farm; prosperity and a move to town being the end of an era.

2149   WILSON, LOUISE
        This Stranger, My Son: A Mother's Story. New York:
        Putnam, 1968. 247pp.

        When her son is diagnosed as a paranoid schizophrenic,
she is driven to an examination of his past; she tells of his

childhood troubles and her painful doubts about her mothering; she finds conflicting theories of various psychiatrists and therapists disturbing, as is the impact of tension and violence and financial strain on the rest of her family; she closes on a note of cautious hope.

2150   WILSON, MARGERY
       I Found My Way.   Philadelphia: Lippincott, 1956.   296pp.

Describing a "life of sharp contrasts," she tells how she is raised in a southern family with a rich imaginative and intellectual life fed by her father; when the family disperses, she begins performing to aid the family finances; at sixteen she manages a touring theatre company; she moves to Hollywood and works with D. W. Griffith, appearing in and later directing many films; she writes books on charm and religion, and is a consultant and lecturer; she suffers the loss of her husband and young son, remarries, but must adjust again to widowhood.

2151   WILSON, RUTH DANENHOWER (1887-)
       Here Is Haiti.   New York: Philosophical Library, 1957.
       204pp.

She tells of long visits to Haiti in 1950, 1952, and 1955; each time she makes new acquaintances among all classes of people and increases her knowledge of the country, enjoying her "rambles" and explorations; the hospitality of the island's elite is extended to her.

2152   WILSON, SONJA
       Castle on the Prairie.   Boston: Branden, 1972.   (no pagination)

A person who "always wanted to be a cowgirl," she marries at eighteen and settles on a Montana ranch, one of few women in a man's world; in simple prose with much dialogue, she tells of her growing self-reliance, her partnership in ranch chores, her deep love for the "great, powerful country"; she closes with the sudden accidental death of her husband.

2153   WINCHELL, MARY EDNA (1878-)
       Home by the Bering Sea.   Caldwell, Id.:   Caxton, 1951.
       226pp.

A devoted matron and teacher in an Aleutian island village mission school tells of her work there, "always interesting, often discouraging"; in self-contained chapters, she describes the details of her daily life, revealing a warm affection for the children and her colleagues.

2154   Where the Wind Blows Free.   Caldwell, Id.:   Caxton, 1954.
        176pp.

        In this sequel to her earlier volume, she continues to tell of her love of Alaska and her dedication to providing a "happy childhood" for each of her charges at an Aleutian missionary orphanage; each chapter, centered on the children, describes a small characteristic episode.

2155   WINDISCH, IDA ADELAIDE
        My Life in Show Business.   New York: Vantage, 1954.
        67pp.

        Married in 1916 to a circus aerialist, she becomes a member of his act, sharing hard times during years of touring; a son and daughter later join the act; she relishes the excitement of performing and takes great pride in a devoted family life which contributes to show business success.

2156   Room, Board, and Bedlam.   New York: Vantage, 1958.
        113pp.

        The owner, with her husband, of a rooming house in which there is "never a dull moment," she produces lightweight anecdotes of an endless stream of guests with whom she chats and to whom she offers advice.

2157   WINDSOR, WALLIS WARFIELD (1896-   )
        The Heart Has Its Reasons: The Memoirs of the Duchess
        of Windsor.   New York: David McKay, 1956.   372pp.

        An articulate writer, she describes "an ordinary life that became extraordinary" with her marriage to England's King Edward VIII; she describes the "genteel austerity" of her sheltered Baltimore childhood, the "harrowing experience" of a failed first marriage, her enjoyment of sedate London social life with her second husband, and her first meeting with the Prince of Wales in 1930; their relationship brings her notoriety and condemnation, and she argues that she attempts to prevent his abdication; once married and in a kind of exile, she seeks opportunities for service, to soften "a most ambiguous and amorphous position," living a life of enormous self-discipline.

2158   WINSLOW, ANNA J. FRAZER (1848-)
       Jewels from My Casket.   Los Angeles: Nazarene, 1910.
       193pp.

       After her marriage in 1864, a serious illness precipitates
       her religious conversion; she becomes a Quaker minister
       despite her initial feelings of inadequacy and focuses her
       narrative on numerous meetings held throughout the midwest
       and in North Carolina; her pioneer homestead and five chil-
       dren are only briefly mentioned; she retires from preaching
       at sixty-two.

2159   WINSLOW, ELEANOR
       And Away We Went; For the Armchair Tourist.   Philadel-
       phia: Dorrance, 1970.   189pp.

       In a "chatty, informal" style, she tells of her travels
       with her husband, a prosperous businessman, from 1947 to
       1967; they tour Europe, the United States, Mexico, Central
       America, South America, North Africa, and the Far East,
       and she offers pleasant, brief travel notes of their sight-
       seeing and attendance at social functions.

2160   WINSLOW, GRACE COOLIDGE DAVENPORT (1877-)
       My First Day and My Last Day with Grandma Coolidge.
       Cleveland: Lezius-Hiles, 1967.   54pp.

       In a series of random domestic reminiscences dictated
       and later transcribed, she describes her large, close, ex-
       tended family with its roots in old Boston; she reveals a
       great deal about her grandmother, "a woman of great char-
       acter," as she tells of her own childhood and youth up to
       the turn of the century; the volume includes her grandmoth-
       er's own brief childhood memories, prepared in 1896.

2161   WINTER, ELLA (1898-)
       And Not to Yield; An Autobiography.   New York: Harcourt,
       Brace & World, 1963.   308pp.

       A journalist and writer, she tells of her childhood in
       London, her growing political interests as a student at the
       London School of Economics, her work as an aide at the
       Paris Peace Conference; she enjoys an "odd companionship"
       with Lincoln Steffans, describing thirteen years of "our
       brimming life together" during which they settle in Califor-
       nia and work on labor reform issues; after his death, follow-
       ing her belief that "one must fight," she works for the anti-
       Nazi cause, is a Moscow correspondent, and travels in post-
       war Europe, settling there to avoid the cold-war atmosphere
       of the U.S.

2162   WINTER, MARJORIE (pseud.)
        For Love of Martha.   New York: Julian Messner, 1956.
        191pp.

           She writes to expose the need for reform of adoption
        procedures and laws and to share "a miracle of love"; tired
        of bureaucratic bungles, she turns to a private agency and
        adopts a cruelly neglected five-year-old girl; after a har-
        rowing adjustment, the child becomes healthy and happy,
        but the author and her husband endure fear and uncertainty
        when the agency is exposed as corrupt and a relative of the
        child attempts to reclaim her in a dramatic contest of wills;
        she closes her account with the removal of the final legal
        barrier to custody.

2163   WISBESKI, DOROTHY GROSS
        Okee: The Story of an Otter in the House.   New York:
        Farrar, Straus, 1964.   246pp.

           A librarian with a great fondness for animals describes
        in delightful detail her "servitude" when she and her husband
        take in an otter; trusting to common sense and luck, she
        displays endless tolerance for the otter's tireless activity
        and depredations; she uses the otter to teach animal appre-
        ciation to members of the community.

2164   WISER, CHARLOTTE MELINA VIALL
        Behind Mud Walls, 1930-1960.   Berkeley: University of
        California Press, 1963.   249pp.

           She and her husband are missionaries who reside in an
        Indian village for five years (this early period constitutes the
        earlier 1930 edition and covers pages 1 to 134); after her
        husband's death and a hiatus of thirty-two years, she re-
        turns, noting the continuity in family and religious life as
        well as advances in agriculture, health, and education; she
        is a sensitive observer, with warm feelings for "my people. "

2165   WITKER, KRISTI
        How to Lose Everything in Politics Except Massachusetts.
        New York: Mason & Lipscomb, 1974.   230pp.

           She describes her behind-the-scenes work on the McGovern
        presidential campaign in 1972; her initial hopes and ideals
        are slowly eroded as she observes other workers' jockeying
        for position, small conspiracies, staff shakeups, rumors,
        pettiness, financial problems, shifts on the issues; disillu-
        sioned, after his nomination she feels that the campaign is
        "doomed" by cumulative despair.

2166 WITTE, EVA KNOX
      see EVANS, EVA KNOX (1905-   )

2167 WOJCIECHOWSKA, MAIA (1927-   )
      Till the Break of Day: Memories, 1939-1942.   New York:
      Harcourt Brace Jovanovich, 1972.   156pp.

      A young Polish girl of twelve when the war breaks out,
      she recalls the dislocations of war and the pains of adoles-
      cence mingled in the troubled years from 1939 to 1942;
      wishing to be heroic as a "matter of pride" but having lost
      her roots when the family flees to France, she finds sabo-
      tage and resistance an exciting game during the German oc-
      cupation; she settles finally in Washington, D.C. where her
      father works with the Polish embassy, and she struggles to
      make her own inner peace with adulthood.

2168 WOLF, MARGUERITE HURREY
      Vermont Is Always with You.   Brattleboro, Vt.:   Stephen
      Greene, 1969.   121pp.

      In an account suffused with her deep allegiance to Ver-
      mont, she discusses her misadventures with renovation of a
      country home, prize-winning pumpkins, family cats, raising
      pigs and poultry in an "attack of animal husbandry," a de-
      luge of apples, her daughters' horse phase, and country
      Christmas traditions; opening her Vermont home is a purify-
      ing spring ritual for twenty years.

2169 WOLFE, ELLEN
      Aftershock; The Story of a Psychotic Episode.   New York:
      Putnam, 1969.   216pp.

      A wife and mother of two small children describes one
      month in a mental hospital when her "facade of normality"
      gives way; recalling the events which lead to her breakdown,
      she tells of her job aspirations, her father's terminal ill-
      ness, her feeling overwhelmed by her children, her abortion,
      and her treatment by a brusque psychiatrist; she notes the
      effects of shock treatment, and feels "helpless, maimed"
      when she must "re-orient" herself to her home and family,
      learning "how to be a woman without hating yourself for
      being only a woman."

2170 WOLFF, SISTER MARY MADELEVA (MARY EVALINE)
      (1887-1964)   NAWM
      My First Seventy Years.   New York: Macmillan, 1959.
      172pp.

A teacher, administrator, and poet, she tells of her educational pursuits from the University of Wisconsin in 1905 to a Ph. D. from Berkeley in 1925 to advanced studies at Oxford in 1933; having entered the novitiate in 1908, she teaches college classes, establishes a Catholic college for women in Utah, and is the president of St. Mary's College beginning in 1934.

2171   WONG, JADE SNOW (1922-)
        Fifth Chinese Daughter.   New York: Harper & Row, 1950.
        246pp.

A Chinese-American, she writes in the third person about the "significant episodes" in her youth that shape her life; she notes the Chinese characteristics within her family, emphasizing respect and order, as well as the greater value placed on sons; she demands greater freedom from parental domination and pursues a college education which allows her "broadened living," an introduction to Western fine arts, and ultimately a career in pottery as well as writing; she seeks a balance between her two cultures.

2172   No Chinese Stranger.   New York: Harper & Row, 1975.
        366pp.

In this sequel to Fifth Chinese Daughter, she begins her narrative in the third person, describing a family life dominated by her father and telling of her early work as a ceramist; she notes the reception of her first book; after her father's death, she shifts to a first person narrative and tells of marriage, motherhood, and career; the last section describes a trip to China in 1972.

2173   WOOD, DOROTHY WARREN
        A Trailer Goes to See.   New York: Vantage, 1959.   141pp.

She writes a descriptive chronicle of sights seen in three years of leisurely travel in the U.S. as told through the eyes of her trailer.

2174   WOOD, MIRIAM
        All My Dusty Babies; One Week's Visit in New Guinea,
        November 30-December 7, 1970.   Washington, D. C.:   Review and Herald Publishing Association, 1972.   174pp.

A Seventh-day Adventist missionary goes with her husband and experiences her own "conversion to the value of mission service"; she produces a lively description of daily life at the mission, adding details about the schools, local markets, a leprosarium, Sabbath services, and role of missionary wives.

2175   Reluctant Saint, Reluctant Sinner.   Washington, D. C. :   Re-
       view and Herald Publishing Association, 1975.   127pp.

       She provides an exploration of "guilt and grace" in her
       life; having lost her mother at seven, she is raised by
       strict, conservative Adventist grandparents whose theology
       of high expectations and moral rigor leads her to anguished
       adolescence in spite of the enveloping religious certainty of
       her family and Adventist educational institutions; she reaches
       a mature understanding of her earlier immaturity.

2176   Two Hands, No Wings.   Washington, D. C. :   Review and
       Herald Publishing Association, 1968.   192pp.

       In a lively account, she tells of the rewards of having
       "an active part in her husband's work" throughout thirty
       years as the wife of a Seventh-day Adventist minister; she
       enjoys the challenges of homemaking on a shoestring, rais-
       ing "minister's children," engaging in delicate human rela-
       tions with parishioners, and living up to the other obligations
       of her role.

2177   WOOD, PEGGY (1892-)
       Arts and Flowers.   New York: William Morrow, 1963.
       189pp.

       A sequel to How Young You Look!, the account is organ-
       ized thematically and covers the years from 1941 to 1963;
       an actress, she enjoys "the best of television" in a series
       in the 1950's; she describes her success in Blithe Spirit,
       playing in New York, entertaining World War II soldiers,
       touring; she describes a summer of European drama festi-
       vals; she reflects on the state of theatre in the U. S. , on
       her role as president of the American National Theater and
       Academy, on the need for diffusion and financial support of
       the theatre.

2178   WOODFIN, JANE
       Of Mikes and Men.   New York: McGraw-Hill, 1951.   275pp.

       She presents a humorous account of her three years in
       early radio beginning in 1929; totally inexperienced but un-
       daunted, she copes with eccentric and spirited co-workers,
       contacts sponsors, schemes to build the station's popularity.

2179   WOODIN, ANN
       In the Circle of the Sun.   New York: Macmillan, 1971.
       307pp.

Continuing her "childhood traveling patterns," she spends a year traveling with her husband and four teen-age sons "through Old World deserts"; in the Far East, India and North Africa she notes her return "to the core of living experience," concerned with society, food, and shelter; her detailed descriptions and use of historical background lead to broader considerations of truth and value.

2180   WOODLEY, WINIFRED (pseud.)
Two and Three Make One.   New York: Crown, 1956.
167pp.

A novelist, she keeps a journal from 1935 to 1940 and includes additions from 1944 and 1955; although she writes from deep inner necessity, she notes the problems of "the would-be intellectual-and-writer, and the outwardly conventional female"; married and the mother of three, she feels inadequate but earnest as a parent, she notes the strange unreality of suburban existence, and she revels in summertime "authentic family living."

2181   WOODS, CORNELIA WILSON (1879-   )
Reminiscences of a Teacher.   New York: Vantage, 1964.
67pp.

This rambling account tells of her years as a classroom teacher, principal, and tutor of the mentally and physically handicapped, and she recounts stories of various individual pupils; a supporter of phonetic instruction, she begins her career in 1897, earns B.A. and M.A. degrees.

2182   WOODY, REGINA LLEWELLYN JONES (1894-   )
Dancing for Joy.   New York: Dutton, 1959.   223pp.

In a delightful account, she tells of her dreams of becoming a dancer, going to London at fifteen to assess her potential and study dance; taken by "dramatic dancing" rather than ballet, she continues her studies in Paris, enjoying a wildly successful debut and stardom at the Folies Bergère under the stage name of Nila Devi; homesick for the U.S., she returns for a grueling but successful vaudeville tour; an accident halts her career; her marriage and the birth of a son open a new career as "a doctor's wife, mother, and writer."

2183   WOOLLEY, MARY EMMA (1863-1947)   NAW
Life and Letters of Mary Emma Woolley, by Jeannette
Marks.   Washington: Public Affairs Press, 1955.   300pp.

The book consists of excerpts from letters as well as
from "Notes on Autobiography" with much connecting narrative; a teacher at Wheaton, Brown, and Wellesley, she becomes the president of Mt. Holyoke in 1900, a committed
feminist and devoted champion of education for women; her
letters describe a strenuous educational mission to China
in 1921, participation in the Geneva Disarmament Conference
in 1932, constant vigorous fund-raising efforts, and in 1936
the pain and tumult of the Holyoke Trustees' choice of a
male president which she perceives as a betrayal of a great
principle.

2184   WORCESTER, DAISY LEE WORTHINGTON
       Grim the Battles; A Semi-Autobiographical Account of the
       War Against Want in the United States During the First Half
       of the Twentieth Century.   New York: Exposition, 1954.
       410pp.

       A pioneer social worker and researcher with both private
       and public agencies, she draws her narrative from a journal
       kept jointly with her husband of "the long struggle against
       poverty"; in 1907, her investigation of Southern cotton mills
       reveals the horrors of child labor, poverty, and disease,
       shocking her into a major turning point and setting the
       idealistic pattern for the rest of her life; she takes a "fur-
       lough" for motherhood between 1919 and 1923; she marks
       the loss of social work's crusading spirit, describes her
       bitter experience in the Department of Public Welfare, criti-
       cizes the medical profession; her own life story is inextri-
       cably linked with the dynamics of the social movement over
       a period of forty years.

2185   WORKMAN, GLADYS
       Only When I Laugh.   Englewood Cliffs, N.J.:   Prentice-Hall,
       1959.   236pp.

       A "commercial party hostess," she turns to the Oregon
       woods after thirty years of marriage "to find health" for her
       husband; renovating a primitive cabin and becoming a daffodil
       farmer, she tries to soften her reputation as a "snooty old
       gal" by participating in the social activities of the Grange;
       her ceramics hobby becomes a business, the source of a
       newspaper column, and a major social focus, providing her
       with a valley identity.

2186   WOYTINSKY, EMMA SHADKHAN (1893-   )
       Two Lives in One.   New York: Praeger, 1965.   324pp.

       In an introspective account, a Russian Jew of the middle
       class describes her forty-four years of intense intellectual

"teamwork" in international political economics with her husband; "educated" by the chaos and despair of the Russian
Revolution, they combine writing and political activity, serving in diplomatic posts in France and Germany; at the rise
of Hitler, they emigrate to the U.S. in 1935 and work with
New Deal economic policy; their extensive travels include
two world lecture tours; she enjoys a full life characterized
by unity, joy, and work but feels her life is at an end at
her husband's death.

2187   WRIGHT, ALICE PADDOCK
        Half Around the Globe....   New York: Pageant, 1956.
        42pp.

        A librarian and resident of Hawaii, she marries in Paris,
        then travels in Europe and northern Africa; the stilted nar-
        rative shifts inexplicably into and out of the third person.

2188   One Fifth Avenue.   New York: Pageant, 1954.   54pp.

        A librarian reminiscences about her childhood in the
        1890's in Moline, Illinois; the daughter of socially prominent
        parents, she describes her upper middle class neighbors
        and neighborhood in a complacent, self-satisfied third-person
        voice.

2189   Yesterday Was Like This; Greece, Turkey, Tunisia and Al-
        geria.   New York: Hobson, 1947.   136pp.

        She travels with her husband at an unspecified time prior
        to World War II, sightseeing around the Mediterranean; she
        includes her observations on women in each country; she
        writes in a bland, slightly inflated style.

2190   WRIGHT, ANNA MARIA ROSE (1890-1968)
        "The Gentle House," by Anna Perrott Rose.   Boston:
        Houghton Mifflin, 1954.   177pp.

        A widowed schoolteacher with three grown children, she
        offers a home to an orphaned DP student from 1950 to 1954;
        she must cope with his violent temper and wild fears as he
        slowly learns American ways and manners; she reveals a
        wealth of common sense, great physical stamina, emotional
        endurance, understanding, and love as she attempts to pro-
        vide a "gentle house" for him.

2191   Room for One More.   Boston: Houghton Mifflin, 1950.
        272pp.

A family with three children accepts three foster children, one by one, who then want to remain; she describes domestic anecdotes of the adjustments of the new children to the family and of the family to the new children; the first is a disturbed adolescent girl, the second a malnourished boy, the third a crippled boy; the author is also a writer of children's books and magazine articles.

2192   WRIGHT, ANNA MAY (1885?-)
        In the Shadow of Black Rock.   New York: Vantage, 1956.
        284pp.

The daughter of spirited pioneers, she presents rambling anecdotes of her childhood; her first loveless marriage ends when she leaves her drunken husband; her second merely continues her "trials and tribulations"; a third marriage in 1917 finally brings happiness, although it is also marked by health problems, frequent moves, and eventual widowhood; in spite of hardships, she professes "no regrets or bitterness."

2193   WRIGHT, BILLIE
        Four Seasons North: A Journal of Life in the Wilderness.
        New York: Harper & Row, 1973.   278pp.

Accompanying her sociologist husband to the Brooks Range in northern Alaska, she settles in an isolated log cabin and lives like the early Eskimos in a life dominated by the seasonal cycle; she describes the "incredible beauty," her "contentment and well-being," preparations for the long night of winter, subtle relationships with animals, the dramatic changes brought by spring; she notes her own shifts in perceptions and values as she reflects on Eskimo culture.

2194   WRIGHT, CATHARINE WHARTON MORRIS (1899-)
        The Color of Life.   Boston: Houghton Mifflin, 1957.   203pp.

An artist who writes with great sensitivity, she tells of her Philadelphia Quaker background, the daughter of a father who is an editor, artist and writer and a mother who is a writer; she discusses numerous childhood trips to Europe, contacts with artists and art studies which serve her talent and developing artistic values; she struggles for "breathing space, for clarity; always for deeper and broader vision"; later married and the mother of four, she uses the solitude of painting to balance the chaos of being "materfamilias"; an articulate, reflective account.

2195   WRIGHT, CHARLOTTE CROGMAN (1897-1959)
       Beneath the Southern Cross; The Story of an American
       Bishop's Wife in South Africa.   New York: Exposition,
       1955.   184pp.

       She and her husband are black missionaries for the Af-
       rican Methodist Episcopal Church in South Africa from 1936
       to 1940; she describes the government's policy of strict
       apartheid, although she and her husband travel extensively
       to attend religious conferences and to serve the people's
       "need of Christian leadership. "

2196   WRIGHT, COBINA (ELAINE COBB)
       I Never Grew Up.   New York: Prentice-Hall, 1952.   316pp.

       She presents a complex story beginning with her childhood
       on an Oregon ranch; at the death of her father, she is taken
       by a New England aunt to Europe where she studies voice
       and sings opera; she returns to the U.S., marries a novel-
       ist, and struggles unsuccessfully to balance marriage and
       career; divorced, she entertains in France during World
       War I; later she gives up opera for marriage to a wealthy
       businessman, enjoys perfect bliss as a famous socialite but
       continues to be pulled by music; bankrupt after the crash of
       1929 and a second divorce, she becomes a nightclub singer
       and radio personality; she describes her idolatrous attach-
       ment to her daughter, the pain of separation when her daugh-
       ter marries, and her intense pride in her daughter's beauty
       and success.

2197   WRIGHT, MABEL STEELE
       River Ripples.   New York: Vantage, 1959.   52pp.

       The wife of a cattle rancher on the Rio Grande, she of-
       fers random recollections of ranch life, neighbors, hired
       hands, and humorous events.

2198   WRIGHT, OLGIVANNA LLOYD
       Our House.   New York: Horizon Press, 1959.   308pp.

       The wife of architect Frank Lloyd Wright presents a
       series of vignettes written with great simplicity which re-
       veal glimpses of her domestic life at both Taliesin and
       Taliesin West; she notes her wide-ranging discussions with
       her husband which include explorations of the joy of work,
       the devotion to beauty, the existence of genius, her own
       lecturing and writing, and the continuation of her Russian
       tradition to the Taliesin community.

2199   WULF, HELEN HARLAN (1913-   )
       Aphasia, My World Alone.   Detroit: Wayne State University
       Press, 1973.   144pp.

       The victim of a stroke in 1970, she writes with great in-
       sight to provide a "truthful record" about the unique daily
       frustrations, drastic changes, devotion to therapy, and ma-
       jor adjustments caused by her handicap; a wife, the mother
       of four, and business partner of her husband, she portrays
       disconcerting communication tangles, for her writing and
       speech are severely affected; she calls for sensitivity to
       and understanding for the difficulties of an aphasic.

2200   WYCOTT, SARA JEAN CLARK (1924-1960)
       Everywhere God; A Spiritual Autobiography.   New York:
       Greenwich Book Publishers, 1961.   53pp.

       The account consists of journal entries from 1942 to 1946
       compiled after her death by her mother; she is "a dreamer
       and idealist" with a deep desire to record her innermost
       feelings; she dwells on World War II, her college aspira-
       tions, her love for her family, her closeness to God, and
       her joy at the war's end.

2201   XAN, ERNA OLESON (1898-)
         Wisconsin My Home, as told by Thurine Oleson.   Madison:
         University of Wisconsin Press, 1950.   224pp.

     The first child of her Norwegian immigrant parents to be
born in the U.S., she tells of pioneer life on a Wisconsin
farm, full of unexpected hardships and simple but refined;
she describes domestic details, church activities, and the
hospitality of neighbors and relatives; a spirited woman, she
later marries and raises eight children, continuing rural
traditions; her account is recorded by a daughter.

2202 YEN, LIANG (pseud.)
see BRIGGS, MARGARET YANG (1917-)

2203 YODER, ROSELYN
Play It by Ear; Highlights and Sideviews of True Life Experiences. Miami Beach, Fla. : Charles Hansen Educational Music and Books, 1965. 176pp.

In a disjointed account, she raises her objections to media images of the housewife and takes pride in the joys of domesticity; she studies dietetics in Boston, marries, and keeps house in Chicago and Florida; she accompanies her husband to summer music camps and travels in Europe; her book includes verses.

2204 YOUNG, ESTELLE
Gone to Europe. New York: Richard R. Smith, 1952.
241pp.

She describes her voyage on the Queen Elizabeth to Europe and her subsequent travels for six weeks in France, Italy, Switzerland, Germany, and England, including visits to such World War II landmarks as Normandy Beach and Anzio Beach.

2205 YOUNG, JANETTE LEWIS (1858-1887)
An Oregon Idyl, by Nellie May Young. Glendale, Cal. :
Clark, 1961. 111pp.

Going to work with her husband in the home mission field in Oregon, she travels by train from Pennsylvania in 1883; she describes the details of daily domestic activities, her church work, her acquaintances; leaving Oregon for her health, she dies at twenty-nine; editor's comments are interspersed throughout the narrative.

2206 YOUNG, LORETTA (1913-)
The Things I Had to Learn, as told to Helen Ferguson. Indianapolis: Bobbs-Merrill, 1961. 256pp.

An actress reflects on her experiences of learning and growth; she expresses her love, admiration, and gratitude for her mother's subtle wisdom; she chooses Colleen Moore (see entry #1462) as a role model, her career flourishes, and she thanks acting colleagues from whom she has learned much; she is highly enthusiastic about her television work; she comments on religion, adolescence, fashion, beauty, and charm.

2207   YURKA, BLANCHE (1887-1974)   NAWM
       Bohemian Girl: Blanche Yurka's Theatrical Life.   Athens,
       Ohio: Ohio University Press, 1970.   306pp.

She describes sixty years as a professional actress; she is born in Minnesota of Czech parents; her family's move to New York in 1900 opens the way to her career; aspiring to opera, she reluctantly settles for the stage and becomes an established star by 1928, continuing in films and on one-woman tours; she maintains close family ties throughout her life; she discusses various successful and unsuccessful roles, from classical drama to Ibsen.

2208   ZAHARIAS, MILDRED ELLA (BABE) DIDRIKSON (1911-
1956)   NAWM
This Life I've Led: My Autobiography, as told to Harry
Paxton. New York: A. S. Barnes, 1955. 242pp.

Her anecdotal account is written from taped conversations;
raised in a poor but close-knit Texas family, she describes
her early commitment to excel in athletics; intensely competitive, she plays basketball and competes in the 1932 national track championships and the 1932 Olympics; she marries in 1938; she is barred from tennis as a professional,
but competes as a professional and an amateur golfer, winning many golf titles in the U. S. and England; she works in
the late 1940's to build the women's pro golf tour; in 1953
she overcomes cancer to return to tournament golf.

2209   ZELAYETA, ELENA EMILIA (1897-)
Elena. Englewood Cliffs, N. J.: Prentice-Hall, 1960.
246pp.

Born in Mexico of Spanish parents, she settles in the
U. S. at nine, assuming family responsibilities due to her
knowledge of English and her headstrong personality; married, she is a "dutifully deferring wife" until her success
in the restaurant business undermines her home life; when
she becomes blind, she is first anguished and suicidal but
then is determined to be independent within a happy second
marriage; she teaches cooking classes for the blind, publishes several cookbooks, lectures, and joins her two adult
sons in a food business, a model of courage and self-
reliance.

2210   ZIEGFELD, PATRICIA (1916-)
The Ziegfelds' Girl: Confessions of an Abnormally Happy
Childhood. Boston: Little, Brown, 1964. 210pp.

In a highly amusing account, the daughter of Florenz
Ziegfeld and Billie Burke (see entry #315) tells of her parents' courtship and of her childhood on an extravagant country estate, a "twentieth century Peaceable Kingdom"; she
grows up normally in "a wacky, Arabian Nights sort of way"
with summer camping in Canada, winters in Palm Beach,

surrounded by love, far away from her parents' theatrical lives.

2211   ZIMMER, JILL SCHARY (1936?-)
With a Cast of Thousands; A Hollywood Childhood. New York: Stein and Day, 1963. 252pp.

The eldest daughter of Dore Schary describes growing up with a "princess complex," portraying her warm relationships with her father and mother; she tells of Hollywood children's parties, various private schools, summer holidays, adolescent snobbishness about being Jewish, her quest for independence, films in the family projection room, her courtship and marriage to a naval officer; her story is told in a lively, slightly ironic style.

2212   ZIMMER, MAUDE FILES
A Time to Remember. New York: Robert Speller, 1963. 152pp.

In a nostalgic account focused on her childhood in "a very small southern village," she tells of the security of having her mother "always within reach," of eight siblings, of her blissful unawareness of their "under-privileged" status; she is influenced by her mother's concern for new perspectives and broad tolerance; she recalls clothing, etiquette, hospitality, family pets, a Christmas celebration, and the benevolently despotic cook; she revisits her old home after half a century.

2213   A Village So Small. New York: Robert Speller, 1965. 213pp.

In a delightful description of her childhood in a Louisiana village, she maintains a child's perspective on the world, telling of the benevolent chaos of her large family; with a wealth of detail, she portrays her family's love of the land, her neighbors, the school, lyceum programs, church, Sunday school, and local entertainments; her account is colored by nostalgia for times of community-wide affection and security.

2214   ZINER, FEENIE
A Full House. New York: Simon and Schuster, 1967. 223pp.

A delightfully wry and articulate book about a writer's career and domestic life; married to an artist, she plays "second fiddle to a paintbrush" and describes her monstrous suburban home with exaggerated despair; already the mother of two small sons, the birth of triplets presents logistical and emotional challenges, made more complex by their move to New York and another huge "demented dwelling"; she lives "under the shadow of the rolled-up sleeve" of a flamboyant Polish maid, dreaming of her "private necessity"-- her writing career.

2215 ZISTEL, ERA
      The Good Year. New York: Crowell, 1959. 199pp.

      Taking advantage of a tolerant husband and a country house, she goes "hog-wild" over animals, gradually acquiring as pets cats, chipmunks, rabbits, goats, raccoons, and a dog; her decision to stay year-round in the country for the sake of the animals changes "our whole way of life."

2216 ZWINGER, ANNE HAYMOND
      Beyond the Aspen Grove. New York: Random, 1970.
      368pp.

      With her husband and three daughters, she settles in the "wild mountain land" of Colorado, feeling she belongs to the land she gains "openness and freedom"; writing of nature with perception and sensitivity, she tells of her special experiences and associations with the lakes, streams, meadows, forests, and their seasonal variations.

2217 Run, River, Run; A Naturalist's Journey Down One of the
      Great Rivers of the West. New York: Harper & Row,
      1975. 317pp.

      Traveling by canoe and river raft on the Green River in Wyoming, Colorado, and Utah from its source to its end, she develops great respect for the force and power of the river and its dramatic canyons and rapids; observing and recording in detail the flora, fauna, geological formations, weather, and moods of the river along the way, she comes to feel that "the river becomes a way of thinking."

Brigham, Gertrude Richardson
Chicago, Judy
Comstock, Anna Botsford
de Angeli, Marguerite Lofft
Dorcy, Sister Mary Jean
Foote, Mary Hallock
Foster, Dorothy F.
Goldberg, Dorothy Kurgans
Granger, Kathleen Buehr
Hale, Nancy
Hathaway, Katharine Butler
Hoffman, Helen
Kent, Adaline
Kligman, Ruth
Langseth-Christensen, Lillian
Lenski, Lois
Locke, Elizabeth N.
Luquer, Eloise Payne
Rizzi, Marcia Salo
Robinson, Ione
Seeman, Elizabeth
Stark, Elizabeth Worthington
    Philip

Athlete

Baranet, Nancy Neiman
Connolly, Olga Fikotova
Gibson, Althea
Hart, Doris
Huey, Lynda
King, Billie Jean
Marble, Alice
Zaharias, Mildred Ella (Babe)
    Didrikson

Auctioneer

Bailey, Emma

Aviator

Bernheim, Molly
Cobb, Jerrie
Cochran, Jacqueline
Hart, Marion Rice
Lindbergh, Anne Morrow
Lussier, Betty
Mock, Jerrie
Nichols, Ruth Roland
Pellegreno, Ann Holtgren

Biographer

Adams, Cindy Heller

Benét, Laura
Bowen, Catherine Shober Drinker
Burton, Katherine Kurz
Caruso, Dorothy Park Benjamin
Comstock, Anna Botsford
Elliot, Elisabeth
Marshall, Catherine Wood
Stern, Madeleine Bettina
Wayman, Dorothy Godfrey

Biologist

Hamerstrom, Frances

Bookseller

Hard, Margaret Steel
Rostenberg, Leona
Russ, Lavinia
Stern, Madeleine Bettina
Widdemer, Margaret

Bootlegger

Lockwood, Gertrude M.
Lythgoe, Gertrude C.

Botanist

Clements, Edith Gertrude Schwartz
Luquer, Eloise Payne
Parsons, Frances Theodora Smith
    Dana
Westcott, Cynthia

Broadcaster

Aimi, Marguerite Sitgreaves
Anthony, Susan Brownell
Barrett, Rona
Berg, Gertrude
Dickerson, Nancy
Falkenburg, Jinx (Eugenia)
Fuldheim, Dorothy
Graham, Virginia
Harris, Radie
Higby, Mary Jane
Howar, Barbara
Klose, Virginia Taylor
McBride, Mary Margaret
Margolies, Marjorie
Perkins, Faith
Price, Eugenia
Quinn, Sally

Congresswoman

Abzug, Bella
Chisholm, Shirley

Conservationist

Buyukmihci, Hope Sawyer
Hoover, Helen
Murie, Margaret E.
Taber, Gladys Bagg

Cookbook Author

Bailey, Pearl
Bracken, Peg
Cannon, Poppy
Kent, Louise Andrews
Langseth-Christensen, Lillian
Makanowitzky, Barbara Norman
Murphy, Patricia
Toklas, Alice Babette
Zelayeta, Elena Emilia

Critic

Bogan, Louise
Davenport, Marcia Gluck
Helburn, Theresa
McCarthy, Mary
Mannes, Marya
Meyer, Annie Nathan
Strainchamps, Ethel Reed

Cruise Director

Saunders, Jeraldine

Dancer

Angelou, Maya
Braggiotti, Gloria
Castle, Irene Foote
DeMille, Agnes George
Duncan, Irma
Duncan, Isadora
Dunham, Katherine
Geva, Tamara
Gilbert, Virginia Johnson
Hight, Gladys
Humphrey, Doris
Kitt, Eartha
MacLaine, Shirley

Martin, Mary
Miller, Ann
Roberts, Joan
Sherman, Jane
Woody, Regina Llewellyn Jones

Daughter of Famous Man

Allilueva, Svetlana
Armstrong, April Oursler
Barrymore, Diana
Boone, Shirley
Bowles, Cynthia
Clemens, Clara
de Rachewiltz, Mary
Finletter, Gretchen Damrosch
Frémont, Jessie Ann Benton
Frost, Lesley
Geld, Ellen Bromfield
Harriman, Margaret Case
James, Alice
Quincy, Eliza Susan
Quincy, Maria Sophia
St. Johns, Adela Rogers
Sandburg, Helga
Skinner, Cornelia Otis
Smith, Corinna Haven Putnam Lindon
Truman, Margaret
Waterston, Anna Cabot Lowell Quincy
Ziegfeld, Patricia
Zimmer, Jill Schary

Daughter of Famous Woman

Barrymore, Diana
Carey, Ernestine Moller Gilbreth
Davenport, Marcia Gluck
de Rachewiltz, Mary
Lane, Rose Wilder
Truman, Margaret
Ziegfeld, Patricia

Diplomat

Mesta, Perle Skirvin
Woytinsky, Emma Shadkhan

Diplomat's Wife

Alsop, Susan Mary
Curzon, Grace Elvina Trilla Hinds Duggan

Entertainer--see also Actress,
          Broadcaster, Circus
          Performer, Dancer,
          Mime Artist, Popular
          Singer

Ethnologist

Factory Worker

Farmer/Farm Wife

Fashion Designer

Federal Official

Feminist

Kane, Paula
Keller, Helen Adams
Kennedy, Florynce R.
King, Billie Jean
Louchheim, Katie Scofield
Martin, Del
Mesta, Perle Skirvin
Millett, Kate
Nevelson, Louise Berliawsky
Nin, Anaïs
Olender, Terrys T.
Rizzi, Marcia Salo
Rollin, Betty
Schwartz, Helene E.
Smith, Hannah Whitall
Stern, Susan Harris
Sullivan, Judy
Van Hoosen, Bertha
Woolley, Mary Emma

Filmmaker

Cussler, Margaret

First Lady

Adams, Abigail Smith
Grant, Julia Dent
Johnson, Lady Bird
Roosevelt, Eleanor
Wilson, Ellen Axson

Flight Attendant

Baker, Trudy
Chase, Lucille
Kane, Paula
Waterman, Sherry

Food Editor

Paddleford, Clementine

Forest Service Member

Hardy, Martha

Granddaughter of Famous Man

Steichen, Paula

Historian

Davis, Julia

Horsewoman

Bloodgood, Lida Fleitmann

Hospital Administrator

Pember, Phoebe Yates

Hostess

Maxwell, Elsa
Mesta, Perle Skirvin
Workman, Gladys

Hotel/Innkeeper

Edwards, Anne
Morse, Theresa A.
Shand, Margaret Clark
Springer, Francesca
Weaver, Adelaide
Windisch, Ida Adelaide

Housekeeper

Nesbitt, Victoria Henrietta Kugler
Parks, Lillian Rogers
Rasmussen, Anne-Marie

Ichthyologist

Clark, Eugenie

Illustrator--see Artist

Immigrant

Adler, Polly
Agnelli, Susanna
Aladjem, Henrietta
Allilueva, Svetlana
Anderson, Mary

Baum, Vicki
Belmont, Eleanor Robson
Berkowitz, Sarah Bick

Interior Decorator

Parsons, Louella Oettinger
Parton, Margaret
Patterson, Grace Daniel
Paul, Charlotte
Paxton, June LeMert
Peden, Rachel
Perkins, Faith
Popkin, Zelda
Prewett, Virginia

Quinn, Sally

Rama Rau, Santha
Roberts, Katherine

St. Johns, Adela Rogers
Salisbury, Charlotte Y.
Sargent, Wyn
Scherman, Bernardine Kielty
Schuyler, Philippa Duke
Sermolino, Maria
Shepard, Elaine
Sibley, Celestine
Siddons, Anne Rivers
Solomon, Barbara Probst
Spriggs, Edyth Elizabeth Jones
Stout, Ruth
Strainchamps, Ethel Reed
Strong, Anna Louise
Stuhldreher, Mary A.

Tarry, Ellen
Taves, Isabella
Taylor, Rosemary Drachman
Thompson, Era Bell
Thompson, Goldianne Guyer
Thompson, Nora Belle
Tornabene, Lyn
Torre, Marie
Treviño, Elizabeth Borton
Turner, Gladys Vanderburg

Underwood, Agness

Van Leer, Twila

Waitzmann, Dorothea
Walters, Barbara
Warfield, Frances
Wason, Betty
Wayman, Dorothy Godfrey
Wertenbaker, Lael Tucker
Wier, Delight Bobilya
Winter, Ella
Workman, Gladys
Wright, Anna Maria Rose

Judge

Allen, Florence Ellinwood

Labor Leader

Anderson, Mary
Mason, Lucy Randolph
Nestor, Agnes
O'Neal, Mary T.
Pesotta, Rose
Robins, Margaret Dreier
Schneiderman, Rose

Lawyer

Allen, Florence Ellinwood
Campbell, Litta Belle Hibben
Densen-Gerber, Judianne
Dodd, Bella Visono
Farrow, Tiera
Kennedy, Florynce R.
McClanahan, Alice M.
Murray, Pauli
Olender, Terrys T.
Schwartz, Helene E.

Lecturer

Baldrige, Letitia
Bjorn, Thyra Ferré
Bowne, Elizabeth
Brown, Eleanor Gertrude
Brown, Helene

Chou, Cynthia L.
Clapper, Olive Ewing
Clemens, Marie Louise
Clifton, Bernice

Davidson, Jaquie

Ethridge, Willie Snow

Farrington, Sara Houston Chisholm
Fuldheim, Dorothy

Garden, Mary

Hall, Eva Lichtfield
Haney, Germaine
Hege, Ruth
Hungerford, Katherine L.
Hunter, Frances Gardner

Kligman, Ruth
Morgan, Kay Summersby
Pierce, Deborah
Renay, Liz
Saunders, Jeraldine

Mother of Famous Man

Adams, Abigail Smith
Cassini, Marguerite
Kennedy, Rose Fitzgerald
Pinckney, Elizabeth Lucas
Williams, Edwina Dakin

Mountaineer

Petzoldt, Patricia

Musician--see also Composer,
          Concert Singer, Organist,
          Pianist, Popular Singer,
          Opera Singer, Violinist

Baum, Vicki
Beck, Daisy Woodward
Carlson, Betty
Kahn, Frida
Lenihan, Mina Ward
MacDonald, Susanne Rike
McKelvie, Martha Groves
Previn, Dory Langan
Reichert, Florian, Sister
Reis, Claire Raphael
Trapp, Maria Augusta von
Truman, Margaret
Turnor, Mae Caesar
Van Nuys, Laura Bower

Naturalist

Arny, Mary Travis
Carrighar, Sally
Comstock, Anna Botsford
Crisler, Lois
Goin, Olive Bown
Guild, Caroline
Kellner, Esther
Murie, Margaret E.
Stanwell-Fletcher, Theodora
    Morris Cope
Zwinger, Ann Haymond

Novelist

Beebe, Elswyth Thane Ricker
Bond, Mary Wickham
Buck, Pearl Sydenstricker

Calisher, Hortense
Carroll, Gladys Hasty
Cather, Willa Sibert
Coatesworth, Elizabeth Jane
Cuthrell, Faith Baldwin

Davenport, Marcia Gluck
Davis, Julia
Dykeman, Wilma

Eaton, Evelyn Sybil Mary
Edwards, Anne
Elliot, Elisabeth
Enters, Angna
Erdman, Loula Grace

Felps, Jettie Irving
Ferber, Edna
Fletcher, Inglis Clark
Foote, Mary Hallock
Frankau, Pamela
Franken, Rose

Glasgow, Ellen Anderson Gholson
Goodspeed, Bernice I.
Green, Anne
Grissom, Irene Welch

Harris, Bernice Kelly
Hobart, Alice Tisdale Nourse
Hurst, Fannie

Keyes, Frances Parkinson Wheeler
Klass, Sheila Solomon

Lane, Rose Wilder
Loos, Anita

McCarthy, Mary
McCloskey, Eunice Mildred
Mackay, Margaret Mackprang
Meriwether, Elizabeth Avery
Meyer, Annie Nathan
Mitchell, Margaret

Nin, Anaïs
Norris, Kathleen Thompson

Ovington, Mary White

Paul, Charlotte
Plath, Sylvia

Nun

Nurse

Opera Singer

Orchestral Manager

Organist

Painter

Berkeley, Mary Emlen Lloyd
Bush, Marian Spore
Greenman, Frances Cranmer
Langseth-Christensen, Lillian
Lasky, Bessie Mona Garness
McCloskey, Eunice Mildred
Moses, Anna Mary Robertson
Pillét, Nettie Ethel Leist
Turnbull, Grace Hill
Wright, Catharine Wharton Morris

Philanthropist

Aldrich, Margaret Chanler
Balsan, Consuelo Vanderbilt
Bowen, Louise Hadduck deKoven
Havemeyer, Louisine Waldrone
   Elder
Ileana, Princess of Romania
Meyer, Agnes Elizabeth Ernst
Oliver, Susan Lawrence
Rockefeller, Abby Greene Aldrich
Rubinstein, Helena
Solomon, Hannah Greenebaum
Whitney, Eleanor Searle

Philosopher

Turnbull, Grace Hill

Photographer

Armer, Laura Adams
Baus, Ruth
Bourke-White, Margaret
Chapelle, Dickey
Hungerford, Katherine L.
Johnson, Osa Helen Leighty
LaBastille, Anne

Pianist

Chanler, Margaret Terry
Cornish, Nellie Centennial
Dana, Ethel Nathalie Smith
Hughes, Adella Prentiss
Resnick, Rose
Schuyler, Philippa Duke
Slenczynska, Ruth
Towne, M. Carola, Sister
Van Nes, Mary Felts

Pilot--see Aviator

Playwright

Franken, Rose
Goodspeed, Bernice I.
Hanff, Helene
Hansberry, Lorraine
Harmon, Charlotte
Helburn, Theresa
Hellman, Lillian
Kerr, Jean Collins
Meyer, Annie Nathan
O'Hara, Constance Marie
Ovington, Mary White
Sheklow, Edna

Poet

Aldrich, Margaret Chanler
Angelou, Maya

Benét, Laura
Bevington, Helen Smith
Bogan, Louise
Brooks, Gwendolyn

Caskey, Jessie Jane Hussey
Clifton, Lucille
Coatesworth, Elizabeth Jane
Crosby, Caresse Jacob
Cuthrell, Faith Baldwin

de Pierrefeu, Elsa Tudor
Dickenson, Emily
Djerassi, Norma Lundholm
Duffee, Mary Gordon

Eaton, Evelyn Sybil Mary

Giovanni, Nikki
Goodwin, Ruby Berkley
Grissom, Irene Welch

Hall, Mabel Wilson
Helburn, Theresa

Lazarus, Emma
Leitch, Mary Sinton Lewis
Levertov, Denise
Lind, Miriam Seiber

McCloskey, Eunice Mildred
MacDonald, Susanne Rike
McGinley, Phyllis
Maryanna, Sister
Millay, Edna St. Vincent
Morton, Lena Beatrice
Murray, Pauli

Nicholson, Martha Snell

Paxton, June LeMert
Peck, Clara Temple Boardman
Plath, Sylvia
Potts, Abbie Findlay

Quick, Dorothy

Randall, Margaret

Sarton, May
Sebastian, Fannie B.
Succop, Margaret Phillips

Thaxter, Celia Laighton
Tobin, Agnes

Untermeyer, Jean Starr

Walker, Margaret
Welles, Winifred Hale
Widdemer, Margaret
Williams, Rose Berthenia Clay
Wolff, Sister Mary Madeleva

Police Officer

Abrecht, Mary Ellen
Cirile, Marie
Schnabel, Martha

Political Radical

Davis, Angela
Day, Dorothy
Dodd, Bella Visono
Flynn, Elizabeth Gurley
Goldman, Emma
Lang, Lucy Fox Robins
Massing, Hede
Randall, Margaret
Robinson, Ione
Stern, Susan Harris
Strong, Anna Louise
Utley, Freda

Politician--see also Congress-
woman, Federal Official

Abzug, Bella
Bass, Charlotta A. Spears
Brookter, Marie
Chisholm, Shirley
Crawford, Dorothy Painter

Louchheim, Katie Scofield
Mesta, Perle Skirvin
Moore, Martha Edith Bannister
Noble, Cora Moore
Pellet, Elizabeth Eyre
Priest, Ivy Maude Baker
Sanders, Marion K.
Snorgrass, Wanda
Stanford, Sally
Witker, Kristi

Politician's Wife

Adams, Rachel White
Ames, Blanche Butler
Barkley, Jane Rucker
Dirksen, Louella Carver
Keyes, Frances Parkinson Wheeler
McCarthy, Abigail Quigley
McGovern, Eleanor
McKelvie, Martha Groves
Magruder, Gail
Proxmire, Ellen
Slayden, Ellen Maury
Sparkman, Ivo Hall
Wallace, Cornelia

Popular Singer

Baez, Joan
Bailey, Pearl
Boone, Shirley
Bryant, Anita
Cole, Maria Ellington
Dandridge, Dorothy
Holiday, Billie
Horne, Lena
Jackson, Mahalia
Kitt, Eartha
Lynn, Loretta Webb
Merman, Ethel
Picon, Molly
Riddle, Almeda
Ritchie, Jean
Rogers, Dale Evans
Scott, Toni Lee
Smith, Kate
Traubel, Helen Francesca
Waters, Ethel
Wright, Cobina

Potter

Wildenhain, Marguerite
Wong, Jade Snow
Workman, Gladys

Schiff, Jaquie Lee
Simkhovitch, Mary Melinda Kingsbury
Thompson, Era Bell
Vester, Bertha Hedges Spafford
Washington, Vivian Edwards
Worcester, Daisy Lee Worthington

Sociologist

Cussler, Margaret
Ovington, Mary White

Sports Figure--see Athlete

Sport Fisher

Farrington, Sara Houston Chisholm

Spy/Secret Agent

Bentley, Elizabeth
Brown, Julia Clarice
Massing, Hede
Miller, Marion Freed
Phillips, Claire

Stenographer

Fox, Lydia Mantle
Ruby, Edna R.

Stewardess--see also Flight Attendant

Rodrigue, Rosalie

Suffragist

Aldrich, Margaret Chanler
Allen, Florence Ellinwood
Balsan, Consuelo Vanderbilt
Bowen, Louise Hadduck deKoven
Havemeyer, Louisine Waldrone
    Elder
Katzenstein, Caroline
Langhorne, Orra Henderson
    Moore Gray
Meriwether, Elizabeth Avery
Nestor, Agnes
Park, Maud May Wood
Pellet, Elizabeth Eyre
Robins, Margaret Dreier

Superintendant of Orphanage

Burmeister, Eva
Hartman, May Weisser

Teacher

Adams, Effie Kay
Adams, Lillian Loyce
Anderson, Rosa Claudette
Andrews, Fannie Fern Phillips
Andrews, Grace Eleanor
Arnold, Mary Ellicott
Austin, Ethel L.

Baird, Margaret E.
Baker, Louise Maxwell
Barber, Olive
Bard, Lori
Barlow, Leila Mae
Barrett, Raina
Bauer, Hanna
Beam, Lura
Bernheim, Molly
Berry, Ruth Muirhead
Berto, Hazel Dunaway
Bevington, Helen Smith
Blaustein, Esther Gordon
Bohner, Olivine Nadeau
Bourne, Emma Guest
Bourne, Eulalia
Brooks, Gwendolyn
Brown, Eleanor Gertrude
Brown, Estelle Aubrey
Brown, Mary Jane
Browne, Rose Butler

Campbell, Elizabeth Warder Crozer
Carlson, Betty
Carpenter, Edna Turley
Carr, Lorraine
Cattell, Ann
Caulfield, Genevieve
Chicago, Judy
Chou, Cynthia L.
Clark, Septima Poinsette
Clawson, Bertha Fidelia
Comstock, Anna Botsford
Cone, Virginia S.
Corben, Mulaika
Cornish, Nellie Centennial
Cotton, Ella Earls
Cox, Eugenia M.
Craig, Eleanor
Craig, Lillian K.
Crawford, Dorothy Painter
Culbertson, Manie
Cummings, Evangeline Haas

Rogers, Dorothy
Rothman, Esther P.
Russell, Lucy Phillips
Rutherford, Blanche Scott

Sanford, Agnes Mary White
Sanford, Mollie Dorsey
Sarton, May
Schwartz, Helene E.
Sebastian, Fannie B.
Seibels, Fanny Marks
Sheppard, Lila
Sibley, Agnes Marie
Skrjabena, Elena
Smith, Ethel Sabin
Smith, Ruth
Snyder, Grace McCance
Stanfield, Mattie Cole
Stern, Carolyn
Steurt, Marjorie Rankin
Strainchamps, Ethel Reed
Stull, Ruth O.
Sullivan, Judy
Svendsen, Gro Nilsdatter

Trobisch, Ingrid Hult
Turk, Midge
Turnor, Mae Caesar

Van Dyke, Phyllis
Van Hoosen, Bertha
Vining, Elizabeth Gray

Wallace, Elizabeth
Washington, Vivian Edwards
Williams, Celia Ann
Williams, Rose Berthenia Clay
Williamson, Myrtle
Winchell, Mary Edna
Wolff, Sister Mary Madeleva
Woods, Cornelia Wilson
Woolley, Mary Emma
Wright, Anna Maria Rose

Zelayeta, Elena Emilia

Theatrical Producer/Director

Angier, Vena
Cullman, Marguerite
Dalrymple, Jean
Harmon, Charlotte
Helburn, Theresa
LeGallienne, Eva
Webster, Margaret

Transexual

Jorgensen, Christine

Translator

Bogan, Louise
Meyer, Agnes Elizabeth Ernst
Peterson, Virgilia
Untermeyer, Jean Starr

Violinist

Pillêt, Nettie Ethel Leist
Seibels, Fanny Marks

Wife of Famous Man

Akeley, Mary Lee Jobe
Anderson, Elizabeth

Backus, Henny
Barrymore, Elaine Jacobs
Boone, Shirley
Boulton, Agnes
Bourke-White, Margaret
Brooks, Gladys Rice Billings
Brown, Lilian MacLaughlin
Burke, Billie

Cannon, Poppy
Caruso, Dorothy Park Benjamin
Castle, Irene Foote
Chaplin, Lita Grey
Clark, Maurine Doran
Cole, Maria Ellington
Crater, Stella Wheeler
Crosby, Caresse Jacob
Crosby, Kathryn
Custer, Elizabeth Bacon

Davis, Varina Anne Howell
Day, Laraine
Dean, Maureen
Dreiser, Helen Patges

Emerson, Ellen Louisa Tucker
Evers, Myrlie Beasley

Fermi, Laura
Frémont, Jessie Ann Benton

Gable, Kathleen Williams
Gehrig, Eleanor Twitchell
Geva, Tamara

Goldberg, Dorothy Kurgans
Grant, Jane Cole

Haymes, Nora Eddington Flynn
Hemingway, Mary Welsh
Hersey, Jean

King, Coretta Scott

Lasky, Bessie Mona Garness
Lewis, Grace Hegger
Lindbergh, Anne Morrow
Longfellow, Fanny Appleton

McCormack, Lily Foley
Marshall, Katherine Tupper

Peale, Ruth Stafford
Pickford, Mary
Pike, Diane Kennedy
Powers, Barbara Moore
Previn, Dory Langan

Rasmussen, Anne-Marie
Roberts, Evelyn
Rockefeller, Abby Greene Aldrich
Rodzinski, Halina
Rogers, Dale Evans
Roosevelt, Eleanor Butler Alexander
Roosevelt, Patricia Peabody
Rosenberg, Ethel Greenglass
Ruth, Claire Merritt

Salisbury, Charlotte Y.
Simon, Charlie May Hogue
Sinclair, Mary Craig
Snow, Lois Wheeler
Stevenson, Frances Van de Grift

Thomas, Mary Pryor
Tillich, Hannah

Van Doren, Dorothy Graffe
von Mises, Margit

Windsor, Wallis Warfield
Wright, Olgivanna Lloyd

Witch

Heather
Leek, Sybil

Writer--see also Biographer,
    Children's Author, Cook-
    book Author, Critic,

Journalist, Novelist, Play-
    wright, Poet, Translator

Abdalian, Zabel
Acosta, Mercedes de
Adams, Cindy Heller
Alsop, Gulielma Fell
Alta
Ames, Evelyn Perkins
Anderson, Margaret Carolyn
Andrews, Fannie Fern Phillips
Angelou, Maya
Angier, Vena
Anthony, Susan Brownell
Armer, Laura Adams
Armstrong, April Oursler
Atkinson, Oriana Torrey

Baker, Louise Maxwell
Balch, Emily Tapscott Clark
Barber, Olive
Bard, Mary
Barkins, Evelyn Werner
Bartell, Jan Bryant
Baum, Vicki
Beers, Lorna Doone
Bengis, Ingrid
Berg, Gertrude
Bevington, Helen Smith
Bjorn, Thyra Ferré
Boulton, Agnes
Bowen, Catherine Shober Drinker
Bowne, Elizabeth
Brennan, Maeve
Brooks, Gwendolyn
Brown, Eleanor Gertrude
Bryant, Anita
Buck, Pearl
Burton, Katherine Kurz
Burton, Naomi

Calisher, Hortense
Campion, Rosamond
Carey, Ernestine Moller Gilbreth
Carrighar, Sally
Carroll, Gladys Hasty
Caskey, Jessie Jane Hussey
Cather, Willa Sibert
Chase, Ilka
Chase, Mary Ellen
Chou, Cynthia L.
Clapp, Estelle Barnes
Clapper, Olive Ewing
Clements, Edith Gertrude Schwartz
Comstock, Anna Botsford
Comstock, Clara Mabel Haggard
Cuthrell, Faith Baldwin

Index of Narratives by Subject Matter

In the case of an author with multiple entries, the numbers in parentheses refer the reader to the narratives appropriate to the index category only.

Alcohol/Drug Addiction

Anthony, Susan Brownell (1), (2)
Astor, Mary (2)
Berg, Norah Sullivan
Burns, Elizabeth
Clark, Janet (pseud.)
Fisher, Florrie
Hall, Pamela
Holiday, Billie
Horn, Jane (pseud.)
Leah
McNeal, Violet
Mileto, Cecile
Nadler, Susan
Painter, Charlotte (1)
Patterson, Bonnie
Quinn, Barbara
Roth, Lillian (1), (2)

American Indian Woman's Experience

Bennett, Kay
Cuero, Delfina
Lone Dog, Louise
Lowry, Annie
Mountain Wolf Woman
Pollard, Ellen H.
Pretty-Shield
Sekaquaptewa, Helen
Shaw, Anna Moore

Back-to-the-land Experience

Allen, Gina
Alsop, Gulielma Fell (1)
Anderson, Olive
Angier, Vena
Beebe, Elswyth Thane Ricker
   (2), (3)
Beers, Lorna Doone
Bell, Clare

Coatesworth, Elizabeth Jane (1),
   (2)
Crowell, Marnie Reed
Dillard, Annie
Dimock, Gladys Gouverneur Ogden
Ethridge, Willie Snow (4)
Evans, Eva Knox
Granger, Kathleen Buehr
Hilles, Helen Train
Hobbs, Lisa (3)
Hoover, Helen (1), (2), (3)
McCully, Ethel Walbridge
McEwen, Inez Puckett
Mather, Melissa
Moxley, Verna
Nicholds, Elizabeth
Paxton, June LeMert
Pochmann, Ruth Fouts
Price, Gladys Bibee
Robinson, Bernice Nelke
Seeman, Elizabeth
Selby, Hazel Barrington
Sibley, Celestine
Teal, Marion Pedersen

Black Woman's Experience

Anderson, Marian
Anderson, Rosa Claudette
Angelou, Maya

Bailey, Pearl
Barlow, Leila Mae
Barnett, Ida B. Wells
Bass, Charlotta A. Spears
Bates, Daisy Lee Gatson
Brooks, Gwendolyn
Brookter, Marie
Brown, Julia Clarice
Browne, Rose Butler

Chisholm, Shirley
Clark, Septima Poinsette

Catholic Conversion Experience

Civil War Experience

Communist/Ex-Communist Experience

Concentration Camp Experience

Gardner, Jeanne Francis
Lone Dog, Louise
Mann, Stella Terrill
Martin, Wanda
Montgomery, Ruth Shick
Peterson, Flora Culp
Rhodes, Harrie Vernette
Smith, Susy

Religious Reflections

Aldrich, Dorothy Coffin
Berry, Ruth Muirhead
Bryant, Anita (1), (2), (3), (4),
  (5), (6)
Bulle, Florence
Cuthrell, Faith Baldwin (2), (4),
  (5), (6)
Holmes, Marjorie (2)
Jacobs, Margaret Branch Moore
Jeffcoat, Gladys Neill
Lockerbie, Jeanette W.
Mollenkott, Virginia Ramey
Perkins, Mary
Rinker, Rosiland
Rogers, Dale Evans (1)
Schneider, Frieda Johnetta
Strong, June

Spiritual Autobiography/Awakening

Anthony, Alba Riek
Anthony, Susan Brownell
Boone, Shirley
Chambers, Mary Jane
Dunford, Katherine
Leah
Marshall, Catherine Wood (1)
Montgomery, Ruth Shick
Morgan, Geraldine
Neal, Emily Gardiner
O'Hara, Constance Marie
Pratt, Marsha Whitney
Price, Eugenia
Robinson, Mary Ann
Rogers, Dale Evans (2)
Selvey, Virginia F.
Stackhouse, Mildred Orr
Teillard, Dorothy Lamon
Whitney, Eleanor Searle
Wigoder, Devorah
Winslow, Anna J. Frazer
Wycott, Sara Jean Clark

Travel/Householding Abroad

Adams, Abigail Smith (1)
Adams, Cindy Heller
Adams, Effie Kay
Adams, Lillian Loyce
Akeley, Mary Lee Jobe
Alireza, Marianne
Alsop, Susan Mary
Ames, Evelyn Perkins (2), (3)
Anderson, Rosa Claudette
Andrews, Fannie Fern Phillips
Armstrong, Joanna Neuman
Armstrong, Ruth Gallup
Arnett, Jean
Astor, Brooke Russell
Athas, Daphne
Atkinson, Oriana Torrey (2), (3)
Aye, Lillian

Baer, Jean L.
Baker, Trudy (pseud.) (1), (2)
Baldrige, Letitia (2), (3)
Ballentine, Frances Griswold
Barbosa, Dian Ruy
Bard, Lori
Barnard, Maude Edmundson Banister
Bartholomew, Carol
Baus, Ruth
Baxter, Anne
Beach, Marjorie Marshall
Beadle, Muriel (1)
Belfrage, Sally (2)
Bengis, Ingrid (2)
Berkeley, Mary Emlen Lloyd
Berry, Katherine Fiske
Bertrande, Sister
Bevington, Helen Smith (2)
Blair, Maude Hall
Bodell, Mary
Bodger, Joan
Bond, Mary Wickham
Borland, Mary Bernice
Borowsky, Marcia C. R.
Bowles, Cynthia
Bowne, Elizabeth (1), (2)
Bracken, Peg (1)
Braidwood, Linda S.
Brigham, Gertrude Richardson
Bristow, Katie S.
Brown, Clara Lee (1), (2),
Brown, Lilian MacLaughlin (1),
  (2), (3)
Brown, Margery Finn
Brown, Mary Jane
Brown, Opal Hartsell
Buck, Pearl Sydenstricker (1), (3)
Burnham, Eleanor Waring

Wilderness Living

Numbers in the index refer to entry number, not page number.